Data Analysis and Mining

Data Analysis and Mining

Editors

Stefanos Ougiaroglou
Dionisis Margaris

Basel • Beijing • Wuhan • Barcelona • Belgrade • Novi Sad • Cluj • Manchester

Editors
Stefanos Ougiaroglou
Department of Information and
Electronic Engineering
International Hellenic University
Sindos, Thessaloniki
Greece

Dionisis Margaris
Department of Digital Systems
University of the Peloponnese
Kladas, Sparta
Greece

Editorial Office
MDPI
St. Alban-Anlage 66
4052 Basel, Switzerland

This is a reprint of articles from the Special Issue published online in the open access journal *Applied Sciences* (ISSN 2076-3417) (available at: www.mdpi.com/journal/applsci/special_issues/data_analysis_mining).

For citation purposes, cite each article independently as indicated on the article page online and as indicated below:

Lastname, A.A.; Lastname, B.B. Article Title. *Journal Name* **Year**, *Volume Number*, Page Range.

ISBN 978-3-0365-9503-0 (Hbk)
ISBN 978-3-0365-9502-3 (PDF)
doi.org/10.3390/books978-3-0365-9502-3

© 2023 by the authors. Articles in this book are Open Access and distributed under the Creative Commons Attribution (CC BY) license. The book as a whole is distributed by MDPI under the terms and conditions of the Creative Commons Attribution-NonCommercial-NoDerivs (CC BY-NC-ND) license.

Contents

About the Editors vii

Preface ix

Magdalena Garvanova, Ivan Garvanov, Vladimir Jotsov, Abdul Razaque, Bandar Alotaibi, Munif Alotaibi and Daniela Borissova
A Data-Science Approach for Creation of a Comprehensive Model to Assess the Impact of Mobile Technologies on Humans
Reprinted from: *Appl. Sci.* **2023**, *13*, 3600, doi:10.3390/app13063600 1

Michail Salampasis, Alkiviadis Katsalis, Theodosios Siomos, Marina Delianidi, Dimitrios Tektonidis, Konstantinos Christantonis, et al.
A Flexible Session-Based Recommender System for e-Commerce
Reprinted from: *Appl. Sci.* **2023**, *13*, 3347, doi:10.3390/app13053347 21

Marina Delianidi, Konstantinos Diamantaras, Dimitrios Tektonidis and Michail Salampasis
Session-Based Recommendations for e-Commerce with Graph-Based Data Modeling
Reprinted from: *Appl. Sci.* **2023**, *13*, 394, doi:10.3390/app13010394 45

Evangelos Tsagalidis and Georgios Evangelidis
Exploiting Domain Knowledge to Address Class Imbalance in Meteorological Data Mining
Reprinted from: *Appl. Sci.* **2022**, *12*, 12402, doi:10.3390/app122312402 61

Ming Liu, Lei Chen and Zihao Zheng
Similarity Calculation via Passage-Level Event Connection Graph
Reprinted from: *Appl. Sci.* **2022**, *12*, 9887, doi:10.3390/app12199887 73

Christos Orovas, Eirini Orovou, Maria Dagla, Alexandros Daponte, Nikolaos Rigas, Stefanos Ougiaroglou, et al.
Neural Networks for Early Diagnosis of Postpartum PTSD in Women after Cesarean Section
Reprinted from: *Appl. Sci.* **2022**, *12*, 7492, doi:10.3390/app12157492 95

Monia Hamdi, Inès Hilali-Jaghdam, Manal M. Khayyat, Bushra M. E. Elnaim, Sayed Abdel-Khalek and Romany F. Mansour
Chicken Swarm-Based Feature Subset Selection with Optimal Machine Learning Enabled Data Mining Approach
Reprinted from: *Appl. Sci.* **2022**, *12*, 6787, doi:10.3390/app12136787 111

Alicia Huidobro, Raúl Monroy and Bárbara Cervantes
A High-Level Representation of the Navigation Behavior of Website Visitors
Reprinted from: *Appl. Sci.* **2022**, *12*, 6711, doi:10.3390/app12136711 127

Amira Abdelwahab and Mohamed Mostafa
A Deep Neural Network Technique for Detecting Real-Time Drifted Twitter Spam
Reprinted from: *Appl. Sci.* **2022**, *12*, 6407, doi:10.3390/app12136407 149

Mayur Kishor Shende, Sinan Q. Salih, Neeraj Dhanraj Bokde, Miklas Scholz, Atheer Y. Oudah and Zaher Mundher Yaseen
Natural Time Series Parameters Forecasting: Validation of the Pattern-Sequence-Based Forecasting (PSF) Algorithm; A New Python Package
Reprinted from: *Appl. Sci.* **2022**, *12*, 6194, doi:10.3390/app12126194 169

Jonathan Ayebakuro Orama, Assumpció Huertas, Joan Borràs, Antonio Moreno and Salvador Anton Clavé
Identification of Mobility Patterns of Clusters of City Visitors: An Application of Artificial Intelligence Techniques to Social Media Data
Reprinted from: *Appl. Sci.* **2022**, *12*, 5834, doi:10.3390/app12125834 . . . . **189**

Zichao He, Chunna Zhao and Yaqun Huang
Multivariate Time Series Deep Spatiotemporal Forecasting with Graph Neural Network
Reprinted from: *Appl. Sci.* **2022**, *12*, 5731, doi:10.3390/app12115731 . . . . **207**

Amira Abdelwahab and Nesma Youssef
Performance Evaluation of Sequential Rule Mining Algorithms
Reprinted from: *Appl. Sci.* **2022**, *12*, 5230, doi:10.3390/app12105230 . . . . **229**

Yu Liu and Bai Wang
User Trust Inference in Online Social Networks: A Message Passing Perspective
Reprinted from: *Appl. Sci.* **2022**, *12*, 5186, doi:10.3390/app12105186 . . . . **251**

Jing Wang and Xiongfei Li
Parallel Frequent Subtrees Mining Method by an Effective Edge Division Strategy
Reprinted from: *Appl. Sci.* **2022**, *12*, 4778, doi:10.3390/app12094778 . . . . **281**

Guangyi Man and Xiaoyan Sun
Interested Keyframe Extraction of Commodity Video Based on Adaptive Clustering Annotation
Reprinted from: *Appl. Sci.* **2022**, *12*, 1502, doi:10.3390/app12031502 . . . . **297**

Zhongxue Chen
Optimal Tests for Combining *p*-Values
Reprinted from: *Appl. Sci.* **2022**, *12*, 322, doi:10.3390/app12010322 . . . . **315**

About the Editors

Stefanos Ougiaroglou

Stefanos Ougiaroglou is an assistant professor in the Department of Information and Electronic Engineering at the International Hellenic University, where he teaches courses on programming, databases, web application development, and data mining. He received a B.Sc. in Computer Science (2004) from the Department of Informatics at the Alexander TEI in Thessaloniki, Greece; an M.Sc. in Computer Science (2006) from the Department of Computer Science at Aristotle University in Thessaloniki, Greece; and a PhD in Computer Science (2014) from the Department of Applied Informatics at the University of Macedonia, Greece. His research interests include data mining algorithms, data reduction, data streams, data management for mobile computing, databases, algorithms and data structures, educational technology, and web application development. He has published several papers in peer-reviewed international journals and conferences proceedings.

Dionisis Margaris

Dionisis Margaris is an assistant professor in the Department of Digital Systems, University of the Peloponnese, Greece, where he teaches courses on programming, operating systems, software technology, and information systems. He received his B.Sc., M.Sc., and Ph.D. from the Department of Informatics and Telecommunications, University of Athens, Greece, in 2007, 2010, and 2014, respectively. He has published more than 70 papers in peer-reviewed international journals, books, and conferences proceedings. His research interests include information systems, personalization, recommender systems, business processes, and web services and data mining.

Preface

To date, data analysis and mining is being used in numerous everyday tasks to solve practical problems. This research field has attracted the interest of both academia and industry. The research community has developed algorithms, techniques, and tools for the prediction of future situations, discovery of clusters with similar data, association rules in mining, and pattern recognition, among others, all of which have found applications in many domains, such as medicine, finance, business, biology, marketing, and education. In this reprint, 17 papers are published on different topics of the broad research field of data analysis and mining. Each of the included papers presents new data mining algorithms and techniques, as well as applications of data analysis and mining in real-world domains. These papers have been carefully selected based on a vigorous peer-review process involving several respectful reviewers organized by *Applied Sciences*. It is our sincere hope that these papers will provide new inspiration for the development and application of data analysis and mining. We would like to thank all the authors and reviewers who contributed to this reprint.

Stefanos Ougiaroglou and Dionisis Margaris
Editors

Article

A Data-Science Approach for Creation of a Comprehensive Model to Assess the Impact of Mobile Technologies on Humans

Magdalena Garvanova [1,*], Ivan Garvanov [1], Vladimir Jotsov [1,2], Abdul Razaque [2,*], Bandar Alotaibi [3], Munif Alotaibi [4] and Daniela Borissova [1,5]

1. Department of Information Systems and Technologies, University of Library Studies and Information Technologies, 1784 Sofia, Bulgaria
2. Department of Cybersecurity, International Information Technology University, Almaty 050000, Kazakhstan
3. Department of Information Technology, University of Tabuk, Tabuk 47731, Saudi Arabia
4. Department of Computer Science, Shaqra University, Shaqra 11961, Saudi Arabia
5. Department of Information Processes and Decision Support, Institute of Information and Communication Technologies, Bulgarian Academy of Sciences, 1113 Sofia, Bulgaria
* Correspondence: m.garvanova@unibit.bg (M.G.); a.razaque@iitu.edu.kz (A.R.)

Abstract: Mobile technologies are an essential part of people's everyday lives since they are utilized for a variety of purposes, such as communication, entertainment, commerce, and education. However, when these gadgets are misused, the human body is exposed to continuous radiation from the electromagnetic field created by them. The communication services available are improving as mobile technologies advance; however, the problem is becoming more severe as the frequency range of mobile devices expands. To solve this complex case, it is necessary to propose a comprehensive approach that combines and processes data obtained from different types of research and sources of information, such as thermal imaging, electroencephalograms, computer models, and surveys. In the present article, a complex model for the processing and analysis of heterogeneous data is proposed based on mathematical and statistical methods in order to study the problem of electromagnetic radiation from mobile devices in-depth. Data science selection/preprocessing is one of the most important aspects of data and knowledge processing aiming at successful and effective analysis and data fusion from many sources. Special types of logic-based binding and pointing constraints are considered for data/knowledge selection applications. The proposed logic-based statistical modeling method provides both algorithmic as well as data-driven realizations that can be evolutionary. As a result, non-anticipated and collateral data/features can be processed if their role in the selected/constrained area is significant. In this research, the data-driven part does not use artificial neural networks; however, this combination was successfully applied in the past. It is an independent subsystem maintaining control of both the statistical and machine-learning parts. The proposed modeling applies to a wide range of reasoning/smart systems.

Keywords: signal processing; smart device; electromagnetic field; non-ionizing radiation protection; SAR; ANOVA; data science; selection; constraint satisfaction; preprocessing; mobile technology; machine learning; statistics

1. Introduction

The methods used in data science show ways to find solutions to a specific problem [1]. With the development of technology, the types of data to be analyzed are diverse and heterogeneous [2]. Having many and varied sensors to register an event or phenomenon is a great advantage in data processing and decision making but also a great challenge for data analysts [3]. The processing, aggregation, and analysis of disparate data is a complex process that can be facilitated by the use of intelligent solutions [4].

The study of the issue of the effects of smart devices on humans is an extremely recent scientific task that requires the processing and analysis of diverse data sets obtained from numerous measurements [5]. It is not possible to give an unambiguous answer to this question when conducting the same type of research. Smart technologies are all around us and, in the near future, their number will increase many times over [6]. One of the most popular and currently used smart devices is the smartphone, which is used for both work and entertainment [7].

In recent years, this type of device has been increasingly used, and children and early teens own and use smartphones. These devices are used for communication, work, games, entertainment (watching movies and listening to music), visiting social networks, and more. At the same time, there are studies and analyses of the impact of these technologies on humans, and these effects are both psychological and biophysical in nature [8]. The smartphone is close to its owner, and the amount of time spent with this device is constantly increasing [9]. This process is difficult to interrupt or limit; however, if the consequences of overuse are studied and properly analyzed, the question of how to reduce the harmful effects on humans can be answered [10].

The psychological effects of smart technologies are the result of their long-term use and merging of the real and virtual worlds, which leads to social alienation, psychological loneliness, personal anxiety, low self-esteem, and hence to depressive states. More specific questions are related to: what is internet addiction and what physical and mental symptoms characterize this condition, the types of addictions, the extent to which they spread in society and what are the main areas affected, which is the most at-risk group among the population, what are the consequences, and—last but not least—the mechanisms of therapy and prevention.

Among the most commonly used methods of analysis are statistics from consulting agencies, content analysis of sites and blogs, and data from empirical studies and psycho diagnostic tests. The data analytics processes can be successfully combined with logic-based modeling instruments with the aim to create more medical applicable, versatile, and universal decisions.

Some experts find that dependence on smart technologies, and in particular on the services they offer, is not a separate behavioral disorder but a syndrome of a serious socio-psychological problem. The majority of researchers believe that the combination of addiction to cyberspace, together with electromagnetic radiation from smart devices, is a risk factor with dangerous consequences for the mental and physical health of an individual. Most smart devices communicate with each other using electromagnetic signals, which are a serious threat to human life and pollute the environment with invisible "electrosmog".

This article discusses the data-science approach to creating a comprehensive model for assessing the impact of mobile technologies on humans. The aim is to propose a data-science concept for the preprocessing, processing, and postprocessing of disparate data obtained from various sensors, measuring devices, and computer models for assessing the impact of mobile technologies on humans.

1.1. Paper Organization

The remainder of this paper is organized as follows. Section 2 presents the salient features of existing works. Section 3 presents the main statistical data processing methods. Section 4 shows the results from measuring the electromagnetic field, which reveal that, under certain conditions, mobile devices emit high-frequency electromagnetic waves and can cause various negative effects on humans. Section 5 discusses the most popular dosimetric values that estimate the levels of absorption of electromagnetic fields by the human body.

Modeling for SAR is used to mimic and illustrate the process of electromagnetic field absorption by the human head in Section 6. The collection and processing of thermal images are shown in Section 7. In Section 8, the experimental results and discussion are presented related to the change of brain activity of a mobile phone user. Section 9 proposes the use of complex data preprocessing, postprocessing, deep modeling, and analysis models by using intelligent methods. Finally, in Section 10, the paper is concluded.

1.2. Research Methodology

Extensive investigation, familiarity, and evaluation are crucial components in laying the groundwork for our suggested strategy. In order to handle and analyze heterogeneous data, we developed a sophisticated model based on mathematical and statistical techniques, and we then compared it to current state-of-the-art algorithms. In order to obtain these results, libraries were employed with existing algorithms. We reviewed the literature for a variety of study subjects and datasets and published the findings. These findings show that some of the outcomes are comparable to our suggested methodology.

The purpose of our study is to understand how mobile phones affect people in order to forward our efforts, which are described in this paper. In conclusion, because of the nature of the problem and the datasets that the algorithms are intended for, a true comparison is fairly challenging. In other terms, one may do better than the other in some situations, while the opposite results may occur in others. This article's focus does not enable for a thorough analysis and experimental investigation of each. A thorough evaluation of different methods is provided. Furthermore, it can be said that a more complex approach is required to solve the research issue, one that involves performing various experimental measurements, compiling statistical data, and using a computer model to explain some physiological effects brought on by electromagnetic wave exposure to the human head.

2. Related Work

This section discusses the main contributions of the current works. An assessment of the environmental and human health implications of base station and mobile phone radiation is provided [11]. A key invention that has changed people's lifestyles is the cell phone. With the widespread use of mobile phones in everyday life, the standard of living has significantly improved around the world. There have always been concerns about the effects of radio frequency radiation on humans, plants, and animals. Furthermore, it is alleged that the radiation emitted by mobile phones damages human health and jeopardizes the enjoyment and convenience derived from using the devices. The authors in [12] analyzed the changes that these smart phone technologies can bring to human–nature interactions while focusing on the outdoor behaviors of experienced outdoor users.

GHz [13] presented that the exposure of the human body to electromagnetic fields (EMF) with different frequencies can cause different biophysical effects. Thermal effects are typically minimal with frequencies less than 100 kHz; however, effects appear when increasing the frequencies. Smartphones communicate via high-frequency signals, and extended use of the generated electromagnetic field affects the skull. Additionally, irritability, memory impairment, weariness, anxiety, headaches, and disrupted sleep are primary indicators of changes in the body. It is believed that the changes caused by EMF are able to accumulate in the body under conditions of prolonged exposure.

As a result, pathologies, such as leukemia, brain tumors, and hormonal diseases, can develop. Research has investigated memory loss, Parkinson's and Alzheimer's disease, amyotrophic sclerosis, AIDS, and an increase in suicides in relation to EMF exposure [14]. Another consequence of exposure to EMF in people is the syndrome of premature aging of the body. Despite extensive investigations, there remain a variety of unknown and undiagnosed addictions in people induced by EMF. All of these impacts have been recorded using various research approaches.

These include the processing of thermal pictures to analyze thermal effects and the processing of EEG signals to assess brain activity [15]. To obtain a unified thorough evaluation of the impact of smart technology on humans, an intelligent approach for assessing various data is presented. To that end, this study proposes a framework for combining disparate data sets in order to assess the impact of smart technology on humans. Additionally, new methods for acquiring and evaluating empirical and experimental data are required to overcome the problem. A proposed paradigm for unification and intelligent solutions is effectively evaluated in this research for addressing difficulties.

3. Statistical Data Processing

It is feasible to collect data on the impacts of mobile devices on the psychological and physical health of the users to measure the impacts of active usage of smart technology. Correlation analysis was used to establish the relationships and the degree of dependence between individual variables. The most commonly used correlation coefficient is the Pearson coefficient (r) for linear correlation, which is calculated by the formula [16]:

$$r = \frac{P}{S_X S_Y} \quad (1)$$

where P—moment of the products; S_X—standard deviation of the variable X; and S_Y—standard deviation of the variable Y. The moment of the products (P) is calculated as:

$$P = \frac{\sum XY}{n-1} - \frac{\sum X \sum Y}{n(n-1)} \quad (2)$$

where $\sum X$—sum of X values; $\sum Y$—sum of Y values; $\sum XY$—sum of products of X and Y; and n—sample size.

Another statistical criterion that is successfully used to determine changes in the responses and/or conditions of subjects as a result of an experimental intervention is Student's t-test for related samples, which involves research design "before-and-after". It has the ability to work with small volumes of data, and there is measurement "before the intervention", measurement "after the intervention", and the recording of statistically significant differences in the values of the tested variables. The empirical value of the t-test is calculated by the formula [16]:

$$t_E = \frac{|\bar{d}|}{\sqrt{\frac{\sum d^2 - n\bar{d}^2}{n^2 - n}}} \quad (3)$$

where $d = X_2 - X_1$ is the difference between two measured values of each object, n is the number of observed objects, and df are the degrees of freedom $df = n - 1$.

Among the most powerful statistical techniques for studying causal relationships is ANOVA (Analysis of Variance). One-way ANOVA provides analysis of the variation of a quantitatively dependent variable—for example, the degree of internet addiction caused by an independent qualitative or quantitative variable—for example, the age group. According to the null hypothesis, ANOVA is used to test the assumption of whether several means are equal, allowing determination of not only the differences between them but also which exact mean values differ from the others.

Table 1 shows the formulas for calculating the one-way ANOVA. The notations are as follows: SSb—sum of between-group squares; SSw—sum of within-group squares; SST—total sum of squares; K—degrees of freedom; nj—size (number of measurements) for each of the k samples (groups); $\bar{x}_j$—sample mean for the j-th group; $\bar{x}$—total mean; $\bar{x}_{ij}$—mean of the i-th individual from the j-th group; and n—total sample size. From the presented Table 1, it is clear that the F-ratio is obtained by dividing the between-group mean square MS_b by the within-group mean square MS_w:

$$F = \frac{MS_b}{MS_w} \quad (4)$$

Therefore, the logic of ANOVA is based on the decomposition of the total variance of the variable into two key components: the between-group variance (deviations of the group means from the total arithmetic mean) and within-group variance (individual deviations of the values from the mean within a category (group)).

Table 1. One-way ANOVA [16].

Variance	Sum of Squares (SS)	K	Mean Square (MS)	F-Ratio
Between groups	$SS_b = \sum_{j=1}^{k} n_j (\bar{x}j - \bar{x})^2$	$k-1$	$MS_b = \frac{SS_b}{k-1}$	$F = \frac{MS_b}{MS_w}$
Within groups	$SS_w = \sum_{j=1}^{k} \sum_{i=1}^{n_j} (\bar{x}ij - \bar{x}j)^2$	$n-k$	$MS_w = \frac{SS_w}{n-k}$	
Total	$SS_T = \sum_{j=1}^{k} \sum_{i=1}^{n_j} (x_{ij} - \bar{x})^2$	$n-1$		

The Fisher's F-test is checked according to the significance level α (usually equal to or less than 0.05) and the degrees of freedom K, as follows: for the between-group variance $K_1 = k - 1$, where k is the number of groups compared (degrees of freedom of the numerator); and for the within-group variance $K_2 = n - k$, where n is the sample size (degrees of freedom of the denominator).

4. Measuring the Electromagnetic Field from a Smartphone

These measurements show the presence of electromagnetic fields generated by different models of GSM devices in different operating modes. Depending on where the measurements are made—outdoors or indoors, the results differ. The obtained values additionally vary depending on how far the smartphone is from the measuring equipment or from the distance to the base station, as well as what additional radio sources are nearby. For this purpose, experimental measurements were performed in which the GSM device was positioned at distances of 1 and 10 cm from the smartphone. The average measurement results are shown in Table 2. Measurements were obtained with Gigahertz HFE35C.

Table 2. EMF values generated by a GSM device.

GSM Operating Mode	Distance between GSM and HFE35C [μ W/m^2]	
	1 cm	10 cm
Outdoor		
Passive mode	2	2
Search mode	520	150
Conversation mode	515	230
Indoor (Second floor of a building)		
Passive mode	2	2
Search mode	640	220
Conversation mode	1550	530
Indoor (underground floor)		
Passive mode	2	2
Search mode	860	310
Conversation mode	Over 2000	1450

The data in Table 2 show that, in search and talk mode, the emission levels are many times higher than in passive mode. When ringing, the signal level is high for the first 20 s, and then decreases significantly. Depending on the location of the smartphone, the signal levels are different, and when indoors, the signal level may be above the normal values. The measurements were performed both indoors and in underground rooms, where the signal source from the base station was extremely weak, and, in order to achieve successful communication, the radiation level of the GSM device was at the maximum value to compensate for attenuation and to not let the conversation fail.

Studies have shown that the level of the electromagnetic field in urban conditions is many times higher than in rural areas. This confirms the assumption that the presence of different types of electrical devices and transmitters will lead to a significant increase in the background electromagnetic field. With the development of technology, this problem will deepen and become more relevant. One of the most serious generators of electromagnetic fields is the smartphone. The level of the electromagnetic field generated by these strongly depends on the mode of operation and the environment in which the phone is located. In some cases, the levels of electromagnetic fields exceed the regulated permissible levels. The proximity of these devices to the human head requires in-depth study of the influence of electromagnetic fields on the possible effects on the human body.

5. Specific Absorption Rate

The specific absorption rate (SAR) shows how much radiation is absorbed by human tissues when irradiated by an electromagnetic field. The SAR is a measure of the rate at which the radio-frequency energy from a mobile phone is absorbed by the human body [17].

The local SAR is calculated as the power loss dP_l absorbed in an infinitesimal mass dm in the following way:

$$SAR = \frac{dP_l}{dm} = \frac{\sigma_{eff} E_{rms}^2}{\rho} = \frac{J_{rms}^2}{\rho \sigma_{eff}} \quad (5)$$

where E_{rms} is the root mean square value of the electric field, J_{rms} is the current density. σ_{eff} is the effective conductivity of human brain tissue, and ρ is the tissue density. Therefore, the SAR unit of measurement is W/kg. Energy from electromagnetic fields is absorbed into the human tissues and warms them. This leads to another definition of SAR, namely:

$$SAR = c_p \frac{\Delta T}{\Delta t} \quad (6)$$

where c_p is the specific heat capacity of the tissue and ΔT is the change in temperature over a period of time Δt.

A distinction should be made between the instantaneous SAR and the permissible SARs, where an average value is measured for a given mass of tissue and a specified period of time. It is best to use a computer model to study the SAR and the thermal effects. The benefit of the model is that it visualizes the processes in depth.

6. Modeling for SAR Simulation

With the use of a computer model, it is feasible to thoroughly analyze SAR in the human body. This model may be used to research the effects of mobile phones on the human head since it can be used to visualize the processes of tissue absorption and heat deep within the human body. The characteristics of human tissues can be altered to imitate various age groups. The numerous tissues and bones that make up the human head model each have unique electromagnetic energy-absorption properties.

A mobile phone's characteristics can be changed to emulate various GSM device models. Numerous factors, including the antenna radiation pattern, transmitted signal strength, and signal frequency, are modifiable. The computer model's ability to see the depth of the human head, which can be utilized to analyze the absorption and warming processes in depth, is its most important feature.

For the proper functioning of the model, it is essential to know the biological characteristics of human tissues. The human body is composed of many organs and characterized by specific biological parameters that must be taken into account correctly in the model. The electromagnetic characteristics of the dielectric constant, magnetic permeability, and conductivity [18] should be properly defined for each modeled organ. The created computer model uses parameters that characterize the biological tissues of an adult. The shape of the human head was applied by the IEEE library and was loaded into the COMSOL Multiphysics software. The model was imported from a file named sar_in_human_head.mphbin [19,20].

The source of electromagnetic radiation was a model of a smartphone that was manually added. In the considered model, the location of the device was chosen to be on the left side of the head in order to facilitate the comparison of the obtained results with thermal images from our previous experimental studies. The mobile device was modeled at a distance of 1 cm from the head as shown in Figure 1.

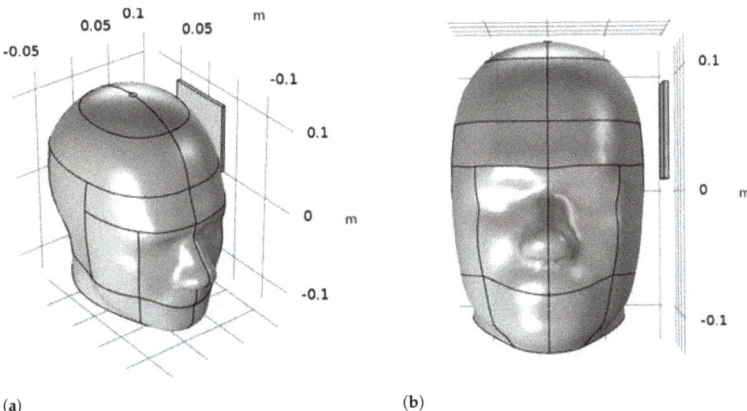

Figure 1. (a) and (b) Human head model and mobile device.

The electromagnetic parameters of the biological tissues of the human head were modeled through an interpolation function that uses the characteristics of the tissue inside the human head. The output for this function is directly taken from a file named sar_in_human_head_interp.txt. After simulation of the model, it is possible to estimate the SAR on any shape and tissue of the human body. When designing mobile devices, it is important to determine the amount of radiation that can be absorbed by the human body. The use of COMSOL Multiphysics and its radio frequency module allows a faster and more-efficient approach in the design of wireless devices that meet certain safety requirements. The local SAR value in the human head, calculated using the 900 MHz frequency equation, is shown in Figure 2.

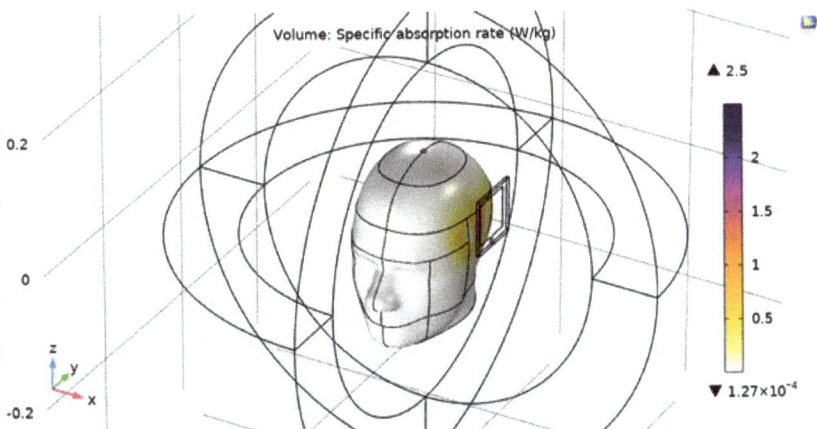

Figure 2. SAR visualization.

When talking to a mobile phone, the human head is very close to the phone, and the power of the emitted electromagnetic field is very high. Penetrating into a person's head, the electromagnetic field releases some of its energy, and the tissues in the head absorb this energy. Electromagnetic energy affects the particles in the tissue due to the electrical and magnetic components of the electromagnetic field. Visualization of the effects of penetration of the electromagnetic wave into the human head can be shown by means of incisions of the head at certain levels (Figure 3).

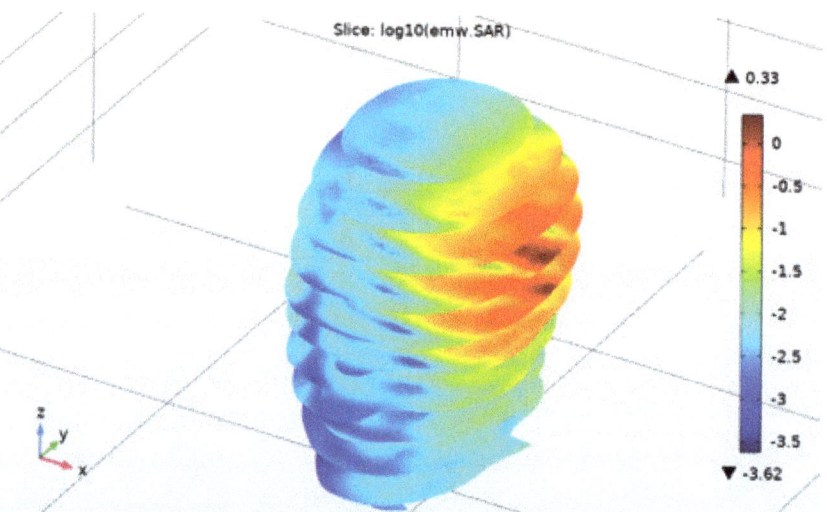

Figure 3. SAR visualization at different levels in the human head.

The strongest influence of the electromagnetic waves is in the head area, located in the immediate vicinity of the mobile device [17]. The greatest amount of energy is absorbed in this area, and the penetration into the human head is the greatest. The effects of exposure of the human body to radio frequency radiation mainly depend on the exposure time and the strength of electromagnetic fields. The penetration of the electromagnetic field into the depths of the human head depends on the frequency of the carrier signal. The higher this frequency, the faster it attenuates in space and the less it penetrates the human head. The highest values of absorption are observed on the surface of the human head. The developed model calculated only the local values of the SAR parameter. The maximum local SAR value is always higher than the maximum mean SAR value.

The amount of energy absorbed by the human head affects the temperature to which the tissues of the head are heated. The study of the processes of temperature distribution in the human head and on its surface is possible with the help of the created computer model using the COMSOL Multiphysics software. The frequency of the signal of the mobile device was selected to be 900 MHz. The transformation of the absorbed energy into heat was conducted with a biothermal equation. The change in temperature is a function of the physiological properties of biological tissues and blood circulation in the human body [21]. The thermal effects on and in the human head are shown in Figure 4.

Due to the created computer model, it is possible to study the processes of penetration of the electromagnetic field into the human head and the effects caused by this, thus, thoroughly simulating different situations and different characteristics of the head model and mobile phone characteristics. The visualization capabilities of the COMSOL Multiphysics software are impressive and allow a detailed view of the simulation results.

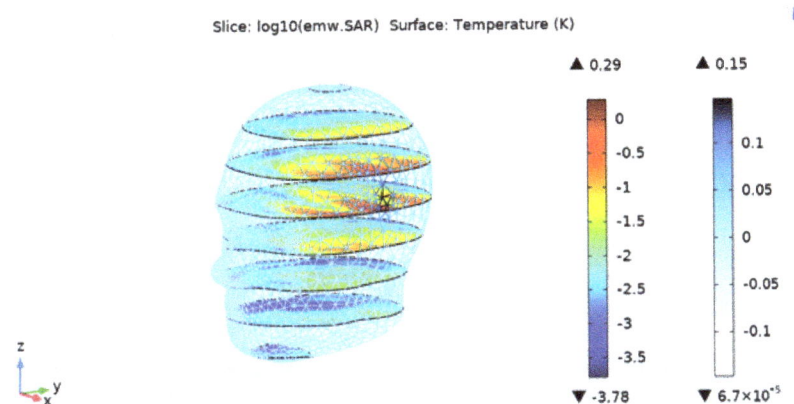

Figure 4. Visualization of the thermal effects in the human head for several horizontal layers.

7. Collection and Processing of Thermal Images

The impacts of the use of GSM devices on the physical condition of a person can be assessed by the thermal effects caused by the electromagnetic waves emitted by GSM devices. The experimental scenario includes a speaker with a GSM device for 20 min and a FLIR P640 thermal camera to capture their head in profile and full face. During the conversation, the GSM device was located about 1 cm from the head of the participant in the experiment, and the thermal camera was about 2 m away, focused on their head. The average room temperature was around 22 °C.

As a result of the 20 min conversation and the irradiation with the electromagnetic waves from the GSM device, the head of the participant in the experiment warms up by about 1–2 °C as can be seen from Figure 5. The increase in head temperature depends on the duration of the conversations. When talking for up to 30 s, no change in intracranial temperature is observed; however, when talking for more than 2 min, first, the ear begins to warm up and then the soft tissues around the ear. The increase in temperature is a result of prolonged irradiation of the human body with high-frequency radio signals from the GSM device.

The obtained results show that the temperature on the surface of the head is the highest and decreases in depth. The temperature change near the mobile phone is on the order of 0.6 °C and decreases rapidly inside the head. The thermal effects obtained from the model largely coincide with the results of a real experiment conducted with a thermal camera (Figure 5).

Averaging the temperature of the head before and after the experiment resulted in a temperature difference of about 1.3 °C. After checking the number of pixels exceeding the temperature of 34 °C before and after the experiment, we found that, after the experiment, the area heated above this value was three-times larger than before the experiment. The thermal images were processed using MATLAB. The study found that the temperature of the head on the side of the GSM device heated up much more than the other side. The areas around the ear, forehead, and neck heated up much more than the rest of the head.

The study of the processes of penetration of the electromagnetic field into the human head and the effects caused by this is an extremely important scientific task. The interaction between the human head and the electromagnetic radiation caused by cell phones can cause electric currents and electric fields in the human head, which can lead to negative health effects.

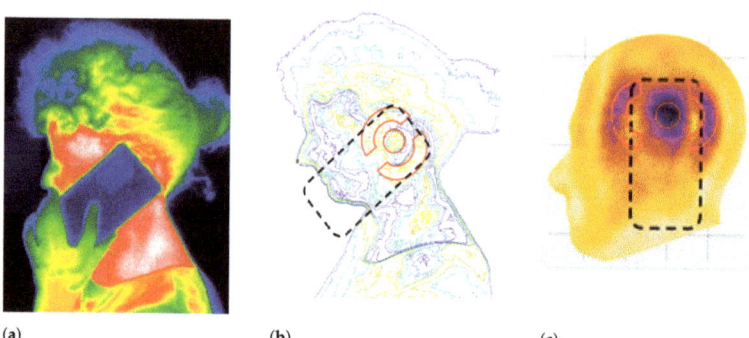

Figure 5. (a) Visualization of thermal effects in a human head before use of a GSM device; (b) visualization of thermal effects in a human head during use of a GSM device; and (c) visualization of thermal effects in a human head after use of a GSM device.

8. Experimental Results and Discussion

Electroencephalographs (EEGs), which measure electrical signals generated by the brain (brain waves), are used to study a person's brain activity. EEG signals are obtained as a result of the work of neurons in the human brain and can be intercepted using electrodes attached to the surface of the scalp [22–24].

A series of experiments were conducted to analyze the possible effects of the electromagnetic fields generated by smartphones on the activity of the human brain. Thirty volunteers (16 men (53.3%) and 14 women (46.7%) with an average age of 45.2 years) participated in the studies; however, we plan to increase these numbers in future studies among adults and children. The participants in the study stated that they were physically and mentally healthy, that they had not taken any medication before the tests, and that they were voluntarily undergoing these tests. The experiments were conducted in two stages.

The first stage involved studying the EEG signals of the subjects without using a mobile phone. The second stage of the experiment was performed while the subjects used a mobile phone (Figure 6). The EEG recordings from the two experiments were processed in the MATLAB environment in the time and frequency domain of the signal. The aim was to make a comparative analysis of the signal spectra from the two experiments.

Measures to reduce any other brain activity have been taken to assess the effect of cell phone electromagnetic radiation on a person's brain activity. The experiments were conducted in a quiet and cozy room, with the test subjects placed in comfortable armchairs with their eyes closed to reduce side stimuli. During the experiments, participants held the phone at a distance of about 1 cm away from the head, listening to a quiet countdown from one to one hundred, which was started by a researcher in another room. The aim of the experiment was to be as close as possible to a real conversation as shown in Figure 6.

A mobile phone with a SAR of 0.36 W/kg was used during the experiment. The experiment lasted about an hour with the first 30 min without a phone and the second 30 min with a phone. The obtained signals were filtered and divided into frequency ranges, respectively: delta δ (1–4 Hz), theta θ (4–8 Hz), alpha α (8–13 Hz), and beta β (13–32 Hz). With the help of the Pwelch function of the MATLAB program, the spectra of the signals before and after a call with a mobile device were obtained. The spectra of the two experiments for all electrodes were compared, and differences in the spectra were found at several measurement points (Figure 7).

Figure 6. Participant during the experiment.

At the points with the numbers T3, T5, and F7, which are the closest to the mobile phone, a significant change in the spectral activity of the brain was found. The largest change in the spectrum was found in T3, where the changes were in the theta, alpha, and beta frequency ranges. The changes in the spectra at points T5 and F7 were only in the theta and alpha ranges. Interestingly, this dependence was found in all participants in the experiments but to varying degrees.

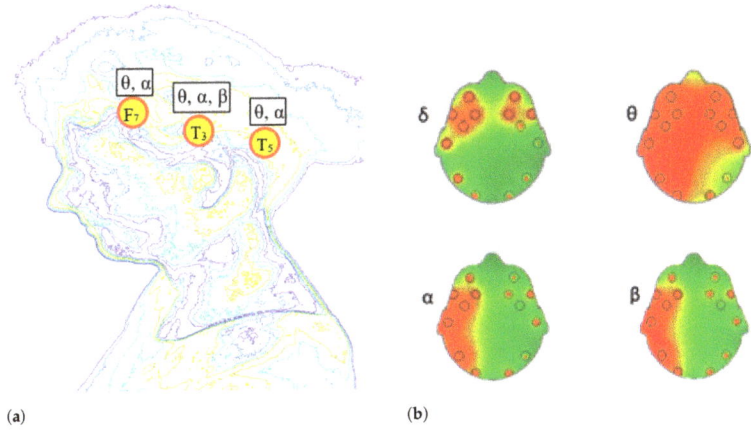

Figure 7. (**a**) Differences in the spectra by range and (**b**) different GSM ranges for delta, theta, alpha, and beta.

To compare the average spectral exposure with and without GSM for the ranges of delta δ (1–4 Hz), theta θ (4–8 Hz), alpha α (8–13 Hz), and beta β (13–32 Hz), Student's t-test for related samples was used (Howard, 2008). Statistically significant differences, where $p < 0.05$, are visualized in Figure 7.

The change in brain activity in a person's head on the side of a mobile phone has a short-term effect that is shown to be due to the operation of a mobile phone. If the *SAR* is studied and analyzed in more detail using a computer model, we expect that the changes in brain activity will be closely related to the location and amount of absorbed electromagnetic energy. This relationship has not been studied in sufficient depth and requires further research into the body's biophysical responses; thus, this is of interest for future research.

Accuracy

The degree of similarity between a measurement and its real value is referred to as accuracy. A limited number of EEG channels recorded concurrently can improve the accuracy. Two distinct types of tests were conducted to evaluate brain activity and lasted 30 min. The first experiment was performed without a cell phone (GSM); however, the second experiment included a mobile phone while subtracting brain activity. Interesting discoveries were made, and it was revealed that, while utilizing a cell phone, the accuracy was somewhat reduced.

Figure 8 demonstrates the accuracy and compares the average spectrum exposure with and without GSM for the ranges of delta (1–4 Hz), theta (4–8 Hz), alpha (8–13 Hz), and beta β (13–32 Hz). Figure 8a indicates that the accuracy without a mobile phone was 99.95%, whereas the accuracy with a mobile phone was 99.78% utilizing a delta range of (1–4 Hz). Figure 8b shows that, with the theta (4–8 Hz) frequency range, 99.88% accuracy was obtained without a mobile phone, whereas 99.69% accuracy was obtained with a mobile phone.

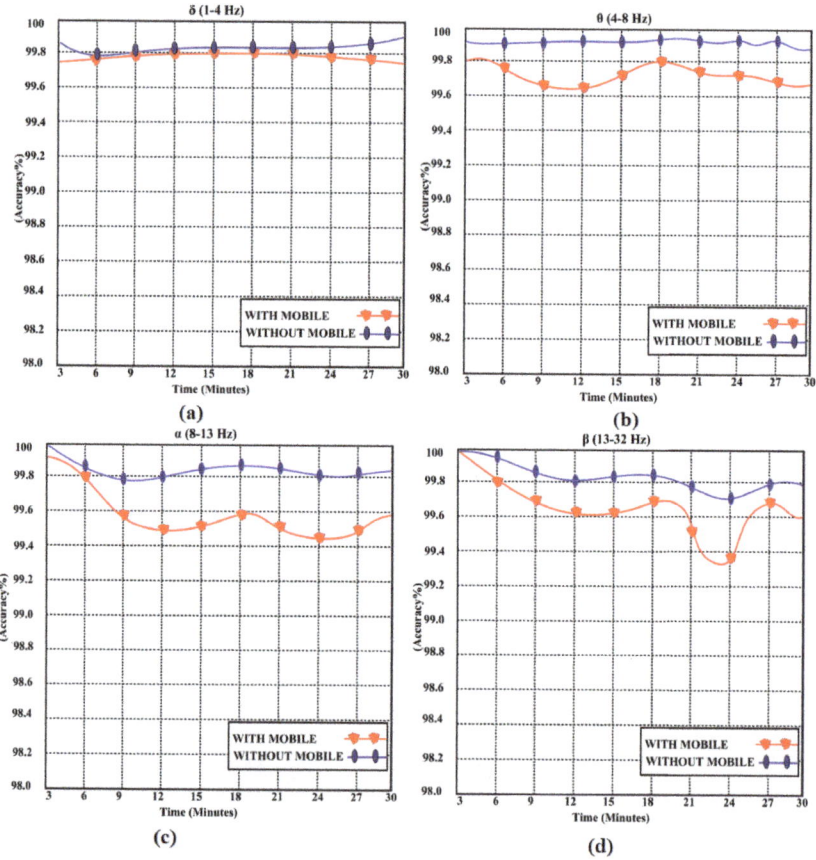

Figure 8. (**a**) The accuracy of the average spectrum exposure with and without GSM using the frequency range of delta δ (1–4 Hz). (**b**) The accuracy of the average spectrum exposure with and without GSM using the frequency range of theta ϑ (4–8 Hz). (**c**) The accuracy of the average spectrum exposure with and without GSM using the frequency range of alpha α (8–13 Hz). (**d**) The accuracy of the average spectrum exposure with and without GSM using the frequency range of beta β (13–32 Hz).

Figure 8c depicts the 99.81% accuracy with the alpha (8–13 Hz) range in the absence of a mobile phone. A cell phone, on the other hand, achieved 99.58% accuracy in the same frequency band. Figure 8d exhibits 99.80% accuracy without a mobile phone utilizing a beta (13–32 Hz) frequency range and 99.59% accuracy with a mobile phone. It was shown that the GSM had a negligible impact on the signal accuracy while monitoring brain activity.

9. Processing of Complex Data Analysis Models Using Intelligent Methods

Intelligent methods are the processes of gathering, modeling, and analyzing data in order to derive insights that may be used to make decisions.

9.1. Deep Knowledge Modeling and Constraint-Based Fast Preprocessing

The preprocessing of data is effectively utilized in different domains, such as number theory, cryptography, intelligent measurement, education, and bioinformatics. The chances of making an improvement will be quite slim without a comprehensive description of the surroundings. It is clear from working with description logic that logic-based modeling is challenging to control, that it is challenging to merge the logical and statistical phases of the data science cycle, and that their algorithmic complexity is often considerable.

On the other hand, it is possible to reason using the body of knowledge, and this capability enables the development of knowledge- and data-driven open systems. It is simple to combine the suggested study with the mentioned non-classical logical methodologies. More information is available in [25]. When discussing data-driven methodologies, artificial neural networks (ANNs), such as deep learning, are frequently used. In order to enhance the quality of human-like reasoning, this paper investigated a novel data-driven methodology that makes use of modeling and constraint fulfillment characteristics.

The constraint satisfaction methods are frequently used in data-preprocessing issues. A selection of data was applied aiming to complete preprocessing more efficiently, and the considered deep-modeling constraint satisfaction methods significantly improved this process. Currently, the following groups of novel logically-inspired constraints have been investigated in [25–27]. The mema method for control is named Puzzle but it significantly differs from the methods constructed for solving puzzles, such as [26–29].

The latter are ineffective because of the usage of random number strategies. The proposed Puzzle approach is easily combined with these and other methods [30] with the aim to increase their efficiency. Initially the classical constraint satisfaction methods can be applied with the purpose to form a closed focus area where certain data may be logically connected.

Let us focus on the considered two objects, ones of the many enclosed in the area from Figure 9. The closed 'focus/selection area' helps to reveal new knowledge concerning the enclosed objects. The data analysis concerning this case can reveal new knowledge, for example, that M implies N or that M has some relationship to N. The second case is the result of the classical link analysis and/or corresponding data mining applications. Some general disadvantages: the classical approach works with a priori given data and is not intended for the elaboration of open systems.

In practice, the constraints should be dynamically changed depending on the current knowledge/data. This becomes possible after the introduction of new types of non-classical constraints. Generally speaking, there should be new types of constraints introduced. Constraint violation is impossible in the classical case but this case should be reconstructed. Every rule/constraint could be defeated depending on the conditions. The new types of constraints make it possible. Somebody who exposed their body to radiation generally does not think about cancer that could occur 20 years later. Many other application problems arise in medical practice where the problems are gradually accumulating.

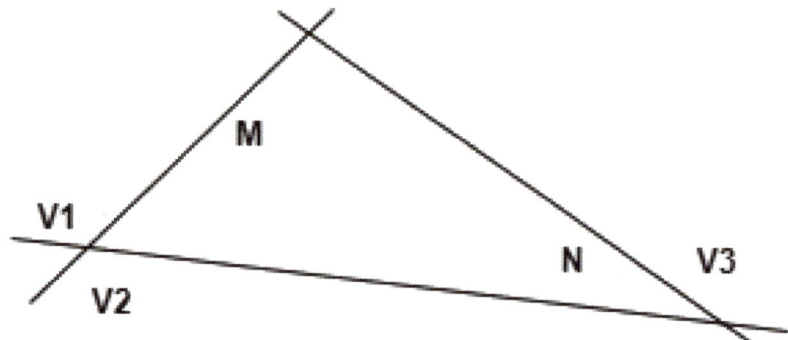

Figure 9. A set of three linear constraints constructs a closed area focusing on objects M and N.

With new conditions, additional questions arise: **why** the constraints are imposed, **what** and when violates it, **where** it could be defeated, and other use cases.

Binding, pointing, and crossword are the new groups of constraints. There exist many binding situations, and some of them have been researched in this article. The first case is when the maximum binding possibility is concentrated in the center of the area, and the distance from it is a function diminishing its value. The proposed research revealed that the binding may depend on certain conditions, and it may also influence the features of all objects contained in its area: the linearity/range/the region of the usage and/or other properties could be defeated. The general case is depicted in Figure 10 where curves B and D are the bindings concerning the searched goal $G1$.

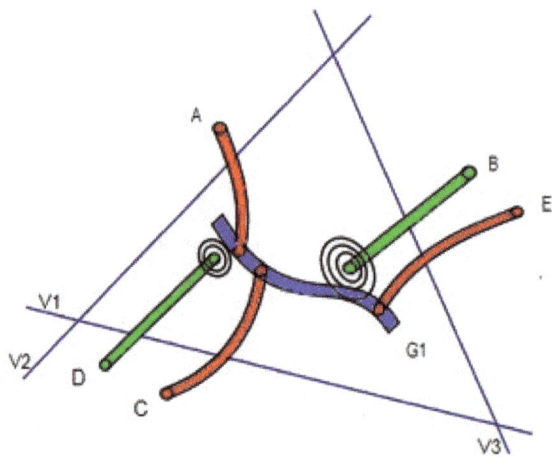

Figure 10. A set of nonlinear constraints in combination with the proposed three groups of logically-based constraints.

Association methods are generalized in binding constraint theories [31–36]. Associations are purposed for finding implicative classical form of rules, while the binding constraints explore any form of causal relationships. We investigated only a few binding constraint groups but they were very useful as a data-science modeling tool.

1. Denote A is bound to B if there is proven evidence of any form of causal relationship between them. The implication is also included in this case.

    Should the type of the causal form should be described in special forms of meta-knowledge attached to the corresponding binding case? For example, some people are very sensitive to long phone calls. The personal binding constraint 'phone call > 10 min'—>'tired' or 'noise in the head' should be added to the modeling case. The metaknowledge should include the complex of disease history, a nervous state, a history of complaints, and corresponding factors. Semantic reasoners are very helpful in binding information processing.

2. A frequently used form of binding is 'the solution to the problem is somewhere here'. This case is depicted in B and D areas in Figure 9. In this case, type-1 fuzzy systems are effectively used in combination with binding constraint modeling. The most possible solution zone is situated in the binding very center. Accordingly, the distance from the center diminishes the possibility to bind the corresponding features. For example, the center of this binding area could be the area where is the pain located.

3. The above quoted cases did not influence the other modeling methods schematically depicted in Figures 9 and 10. In many cases, this is not enough. In this case, the application of the binding zone introduces defeasible reasoning in the zone and/or around it. The proposed forms of defeasible reasoning are discussed in [37], and the introduction to this research is briefly presented below. In our medical modeling practice, every part of knowledge could be defeated and/or exchanged with other knowledge forms.

4. The cases 1–3 are unconditional cases. In practice, many binding relations exist only in some special conditions: if $|T_1 \star T_2 \cdots T_k$ are true, then A is bound with type 1, 2 or 3 to B, where $\star$ denotes a logical operation conjunction or disjunction. The corresponding T_i are a priori given.

5. The variant of type-4 binding was considered where the binding control is data-driven and C_i are formed by using ANNs.

6. Binding areas where the constraint satisfaction rules could be defeated are shown below.

In Figure 11, an example is shown where the linearity of a classical constraint satisfaction case is fuzzified/defeated in the considered binding constraint area.

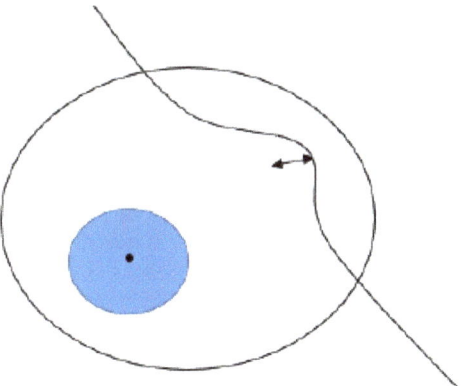

Figure 11. Type-6 binding constraint and its influence on classical linear constraints.

Agents, especially in health-oriented systems, can not effectively behave using a set of algorithms. In certain conditions, every solution may be modified or changed. One of the frequent forms of change is defeasible reasoning. In practice, the software agent should defeat its goals aiming at better performance. Every rule should be gradually improved and modified and/or suddenly changed depending on the situation in a data-driven way. The defeasible scheme controls the usage of many unified exclusions and other defeasible knowledge forms.

Let a Horn clause describe Rule (7).

$$B \leftarrow \wedge_{i \in I} A_i \tag{7}$$

where the form of the rule is suitable for the backward chaining. This rule is changed when an exclusion $E(C, Ak)$ is attached to Equation (7): if C is true, the corresponding Ak is defeated, which means that its truth value is reverted Equation (8) or it disappears from the antecedent Equation (9) because its significance for 'B is true' is defeated to zero. Furthermore, the variant Equation (10) is researched where the defeated value is changed by another formula.

$$\frac{B \leftarrow \wedge_{i=1}^{z} A_i, C, E(c, A_k), \neg A_k \leftarrow C}{B \leftarrow A_1 \wedge A_2 \wedge \cdots A_{k-1} \wedge \neg A_k \wedge \cdots A_z} \tag{8}$$

$$\frac{C, B \leftarrow \wedge_{i=1}^{z} A_i, E(C, A_k)}{B \leftarrow A_1 \wedge \cdots A_{k-1} \wedge A_{k+1} \wedge \cdots A_z} \tag{9}$$

$$\frac{C, B \leftarrow \wedge_{i=1}^{z} A_i, E(C, A_k)}{B \leftarrow A_1 \wedge \cdots A_{k-1} \wedge (A_k \forall C) \wedge A_{k+1} \cdots A_z} \tag{10}$$

One of the frequently used health cases is where both antecedent and consequent are changed in the defeated rule. The other frequent case produces a fact from the defeated rule, and this fact contains a non-implicative relation. The defeasible process explores non-classical rule forms, one of them is 'Ak is defeated if C is true in $E(C, Ak)$'. Detailed information concerning this topic is given in book chapter [25].

The defeasible reasoning is applied to test the strength of the investigated process and of its significant features. The quoted binding and pointing constraints significantly improve the defeasible processes. The pointing (indicating) constraints are applied in order to determine both the distance to the goal and the direction of the research. Furthermore, the history of the research process can influence on the pointing direction.

The group of pointing constraints can be considered as a generalization of the classical systems of goal/target or fitness functions. In contrast to the classical cases, pointing constraints are data-driven by nature and revert to being direction-driven with accumulated data. For example, if there is information that there was a pain, the data on its coordinates are probably no longer valid. In this case, the exact conclusion is in doubt until enough proof is accumulated.

The third researched constraint is named 'crossword'. It is depicted by the triple $\{A, C, E\}$ in Figure 10. This type models the process of reasoning on the unknown things based on the accumulated knowledge. In such a way, parts of the searched goal have been found, and by using original evolutionary Puzzle method, a trial to complete the whole solution is attempted. The internal links between the elements of $\{A, C, E\}$ are studied using different combinations of the quoted binding and pointing modeling.

Many algorithms and data-driven approaches were investigated with the aim to find any binding or pointing solution enlarging the set of the known part from $G1$. Generally speaking, every pointing constraint was used aiming to diminish the set of selected/processed data and knowledge: the 'selection focus' should be narrowed. Pointing to a certain part of the binding area improves the reasoning process.

- Type 1: this pointing constraint is based on a priori given special conditions: if $T_1 \star T_2 \cdots \star T_n$ are true, then pointing value of Y is formed, where $\star$ denotes a logical operation conjunction or disjunction.
- Type 2: this pointing constraint is based on conditions: if $T_1 \star T_2 \cdots T_n$ are true, then pointing value of Y is formed, and T_i have been formed in a data-driven manner. Y is gradually changing its direction and value.

On the other hand, in mobile signal processing applications, the pointing constraints show to the center of corresponding binding area. The binding cases frequently concern best signal processing practice, good medical practice, and many analogical examples. In many cases, little but important signal changes may be traced in this way, where neuro-fuzzy deep learning methods are successfully able to be combined with binding approaches. For example, the pointing constraints have been used for descriptions and maximization of the effectiveness of specific brain–computer interface features and communications to other medical procedures and devices.

Please note that the good practice examples were researched in coordination with possible bad practice situations, where they are described by using a combination of pointing and binding constraints. The considered novel modeling by using constraints does not change, in any direction, the considered biomedical research schemes but improves the effectiveness.

9.2. Analysis on Preprocessing and Postprocessing Features

The pointing constraints in this article concern the research on interconnection of electromagnetic and thermal influence, the influence of thermal-located radiation on skin/brain aging, an exploration of possibilities of overreaction to mobile radiation in small groups of people, and the influence of emotional state of researched people to their reaction. Noise in the head, forgetting, loss of concentration, bad mood, and slight disorientation symptoms after the call are not the factors of the binding process but they should be further investigated one by one of in a group with other medical data.

The binding constraints aim to model the facts how the size of the overheated area is connected to the damage effect, why the spots T3, T5, and F7 are the most promising places to estimate the aging affects, and the possible influence of radiation and fields on brain tissue processes, some of them presumably unknown. Other binding modeling options concern the research on mobile radiation in smoke, wet, and dirty air environments, and the binding of high-level SAR signals to the spectral power of EEG/electromagnetic field absorbtion.

Human health problems are a result of long-term dynamic process in nonlinear, and dispersive tissues. Potentially important outcomes may be obtained during long-term research on the accumulated effects on humans after 20, 30, and even 50 years of mobile phone usage. This type of work could not be executed manually, Deep Learning (DL) should be applied instead. The proposed deep modeling approaches should help to trace and process tiny changes and gradually re-evaluate their significance.

Significant ANOVA variables should be reinforced by the proposed types of pointing and binding constraints aiming to improve the constant knowledge elicitation, accumulation and processing possibilities. In this way the principles of open systems had been applied to statistical type of research making it more data-driven. The good practice database contains facts that many people are using hands-free,microphone,Bluetooth and other options where the mobile device is far from the head. This does not mean that the problem has an easy solution: the same sort of radiation still remains just near the human body.

Aiming at long-term search the binding constraints are set to search allergic reactions, oncology-like or blood problems, stomach infections, pain picture, influenza history, and Alzheimer symptoms. The history before and after the active start of the mobile era should be compared. The earlier history of PC usage also is included in the research. As a result, human-like reasoning is inspired: the radiation implies slightly higher temperatures in skin and tissue, and how high should be this difference to be physically noticed by the patient in very cold or cold environment.

This is an experimental attempt to bind the mobile radiation to any noticeable influence on the human body. In the positive case the binding/pointing areas may be enlarged by using other types of constraints. If the patient has any specific problems just after the long calls, he should be analyzed in the lab aiming to bind the problem to mobile radiation as a research hypothesis.

The aging and other human body features depend on many personal factors and history. This is frequently used to oppose to many of the medical research data in the field. As a whole it is rather easy to prove or destroy any hypothesis from the scope in a narrow research concentrated only to one group of facts and features. The proposed deep modeling options helped us to escape from this situation.

The complex research involving DL in perspective will be processed by software agents. In such a way, the types of constraints should be changed depending on the situation. As a result, powerful data science will analyze symptoms in each case by using the accumulated medical data and knowledge. The early eradication of irrelevant medical facts and hypotheses should be preserved by the use of software agents.

The use of the proposed data-science techniques opens up the prospect of greatly reducing manual effort and paving the way for intelligent medical research that focuses on combinations made up of minor and ancillary aspects. Sometimes little details might alter the overall course of the investigation.

10. Conclusions

We developed a novel data-science technique to identify the detrimental impacts of electromagnetic radiation from mobile devices on the human body. The proposed method for analyzing heterogeneous data is based on mathematical and statistical methodologies (thermal imaging and electroencephalograms). The proposed solution combines the ANOVA statistical method with deep modeling and rapid preprocessing approaches, such as binding/pointing/crossword constraints. Several tests were conducted utilizing the Pwelch function of MATLAB software, both with and without a mobile device. Each experiment was 30 min long.

The resulting signals were filtered and classified into four frequency ranges: delta (1–4 Hz), theta (4–8 Hz), alpha (8–13 Hz), and beta (13–32 Hz). The accuracy was determined for each frequency range with and without a mobile device based on the collected signals. The findings demonstrate that the emission of electromagnetic radiation from mobile devices has an effect on the signal frequency range accuracy. The presence of irradiation leads to an increase in the amplitude of brain signals in different frequency ranges. Furthermore, the results show that improved accuracy was reached without the use of a mobile device for each frequency band.

The proposed approach has limitations because it increases the computational complexity due to obtaining heterogeneous data. However, this issue can be resolved using a data-mining approach. In the future, different Quality-of-Service parameters (e.g., energy consumption, time complexity, and reliability) will be examined in the future. Furthermore, the proposed approach will also be compared to state-of-the-art approaches: IoT based mobile monitoring framework for hyper-local PM2 [1], and cognitive emotion pre-occupation method [38].

Author Contributions: M.G., conceptualization, writing, idea proposal, methodology, and results; V.J. and I.G., data curation, software development, and preparation; A.R., Writing, results, software development, preparation, submission, review and editing; M.A. and B.A., review, manuscript preparation, and visualization; D.B. review and editing. All authors have read and agreed to this version of the manuscript.

Funding: This work is supported by the Bulgarian National Science Fund, project title "Synthesis of a dynamic model for assessing the psychological and physical impacts of excessive use of smart technologies", KP-06-N 32/4/07.12.2019, led by Magdalena Garvanova.

Institutional Review Board Statement: Not applicable.

Informed Consent Statement: Not applicable.

Data Availability Statement: The data that supports the findings of this research is publicly available as indicated in the reference.

Acknowledgments: This work was supported by the Bulgarian National Science Fund, project title "Synthesis of a dynamic model for assessing the psychological and physical impacts of excessive use of smart technologies", KP-06-N 32/4/07.12.2019, led by Magdalena Garvanova.

Conflicts of Interest: The authors declare no conflict of interest.

References

1. Swaminathan, S.; Guntuku, A.V.S.; Sumeer, S.; Gupta, A.; Rengaswamy, R. Data science and IoT based mobile monitoring framework for hyper-local PM2. 5 assessment in urban setting. *Build. Environ.* **2022**, *225*, 5–34. [CrossRef]
2. ur Rehman, M.H.; Liew, C.S.; Wah, T.Y.; Khan, M.K. Towards next-generation heterogeneous mobile data stream mining applications: Opportunities, challenges, and future research directions. *J. Netw. Comput. Appl.* **2017**, *79*, 1–24 [CrossRef]
3. Razaque, A.; Rizvi, S.S. Secure data aggregation using access control and authentication for wireless sensor networks. *Comput. Secur.* **2017**, *70*, 532–545. [CrossRef]
4. Liu, X.; Chen, Y. Group effect-based privacy-preserving data aggregation for mobile crowdsensing. *Comput. Netw.* **2023**, *222*, 109507. [CrossRef]
5. Chen, Z.; Li, P.; Jin, Y.; Bharule, S.; Jia, N.; Li, W.; Song, X.; Shibasaki, R.; Zhang, H. Using mobile phone big data to identify inequity of aging groups in transit-oriented development station usage: A case of Tokyo. *Transp. Policy* **2023**, *132*, 65–75. [CrossRef]
6. Shah, I.A.; Jhanjhi, N.Z.; Amsaad, F.; Razaque, A. The Role of Cutting-Edge Technologies in Industry 4.0. In *Cyber Security Applications for Industry 4.0*; Chapman and Hall/CRC: Boca Raton, FL, USA, 2022; pp. 97–109.
7. Ma, T.; Wang, H.; Wei, M.; Lan, T.; Wang, J.; Bao, S.; Ge, Q.; Fang, Y.; Sun, X. Application of smart-phone use in rapid food detection, food traceability systems, and personalized diet guidance, making our diet more health. *Food Res. Int.* **2022**, *152*, 110918. [CrossRef]
8. Jwo, J.S.; Lin, C.S.; Lee, C.H. Smart technology–driven aspects for human-in-the-loop smart manufacturing. *Int. J. Adv. Manuf. Technol.* **2021**, *114*, 1741–1752. [CrossRef]
9. Hareem, A.; Dahri, S.; Hafiz, M.Y. Phrase of attentiveness: Use of smart phone applications for mental health concerns. *Ann. Med. Surg.* **2022**, *82*, 104783.
10. Jayaraju, N.; Kumar, M.P.; Sreenivasulu, G.; Prasad, T.L.; Lakshmanna, B.; Nagalaksmi, K.; Madakka, M. Mobile phone and base stations Radiation and its effects on Human health and environment: A Review. *Sustain. Technol. Entrep.* **2022**, *114*, 100031. [CrossRef]
11. Irma, A.; Fischer, A.; Duckett, D.; Wal, R.V.D. Information technology and the optimisation of experience—The role of mobile devices and social media in human-nature interactions. *Geoforum* **2021**, *122*, 55–62.
12. Garvanova, M.; Shishkov, B.; Vladimirov, S. Mobile devices: Effect on human health. In Proceedings of the Seventh International Conference on Telecommunications and Remote Sensing, New York, NY, USA, 22–26 April 2018; pp. 101–104.
13. Directive 2013/35/EU on Electromagnetic Fields. 2014. Available online: https://ncpha.government.bg/ (accessed on 3 January 2023).
14. Masomeh, B.; Riahi, S.M.; Bazrafshan, N.; Gamble, H.R.; Rostami, A. Toxoplasma gondii infection and risk of Parkinson and Alzheimer diseases: A systematic review and meta-analysis on observational studies. *Acta Trop.* **2019**, *196*, 165–171.
15. Kim, J.H.; Yu, D.H.; Huh, Y.H.; Lee, E.H.; Kim, H.G.; Kim, H.R. Long-term exposure to 835 MHz RF-EMF induces hyperactivity, autophagy and demyelination in the cortical neurons of mice. *Sci. Rep.* **2017**, *7*, 41129. [CrossRef] [PubMed]
16. Garvanova, M. Statistical data processing and data analysis with SPSS. In *Sofia: Za Bukvite—O Pismeneh*; Institute of Balkan Studies with Center for Tracology—Bulgarian Academy of Sciences: Sofia, Bulgaria, 2014.
17. Stanković, V.; Jovanović, D.; Krstić, D.; Cvetković, N. Electric field distribution and SAR in human head from mobile phones. In Proceedings of the ninth International Symposium on Advanced Topics in Electrical Engineering (ATEE), Bucharest, Romania, 7–9 May 2015; IEEE: New York, NY, USA, 2015; pp. 392–397.
18. Stanković, V.; Jovanović, D.; Ilie, S.; Marković, V. *Electric Field Distribution in Human Head*; CEMEMC: Timisoara, Romania, 2014.
19. Griesmer, F. Specific Absorption Rate (SAR) in the Human Brain. Available online: https://www.comsol.com/blogs/specific-absorption-rate-sar-human-brain/ (accessed on 12 June 2022).
20. Patel, D. Measuring the SAR of a Human Head Next to a Wi-Fi Antenna. Available online: https://www.comsol.com/blogs/measuring-the-sar-of-a-human-head-next-to-a-wi-fi-antenna/ (accessed on 12 June 2022).
21. Zaretsky, D.V.; Romanovsky, A.A.; Zaretskaia, M.V.; Molkov, Y.I. Tissue oxidative metabolism can increase the difference between local temperature and arterial blood temperature by up to 1.3 oc: Implications for brain, brown adipose tissue, and muscle physiology. *Temperature* **2018**, *5*, 22–35. [CrossRef] [PubMed]
22. Garvanova, M.; Garvanov, I.; Borissova, D. The influence of electromagnetic fields on human brain. In Proceedings of the 2020 21st International Symposium on Electrical Apparatus & Technologies (SIELA), Bourgas, Bulgaria, 3–6 June 2020; IEEE: New York, NY, USA, 2020; pp. 1–4.
23. Garvanova, M.; Garvanov, I.; Trapkova, D.; Nedelchev, K.; Borissova, D.; Dimitrov, G.; Nurassyl Kerimbayev, Galina Tkach, Zeinullayeva, I. Effects of Mobile Phone Electromagnetic Fields on Human Brain Activity. In Proceedings of the tenth International Conference on Telecommunications and Remote Sensing, Online, 15–16 November 2021; pp. 31–36.

24. Garvanova, M.; Garvanov, I.; Jotsov, V. Data Science Modeling and Constraint-Based Data Selection for EEG Signals Denoising Using Wavelet Transforms. In *Advances in Intelligent Systems Research and Innovation*; Springer: Cham, Switzerland, 2022; pp. 241–267.
25. Jotsov, V.S. Proposals for Knowledge Driven and Data Driven Applications in Security Systems. In *Innovative Issues in Intelligent Systems*; Springer: Cham, Switzerland, 2016; pp. 231–293.
26. Makridis, M.; Papamarkos, N. A new technique for solving puzzles. *IEEE Trans. Syst. Man Cybern. Part B* **2009**, *40*, 789–797. [CrossRef]
27. Levitin, A. Algorithmic puzzles: History, taxonomies, and applications in human problem solving. *J. Probl. Solving* **2017**, *10*, 1. [CrossRef]
28. Alajlan, N. Solving square jigsaw puzzles using dynamic programming and the hungarian procedure. *Am. J. Appl. Sci.* **2009**, *6*, 1941. [CrossRef]
29. Jun, S.; Kochan, O.V.; Jotsov, V.S. Methods of reducing the effect of the acquired thermoelectric inhomogeneity of thermocouples on temperature measurement error. *Meas. Tech.* **2015**, *58*, 327–331. [CrossRef]
30. Jotsov, V.S.; Iliev, E. Applications of advanced analytics methods in SAS enterprise miner. In *Intelligent Systems' 2014*; Springer: Cham, Switzerland, 2015; pp. 413–429.
31. Jotsov, V.S. Machine self-learning applications in security systems. In Proceedings of the sixth IEEE International Conference on Intelligent Data Acquisition and Advanced Computing Systems, Prague, Czech Republic, 15–17 September 2011; IEEE: New York, NY, USA, 2011; Volume 2, pp. 727–732.
32. Abhinav, D.; Aroyo, A.M.; Dautenhahn, K.; Smith, S.L. A survey of multi-agent Human—Robot Interaction systems. *Robot. Auton. Syst.* **2023**, *161*, 1043356.
33. Jotsov, V.; Sgurev, V. Applications in intelligent systems of knowledge discovery methods based on human–machine interaction. *Int. J. Intell. Syst.* **2008**, *23*, 588–606. [CrossRef]
34. Marinova, I.; Jotsov, V. Node-based system for optimizing the process of creation ff intelligent agents for intrusion detection and analysis. In Proceedings of the 2018 International Conference on Intelligent Systems (IS), Funchal, Portugal, 25–27 September 2018; IEEE: New York, NY, USA, 2011; pp. 557–563.
35. Agrawal, R.; Imieliński, T.; Swami, A. Mining association rules between sets of items in large databases. In Proceedings of the 1993 ACM SIGMOD International Conference on Management of Data, Washington, DC, USA, 25–28 May 1993; pp. 207–216.
36. Webb, G.I. OPUS: An efficient admissible algorithm for unordered search. *J. Artif. Intell. Res.* **1995**, *3*, 431–465. [CrossRef]
37. Jotsov, V.; Kochan, O.; Jun, S. Decreasing Influence of the Error Due to Acquired Inhomogeneity of Sensors by the Means of Artificial Intelligence. In *Practical Issues of Intelligent Innovations*; Springer: Cham, Switzerland, 2018; pp. 89–130.
38. Jianxun, C.; Qaisar, S.; Shah, Z.; Jalil, A. Attention or distraction? The impact of mobile phone on users' psychological well-being *Front. Psychol.* **2021**, *12*, 612127.

Disclaimer/Publisher's Note: The statements, opinions and data contained in all publications are solely those of the individual author(s) and contributor(s) and not of MDPI and/or the editor(s). MDPI and/or the editor(s) disclaim responsibility for any injury to people or property resulting from any ideas, methods, instructions or products referred to in the content.

Article

A Flexible Session-Based Recommender System for e-Commerce

Michail Salampasis [1,*], Alkiviadis Katsalis [1], Theodosios Siomos [1], Marina Delianidi [1], Dimitrios Tektonidis [1], Konstantinos Christantonis [1], Pantelis Kaplanoglou [1], Ifigeneia Karaveli [1], Chrysostomos Bourlis [2] and Konstantinos Diamantaras [1]

1 Department of Information and Electronic Engineering, International Hellenic University, 57400 Sindos, Greece
2 Arx.NET S.A., Leontos Sofou 18, 54626 Thessaloniki, Greece
* Correspondence: msa@ihu.gr

Abstract: Research into session-based recommendation systems (SBSR) has attracted a lot of attention, but each study focuses on a specific class of methods. This work examines and evaluates a large range of methods, from simpler statistical co-occurrence methods to embeddings and SotA deep learning methods. This paper analyzes theoretical and practical issues in developing and evaluating methods for SBSR in e-commerce applications, where user profiles and purchase data do not exist. The major tasks of SBRS are reviewed and studied, namely: prediction of next-item, next-basket and purchase intent. For physical retail shopping where no information about the current session exists, we treat the previous baskets purchased by the user as previous sessions drawn from a loyalty system. Mobile application scenarios such as push notifications and calling tune recommendations are also presented. Recommender models using graphs, embeddings and deep learning methods are studied and evaluated in all SBRS tasks using different datasets. Our work contributes a number of very interesting findings. Among all tested models, LSTMs consistently outperform other methods of SBRS in all tasks. They can be applied directly because they do not need significant fine-tuning. Additionally, they naturally model the dynamic browsing that happens in e-commerce web applications. On the other hand, another important finding of our work is that graph-based methods can be a good compromise between effectiveness and efficiency. Another important conclusion is that a "temporal locality principle" holds, implying that more recent behavior is better suited for prediction. In order to evaluate these systems further in realistic environments, several session-based recommender methods were integrated into an e-shop and an A/B testing method was applied. The results of this A/B testing are in line with the experimental results, which represents another important contribution of this paper. Finally, important parameters such as efficiency, application of business rules, re-ranking issues, and the utilization of hybrid methods are also considered and tested, providing comprehensive useful insights into SBRS and facilitating the transferability of this research work to other domains and recommendation scenarios.

Keywords: next-item and next-basket recommendations; graph-based recommendations; purchase intent; e-commerce; LSTM-RNN

1. Introduction

A pleasant online shopping experience depends on factors such as convenience, comfort, product findability. Some of these constituents of success rely on researchers conducting usage analysis of an e-commerce application in order to improve its design [1], with these factors ranging from good typography, product photography and elegant and clean checkout forms, to personalized website structure [2]. Others, such as managing information overload, finding interesting, and related or alternative products in e-commerce sites, depend on good retrieval and recommendation methods [3]

As a response to this last need, recommender systems (RS) have become fundamental tools for conducting effective e-commerce. They provide customers with personalized recommendations in searching for additional products. RS collect and model past user transactions, and potentially other features such as location, demographic profiles and other people's preferences. Several models for RS of that conventional type have been proposed and proved their efficacy. Some examples are content-based [4] and collaborative filtering [5] systems. These research methods make use of the long-term user profiles that are logged every time customers visit an e-commerce site.

However, these conventional RS methods have some important limitations. Firstly, in many e-commerce applications, long-term user models are simply not viable for several reasons: new users visiting for the first-time, or not being required to have user IDs, or choosing not to login for privacy or transaction speediness reasons will disrupt the functioning of these models. However, there are more drawbacks. Focusing on a community's long-term preferences ignores short-term transactional patterns, interest, and temporal shifts. This generally degrades ability to understand the intrinsic nature of a user's behavior in her/his current ongoing session.

To address these issues, session-based recommender systems (SBRS) have emerged. In the context of e-commerce, a session can be seen as a single episode that includes visiting several web pages and viewing items, ending potentially with multiple purchased items in one shopping transaction. The same idea can equally serve other domains such as in linear TV programming [6], next point of interest assessments (POI), or movie and next song recommendations. SBRS solely rely on session-specific information and the user's most recent activities. The most recent interactions the user has had with the web application, or other sorts of information that may be acquired or inferred during a session, should thus be the basis for successful suggestions. These details may include, for example, how a user arrived at the website, how long they stayed on previous pages, short-term community popularity patterns [7], browsing patterns [8] or the ability to predict a customer's intent in real time [9]. A simpler SBRS strategy is to merely utilize the currently available item and community-observed patterns, i.e., suggestions in the form of "people who viewed/bought this item also viewed/bought this item". However, more advanced session-based methods should consider all of the user's previous session activities in addition to the most recent item they have viewed. A thorough study of a current session may be performed by considering the possibility that additional action categories, such as searching, clicking, and cart viewing, were also included in these earlier acts.

The context we described above defines how to recommend in these scenarios. Another important consideration is to inquire what the main tasks are within these scenarios, in other words what can be recommended. The next-item or the next-basket recommendations are candidate tasks, depending on whether the recommended items are for the current running session or for the next one, respectively, if session boundaries are defined. The following events or actions should be recommended if there are not any obvious session boundaries, as in music listening apps (recommend the next movie to be watched).

Another important task in e-commerce is to establish a model of how customers behave, and to predict during a session whether the user has real purchase intent or to determine the cart abandonment probability in real time. If these events could be predicted effectively, then conversion rates would be improved if marketing would be applied and incentives would be offered. Examples of such stimuli are coupons, price discounts that are valid for a short period, and other incentives. In fact, various recommendation tasks can run complementarily to preference assessments.

Flexible recommendation systems (FRES) https://www.fres-project.gr/, accessed on 20 February 2023, refer to a three-year research project that was funded to investigate the effectiveness of several methods and algorithms for SBRS in e-commerce, retail and web services. Several datasets and settings were used to test the effectiveness and the robustness of various SBRS methods in various tasks, namely in establishing next-item, next-basket and purchase intent [10]. Additionally, a testing component was integrated into an e-commerce site to allow evaluation in a realistic environment. Additionally, several recommenders have been tested in mobile applications. Another aim was also to study the efficiency and other practical parameters, such as the training parameters, processing, and maintenance costs of different SBRS methods.

At the beginning of the project, we studied the concept of modeling anonymous sequential interactions in e-commerce and reviewed relevant prior work. Afterwards, we implemented and tested various forms of SBRS methods. Several types of recurrent neural networks (RNN/LSTM) were created, and their models were evaluated alongside those of other session-based recommenders that utilize various embedding techniques to represent items (Item2Vec, Doc2Vec). Furthermore, we proposed a framework to enable the hybrid application of text and product views sequences. Additionally, the core LSTM model was extended by adding an embedding layer before the LSTM layer. Finally, we used various reranking methods to improve the results of the basic recommenders using item categories.

To investigate reports claiming that recommendation methods using relatively simple statistical co-occurrence analysis are quite effective, we also developed a graph-based model for item recommendations. This method exemplifies a balance between the data processing and management requirements and the effectiveness of the recommendations produced.

Another challenge we examined during the project was the prediction of the shopping intent of e-commerce users using only the short-term browsing pattern of a user. LSTMs have been used recently in the e-commerce domain to improve recommendations; however, they have been barely used to predict a user's buying intention. In that regard, our study contributes to a better understanding of the LSTM approach for predicting the purchase intent. More precisely, we examined whether the e-commerce scenarios in which RNN-LSTM could provide better results in comparison to more conventional ML techniques, which have been considered as the SotA for the purchase intent task.

This paper presents the main results of the FRES project. The methodology of our approach is outlined in Figure 1. The major challenges and problems of SBRS that are addressed by our research work are the following:

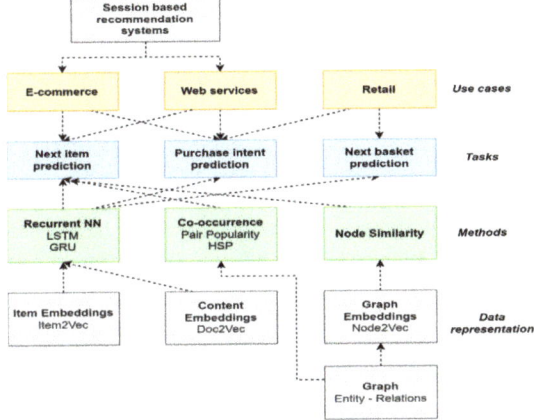

Figure 1. The methodology of a flexible recommendation system. It involves the use cases of "e-commerce", "web services" and "physical retail store" (yellow boxes). The relevant tasks for each case are shown in blue boxes. They are the prediction of the next item in an online session, the prediction of the intent to purchase, and the prediction of the next basket. The arrows indicate the relationship between the tasks and the corresponding use cases. The methods used to solve these tasks are shown in the green boxes. These include recurrent neural networks and graph-based methods using either statistical co-occurrence analysis or node similarity assessments. The methods are in turn based on the representation of the data. The representation can be used to make additional determinations.

The development of a flexible SBRS system that is based on a common set of principles and methods to address the variety of problems in session-based recommendation systems and physical retail shops. These problems/tasks are next-item recommendation, purchase intent prediction and next-basket recommendation.

The performance of a comparative study of SotA methods from different domains, including neural networks and graph methods.

The identification of a set of efficient and general methods for representing the history of user activity such as session data and basket data history.

The paper is structured as follows: Section 1 discusses earlier work. We go through the tasks and the methods we propose to solve them with in Section 2. The numerous datasets we produced to assess our techniques are shown in Section 3. We provide a description of the experiments, as well as a report and discussion of the findings, in Section 4. In Section 5, we summarize the results, point out challenges and issue a plan for the advancement of SBRS in the future.

2. Methods and Literature Review

In this section, we present the tasks that are addressed in this paper and the tools and methodologies that were used to tackle problems and challenges related to these tasks. For all these methods, we discuss major relevant literature that shows how each method has been developed and what the current state of the art. In particular, Section 2.1 describes the task of predicting the next item and the last item in a session using the prior user behavior within this session. Section 2.2 discusses graph representations methods for recommendation systems. Section 2.3 discusses the task of purchase intent, which seeks to explicitly determine whether the intent of the user in the current session is to purchase some product or not. Section 2.4 describes the evaluation metrics used in the subsequent experiments. Section 2.5 presents the SBRS methods that we employed in various practical scenarios.

2.1. Next-Item, Last-Item Tasks

Early recommendation methods used simple pattern mining techniques. These techniques are easy to implement and lead to interpretable models. However, the mining process is usually computationally demanding. Furthermore, several parameters of an algorithm should be fine-tuned, and this might be difficult. Moreover, in some application domains, frequent item sequences do not lead to better recommendations than when using much computationally simpler co-occurrence patterns [11].

After these first experiments, more complex approaches based on context trees [12], [13] reinforcement learning [14], and Markov decision processes [15] were developed. The number of prior interactions (i.e., history window) that should be taken into account while estimating the following interaction was a parameter used in these recommender models.

Word2Vec/Doc2Vec methods were developed for use in linguistic tasks, but they can also be applied in recommender methods for CF [16]. Word2Vec is a two-layer neural network which is trained to represent words as vectors in such a way that words that share common contexts in the training corpus are located in close proximity to one another in the space. These representation vectors are known as embeddings. There are two varieties of Word2Vec called CBOW and skip-gram, with the second one being the most common approach. Skip-gram predicts the context of a word, w, given w as the input. Doc2Vec is based on Word2Vec with the aim of creating vector representations of documents rather than single words. Doc2Vec creates paragraph vectors by training a neural network to predict the probability distribution of words in a paragraph given a randomly selected word from it.

Word2Vec can be generalized to represent items with vectors based on their context (i.e., other items in the same session or basket) in a very similar fashion to its means of assigning vector representations to words. It can infer item–item relationships even in the absence of user ID information. The item-to-item recommender system (Item2Vec) is initially trained using the item sequences from prior anonymous user sessions. Then, when the system is actually applied, it accepts the currently selected item as input and produces a group of related things based on the input. In fact, when compared to SVD and other sequence-based CF approaches, this method yields results that are competitive [17,18].

Deep neural networks have recently been suggested for recommender systems. In particular, recurrent neural networks (RNN) have been very effective models for session data of user interactions. Recurrent neural networks are extensions of feedforward networks with additional internal memory. They are created by adding a feedback loop from the output back to the input of the network. As a result, the current output depends on both the input and the previous output. The fundamental benefit of RNNs over other approaches for recommendation is that they can naturally and incrementally model series of user interactions. After creating a predictive model, RNNs offer more effective recommendations than other sequence-based conventional techniques [19,20].

2.2. Graph-Based Methods

The use of graph databases (GDBs) is a new approach for data modeling [21]. A graph database represents data entities as nodes and their relationships as directed connections between nodes. Neo4j is an open source graph database tool that supports semi-structured hierarchically organized data [22,23]. The graph using this method is used to represent sequences of items in a session using node relationships. Thus, it becomes another way to represent item sequences.

Neo4j was used for creating various recommendation systems, making recommendations of friends, movies, and objects, and also in the field of e-commerce. Konno [24] developed a recommendation system based on data-driven rules. They applied a two-layer approach to retail business transaction data for business information query and reasoning. Another graph-based and rule-based recommendation system approach was described by [25]. Delianidi [26] presented another graph-based recommender using Neo4j in which emphasis was given to efficiency. In this work, nodes and relationships between the nodes were defined using session training data. The system finds all pairs of co-occurring items in the current session by running cypher queries. Then, the similarity between the items of the pair can be calculated using these co-occurrence frequencies.

2.3. Purchase Intent Task

In all likelihood, the first techniques tested to determine whether or not a user session in an e-commerce application is likely to end with a purchase were multilayer perceptron classifiers and simple Bayes classifiers [27]. Suchacka [28] used data from an online bookstore to evaluate SVM using a variety of factors (23), with a similar goal of classifying user sessions as either browsing-only or purchasing-related. The most effective SVM classifier showed high performance. It achieved a likelihood of predicting a purchasing session of about 95% and an overall prediction accuracy of 99%.

Association rules and a k-nearest neighbor (k-NN) classifier were used by [29] to enhance their study and estimate the likelihood of a purchase. To predict purchase likelihood for two client groups—traditional consumers (accuracy 90%) and more diverse–novel customers—they employed basic association rule mining and other behavioral knowledge (accuracy 88%).

The hidden Markov model (HMM) is another method that was tested. In fact, there are many web usage mining research efforts that have considered HMM to predict user behavior in several settings and for different tasks. Examples of its uses include deciding if a web search session was successful or not, establishing recommender systems [13], or making suggestion for the next point of interest in tourism websites. Ding [2] presented a research study that was more related to our work; however, it primarily made use of HMM to understand customer intent in real-time in order to make web page adaption.

Using user activity data, participants in the RecSys2015 competition attempted to estimate the assortment of goods that would be purchased during a session. The state-of-the-art (SotA) solution for this issue remains the two-stage classifier provided by the competition winners [30]. While the second classifier predicts the things that will be purchased, the first classifier predicts whether at least one item will be purchased during the session or not. In this work, the session and click dates, click counts for individual things, and other category features of the sessions and objects were employed.

Recurrent neural networks (RNN) were utilized by [31] to capture event dependencies and connections for user sessions of arbitrary length, both within and across datasets. Results from the RecSys15 challenge indicate that their solution performed admirably well. The key benefit of their approach is that it needs reduced domain- or dataset-specific feature engineering.

Another RNN-LSTM-based system for analyzing online shopping behavior was present-ed by [9]. It had two parallel-operating components. The first predicted consumers' tendency to shop; however, this module employed machine learning classifiers such as random forest, support vector machines, and multilayer perceptron. RNN-LSTM is only used in the second module, which predicts the likelihood that users would leave a website without buying anything. In relation to the SotA, their purchasing intent module performed much worse. The accuracy of the second module, which predicted website desertion after a short window of three-user action, was almost 75%.

A full connected long short-term network (FC-LSTM) for modeling the interactions between customers was tested by [32]. The same network models the nonlinear sequence correlations and cumulative effects between customer's browsing behavior. However, to attain better predictions, they use more features from user profiles, including purchase history and demographics.

2.4. Evaluation Metrics

One of the most common evaluation metrics used was the mean reciprocal rank (MRR). Its calculation formula is:

$$MRR = \frac{1}{Q} \sum_{x}^{Q} \frac{1}{\text{rank}(x)} \quad (1)$$

where Q is the number of queries we are considering, and rank is the position of the correct answer x among the returned values, with $\text{rank}(x) = 1$ if x is the first item in the recommendation list. When there is no correct answer within the recommendation list, then we set $\text{rank}(x) = \infty$ and the reciprocal rank $1/\text{rank}(x)$ equals zero. In our case, the MRR varies between 0.017 and 0.03 depending on the number of responses we return.

Another evaluation metric used in our experiments is the F1 score @ k, which equals the F1 score of the recommendation list containing k items. The F1 score is the harmonic mean between the precision and the recall, defined as

$$F1 = \frac{precision \cdot recall}{(precision + recall)/2} \quad (2)$$

where $precision = \frac{tp}{tp+fp}$, $recall = \frac{tp}{tp+fn}$, and tp = true positives, fp = false positives and fn = false negatives.

2.5. Tested SBRS Methods and Practical Scenarios

2.5.1. Content-Based SBRS Using Doc2Vec Embeddings

This approach is similar to traditional content-based systems in that it suggests products that are pertinent to previous "liked" things by the user [4]. The similarity is calculated on basis of the text content or other attributes of the items liked by the user. Note that the term "liked" can take several interpretations depending on the domain, application, or other context. In the context of SBRS, the items visited in the current ongoing session provide input content to the recommender.

In our project, we created a vector for each product item using the title, color, and extended description. A fixed dimension vector for every item was produced using the

Doc2Vec model. We created an n-dimensional vector for each item after training the Doc2Vec model using the textual descriptions of the products. Following multiple experiments, vector sizes of 500 for the next-item dataset and 100 for the last-basket dataset were chosen. In this method, the similarities to all other things are computed for each viewed item during an ongoing session to suggest the next item. The cosine similarity measure gave slightly better results in all the datasets we tested.

2.5.2. Item-Based SBRS Using Item2Vec Embeddings

This approach is a Word2Vec technique transfer to the SBRS problem. To learn distributed representations of words, the Word2Vec approach was first used in natural language processing.

Item2Vec provides embeddings to things in a manner that is very similar to providing embeddings to words [16]. The underlying idea is that it can be used in the sense of collaborative filtering to provide recommendations, despite user IDs not being available. The Item2Vec method uses item views like Word2Vec to process the sequence of words; in this process, the word sequences match to the users' sessions while they browse an online store (sentences). Our technique utilizes Word2Vec's skip-gram variety of Word2Vec. As such, the underlying assumption is that, given a sequence of previously visited items in an ongoing session, the task is to predict the next item(s).

We tested several embeddings by increasing the sizes of vector dimensions, but the best sizes were 30 for the next-item task/dataset and 100 for the next-basket task/dataset. L2 norm achieves better results when measuring the similarity between items in the first dataset, whereas cosine similarity produced better results in the second dataset.

2.5.3. SBRS Methodology Using Embeddings

When implementing recommendation methods relying solely on the ongoing session, there are several decisions that should be considered on how to execute such operation. For example, how many previous actions of the ongoing session should be accounted for in the prediction? Or, how the previous actions will be summarized of the ongoing session to represent the behavior so far? The following list outlines all these steps and the parameters that are typically involved.

1. Obtain the embeddings of the most recent n items a user has visited in their current session (or purchased in previous n baskets in the next-basket task). This parameter affects how well these recommenders function.
2. Use these embeddings to calculate the average vector, u.
3. Calculate the L2 norm or the cosine similarity between the vector u and each of the other dataset items' embeddings
4. The user's recommendations are the top k most similar items.

We conducted several experiments in our project to assess how these criteria might affect the results. In order to obtain the vector u, we averaged the embeddings of either the last n items the user viewed during a current session or all of the products they purchased in the previous n baskets. We conducted a number of tests and found that the "temporal locality principle" typically holds. Results are improved when only the most recent items are taken into account; in other words, recent behavior greatly outperforms activity from the session's very beginning in terms of predicting the next action. In general, all SBRS approaches perform better when a smaller memory of the user activities is taken, as we shall demonstrate later.

2.5.4. Hybrid Methods

Systems aggregating both collaborative filtering and content-based methods are called hybrid recommenders [33]. In our research, we explored if the two embedding techniques we created could be used together to operate a hybrid usage of text and item sequences. In particular, our system combines the browsing patterns of all sessions, together with the model that is developed based on item's text, using the Item2Vec and the Doc2Vec methods, respectively.

The two methods produce their predictions inside their vector space. The vectors generated by the Item2Vec method are located in one vector space, whereas those generated by the Doc2Vec method are found in the other. Both techniques estimate item similarity using the cosine similarity. The range of cosine similarity is [0, 1]. Therefore the closer the value is to 1, the stronger the similarity and prediction will be. Given that cosine similarity has a range of [0, 1], the stronger the similarity and pre-diction is, the closer the result will be to 1. In our hybrid approach, we compute the combined prediction using v = [1-CosineSimilarity]. The values' range is still [0, 1] in this instance, but the prediction is now greater the closer a value is to 0.

For each of the two methods, we multiplied the value of v with the rank of the item in the recommendations list. The product indicates the confidence each method gives the recommendation. Finally, we combined the Item2Vec and Doc2Vec confidences to calculate the final prediction value.

2.5.5. Graph-Based SBRS

In our project we implemented two SBRS methods using Neo4j. The first method, called pair popularity, models in the graph all item co-occurrences found anywhere in the same session. Having recorded the item P viewed by the user at session step t, the method recommends a list of items for step t+1 based on how often the items co-appeared with P in the training sessions. Later, we proposed the hierarchical sequence popularity (HSP) recommendation method. This method uses a hierarchical representation of item sequences in user sessions to further improve the results and produces significantly better results. To recommend an item, we looked at its frequency of appearance as well as the history of sequences of length 1 or 2 in which this item participated during the training sessions. In the absence of history (i.e., in the first step of a session), items were recommended based on their popularity. Both recommendation approaches can be applied to a wide variety of e-shops regardless of the type of items. The item recommendations that the methods offer can be used as an essential component to automate and improve the identification of related items for the online customer.

The main advantage of graph-based recommenders is that they quite are effective, but at the same time are efficient when considering the complete operation cycle of SBRS (data gathering, modeling, processing, analysis, filtering). Graph-based SBRS, due to their underlying architecture, can incrementally collect data from an e-commerce website from all ongoing user sessions. Moreover, these data are immediately available to the recommendation algorithm because no training phase is required. Finally, it is easy to integrate new business rules and constraints on demand, something that is more difficult to inherently implement using ML methods.

Generally, scalability is a critical issue that should be very carefully considered, especially when building SBRS for big data. If a method is very effective, but it requires a substantial amount of training time exceeding the periodic time in which the recommender prediction model should be updated (every day or every week), it is not applicable.

2.5.6. SBRS Methodology Using LSTMs

In a typical architecture of an LSTM recommender, the recently visited item(s) of the ongoing user's session are the input. The output is the next item to be recommended using the system's one-hot encoding. Compared to all the other methods, this one has actually produced strong results. At the conclusion of the model's 20-epoch training process, we obtained the best score by utilizing 200 hidden units for the LSTM layer and a Softmax layer with a size of 1097 units for categorical cross-entropy loss. Figure 2 shows the architecture of this recommender.

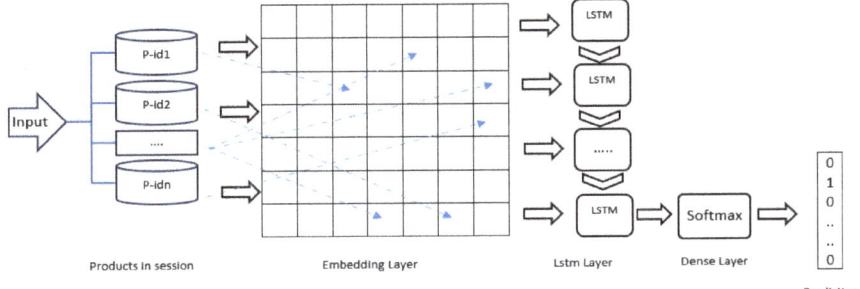

Figure 2. LSTM design in the next-item task.

For the last-basket job, the user's previous baskets provided the input. The average Doc2Vec vector of the items inside each basket was used to represent each basket. We received a sorted list of all the probabilities for each item as the result. The best F1@2 score for the model's hyperparameters was obtained using 300 LSTM units, 100-dimensional Doc2Vec vectors, and 100 epochs.

An additional embedding layer was added to the LSTM recommenders to improve their performance (Figure 3). In particular, we expanded the approach by using the vectors we trained with Doc2Vec as the initializing weights of the LSTM. As compared to our basic LSTM approach and our hybrid technique (which combines Item2Vec and Doc2Vec), this expansion provided an overall improvement in MRR of up to 10% and up to 100%, respectively.

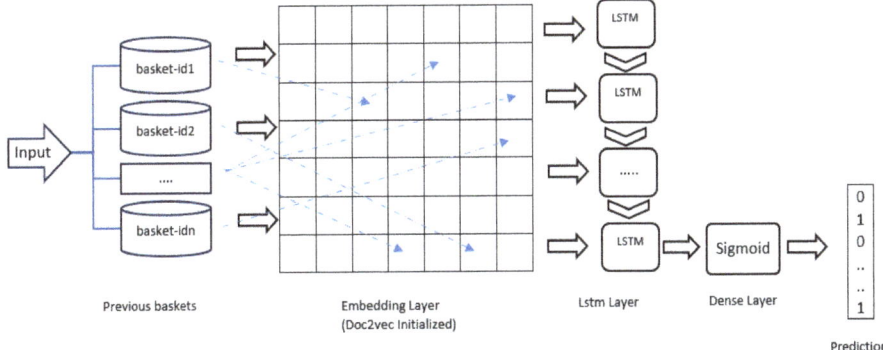

Figure 3. LSTM architecture used in the last-basket task.

2.5.7. SBRS and the Purchase Intent Task

Our method for predicting purchase intent modeled all user actions as a sequence like in our recommenders. However, it differed in that we applied extra features. Specifically, one such feature was the time (in seconds) the user spent in each action. We also used four other features (season, day, working hours, origin). These extra features were important for an e-commerce application as other studies have shown that buying behavior changes over time [30]. The feature Season specifies a high season (autumn/winter for leather apparel) or not. We also know that a purchase is more likely to be made on the weekend, and that visiting an e-commerce application in midday hours usually results more purchases than in the night hours.

Nevertheless, the main difference in the purchase intent task is that we retrieved and modeled all user actions, and not only the View Item actions, as we did in our recommenders. All user actions belong in one out of the twelve action types. These twelve action types include all potential actions that customers do in e-commerce web applications. As such, hence they may be seen as a "standard" set of action types for other studies in the e-commerce domain. Table 1 shows all user action types modeled and their frequency in the dataset and in each of the two session types we wanted to predict. Most of them are self-explanatory. The action type "Concerned" means that a user has visited a web page reflecting a customer concern about privacy policy, payment security or product shipping and returns. The "Recommend Product" action signals the recommendation of a product to another person by sending an email message.

Table 1. User action types.

	All Sessions (21.896)		Purchase Sessions (689)		Cart Abandonment Sessions (1305)	
	Occurs	Frequency	Occurs	Frequency	Occurs	Frequency
CATEGORY	141,561	54.8%	2760	20.5%	9956	40.6%
VIEW PRODUCT	83,299	32.3%	3149	23.4%	6511	26.5%
HOME	6139	2.4%	316	2.3%	360	1.5%
ASK QUESTION	4027	1.6%	150	1.1%	479	2.0%
ORDER	730	0.3%	730	5.4%	0	0.0%
CONTACT	4264	1.7%	42	0.3%	133	0.5%
ADD CART	3380	1.3%	1113	8.3%	2267	9.2%
VIEW CART	10,722	4.2%	5011	37.2%	4483	18.3%
SEARCH	69	0.0%	0	0.0%	0	0.0%
CONCERNED	1172	0.5%	115	0.9%	183	0.7%
ACCOUNT	2068	0.8%	75	0.6%	155	0.6%
RECOMMEND	670	0.3%	5	0.0%	9	0.0%
	258.101	100%	13.466	100%	24.536	100%

In this task, each event is represented with a vector and each session is modeled as a sequence of events. A sliding window, starting from the first session action, designates the context of each user movement and it is exactly this context window that it used as a sample for training (Figure 4). The length of the window (N) is a parameter of our method. If the window ends inside the first N-1 events, the previous navigation steps apparently remain fewer than the size of window. In this case, the empty slots are taken as zeroed events.

Similarly, for each input instance, the output is computed using the remaining events. Specifically, for every occurring event, E_i, our method calculates the outcome after considering all the remaining events until the end of the session. The target is modeled as a 2-digit enumeration structure. Each binary digit independently represents one of the two actions of interest (i.e., add cart, make order). Thus, in total there are four outputs possible. Two of them, [1, 0] and [0, 1], signify that at least one add-cart or one purchase event occurred, respectively. The existence of both events is the output [1, 1]. If both these two events do not occur in the remaining segment of a session, the output is coded as [0, 0].

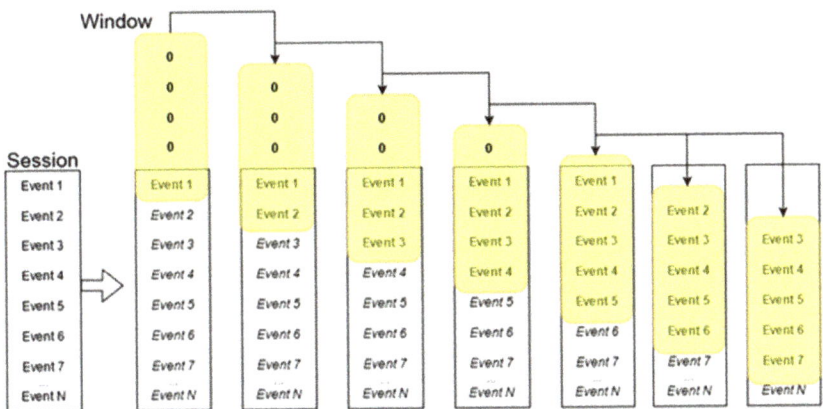

Figure 4. Operation of our purchase intent method with the sliding window running from the start to the end of each session to obtain instances for training purposes.

To summarize, our purchase intent system is modeled as a multilabel classification problem that determines, for each session action, the result of the rest session. The following four scenarios outline four different outputs:

1. A user adds item(s) to her/his cart but does not make a purchase finally. This is the cart abandonment scenario.
2. A user adds item(s) to the cart and makes a purchase (purchase scenario).
3. None of the add-item and make-order events happens (browse-only scenario).
4. A user makes a purchase.

2.5.8. Last-Item (Calling Tune Recommendation) Task Using the Node2Vec Method

In this task, we used a different method called Node2Vec, inspired from bio-informatics. The Node2Vec framework learns low-dimensional representations for nodes of a graph using random graph walks starting at a target node. This method requires the creation of a graph where the associations between the various entities—in our application, the main entities were users, songs, artists, genres—are represented as arcs. After creating the graph by applying 2nd-order random walks, numerical representations for each node within the graph can be produced. These representations are finally used as input to the classic word2vec algorithm (skip-gram model with negative sampling) to derive the final embeddings of each node. In essence, the resulting embeddings preserve the structure of the original network in the sense that related nodes have similar representations.

The key characteristic of 2nd-order random walks is that each transition to a neighboring node is accompanied by a probability, defined as a hyper-parameter, different from that of returning to the previous node. This particular methodology requires the user to define a series of hyper-parameters that control the process mainly in terms of complexity. These basic hyper-parameters are the following: number of walks, walk length, return value to the previous node (return hyper parameter—p), and transition value to a new node (in-out hyper parameter—q). The last two parameters concern the transition between nodes during the random walks phase.

When implementing this method, we had to solve several efficiency and scalability challenges. Initially we used the python library NetworkX to create the graph. NetworkX is the most common open source package for creating and editing graphs in python. Nevertheless, the specific method in its basic implementation, although highly effective, is not scalable enough due to memory (RAM) problems. This is because 2nd-order transitions increase the number of total transition probabilities quadratically with respect to the number of edges within the graph. For this reason, another implementation of this method called PecanPy was used which largely solves memory sufficiency problems. In essence,

PecanPy solves the problem of parallelizing the two otherwise parallel processes, i.e., the preprocessing of the transition probability from each node, as well as the random walk application.

3. Datasets

In terms of data, the problem of SBRS becomes complex. There are several data items and certain feature selection, and session and feature engineering will be needed. The item (product, movie, tune, etc.) is the central concept, however the presence of the session concept and the potentially different domains, bring extra complexity. For example, selected past sessions may be characterized as irrelevant to the current ongoing session. The item concept in e-commerce will normally be a tangible product. However, item in the music domain will be a song. Additionally, tasks like the purchase intent or the requirement to address the temporal locality principle (i.e., make recommendations that predominantly reflect recent behavior) bring even more complexities.

Furthermore, a dataset in SBRS research should have a clear session structure. The session structure may also present a clear ordering of the events that occur within a session. If a sequence of the events is explicit in the dataset, then this dataset is best fitted for next-item tasks. Sometimes, session boundaries may be clear; however, the sequence of events within the session are not specified. For example, in a shopping cart dataset, each shopping basket has clear session boundaries which distinguish it from all the other baskets, and so it naturally represents a session. The recommendation tasks on such dataset can be next-item(s) or next-basket recommendations. However, it should be noted that the entire basket session should be considered in its entirety. This because we do not know the sequence in which a user has put these items into the basket. For all these reasons, such a dataset is better suited for the next-basket task and is totally unsuitable for the purchase intent task.

Our experimental work in the project was driven in part by the views we discussed above, but mainly by the funding requirements to deploy, apply, and evaluate our developed methods in real e-commerce environments for a long duration.

Many experiments reported in this paper used data that were extracted from the web server logs of an apparel e-commerce website for a relatively long period of time (a few months). The log data were analyzed to identify sessions, session length, user actions in each session, actions' related items, item categories, and time spent on each action. As a result of this preprocess, the first dataset we produced (Dataset A) consisted of 24,111 sessions that altogether counted 312,912 user actions. Twelve different action types exist overall, but all the events were utilized only in the purchase event task. The 728 sessions ending in purchases represent a 3% conversion rate. In 22,008 sessions, users did not have any items in their shopping cart when they exited, meaning that 91.2% sessions were browse-only. The rest of the sessions had items in their shopping cart when they finished, but these never turned into purchases. In the next-item experiments reported in Section 5, we included only the "View Product" user actions and only the sessions holding at least two different item views, finally collecting a number of 12,128 applicable sessions consisting of 67,101 "View Product" user actions.

The above dataset was further processed to create another variation (Dataset B) suitable for the purchase intent task. In this second dataset, we used all event types listed in Table 2, but we kept the sessions that had at least 3 behavior sequences. This preprocessing led to the final dataset containing 21.896 sessions, including 258.101 user actions (the size of each session was 11.7 actions in average and the Median was 8). The average size of Browsing, Cart Abandonment and Purchase sessions are 11, 18.8, and 19.5, respectively. The 689 purchase sessions make a conversion rate of 3.14%. In 90.9% of sessions (19.902), users did not add any items to their shopping cart. In 1305 sessions, users added items to their shopping cart, albeit without completing a purchase. Table 2 shows all user action types and their frequency in the complete dataset.

Table 2. Results of all recommender methods for next-item and next-basket task.

Method	Next-Item Recommendation (e-Commerce Site)		Next-Basket Recommendation Task (Almapet)	
	MRR/last	MRR/all	F1@2/7	F1@2/all *
Doc2Vec	0.101	0.062	0.154	0.114
Doc2Vec + reranking	0.123	0.079	0.143	0.105
Item2Vec	0.087	0.079	0.221	0.167
Item2Vec + reranking	0.111	0.093	0.182	0.148
Fusion method	0.112	0.078	0.216	0.167
Fusion method + reranking	0.126	0.089	0.184	0.151
LSTM (random init)	-	0.265	0.208	0.205
LSTM (Doc2Vec init)	-	0.268	0.218	0.219

* all (column 5) denotes a session "history" of 35 items max.

The third dataset we created (Dataset C) reproduces the next-basket scenario and it is also built on a real application. It contains purchased items (in baskets) from a petshop store. The dataset has 40,203 transactions (baskets) belonging to 1493 users of which 1408 two or more baskets, i.e., they can be included in the experiment. The dataset contains 6626 items in total. The average length of all baskets is 2.26, therefore we calculate F1@2 in our results. Another parameter that we tested was the number of previous baskets to consider in predicting the last-basket content.

In later phases of the project, we installed a logging component into an e-commerce web application, and we collected data, although this time not from the web server logs but directly by logging specific user actions. For the experiments we report in the next section, this dataset (Dataset D) was processed to obtain only the sessions that contain the "View Item" and "Add to Cart" actions, resulting in 102.024 records. A typical split into train (80%) and test (20%) datasets was performed. Thus, the train sessions are 81.651 and the test sessions 20.373. The total number of unique sessions is 19.236 which corresponds to 15.388 sessions in the train set and 3.848 unique sessions in the test set. The dataset contains 1448 unique items, of which 1429 appear in the train set and 1296 in the test set.

One last dataset we used was the one for the calling tune recommendation task using the Node2Vec method (Dataset E). The data for this task fall into one of these entities: user, song, artist, and genre of music (user_id, item_id, artist_id, genre_id). Initially, the construction of the graph required in Node2Vec was carried out by connecting all the correlations of the above fields with the central entity, which is that of the song/tune (item_id). Specifically, the following associations were added to the graph: item_id->user_id, item_id->artist_id, item_id->genre_id. It is worth noting that a graph created in this way is neither directed nor weighted. The initial dataset contained 662,698 instances. Many of the users appeared more than once and were the customers of interest to our method because users with a single transaction cannot be tested. For this reason, all records having users with just one transaction (tune) were removed and the final size of the dataset was reduced to 570,533 transactions. Then, to configure the train and test set, the following procedure was followed. The train set comprised all user tune records except for the last one, which was put in the test set. For example, if a user has 4 transactions, the first 3 are included in the train set while the fourth ends up in the test set. The size of the two resulting sets was 478,572 for the train set and 91,961 for the test set. The total training time of the model was in the order of minutes (5–10), which gives more value to this method.

4. Results and Discussion

Before discussing the results of each technique, we need make a few clarifications based on the experimental setting. Section 4 provides a description of the datasets. In the next-item task, we created a list of recommended things that executed all methods for each item in each test session.

If a method needs the sequence of the item(s) viewed hitherto, then this sequence is provided to the method. We estimate the reciprocal rank for each list that each method returns, which is a ranked list of n recommended item(s) (RR). In this manner, the RR for each test session's action is computed.

The mean reciprocal rank (MRR) of the entire session may then be calculated. Finally, the MRR of the approach can be calculated by averaging the MRR of all sessions that have been tested. The reason we choose MRR as the evaluation measure is because it expresses the effectiveness of a method to recommend the next-item as highly as possible in the recommendation list. If a method achieves an MRR of 0.25, then a recommender would require showing 4 recommended items to effectively include an item that could be selected with high probability.

The experiments described below were executed on a computer with an AMD Ryzen-9 CPU @ 4.9 GHz, 32GB memory, and a NVIDIA Titan Xp GPU card. The neural network models were executed on the tensorflow-2 platform, while Neo4j was used for the graph-based algorithms.

4.1. Results of the Next-Item and Next-Basket Tasks

In these experiments, 90% of dataset A was used for training and the remaining 10% for testing. A random split was repeated five times. The results reported here are the average of the results produced from each split. In the last-basket task, all available baskets were used both for training and testing. Specifically, all baskets, except for the last one, were used to train the last-basket prediction model. Then, the last basket of each user's baskets was predicted and compared to the actual last basket the user purchased.

The post-prediction reranking was inspired by the knowledge that several product categories dominate each customer's purchases. To apply this reranking method, we define the dominant category as the one with the most "hits" from the session's start. Once the prevailing category is determined after each user action, all the recommended items in the dominant category are top-ranked. In the table summarizing the results, this method is indicated as "with reranking".

The results of each method for the next-item (MRR) and the last-basket (F1@2) tasks are presented in Table 2. The column "last" shows the results if only the last item was taken as the context. The column indicated as "all" presents the results when the entire user behavior sequence, from the session start until the current item, is taken into account.

The LSTM methods produced considerably better results. The MRR was 0.265 when we initialized the LSTM recommender using random weights. The embedded layer which we added improved the performance only marginally. The Doc2Vec method was the best from the embeddings that we tested, attaining an MRR of 0.101. The Item2Vec method performed less effectively, having an MRR of 0.087. When the content-based and the item sequence embeddings were combined, they produced better results. Finally, our experiments confirmed the intuitive assumption that category-driven reranking improves the results, except in the LSTM method. We believe this occurs because LSTMs already capture the focus on specific product categories.

Table 3 also illustrates the results of the last-basket prediction task. Column 4 presents the F1@2 results, considering seven previous baskets as the purchase history. Column 5 illustrates the results when all the purchases are considered. In these experiments, the results are quite different from the next-item task. In the reverse of what happens in the next-item task, the Item2Vec method in this task performs much better than the Doc2Vec. This is due to the smaller textual information available in the items in this dataset. Quite surprisingly, Item2Vec outperforms the LSTM method when only seven baskets are considered; however, the performance order is marginally reversed with larger purchase history. Generally, all methods produce better results when a shorter purchase history is used. It seems that a principle of locality consistently holds which states that the next user action is influenced more intensively by its immediate surroundings. Another interesting result is that category-based reranking negatively affects all methods. We believe this outcome relates to the organization of the dataset which has very few categories.

Table 3. Accuracy Results (Window size = 10).

Model	Units	Features Used	Accuracy
LSTM	500	First 12	97
LSTM	500	All 16	97.3
LSTM + GRU	500 × 300	First 12	97.2
LSTM + GRU	500 × 300	All 16	97.6

4.2. Results of the Purchase Intent Task

Dataset C was used in this task. A 10-fold stratified cross-validation procedure was applied. We found that the optimal settings are a 0.2 dropout rate, Adam optimizer and 500 LSTM units. Table 3 shows the results using window size N = 10. When we combined LSTM with a GRU layer, the performance was better in comparison to result obtained using one LSTM layer. This finding is in accordance with other studies on sequence modeling (Chung et al, 2014), in which combinations of LSTM and GRU variants outperform standard RNNs. At the end of the architecture, we used a dense layer with sigmoid function to deliver the final probabilities for multilabel prediction.

The results produced by our fine-tuned method are better than those from other similar research reported in the literature using RNN-LSTM. Additionally, the results are comparable to the accuracy results that SotA methods have achieved (Section 2.3).

The window size, i.e., the size of previous items considered as "history", is an important parameter for our method. To that end, we performed further experiments to test our model using different window sizes. The cart abandonment sessions are of particular economic interest for e-commerce applications because the user adds item(s) into the cart, but s/he does not complete a purchase in the end. An e-commerce application will benefit remarkably if these sessions are predicted during a session as early as possible. Table 4 presents the accuracy results as a function of multiple window sizes in two different conditions. The first includes all sessions, and the second considers only the "Cart Abandonment" sessions. The prediction of the cart abandonment sessions is less effective. Similar findings have been observed in other studies as a result of datasets containing many sessions that did not conclude with a purchased basket, and very few cart abandonment and purchase sessions.

Table 4. Accuracy results as a function of Window size.

Window Size	Binary Accuracy (Including All Sessions)	Binary Accuracy (Cart Abandonment Only)
4	94.64	56.40
8	96.35	71.00
11	97.45	78.60
14	97.82	81.17
20	98.15	83.16
25	98.14	82.65
30	98.12	83.30

4.3. Results of Our Graph-Based SBRS

Table 5 presents the MRR results of the proposed hierarchical sequence popularity recommendation method in comparison to the "simple" pair popularity graph-based recommendation approach and other recommendation methods using machine learning models (Item2Vec, Doc2vec and LSTM) in Dataset D.

Table 5. Results of the next-item task using the graph-based methods for SBRS vs. other ML/DL methods.

Method	MRR (Excluding Cold Start)
Doc2Vec	0.205
Item2Vec	0.197
LSTM	0.291
Pair Popularity	0.273
Hierarchical Sequence Popularity (HSP)	0.283

Between the two graph-based methods, the new HSP approach outperforms the pair popularity approach in both next-item recommendation scenarios by 3–4%. In terms of comparison with the machine learning methods tested, in the case of the Item2Vec and Doc2vec models, the HSP method prevails by a significant margin.

According to the experimental results, the method that produces the best results is the LSTM machine learning model. The HSP makes recommendations based on limited history and using a quite small memory window extending up to only two previous items. Nevertheless, the performance of the HSP method is very close to the LSTM performance. This is surprising because the LSTM is one of the most powerful models and is equipped with infinite memory capability, enabling maximal exploitation of the history data in a session to produce good recommendations.

4.4. Results for the Calling Tune Recommendation Task using Node2Vec

In the experiments using Dataset E, after fine-tuning, the final values of the hyperparameters discussed in 3.8 are the following: number of runs = 10, length of runs = 100, p value = 0.5, Q-value = 1.

A disadvantage of the way we implemented the Node2Vec method in this problem was that most nodes represented users. As a consequence, recommendations with the most "relevant" nodes always returned a large number of users. For this reason, there was a risk that, if the list of recommendations we requested from the graph was relatively small (of the order of hundreds), we would not receive recommendations concerning calling tunes. This was also the reason why MRR attained very low values. Table 6 shows how the MRR is shaped in relation to the number of recommendations and how many queries end up not returning any music as an answer.

Table 6. MRR results for the calling tune recommendation task.

Mean Reciprocal Rank	Length of Recommendation List	Empty Results (Total 91,961)
0.017	1k	19,080
0.020	2k	7652
0.022	3k	4015
0.026	5k	1429
0.030	10k	183

In summary, the Node2Vec recommendation method solves the problem of tune recommendation, but at the same time it is a method that does not require high computational costs. Its evaluation, although it does not seem very impressive, in reality should be considered highly satisfactory for this type of problem. Its qualitative evaluation showed that there is indeed a great relevance between the suggested tunes and the history of the user, regardless of whether s/he had not selected them up to that point in time.

4.5. Push (Offers) Notifications Task

The widespread use of mobile applications developed specifically for use on small, wireless computing devices, such as smartphones and tablets, has developed the need for recommender systems that can execute the core task of sending push notifications. A push notification is a message that is "pushed" from a back-end server or application to a mobile application. However, although some aspects are similar, push notifications cannot be managed in the same way that next-item or next-baskets recommendations are created in e-commerce. This is mainly because push notifications have to take into account several other factors that will determine the type of the message or the items that may be recommended inside the delivered message. Such parameters may include the need not to disturb the customer receiving the notification, but also other marketing strategies like promoting specific brands and marketing goals (Figure 5). Additionally, the situation for managing push notification messages is quite different, e.g., push messages may be ignored completely by the user, without even reading them. The final aim in assessing and criteria to evaluate a push notification strategy is the capacity to create push notifications that will be not rejected, will be read by users, but most importantly will activate links or recommended actions. In other scenarios, the aim is to lower customer churn, i.e., the rate at which customers will stop using an app or purchasing items with a company's e-shop over a given period of time.

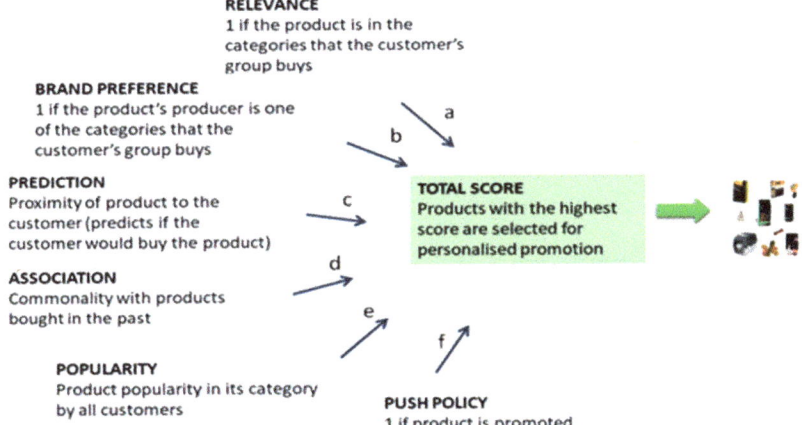

Figure 5. Parameters determining a push notification policy.

In our research project, we implemented a push notification subsystem for a pet-shop (Almapet, refers to Dataset C in Section 4) and for a mobile lottery application. In the Almapet case study, the first objective was the exploratory analysis of the purchasing behavior of the pet-shop customers based on the history of their purchases from a physical store. The second objective was the prediction of the next purchases in order to recommend products that are relevant to a customer and can be the subject of personalized offers using notification messages. The training set included 1408 customers having more than 1 basket, a total of 40,203 baskets and approximately 6400 products. Two methods were used to categorize products. The first method was codenamed cat01 and used product categories (32 exist). The second method was named cat02 and was based on the producer. From the purchase history of each user, a vector representing the user's profile was created. Additionally, clustering revealed 10 customer groups and their preferences according to the animals they own, the items they buy most often and the brands they prefer. The output of the clustering algorithm was used to produce a personalized prediction of the product categories each user buys (category relevance, see next paragraph) and the producers/brands they prefer (brand relevance, see next paragraph again).

The method overall takes as an input a user id and calculates: category relevance, brand relevance, items composing the next-basket, associated items (items purchased together), recent sales trends and finally the push policy, i.e., items and/or categories that are selected for promotion. Using a weighted scheme to assign a weight to each selection parameter, the management can decide its marketing strategy. For example, the aim to increase weights for category relevance, brand relevance and items composing the next-basket places the emphasis on a customer's purchase needs. On the other hand, increased weights for the parameters associated items, sales trends and the push policy, increases the diversity, novelty and serendipity of the purchase behavior.

The second scenario regarding this push notification task builds around a mobile lottery application. The basic aim is to send push-promotion messages to increase the use of the lottery application. The strategy we used was to suggest new lottery games to mobile application users that were considered most likely to engage the recipient, with the following objectives:

1. Optimizing the effectiveness of promotional messages, which is expressed as (a) the probability that the message will be read and not rejected and (b) the probability that the recipient will respond to the purpose of the message, i.e., click on the link contained.
2. Reducing the annoyance and negative reaction that may be caused by sending promotional messages with content which the recipient is indifferent to or which is even annoying to the recipient.

This notification message component takes as its input the historical sequence of games that a user has played in the past and produces a recommendation about a game that a user has not played before. For this type of recommendation, we used the Word2Vec method. The training sessions, with each sequence of games played on by users being regarded as a session, are used to create and assign embeddings vectors for each game in the lottery application. Games that are played jointly by users (i.e., co-exist in the history of multiple users) are close to the vector space. Thus, by calculating the mean vector of the vectors of a user's games we can say that we are vectorizing the user's preference in the space of lottery games. Then, the Euclidean distance of the user's preference with all the vectors of the games s/he did not play is calculated. The game with the shortest distance from the user's preference vector becomes the recommended game for them that is sent through a push notification message.

4.6. A/B Testing Results

One of our research objectives and a deliverable aim of our project was to test session-based recommendations in the real environment of an online shop. For this purpose, we integrated all the SBRS methods that we analyzed in this paper and created a demonstrator to enable evaluations using different recommenders in a real environment and with real users. One target was to measure the effectiveness of SBRS, but we also wanted to consider other practical issues such as efficiency and adaptation to business rules.

We utilized A/B testing to conduct the study. A/B testing is a quantitative evaluation technique that compares two real versions of a web page or a component of a web application in general to examine which version performs better. These variations, known as A, B, etc., are selected randomly to each new user entering the website. Some of them will be directed to the first version, more rest to the second, and so on. Hence, product recommendations are made to each group of users by a different SBRS method. The division of users into groups is performed with a rotation function. Once users connect to any website, a unique alphanumeric is given which identifies the session id of each user. The session id remains the same for each user until they leave the site. So, the user's session id can be fed into the rotation function and a different recommendation method is selected for the entire session of a user.

Using A/B testing, we were able to test and verify in a real e-shop which recommender method produces more clicks for recommended products, creates more purchases, and so on. Three SBRS methods were applied, specifically, RNN-based, graph-based, and Item2Vec. Additionally, we used an extra "random" algorithm which made suggestions using only the product category that the visitor was currently viewing.

The recommender component was integrated into an e-shop (leather apparel). When a product is viewed, it shows more recommended products to the visitor, aiming to provide them with a better experience. If this aim is realized, then longer user sessions should be expected, more customer satisfaction, hopefully leading to better conversion rates. Web usage data were recorded to enable calculation of several evaluation metrics (All data and statistics of our A/B testing are accessible in this URL: https://fresanalytics.cntcloud.eu/, accessed on 20 February 2023). All methods have been evaluated for their success based on the number of clicks on recommended products.

Figure 6 shows the number of clicks made by users for an equal number of user sessions, using each algorithm for a period of time. Thus, based on the results, the RNN method produced more recommendations (4768 in number) while the Graph DB-Neo4J algorithm was the second most effective method (4451 clicks). The Item2Vec algorithm was the third best performing method. It is also important to note that the clicks produced by the "random" algorithm were almost half those of the other algorithms. From these results, one can easily infer that the three algorithms were more effective than the recommendations that were made solely based on category. In other words, the success of the recommendation engine, regardless of the algorithm used, is far greater than the most widely used practice, which is to recommend products coming from the same category as the current viewed product.

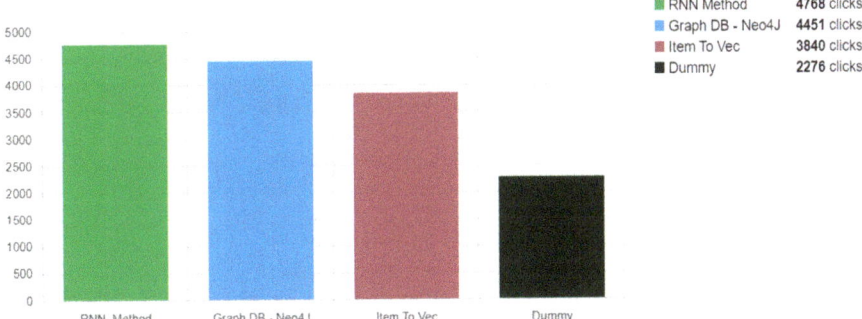

Figure 6. Number of clicks produced by each recommender method.

The most important metric that highlights the effectiveness of a recommendation engine not only scientifically but also commercially, however, is the click-through rate, i.e., the number of clicks that the e-shop users did as a proportion of the total item recommended (Figure 7).

However, the findings, as presented in Figure 7 below, are very encouraging as the click-through rate of the proposals that came from the recommendation engine exceeded 3%. The above percentage would be much higher if the panel of recommended products was higher on the product view web page. However, it was not possible to do this based on an agreement made with the company owning the e-shop. Another interesting finding was the significant improvement in terms of the bounce rate which was recorded in the Google Analytics of the e-shop after we installed the recommendation component, showing the success of the recommendation engine. Of course, several parameters have been identified that can be improved and would potentially lead to better results. One further experiment we intend to perform will test different layouts of the recommended products in order to increase the utility of the recommendation process and ultimately increase session time and user satisfaction.

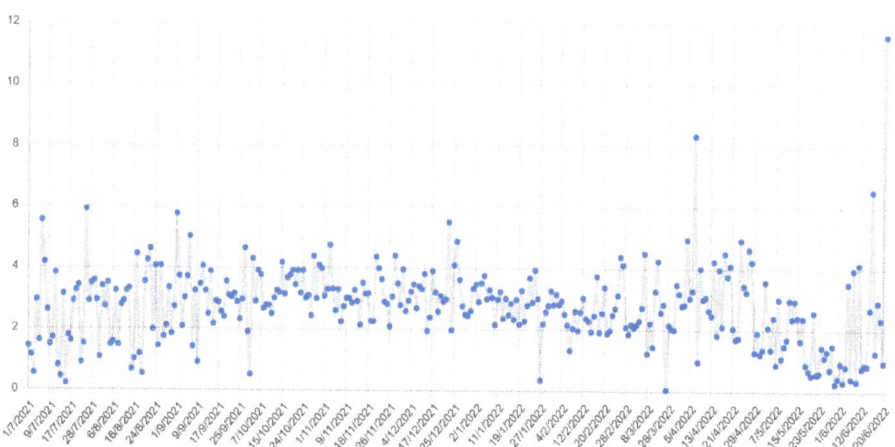

Figure 7. Click-through rate achieved by our recommender method.

5. Conclusions and Future Directions

Nowadays, many retail sales come from e-commerce web applications. Furthermore, e-commerce exploded during the pandemic, a business trend which is expected to last. Subsequently, the effectiveness of e-commerce solutions has become an important challenge for successful e-businesses. For large e-businesses that have tens of thousands or millions of users making repetitive visits and purchases, conventional recommender systems that rely on user ID and products views information are viable and very effective. However, these conventional systems cannot sufficiently address other widespread scenarios such as:

Smaller e-businesses, in which it is difficult to collect user ID information for privacy and other reasons.

More dynamic shopping environments that need to understand the user's intent and preferences at a certain time point, without being obscured in long-term historical shopping behaviors.

Capture a short temporal preference shift in user buying behavior that is represented only in the intrinsic nature of each specific session.

The scenarios outlined above show the need for SBRS. In other words, in many e-commerce applications and environments, it is necessary to learn user behavior patterns using sessions as the main transaction unit. Having identified the main requirements of SBRS and the main tasks, our work in the FFRES project was driven by the need to investigate, develop and evaluate several methods for SBRS. After many lab experiments using our SBRS methods, but also testing their operation in real e-commerce application, our main conclusions related to the next-item and next-basket recommender tasks are as follows:

1. When used in next-item recommendations based on sessions, LSTMs perform noticeably better than embedding approaches. Furthermore, these approaches do not require adjusting and are simpler to implement. Additionally, these methods are easier to apply without much tuning. Furthermore, their dynamic nature, inherently models the behavior of explorative browsing that usually occurs in e-commerce applications; therefore, they are better suited for this task.

2. In our investigation, we used LSTMs, although they were not as effective at predicting the last basket. The performance of Item2Vec was just slightly superior to our best LSTM implementation (the one that uses the extra embedding layer tailored to RNNs).

Additionally, LSTM approaches exceeded Word2Vec performance, albeit not on the same level as in the next-item task.

3. Combining several approaches has not always produced satisfying results. It significantly depends on whether textual data (Doc2Vec) can enhance the value of item-based recommendations. This observation inspires the concept of customized and pluggable recommenders that select the most appropriate recommendation algorithm in real time (for example, between Item2vec or LSTM). For each user action, we think a model may be trained to dynamically select one recommender technique, or possibly a combination of recommenders. We intend to go deeper into this topic.
4. Practical practices like category-based re-ranking could be useful, but only if recommenders perform poorly.
5. Graph-based methods can be a good compromise between effectiveness and efficiency. They can collect data from ongoing user sessions continually and make them available to the recommendation algorithm directly without any training phase.
6. Efficiency and scalability are critical issues that should be very carefully considered, especially in large-scale applications. Additionally, there is a need for methods supporting incremental training. We plan to investigate this issue further in future research.
7. During our collaboration with the e-shop top produce as our demonstrator, we realized that an important functional requirement for SBRS is to accommodate business rules that are required by the management of an e-commerce application.

These conclusions we believe make it clear that designing a SBRS is a complex problem that has practical constraints. Recommendations must be effective, i.e., propose relevant items but also deliver next-item recommendations as highly as possible in the list of suggestions. At the same time, the operation of a recommender (i.e., data gathering, data curation and modeling, processing, analysis, filtering) should be executed efficiently and in a way that allows operators to frequently update the recommender models. This is one direction that we plan to explore in our future research.

Besides the work we conducted on next-item and next-basket recommendations, we also worked on the purchase intent problem. This study was mainly motivated by the idea that e-commerce applications should have components for continuously monitoring users during their navigation. We believe that the key features such components can deliver into e-commerce applications are proactive stimuli actions, offering buying incentives to the user.

In conclusion, we believe that by completing the FRES project we have demonstrated the importance of SBRS for e-commerce applications. Furthermore, we have developed and tested many methods to effectively execute all the main tasks and predictions of an SBRS: next-item and next-basket recommendations, as well as purchase intent. The most effective method in all these tasks was RNN-LSTM. This method could become the cornerstone for developing more complex frameworks for e-commerce applications that will aim at higher conversion rates and better profitability.

Author Contributions: Conceptualization, M.S. and K.D.; methodology, M.S., A.K., T.S., M.D., P.K. and K.D.; software, A.K., T.S., D.T., P.K., K.C. and M.D.; validation, A.K., T.S., P.K., C.B and M.D.; formal analysis, A.K., T.S., K.C., M.D., D.T, P.K.; investigation, M.D. and I.K.; resources, C.B. and K.D.; data curation, M.S., P.K. and D.T.; writing—original draft preparation, M.S. and I.K.; writing—review and editing, M.S and I.K.; visualization, D.T.; supervision, M.S. and K.D.; project administration, K.D.; funding acquisition, K.D and C.B. All authors have read and agreed to the published version of the manuscript.

Funding: This research work received funding by the European Regional Development Program of the European Union and also by the Greek state through the Program RESEARCH–CREATE–INNOVATE (project code: T1EDK-01776).

Informed Consent Statement: Not applicable.

Data Availability Statement: Restrictions apply to the availability of these data. Data was obtained from on leather apparel e-shop and are available from the authors with the permission of the leather apparel e-shop.

Conflicts of Interest: The authors declare no conflict of interest.

Notations and Abbreviations

Abbreviation	Meaning
CF	collaborative filtering
DL	deep learning
GDB	graph database
GRU	gated recurrent unit
HMM	hidden Markov models
HSP	hierarchical sequence popularity
LSTM	long short-term memory
ML	machine learning
MRR	mean reciprocal rank
RNN	recurrent neural networks
RS	recommender systems
SBRS	session-based recommender systems
SotA	state of the art
SVD	singular value decomposition

References

1. Carmona, C.J.; Ramírez-Gallego, S.; Torres, F.; Bernal, E.; del Jesus, M.J.; García, S. Web usage mining to improve the design of an e-commerce website: OrOliveSur.com. *Expert Syst. Appl.* **2012**, *39*, 11243–11249. [CrossRef]
2. Ding, A.W.; Li, S.; Chatterjee, P. Learning User Real-Time Intent for Optimal Dynamic Web Page Transformation. *Inf. Syst. Res.* **2015**, *26*, 339–359. [CrossRef]
3. Altulyan, M.; Yao, L.; Wang, X.; Huang, C.; Kanhere, S.S.; Sheng, Q.Z. A survey on recommender systems for Internet of Things: Techniques, applications and future directions. *Comput. J.* **2022**, *65*, 2098–2132. [CrossRef]
4. Aggarwal, C.C. Content-based recommender systems. In *Recommender Systems*; Springer: Bangkok, Thailand, 2016; pp. 139–166.
5. Schafer, J.B.; Frankowski, D.; Herlocker, J.; Sen, S. Collaborative filtering recommender systems. In *The Adaptive Web*; Springer: Berlin/Heidelberg, Germany, 2007; pp. 291–324.
6. Bogina, V.; Variat, Y.; Kuflik, T.; Dim, E. Incorporating time-interval sequences in linear TV for next-item prediction. *Expert Syst. Appl.* **2021**, *192*, 116284. [CrossRef]
7. Jannach, D.; Ludewig, M.; Lerche, L. Session-based item recommendation in e-commerce: On short-term intents, reminders, trends and discounts. *User Model. User-Adapt. Interact.* **2017**, *27*, 351–392. [CrossRef]
8. Awad, M.A.; Khalil, I. Prediction of user's web-browsing behavior: Application of markov model. *IEEE Trans. Syst. Man Cybern. Part B Cybern.* **2012**, *42*, 1131–1142. [CrossRef] [PubMed]
9. Sakar, C.O.; Polat, S.O.; Katircioglu, M.; Kastro, Y. Real-time prediction of online shoppers' purchasing intention using multilayer perceptron and LSTM recurrent neural networks. *Neural Comput. Appl.* **2018**, *31*, 6893–6908. [CrossRef]
10. Salampasis, M.; Siomos, T.; Katsalis, A.; Diamantaras, K.; Christantonis, K.; Delianidi, M.; Karaveli, I. Comparison of RNN and Embeddings Methods for Next-item and Last-basket Session-based Recommendations. In Proceedings of the ICMLC Conference, Shenzhen, China, 26 February–1 March 2021.
11. Bonnin, G.; Jannach, D. Automated Generation of Music Playlists: Survey and Experiments. *ACM Comput. Surv.* **2014**, *47*, 1–35. [CrossRef]
12. Garcin, F.; Faltings, B. A personalized news recommender systems framework. In Proceedings of the 2013 International News Recommender Systems Workshop and Challenge, Kowloon, Hong Kong, 13 October 2013.
13. Hosseinzadeh Aghdam, M.; Hariri, N.; Mobasher, B.; Burke, R. Adapting recommendations to contextual changes using hierarchical hidden Markov models. In Proceedings of the 9th ACM Conference on Recommender Systems, Vienna, Austria, 16–20 September 2015; pp. 241–244.
14. Hussein, A.S.; Omar, W.M.; Li, X.; Ati, M. Efficient chronic disease diagnosis prediction and recommendation system. In Proceedings of the 2012 IEEE-EMBS Conference on Biomedical Engineering and Sciences, Langkawi, Malaysia, 17–19 December 2012.
15. Shani, G.; Heckerman, D.; Brafman, R.I.; Boutilier, C. An MDP-based recommender system. *J. Mach. Learn. Res.* **2005**, *6*, 1265–1295.
16. Barkan, O.; Koenigstein, N. Item2vec: Neural item embedding for collaborative filtering. In Proceedings of the IEEE 26th International Workshop on Machine Learning for Signal Processing (MLSP), Salerno, Italy, 13–16 September 2016; pp. 1–6.
17. Sun, M.; Min, T.; Zang, T.; Wang, Y. CDL4CDRP: A Collaborative Deep Learning Approach for Clinical Decision and Risk Prediction. *Processes* **2019**, *7*, 265. [CrossRef]

18. Phi, V.T.; Chen, L.; Hirate, Y. Distributed representation-based recommender systems in e-commerce. In Proceedings of the DEIM Forum, Online, 29 February–2 March 2016.
19. Devooght, R.; Bersini, H. Long and short-term recommendations with recurrent neural networks. In Proceedings of the 25th Conference on User Modeling, Adaptation and Personalization, Bratislava, Slovakia, 9–12 July 2017; pp. 13–21.
20. Hidasi, B.; Karatzoglou, A. Recurrent neural networks with top-k gains for session-based recommendations. In Proceedings of the 27th ACM International Conference on Information and Knowledge Management, Turin, Italy, 22–26 October 2018; Association for Computing Machinery: New York, NY, USA, 2018; pp. 843–852.
21. Wang, S.; Hu, L.; Wang, Y.; He, X.; Sheng, Q.Z.; Orgun, M.A.; Cao, L.; Ricci, F.; Yu, P.S. Graph learning based recommender systems: A review. In Proceedings of the Thirtieth International Joint Conference on Artificial Intelligence Survey Track, Montreal, Canada, 19–27 August 2021; pp. 4644–4652.
22. Guia, J.; Soares, V.G.; Bernardino, J. Graph Databases: Neo4j Analysis. In Proceedings of the ICEIS, Porto, Portugal, 26–29 April 2017; pp. 351–356.
23. Miller, J.J. Graph database applications and concepts with Neo4j. In Proceedings of the southern association for information systems conference, Atlanta, GA, USA, 23–24 March 2013; Volume 2324.
24. Konno, T.; Huang, R.; Ban, T.; Huang, C. Goods recommendation based on retail knowledge in a Neo4j graph database combined with an inference mechanism implemented in jess. In Proceedings of the 2017 IEEE SmartWorld, Ubiquitous Intelligence Computing, Advanced Trusted Computed, Scalable Computing Communications, Cloud Big Data Computing, Internet of People and Smart City Innovation (Smart-World/SCALCOM/UIC/ATC/CBDCom/IOP/SCI), San Francisco, CA, USA, 4–8 August 2017; pp. 1–8.
25. Sen, S.; Mehta, A.; Ganguli, R.; Sen, S. Recommendation of influenced products using association rule mining: Neo4j as a case study. *SN Comput. Sci.* **2021**, *2*, 1–17. [CrossRef]
26. Delianidi, M.; Salampasis, M.; Diamantaras, K.; Siomos, T.; Katsalis, A.; Karaveli, I. A Graph-based Method for Session-based Recommendations. In Proceedings of the 24th Pan-Hellenic Conference on Informatics, Athens, Greece, 20–22 November 2020; Association for Computing Machinery: New York, NY, USA, 2020; pp. 264–267.
27. Budnikas, G. Computerised Recommendations on E-Transaction Finalisation by Means of Machine Learning. *Stat. Transit. New Ser.* **2015**, *16*, 309–322. [CrossRef]
28. Suchacka, G.; Skolimowska-Kulig, M.; Potempa, A. Classification of E-Customer Sessions Based On Support Vector Machine. *ECMS* **2015**, *15*, 594–600.
29. Suchacka, G.; Chodak, G. Using association rules to assess purchase probability in online stores. *Inf. Syst. e-Bus. Manag.* **2017**, *15*, 751–780. [CrossRef]
30. Romov, P.; Sokolov, E. RecSys Challenge 2015: Ensemble learning with categorical features. In Proceedings of the 2015 International ACM Recommender Systems Challenge (RecSys '15 Challenge), Vienna, Austria, 16–20 September 2015.
31. Sheil, H.; Rana, O.; Reilly, R. Predicting purchasing intent: Automatic feature learning using recurrent neural networks. *arXiv* **2018**, arXiv:1807.08207.
32. Ling, C.; Zhang, T.; Chen, Y. Customer purchase intent prediction under online multi-channel promotion: A feature-combined deep learning framework. *IEEE Access* **2019**, *7*, 112963–112976. [CrossRef]
33. Liu, G.; Wu, X. Using collaborative filtering algorithms combined with Doc2Vec for movie recommendation. In Proceedings of the 2019 IEEE 3rd Information Technology, Networking, Electronic and Automation Control Conference (ITNEC), Chengdu, China, 15–17 March 2019; pp. 1461–1464.

Disclaimer/Publisher's Note: The statements, opinions and data contained in all publications are solely those of the individual author(s) and contributor(s) and not of MDPI and/or the editor(s). MDPI and/or the editor(s) disclaim responsibility for any injury to people or property resulting from any ideas, methods, instructions or products referred to in the content.

Article

Session-Based Recommendations for e-Commerce with Graph-Based Data Modeling

Marina Delianidi, Konstantinos Diamantaras *, Dimitrios Tektonidis and Michail Salampasis

Department of Information and Electronic Engineering, International Hellenic University, 57400 Thessaloniki, Greece
* Correspondence: kdiamant@ihu.gr

Abstract: Conventional recommendation methods such as collaborative filtering cannot be applied when long-term user models are not available. In this paper, we propose two session-based recommendation methods for anonymous browsing in a generic e-commerce framework. We represent the data using a graph where items are connected to sessions and to each other based on the order of appearance or their co-occurrence. In the first approach, called Hierarchical Sequence Probability (HSP), recommendations are produced using the probabilities of items' appearances on certain structures in the graph. Specifically, given a current item during a session, to create a list of recommended next items, we first compute the probabilities of all possible sequential triplets ending in each candidate's next item, then of all candidate item pairs, and finally of the proposed item. In our second method, called Recurrent Item Co-occurrence (RIC), we generate the recommendation list based on a weighted score produced by a linear recurrent mechanism using the co-occurrence probabilities between the current item and all items. We compared our approaches with three state-of-the-art Graph Neural Network (GNN) models using four session-based datasets one of which contains data collected by us from a leather apparel e-shop. In terms of recommendation effectiveness, our methods compete favorably on a number of datasets while the time to generate the graph and produce the recommendations is significantly lower.

Keywords: recommender systems; session-based recommendations; e-commerce; data and web mining; item co-occurrence; graph data model

Citation: Delianidi, M.; Diamantaras, K.; Tektonidis, D.; Salampasis, M. Session-Based Recommendations for e-Commerce with Graph-Based Data Modeling. *Appl. Sci.* **2023**, *13*, 394. https://doi.org/10.3390/app13010394

Academic Editor: Keun Ho Ryu

Received: 20 November 2022
Revised: 13 December 2022
Accepted: 24 December 2022
Published: 28 December 2022

Copyright: © 2022 by the authors. Licensee MDPI, Basel, Switzerland. This article is an open access article distributed under the terms and conditions of the Creative Commons Attribution (CC BY) license (https://creativecommons.org/licenses/by/4.0/).

1. Introduction

Intelligent recommendations and their application in e-business systems are increasingly attracting the interest of researchers and companies. Particularly, the use of the recommendations systems in e-commerce aims at increasing conversion rate, profit and customer engagement and satisfaction. Today, online sales are often made by non-registered users, and therefore there is no historical user data recorded by the e-shop platforms. In these cases, the only data that can be stored is information concerning the duration of a session, the actions performed in each session's step, the items (i.e., products) viewed, and other activities of the online customers. This information will be recorded to later generate recommendations in real time for other users visiting similar or related items. These are session data [1] and can be collected while users navigate in the e-shop platform.

There is a variety of methods used in recommendation systems, such as association rules [2], matrix factorization [3] or machine learning techniques [4], etc. Other methods recently used in recommendation systems are based on graphs [5]. Graphs can efficiently model user–item interactions within sessions enabling the easy generation of new session data in near-real-time. The most frequent items that users visit are easily found using the current complete graph where nodes represent items and edges represent the "next-item-in-session" relationship between the nodes. Additionally, the combination of consecutive item appearances during user navigation in the online store is easily identified through the graph structure. Implementing a standard co-occurrence method using graphs, a session-based recommendation method, called Pair Popularity, based on item co-appearances anywhere in the same session was presented in [6]. Having recorded the item x viewed by the user at session step t, the method recommended a list of items for step $t + 1$ based on the number of times the items co-appear with x in the training sessions. Session-based recommendation with Graph Neural Networks such as SR-GNN [7], GCE-GNN [8] and IC-GAR [9] have become very popular recently because of their very good performance that often represents the state-of-the-art. However, there are also a number of drawbacks regarding GNN approaches:

- Large computational complexity and large memory requirements during training. Most GNN models require very large training times and large amounts of memory even for medium-size datasets and even with special GPU acceleration hardware;
- Difficulty with cold-start recommendations. Most GNN models base their predictions on previous items visited in the session, so it is difficult to recommend new items or make recommendations without session data;
- Relatively reduced performance when the same item never appears repeatedly in consecutive session steps. This indicates that these models have difficulty in introducing novelty and diversity in the recommendations.

The motivation behind this work is to address these problems by introducing improved graph-based recommendation models which are simple, therefore computationally efficient. Moreover, they should be able to exploit the cold-start probabilities of items when there is no available co-occurrence with other items in the session and should be able to offer novel and diverse recommendations. To that end, we propose two new session-based recommendation methods—the Hierarchical Sequence Probability (HSP) and the Recurrent Item Co-occurrence (RIC). The HSP method extends the Pair Popularity graph-based approach to improve the results by using item sequences in user sessions to produce the hierarchical recommendation list, while the Recurrent Item Co-occurrence recommendation approach focuses on the co-occurrence of the products by giving weight to the count of item appearances in the corresponding sessions.

The goal is to produce the optimal item recommendation list at time step $t + 1$ according to the items observed by the user up until the current time step t. The contributions of our work are:

- The proposition of two simple yet efficient session-based recommendation methods based on the "Next" relationship and the co-occurrence relationship between items in the data representation graph;
- The comparison of the proposed methods with state-of-the-art Graph Neural Network models using four different datasets. One of the two proposed methods outperforms the GNN models in two cases while achieving close performance in the other two;
- The study of item sequences of the recent user browsing history vs. the simple item co-occurrence. We show that the method using co-occurrence statistics can achieve considerably better results than the one using the recent item sequences data;
- Attention to the efficiency aspect, showing that the proposed methods are significantly less computationally expensive than the compared GNN approaches even though the GNN models take advantage of a special GPU accelerator hardware to be trained.

The rest of the paper is organized as follows. In Section 2, we present an overview of the existing research related to the session-based recommendation problem. The data model analysis for the proposed recommendation methods and the algorithmic details are presented in Section 3. Section 4 presents the datasets used in our experiments. In Section 5, we describe the experimental procedure and discuss the results of the proposed recommendation methods. Section 6 concludes the paper.

2. Literature Review

There is a large number of recommendation methods used for different purposes such as recommending friends, destinations, movies, products, etc [10]. These systems use, in addition to previous user transactions, features such as location, demographic profile, and user preferences to identify items that are similar to one another. The role of recommendation systems (RS) has become increasingly crucial, especially in e-commerce, due to the availability of a large group of items from which the user can choose. Users of e-commerce sites are given tailored recommendations for products that they might find interesting. After applying desired business criteria that can be applicable, RSs finally offer a list of the top n recommended products for each targeted user action. If they do exist, long-term user profiles are prominently used in RS techniques. Such long-term user models, however, are usually unavailable in many applications for privacy-related reasons [11].

Session-based recommendation approaches (SBR) are recommendation techniques that only consider the user's in-session behavior and other session-specific information as well as the sequential order of items in sessions [12]. They adjust their recommendations to the user's most recent actions, and their main objective is to predict and suggest the next item(s) during every active user session [1].

A general method for developing recommendation systems is matrix factorization [13,14]. A user–item rating matrix must be factorized into two low-rank matrices, each of which reflects the latent factors of users or objects. In [3], the authors propose a matrix factorization approach for session-based recommendations which is based on solving a least squares optimization problem involving item–item similarities and session–item weights. The method achieves results comparable to the state-of-the-art; however, its complexity increases quickly with the size of the itemset. The item-based neighborhood approaches [15], in which item similarities are determined by the co-occurrence within the same session, could be a rational solution by taking into account the sequential order of the objects instead of generating predictions relying on the most recent click. The sequential Markov chain approaches are suggested to be used to predict users' future actions based on their past actions [16,17]. The weakness of Markov-chain-based models is that they independently recombine the previous components. Such a significant assumption of independence affects the prediction's accuracy.

Recommendation systems using graphs have also been quite actively studied recently. In fact, graph databases (GDBs) are one of the latest approaches in data modeling [5]. In a graph model, the data entities are represented as nodes and their relationships as directed or undirected connections between the nodes; thus, any data relationship can be represented on a corresponding graph [18]. The Neo4j [19] is a popular graph database tool used for creating various recommendation systems for friends, movies and items, as well as in e-commerce and loyalty-based retail businesses [20,21]. It uses the Cypher declarative graph query language, which is similar to SQL allowing efficient creation, reading, updating and querying of the graph data [22].

A session-based recommendation solution developed using the Neo4j graph database is presented in [6]. In this paper, the authors demonstrate an efficient method for session-based next-item recommendations. This recommendation system has been developed for an e-commerce retail store. With the appropriate data modeling, by defining nodes and relationships between the nodes and executing cypher queries, the system identifies the co-occurring paired items anywhere in the same session. The frequency of co-occurring item pairs determines the degree of similarity between these items. In practice, the next-item recommendation method uses these similarities for building the model.

Deep Learning (DL) models based on Recurrent Neural Networks (RNN) have been recently proposed for session-based recommendation solutions. The work in [23] proposes the Recurrent Neural Network approach for session-based recommendations, called GRU4REC, which employs multiple layers of the GRU model and uses only item sequences. In [24], the authors propose a hierarchical Recurrent Neural Network based again on the GRU model for session-based recommendations using user information. The work presented in [25] extends the GRU4REC method by introducing data augmentation, and [26] proposes NARM which is an integration of a stacked GRU encoder attention mechanism to capture more representative item transition information of SBR. In [27], the authors mix the sequential patterns and co-occurrence signals by combining together the recurrent method and the neighborhood-based method to enhance the performance of the GRU4REC recurrent model. One more DL recommendation method is based on mixture-channel purpose routing networks (MCPRNs) [28]. To handle multi-purpose sessions, the authors suggest a mixture-channel model. To model the dependencies between items within each channel for a specified purpose, they create a purpose-specific recurrent network (PSRN), a variation of the GRU RNN model. The authors of [29] introduce an RNN model named Hierarchical Attentive Transaction Embedding (HATE), which exploits the attention mechanism to predict the next item by modeling dependencies in transactional data. The HATE model consists of two parts, the Inter-transaction Context Embedding part for the item representation, and the Intra-transaction Context Embedding part for the representation of multiple chosen items in the current transaction, integrating these embeddings using Intra-transaction attention.

Graph Neural Network (GNN) models implement recommendation systems of various scenarios such as Social Recommendation, Sequential Recommendation, Session-based Recommendation, Bundle Recommendation, Cross-Domain Recommendation or Multi-behavior Recommendation [30]. Additionally, GNN models adopt machine learning and deep learning techniques, such as Convolutional Networks, Attention Mechanism or Embeddings representation to create recommendation systems in different domains [5]. Several next-item Graph Neural recommendation models have been proposed recently for the case of e-commerce scenarios using session-based datasets. One of Graph Neural Network's next-item recommendation approaches, named the Heterogeneous Mixed Graph Learning (HMGL) framework [31], was constructed to learn the complex local and global dependencies for next-item recommendations. HMGL encodes both session information and item attribute information into one unified graph modeling both local and global dependencies to better prepare for the next-item recommendations. In SR-GNN (https://github.com/CRIPAC-DIG/SR-GNN, accessed on 15 March 2022) [7], the session sequences are modeled as graph-structured data. Each session is represented as the composition of the global preference and the current interest of the session. An attention network is used to learn item embeddings on the session graph, and then obtain a representative session embedding which is calculated according to the relevance of each item to the last one. The GCE-GNN (https://github.com/CCIIPLab/GCE-GNN, accessed on 10 May 2022) [8] extends the previous approach by employing a session-aware attention mechanism to recursively incorporate the neighbors' embeddings of each node on the global graph. First, the session sequences are converted into session graphs to construct a global graph. The GCE-GNN learns two levels of item embeddings from the session graph by modeling pairwise item-transitions within the current session and the global graph which is to learn the global-level item embedding by modeling pairwise item-transitions over all sessions. Another recent GNN model, called IC-GAR (https://github.com/Taj-Gwadabe/IC-GAR, accessed on 10 October 2022) [9], models current session representations with session co-occurrence patterns, using a modified variant of Graph Convolutional Network (GCN). The Prediction Module of the IC-GAR separates global preference, local preference, and session co-occurrence in order to estimate the probability scores of candidate items. The global and local preferences model user interest in the current session, whereas the session co-occurrence representation aggregates the higher-order transition patterns of all the items in the training sessions. IC-GAR generates a single undirected graph for every training session. The SR-GNN, CGE-GNN and IC-GAR are the most recent state-of-the-art GNN RS models for SBR where one enhances the other with additional modules in order to more accurately predict the next item. The summary of the reviewed recommendation methods is presented in Table 1.

In the present work, we focus on graph-based recommendation systems in the e-commerce domain by proposing recommendation models that compete with recent state-of-the-art GNN based recommendation models. We propose two different methods called Hierarchical Sequence Probability (HSP) and Recurrent Item Co-occurrence (RIC) which create the recommendation list using the item–item relationships: "next" and "in-same-session", respectively. Related to these two methods, the aim of this paper is to answer the following research questions:

RQ1 Can HSP and RIC models achieve a state-of-the-art performance?
RQ2 How robust are these methods, i.e., how do they perform on different datasets?
RQ3 What is the effect of the item sequences and co-occurrences on the performance of HSP and RIC?
RQ4 What computational resources are required to perform each experiment and how time-consuming is it?

Table 1. Summary of reviewed methods.

Method	Approach	Citation
Probabilistic Matrix Factorization (PMF)	Matrix Factorization	[13]
SLIS, SLIT, SLIST	Matrix Factorization, Linear item–item recommendation	[3]
Matrix Factorization	Item-based Collaborative filtering	[15]
MDP-Based Recommender Model	Markov models	[16]
FPMC	Markov chain, Matrix Factorization	[17]
Recommendation of Influenced Products Using Association Rule Mining	Neo4j, Association rules	[20]
Goods Recommendation	Neo4j, Knowledge Graph database	[21]
Pair Popularity	Neo4j, Collaborative filtering	[6]
GRU4REC	RNN	[23]
HRNN	RNN	[24]
M{1,2,3,4}(GRU Size)	RNN, Data augmentation	[25]
NARM	GRU RNN, Attention mechanism	[26]
WH (KNN, GRU)	GRU RNN, k-NN	[27]
PSRN	GRU RNN, Mixture-channel Purpose Routing Networks (MCPRNs)	[28]
HATE	Attention mechanism, Item embeddings	[29]
HMLG	Gated Graph neural network, Path-based matrix factorization model	[31]
SR-GNN	Graph neural network, Attention mechanism, Item embeddings	[7]
GCE-GNN	Graph Neural Network, Session-aware attention mechanism, Neighbors' embeddings	[8]
IC-GAR	Graph neural network, Session co-occurrence patterns	[9]

3. Recommendation Methods

In this section, we describe two session-based recommendation methods called Hierarchical Sequence Probability (HSP) and Recurrent Item Co-occurrence (RIC), respectively. For both methods, we use graphs to represent data. These graph methods can be applied in e-shop platforms that allow anonymous access from non-registered users. The difference between the two recommendation methods is that HSP exclusively uses the sequence of items appearing in the session, while in the case of RIC, the recommendation list is based primarily on the items' co-occurrences extracted from session data. In detail, the two methods are described below.

3.1. The Graph Models

In both proposed methods, the graphs consist of two types of nodes which represent sessions and items. In the HSP graph, the connections between the nodes represented relationships as follows:

- Item o appearing in session s is connected with s via the *ItemInSession* relationship;
- An item o_1 appearing in session step t and an item o_2 appearing in the same session in step $t+1$ are connected with the relationship *Next*.

Thus, the graph data provide sequence information about items in sessions. Figure 1a shows part of the data graph including the *ItemInSession* and the *Next* relationships between the items and the sessions.

In the RIC method, similar to the HSP, the graph has two types of nodes, for the items and sessions representations and also two types of following connections:

- The *ItemInSession* relationship as in the HSP method, and
- The *InSameSession* relation connects the items' co-occurrences in the same session independently to the sequence they appeared in. This is an undirected relationship.

In this case, the graph data model does not provide the sequence information about items in sessions. Figure 1b shows part of the data graph including the *ItemInSession* and the *InSameSession* relationships between the items and the sessions.

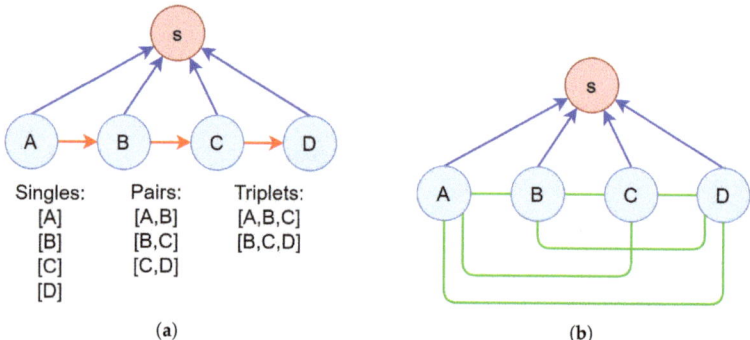

Figure 1. Representation of items (light blue nodes), sessions (pink nodes) and the relationships *ItemInSession* (blue edges), *Next* (red edges), *InSameSession* (green edges). (a) The HSP Graph Model, (b) The RIC Graph Model.

3.2. Hierarchical Sequence Probability Method—HSP

The Hierarchical Sequence Probability approach is an item–item collaborative filtering recommendation method where the list of recommended items arises from the items' sequential appearances during session navigation. We consider t the current time instance and $item_t$ the item that appears to a user in time t during the session s. To recommend the next item at time instance t during s, we introduce the concept of *"item sequence probability"*. This term derives from the visiting frequency of the item by users during the sessions on the e-shop platform. All the items have the *single item probability*, *pair sequence probability* and *triplet sequence probability* as follows:

- $P_0(A)$—*single item probability*, or *cold-start probability* is the number of appearances of item A in all sessions divided by the total number of appearances of all items:

$$P_0(A) = \frac{\text{number of appearances of } A}{\text{number of appearances of all items}} \quad (1)$$

The *single item probability* is derived from the relationship *ItemInSession* of the graph;

- $P_1(A, B)$—*pair sequence probability*, the number of appearances of the item pair (A,B) in successive instances in all sessions, i.e., $item_{t-1} = A$, $item_t = B$ divided by the number of appearances of item A

$$P_1(A, B) = \frac{\text{number of appearances of consecutive pair } A, B}{\text{number of appearances of item } A}$$
$$= P(item_t = B | item_{t-1} = A) \quad (2)$$

This function is created for all pairs of items using the *Next* relationship;

- $P_2(A, B, C)$—*triplet sequence probability*, the number of appearances of the item triplet (A,B,C) in successive steps in all sessions, i.e., $item_{t-2} = A$, $item_{t-1} = B$, $item_t = C$ divided by the number of consecutive pairs A, B

$$P_2(A, B, C) = \frac{\text{number of appearances of consecutive triplet } A, B, C}{\text{number of appearances of consecutive pair } A, B}$$
$$= P(item_t = C | item_{t-2} = A, item_{t-1} = B) \quad (3)$$

This function is created for all triplets of items connected by the *Next* relationship in a chain $A \rightarrow B \rightarrow C$.

The probabilities P_1 and P_2 are closely related to the confidences of the association rules $(A \Rightarrow B)$ and $(A, B \Rightarrow C)$ under the additional constraint that A, B, and C must be consecutive items [32].

The Algorithm

The Hierarchical Sequence Probability (HSP) recommendation method is based on item sequences observed through the users' actions in the sessions. To recommend an item, we look at its probability of appearance as well as the history of sequences of length 1 or 2 in which this item has participated during the training sessions. In the absence of a history (i.e., in the first step of a session), items are recommended based on their probability. Thus, the recommendation of the next item is based on the following cases:

1. The item recommendation list at step $t = 1$ (cold start case) contains the most frequently visited items ordered according to decreasing single item probability value P_0. We call this the "0-history" prediction since no previous session steps are required;
2. For step $t = 2$, the item recommendation list is compiled using navigation history of length 1. In particular, the recommendation list contains the items B that have a nonzero pair-sequence-probability value $P_1(item_1, B)$ with $item_1$ appearing at step $t = 1$. The list is ordered by decreasing the P_1 value. Since $item_1$ may be unpopular, it is likely that there are very few items B with the non-zero $P_1(item_1, B)$ value. For this reason, the recommendation list is completed with "0-history" predictions, i.e., appending the most popular items according to P_0, excluding those that are already included in the list;
3. For steps $t \geq 3$, the recommendation is compiled looking at the session history of length 2. In particular, the recommendation list contains the items C that have a nonzero triplet-sequence-probability value $P_2(item_{t-2}, item_{t-1}, C)$ ordered by decreasing value. Again, due to scarcity reasons, the recommendation list is complemented with predictions made using a history of length 1: we append the items B that have a nonzero pair-sequence-probability value $P_1(item_{t-1}, B)$, ordered by decreasing P_1 value, unless they are already included in the list. If that is still not sufficient, the list is finally completed with "0-history" predictions, i.e., with all the items A ordered by decreasing single item probability value $P_0(A)$, excluding those already in the list.

Figure 2 summarizes the flowchart of the proposed algorithm. In general, the recommended items appear only once in the final list following the hierarchy "*triplet sequence probability*" (2-length history), followed by "*pair sequence probability*" (1-length history), and followed by "*single item probability*" (0-length history).

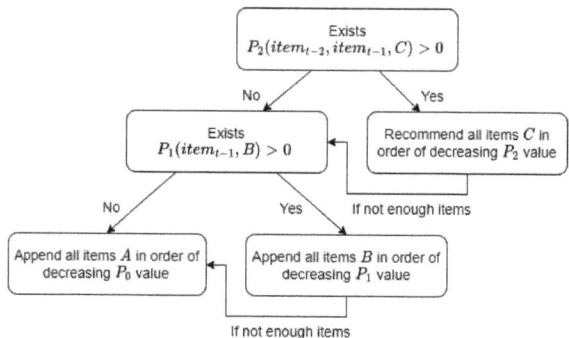

Figure 2. The flowchart of the proposed Hierarchical Sequence Probability (HSP) algorithm. Whenever appending an item in the recommendation list, we make sure it is not already included to avoid duplicate recommendations.

3.3. Recurrent Item Co-Occurrence Algorithm

Whereas HSP is based primarily on the *Next* relationship to determine the list of recommended items, our second proposed method is based primarily on the *InSameSession* relationship, which neglects the relative position of the items in the session. Let $\mathcal{I} = \{o_1, \ldots, o_N\}$ be the set of all the items. Given a current item x we define the confidence weight $\gamma(x|o_i)$ of any other item o_i as the ratio of all the *InSameSession* relations involving both x and o_i divided by the number of the *ItemInSession* relations involving x and any session s:

$$\gamma(o_i|x) = \frac{\text{count}(InSameSession(x, o_i))}{\text{count}(ItemInSession(x, s))}. \quad (4)$$

This is equivalent to the confidence value $\text{conf}(x \Rightarrow o_i)$ of the association rule $x \Rightarrow o_i$ [32]:

$$\text{conf}(x \Rightarrow o_i) = P(s \ni o_i | s \ni x) = \frac{P((s \ni x) \cap (s \ni o_i))}{P(s \ni x)}$$
$$= \frac{\text{number of sessions containing both } x \text{ and } o_i}{\text{number of sessions containing } x}. \quad (5)$$

A naive approach would be to build the recommendation list by simply sorting items by decreasing confidence $\gamma(o_i|x)$. This approach, however, has two major drawbacks:

(a) it poorly treats the case where there is no co-occurrence of x and o_i in any session. As it happens, this is a very common situation where, obviously, $\gamma(o_i|x) = 0$. Since all such items are put in the same ranking position, they will be randomly sorted;

(b) it is a memoryless approach since the recommendation list is built based solely on x, ignoring any other items viewed prior to x.

To alleviate these problems, we define a new confidence value c_i for item o_i which is equal to $\gamma(o_i|x)$ if x and o_i co-occur in at least one session; otherwise, c_i is equal to the cold-start probability $P_0(o_i)$ defined in Equation (1):

$$c_i = \begin{cases} \gamma(o_i|x) & \text{if } \gamma(o_i|x) > 0 \\ P_0(o_i) & \text{otherwise} \end{cases} \quad (6)$$

With this approach, items with no history of co-occurrence with x are placed in decreasing cold-start probability.

In order to introduce memory to the system, we further propose a simple, first order recurrent model that generates the item weights which will be used to build the recommendation list. Let $x = item_t$ be the item viewed at step t in some session s and $c_i(t)$ be the confidence value of any item o_i based on $item_t$ as described in Equation (6). Then, the weight $w_i(t)$ of this item at time t will be defined by the recurrent model:

$$w_i(t) = \alpha w_i(t-1) + (1-\alpha)c_i(t). \tag{7}$$

The initial condition is again the cold-start probability $w_i(0) = P_0(o_i)$. The recommendation list at any time step t is built using the top n items with the largest weights $w_i(t)$. Since the weights are computed independently for different items, the process can be easily parallelized using the vectors $\mathbf{w}_t = [w_1(t), \ldots, w_N(t)]$, $\mathbf{c}_t = [c_1(t), \ldots, c_N(t)]$, where now: $\mathbf{w}_t = \alpha \mathbf{w}_{t-1} + (1-\alpha)\mathbf{c}_t$.

The parameter $1 - \alpha$ ($0 \leq \alpha \leq 1$) is the "forgetting factor," which determines the memory length of the system. For $1 - \alpha = 0$ the system has infinite memory, the confidence $c_i(t)$ based on $item_t$ is ignored and $w_i(t)$ maintains a constant initial value through-out the session. If $1 - \alpha = 1$ the model becomes memoryless and $w_i(t) = c_i(t)$. The parameter α is set by the user and determines the effect that the previous items $item_{t-1}, item_{t-2}, \ldots$ have on the current decision. Figure 3 depicts the schematic diagram of the proposed recurrent system.

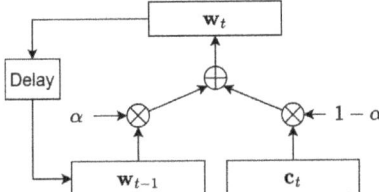

Figure 3. In the RIC method, the item weight vector $\mathbf{w}_t$ at any time step t is generated by a first order linear recurrent model. The input to the model is the current confidence vector $\mathbf{c}_t$.

Depending on how the sessions are recorded, it is possible to have repeated consecutive entries of the same item, for example, the item sequence could be A, B, B, C. In some datasets this is a frequent situation, whereas in other datasets this case never appears. We offer two-flavors of the RIC algorithm:

(a) Plain RIC where the recommendation list is provided as described above. In this case, the current item $x = item_t$ is very likely to be in the top position since $c_x = \gamma(x|x) = 1$;

(b) Current-item-Last (CiL) RIC, in which the current item is specifically moved to the last position in the list of all items, practically making it disappear from the top-n recommendation list.

4. The Datasets

We applied the experimentation on four session-based datasets: Leather (https://github.com/delmarin35/Graph-Probability-Rec-Sys/tree/main/data, accessed on 19 November 2022), Yoochoose1/64 (http://2015.recsyschallenge.com/challege.html, accessed on 3 April 2022), Diginetica (http://cikm2016.cs.iupui.edu/cikm-cup, accessed on 3 April 2022), eElectronics (https://www.kaggle.com/datasets/mkechinov/ecommerce-events-history-in-electronics-store, accessed on 18 June 2022).

Leather: The data of the Leather dataset obtained from the processing of web server log records of an e-shop with leather apparel, jackets, furs and accessories. This is real data that emerged from the log files that were recorded implicitly during the users' navigation actions in the e-shop platform for the time period of six months from March to August of 2021. The log data were preprocessed by identifying sessions, session length, user actions in each session, and the items targeted by the actions. We consider as a session step every user action during the session, for example, viewing an item or adding an item to the basket. The dataset was processed to obtain only the sessions that contain at least two behavior sequences, *"view item"* and *"add to cart"*, resulting in 102,024 records. The dataset was split into train (80%) and test (20%) sets. Thus, the number of records of the train and test sets are 81,651 and 20,373 respectively. The total number of unique sessions is 19,236 which corresponds to 15,388 unique sessions of the train set and 3848 unique sessions of the test set. In addition, the dataset contains 1448 unique items, of which 1429 appear in the train set and 1296 in the test set. The same item never appears in two consecutive steps in any session.

Yoochoose1/64: It is a public benchmark session-based dataset that has been commonly used to evaluate recommendation system performance. This dataset has 17,740 unique items, of which 17,371 appear in the train set and 6745 in the test set. In addition, 369 items of the test set do not appear in the train set, while 10,995 train set items do not exist in the test set. Moreover, 16.183% of the item pairs in the train sessions and 14.938% of the item pairs in the test sessions, respectively, contain the same item twice.

Diginetica: similarly to the Yoochoose1/64 dataset, the Diginetica dataset is often used as a benchmark for testing recommendation systems' performances. This dataset contains 43,097 items. All the items appear in the train set, but only 21,129 appear in the test set. The percentage of consecutive item pairs with a repeated item is less than in Yoochoose1/64, being approximately 9% in both train and test sets.

eElectronics: this dataset contains user behavior data recorded for a period of 5 months (October 2019–February 2020) from a large electronics online store. After removing the sessions with only one item, and splitting the total number of 68,973 sessions into train (80%) and test (20%) sets, 55,089 sessions were used for training and 13,884 sessions were used for testing. Additionally, there are 33,130 unique items, 29,917 of which appear in the train test and 14,482 appear in the test set. Furthermore, 3213 test set items are not in the train set and 1848 train test items do not appear in the test set.

The description of statistical information of the datasets is presented in Table 2. All the datasets have items that exist in the test set and do not exist in the train set or vice versa. No item was removed from either the train or the test sets.

Table 2. Datasets statistics.

Dataset	# Sessions in		% Repeated Item Pairs in		# Items
	Train Set	Test Set	Train Set	Test Set	
Leather	15,388	3848	0.000	0.000	1448
Yoochoose1/64	116,167	15,324	16.183	14.938	17,740
Diginetica	186,670	15,963	9.199	9.143	43,097
eElectronics	55,089	13,884	0.000	0.000	33,130

5. The Experimentation Procedure and Results

In this section, we first describe the evaluation metric for performance evaluation. We then intend to answer the research questions posed in Section 2.

5.1. Evaluation Metrics

The metrics that we used to evaluate the methods were the Mean Reciprocal Rank (MRR)@K and the Recall@K. The MRR is an appropriate metric for measuring the performance of recommendation algorithms on a session-based dataset as well as a good measure of the effectiveness of next-item recommendation [33]. It evaluates the accuracy of the recommended top-k list and is defined as:

$$MRR@k = \frac{1}{N} \sum_{x} \frac{1}{\text{rank}(x)},$$

where x is the next item to be predicted and $\text{rank}(x)$ is the position of x in the recommendation list, starting from position 1 for the first item. If x is not in the recommendation list, we set $\text{rank}(x) = \infty$. The value of MRR is between 0 and 1 and the higher the value, the more effective the quality of the recommendations. Assuming, as is often the case, that at least five recommended items appear on the user's screen, an MRR ≥ 0.2 indicates that the method is quite successful, since the next item chosen by the user is—on average—among the top five recommended.

The Recall@k is defined as the percentage of the target items that were actually included in the top-k recommendation list. Specifically, given a sequence of N top = k recommendation lists L_i with corresponding target items x_i, the Recall@k is defined as [29]:

$$\text{Rec@}k = \frac{1}{N}\sum_{i=1}^{N}|L_i \cap \{x_i\}|,$$

where $|L_i \cap \{x_i\}|$ denotes the cardinality of the intersection set between L_i and $\{x_i\}$ which, in this case, can either take the value 0, if the intersection is empty (i.e. $x_i \notin L_i$), or 1, if $x_i \in L_i$.

In all experiments, we used the train sets to construct the data representation graphs or to train the neural models. The evaluation of the algorithms was performed on the test sets.

5.2. The Experiments

The same session-based datasets were used for all the experimental implementations and recorded the results for MRR@k and Rec@k for the top items $k = \{10, 20, 30\}$. More specifically,

- We compared our methods against three state-of-the-art GNN recommendation models, namely, SR-GNN [7], GCE-GNN [8], and IC-GAR [9]. We trained the models using the code available from the respective GitHubs and recorded the time from the moment the training starts to receiving the results. For each model, we used the hyperparameters proposed in the corresponding Github codes. We executed the GNN models in the Google colab environment with a Tesla T4 GPU accelerator (16 GB) and Intel Xeon CPU @ 2.2 GHz;
- We also performed the same experiments using HSP and RIC and recorded the execution times from the moment we read the data until the generation of the results. The HSP method has no hyper-parameter that requires adjustment. It is worth mentioning that the HSP method extends the Pair Popularity approach and achieves better results. For the RIC method, the values of the parameter α were set to 0.1, 0.3, 0.5, 0.7 and 0.9 during the experiments. Table 3 shows the optimal parameter value per dataset. Our models were executed in Google colab in a CPU-only machine with an Intel Xeon CPU @ 2.2 GHz;
- Additionally, we run the experiments for the Pair Popularity algorithm [6] in the same scenarios of the top k recommendation items.

Table 3. Optimal values of the α parameter in the RIC method.

Dataset	α
Leather	0.3
Yoochoose1/64	0.1
Diginetica	0.7
eElectronics	0.7

5.3. Results and Discussion

The experimentation results show that the effectiveness of a model is affected by the dataset. Table 4 shows that the RIC-CiL recommendation method has a better MRR@k performance for any k in the case of the Leather and Electronics datasets. In these datasets, there is no session with repeated items in consecutive steps. The RIC-CiL variant achieves these results by transferring the current item to the end of the recommendation list, thus essentially excluding it from the top-k recommendations. This technique does not bring desired results in the Yoochoose1/64 and Diginetica datasets due to the existence of repeated consecutive items in the train and test sets. In these cases, the plain RIC variant works better and, especially in the Diginetica case, outperforms SG-NN and IC-GAR with respect to the MRR@*k* metric. HSP also has a very good MRR performance, outperforming the GNN models on the Leather dataset (falling only behind RIC CiL).

On the other hand, the GCE-GNN and SR-GNN models achieve a better MRR performance in the Diginetica dataset while all three GNN models have better MRR performance on the Yoochoose1/64 dataset. In both of these datasets, repeated consecutive items appear in many sessions. As shown in Table 2 the Yoochoose dataset has a very large percentage of repeated item pairs (15–16%), even higher than the Diginetica dataset (~9%). This indicates that the GNN models have difficulty predicting the next item in a high ranking position in the recommendation list unless the next item is identical to the current one. In other words, they are not as efficient in identifying novelty. We stipulate that this phenomenon is due to overfitting, considering that these models have a lot of parameters that allow them to achieve very good fit on the training data but may not generalize as efficiently on the test data. Here, it is worth noting that online store users may not appreciate getting recommendations including the same item they are currently visiting. It seems more natural to exclude the current item from the recommendation list. However, in our experiments, we still use the Diginetica and Yoochoose1/64 datasets because they are common benchmarks studied in many papers in the field.

Table 4. Comparison results of our methods against three state-of-the-art Graph Neural Network recommendation models. The MRR@{10,20,30} and Recall@{10,20,30} are used as evaluation metrics. The best performance for each dataset and corresponding metric is marked by bold-face numbers.

Dataset	Method	Rec@10	MRR@10	Rec@20	MRR@20	Rec@30	MRR@30
Leather	SR-GNN	0.5007	0.2723	0.6028	0.2793	0.6574	0.2814
	GCE-GNN	**0.5391**	0.2686	**0.6452**	0.2760	**0.6994**	0.2781
	IC-GAR	0.4744	0.2675	0.5654	0.2734	0.6171	0.2754
	Pair Popularity	0.4776	0.2605	0.5678	0.2667	0.6206	0.2688
	HSP	0.4878	0.2837	0.5632	0.2892	0.6028	0.2905
	RIC CiL	0.5308	**0.2986**	0.6175	**0.3046**	0.6683	**0.3066**
	RIC plain	0.5083	0.1984	0.6062	0.2053	0.6594	0.2074
Yoochoose1/64	SR-GNN	0.6013	**0.2990**	0.7059	**0.3070**	0.7546	**0.3080**
	GCE-GNN	**0.6113**	0.2966	**0.7117**	0.3040	**0.7660**	0.3060
	IC-GAR	0.5776	0.2947	0.6803	0.3018	0.7310	0.3039
	Pair Popularity	0.4266	0.2108	0.5227	0.2176	0.5715	0.2196
	HSP	0.5455	0.2766	0.6409	0.2833	0.6835	0.2850
	RIC CiL	0.4365	0.2147	0.5366	0.2217	0.5865	0.2237
	RIC plain	0.5693	0.2755	0.6791	0.2832	0.7307	0.2853
Diginetica	SR-GNN	0.3877	0.1697	0.5160	0.1788	0.5945	0.1819
	GCE-GNN	**0.4104**	**0.1812**	**0.5426**	**0.1900**	**0.6193**	**0.1932**
	IC-GAR	0.3581	0.1572	0.4838	0.1659	0.5631	0.1691
	Pair Popularity	0.2664	0.1078	0.3685	0.1149	0.4271	0.1173
	HSP	0.2742	0.1225	0.3414	0.1273	0.3692	0.1283
	RIC CiL	0.3190	0.1406	0.4295	0.1483	0.4944	0.1509
	RIC plain	0.3931	0.1777	0.5134	0.1860	0.5806	0.1868
eElectronics	SR-GNN	0.4041	0.1958	0.4957	0.2023	0.5453	0.2043
	GCE-GNN	**0.4553**	0.2116	**0.5555**	0.2185	**0.6037**	0.2204
	IC-GAR	0.3868	0.2004	0.4730	0.2057	0.5188	0.2075
	Pair Popularity	0.3842	0.1872	0.4697	0.1931	0.5100	0.1948
	HSP	0.3668	0.2068	0.4243	0.2109	0.4491	0.2119
	RIC CiL	0.4525	**0.2382**	0.5421	**0.2444**	0.5892	**0.2463**
	RIC plain	0.4390	0.1685	0.5356	0.1752	0.5854	0.1772

Additionally, our experiments show that the GCE-GNN model achieves the best Recall@k for any k in all the datasets. In combination with the previous observations, we conclude that the GCE-GNN model is the most efficient one in finding the next item somewhere in the top-k list. However, it has still some difficulty in placing the next item in a high ranking position unless it is the same item as the current one. This is more obvious when studying the top 10 recommendations in the Leather and eElectronics datasets. In this case, we note that, although Rec@10 is almost identical for GCE-GNN and RIC-CiL, GCE-GNN has a significantly lower MRR@10 (between 2.5–3%)

Comparing HSP and RIC with each other, we find that HSP is inferior to RIC-CiL in the case of the non-repeating datasets (Leather and eElectronics) and inferior or very close to the performance of RIC-plain in the item-repeating datasets (Diginetica and Yoochoose1/64). Especially in the case of Yoochoose1/64, the HSP and RIC-plain are almost equivalent in terms of MRR performance although HSP is inferior in terms of the Rec@k metric. In the case of the Diginetica dataset, the performance of HSP is inferior to both versions of RIC. The difference between our two proposed methods is that, in HSP, we are basing it on the *Next* relationship, taking into account the sequence of items, while in RIC, we are basing it on the *InSameSession* taking into account the items' co-occurrence. The performance superiority of RIC against HSP indicates that focusing on item co-occurrence is more beneficial than looking strictly at the recent item sequence.

Based on these findings, we can claim that the structure of a dataset affects the performance of the recommendation models regardless of the way the recommendation model is constructed, i.e., with or without the use of neural networks. Assuming that we do not recommend the current item to the online user, the RIC-CiL variation achieves the best MRR performance compared against state-of-the-art GNN models.

Regarding the execution time, the proposed HSP and RIC methods differ significantly in the production of the recommendations list from the initial stage. In addition, simple CPU execution is sufficient for the studied datasets to quickly implement the training process or the calculations of the possible recommended items. The time it took for the entire experimental process per recommendation method and dataset, from the beginning to the appearance of the results, is shown in Table 5 and schematically illustrated in Figure 4. Despite the fact that, for the training of the state-of-the-art GNN methods, a GPU is necessary to complete the experiments in the time indicated in Table 5, for our HSP and RIC methods, significantly less time was consumed without the use of a GPU.

Table 5. The approximate experimentation execution time in minutes.

Dataset	SR-GNN 30 Epochs	GCE-GNN 20 Epochs	IC-GAR 10 Epochs	HSP	RIC
Leather	25	30	20	1	1
Yoochoose1/64	240	500	190	6	10
Diginetica	210	400	380	20	18
eElectronics	210	920	80	5	5

During the training process on the eElectronics dataset, we reduced the batch size to eight to avoid the out-of-memory problem. For the other datasets, we kept the batch size to 100 as defined in the methods' GitHub.

Based on the above findings, the proposed HSP and RIC methods are sufficiently competent against more complex, state-of-the-art methods, and can be applied in real e-commerce environments without requiring special equipment for their productive operation.

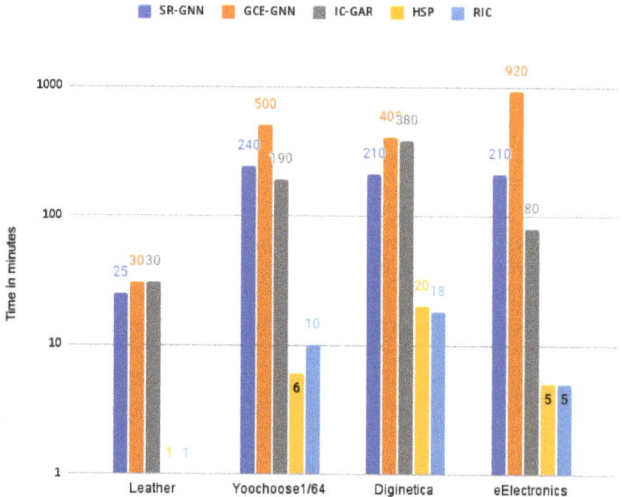

Figure 4. The execution time in minutes for all methods and each dataset. Our proposed methods are between 10× and 180× times faster than GNN models.

6. Conclusions

We have presented two graph-based methods for session-based recommendations in a generic e-commerce environment without employing user history, i.e., suitable for anonymous browsing. The methods are called Hierarchical Sequence Probability (HSP) and Recurrent Item Co-occurrence (RIC). HSP is based on the statistics of the *Next* relationship between items computing the probabilities of triplets, pairs and single items, which are then used—in that order—to determine the position of each item in the recommendation list. The RIC method is primarily based on the *InSameSession* relationship, which determines the co-occurrence of pairs of items in the same session. We introduce memory to RIC by incorporating a simple recurrent formula to determine the weight of each item which is subsequently used to place the item in its proper position in the recommendation list. Setting the value of the forgetting factor of this recurrent formula allows us to balance the effect on our current decision of previously visited items in the session.

Both proposed methods have been compared to state-of-the-art Graph Neural Network models. Our experiments, which involve four diverse datasets, show that RIC can outperform the GNN models in two cases and achieve a performance quite close to that of the winner model in the other two. The HSP approach is typically inferior to RIC, indicating that the *Next* relationship is not so important compared to the *InSameSession* relationship when building the recommendation list.

Additionally, both HSP and RIC methods are very fast compared to the GNN models. This happens despite the fact that the execution time of the GNN models is reduced thanks to the presence of a GPU accelerator, whereas the times recorded for our models are measured on a simple CPU-based machine.

In future work, we plan to investigate the improvement of the RIC method by automatically determining the optimal parameter α and also to determine whether the current item should be first or last in the recommendation list. Another important aspect of the algorithm which is worth investigating is the graph update as new data are collected in such a way that the computational cost of updating the new confidence vectors, cold-start probabilities and weight vectors is minimized.

Author Contributions: Conceptualization, M.D. and K.D.; methodology, M.D. and K.D.; software, K.D.; validation, M.D. and K.D.; formal analysis, M.D. and K.D.; investigation, M.D. and K.D.; resources, D.T. and M.S.; data curation, D.T., M.D., K.D. and M.S.; writing—original draft preparation, M.D. and K.D.; writing—review and editing, K.D., M.D. and M.S.; visualization, K.D.; supervision, K.D.; project administration, K.D. All authors have read and agreed to the published version of the manuscript.

Funding: This research was funded by RESEARCH–CREATE–INNOVATE call (project code: T1EDK-01776).

Institutional Review Board Statement: Not applicable.

Informed Consent Statement: Not applicable.

Data Availability Statement: Data for this study are available on request from the corresponding authors.

Acknowledgments: This research has been co-financed by the European Regional Development Fund of the European Union and Greek national funds through the Operational Program Competitiveness, Entrepreneurship and Innovation, under the call RESEARCH–CREATE–INNOVATE (project code:T1EDK-01776).

Conflicts of Interest: The authors declare no conflict of interest.

References

1. Wang, S.; Cao, L.; Wang, Y.; Sheng, Q.Z.; Orgun, M.A.; Lian, D. A survey on session-based recommender systems. *ACM Comput. Surv. CSUR* **2021**, *54*, 1–38. [CrossRef]
2. Han, J.; Kamber, M. *Data Mining: Concepts and Techniques*, 2nd ed.; University of Illinois at Urbana Champaign: Champaign, IL, USA; Morgan Kaufmann: Burlington, MA, USA; Elsevier: Amsterdam, The Netherlands, 2006.
3. Choi, M.; Kim, J.; Lee, J.; Shim, H.; Lee, J. Session-aware linear item–item models for session-based recommendation. In Proceedings of the Web Conference 2021, Ljubljana, Slovenia, 19–23 April 2021; pp. 2186–2197.
4. Chakraborty, S.; Hoque, M.; Rahman Jeem, N.; Biswas, M.C.; Bardhan, D.; Lobaton, E. Fashion Recommendation Systems, Models and Methods: A Review. *Informatics* **2021**, *8*, 49. [CrossRef]
5. Wang, S.; Hu, L.; Wang, Y.; He, X.; Sheng, Q.Z.; Orgun, M.A.; Cao, L.; Ricci, F.; Yu, P.S. Graph learning based recommender systems: A review. In Proceedings of the Thirtieth International Joint Conference on Artificial Intelligence, Montreal, QC, Canada, 19–27 August 2021; pp. 4644–4652.
6. Delianidi, M.; Salampasis, M.; Diamantaras, K.; Siomos, T.; Katsalis, A.; Karaveli, I. A Graph-Based Method for Session-Based Recommendations. In Proceedings of the 24th Pan-Hellenic Conference on Informatics, Athens, Greece, 20–22 November 2020; Association for Computing Machinery: New York, NY, USA, 2020; pp. 264–267. [CrossRef]
7. Wu, S.; Tang, Y.; Zhu, Y.; Wang, L.; Xie, X.; Tan, T. Session-based recommendation with graph neural networks. *AAAI Conf. Artif. Intell.* **2019**, *33*, 346–353. [CrossRef]
8. Wang, Z.; Wei, W.; Cong, G.; Li, X.L.; Mao, X.L.; Qiu, M. Global context enhanced graph neural networks for session-based recommendation. In Proceedings of the 43rd International ACM SIGIR Conference on Research and Development in Information Retrieval, Virtual, 25–30 July 2020; pp. 169–178.
9. Gwadabe, T.R.; Liu, Y. IC-GAR: Item co-occurrence graph augmented session-based recommendation. *Neural Comput. Appl.* **2022**, *34*, 7581–7596. [CrossRef]
10. Roy, D.; Dutta, M. A systematic review and research perspective on recommender systems. *J. Big Data* **2022**, *9*, 1–36. [CrossRef]
11. Ludewig, M.; Jannach, D. Evaluation of session-based recommendation algorithms. *User Model. User Adapt. Interact.* **2018**, *28*, 331–390. [CrossRef]
12. Wang, S.; Hu, L.; Wang, Y.; Cao, L.; Sheng, Q.Z.; Orgun, M. Sequential recommender systems: Challenges, progress and prospects. *arXiv* **2019**, arXiv:2001.04830.
13. Mnih, A.; Salakhutdinov, R.R. Probabilistic matrix factorization. In *Advances in Neural Information Processing Systems*; Curran Associates Inc.: Red Hook, NY, USA, 2007; Volume 20.
14. Koren, Y.; Rendle, S.; Bell, R. Advances in collaborative filtering. In *Recommender Systems Handbook*; Springer: Boston, MA, USA, 2022; pp. 91–142.
15. Sarwar, B.; Karypis, G.; Konstan, J.; Riedl, J. Item-based collaborative filtering recommendation algorithms. In Proceedings of the 10th International Conference on World Wide Web, Hong Kong, China, 1–5 May 2001; pp. 285–295.
16. Shani, G.; Heckerman, D.; Brafman, R.I.; Boutilier, C. An MDP-based recommender system. *J. Mach. Learn. Res.* **2005**, *6*, 1265–1295.
17. Rendle, S.; Freudenthaler, C.; Schmidt-Thieme, L. Factorizing personalized markov chains for next-basket recommendation. In Proceedings of the 19th International Conference on World Wide Web, Raleigh, NC, USA, 26–30 April 2010; pp. 811–820.
18. Jyothi, D.N. Book Recommendation System using Neo4j Graph Database. *Int. J. Anal. Exp. Modal Anal.* **2020**, *12*, 498–504.

19. Neo4J. Graph Database Platform | Graph Database Management System. 2021. Available online: https://neo4j.com (accessed on 10 June 2021).
20. Sen, S.; Mehta, A.; Ganguli, R.; Sen, S. Recommendation of Influenced Products Using Association Rule Mining: Neo4j as a Case Study. *SN Comput. Sci.* **2021**, *2*, 1–17. [CrossRef]
21. Konno, T.; Huang, R.; Ban, T.; Huang, C. Goods recommendation based on retail knowledge in a Neo4j graph database combined with an inference mechanism implemented in jess. In Proceedings of the 2017 IEEE SmartWorld, Ubiquitous Intelligence & Computing, Advanced & Trusted Computed, Scalable Computing & Communications, Cloud & Big Data Computing, Internet of People and Smart City Innovation (SmartWorld/SCALCOM/UIC/ATC/CBDCom/IOP/SCI), San Francisco, CA, USA, 4–8 August 2017; pp. 1–8.
22. Yi, N.; Li, C.; Feng, X.; Shi, M. Design and implementation of movie recommender system based on graph database. In Proceedings of the 2017 14th Web Information Systems and Applications Conference (WISA), Liuzhou, China, 11–12 November 2017; pp. 132–135.
23. Hidasi, B.; Karatzoglou, A.; Baltrunas, L.; Tikk, D. Session-based recommendations with recurrent neural networks. *arXiv* **2015**, arXiv:1511.06939.
24. Quadrana, M.; Karatzoglou, A.; Hidasi, B.; Cremonesi, P. Personalizing session-based recommendations with hierarchical recurrent neural networks. In Proceedings of the Eleventh ACM Conference on Recommender Systems, Como, Italy, 27–31 August 2017; pp. 130–137.
25. Tan, Y.K.; Xu, X.; Liu, Y. Improved recurrent neural networks for session-based recommendations. In Proceedings of the 1st Workshop on Deep Learning for Recommender Systems, Boston, MA, USA, 15 September 2016; pp. 17–22.
26. Li, J.; Ren, P.; Chen, Z.; Ren, Z.; Lian, T.; Ma, J. Neural attentive session-based recommendation. In Proceedings of the 2017 ACM on Conference on Information and Knowledge Management, Singapore, 6–10 November 2017; pp. 1419–1428.
27. Jannach, D.; Ludewig, M. When recurrent neural networks meet the neighborhood for session-based recommendation. In Proceedings of the Eleventh ACM Conference on Recommender Systems, Como, Italy, 27–31 August 2017; pp. 306–310.
28. Wang, S.; Hu, L.; Wang, Y.; Sheng, Q.Z.; Orgun, M.; Cao, L. Modeling multi-purpose sessions for next-item recommendations via mixture-channel purpose routing networks. In Proceedings of the International Joint Conference on Artificial Intelligence, Macao, China, 10–16 August 2019.
29. Wang, S.; Cao, L.; Hu, L.; Berkovsky, S.; Huang, X.; Xiao, L.; Lu, W. Hierarchical attentive transaction embedding with intra-and inter-transaction dependencies for next-item recommendation. *IEEE Intell. Syst.* **2020**, *36*, 56–64. [CrossRef]
30. Gao, C.; Zheng, Y.; Li, N.; Li, Y.; Qin, Y.; Piao, J.; Quan, Y.; Chang, J. A Survey of Graph Neural Networks for Recommender Systems: Challenges, Methods, and Directions. *ACM Trans. Rec. Sys* **2022**, *55*, 97.
31. Wang, N.; Wang, S.; Wang, Y.; Sheng, Q.Z.; Orgun, M. Modelling local and global dependencies for next-item recommendations. In *International Conference on Web Information Systems Engineering*; Springer: Cham, Switzerland, 2020; pp. 285–300.
32. Agrawal, R.; Imieliński, T.; Swami, A. Mining association rules between sets of items in large databases. *ACM SIGMOD Record* **1993**, *22*, 207–216. [CrossRef]
33. Chen, M.; Liu, P. Performance evaluation of recommender systems. *Int. J. Perform. Eng.* **2017**, *13*, 1246. [CrossRef]

Disclaimer/Publisher's Note: The statements, opinions and data contained in all publications are solely those of the individual author(s) and contributor(s) and not of MDPI and/or the editor(s). MDPI and/or the editor(s) disclaim responsibility for any injury to people or property resulting from any ideas, methods, instructions or products referred to in the content.

Article

Exploiting Domain Knowledge to Address Class Imbalance in Meteorological Data Mining

Evangelos Tsagalidis [1] and Georgios Evangelidis [2,*]

[1] Hellenic Agricultural Insurance Organization, Meteorological Applications Centre, International Airport Makedonia, 551 03 Thessaloniki, Greece
[2] Department of Applied Informatics, School of Information Sciences, University of Macedonia, 546 36 Thessaloniki, Greece
* Correspondence: gevan@uom.edu.gr

Abstract: We deal with the problem of class imbalance in data mining and machine learning classification algorithms. This is the case where some of the class labels are represented by a small number of examples in the training dataset compared to the rest of the class labels. Usually, those minority class labels are the most important ones, implying that classifiers should primarily perform well on predicting those labels. This is a well-studied problem and various strategies that use sampling methods are used to balance the representation of the labels in the training dataset and improve classifier performance. We explore whether expert knowledge in the field of Meteorology can enhance the quality of the training dataset when treated by pre-processing sampling strategies. We propose four new sampling strategies based on our expertise on the data domain and we compare their effectiveness against the established sampling strategies used in the literature. It turns out that our sampling strategies, which take advantage of expert knowledge from the data domain, achieve class balancing that improves the performance of most classifiers.

Keywords: meteorological data mining and machine learning; class imbalance; classification; randomized undersampling; SMOTE oversampling; undersampling using temporal distances

Citation: Tsagalidis, E.; Evangelidis, G. Exploiting Domain Knowledge to Address Class Imbalance in Meteorological Data Mining. *Appl. Sci.* **2022**, *12*, 12402. https://doi.org/10.3390/app122312402

Academic Editor: Yosoon Choi

Received: 27 October 2022
Accepted: 2 December 2022
Published: 4 December 2022

Publisher's Note: MDPI stays neutral with regard to jurisdictional claims in published maps and institutional affiliations.

Copyright: © 2022 by the authors. Licensee MDPI, Basel, Switzerland. This article is an open access article distributed under the terms and conditions of the Creative Commons Attribution (CC BY) license (https://creativecommons.org/licenses/by/4.0/).

1. Introduction

Imbalanced or skewed training datasets make predictive modeling challenging since most of the classifiers are designed assuming a uniform distribution of class labels among the examples. There are classification problems that must deal with various degrees of imbalance. The goal is to improve the quality of the training dataset, i.e., make it more balanced, in order for the classifiers to achieve better predictive performance, specifically for the minority class. Usually, the minority class is more important and, hence, the classifier should be more sensitive to classification errors for the minority class than the majority class [1]. A typical approach in the literature is the application of techniques for transforming the training dataset to balance the class distribution including data oversampling for the minority examples, data undersampling for the majority examples and combinations of these techniques [1,2].

We attempt to enhance existing pre-processing sampling strategies by exploiting expert knowledge from the domain of Meteorology. We use the European Centre for Medium-Range Weather Forecasts (ECMWF) Reanalysis 40-years dataset (See https://www.ecmwf.int/en/forecasts/dataset/ecmwf-reanalysis-40-years, accessed on 29 November 2022, for details) (also known as ERA-40) and a dataset with the historical observations of the meteorological station of Micra, Thessaloniki, Greece and we attempt to predict the occurrence of precipitation on the ground at the meteorological station. We use various data pre-processing strategies (based on oversampling and undersampling) for the selection of the appropriate training dataset, and, we test their effectiveness on various classifiers.

The input dataset consists of imbalanced data regarding the precipitation class variable, where the minority class is only the 16.1% of the cases. It is known that such situations degrade the performance of data mining or machine learning classifiers. In [3], we determined the minimum training dataset size that can ensure effective application of data mining techniques specifically on meteorological data. The performance of various classifiers did not increase significantly for training dataset sizes of more than 9 years. Also, the results were not affected by the way we chose the training dataset examples, i.e., randomly isolated examples totalling nine years versus nine entire yearly sets of examples randomly selected. In this paper, we take advantage of the above finding by choosing appropriately large training datasets for the tested classifiers.

The contribution of this study is the proposal of effective sampling strategies on meteorological training datasets that are based on our expertise on the data domain. In our experimental study, we compare common sampling strategies from the literature and the proposed new strategies and show that the newly proposed strategies improve the performance of most classifiers.

The remainder of the paper is organized as follows. Section 2 discusses the problem of class imbalance, reviews recent works that address it using domain knowledge, and, describes the sampling strategies used in the literature as well as the novel sampling strategies we propose. Section 3 describes the datasets we used for applying the sampling strategies on the training dataset and the classifiers that we compared. Section 4 discusses the methodology used in the experiments. In Section 5, we present the analysis and the results, and, finally, we conclude in Section 6.

2. The Problem of Class Imbalance

A very good introduction to the problem of class imbalance and the related research efforts is given in [4,5]. Ref. [4] provides a comprehensive review of the subject and discusses the initial solutions that were proposed to deal with the problem of class imbalance. Ref. [5] discusses the role that rare classes and rare cases play in data mining, the problems that they can cause and the methods that have been proposed to address these problems.

Over the years the problem of class imbalanced has been studied extensively. There exist numerous papers that use standard data agnostic oversampling and undersampling techniques to create balanced training datasets. Regarding meteorological data, ref. [6] first applies oversampling to increase thunderstorm examples in the training dataset and then uses deep neural networks to predict thunderstorms. Similarly, ref. [7] applies standard oversampling techniques on radar image data to improve rainfall prediction, while [8] presents a framework for predicting floods, in which it embeds re-sampling to address class imbalance. Finally, ref. [9] does not apply any sampling strategies but experiments with various classifiers and concludes that Self-Growing Neural Networks perform better when predicting fog events using data with class imbalance.

Various research works attempt to exploit domain knowledge to address the class imbalance problem, but not in the meteorological domain. Ref. [10] addresses the problem of noisy and borderline examples when using oversampling methods, while [11] deals simultaneously with the problems of class imbalance and class overlap. Ref. [12] uses domain specific knowledge to address the problem of class imbalance in text sentiment classification. Finally, ref. [13] exploits domain knowledge to address multi-class imbalance in classification tasks for manufacturing data.

In our study, we use the most common sampling strategies found in the literature to address the class imbalance problem, namely, the randomized undersampling and the SMOTE oversampling methods and their combination. SMOTE stands for Synthetic Minority Oversampling Technique [14]. Besides the natural distribution, we employ the commonly used 30% and 50% (or balanced) distributions regarding the minority class [1]. We also examine the within-class distribution in addition to the between-class distribution [15], using a combination of the randomized undersampling and the SMOTE oversampling methods in both minority and majority examples.

In an effort to take into account the peculiarities of the data domain when sampling the training datasets and to examine how these could affect the performance of the classifiers, we applied two novel strategies when constructing balanced datasets, i.e., datasets where the number of majority and minority examples is equal. In the first strategy, we applied the k-Means clustering algorithm using "classes to clusters" evaluation to select only the most homogeneous majority examples. In the second strategy, we rejected the majority examples that were closer to the minority examples with respect to their temporal distance in days using three different values for the distance. Then, we further reduced the number of majority examples to achieve a balanced distribution using the randomized undersampling method. We are not aware of any other attempt that uses large meteorological databases and at the same time domain specific sampling techniques to address the class imbalance problem.

We used five different classifiers to build models for predicting our class variable. The training/test set method was used to evaluate the models and to reveal the best sampling strategy for meteorological data. As an evaluation metric, we used the Area Under the ROC (Receiver Operating Characteristics) Curve (AUC) [5,16].

3. Datasets
3.1. ERA-40 Dataset

The European Centre for Medium-Range Weather Forecasts (ECMWF) Reanalysis 40-years dataset (ERA-40) is a global atmospheric analysis of many conventional observations and satellite data streams for the period of September 1957 to August 2002. Reanalysis products are used increasingly in many fields that require an observational record of the state of either the atmosphere or its underlying land and ocean surfaces. There are numerous data products that are separated into dataset series based on resolution, vertical coordinate reference, and likely research applications. In this study, we used the ERA-40 2.5 degree latitude-longitude gridded upper air analysis on pressure surfaces. This dataset contains 11 variables on 23 pressure surfaces on an equally spaced global 2.5 degree latitude-longitude grid. All variables are reported four times a day at 00, 06, 12 and 18UTC for the entire period [17].

We created our initial dataset choosing the values of 10 variables on 7 pressure surfaces on one node. We used only the data from the node with geographical coordinates 40° N latitude and 22.5° E longitude, which is the closest node to the Meteorological Station of Micra, Thessaloniki, Greece located at 40.52° N, 22.97° E and altitude of 4m. We omitted the 11th variable of the Ozone mass mixing ratio. The 1000 hPa, 925 hPa, 850 hPa, 700 hPa, 500 hPa, 300 hPa and 200 hPa are the 7 pressure surfaces we chose, because these are the ones that are mainly used by the meteorology forecasters operationally. In addition, the values of the barometric pressure on mean sea level in Pa supplement the initial dataset that consists of 71 variables.

Furthermore, the initial values of most of the variables for each pressure surface and the pressure on mean sea level were transformed to make them easier to understand or to express them in the same metric units as used operationally by the meteorologists. More specifically, specific humidity initially expressed in $kg \cdot kg^{-1}$ was converted to $g \cdot kg^{-1}$ and vertical velocity in $Pa \cdot s^{-1}$ to $hPa \cdot h^{-1}$. The relatively small values of both vorticity (relative) in s^{-1} and divergence also in s^{-1} were multiplied by 10^6, and the value of potential vorticity in $K \cdot m^2 \cdot kg^{-1} \cdot s^{-1}$ by 10^8. Regarding the wind, wind direction in azimuth degrees and wind speed in knots were calculated using the U and V velocities in m^{-1}. Also, the azimuth degrees for the wind direction were assigned into the eight discrete values of north (N), northeast (NE), etc., used in meteorology. The geopotential in $m^2 \cdot s^{-2}$ was divided by the World Meteorological Organization (WMO) defined gravity constant of 9.80665 $m \cdot s^{-2}$, thus, it was transformed to geopotential height in gpm. Finally, the values of barometric pressure on mean sea level were expressed in hPa, and only the values of temperature in K and relative humidity as percentage (%) on pressure surfaces remained unchanged.

3.2. Class Variable

The 6-hourly main synoptic surface observation data of the Meteorological Station of Micra, Thessaloniki, Greece completed our initial dataset. More specifically, we collected the recorded precipitation data of the period 1 January 1960 00UTC–31 December 2001 18UTC. We assigned the value 'yes' to the 6-hourly records of rain, drizzle, sleet, snow, shower at the station or the records of thunderstorm at the station or around it, and the value 'no' to the rest of the records, thus, creating the class variable of our study. Our purpose is to use the ERA-40 atmospheric analysis data at node 40° N, 22.5° E to predict the precipitation at the station. We mention that the determination of the recorded precipitation is taking into account both the present and past weather of the synoptic observation, and that snow or thunder have priority over rain. Tables 1 and 2 depict the distribution of the precipitation types that had been recorded in the Meteorological Station according to the defined sub-clusters.

Table 1. Natural distribution of values within the minority class variable (precipitation 'yes').

Rain/Drizzle	Snow/Sleet	Thunder	Total 'Yes'
7154	547	2181	9882
11.66%	0.89%	3.55%	16.1%

Table 2. Natural distribution of values within the majority class variable (precipitation 'no').

Fog	Fair/Cloudy	Total 'No'
1395	50,087	51,482
2.27%	81.62%	83.9%

3.3. Predictor Variables

In the pre-processing phase we applied data reduction using the Principal Component Analysis (PCA) extraction method to remove highly correlated variables from the ERA-40 dataset. We used the SPSS statistical software package to process the entire ERA-40 dataset and to produce a new one that consisted of a reduced number of uncorrelated variables.

After applying PCA and examining the component matrix of loadings and the variable communalities, we deleted a total of 36 variables from our initial dataset that consisted of 71 variables. The component model was re-specified six times with a final outcome of 35 variables and 9 components with eigenvalues greater than 1. This is exactly the same methodology we used in a previous work of ours [18]. The analysis revealed the findings of Table 3.

Table 4 displays the variance explained by the rotated components and additionally the corresponding nine most highly correlated variables. The Total column gives the eigenvalue, or amount of variance in the original variables accounted for by each component. The % of Variance column gives the ratio of the variance accounted for by each component to the total variance in all of the variables (expressed as a percentage). The % Cumulative column gives the percentage of variance accounted for by the first 9 components.

The first nine rotated components explain nearly 85.2% of the variability in the original variables and it is possible to considerably reduce the complexity of the data set by using these components, with a 14.8% loss of information. As a result, we can reduce the size of the ERA-40 dataset by selecting the 9 most highly correlated variables with the 9 principal components [18,19]. These meteorological parameters could express the state of the troposphere where precipitation is created and reaches the ground. The reduced ERA-40 dataset with the 9 chosen variables, as predictors, and the precipitation, as class variable, comprised our experimental dataset with 61,364 examples. The size of the dataset is explained by the fact that we have four daily examples (one every 6 h) for a period of 42 years ($42 \times 365 \times 4 = 61{,}320$ examples plus $11 \times 4 = 44$ examples for the 11 extra leap year days of that period).

Table 3. Most highly correlated variables to the rotated components.

Component	Most Highly Correlated Initial Variable	Other Highly Correlated Initial Variables
1st	geopotential height on 200 hPa	geopotential height in the upper levels, the temperature almost in all levels, and the specific humidity in low levels of the atmosphere
2nd	relative vorticity on 1000 hPa	relative vorticity in low levels, the geopotential height on 925 hPa, and the pressure at mean sea level
3rd	wind direction on 300 hPa	wind direction in middle and upper levels
4th	wind speed on 300 hPa	wind speed in upper levels
5th	wind speed on 925 hPa	wind speed in low levels
6th	divergence on 300 hPa	vertical velocity in the upper levels
7th	temperature on 200 hPa	relative vorticity on 200 hPa
8th	potential vorticity on 500 hPa	relative vorticity on 500 hPa
9th	wind direction on 925 hPa	wind direction in low levels

Table 4. Variance explained by rotated components and the representative variables.

Component	Variable	Total	% of Variance	% Cumulative
1st	geopotential height 200 hPa	9.8	28	28
2nd	relative vorticity 1000 hPa	4.2	11.9	39.9
3rd	wind direction 300 hPa	2.9	8.4	48.3
4th	wind speed 300 hPa	2.6	7.5	55.7
5th	wind speed 925 hPa	2.4	7	62.7
6th	divergence 300 hPa	2.3	6.7	69.4
7th	temperature 200 hPa	2.1	6	75.4
8th	potential vorticity 500 hPa	1.8	5	80.4
9th	wind direction 925 hPa	1.7	4.8	85.2

4. Methodology

Since the focus of our study was to address the class imbalance problem, we used a number of sampling strategies in order to balance the training datasets used in the classification task.

Besides the training dataset with the natural distribution of the precipitation values that are shown in Tables 1 and 2 (Strategy 1), we created nine more balanced training datasets following different strategies (Strategies 2–10) (Table 5). Two of them followed the 30% distribution regarding the minority class variable and the other seven the balanced distribution (50%). In the following we describe Strategies 2 through 10.

In the second and third strategies, we used the randomized undersampling method to remove examples producing two datasets with a 30% (U30) and a 50% (U50) distribution of the minority class, respectively [5].

Likewise, in the fourth and fifth strategies, we used a combination of the SMOTE oversampling method to create new examples of the minority class and the randomized undersampling method to remove examples from the majority class, achieving a 30% (SU30) and a 50% (SU50) distribution of the minority class, respectively. We ran the SMOTE oversampling method in the WEKA environment, using 3 nearest neighbors [14,20,21].

In the sixth strategy (BW), we formed balanced datasets not only between-classes but also within-classes [15]. Thus, we employed the randomized undersampling method to reduce the number of the examples for the large clusters of 'Rain/Drizzle' and 'Fair/Cloudy' and the SMOTE oversampling method to increase the number of the examples for the small clusters of 'Snow/Sleet', 'Thunder' and 'Fog'. Thus, the sum of the 'Rain/Drizzle', 'Snow/Sleet' and 'Thunder' examples that belong to the minority class became equal to the sum of the 'Fair/Cloudy' and 'Fog' examples of the majority class achieving the between-class balance. Moreover, the number of the 'Rain/Drizzle', 'Snow/Sleet' and 'Thunder' examples became equal to each other, and, similarly, the number of 'Fair/Cloudy' and 'Fog' examples became equal to each other achieving the within-class balance.

Table 5. Description of used sampling strategies.

Strategy	Acronym	Description
1	UN	Initial unbalanced dataset
2	U30	Randomized Undersampling 30%
3	U50	Randomized Undersampling 50%
4	SU30	SMOTE Oversampling + Randomized Undersampling 30%
5	SU50	SMOTE Oversampling + Randomized Undersampling 50%
6	BW	Balanced between-classes and within subclasses
7	CU	Remove majority examples that cluster with minority ones + Randomized Undersampling
8	D1U	Select only majority examples > 1 day away from minority ones + Randomized Undersampling
9	D2U	Select only majority examples > 2 days away from minority ones + Randomized Undersampling
10	D4U	Select only majority examples > 4 days away from minority ones

Strategies 7 through 10 are newly proposed sampling strategies that take into consideration the nature of the data at hand. More specifically, in the seventh strategy (CU), we applied the k-means clustering algorithm to the entire dataset using WEKA. We set the number of clusters equal to five and chose the "classes to clusters" evaluation in WEKA to evaluate each cluster according to the five classes of precipitation (Tables 1 and 2). In the first step, we selected only the majority examples of the 'Fair/Cloudy' and 'Fog' labeled clusters. In this manner, we rejected all the majority examples that clustered in the three clusters that corresponded to the three minority classes. The idea is that these examples are not good majority representatives since they cluster with minority examples and the classifiers would suffer to distinguish between them. Then, we employed the randomized undersampling method to further reduce the number of majority examples in order to achieve a balanced distribution.

Finally, we introduced three more strategies to reduce the excessive number of majority examples that comprise the majority class. For each majority example, we added a new attribute that expressed its temporal distance to the closest minority example. Then, we selected only the majority examples that had a temporal distance greater than one day (D1U), or two days (D2U), or four days (D4U). And finally, similarly to strategy CU, we employed in the D1U and D2U strategies the randomized undersampling method to further reduce the number of majority examples and achieve a balanced distribution. In the case of the D4U strategy, the number of the majority examples after the reduction was very close to the number of the minority examples. The idea of the temporal distance arose from the fact that during the precipitation episodes there may be some intervals without precipitation on the ground, while the meteorological factor for the precipitation still exists. It is possible that the classifiers can not distinguish these cases of majority class from a minority one leading to a degradation of their performance.

In Section 5, we provide the corresponding number of examples for each strategy and the details regarding the sub-clusters of the precipitation class variable. The training datasets were the input to five classifiers, namely, the Decision tree C4.5, the k-Nearest Neighbor, the Multi-layer Perceptron with back-propagation, the Naïve Bayesian and the RIPPER (Repeated Incremental Pruning to Produce Error Reduction) [21].

We evaluated the resulting models on separate test datasets that followed the natural distribution regarding the clusters of precipitation (Tables 1 and 2). The Area Under the ROC Curve, or simply AUC, was the evaluation metric we used. The AUC measures the performance of the classifiers as a single scalar. ROC graphs are two-dimensional graphs in which the True Positive Rate (the percentage of minority cases correctly classified as belonging to the minority class) is plotted on the Y axis and the False Positive Rate (the percentage of majority cases misclassified as belonging to the minority class) is plotted on the X axis. An ROC graph depicts relative trade-offs between benefits (true positives) and costs (false positives). The AUC is a reliable measure especially for imbalanced datasets to get a score for the general performance of a classifier and to compare it to that of another classifier [5,16].

5. Experiments and Results

5.1. Training/Test Datasets

The training/test set method was used to build and evaluate the data mining models. The initial dataset of 61,364 examples was divided into 10 non-overlapping folds. By taking each one of the 10 folds as a test set and the remaining 9 as a pool of examples for choosing the training datasets, we formed 10 groups with 55,228 training examples and 6136 test examples. Every fold was chosen randomly, but it followed the natural distribution according to the clusters within the precipitation class variable, as shown in Tables 1 and 2. Thus, we produced 10 test datasets with 6136 examples following the natural distribution that covered the entire initial dataset. In our experiments we always used the above test datasets without introducing any synthetic examples.

We created 100 training datasets by randomly taking 10 samples with replacement consisting of 17,788 examples from the training examples of each one of the 10 groups. Furthermore, we joined the same test dataset 10 times to the corresponding 10 training datasets of each group and formed 100 training/test datasets with 23,924 examples (17,788 training and 6136 test examples, 74.35–25.65%). It is noted that in the strategy of D4U, where we used the four days restriction and reduced the number of majority examples close to the number of minority examples, we formed only a total of 10 training datasets, one for each group.

The different methodologies used to generate a training dataset, characterize the different strategies that we followed to address the class imbalance problem. We employed nine new training datasets according to the strategies that we described in Section 4.

Table 6 shows the number of examples of each of the five different types of precipitation for: (a) the initial file (Initial), (b) the 10 groups (Groups), (c) the 10 folds or test sets (Folds), and, (d) the sampled training datasets produced by the nine strategies. Notice that for all strategies, we generated 10 samples per Group for a total of 100 samples of 17,788 examples. The exception was D4U, where the generated testing datasets had an almost balanced distribution of the majority and minority classes, hence, we generated a single sample per Group for a total of 10 samples of 17,625 examples.

In Table 6, we observe that the total number of minority examples in the original training datasets (Groups of 9 folds) was 8894. Hence, in order to produce a 50% balanced training dataset, one needs to choose the same number of majority examples out of the 46,334 available ones. This is the reason we chose 17,788 as the size of the sampled training dataset. These examples correspond to about 12 years of data that is an acceptable amount of data for classification purposes according to our previous research [3], as we explained in Section 1.

5.2. Algorithm Runs

To recap, we tested each one of the first nine strategies with 100 training/test datasets (UN, U30, U50, SU30, SU50, BW, CU, D1U and D2U) and the tenth strategy with 10 training/test datasets (D4U), for a total of 910 training/test datasets.

These datasets comprised the input to the five classifiers that were run and evaluated using WEKA. The classifiers were the decision tree C4.5 without pruning and Laplace estimate (DT), the k-Nearest Neighbors with k = 5 and Euclidean distance (kNN), the RIPPER (RIP), the Naïve Bayesian (NB), and the Multilayer Perceptron neural network with back-propagation (MP).

Table 6. The natural distribution and the number of examples within the precipitation class variable of the training datasets generated by the various sampling strategies.

	Precipitation 'Yes'				Precipitation 'No'			
	Rain/Drizzle 11.66%	Snow/Sleet 0.89%	Thunder 3.55%	Total 'Yes' 16.10%	Fog 2.27%	Fair/Cloudy 81.62%	Total 'No' 83.90%	Total 100.00%
Initial	7154	547	2181	9882	1395	50,087	51,482	61,364
Groups	6438	493	1963	8894	1256	45,078	46,334	55,228
Folds	715	55	218	988	140	5008	5148	6136
Strategy								
UN	2069	171	639	2879	443	14,466	14,909	17,788
U30	3863	296	1177	5336	362	12,090	12,452	17,788
U50	6438	493	1963	8894	250	8644	8894	17,788
SU30	3863	296	1177	5336	362	12,090	12,452	17,788
SU50	6438	493	1963	8894	250	8644	8894	17,788
BW	2965	2964	2965	8894	4447	4447	8894	17,788
CU	6438	493	1963	8894	250	8644	8894	17,788
D1U	6438	493	1963	8894	250	8644	8894	17,788
D2U	6438	493	1963	8894	250	8644	8894	17,788
D4U	6438	493	1963	8894	193	8538	8731	17,625

The last three classifiers were run using the default settings of WEKA. Thus, we performed 4550 runs in the WEKA environment and we present the results in Table 7 and in Figures 1 and 2. Table 7 shows the mean value and the standard deviation of AUC of the 100 or 10 (for D4U) runs for each strategy and classifier.

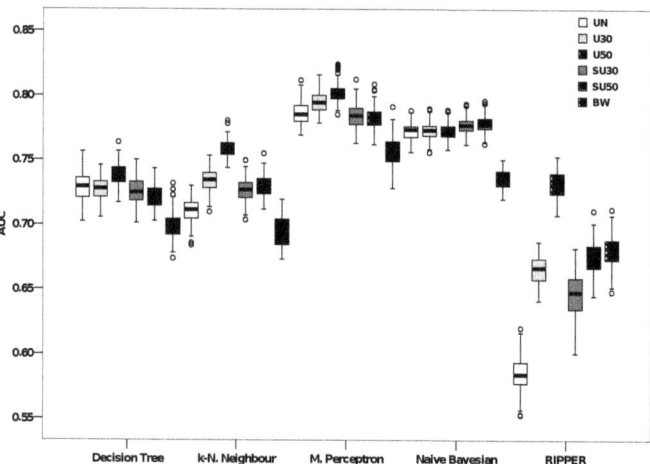

Figure 1. Box-plots of AUC values for strategies UN, U30, U50, SU30, SU50, BW and all classifiers.

Since it is impossible to plot all the box plots for all strategies and classifiers in a single figure, we decided to use two figures. In the first figure, we compare the strategies commonly used in the literature (2 through 6) against UN (strategy 1 that simply uses the initial unbalanced dataset). In the second figure, we compare the newly proposed strategies (7 through 10) against UN and the best strategy of the first figure.

Thus, Figure 1 depicts the box-plots of the corresponding AUC values for the first six strategies. The white box-plots correspond to the UN strategy, the light gray box-plots to the U30 strategy, the light gray box-plots with a pattern of black dots to the U50 strategy, the dark gray box-plots to the SU30 strategy, the dark gray box-plots with a pattern of black dots to the SU50 strategy and the white box-plots with a pattern of black dots to the BW strategy.

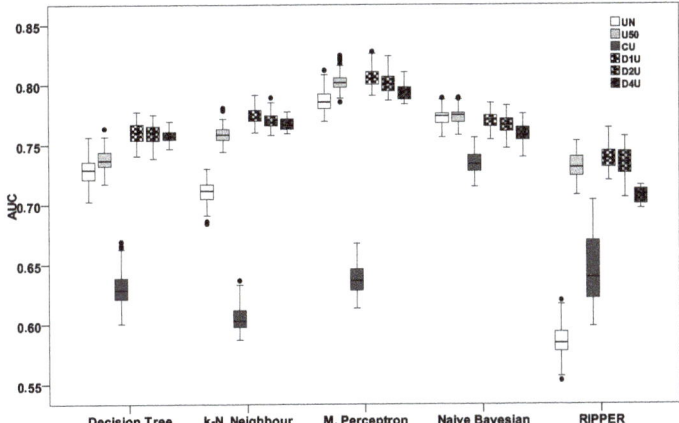

Figure 2. Box-plots of AUC values for strategies UN, U50, CU, D1U, D2U, D4U and all classifiers.

Table 7. Mean value and standard deviation (SD) of AUC. The top three strategies per classifier are shown in red text.

		Classifier				
Strategy		DT	kNN	MP	NB	RIP
UN	Mean	0.728	0.711	0.786	0.773	0.586
	SD	0.011	0.009	0.009	0.008	0.014
U30	Mean	0.727	0.734	0.795	0.773	0.665
	SD	0.009	0.009	0.009	0.008	0.012
U50	Mean	0.737	0.759	0.803	0.774	0.732
	SD	0.008	0.007	0.008	0.008	0.01
SU30	Mean	0.725	0.726	0.785	0.778	0.647
	SD	0.01	0.009	0.009	0.008	0.016
SU50	Mean	0.722	0.73	0.783	0.779	0.676
	SD	0.009	0.009	0.009	0.008	0.013
BW	Mean	0.699	0.71	0.757	0.735	0.68
	SD	0.011	0.012	0.012	0.008	0.012
CU	Mean	0.631	0.607	0.638	0.735	0.644
	SD	0.015	0.012	0.013	0.011	0.028
D1U	Mean	0.76	0.774	0.806	0.77	0.739
	SD	0.008	0.007	0.008	0.008	0.01
D2U	Mean	0.759	0.77	0.802	0.766	0.735
	SD	0.008	0.006	0.008	0.009	0.012
D4U	Mean	0.757	0.768	0.795	0.759	0.706
	SD	0.007	0.006	0.008	0.009	0.007

We notice that the best strategy for each classifier, with the exception of Naïve Bayesian, is the Randomized Undersampling with the balanced distribution (U50). Also, the classifier with the highest AUC value is the Multilayer Perceptron with back-propagation Neural Network. Regarding the Naïve Bayesian classifier, all strategies perform about equally and it seems that only the combination of the SMOTE Oversampling and Randomized Undersampling strategies (SU30, SU50) slightly improve the AUC metric. For the k-Nearest Neighbor and RIPPER classifiers, the U30, U50, SU30 and SU50 strategies significantly improve the performance on AUC, and, especially, the U50 strategy. For the Decision Tree C4.5, only the U50 strategy performs slightly better than the Natural one (UN), and, for the Multilayer Perceptron, the U50 strategy performs better than the Natural one (UN) and the U30 strategy slightly better. The balanced distribution in both the between and within-classes (BW) strategy gave the worst results on AUC with the exception of the RIPPER classifier.

Likewise, Figure 2, depicts the box-plots of the corresponding AUC values for the proposed four strategies (CU, D1U, D2U, D4U), and, additionally, the UN and U50 strategies for comparison. The U50 strategy was chosen because of its performance shown in Table 7 and Figure 1. The white box-plots correspond to the UN strategy, the light gray box-plots to the U50 strategy, the dark gray box-plots to the CU strategy, the white box-plots with a pattern of black dots to the D1U strategy, the light gray box-plots with a pattern of black dots to the D2U strategy, and the dark gray box-plots with a pattern of black dots to the D4U strategy.

In both Figure 2 and Table 7 that highlights the top three performing strategies per classifier, we notice that the strategies with the temporal distance restriction of each minority example from the closer majority one (D1U, D2U and D4U) perform better than the UN strategy on all classifiers with the exception of the Naïve Bayesian classifier. In addition, they perform better than the U50 strategy in the case of the Decision Tree C4.5 and the k-Nearest Neighbor classifiers. Regarding the Multi-layer Perceptron, Naïve Bayesian and RIPPER classifiers, the D1U strategy performs about equally to or slightly better than the U50 strategy, while it performs better than the D4U strategy. Finally, the CU strategy gave very poor results on AUC and only in the RIPPER classifier it outperformed the UN strategy.

6. Conclusions

We applied Principal Component Analysis to reduce the 71 initial chosen variables of the ERA-40 dataset to 9 variables that were uncorrelated to each other, which explain nearly 85.2% of the variability in the original variables. The reduced ERA-40 dataset and the historical precipitation records of the Meteorological Station of Micra, Thessaloniki, Greece were then input into five data mining and machine learning classifiers we used to build models that predict the occurrence of precipitation at the station.

The Multilayer Perceptron with back-propagation neural network classifier outperforms all other classifiers on AUC, revealing the most effective classifier in this meteorological domain.

Moreover, the proposed new strategy D1U with the balanced distribution resulting from the combination of the one day restriction and the Randomized Undersampling method is the recommended strategy to address the class imbalance problem for the Multilayer Perceptron with back-propagation neural network, Decision Tree C4.5, k-Nearest Neighbor and RIPPER classifiers. Alternatively, the Randomized Under-sampling with the balanced distribution strategy U50 could also be used for the Multilayer Perceptron with back-propagation neural network and RIPPER classifiers. Finally, regarding the Naïve Bayesian classifier, the proposed sampling strategies did not improve its performance when compared to the natural distribution. We observe that in the class imbalance problem, the application of sampling strategies based on the expertise on the data domain can improve the effectiveness of some classifiers.

Author Contributions: Conceptualization, E.T. and G.E.; Methodology, E.T. and G.E.; Software, E.T.; Validation, E.T. and G.E.; Formal analysis, E.T. and G.E.; Investigation, E.T.; Resources, E.T.; Data curation, E.T.; Writing—original draft, E.T.; Writing—review & editing, E.T. and G.E.; Visualization, E.T. and G.E.; Supervision, G.E. All authors have read and agreed to the published version of the manuscript.

Funding: This research received no external funding.

Institutional Review Board Statement: Not applicable.

Informed Consent Statement: Not applicable.

Data Availability Statement: Not applicable.

Acknowledgments: We wish to thank the European Centre for Medium-Range Weather Forecasts and the Greek National Meteorological Service for providing us with the meteorological data. We would also like to thank our colleagues Demetrios Papanastasiou and Leonidas Karamitopoulos for their valuable suggestions and comments.

Conflicts of Interest: The authors declare no conflict of interest.

References

1. Brownlee, J. *Imbalanced Classification with Python: Better Metrics, Balance Skewed Classes, Cost-Sensitive Learning*; Machine Learning Mastery: San Juan, PR, USA, 2020.
2. Lemaître, G.; Nogueira, F.; Aridas, C.K. Imbalanced-learn: A python toolbox to tackle the curse of imbalanced datasets in machine learning. *J. Mach. Learn. Res.* **2017**, *18*, 559–563.
3. Tsagalidis, E.; Evangelidis, G. The Effect of Training Set Selection in Meteorological Data Mining. In Proceedings of the IEEE 14th Panhellenic Conference on Informatics (PCI 2010), Tripoli, Greece, 10–12 September 2010; pp. 61–65. [CrossRef]
4. Chawla, N.V.; Japkowicz, N.; Kotcz, A. Editorial: Special issue on learning from imbalanced data sets. *ACM SIGKDD Explor. Newsl.* **2004**, *6*, 1–6. [CrossRef]
5. Weiss, G.M. Mining with rarity: A unifying framework. *ACM SIGKDD Explor. Newsl.* **2004**, *6*, 7–19. [CrossRef]
6. Healy, D.; Mohammed, Z.; Kanwal, N.; Asghar, M.N.; Ansari, M.S. Deep Learning Model for Thunderstorm Prediction with Class Imbalance Data. In Proceedings of the 15th International Conference on Information Technology and Applications, Dubai, United Arab Emirates, 13–14 November 2021; Ullah, A., Anwar, S., Rocha, Á., Gill, S., Eds.; Springer Nature: Singapore, 2022; pp. 195–205.
7. Bouget, V.; Béréziat, D.; Brajard, J.; Charantonis, A.; Filoche, A. Fusion of Rain Radar Images and Wind Forecasts in a Deep Learning Model Applied to Rain Nowcasting. *Remote Sens.* **2021**, *13*, 246. [CrossRef]
8. Wang, D.; Ding, W.; Yu, K.; Wu, X.; Chen, P.; Small, D.L.; Islam, S. Towards Long-Lead Forecasting of Extreme Flood Events: A Data Mining Framework for Precipitation Cluster Precursors Identification. In Proceedings of the 19th ACM SIGKDD International Conference on Knowledge Discovery and Data Mining (KDD'13), Chicago, IL, USA, 11–14 August 2013; Association for Computing Machinery: New York, NY, USA, 2013; pp. 1285–1293. [CrossRef]
9. Nugroho, A.; Kuroyanagi, S.; Iwata, A. Fog forecasting using self growing neural network "CombNET-II"—A solution for imbalanced training sets problem. In Proceedings of the IEEE-INNS-ENNS International Joint Conference on Neural Networks. IJCNN 2000, Neural Computing: New Challenges and Perspectives for the New Millennium, Como, Italy, 27–27 July 2000; Volume 4, pp. 429–434. [CrossRef]
10. Li, J.; Zhu, Q.; Wu, Q.; Zhang, Z.; Gong, Y.; He, Z.; Zhu, F. SMOTE-NaN-DE: Addressing the noisy and borderline examples problem in imbalanced classification by natural neighbors and differential evolution. *Knowl. Based Syst.* **2021**, *223*, 107056. [CrossRef]
11. Li, Z.; Qin, J.; Zhang, X.; Wan, Y. Addressing Class Overlap under Imbalanced Distribution: An Improved Method and Two Metrics. *Symmetry* **2021**, *13*, 1649. [CrossRef]
12. Li, Y.; Guo, H.; Zhang, Q.; Gu, M.; Yang, J. Imbalanced text sentiment classification using universal and domain-specific knowledge. *Knowl. Based Syst.* **2018**, *160*, 1–15. [CrossRef]
13. Hirsch, V.; Reimann, P.; Mitschang, B. Exploiting Domain Knowledge to address Multi-Class Imbalance and a Heterogeneous Feature Space in Classification Tasks for Manufacturing Data. *Proc. VLDB Endow.* **2020**, *13*, 3258–3271. . [CrossRef]
14. Chawla, N.V.; Bowyer, K.W.; Hall, L.O.; Kegelmeyer, W.P. SMOTE: Synthetic Minority Over-sampling Technique. *J. Artif. Intell. Res.* **2002**, *16*, 321–357. [CrossRef]
15. Jo, T.; Japkowicz, N. Class imbalances versus small disjuncts. *ACM SIGKDD Explor. Newsl.* **2004**, *6*, 40–49. [CrossRef]
16. Batista, G.E.A.P.A.; Prati, R.C.; Monard, M.C. A study of the behavior of several methods for balancing machine learning training data. *ACM SIGKDD Explor. Newsl.* **2004**, *6*, 20–29. [CrossRef]
17. Kållberg, P.; Simmons, A.; Uppala, S.; Fuentes, M. *The ERA-40 Archive*; ECMWF: Reading, UK, 2004; p. 31.
18. Tsagalidis, E.; Evangelidis, G. Pre-processing of Meteorological Data in Knowledge Discovery. In Proceedings of the 10th International Conference of Meteorology, Climatology and Atmospheric Physics, COMECAP 2010, Patras, Greece, 25–28 May 2010.

19. Hair, J.; Black, W.; Babin, B.; Anderson, R. *Multivariate Data Analysis*; Always Learning; Pearson Education Limited: New York, NY, USA, 2013.
20. Hall, M.A.; Frank, E.; Holmes, G.; Pfahringer, B.; Reutemann, P.; Witten, I.H. The WEKA data mining software: An update. *ACM SIGKDD Explor. Newsl.* **2009**, *11*, 10–18. [CrossRef]
21. Witten, I.H.; Frank, E.; Hall, M.A. *Data Mining: Practical Machine Learning Tools and Techniques*, 3rd ed.; Morgan Kaufmann, Elsevier: Amsterdam, The Netherlands, 2011.

Article

Similarity Calculation via Passage-Level Event Connection Graph

Ming Liu [1,2,3,4], Lei Chen [4,*] and Zihao Zheng [2]

[1] State Key Laboratory of Communication Content Cognition, People's Daily Online, Beijing 100733, China
[2] Harbin Institute of Technology, School of Computer Science and Technology, Harbin 150001, China
[3] Peng Cheng Laboratory, Shenzhen 518055, China
[4] International Business and Management Research Center, Beijing Normal University, Zhuhai 519087, China
* Correspondence: chenlei@bnuz.edu.cn

Abstract: Recently, many information processing applications appear on the web on the demand of user requirement. Since text is one of the most popular data formats across the web, how to measure text similarity becomes the key challenge to many web applications. Web text is often used to record events, especially for news. One text often mentions multiple events, while only the core event decides its main topic. This core event should take the important position when measuring text similarity. For this reason, this paper constructs a passage-level event connection graph to model the relations among events mentioned in one text. This graph is composed of many subgraphs formed by triggers and arguments extracted sentence by sentence. The subgraphs are connected via the overlapping arguments. In term of centrality measurement, the core event can be revealed from the graph and utilized to measure text similarity. Moreover, two improvements based on vector tunning are provided to better model the relations among events. One is to find the triggers which are semantically similar. By linking them in the event connection graph, the graph can cover the relations among events more comprehensively. The other is to apply graph embedding to integrate the global information carried by the entire event connection graph into the core event to let text similarity be partially guided by the full-text content. As shown by experimental results, after measuring text similarity from a passage-level event representation perspective, our calculation acquires superior results than unsupervised methods and even comparable results with some supervised neuron-based methods. In addition, our calculation is unsupervised and can be applied in many domains free from the preparation of training data.

Keywords: text similarity calculation; passage-level event connection graph; vector tuning; graph embedding

1. Introduction

The fast advance of web technology causes an explosive increase of web data. Text is one of the most prevailing data formats across the web, which enables lots of text-based analysis tools to be provided to help users ease the way to process texts. Text similarity calculation is one of the fundamental text processing tasks, which is also the bottleneck of many web applications, such as news recommendation, Q&A system, etc. Traditional text similarity calculations can be roughly divided into two classes. One is supervised based, which maps two texts into a high-dimensional space and finally makes two similar texts close in the form of vector representation. The other one is unsupervised based, which often treats text as a sequence of word pieces and scores the similarity between two texts in terms of word concurrence plus the order of the sequence or ignoring it. Except word concurrence, some other statistical features are also utilized such as TF/IDF or Mutual Information. Between the two kinds of calculations, supervised ones always own high performance, since they can accurately draw the boundary between similar texts and dissimilar texts with the help of training data. The emergence of neural-based algorithm enhances the performances of supervised methods to a higher level, which gain a huge advantage beyond unsupervised ones. Accordingly, their high-quality results are over dependent on training data. When the domain changes, the performances of supervised ones degrade sharply. Unsupervised ones do not suffer from this limitation, since they do not refer to any transcendental knowledge and are free from training data. Thus, they do not fear domain transferring. The types of texts across the web are countless. We cannot collect all types of texts as training data to let supervised methods go through at advance. Therefore, it is reasonable to design an unsupervised similarity calculation, which can be applied in any domain.

Text is often used to record events. Reading text, we know what is happening and what is the end. An event just indicates something happens in some place at some time. Traditional event extraction tasks, like ACE [1] and FrameNet [2], treat events occurring in sentence-level (which means event is fine-grained). The events stated by different sentences are independent. Events extracted at sentence level cannot be directly utilized to deal with passage-level task. Text similarity calculation is a typical passage-level task. The similarity between two texts depends on their overall content similarity. We should take a high-level view over all the events mentioned in one text. Such as one text has one main topic, from passage-level, though there are many events stated by the sentences in one text, one text only has a core event. The other events serve the core event, as explaining the core event or completing the details of the core event. That indicates the core event mostly decides the similarity between two texts, and the other events play an auxiliary role. For example, the similarity between two following articles (Two articles are, respectively, https://www.reuters.com/article/us-asia-storm/super-typhoon-slams-into-china-after-pummeling-philippines-idUSKCN1LW00F, and https://www.wunderground.com/cat6/Typhoon-Mangkhut-Causes-Heavy-Damage-Hong-Kong-China-and-Macau, accessed on 17 May 2022. These two articles can be accessed till the pages are deleted) is high, since both take the event of the damage of "Mangosteen" typhoon as the core event, though one details the degree of the damage and the other does not.

As text similarity calculation is a passage-level task and concerns whether two texts stress the same core event or not, we should take the entire text into consideration to locate the core event. Anyway, most of events cannot be fully stated by only one sentence. They may cross several sentences, even the nonadjacent sentences. Like financial events, e.g., investment and debt, the arguments of those events spread all over the entire text. For this reason, traditional sentence-level event extraction methods are not appropriate to extract the core event from a passage level. This paper just constructs a graph, namely event connection graph, to cover the multiple relations among the events mentioned in one text. This graph is composed of a set of polygons. Each polygon is formed by one trigger as its center and some arguments surrounding this center. The trigger and the arguments are extracted by a sentence-level event extraction method. To value the nodes in the graph, PageRank is adopted. The nodes of the largest values are treated as the core event, and text similarity is calculated according to the correlation between two core events, respectively, extracted from two texts. Moreover, two improvements based on vector tuning are proposed to better model the event connection graph. One is to detect the semantically similar triggers and link them to fully cover the relations among events. The other is to embed the global content carried by the entire event connection graph into the core event to let text similarity be partially guided by the full-text content.

To sum up, the contributions of this paper can be summarized as follows:

1. This paper proposes a novel event connection graph to model the events and their mutual relations mentioned in one text. This graph is composed of some polygons, and each polygon represents a sentence-level event. Via PageRank, the core event can be extracted to represent the main content of the text, and further utilized to calculate text similarity.

2. Two improvements are provided to enhance the completeness and effectiveness of the constructed event connection graph. One is to tune the vector representation of

the trigger to find and link more related events, which enables the generation of a more comprehensive event connection graph. The other is to embed the information carried by the entire event connection graph into the core event to make similarity result more rational.

3. As shown by experimental results, our similarity calculation obtains superior results than unsupervised methods by a large margin, and even comparable results with supervised neuron-based methods. Typically, our calculation is unsupervised. It can be applied in any domain without the dilemma of domain transferring.

Though our similarity calculation can combine the merits from supervised and unsupervised similarity calculations. Our calculation has time issues needed to be further solved. In particular, our calculation needs to form a passage-level event representation. This kind of operation needs extra time. Thus, though our calculation has higher accuracy, it is not fit to online applications, especially some time-insensitive applications.

Our paper has six sections. Section 1 is introduction, which briefly introduces the motivation of our work and summarizes its contributions. Section 2 shows some related research. Section 3 gives a brief overview of our work at first, and then details the process used to construct the event connection graph and the approach used to value the nodes in the graph. Section 4 tells two improvements on our event connection graph based on vector tuning. Section 5 designs some experiments to illustrate the high quality of our similarity calculation. Section 6 presents the conclusions and gives some future works.

2. Related Work

The rapid advance of internet technology brings the explosive increase of web data. Facing the massive amount of data, internet users require automatic data analysis and processing tools. Text is one of the most prevailing data formats on the web. Thus, many web applications are designed aiming at processing textual data. Almost all the text related applications treat text similarity calculation as their fundamental module. Such as text clustering [3], machine dialogue [4], product recommendation [5], Q&A [6], those applications take text similarity calculation as the key component. In general, the methods for text similarity calculation can be partitioned into two categories. One is supervised based which is guided by annotated training samples. The other one is unsupervised based free from annotations.

Supervised type often treats texts as points mapping to the high-dimensional space. A classification function is trained to separate points into similar and dissimilar two groups. Some other methods turn classification to a rank problem, which learn score functions to discriminate similar points from dissimilar ones. The advantage of supervised type is brought from the guidance of training data. Due to training process, supervised type often acquires high performance. Text is encoded as a vector for calculating convenience. Before the appearance of deep neuron network, one-hot vector is widely used. Only one entry has non-zero value. This kind of encoder generates high-dimensional and sparse vectors, which degrades the quality of many text-oriented applications [7]. The proposal of word embedding changes this dilemma. Word embedding compresses one-hot vector into a densely distributional vector with low dimension. Skip-gram [8], CBOW [9], GloVe [10], ELMo [11] are typical exemplars. The neuron-based models, such as CNN [12], GRU [13], LSTM [14], or the pre-trained language models such as Transformer [15], GPT [16], BERT [17], XL-NET [18], Roberta [19] can produce more reasonable text representation on the basis of word embedding. The overlapping degree decides the similarity between texts, whereas, only depending on word concurrence or word alignment cannot fully express the semantic similarity between texts. To better model the interaction between texts, attention mechanism is taken, which considers the relevance of non-aligned parts across the input sequences. The widely applied attentions are multiple layer attention in [20] and co-attention in [21]. Basically, supervised text similarity calculations own high performance, especially after the application of neuron-based models. However, they are easily distorted by training data. They have to make a hypothesis about the distribution of input data in terms of the transcendental knowledge implicitly provided by training data. There is no way to collect enough training data to let supervised calculations go through in advance, especially for the neural-based methods, since their explosive parameters require massive data for fully training. For this reason, supervised calculations are appropriate to deal with domain data and can hardly be transferred. In our paper, we hope to design a text similarity calculation, which can fit to the texts in any type and from any domain. Therefore, we try to design an unsupervised text similarity calculation.

Unsupervised similarity calculations free from training data. They model input data all by their natural distribution. Some untrained score functions are taken to measure text similarity based on distribution similarity. Euclidean distance [22], KL divergence [23], and Entropy [24] are some widely used score functions. Joint functions are also proposed to integrate previous scores [25,26]. Due to missing training data, the features used by score functions are some statistical values provided by raw texts after word segmentation and stemming, such as TF/IDF [27], TextRank [28], and LDA [29]. Some recent works try to turn unsupervised similarity calculation into a supervised task. An iterative process is adopted to take the output cases as training data in turn [30]. This kind of calculations suffers from cold-starting issue, which needs to set initial similarity values beforehand, and the final results drop a lot on the inappropriate initialization.

Table 1 just summarizes the difference between supervised text similarity calculation and unsupervised text similarity calculation.

Table 1. Comparison of supervised and unsupervised similarity calculation.

Feature/Method	Supervised	Unsupervised
Training data	Results derived from training data	Free from training data
Performance	Higher performance	Lower performance
W/O semantics	Semantic embedding via representation	Lack of understanding semantics
Domain transfer	Hard	Easy

As indicated by the pervious table, it can be observed that these two kinds of similarity calculations both have corresponding merits and drawbacks. Supervised methods have higher performances due to its importing of training data. However, using training data is hard to alter domain. This situation causes that the performances of supervised methods drop sharply when domain changes. On the contrary, unsupervised methods have lower performances, while their performances do not drop along with domain alteration. In this situation, we try to propose an unsupervised similarity calculation to combine both merits of supervised and unsupervised methods.

Features taken by previous calculations are words or word spans which contribute mostly to score functions (applied in supervised ones) or own some prominent distribution compared with other features (applied in unsupervised ones). Though among supervised calculations, some algorithms may learn a semantic embedding on word level or text level in terms of training data to help model the semantics in input text [31–33]. They all ignore a fact that most of web texts are used to record events. One text should tell one core event. The other mentioned events either help explain the core event or provide some details of the core event (such as time, place, or related events). In fact, the core event mostly decides the similarity between two texts. In other words, if one event is stressed by two texts meanwhile, these two texts are similar at a high possibility. Thus, the task of calculating text similarity can be fulfilled by comparing the discrepancy of the core events, respectively, extracted from two texts. The core event represents the main content of one text. It should be extracted from a passage-level viewpoint.

Event extraction and representation have been studied during a long time. As the most famous event extraction tasks, MUC (Message Understanding Conference) [34] and ACE (Automatic Content Extraction) [35] have been held for about 30 years. The definition of event in MUC and ACE is sentence-level with trigger as key element and arguments as supplementary details. Traditional event extraction tasks assume that an event can be fully expressed by a single sentence. It can be extracted without taking other sentences into consideration. Since an event can be formatted as trigger and arguments, traditional sentence-level event extraction methods can be separated into two successive steps. The former step is called event detection (or trigger extraction), which aims to detect events and classify event type. The latter step is called argument extraction, which aims to acquire the arguments related to the trigger, such as time, location, subject, and object, etc. The algorithms designed for sentence-level event extraction are not appropriate to extract passage-level events, since they aim to learn a better representation for single sentences [36,37] and not to model the relations among events across sentences.

As told before, traditional event extraction methods treat sentences independently and extract events from a single sentence. Though it has been proposed something called cross-sentence event extraction methods. While their object is still to extract events from a single sentence, their highlight is to take the adjacent sentences in a sliding window into consideration during extracting process [38,39]. Obviously, the cross-sentence event extraction methods are not suitable to extract core events, since they also miss the operation of modeling the relations among events from a passage angle. Therefore, this paper designs an event connection graph to cover the relations among all the events mentioned in one text. Via graph centrality measurements, the core event can be extracted and used to calculate text similarity.

3. Model Details
3.1. Task Overview

The objective of text similarity calculation is easy to be defined. As given two texts s_1 and s_2, we hope to obtain the similarity value between s_1 and s_2. Different from traditional calculations, this paper aims to calculate text similarity in terms of measuring whether s_1 and s_2 mention the same core event or not. A graph, noted as $G(V, E)$, is constructed to model the relations among events, where V is node set and E is arc set. It is called event connection graph. The nodes in V are just triggers and arguments. Those triggers and arguments are extracted sentence by sentence to represent a serial of sentence-level events [40]. While the arcs in G represent the relations among events. Since the core event represents the main content of one text, it should be surrounded by the other events. As turning events to nodes and relations among events to arcs to form a graph, the nodes, which represent the core event, should locate at the graph's center. Via some graph centrality measurement, such as PageRank, we can easily locate the core event. It is worth noting that comparing the nodes (extracted by sentence-level event extraction methods), the arcs play an important role to decide the quality of similarity results. As shown in the experiments, we adopt several popular sentence-level event extraction methods, but it can hardly see the difference in accuracy. Therefore, we provide two improvements based on vector tuning to complete the constructed event connection graph to involve more arcs.

3.2. Graph Construction

This section details the approach used to construct the event connection graph. Here we borrow the method shown in [40] to extract fine-grained sentence-level events. Each sentence-level event is formed as a polygon with trigger as its center and arguments as its surrounding nodes. The arguments are listed in the order how they appear in the sentence. The trigger and the arguments are connected by arcs. Figure 1 is an example of one polygon formed from the sentence "The President of USA communicates with Chinese Leader on the phone about North Korea issue". It is straightforward that trigger is the key element, since event type and argument template are both decided by trigger. Therefore, we put trigger at the center of the polygon to represent its pivotal position and put the arguments surrounding the trigger. As shown in Figure 1, the trigger "communicate" (after stemming) is put at the center of the polygon and the arguments related to this trigger are put surrounding the center in the order how they appear in the sentence.

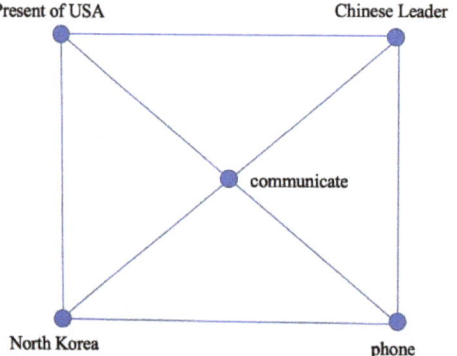

Figure 1. The polygon formed from the example sentence.

To model the relations among events, we just simply connect the polygons via the overlapping arguments to form an event connection graph. Figure 2 shows an example event connection graph formed from the following four sentences. In Section 4, we further propose a way to find semantically similar triggers to reveal deeper relations among events.

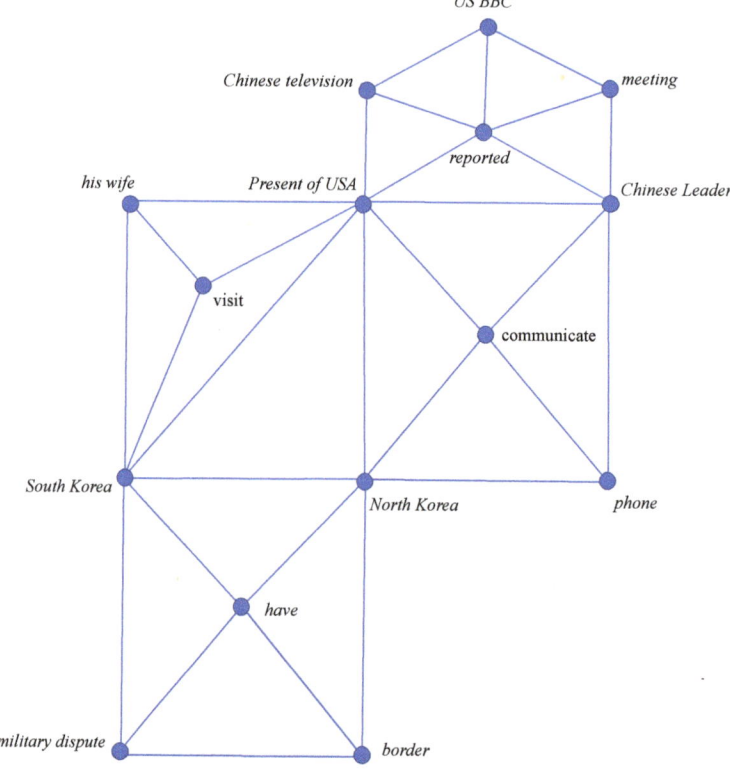

Figure 2. The event connection graph formed from given sentences.

"South Korea and North Korea have a military dispute on the border."
"The President of USA visits South Korea with his wife."

"The President of USA communicates with Chinese Leader on the phone about North Korea issue."

"Chinese television and US BBC reported the meeting between the US president and Chinese leader respectively."

3.3. Node Evaluation

Typically, "If one author emphases a topic (or a clue), everything in his article is related to this topic (or clue)" [41,42]. It is straightforward to make an assumption that the core event in one text should be supported by the other events. If we project all the events mentioned in one text to a plane, the core event will be the point surrounded by the other event. In our paper, we just project events to a plane, while treating the event as a polygon which includes several nodes (i.e., trigger and arguments). Trigger is the key element in the event and decides event type. Thus, we put trigger at the center of the polygon. These two situations ensure that the center of the graph should be the core event. The remaining job becomes how to locate the center of the graph. PageRank, a popular centrality measurement, is chosen to fulfil this task. PageRank is proposed by Google and used to rank web pages in searching engine. The principle behind PageRank is random walk [43]. When one surfer randomly surfs on a graph, the node visited most frequently should be the central node (owning the largest PageRank value).

We just follow the traditional PageRank measurement. The only difference is to use the transition matrix (noted as A) formed from our event connection graph. The size of A is $v * v$. v denotes the number of nodes in the graph. Each entry in A is the transition probability from one node in the row to another node in the column. For example, given a surfer who travels on the event connection graph, if (i,j) is an arc, A_{ij} denotes the transition probability that this surfer visits j by jumping from i, and can be set as the reciprocal of the out degree of node i. On the opposite, if (i,j) is not an arc, this probability is 0.

Via PageRank, each node in the event connection graph has a value. This value indicates the importance of the node in the graph, which can be utilized to locate the core event. There are two kinds of nodes in the graph, i.e., trigger and argument. If the node of the largest PageRank value is a trigger, we then extract the trigger and the arguments belonging to this trigger as the core event. This way just treats the nodes in the polygon which takes the trigger of the largest value as its center as the core event. Otherwise, if the node of the largest value is an argument, we then output the nodes in all the polygons which take this argument as their intersection node. Figure 3 gives the PageRank values of the nodes in Figure 2. In this figure, the node "President of USA" owns the largest value (marked in red color). Since "President of USA" is an argument, we output the nodes in the polygons which take "President of USA" as their intersection node. The chosen nodes are marked in a yellow color in Figure 3. These nodes just indicate the core event expressed by the previous paragraph with four sentences. However, the chosen event is not accurate, since the main meaning of this paragraph is about the meeting of two leaders in USA and China.

Let S_i and S_j, respectively, denote the two sets which include the chosen nodes in the event connection graphs formed from the given texts, $text_i$ and $text_j$. To calculate the similarity between $text_i$ and $text_j$, we can form a matrix, noted as TS_{ij}. Each element in this matrix denotes the similarity between two chosen nodes in S_i and S_j, respectively. Since the node in the graph is either trigger word or argument word, it can be represented as vector via GloVe [10]. Their similarity can be measured by vector similarity via Cosine. Some triggers or arguments may be phrase (composing of several words). We then average the vectors of the words in that phrase as its vector representation. We take the mean of all the elements in TS_{ij} as the similarity between $text_i$ and $text_j$. The formula is shown as follows:

$$sim(text_i, text_j) = \sum_{k=1}^{n} TS_{ij}(k)/n \qquad (1)$$

where n denotes the number of all the elements in TS_{ij}, and $TS_{ij}(k)$ denotes one element in TS_{ij}.

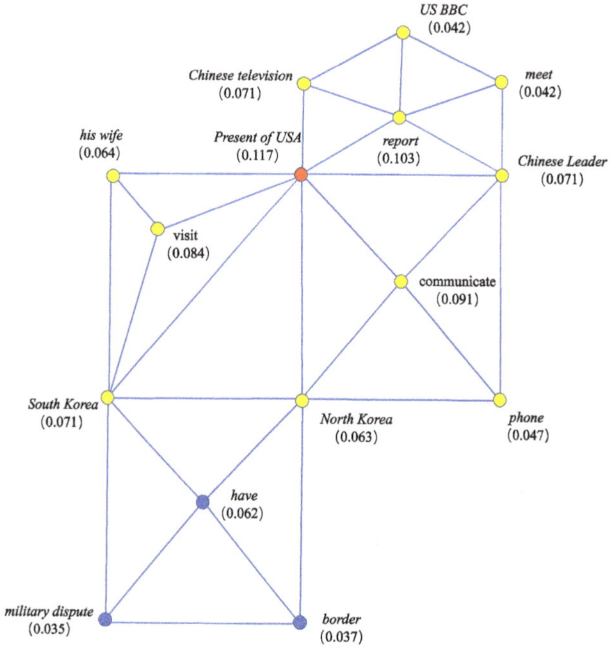

Figure 3. PageRank values of the nodes in the event connection graph.

The previously constructed event connection graph has two flaws. One is that it only uses the overlapping arguments shared by polygons to model the relations among events. This kind of relation is too vague and not sufficient, since the relations among events are mainly caused by triggers. We should provide a way to detect deeper relations among events. The other is that only the node of the largest value and its adjacent nodes are chosen as text representation. These nodes can cover the information expressed by the core event and some other events highly related to the core event. The rest of the events mentioned in the text can also add some supplementary details. These details also need to be considered in similarity calculation. For this reason, two improvements are made. One is to fine-tune the trigger vector to detect and connect more related events. The other is to tune the vectors of the nodes in the core event to let them integrate the information carried by the entire graph.

4. Two Improvements Made on Our Event Connection Graph

4.1. Tuning Trigger Words

The relations among events are mainly caused by trigger words. We should provide a way to find semantically similar triggers and link them in the event connection graph to involve more relations among events. It has been counted that about ninety percent of trigger words are nouns and verbs (or noun and verb phrases) [44,45]. The pre-trained word embedding injects semantics in vector representation and obtains this representation counting on whether two words own the similar contexts or not. However, in event related tasks, we cannot merely depend on pre-trained word embedding to reveal semantic similarity between triggers. Trigger and its arguments have some commonly used collocations, e.g., "kick football" and "play basketball". That causes two trigger words which have high semantic similarity may have different contexts.

To find semantically similar trigger words, we can borrow the help from some synonym dictionaries, like VerbNet and WordNet, two manually formed synonym dictionaries. These two dictionaries put semantically similar words in one synset. The synsets are organized in hierarchy. Unfortunately, dictionary cannot cover all the possible semantically similar trigger pairs. Anyway, it is time-consuming and laborious to manually construct such kind of dictionary. Therefore, we should provide a way to find semantically similar triggers independent of manual dictionary. In this paper, we try to fine-tune the vector representations of the trigger words to let semantically similar triggers own close vector representations. Two triggers whose cosine similarity is beyond the threshold (0.8) are connected through an arc to involve more rational relations among events. Figure 4 shows the event connection graph after connecting similar triggers, i.e., visit and communicate, and report and communicate. Regarding the threshold (0.8), it is set based on sufficient experimental results shown in the experimental section. GloVe [10] trained on wiki data is used as the basic trigger embedding.

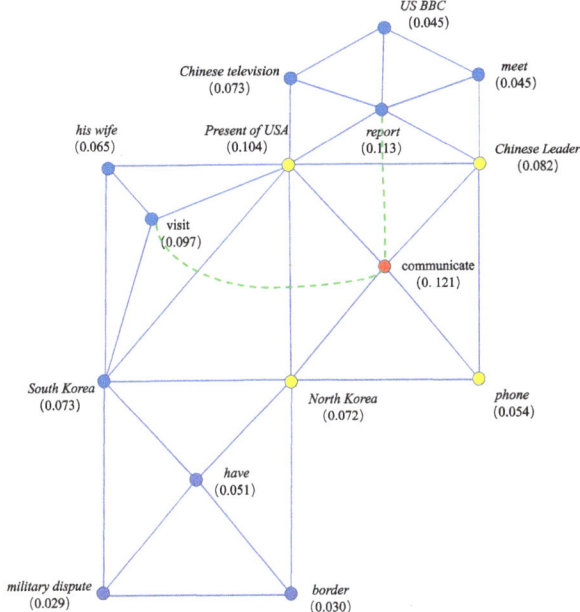

Figure 4. The event connection graph by linking semantically similar triggers.

As shown in Figure 4, with the inserted arc, dotted line with green color, the node of the largest value changes to "communicate". That indicates, after involving novel relation, the core event can be revealed more correctly.

Let B_c denote the set including the synonymous trigger pairs sampled from VerbNet and WordNet. We tune the vector representations of the triggers according to the following formulas:

$$min\ O(B_c) = min(O_c(B_c) + R(B_c)) \tag{2}$$

$$O_c(B_c) = \sum\nolimits_{(x_l, x_r) \in B_c} [\tau(att + x_l t_l - x_l x_r) + \tau(att + x_r t_r - x_l x_r)] \tag{3}$$

$$R(B_c) = \sum\nolimits_{x_i \in B_c} \lambda \parallel x_i(int) - x_i \parallel_2 \tag{4}$$

where (x_l, x_r) denotes a synonymous word pair in B_c. t_l is one word, randomly sampled from the synset which x_l and x_r are not in. So is to t_r. att denotes the predefined deviation between the semantically similar word pair and the dissimilar one. It is set to 0.6. τ denotes max margin loss, noted as $max\ \tau(0, x)$. $x_i(int)$ denotes the pre-trained GloVe vector. λ is a predefined regression parameter and is set to 0.0006. The predefined parameters are set according to [45].

As shown in Equation (2), the tuning formula has two parts. The former part (noted as $O_c(B_c)$) refers to Equation (3), which makes similar triggers own similar vector representations. The latter part (noted as $R(B_c)$) refers to Equation (4), which keeps the tuned vectors not far away from their pre-trained results. Since the pre-trained vectors are acquired from a large-scale corpus, we certainly do not want the tuned vectors to deviate from the pre-trained ones. If one trigger in the event connection graph is tuned, we then replace its original vector representation by the tuned one. In our tuning method, we only tune the vectors of the words included by VerbNet and WordNet, and do not extend the range outside the dictionaries. The reason is that the pre-trained vector representations are acquired from a large-scale corpus. Thus, they are credible until we have enough evidence to support that the pre-trained vector representations cannot calculate word similarity accurately. If one trigger is a phrase, we simply take the mean of the vectors through all the words in that phrase as its representation.

In English, the synonymous word pairs in VerbNet and WordNet can be used as training data. For the other languages, it is hard to find such kind of dictionary. We then use these two dictionaries as bridge to construct training data. We take VerbNet and WordNet as pivot dictionaries and utilize Google translation to translate the words in them into any language. However, one word in English can be translated to many words in the other language. Taking the synonymous word pair "undo" and "untie" in VerbNet for example, "undo" can be translated to five words in Chinese like "打开 (open)", "解开 (untie)", "拆开 (open)", "消除 (remove)", "取消 (cancel)", while "untie" can be translated to "解开 (untie)" and "松开 (loosen)". We finally obtain the possible translated word pairs in the number of 9 (except the duplicated one "解开 (untie)" and "解开 (untie)"). Among them, only the word pair "解开 (untie)" and "松开 (loosen)" is a rational synonym. To avoid incorrect translation, we introduce back translation, extensively used in unsupervised translation task to avoid semantic drift [46]. Following the idea of back translation, we only remain the translated word pairs which can be back translated to the exact same words in English. Also taking the word pair (undo, untie) for example, when we translate them in Chinese, we only remain the word pair (解开, 松开), since these two words can be translated back to undo and untie in English, respectively.

4.2. Node Representation via Graph Embedding

In Section 3, we only choose the nodes which can represent the core event as text representation to calculate text similarity. On one side, except the core event, the information carried by the other events (we call them supplementary events) also provide some useful information. We should not simply abandon them. On the other side, the information carried by the supplementary events is trivial compared with the core event. Thus, there is no need to choose nodes from the event connection graph to represent them. For this reason, we apply graph embedding to integrate the information carried by the supplementary events into the chosen nodes.

Graph embedding is conducted to embed the graph structure into node representation [47], which can make one node in the graph integrate the information carried by the entire graph. Graph embedding often has a clear target to achieve and the vector representations of the nodes are formed via a bunch of training data, while in our setting, we do not have a clear target to set objective function (to integrate information into the chosen nodes is not a clear target to set objective function) and certainly do not have any training data either. In this situation, we follow self-training approach used in word2vec, as shown in [48]. We take random walk to generate a set of paths and take these paths as contexts to adjust the vector representations of the nodes. The graph embedding process used to acquire node representation is shown as follows:

1. Taking $G_i(V, E)$ for example, the event connection graph formed from $text_i$, we treat one node in V as the starting point and choose the successive node via randomly

jumping to one of the adjacent nodes. Repeat this jump for l times. A path of length l can be obtained.
2. Repeat step 1 for m times on each node in V. We then get a path set (noted as PH) whose size is nm, where n denotes the size of V.
3. Each path in PH is treated as one training sample.

Let $v_1, v_2, \ldots, v_{i-1}, v_i, v_{i+1}, \ldots, v_{l-1}, v_l$ denote one path. The values of m and l are set according to [48]. Following self-training setting, we learn a vector representation for v_i to predicate the context of v_i. The loss function for it is:

$$\max P(v_{i-2}, v_{i-1}, v_{i+1}, v_{i+2}|v_i) = \max \prod_{j=1}^{2} P(v_{i\pm j}|v_i) \qquad (5)$$

where $v_{i-2}, v_{i-1}, v_{i+1}, v_{i+2}$ denote the context of v_i. Two fully-connected layers are used to train the node representation. Softmax is adopted as the output layer. During the training process, for the first iteration, the node v_i integrates the representations of its adjacent nodes, i.e., $v_{i-2}, v_{i-1}, v_{i+1}, v_{i+2}$. For the second iteration, v_i integrates the representations of the nodes which can be linked to v_i through the path whose length is less than 4. As the training process continues, the information carried by the entire graph can be integrated into v_i. After graph embedding, we replace the original vector representations of the nodes in the core event by the tuned ones to let the core event integrate the information carried by the entire text and recalculate the similarity between two texts using Equation (1).

5. Experiments and Analyses

5.1. Experimental Setting

Our similarity calculation aims to obtain the similarity value between two texts from a viewpoint of passage-level event representation. One text may mention several related events. An event connection graph is then constructed to model the relations among those events. In addition, two improvements based on vector tuning are provided to help better construct the event connection graph. Finally, the nodes, indicating the core event mentioned in one text, are chosen to represent the graph. It is worth noting that our calculation is unsupervised. It is not limited on any particular language and any particular domain. To test its compatibility in different languages and different tasks, we build testing corpora in three languages, i.e., English, Chinese, and Spanish. For English, there are many open tasks about text similarity measurement, such as paraphrase and query match in NLU (natural language understanding) [49,50]. We just choose these two tasks to test the performance of our similarity calculation. Ten thousand text pairs are sampled from the corpora for these two tasks. One half includes similar text pairs, and the other half includes dissimilar text pairs. The corpora for these two tasks only contain short sentences. Most of short sentences only mention one event. Our similarity calculation is designed on a passage-level representation perspective and chooses the core event to help accurately measure the similarity between two texts. It is more suitable to handle long text which mentions several events. The former two tasks cannot fully demonstrate the advantage of our calculation on dealing with long text. For this reason, we manually annotate a testing corpus including two thousand long text pairs from Daily news published in the latest one month. For Chinese, we build two testing corpora, one for short text and one for long text. The one for short text is provided by Alibaba company for query match task. The one for long text is manually annotated including two thousand long text pairs from Tencent news also published in the latest one month. For Spanish, there is no suitable open corpus for testing. We have to manually annotate one corpus including two thousand long text pairs from kaggle contest. Among all the manually annotated corpora, we set one half including similar text pairs and the other half including dissimilar text pairs.

The criterion used for evaluation is F1. The formulas are shown as follows:

$$P = \frac{r(n)}{t(n)} \qquad (6)$$

$$R = \frac{r(n)}{a(n)} \tag{7}$$

$$F1 = 2 * \frac{P * R}{P + R} \tag{8}$$

where P is precision, which is measured by the correctly calculated similar text pairs (noted as $r(n)$) compared with the totally similar text pairs (noted as $t(n)$). R is recall, which is measured by the correctly calculated similar text pairs compared with the totally noted similar text pairs (noted as $a(n)$). F1 combines precision and recall together.

There are two kinds of corpora in the experiments. One kind is collected from open tasks, such as paraphrase and query match, with a large number. Sufficient annotated texts enable us to compare our calculation with some supervised similarity calculations. The other kind includes the manually collected long texts, which can be used to demonstrate the advantage of our calculation particularly on dealing with long texts. Regarding the large-scale corpora, we separate them into 8:1:1 for training set, development set, and test set. Three neuron-based algorithms are adopted as baselines in the following experiments. They are textCNN (one convolutional layer, one max-pooling layer, and one softmax output layer), Bi-LSTM (taking Bi-LSTM to encode text and softmax to output similarity value), Bi-LSTM+Bidirectional attention (taking Bi-LSTM to encode text and adding a Bidirectional attention layer to model the interaction between two input texts). In detail, we encode text via textCNN, Bi-LSTM, and Bi-LSTM+Bidirectional attention, respectively. Softmax layer is utilized to output a value to indicate the similarity between two texts. The pre-trained model, i.e., BERT base, is also taken as baseline (like machine reading, one of the fine-tuning tasks in BERT, we input two texts into BERT with a segmentation tag [SEP] and add a softmax layer on [CLS] to output similarity value).

Our calculation is unsupervised. Therefore, we also bring in some unsupervised baselines. We represent input text as vector via the following methods and apply Cosine as similarity function to calculate vector similarity as text similarity.

The applied unsupervised vector representations are listed as follows:
(1) Average: the mean of all the word vectors in the input text.
(2) TextRank+Average: take TextRank to choose keywords from input text and then treat the mean of the chosen keyword vectors as representation.
(3) TextRank+Concatenation: take TextRank to choose keywords and concatenate the word vectors of the chosen keywords to form a long vector.

All the word vectors are set via GloVe.

We also bring in two novel and high-performance text similarity calculating methods, Con-SIM [51] and RCMD [52]. They both based on powerful pertained language model. In addition, multi-head attention and cross-attention are both adopted to model deep interaction between two texts. These two algorithms have proved their high accuracy across some text related tasks. Between them, the first one takes context into consideration to model the training gap among different calculations, and the second one models the distance between sentences as the weighted sum of contextualized token distances.

5.2. Experimental Results

The following experiments are conducted in six aspects. Section 5.2.1 shows the experiments to test the rationality of the threshold setting in our calculation. Section 5.2.2 demonstrates the performances of our calculation on the condition that the event connection graph is constructed by different event extraction methods. Section 5.2.3 shows some sampled examples to explicitly demonstrate the ability of our calculation. Section 5.2.4 shows the results of our calculation comparing with the supervised and unsupervised baseline algorithms on the testing corpora. Section 5.2.5 shows the ablation results to see the enhancement brought from two improvements provided in Section 4. In Section 5.2.6, we add an experiment to prove that our calculation is not limited on any particular language and any particular domain.

5.2.1. Testing on Threshold

In Section 4, we provide a vector tunning-based method to find semantically similar triggers and link them to form a comprehensive event connection graph. Two triggers whose semantic similarity value is beyond the threshold (set as 0.8) can be connected in the graph. The following figure just demonstrates and explains the rationality of the threshold setting. It shows F1 values when the threshold changes from 0.1 to 1.0. This experiment is designed to see the rationality of the chosen of the threshold setting.

As shown in Figure 5, the calculating results change along with the variety of the value of the threshold. All the curves have the similar trend across different corpora. They all reach the perk at the value of 0.8 (or close to it). The reason can be explained based on the principle behind word embedding. For most of word pairs, if two words are semantically similar, their pre-trained vector representations are close. The vector representation of trigger is initialized via GloVe, one kind of word embedding; thus, we can take the value between two triggers measured by vector distance to decide whether two triggers are semantically similar or not. Trigger decides event type. Two similar triggers just indicate two related or similar events. However, as indicated in Section 4.1, due to the situation that there are some commonly used collocations in linguistics, the previous conclusion (similar triggers have close vectors) is not always true. Thus, in Section 4.1, we tune the pre-trained vector representations of the triggers via the training data sampled from synonym dictionaries to make semantically similar triggers own close vectors. Based on the tuning operation, finding a threshold to decide whether two triggers are similar becomes feasible. As shown in Figure 5, 0.8 is a reasonable choice, where the performance curves reach the peak through all the testing corpora. When the threshold exceeds 0.8, the performance curves even drop. This is because when the threshold enlarges, some similar triggers are missed to be connected. The relations among events, especially the relations among the semantically similar events, cannot be fully covered by the event connection graph. It finally causes that the extracted event may not be the core event. Furthermore, missing the connections between similar events, the extracted event cannot integrate the information carried by the entire event connection graph. These two situations lead to the drop of the performance curves.

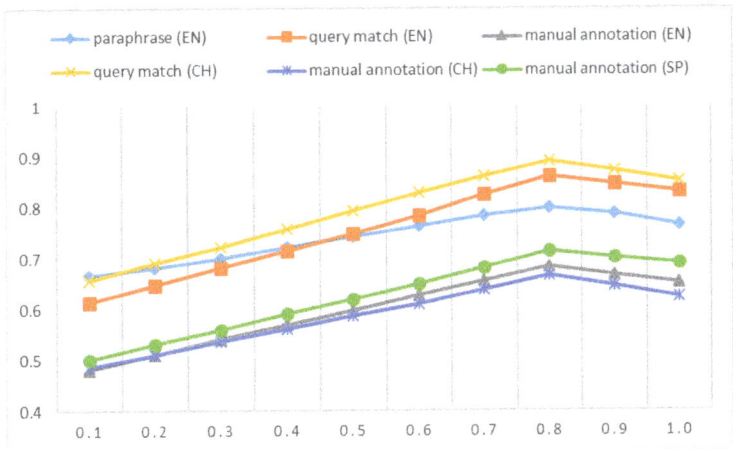

Figure 5. F1 values when we change the threshold from 0.1 to 1.0. The threshold is utilized to decide whether to connect two triggers in the event connection graph or not.

5.2.2. Comparison of Different Event Extraction Methods

Our similarity calculation needs to construct an event connection graph to reveal the core event to calculate text similarity. In our paper, this graph is constructed by the sentence-level event extraction method shown in [40]. We note this method as OneIE as it is called in [40]. There raises a doubt that whether different event extraction methods affect the final calculating results or not. Therefore, we design an experiment to see the similarity calculation results with event connection graphs constructed by different event extraction methods across all the testing corpora. The following table just illustrates the performances of our calculation on the condition that the event connection graph is constructed via several popular sentence-level event extraction methods. The event connection graph includes both trigger and argument; thus, the chosen event extraction methods should jointly extract trigger and argument meanwhile. We choose BeemSearch [53], JointTransition [54], and ODEE-FER [55] as baselines. BeemSearch is one of the classic joint event extraction methods, which encodes text via one-hot feature and applies local and global features to label trigger and argument meanwhile. JointTransition and ODEE-FER are both based on neuron model. The significant difference between them is that JointTransition applies transition model to characterize the relation between trigger and argument, while ODEE-FER integrates latent variable into neuron model to extract open-domain event free from event schema predefinition. Multi-task learning framework is utilized in ODEE-FER to identify trigger and argument concurrently. The corpora for paraphrase, query match, and manually annotated are abbreviated as Para, Q&Q, and MA, which are also used in the following tables.

As shown in Table 2, it can be found that different event extraction methods do not affect the performances of our calculation much. This situation is due to the following two reasons. First of all, the construction of event connection graph is only the first step in our calculation. The extracted triggers and arguments are subsequently measured to indicate their importance via centrality measurement. During the measuring process, the incorrectly extracted triggers and arguments can be eliminated. In Table 2, we also add an extreme case, noted as Extreme listed in the last row, where we treat a verb in the sentence as trigger and noun as argument. If there is more than one trigger in the sentence, we construct polygon for each trigger following the approach shown in Section 3. It can be observed that the result obtained from Extreme is a little different from the ones obtained from the other methods. That indicates we do not need the precise event extraction results, as long as the extracted results contain enough triggers and arguments. Furthermore, two improvements proposed in Section 4 can also help remove the adverse effect brought from the incorrectly extracted triggers and arguments. In detail, one improvement tunes the vector representation of the trigger, and links the semantically similar triggers in the event connection graph. Regarding the triggers incorrectly extracted, they are little related to the core event mentioned in the text. Thus, these triggers do not locate at the center of the event connection graph. After the measuring process, these triggers will be valued with little weights. They will not be chosen as the core event to measure text similarity. The other improvement is to integrate the information carried by the entire text into the chosen nodes via graph embedding. In some cases, even if the incorrectly extracted triggers and arguments are chosen as the core event, after graph embedding, the information carried by the entire text can be integrated into the incorrectly extracted triggers and arguments. This way can also alleviate the adverse effect brought from the incorrect extraction.

Table 2. The results of our calculation obtained on the condition that the event connection graph is constructed via several popular event extraction methods (highest values in bold).

Methods	English			Chinese		Spanish
	Para	Q&Q	MA	Q&Q	MA	MA
BeemSearch	0.81	0.84	0.66	0.85	0.62	0.67
JointTransition	0.79	0.83	0.64	0.84	0.63	0.68
ODEE-FER	**0.82**	0.85	**0.68**	0.86	0.65	**0.71**
OneIE	**0.82**	**0.86**	**0.68**	**0.89**	**0.67**	**0.71**
Extreme	0.77	0.82	0.63	0.82	0.61	0.66

To clearly see the effects brought from different event extraction methods, we also draw a histogram figure to illustrate the calculating results obtained by different sentence-level event extraction methods. In addition, to compare their results in two tasks of text similarity calculation and event extraction, we show the results obtained by different event extraction methods in both tasks in two colors. In this figure, each algorithm corresponds to two columns. The column with blue color indicates the text similarity calculating results, which is averaged across all the corpora including open tasks and manual annotation. The column with orange color indicates the event extracting results, which is averaged across the corpora from ACE and FrameNet, two popular event extraction tasks.

As shown in Figure 6, it is hard to see the performance gap among all the event extraction methods in text similarity calculation task. However, the event extraction methods adopted in the experiment perform differently in the event extraction task. As shown in this figure, ODEE-FER performs much better than the other event extraction methods. Anyway, in this experiment, we also design a simple method called Extreme. This method just simply treats a verb in the sentence as trigger and a noun as argument. It is easy to assume that Extreme should have a poor performance in the event extraction task. The result also proves this assumption. Surprisingly, Extreme obtains almost the same result with the other event extraction methods in the text similarity calculation task. That indicates we do not need the precise event extraction results, as long as the extracted results contain enough triggers and arguments.

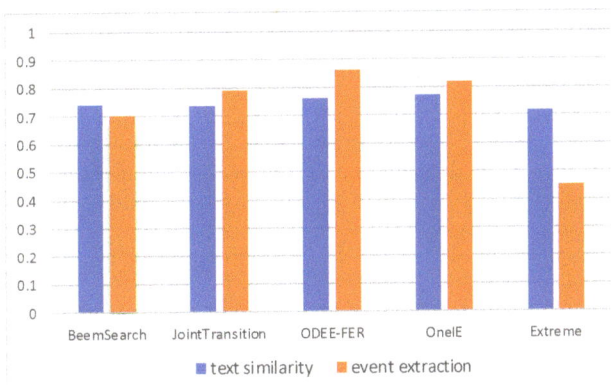

Figure 6. The histogram to see the results obtained by different event extraction methods (blue color indicates text similarity calculation task and orange color indicates event extraction task).

5.2.3. Case Study

In our similarity calculation, we need to extract some nodes from the event connection graph to represent the core event mentioned in the text. In the following table, we just show the extracted nodes (i.e., triggers and arguments) from some sampled texts. We sample 6 texts from our English testing corpora, three for long texts (noted as A1, A2, A3) and three for short texts (noted as S1, S2, S3). The short texts are news caption. The contents of the chosen texts can be found in (A1: https://www.bbc.com/news/technology-52391759; A2: http://news.bbc.co.uk/sport2/hi/football/europe/8591081.stm; A3: https://www.bbc.com/news/business-52467965; S1: https://www.bbc.com/news/uk-51259479; S2: https://www.bbc.com/news/business-44789823; S3: https://www.bbc.com/news/business-52466864 (accessed on 17 May 2022). These texts can be accessed till the pages are deleted). Since keywords can also be treated as the content representation of the text, we also show the keyword extraction results (the top five keywords) obtained by LDA and TextRank, two popular unsupervised keyword extraction algorithms.

As shown in Table 3, among the chosen words, some are the same across different extraction methods while some are distinct. Taking the contents of the sampled texts into consideration, the words extracted by our calculation can exactly cover the core event mentioned in the sampled texts, though the number of extracted words is often less the number from the other two keyword extraction methods. On the contrary, the words extracted by TextRank and LDA are not always related to the core event. This situation is obvious for long texts. For example, for A1, its core event is "Apple iPhone has a software leak on email app". The keywords extracted from this text via TextRank and LDA both include "ZecOps". This word repeats many times in A1. Thus, it is chosen as keyword, whereas this word indicates the source where the news is published. It is not the part of the core event. The reason to this situation is that traditional keyword extraction methods often take the shallow statistics, such as frequency or distribution, to measure word importance. Such an approach causes "ZecOps" to be incorrectly chosen. In our calculation, when measuring the importance of one word, we consider the effect of the event which includes this word. In detail, only if the event is emphasized by one text, the word included by this event can be treated as the representation of this text. In the text of long length, there may mention several events. The frequently occurring words may not be included by the core event, such as the words "ZecOps" and "Rooney" included by A1 and A2. Thus, they may be extracted incorrectly. Regarding the texts of short length, they only include one or two sentences. A few events are mentioned. The frequently occurring words are mostly included by the core event. Thus, among the short texts, the words extracted by the three methods are almost same.

Table 3. The extracted words from the sampled texts (* marks that less than five words can be extracted).

Methods	TextRank	LDA	Ours
		Long Texts	
A1	ZecOps, Apple, mail, leak, hacker	Apple, mobile, ZecOps, bug, hacker	Apple, mail, software, leak, *
A2	Rooney, soccer, Bayern Munich, injury, champion	soccer, Bayern Munich, beat, Man Utd, Rooney	Bayern Munich, beats, Man Utd, *
A3	Barclay, bank, economic, coronavirus, profit	Barclay, coronavirus, bank, pandemic, work	coronavirus, pandemic, costs, £2.1bn, *
		Short Texts	
S1	Carmaker, Tesla, build, factory, Shanghai	Carmaker, Tesla, build, factory, Shanghai	Tesla, build, factory, Shanghai, *
S2	Kobe Bryant, death, BBC, TV news, mistake	BBC, apologize, footage, mistake, *	BBC, apologize, footage, mistake, *
S3	Coronavirus, economy, sink, pandemic, shutdown	Coronavirus, economy, sink, shutdown, *	Economy, sink, pandemic, shutdown, *

5.2.4. Comparison of Different Algorithms

The following table shows the results of comparing our similarity calculation with the supervised and unsupervised baseline algorithms. The supervised baseline algorithms include textCNN, LSTM, LSTM+Bidirectional attention (abbreviated as LSTM+BIA), and BERT-base. They are conducted only on the large-scale testing corpora including short sentences, since these corpora have enough data to form training set. The unsupervised baseline algorithms include Average (abbreviated as AVE), TextRank+Average (abbreviated as TR+AVE), and TextRank+Concatenation (abbreviated as TR+CON). The details of the baseline algorithms are already told at the beginning of Section 5.

For unsupervised similarity calculations, to test their similarity calculating results, we first represent input text as vector. This vector is averaged from all the word vectors through input text, or some chosen word vectors by TextRank algorithm. Then, Cosine similarity is used to decide whether two texts are similar or not. For supervised similarity calculations, we also represent input text as vector, while this vector is formed by different encoder models like LSTM, Bi-LSTM, or pretrained models (BERT or RoBERTa). Then, two vectors obtained by different encoders are sent to MLP layer to output a probability in terms of softmax to indicate similarity results. All the testing algorithms output a value to measure the similarity between two texts. We record the similarity values of all the text pairs in the testing corpora via the given algorithms and take the mean of all the values as the threshold to decide whether two texts are similar or not. To make the obtained results more persuasive, we add significant test. We separate each testing corpus into ten parts, and record calculating results in each part. Two-tail paired t-test is applied to determine whether the results obtained by different algorithms over the ten times' calculations are significantly different or not. We set three significant levels as 0.01, 0.05, and 0.1 (labelled as ***, **, and *).

As shown in Table 4, we list the results obtained in different languages and in different tasks. It can be found that supervised algorithms overwhelm unsupervised algorithms by a large margin in all the testing corpora. The reason is straightforward, since supervised algorithms can utilize training data to obtain a reasonable hyperplane to separate similar text pairs from dissimilar ones. Correspondingly, unsupervised algorithms cannot acquire any transcendental guidance to help model the discrimination between similar and dissimilar text pairs. They only depend on data's natural distribution, thus, obtain lower performance. Anyway, unsupervised algorithms only choose some words with prominent distribution or aggregate all the words in the text to generate text representation, whereas long text has many words which are little related to the main content. This situation causes unsupervised algorithms obtain extremely lower performances on the manually annotated corpora which include only long texts. It can be found that our calculation obtains comparable results with supervised baseline algorithms and performs much better than unsupervised baseline algorithms especially on the corpora including long texts. The reason is totally due to our event connection graph. Based on this graph, the nodes (or words), which can represent the core event mentioned in one text, can be finally extracted. The unrelated noisy words are ignored when calculating text similarity. For this reason, we can acquire accurate similarity results on both long and short texts. Besides, to further improve performance, graph embedding is used to encode the information carried by the entire graph into the chosen nodes to make the chosen nodes carry the global information expressed by entire text. The significant test results also prove the reliability of the high performance of our calculation.

Table 4. The comparison of our calculation with the baseline algorithms (highest values in bold. ***, **, and * indicate three significant levels as 0.01, 0.05, and 0.1.).

Methods		English			Chinese		Spanish
		Para	Q&Q	MA	Q&Q	MA	MA
supervised	TextCNN	0.84 ***	0.82 **	—	0.86 ***	—	—
	LSTM	0.83 **	0.84 **	—	0.83 **	—	—
	LSTM+BIA	0.83 ***	0.87 **	—	0.89 ***	—	—
	BERT-base	0.85 ***	0.89 ***	—	0.91 ***	—	—
	Con-SIM	0.87 ***	0.90 ***	—	0.92 ***	—	—
	RCMD	**0.90** ***	**0.92** ***	—	**0.93** ***	—	—
unsupervised	AVE	0.58 *	0.61 **	0.42 *	0.63 **	0.49 *	0.48 **
	TR+AVE	0.65 **	0.66 **	0.49 **	0.68 **	0.55 **	0.59 **
	TR+CON	0.69 *	0.71 ***	0.53 **	0.66 **	0.53 **	0.57 **
	Ours	**0.82** ***	**0.86** ***	**0.68** ***	**0.89** ***	**0.67** ***	**0.71** ***

In the experiments, there are also two SOTA text similarity calculations, Con-SIM and RCMD. They both obtain extraordinary results. Moreover, it can be observed that RCMD even obtains over 90% F1 value across all the testing corpora. These two methods both have two layers. The lower layer is text encoder, where Con-SIM takes BERT as the encoder and RCMD takes a more powerful model (RoBERTa) as encoder. The difference is that RoBERTa has more parameters; thus, RCMD obtains higher performance. The upper level is the interaction layer, where Con-SIM takes hierarchical interactive attention and

RCMD takes two matrices to model local interaction (inner sentence) and global interaction (outer sentence) to obtain sentence matching results. As indicated in the experiments, our proposed method obtains lower performance than those SOTA methods. However, it is easy to be explained. Those SOTA methods all take pretrained models to encode input texts with massive parameters. Anyway, those methods need to consume training data to adjust model to deal with domain-specific data. As domain changed, these methods are easy to be distorted as shown in the experiments. Compared with those methods, our proposed method is unsupervised based. Thus, it keeps its performance across domains. Anyway, with the help of passage-level document representation, our proposed method can obtain high performance. Though the performance is lower than the ones with pretrained models, its performance is much higher than the baseline unsupervised methods.

5.2.5. Ablation Results

In Section 4, we provide two improvements on our calculation. One is to detect and link similar triggers to involve the relations among the similar or related events into the event connection graph. The other is node representation via graph embedding, which lets the representations of the chosen nodes integrate the information carried by the entire event connection graph. In the following table, we record the results obtained by our calculation in the following two settings. One is with or without linking similar triggers. The other is with or without node representation.

As shown in Table 5, it can be found that two improvements both enhance the performance of our calculation. Between them, node representation brings more boost. The advance brought from these two improvements is easy to be explained. Regarding the advance brought from the linkage of similar triggers, since we find similar triggers via tuning their vector representations and further link them, our event connection graph can cover more relations among events. Via this comprehensive graph, we can locate the core event more accurately. Regarding the advance brought from node representation, the pre-trained vector representations of the chosen nodes can only express their inherent information, i.e., only representing the local information carried by the chosen nodes. After we tune node representation via graph embedding, the vector representations of the chosen nodes can integrate the information carried by the entire event connection graph. Via these nodes, text similarity can be calculated more accurately. Anyway, the representations of the chosen nodes after graph embedding can cover both the inherent information themselves and the information carried by the global graph. It can bring more boost on the performance than the linkage of similar triggers.

Table 5. The ablation results of our calculation (highest values in bold).

Methods	English			Chinese		Spanish
	Para	Q&Q	MA	Q&Q	MA	MA
Only via graph	0.76	0.80	0.55	0.81	0.56	0.57
+linking triggers	0.78	0.82	0.59	0.85	0.60	0.62
+node representation	0.81	0.84	0.63	0.87	0.65	0.69
+linking triggers and node representation	0.82	0.86	0.68	0.89	0.67	0.71

5.2.6. Task Transferring

Text similarity calculation is a fundamental component of many artificial intelligence applications. We cannot predefine the domain and the task where these applications are applied. We then add a test to compare the capacities of different algorithms in the transferring scenario across different tasks and languages. The testing corpora are collected from different domains and different languages. Regarding supervised algorithms, we train them on one corpus and test them on another corpus. There are three kinds of corpora in English, two in Chinese, and one in Spanish. For English, we combine two corpora as training set and test the algorithms on the remaining corpus. For Chinese, we train the algorithms on one corpus and test them on the other corpus. For Spanish, since we only have one corpus, we do not test the algorithms in this language.

To conduct the experiments on the task transferring scenario, we take supervised algorithms and unsupervised algorithms in two ways. Regarding unsupervised algorithms, since they do not have training stage, we run them directly on each corpus and record the results. Anyway, since both languages (English and Chinese) have the corpus about query match task, we test all the algorithms on this task while training on one language and testing on the other language (noted as E-C and C-E indicating English to Chinese and Chinese to English). In this test, all the algorithms are given cross-lingual word embeddings trained on the corpus formed via sentence alignment [56]. We also add significant test to see the credibility of the obtained results.

As shown in Table 6, it can be found that supervised algorithms degrade much compared with the results shown in Table 4. In Table 4, the results are obtained in the situation that training and testing are performed on the same corpus. This phenomenon indicates that task transferring (or corpus changing) deeply affects the performance of supervised algorithms. The reason is obvious. Since supervised algorithms count on the transcendental knowledge (this knowledge indicates data distribution assumption) derived from training corpus to deal with novel data, they are easy to be distorted by the other corpus which owns diverse distribution. On the contrary, there is no training corpus for unsupervised algorithms. Thus, they do not make any assumption about data distribution, which causes they are not affected by task transferring (or corpus changing). Our calculation is one kind of unsupervised algorithms. It keeps high quality across all the corpora. The significant test results prove the reliability of the high quality of our calculation.

Table 6. The results of all the algorithms in the transferring scenario (highest values in bold. ***, **, and * indicate three significant levels as 0.01, 0.05, and 0.1.).

	Methods	English			Chinese		C-E	E-C
		Para	Q&Q	MA	Q&Q	MA	Q&Q	Q&Q
supervised	TextCNN	0.61 ***	0.60 **	0.49 **	0.47 *	0.51 *	0.31 **	0.27 **
	LSTM	0.56 **	0.59 **	0.51 *	0.54 **	0.52 **	0.23 *	0.22 *
	LSTM+BIA	0.54 **	0.53 **	0.47 *	0.55 **	0.56 **	0.26 *	0.24 *
	BERT-base	0.57 ***	0.55 ***	0.53 **	0.49 ***	0.51 **	0.48 **	0.41 **
	Con-SIM	0.52 ***	0.53 ***	0.51 *	0.47 ***	0.50 *	0.44 **	0.38 **
	RCMD	0.53 ***	0.56 ***	0.54 *	0.46 ***	0.53 **	0.42 **	0.43 **
unsupervised	AVE	0.58 *	0.61 **	0.42 *	0.63 **	0.49 *	0.61 **	0.63 **
	TR+AVE	0.65 **	0.66 **	0.49 **	0.68 **	0.55 **	0.66 **	0.68 **
	TR+CON	0.69 *	0.71 ***	0.53 **	0.66 **	0.53 **	0.71 ***	0.66 **
	Ours	**0.82 ***	**0.86 ***	**0.68 ***	**0.89 ***	**0.67 ***	**0.86 ***	**0.89 ***

6. Conclusions and Future Work

Text similarity calculation is a fundamental task for many high-level artificial intelligence applications, such as text clustering, text summarization, and Q&A. Traditional similarity calculations are conducted in terms of either making two similar texts close in a high-dimensional space (supervised methods) or measuring the number of concurrent words shared by two texts (unsupervised methods). They ignore a fact that, in many scenarios, text is used to record events. Text similarity is mostly decided by whether two texts mention the same core event or not. This paper just proposes a novel text similarity calculation via constructing an event connection graph to disclose the core event mentioned in one text. To better model the relations among events, we tune the vectors of the triggers to detect related events and link them in the event connection graph. This approach can locate the core event more accurately. The nodes which can represent the core event are chosen and utilized to measure text similarity. Moreover, we adopt graph embedding to tune the vectors of the chosen nodes to integrate the global information carried by the entire text into the chosen nodes. This way can further boost the performance of our calculation. Experimental results prove the high performance of our similarity calculation.

Though our paper can combine the merits from supervised and unsupervised similarity calculations and can be applied in many text-related downstream applications which need text similarity as their component. Our calculation has time issue needed to be further solved. In particular, our calculation needs to form a passage-level event representation. This kind of operation needs extra time. Thus, though our calculation has higher accuracy, it is not fit to online applications, especially some time-insensitive applications.

One issue needed to be mentioned is that, to link semantically similar triggers to let our event connection graph cover more relations among events, we need to predefine a threshold to decide whether two triggers are similar or not. As shown in the experiments, this parameter setting is not optimal for some corpus. It is chosen via balancing the results across all the testing corpora. Therefore, in the future work, we hope to set it dynamically. The other work we hope to carry out is to improve efficiency. The process of graph construction is time-consuming. We hope to construct some template graphs at advance. During the calculating stage, we choose the corresponding template graph via some matching score and complete the matched template graph using some specific words chosen from input text.

Author Contributions: M.L. and Z.Z. conceived and designed the study, interpreted the data, and drafted the manuscript. L.C. guided the study and revised the manuscript. All authors critically revised the manuscript, agree to be fully accountable for ensuring the integrity and accuracy of the work, and read and approved the final manuscript before submission. All authors have read and agreed to the published version of the manuscript.

Funding: The research in this article is supported by the National Key Research and Development Project (2021YFF0901600), the Project of State Key Laboratory of Communication Content Cognition (A02101), the National Science Foundation of China (61976073, 62276083), and Shenzhen Foundational Research Funding (JCYJ20200109113441941).

Institutional Review Board Statement: Not applicable.

Informed Consent Statement: Not applicable.

Data Availability Statement: No new data were created or analyzed in this study. Data sharing is not applicable to this article.

Acknowledgments: I would like to express my gratitude to all those who have helped me during the writing of this thesis, including all the co-authors. I also appreciate the help from the reviewers' directions.

Conflicts of Interest: This submission is an extension version of a conference paper written by the same authors in NLPCC, however, I confirm that over 60% part including methods and experiments are added. Besides, the results are improved by the novel proposed method. All authors are aware of the submission and agree to its review. There is no conflict of interest with Associate Editors. The coverage of related work is appropriate and up-to-date.

References

1. Ji, H.; Grishman, R. Refining event extraction through cross-document inference. In Proceedings of the 58th Annual Meeting of the Association for Computational Linguistics, Columbus, OH, USA, 16–18 June 2008; pp. 254–262.
2. Baker, C.; Fillmore, C.; Lowe, J. The berkeley framenet project. In Proceedings of the 36th Annual Meeting of the Association for Computational Linguistics and 17th International Conference on Computational Linguistics, Montreal, QC, Canada, 10–14 August 1998; pp. 86–90.
3. Jacksi, K.; Ibrahim, R.; Zeebaree, S.; Zebari, R.; Sadeeq, M. Clustering documents based on semantic similarity using HAC and K-mean algorithms. In Proceedings of the 2020 International Conference on Advanced Science and Engineering, Duhok, Iraq, 23–24 December 2020; pp. 205–210.
4. Huang, X.; Qi, J.; Sun, Y.; Zhang, R. Mala: Cross-domain dialogue generation with action learning. In Proceedings of the 34th AAAI Conference on Artificial Intelligence, New York, NY, USA, 7–12 February 2020; pp. 7977–7984.

5. Kieu, B.; Unanue, I.; Pham, S.; Phan, H.; Piccardi, M. Learning neural textual representations for citation recommendation. In Proceedings of the 25th International Conference on Pattern Recognition, Milan, Italy, 10–15 January 2021; pp. 4145–4152.
6. Chen, Y.; Zhou, M.; Wang, S. Reranking answers for definitional QA using language modeling. In Proceedings of the 21st International Conference on Computational Linguistics and 44th Annual Meeting of the Association for Computational Linguistics, Sydney, Australia, 17–21 July 2006; pp. 1081–1088.
7. Turian, J.; Ratinov, L.; Bengio, Y. Word representations: A simple and general method for semi-supervised learning. In Proceedings of the 48th Annual Meeting of the Association for Computational Linguistics, Uppsala, Sweden, 11–16 July 2010; pp. 384–394.
8. Mikolov, T.; Sutskever, I.; Chen, K.; Corrado, G.; Dean, J. Distributed representations of words and phrases and their compositionality. In Proceedings of the Advances in Neural Information Processing Systems, Lake Tahoe, NV, USA, 5–10 December 2013; pp. 3111–3119.
9. Mikolov, T.; Chen, K.; Corrado, G.; Dean, J. Efficient estimation of word representations in vector space. In Proceedings of the 1st International Conference on Learning Representations, Scottsdale, AZ, USA, 2–4 May 2013; pp. 1–12.
10. Pennington, J.; Socher, R.; Manning, C. GloVe: Global vectors for word representation. In Proceedings of the 2014 Conference on Empirical Methods in Natural Language Processing, Doha, Qatar, 25–29 October 2014; pp. 1532–1543.
11. Peters, M.; Neumann, M.; Iyyer, M.; Gardner, M.; Clark, C.; Lee, K.; Zettlemoyer, L. Deep contextualized word representations. In Proceedings of the 2018 Conference of the North American Chapter of the Association for Computational Linguistics: Human Language Technologies, New Orleans, LA, USA, 1–6 June 2018; pp. 2227–2237.
12. Chen, J.; Dai, X.; Yuan, Q.; Lu, C.; Huang, H. Towards interpretable clinical diagnosis with Bayesian network ensembles stacked on entity-aware CNNs. In Proceedings of the 58th Annual Meeting of the Association for Computational Linguistics, Online, 5–10 July 2020; pp. 3143–3153.
13. Cho, K.; van Merriënboer, B.; Gulcehre, C.; Bahdanau, D.; Bougares, F.; Schwenk, H.; Bengio, Y. Learning Phrase Representations Using RNN Encoder-Decoder for Statistical Machine Translation. In Proceedings of the 2014 Conference on Empirical Methods in Natural Language Processing, Doha, Qatar, 25–29 October 2014; pp. 1724–1734.
14. Behera, R.K.; Jena, M.; Rath, S.K.; Misra, S. Co-LSTM: Convolutional LSTM model for sentiment analysis in social big data. *Inf. Process. Manag.* **2020**, *58*, 102435. [CrossRef]
15. Vaswani, A.; Shazeer, N.; Parmar, N.; Uszkoreit, J.; Jones, L.; Gomez, A.; Kaiser, L.; Polosukhin, I. Attention is all you need. In Proceedings of the Advances in Neural Information Processing Systems, Long Beach, CA, USA, 4–9 December 2017; pp. 5998–6008.
16. Radford, A.; Narasimhan, K.; Salimans, T.; Sutskever, I. Improving Language Understanding by Generative Pre-Training. 2018. Available online: https://S3-Us-West-2.Amazonaws.Com (accessed on 31 December 2021).
17. Devlin, J.; Chang, W.; Lee, K.; Toutanova, K. BERT: Pre-training of deep bidirectional transformers for language understanding. In Proceedings of the Conference of the North American Chapter of the Association for Computational Linguistics: Human Language Technologies, Minneapolis, MN, USA, 2–7 June 2019; pp. 4171–4186.
18. Yang, Z.; Dai, Z.; Yang, Y.; Carbonell, J.; Salakhutdinov, R.; Le, V. XLNET: Generalized autoregressive pretraining for language understanding. In Proceedings of the Advances in Neural Information Processing Systems, Vancouver, BC, Canada, 8–14 December 2019; pp. 5753–5763.
19. Liu, Y.; Ott, M.; Goyal, N.; Du, J.; Joshi, M.; Chen, D.; Levy, O.; Lewis, M.; Zettlemoyer, L.; Stoyanov, V. RoBERTa: A robustly optimized BERT pretraining approach. *arXiv* **2019**, arXiv:1907.11692.
20. Pan, Y.; Yao, T.; Li, Y.; Mei, T. X-Linear attention networks for image captioning. In Proceedings of the IEEE/CVF Conference on Computer Vision and Pattern Recognition, Seattle, WA, USA, 14–19 June 2020; pp. 10971–10980.
21. Liu, Y.; Zhang, X.; Zhang, Q.; Li, C.; Huang, F.; Tang, X.; Li, Z. Dual self-attention with co-attention networks for visual question answering. *Pattern Recognit.* **2021**, *117*, 107956. [CrossRef]
22. Lee, L.H.; Wan, C.H.; Rajkumar, R.; Isa, D. An enhanced Support Vector Machine classification framework by using Euclidean distance function for text document categorization. *Appl. Intell.* **2011**, *37*, 80–99. [CrossRef]
23. Zhu, H.; Zhang, P.; Gao, Z. K-means text dynamic clustering algorithm based on KL divergence. In Proceedings of the 17th IEEE/ACIS International Conference on Computer and Information Science, Singapore, 6–8 June 2018; pp. 659–663.
24. Huang, A. Similarity measures for text document clustering. In Proceedings of the 6th New Zealand Computer Science Research Student Conference, Hamilton, New Zealand, 14–18 April 2008; pp. 9–56.
25. Atoum, A.; Otoom, A. Efficient Hybrid Semantic Text Similarity using Wordnet and a Corpus. *Int. J. Adv. Comput. Sci. Appl.* **2016**, *7*, 124–130. [CrossRef]
26. Gomaa, W.; Fahmy, A. A survey of text similarity approaches. *Int. J. Comput. Appl.* **2013**, *68*, 13–18.
27. Robertson, S. Understanding inverse document frequency: On theoretical arguments for IDF. *J. Doc.* **2004**, *60*, 503–520. [CrossRef]
28. Mihalcea, R.; Tarau, P. Textrank: Bringing order into text. In Proceedings of the 2004 Conference on Empirical Methods in Natural Language Processing, Barcelona, Spain, 25–26 July 2004; pp. 404–411.
29. Blei, D.; Ng, A.; Jordan, M. Latent dirichlet allocation. *J. Mach. Learn. Res.* **2003**, *3*, 993–1022.
30. Pavlinek, M.; Podgorelec, V. Text classification method based on self-training and LDA topic models. *Expert Syst. Appl.* **2017**, *80*, 83–93. [CrossRef]
31. Sharif, U.; Ghada, E.; Atlam, E.; Fuketa, M.; Morita, K.; Aoe, J.-I. Improvement of building field association term dictionary using passage retrieval. *Inf. Process. Manag.* **2007**, *43*, 1793–1807. [CrossRef]

32. Dorji, T.C.; Atlam, E.-S.; Yata, S.; Fuketa, M.; Morita, K.; Aoe, J.-I. Extraction, selection and ranking of Field Association (FA) Terms from domain-specific corpora for building a comprehensive FA terms dictionary. *Knowl. Inf. Syst.* **2010**, *27*, 141–161. [CrossRef]
33. Malkiel, I.; Ginzburg, D.; Barkan, O.; Caciularu, A.; Weill, J.; Koenigstein, N. Interpreting BERT-based Text Similarity via Activation and Saliency Maps. In Proceedings of the 2022 ACM Web Conference, Lyon, France, 25–29 April 2022; pp. 3259–3268.
34. Grishman, R.; Sundheim, B. Message understanding conference-6: A brief history. In Proceedings of the 16th International Conference on Computational Linguistics, Copenhagen, Denmark, 5–9 August 1996; pp. 466–471.
35. Doddington, G.; Mitchell, A.; Przybocki, M.; Ramshaw, L.; Strassel, S.; Weischedel, R. The Automatic Content Extraction (ACE) program-tasks, data, and evaluation. In Proceedings of the 4th International Conference on Language Resources and Evaluation, Centro Cultural de Belem, Lisbon, 24–30 May 2004; pp. 837–840.
36. Yang, S.; Feng, D.; Qiao, L.; Kan, Z.; Li, D. Exploring pre-trained language models for event extraction and generation. In Proceedings of the 57th Annual Meeting of the Association for Computational Linguistics, Florence, Italy, 28 July–2 August 2019; pp. 169–175.
37. Wang, Z.; Wang, X.; Han, X.; Lin, Y.; Hou, L.; Liu, Z.; Li, P.; Li, J.; Zhou, J. CLEVE: Contrastive pre-training for event extraction. In Proceedings of the 59th Annual Meeting of the Association for Computational Linguistics and the 11th International Joint Conference on Natural Language Processing, Online, 1–6 August 2021; pp. 6283–6297.
38. Du, X.; Cardie, C. Document-Level event role filler extraction using multi-granularity contextualized encoding. In Proceedings of the 58th Annual Meeting of the Association for Computational Linguistics, Washington, DC, USA, 5–10 July 2020; pp. 8010–8020.
39. Hu, Z.; Liu, M.; Wu, Y.; Xu, J.; Qin, B.; Li, J. Document-level event subject pair recognition. In Proceedings of the 9th CCF International Conference on Natural Language Processing and Chinese Computing, Zhengzhou, China, 14–18 October 2020; pp. 283–293.
40. Lin, Y.; Ji, H.; Huang, F.; Wu, L. A joint neural model for information extraction with global features. In Proceedings of the 58th Annual Meeting of the Association for Computational Linguistics, Washington, DC, USA, 5–10 July 2020; pp. 7999–8009.
41. Liao, S.; Grishman, R. Using document level cross-event inference to improve event extraction. In Proceedings of the 48th Annual Meeting of the Association for Computational Linguistics, Uppsala, Sweden, 11–16 July 2010; pp. 789–797.
42. Atlam, E.-S.; Elmarhomy, G.; Morita, K.; Fuketa, M.; Aoe, J.-I. Automatic building of new Field Association word candidates using search engine. *Inf. Process. Manag.* **2006**, *42*, 951–962. [CrossRef]
43. Lai, D.; Lu, H.; Nardini, C. Finding communities in directed networks by PageRank random walk induced network embedding. *Phys. A Stat. Mech. Its Appl.* **2010**, *389*, 2443–2454. [CrossRef]
44. Li, P.; Zhou, G.; Zhu, Q.; Hou, L. Employing compositional semantics and discourse consistency in Chinese event extraction. In Proceedings of the 2012 Joint Conference on Empirical Methods in Natural Language Processing and Computational Natural Language Learning, Jeju Island, Korea, 12–14 July 2012; pp. 1006–1016.
45. Amir, H.; Béatrice, D. Word embedding approach for synonym extraction of multi-word terms. In Proceedings of the Eleventh International Conference on Language Resources and Evaluation, Miyazaki, Japan, 7–12 May 2018; pp. 297–303.
46. Davenport, E.; Cronin, B. Knowledge management: Semantic drift or conceptual shift? *J. Educ. Libr. Inf. Sci.* **2000**, *1*, 294–306. [CrossRef]
47. Grover, A.; Leskovec, J. Node2vec: Scalable feature learning for networks. In Proceedings of the 22nd ACM SIGKDD International Conference on Knowledge Discovery and Data Mining, San Francisco, CA, USA, 13–17 August 2016; pp. 855–864.
48. Sasano, R.; Korhonen, A. Investigating word-class distributions in word vector spaces. In Proceedings of the 58th Annual Meeting of the Association for Computational Linguistics, Online, 5–10 July 2020; pp. 3657–3666.
49. Kennington, C. Enriching language models with visually-grounded word vectors and the lancaster sensorimotor norms. In Proceedings of the 25th Conference on Computational Natural Language Learning, Online, 10–11 November 2021; pp. 148–157.
50. Mysore, S.; Cohan, A.; Hope, T. Multi-vector models with textual guidance for fine-grained scientific document similarity. In Proceedings of the 2022 Conference of the North American Chapter of the Association for Computational Linguistics: Human Language Technologies, Seattle, Washington, DC, USA, 10–15 July 2022; pp. 4453–4470.
51. Sun, X.; Meng, Y.; Ao, X.; Wu, F.; Zhang, T.; Li, J.; Fan, C. Sentence similarity based on contexts. *Trans. Assoc. Comput. Linguist.* **2022**, *10*, 573–588. [CrossRef]
52. Lee, S.; Lee, D.; Jang, S.; Yu, H. Toward interpretable semantic textual similarity via optimal transport-based contrastive sentence learning. In Proceedings of the 60th Annual Meeting of the Association for Computational Linguistics (Volume 1: Long Papers), Dublin, Ireland, 22–27 May 2022; pp. 5969–5979.
53. Li, Q.; Ji, H.; Huang, L. Joint event extraction via structured prediction with global features. In Proceedings of the 51st Annual Meeting of the Association for Computational Linguistics, Sofia, Bulgaria, 4–9 August 2013; pp. 73–82.
54. Zhang, J.; Qin, Y.; Zhang, Y.; Liu, M.; Ji, D. Extracting entities and events as a single task using a transition-based neural model. In Proceedings of the Twenty-Eighth International Joint Conference on Artificial Intelligence, Macao, China, 10–16 August 2019; pp. 5422–5428.
55. Liu, X.; Huang, H.; Zhang, Y. Open domain event extraction using neural latent variable models. In Proceedings of the 57th Conference of the Association for Computational Linguistics, Florence, Italy, 28 July–2 August 2019; pp. 2860–2871.
56. Levy, O.; Søgaard, A.; Goldberg, Y. A strong baseline for learning cross-lingual word embeddings from sentence alignments. In Proceedings of the 15th Conference of the European Chapter of the Association for Computational Linguistics, Valencia, Spain, 3–7 April 2017; pp. 765–774.

Article

Neural Networks for Early Diagnosis of Postpartum PTSD in Women after Cesarean Section

Christos Orovas [1,*], Eirini Orovou [2,3], Maria Dagla [3], Alexandros Daponte [4], Nikolaos Rigas [3], Stefanos Ougiaroglou [5], Georgios Iatrakis [3] and Evangelia Antoniou [3]

1. Department of Product and Systems Design Engineering, Faculty of Engineering, University of Western Macedonia, 50100 Kozani, Greece
2. Department of Midwifery, School of Health, Sciences, University of Western Macedonia, 50100 Kozani, Greece; eorovou@uniwa.gr
3. Department of Midwifery, University of West Attica, 12243 Egaleo, Greece; mariadagla@uniwa.gr (M.D.); nrigas@uniwa.gr (N.R.); giatrakis@uniwa.gr (G.I.); lilanton@uniwa.gr (E.A.)
4. School of Health and Science, Faculty of Medicine, University of Thessaly, 41500 Larisa, Greece; daponte@uth.gr
5. Department of Digital Systems, School of Economics and Technology, University of the Peloponnese, Kladas, 23100 Sparta, Greece; stoug@uop.gr
* Correspondence: chorovas@uowm.gr

Featured Application: Early diagnosis and warning mechanisms are essential in every health condition. The research described in this paper can provide the means for the development of medical assistance applications.

Abstract: The correlation between the kind of cesarean section and post-traumatic stress disorder (PTSD) in Greek women after a traumatic birth experience has been recognized in previous studies along with other risk factors, such as perinatal conditions and traumatic life events. Data from early studies have suggested some possible links between some vulnerable factors and the potential development of postpartum PTSD. The classification of each case in three possible states (PTSD, profile PTSD, and free of symptoms) is typically performed using the guidelines and the metrics of the version V of the Diagnostic and Statistical Manual of Mental Disorders (DSM-V) which requires the completion of several questionnaires during the postpartum period. The motivation in the present work is the need for a model that can detect possible PTSD cases using a minimum amount of information and produce an early diagnosis. The early PTSD diagnosis is critical since it allows the medical personnel to take the proper measures as soon as possible. Our sample consists of 469 women who underwent emergent or elective cesarean delivery in a university hospital in Greece. The methodology which is followed is the application of random decision forests (RDF) to detect the most suitable and easily accessible information which is then used by an artificial neural network (ANN) for the classification. As is demonstrated from the results, the derived decision model can reach high levels of accuracy even when only partial and quickly available information is provided.

Keywords: artificial neural networks; random decision forests; posttraumatic stress disorder; DSM-V; emergency cesarean section; elective cesarean section; postpartum period

1. Introduction

Post-traumatic stress disorder (PTSD) is a mental health problem that can develop after a person goes through a life-threatening event. The disorder can develop even when the person is witnessing an event, exposed through information, or extreme repeated exposure to the workplace [1]. The disorder, regardless of the type of exposure to trauma, causes symptoms of re-experiencing, avoidance, negative cognitions in the mood, and arousal. The duration of symptoms lasts more than a month, not due to the action of any substance or physical condition and causes a significant reduction in the individual's social life [2]. Anyone can develop PTSD at any age. Women, however, are twice as likely to develop PTSD as men, showing how they are most affected by traumatic childbirth experiences, hormonal disorders, stressful life events, and domestic violence [3].

On the other hand, PTSD profile, or partial PTSD, originally used in relation to Vietnam veterans has recently been extended to trauma victims. The PTSD profile includes the most important symptoms of PTSD, but people exposed to trauma do not meet all the diagnostic criteria of the disorder. A correlation has also been found between PTSD profiles with increased rates of suicidal ideation, alcoholism, overuse of health services, and several absences from the work environment as well as a negative reduction of a person's social life [4,5].

For several years, scientists viewed the childbirth experience as a positive experience, regardless of the presence of traumatic events. In recent years, however, birth trauma has increased researchers' interest, as it has been shown that it can develop into PTSD or PTSD profile. Actually, more than 1/3 of mothers experienced their delivery as a traumatic event, while 1/4 of them will experience postpartum PTSD [6]. Some factors can increase the chance that a postpartum mother will have PTSD, such as pathology of gestation, complicated vaginal delivery, personal history of mental disorders, tokophobia, low social support, past PTSD, and cesarean section (CS) [7–10]. Postpartum PTSD symptoms are debilitating and affect the social, professional, psychological, and communication function of the mother–infant bond and her family, as well [10]. However, there are many previous and current surveys that highlight the effect of CS on maternal mental health, especially emergency cesarean section (EMCS) which show a strong correlation with postpartum PTSD compared to other types of births [11–16].

Due to the nature of the current diagnosis procedure, which is in accordance with the (DSM-V), in order to reach a conclusion, it is necessary to wait for a period of six weeks to fill up the necessary questionnaires regarding any symptoms. However, the early detection of the possibility of developing PTSD could offer medical personnel significant information to take increased precautionary measures and alleviate any symptoms in advance.

This observation is behind the motivation of the present work. More specifically, our motivation is to examine if machine learning and especially the artificial neural network (ANNs) models can be applied to predict possible PTSD cases. Our contribution is the development of an ANN model that can detect PTSD cases using a minimum amount of information and produce an early PTSD diagnosis as soon as possible.

The rest of the paper is organized as follows: Section 2 presents the related work. In Section 3, the dataset and the proposed methodology for early diagnosis of PTSD cases are described in detail. Section 4 presents the experimental study which is based on a dataset with 469 cases. Section 5 discusses the results while Section 6 concludes the paper and gives directions for future work.

2. Related Work

An early investigation of the application of ANNs as a clinical diagnostic and a modeling tool, especially for psychiatric disorders has been presented in [17]. Although many successful cases of diagnosis in general medicine, contemporary at the time of that review, have been presented, the lack of evaluation of the impact of the nature of psychiatric data, where most variables derive from dimensional rating scales, is also mentioned. A more detailed consideration of the application of ANN models to clinical decision-making exists in [18] where some issues of psychological assessment using ANNs are discussed as well. The use of ANNs in psychology-related applications, such as personality traits analysis, has also been reviewed in [19]. In general, machine learning can provide a powerful diagnostic toolset as it is demonstrated in [20].

In a similar manner to the work presented in this paper, the use of ANNs in identifying the symptom severity in obsessive–compulsive disorder (OCD) for classification and prediction has been successfully employed in [21]. The importance of timely treatment of

OCD before leading to a chronic disability is also stressed and several significant factors related to this disorder are pointed out with confirmatory factor analysis (CFA).

The potentiality of machine learning approaches with multidimensional data sets in pathologically redefining mental illnesses and also improving the therapeutic outcomes in relation to the Diagnostic and Statistical Manual of Mental Disorders (DSM) and the International Classification of Diseases (ICD) is examined in [22]. An extended related review also exists in [23,24] where open issues for AI in psychiatry are discussed as well.

3. Materials and Methods

This study took place from July to November 2019 to August 2020, at the Midwifery Department of the General University Hospital of Larisa in Greece. It was approved by the University Hospital of Larisa Ethics Commission. Approval: 18838/08-05-2019. To answer the research question, the study was designed as a prospective study between 2 groups of postpartum women (EMCS and Elective Cesarean Section (ELCS)).

3.1. Participants

The participants were all postpartum women who gave birth by the 2 types of CS and gave their written consent for their participation. A total of 469 postpartum women were examined in this research. For each case, several demographics, prenatal health, and mental health variables were collected through questionnaires that were filled through interviews during their hospitalization in the departments and 6 weeks later. The exclusion criteria of the research were difficulties at a cognitive level, other languages than Greek, and underage mothers.

3.2. Data and Measures

The data were collected in 2 stages: the first stage was the 2nd day after CS, and the second stage was the 6th week after CS. During the first stage, from 469 women, we collected medical and demographic data from the socio-demographic questionnaire and past traumatic life events from the Life Events Checklist-5 (LEC-5) of DSM-V and Criterion A from the adapted first Criterion of PTSD. At the second stage, the PTSD symptoms from the Post-Traumatic Stress Checklist (PCL-5) of DSM-V are collected (The dataset that was used can be found in: https://users.uowm.gr/chorovas/appsci/nn_ptsd.html (accessed on 20 June 2022)).

The life events checklist (LEC) is the only measure that individuals can determine different levels of exposure to a traumatic event in their lives [25]. For a PTSD diagnosis, 8 criteria must be met. For the first criterion (Criterion A), the individual must have been exposed to death, threatened death, serious injury, or sexual violence in one of the following ways: (a) direct exposure, (b) witness to the event, (c) information of the event, and (d) exposure in the working space [26]. For this study, Criterion A was adjusted accordingly. The post-traumatic stress checklist (PCL-5) is a self-report scale, which was developed to measure and evaluate PTSD and PTSD Profile symptoms [1,27]. In the present study, the postpartum women replied via telephone to 20 questions during the 6th postpartum week, corresponding to 20 symptoms of the criteria B (re-experiencing), C (avoidance), D (negative thoughts and feelings), and E (arousal and reactivity). All replies are scored on 5-point scales (range zero to four). A score of one or more in the categories of criteria B and C and two or more in categories D and E are considered PTSD symptoms. Depending on the symptoms, the postpartum women were diagnosed with (a) provisional diagnosis of PTSD and (b) PTSD profile [27,28].

The demographics, prenatal health, and mental health variables that were collected are presented in Tables 1–3 (statistical tests with IBM SPSS Statistics v.20).

Table 1. Demographic data. Counts and percentages in corresponding diagnosis.

		Diagnosis						p-Value *
		Free		Profile		PTSD		
		N	%	N	%	N	%	
v1. Residence	1. City	303	81.2%	25	6.7%	45	12.1%	0.665
	2. Village	76	79.2%	9	9.4%	11	11.5%	
v2. Age	1. ≤20	17	77.3%	0	0.0%	5	22.7%	0.08
	2. ≤25	32	76.2%	5	11.9%	5	11.9%	
	3. ≤30	77	76.2%	5	5.0%	19	18.8%	
	4. ≤35	107	80.5%	15	11.3%	11	8.3%	
	5. ≤40	121	83.4%	9	6.2%	15	10.3%	
	6. ≤45	23	95.8%	0	0.0%	1	4.2%	
	7. >45	2	100.0%	0	0.0%	0	0.0%	
v3. Family Status	0. Single	3	100.0%	0	0.0%	0	0.0%	0.551
	1. In relationship	29	72.5%	3	7.5%	8	20.0%	
	2. Married	339	81.7%	30	7.2%	46	11.1%	
	3. Engaged	6	85.7%	0	0.0%	1	14.3%	
	4. Divorced	2	50.0%	1	25.0%	1	25.0%	
v4. Educational Status	0. Primary	29	74.4%	3	7.7%	7	17.9%	0.848
	1. Jr High Sch.	22	73.3%	4	13.3%	4	13.3%	
	2. High Sch.	159	81.1%	14	7.1%	23	11.7%	
	3. Uni	140	82.4%	12	7.1%	18	10.6%	
	4. MSc	23	82.1%	1	3.6%	4	14.3%	
	5. PhD	6	100.0%	0	0.0%	0	0.0%	
v5. Occupation	1. Employee (Pub/Priv)	116	85.3%	7	5.1%	13	9.6%	0.277
	2. Freelance	52	77.6%	5	7.5%	10	14.9%	
	3. Health care	30	78.9%	5	13.2%	3	7.9%	
	4. Educators	35	81.4%	1	2.3%	7	16.3%	
	5. Household	102	82.9%	10	8.1%	11	8.9%	
	6. Unemployed	44	71.0%	6	9.7%	12	19.4%	
v6. Financial Status	1. Low	103	75.7%	11	8.1%	22	16.2%	0.399
	2. Medium	266	83.1%	22	6.9%	32	10.0%	
	3. High	10	76.9%	1	7.7%	2	15.4%	
v8. Nationality	1. Greek	343	81.1%	30	7.1%	50	11.8%	0.887
	2. Other	36	78.3%	4	8.7%	6	13.0%	
v9. Minority	0. No	356	81.7%	31	7.1%	49	11.2%	0.196
	1. Yes	23	69.7%	3	9.1%	7	21.2%	

* p-values refer to Pearson chi-square.

Table 2. Prenatal health variables. Counts and percentages in corresponding diagnosis.

		Diagnosis						p-Value *
		Free		Profile		PTSD		
		N	%	N	%	N	%	
v10. Parity	0. No	158	78.2%	13	6.4%	31	15.3%	0.278
	1. One birth	149	84.2%	12	6.8%	16	9.0%	
	2. >1	72	80.0%	9	10.0%	9	10.0%	
v11. Previous labor	0. No prev. labor	160	78.4%	13	6.4%	31	15.2%	0.013
	1. Vaginal	25	67.6%	3	8.1%	9	24.3%	
	2. C-section	188	85.8%	16	7.3%	15	6.8%	
	3. Vag. and CS	6	66.7%	2	22.2%	1	11.1%	
v12. Type of conception	1. Normal	342	79.7%	33	7.7%	54	12.6%	0.145
	2. IVF	37	92.5%	1	2.5%	2	5.0%	

Table 2. Cont.

		Diagnosis						p-Value *
		Free		Profile		PTSD		
		N	%	N	%	N	%	
v14. Atomic history	0. None	297	80.7%	24	6.5%	47	12.8%	0.05
	1. Thyroid	47	87.0%	3	5.6%	4	7.4%	
	2. C/V	9	75.0%	1	8.3%	2	16.7%	
	3. Neurological	5	71.4%	1	14.3%	1	14.3%	
	4. AutoImm.	7	87.5%	1	12.5%	0	0.0%	
	5. Kidney	1	50.0%	0	0.0%	1	50.0%	
	6. Tubes	1	33.3%	2	66.7%	0	0.0%	
	7. Myopia	5	100.0%	0	0.0%	0	0.0%	
	8. Other	7	70.0%	2	20.0%	1	10.0%	
v15. Gynecologic hist.	0. No	345	81.9%	29	6.9%	47	11.2%	0.39
	1. Intr.fetal demise	21	70.0%	2	6.7%	7	23.3%	
	2. Gynec.cancers	1	100.0%	0	0.0%	0	0.0%	
	3. Prem.ovarian	2	100.0%	0	0.0%	0	0.0%	
	4. Surgeries	2	66.7%	1	33.3%	0	0.0%	
	5. Death infant	5	62.5%	2	25.0%	1	12.5%	
	6. Uterine pathology	3	75.0%	0	0.0%	1	25.0%	
v16. Pathology of gestation	0. No	267	85.3%	26	8.3%	20	6.4%	<0.001
	1. Thromb/hyperem.	5	71.4%	1	14.3%	1	14.3%	
	2. Preeclampsia	38	69.1%	2	3.6%	15	27.3%	
	3. Placenta previa	13	68.4%	0	0.0%	6	31.6%	
	4. Diabetes	42	80.8%	5	9.6%	5	9.6%	
	5. Cervical insuff.	6	75.0%	0	0.0%	2	25.0%	
	6. Infection	3	50.0%	0	0.0%	3	50.0%	
	7. Premature contr.	5	55.6%	0	0.0%	4	44.4%	
v18. Full term	1. Yes	330	84.2%	31	7.9%	31	7.9%	<0.001
	2. Late preterm	43	65.2%	3	4.5%	20	30.3%	
	3. Very preterm	6	54.5%	0	0.0%	5	45.5%	
v19. Type of C-section	1. Emergency	115	63.5%	18	9.9%	48	26.5%	<0.001
	2. Programmed	264	91.7%	16	5.6%	8	2.8%	
v21. Cause of C-section	1. Previous CS	178	87.3%	17	8.3%	9	4.4%	<0.001
	2. Abnormal fet.pos.	46	88.5%	2	3.8%	4	7.7%	
	3. Twins/IVF	29	96.7%	1	3.3%	0	0.0%	
	4. Mother's desire	20	83.3%	2	8.3%	2	8.3%	
	5. Placenta previa	7	43.8%	0	0.0%	9	56.3%	
	6. Heavy med. hist.	12	80.0%	3	20.0%	0	0.0%	
	7. Failure of labor	39	88.6%	4	9.1%	1	2.3%	
	8. Abnormal HR	37	57.8%	5	7.8%	22	34.4%	
	9. Preeclampsia	11	55.0%	0	0.0%	9	45.0%	
v22. Complications after C-section	0. None	365	84.1%	34	7.8%	35	8.1%	<0.001
	1. Bleeding	6	33.3%	0	0.0%	12	66.7%	
	2. Infection	3	50.0%	0	0.0%	3	50.0%	
	3. High blood press.	4	57.1%	0	0.0%	3	42.9%	
	4. Neuro/psychiatric	0	0.0%	0	0.0%	1	100.0%	
	5. Other	1	33.3%	0	0.0%	2	66.7%	
v23. Breastfeeding	0. No	101	66.0%	12	7.8%	40	26.1%	<0.001
	1. Yes	278	88.0%	22	7.0%	16	5.0%	
v24. NICU	0. No	319	86.9%	31	8.4%	17	4.6%	<0.001
	1. Perinatal stress	25	61.0%	1	2.4%	15	36.6%	
	2. Infection	2	50.0%	0	0.0%	2	50.0%	
	3. Prematurity	29	59.2%	1	2.0%	19	38.8%	
	4. IUGR	1	50.0%	0	0.0%	1	50.0%	
	5. Other	3	50.0%	1	16.7%	2	33.3%	

* p-values refer to Pearson chi-square.

Table 3. Mental health variables. Counts and percentages in corresponding diagnosis.

		Diagnosis						p-Value *
		Free		Profile		PTSD		
		N	%	N	%	N	%	
v13. Psych. history	0. None	353	85.9%	20	4.9%	38	9.2%	<0.001
	1. Stress disord.	13	44.8%	5	17.2%	11	37.9%	
	2. Postpartum mental disorders	9	52.9%	5	29.4%	3	17.6%	
	3. Depression	2	25.0%	4	50.0%	2	25.0%	
	4. Psych. syndromes	2	50.0%	0	0.0%	2	50.0%	
v25. Support from partner	0. No	30	44.1%	16	23.5%	22	32.4%	<0.001
	1. Yes	349	87.0%	18	4.5%	34	8.5%	
v26. Expectations	0. No	157	64.1%	33	13.5%	55	22.4%	<0.001
	1. Yes	222	99.1%	1	.4%	1	.4%	
v31. Traumatic C-section	0. No	228	99.1%	2	.9%	0	0.0%	<0.001
	1. Yes	151	63.2%	32	13.4%	56	23.4%	
v32. Criterion A1 Was your life or your child's life in danger?	0. No	328	89.1%	31	8.4%	9	2.4%	<0.001
	1. Child's	35	55.6%	3	4.8%	25	39.7%	
	2. Mother's	10	58.8%	0	0.0%	7	41.2%	
	3. Both	6	28.6%	0	0.0%	15	71.4%	
v33. Criterion A2 Any complications involving you or your child?	0. No	349	87.7%	33	8.3%	16	4.0%	<0.001
	1. Child's	20	44.4%	1	2.2%	24	53.3%	
	2. Mother's	8	50.0%	0	0.0%	8	50.0%	
	3. Both	2	20.0%	0	0.0%	8	80.0%	

* p-values refer to Pearson chi-square.

In total, for each case there were 70 data fields available as it is shown in Table 4.

As mentioned in Section 1, the development of a diagnostic model that could indicate early a possible PTSD case using a minimum amount of information could be very useful to prepare the health personnel for such a scenario so that appropriate measures could be taken in advance. Having this in mind we initially trained an artificial neural network (ANN) [18,23] with all the available information so that we could check whether the traditionally confirmed diagnosis could be replicated. Since that was easily achieved by a two-layered feed-forward ANN (Table 5), the focus was moved to the proper subset of data that could be used to achieve high classification accuracy. Random forest classification [29] was performed with the initial set of 70 data fields (variables). The goal was to derive Gini importance values [30] which could assist with the selection of the proper subset of variables. The criteria for the selection of these variables were the level of their direct availability with the smaller number of questions asked. This procedure resulted in having the sets of data that we used to train the ANNs models. A schematic diagram of the above processing is depicted in Figure 1.

Table 4. The total of 70 available data fields.

Description	Number of Data Fields	Coded Labels
Demographics (as shown in Table 1)	8	v1, v2, v3, v4, v5, v6, v8, v9
Prenatal health variables (as shown in Table 2)	12	v10, v11, v12, v14, v15, v16, v18, v19, v21, v22, v23, v24
Mental health variables (as shown in Table 3)	6	v13, v25, v26, v31, v32, v33

Table 4. Cont.

Description	Number of Data Fields	Coded Labels
Criteria A, B, C, D, E (binary variables)	5	v35, v36, v37, v38, v39
Answers to the twenty questions from DSM-V so that the PTSD score and values of Criteria B, C, D, and E are defined (values in {0,1,2,3,4}. These answers and the corresponding values for Criteria B, C, D, and E are only available six weeks after the birth.	20	v41–v60
The third question related to Criterion A (A3), number of similar stressful experiences. Min = 0, max = 11, median = 0. A Kruskal–Wallis H test showed that there was a statistically significant difference in its values between the three different diagnoses, H = 96.480, df = 2, $p < 0.001$, with a mean rank of 219.32 for free, 249.71 for profile, and 332.31 for PTSD.	1	v34
The seventeen Life Events Checklist (LEC-5) of DSM-V. Values are weighted and summed for each of the four severity options (personal, witness, other, and occupation related with weight 4.0, 3.0, 2.0 and 1.0, respectively)	17	lec_1–lec_17
The total count of LEC-5 answers. Min = 0, max = 11, median = 1. A Kruskal–Wallis H test showed that there was a statistically significant difference in its values between the three different diagnoses, H = 49.636, df = 2, $p < 0.001$, with a mean rank of 214.89 for free, 341.76 for profile, and 306.25 for PTSD.	1	v61

Table 5. The averaged confusion matrix of the initial classification results for the training phase using the complete set of the 70 variables. The accuracy is 99.6%.

	Free	Profile	PTSD	Precision	Recall (Sens.)	Specificity
Free	341.1	0	0	99.9%	100%	99.7%
Profile	0.2	28.8	1.5	100%	94.4%	100%
PTSD	0	0	50.4	97.1%	100%	99.6%

The corresponding results and additional details from the above methodology are presented to the following section.

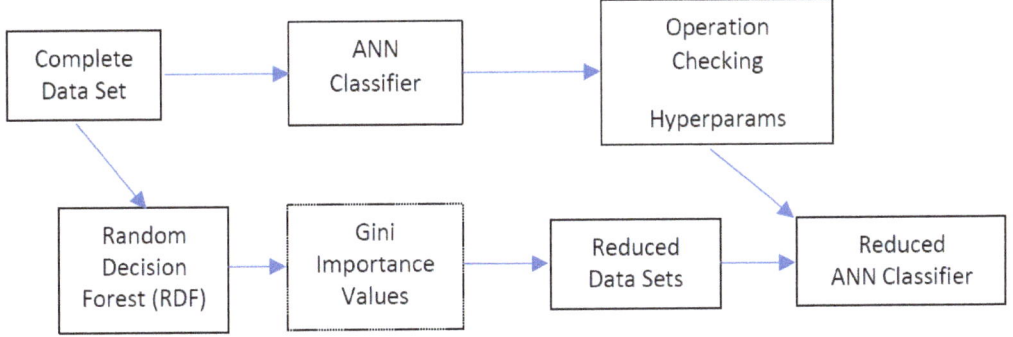

Figure 1. A schematic diagram of the methodology used.

4. Results

4.1. Initial Classification Using the ANN

As mentioned above, the complete set of the data were used initially to examine the feasibility of the reproduction of the original classification according to the DSM-V.

From the 469 cases of the collected data, 379 (80.81%) were manually diagnosed as free of symptoms, 34 (7.24%) had traces and were characterized as profile and 56 (11.94%) were diagnosed as PTSD cases. For the training and testing phases, a stratified ten-fold cross-validation scheme was employed.

The ANN was created using the PyTorch (v1.9.0 + cu11) library in Python and had a structure of seventy input units (in the case of the complete data fields as shown in Table 4), six hidden units, and three output units using three bits for the output where only one of them was set to "1" indicating the diagnosis (one hot coding). The connections were feed-forward from one layer to the next, the Sigmoid function (with $\alpha = 1.0$) was used for activation and the mean squared error (MSE) was employed from the stochastic gradient descent (SGD) optimization algorithm for training. The learning rate was set to 1.0 and the momentum to 0.9. The tuning of the hyperparameters that were used was performed on a trial-and-error base after several initial experimentations.

Initially, we estimated precision, recall, specificity, and accuracy for the complete set of the 70 variables by considering the confusion matrices and these are presented in Tables 5 and 6. Precision estimates how many positive predictions were correct. Recall estimates how many positives are correctly predicted while specificity estimates how many negatives are correctly predicted. Precision is calculated as the fraction $TP/(TP + FP)$, the recall (sensitivity) as $TP/(TP + FN)$, the specificity $TN/(TN + FP)$, and the total accuracy $(TP_1 + TP_2 + TP_3)/(P_1 + P_2 + P_3)$ where TP, FP, TN, and FN are the true and false positives and true and false negatives, respectively.

Table 6. The averaged confusion matrix of the initial classification results for the testing phase using the complete set of the 70 variables. The accuracy is 92,9%.

	Free	Profile	PTSD	Precision	Recall (Sens.)	Specificity
Free	36.9	0.6	0.6	96.8%	97.4%	86.4%
Profile	1.1	1.7	0.6	60.7%	50.0%	97.5%
PTSD	0.1	0.5	4.8	82.8%	88.9%	97.6%

The results for both phases are averaged over ten sessions of the experiments, each one with a different initialization of the weights of the ANN. The averaged learning curve for the training process is depicted in Figure 1.

From Tables 5 and 6 and Figure 2, we can see that the ANN manages to easily learn the classification procedure of the DSM-V. However, we need to perform the same classification with as few variables as possible. Therefore, we employ the RDF importance values.

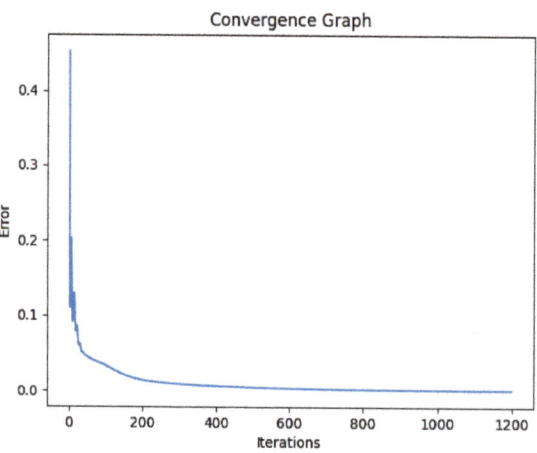

Figure 2. The convergence graph for the training with all the initial data (70 fields).

4.2. Importance Values Using Random Decision Forests

All the data from the initial set (469 × 70) were used with the random decision forests classification which was performed using the function *randomForest* from the library *randomForest* version 4.6-14 in RStudio (v1.3.1093). The number of trees was 500 and the number of variables tried at each split (*mtry*) was 20. These parameters were also selected on a trial-and-error basis. As RDF classification has a stochastic feature in its operation, ten sessions were run, and the average estimated error rate was 1,13%. The average confusion matrix is shown in Table 7.

Table 7. The averaged confusion matrix and the classification errors from the RDF.

	Free	Profile	PTSD	Class. Error	Sd of Class. Error
Free	378	1	0	0.002375	0.001498
Profile	1	31	2	0.097055	0.01421
PTSD	0	1	55	0.017857	3.66×10^{-18}

A powerful feature of RDF classification is that an importance vector is also returned which has the Gini importance values (mean decrease in impurity, MDI) [30] of the variables used. This is very useful for having an idea of what variables contribute more to the classification process as the higher the Gini values the higher the importance of the variables. This is profound in our research as our aim was to reach a competitive level of classification using as less and more directly acquired, variables as possible.

The Gini values for the 70 variables sorted from highest to lowest can be seen in Figure 3 and in Table 8 for more precision.

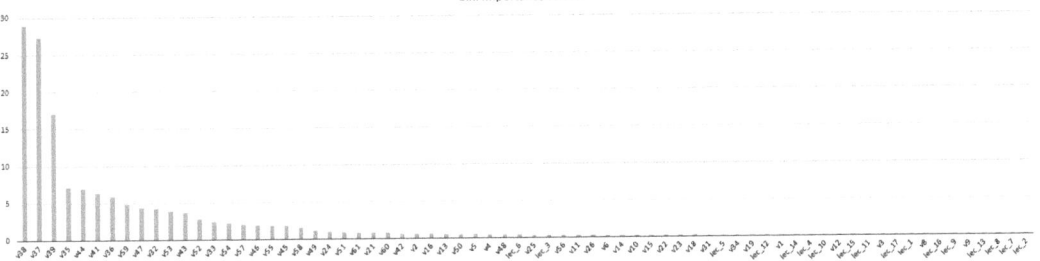

Figure 3. The averaged Gini importance values of the 70 variables in descending order.

Table 8. The averaged Gini importance values of the 70 variables in descending order [1]. Bolded variables are only available after six weeks of birth.

Variable	Gini Value	Variable	Gini Value	Variable	Gini Value	Variable	Gini Value
v38	28.98435	v45	1.8905019	lec_3	0.31930649	lec_4	0.137412479
v37	27.394505	v58	1.5943305	v56	0.30413895	lec_10	0.12593543
v39	17.084163	v49	1.1418203	v11	0.30269473	v12	0.120028475
v35	7.1403067	v24	1.00739209	v26	0.29636865	lec_15	0.107513023
v44	6.971652	v51	0.9250898	v6	0.27196558	lec_11	0.101853315
v41	6.3785479	v61	0.81900432	v14	0.26559605	v3	0.101409277
v36	5.8372447	v21	0.81722037	v10	0.25888349	lec_17	0.094143941
v59	4.8650734	v60	0.81011046	v15	0.2548879	lec_1	0.084016984
v47	4.3128049	v42	0.63748018	v22	0.24198349	v8	0.082011903
v32	4.2619363	v2	0.62349169	v23	0.21767294	lec_16	0.080463707

Table 8. Cont.

Variable	Gini Value	Variable	Gini Value	Variable	Gini Value	Variable	Gini Value
v53	3.8501501	v16	0.60897038	v18	0.1983336	lec_9	0.05289523
v43	3.6749819	v13	0.54351801	v31	0.17640773	v9	0.045091486
v52	2.8472892	**v50**	0.53564906	lec_5	0.17548751	lec_13	0.028551434
v33	2.4381206	v5	0.49679806	v34	0.17496421	lec_8	0.011308693
v54	2.2139708	v4	0.41331847	v19	0.166634565	lec_7	0.008951235
v57	2.0267311	**v48**	0.39974051	lec_12	0.14626491	lec_2	0.004792534
v46	1.9955999	lec_6	0.37660294	v1	0.14314126		
v55	1.8907127	v25	0.36428793	lec_14	0.142114515		

[1] The variable coding scheme is mentioned in Table 4.

4.3. Classification Using a Subset of the Available Data

The values in Table 8 show an expected high level of importance to the variables that are used directly for the typical diagnosis procedure in DSM-V (indicated by bold variable labels). As these are only available after six weeks, our effort is to avoid them and concentrate on what is quickly and easily acquired with as less questions as possible. This gives us the list of candidate variables listed in Table 9.

Table 9. The list of 24 candidate variables for direct diagnosis sorted by Gini importance.

Label	Description	Comments
v35	Criterion A	This is activated upon at least a positive answer in v32 and/or v33 (below). The number of the events (v34 in Table 4) is related to this criterion but is not considered for its activation.
v32	Criterion A1 Was your life or your child's life in danger?	Easy to check in hospital
v33	Criterion A2 Any complications involving you or your child?	Easy to check in hospital
v24	NICU	Easy to check in hospital
v61	The total count of LEC-5 answers	Easy to count from LEC answers
v21	Cause of C-section	Easy to check in hospital
v2	Age	Easy
v16	Pathology of gestation	Info available from surveillance dossier
v13	Psych. history	Info available from surveillance dossier
v5	Occupation	Easy
v4	Educational status	Easy
lec_6	Physical assault	Part of LEC questionary
v25	Support from partner	Easy
lec_3	Transportation accident (car, train, boat)	Part of LEC questionary
v11	Previous labor	Easy
v26	Expectations	Question, subjective
v6	Financial status	Question
v14	Atomic history	Info available from medical history
v10	Parity	Easy
v15	Gynecologic hist.	Info available from medical history
v22	Complications after C-section	Easy
v23	Breastfeeding	Easy but not directly available
v18	Full term	Easy
v31	Traumatic C-section	Easy

All the twenty-four variables that are presented in Table 9 were used to construct eight data sets (called D1–D8) in steps of three. The variables in each dataset and the corresponding sum of the Gini values of these variables can be seen in Table 10.

Table 10. The eight datasets that were created from the variables in Table 9 and the corresponding sum of their Gini values. "1" means the variable is included in the dataset.

	35	32	33	24	61	21	2	16	13	5	4	L6	25	L3	11	26	6	14	10	15	22	23	18	35	
D1	1	1	1																						13.84
D2	1	1	1	1	1	1																			16.48
D3	1	1	1	1	1	1	1	1																	18.26
D4	1	1	1	1	1	1	1	1	1	1	1														19.55
D5	1	1	1	1	1	1	1	1	1	1	1	1	1	1											20.53
D6	1	1	1	1	1	1	1	1	1	1	1	1	1	1	1	1	1								21.37
D7	1	1	1	1	1	1	1	1	1	1	1	1	1	1	1	1	1	1	1	1					22.12
D8	1	1	1	1	1	1	1	1	1	1	1	1	1	1	1	1	1	1	1	1	1	1	1	1	22.72

The results concerning the precision, recall (sensitivity), specificity, and accuracy during the training and testing phases in a stratified ten-fold cross-validation scheme can be seen in Tables 11 and 12 and Figures 4 and 5.

Table 11. The results during the training phase for the eight partial datasets (D1–D8) and for the complete set of the 70 variables (bolded values). Stratified ten-fold cross validation is applied.

	Training Phase									
	PTSD			Profile			Free			
	Prec.	Recall	Spec.	Prec.	Recall	Spec.	Prec.	Recall	Spec.	Acc.
D1	0.63	0.55	0.96	0.00	0.00	1.00	0.86	0.95	0.34	0.84
D2	0.70	0.65	0.96	0.00	0.00	1.00	0.87	0.96	0.41	0.85
D3	0.72	0.70	0.96	0.57	0.12	0.99	0.89	0.96	0.50	0.86
D4	0.74	0.76	0.96	0.66	0.16	0.99	0.90	0.96	0.56	0.88
D5	0.77	0.77	0.97	0.77	0.32	0.99	0.92	0.97	0.64	0.90
D6	0.83	0.83	0.98	0.79	0.35	0.99	0.93	0.97	0.68	0.91
D7	0.83	0.83	0.98	0.79	0.35	0.99	0.93	0.97	0.68	0.91
D8	0.81	0.79	0.97	0.77	0.34	0.99	0.92	0.97	0.66	0.90
All-70	**0.97**	**1.00**	**0.99**	**1.00**	**0.94**	**1.00**	**0.99**	**1.00**	**0.99**	**0.99**

Table 12. The results during the testing phase for the eight partial datasets (D1–D8) and for the complete set of the 70 variables (bolded values). Stratified ten-fold cross validation is applied.

	Testing Phase									
	PTSD			Profile			Free			
	Prec.	Recall	Spec.	Prec.	Recall	Spec.	Prec.	Recall	Spec.	Acc.
D1	0.58	0.52	0.95	0.00	0.00	1.00	0.85	0.94	0.32	0.83
D2	0.61	0.51	0.96	0.00	0.00	1.00	0.86	0.96	0.33	0.83
D3	0.64	0.63	0.95	0.50	0.06	1.00	0.88	0.94	0.43	0.84
D4	0.64	0.64	0.95	0.60	0.09	1.00	0.88	0.94	0.44	0.85
D5	0.67	0.63	0.96	0.38	0.15	0.98	0.89	0.94	0.50	0.85
D6	0.67	0.66	0.96	0.54	0.21	0.99	0.89	0.94	0.52	0.86
D7	0.67	0.66	0.96	0.54	0.21	0.99	0.89	0.94	0.52	0.86
D8	0.65	0.63	0.95	0.43	0.18	0.98	0.89	0.94	0.51	0.85
All-70	**0.83**	**0.89**	**0.98**	**0.61**	**0.50**	**0.97**	**0.97**	**0.97**	**0.86**	**0.93**

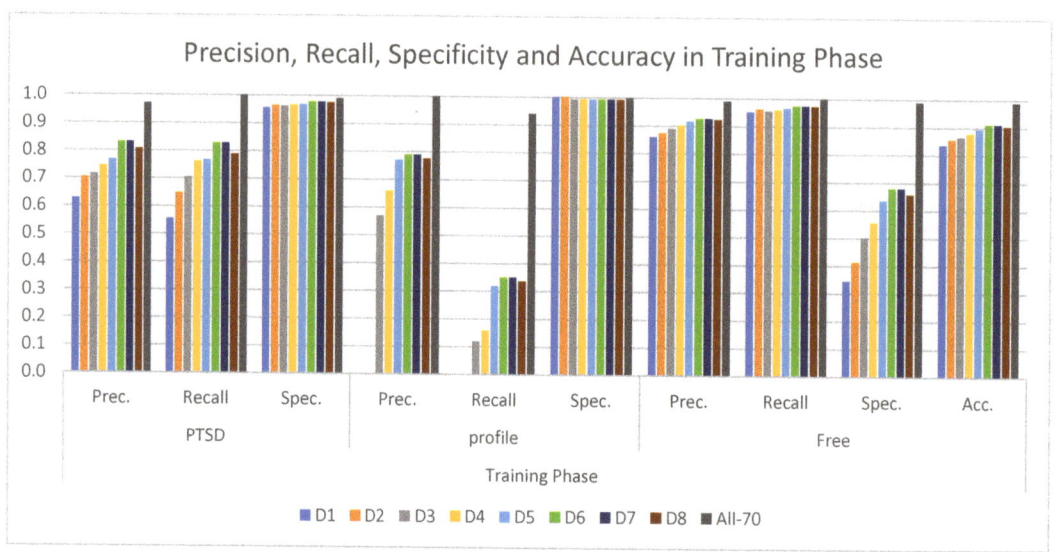

Figure 4. The precision, recall (sensitivity) and specificity for each class and dataset and the accuracy for the training phase.

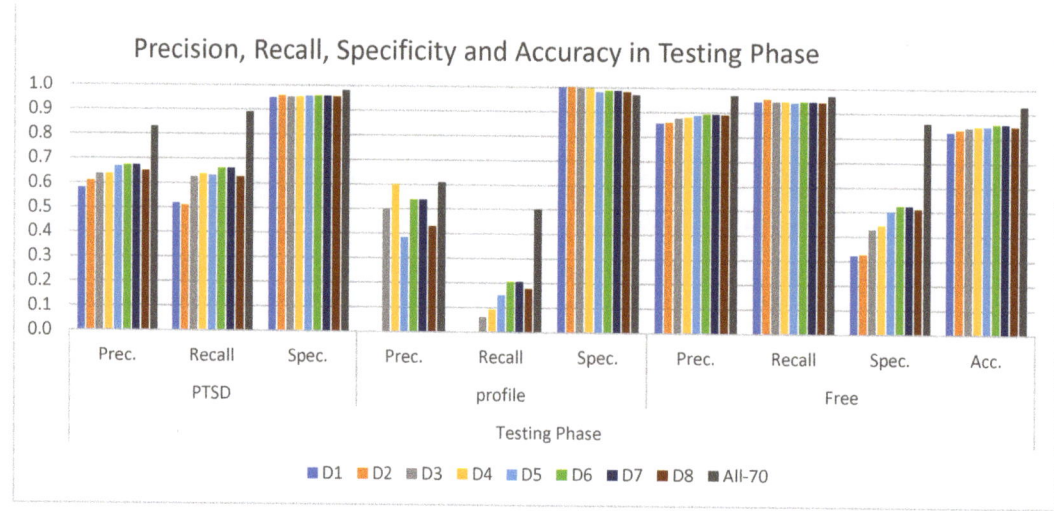

Figure 5. The precision, recall (sensitivity), and specificity for each class and dataset and the accuracy for the testing phase.

In order to have an idea about the best level of classification that could be achieved with RDF using only those variables of the complete set which are not related to DSM-V, (i.e., v41–v60 and v36–v39), ten sessions were run using the complete dataset for training. Comparing the classification errors in Table 13 (which is one recall) with the best values for recall in Table 12 we can observe a slightly better performance from the ANN using datasets D6 and D7 with only 18 and 21 variables, respectively. This is an indication of the validity of the variable selection method that was performed based on Table 8.

Table 13. The averaged confusion matrix and the classification errors from the RDF using the 46 variables remaining after removing the (20 + 4) ones directly related to the DSM-V. The complete dataset is used for the training.

	Free	Profile	PTSD	Class. Error	Sd of Class.Error
Free	357.8	6.6	14.6	0.05594	0.00389
Profile	25.9	6.7	1.4	0.80294	0.03410
PTSD	21.6	0.9	33.5	0.40179	0.02560

5. Discussion

The subject of the present study was to present a model that can produce an early diagnosis to detect and alarm a possible case so that proper measures can be taken as soon as possible. According to our findings, emergency cesarean section, pathology of gestation, preterm birth, the inclusion of neonate in NICU, absence of breastfeeding, psychiatric history, expectations from childbirth, and support from the partner are included in the set of important decision factors.

Additionally, as it can be seen from the results (graphs in Figures 4 and 5, Tables 11 and 12), the ability of the ANN model to arrive at a correct conclusion is demonstrated at a very satisfactory level (around 97% in training and 94% in testing) for the cases which are free of symptoms. For the cases that are PTSD diagnosed, the recognition level reaches 83% in training and 66% in testing. The area in between the above two categories has a low percentage of recognition and it collects the PTSD profile cases. As it can be observed from the results, the PTSD profile cases are the only ones that really need the late questionnaires data (after 6 weeks). According to the above, a policy that could be followed to arrive at a conclusion as soon as possible is to characterize a case that is not classified as free of symptoms as a possible PTSD case. If the case is indeed classified as PTSD, then such a scenario would probably denote an increased potentiality for the appearance of PTSD symptoms after six weeks when the second part of the data is collected. More focused treatment in such a case could be applied and this can start six weeks in advance, providing a beneficial period of medical care.

The use of random decision forests for associating an importance value for each data field is very useful as well. The ordering of the early accessible variables according to their Gini values in Table 9 is the result of that process and it can be noted that this ordering is indeed profound. Criterion A, which constitutes a basic decision factor also in the typical DSM diagnosis, is ranked first and its related parts (A1 and A2) are just after that. Although there is one more datum field related to Criterion A, (v34, number of similar stressful experiences) we decided not to use this as it requires extra effort from the side of the woman in order to be defined. The rest of the data fields that are used for the datasets are all important and this can be shown by the gradual increase in PTSD sensitivity which is noticed in the training phase (Figure 4). This is expected and it denotes the usefulness of the extra information which is added to every dataset. This information increase is also depicted as the sums of the Gini values of the datasets in Figure 6.

Figure 6. The graph of the sums of Gini importance values in the eight datasets (D1–D8) of Table 10.

6. Conclusions

Our aim for this research was to examine whether the use of ANN modeling for describing the classification process of postpartum PTSD could be useful to provide a diagnostic model for the early detection of possible cases. The high accuracy that is obtained using as little and as readily available information as possible demonstrates that this is possible, and this marks a successful scenario for the application of ANNs in psychological data modeling. Future research could incorporate additional machine learning tools for the classification to obtain even more precise classification percentages. The development of mobile device applications to make the process faster would be also desirable. The benefit for the persons that would finally be diagnosed positively is important as well, since the extra period gained could be used in favor of their preliminary treatment.

Author Contributions: Conceptualization, C.O.; methodology, C.O. and S.O.; software, C.O.; validation, M.D., A.D., G.I. and E.A.; formal analysis, C.O.; investigation, E.O., N.R. and E.A.; resources, E.O., N.R. and E.A.; data curation, C.O.; writing—original draft preparation, C.O.; writing—review and editing, M.D., A.D., S.O., G.I. and E.A.; visualization, C.O. and E.O.; supervision, E.A.; project administration, C.O. All authors have read and agreed to the published version of the manuscript.

Funding: This research received no external funding.

Institutional Review Board Statement: This study was approved by the University Hospital of Larisa Ethics Commission. Approval: 18838/08-05-2019.

Informed Consent Statement: Informed consent was obtained from all subjects involved in the study.

Data Availability Statement: Not applicable.

Conflicts of Interest: The authors declare no conflict of interest.

References

1. PTSD Basics—PTSD: National Center for PTSD. Available online: https://www.ptsd.va.gov/understand/what/ptsd_basics.asp (accessed on 29 December 2020).
2. DePierro, J.; D'Andrea, W.; Spinazzola, J.; Stafford, E.; van Der Kolk, B.; Saxe, G.; Stolbach, B.; McKernan, S.; Ford, J.D. Beyond PTSD: Client Presentations of Developmental Trauma Disorder from a National Survey of Clinicians. *Psychol. Trauma* **2019**. [CrossRef] [PubMed]
3. Stein, M.B.; Jang, K.L.; Taylor, S.; Vernon, P.A.; Livesley, W.J. Genetic and Environmental Influences on Trauma Exposure and Posttraumatic Stress Disorder Symptoms: A Twin Study. *Am. J. Psychiatry* **2002**, *159*, 1675–1681. [CrossRef] [PubMed]
4. Breslau, N.; Lucia, V.C.; Davis, G.C. Partial PTSD versus Full PTSD: An Empirical Examination of Associated Impairment. *Psychol. Med.* **2004**, *34*, 1205–1214. [CrossRef] [PubMed]
5. Mylle, J.; Maes, M. Partial Posttraumatic Stress Disorder Revisited. *J. Affect. Disord.* **2004**, *78*, 37–48. [CrossRef]
6. Czarnocka, J.; Slade, P. Prevalence and Predictors of Post-Traumatic Stress Symptoms Following Childbirth. *Br. J. Clin. Psychol.* **2000**, *39*, 35–51. [CrossRef] [PubMed]
7. Sentilhes, L.; Maillard, F.; Brun, S.; Madar, H.; Merlot, B.; Goffinet, F.; Deneux-Tharaux, C. Risk Factors for Chronic Post-Traumatic Stress Disorder Development One Year after Vaginal Delivery: A Prospective, Observational Study. *Sci. Rep.* **2017**, *7*, 8724. [CrossRef] [PubMed]
8. James, S. Women's Experiences of Symptoms of Posttraumatic Stress Disorder (PTSD) after Traumatic Childbirth: A Review and Critical Appraisal. *Arch. Womens Ment. Health* **2015**, *18*, 761–771. [CrossRef]
9. Kessler, R.C.; Sonnega, A.; Bromet, E.; Hughes, M.; Nelson, C.B. Posttraumatic Stress Disorder in the National Comorbidity Survey. *Arch. Gen. Psychiatry* **1995**, *52*, 1048–1060. [CrossRef]
10. Tamaki, R.; Murata, M.; Okano, T. Risk Factors for Postpartum Depression in Japan. *Psychiatry Clin. Neurosci.* **1997**, *51*, 93–98. [CrossRef]
11. Schwab, W.; Marth, C.; Bergant, A.M. Post-Traumatic Stress Disorder Post Partum: The Impact of Birth on the Prevalence of Post-Traumatic Stress Disorder (PTSD) in Multiparous Women. *Geburtshilfe Frauenheilkd* **2012**, *72*, 56–63. [CrossRef]
12. Söderquist, J.; Wijma, B.; Thorbert, G.; Wijma, K. Risk Factors in Pregnancy for Post-Traumatic Stress and Depression after Childbirth. *BJOG Int. J. Obstet. Gynaecol.* **2009**, *116*, 672–680. [CrossRef] [PubMed]
13. Tham, V.; Christensson, K.; Ryding, E.L. Sense of Coherence and Symptoms of Post-Traumatic Stress after Emergency Caesarean Section. *Acta Obstet. Gynecol. Scand.* **2007**, *86*, 1090–1096. [CrossRef] [PubMed]
14. Mahmoodi, Z.; Dolatian, M.; Shaban, Z.; Shams, J.; Alavi-Majd, H.; Mirabzadeh, A. Correlation between Kind of Delivery and Posttraumatic Stress Disorder. *Ann. Med. Health Sci. Res.* **2016**, *6*, 356–361. [CrossRef] [PubMed]

15. Ryding, E.L.; Wijma, B.; Wijma, K. Posttraumatic Stress Reactions after Emergency Cesarean Section. *Acta Obstet. Gynecol. Scand.* **1997**, *76*, 856–861. [CrossRef]
16. Orovou, E.; Dagla, M.; Iatrakis, G.; Lykeridou, A.; Tzavara, C.; Antoniou, E. Correlation between Kind of Cesarean Section and Posttraumatic Stress Disorder in Greek Women. *Int. J. Environ. Res. Public Health* **2020**, *17*, 1592. [CrossRef]
17. Galletly, C.A.; Clark, C.R.; McFarlane, A.C. Artificial Neural Networks: A Prospective Tool for the Analysis of Psychiatric Disorders. *J. Psychiatry Neurosci.* **1996**, *21*, 239–247.
18. Price, R.K.; Spitznagel, E.L.; Downey, T.J.; Meyer, D.J.; Risk, N.K.; El-Ghazzawy, O.G. Applying Artificial Neural Network Models to Clinical Decision Making. *Psychol. Assess.* **2000**, *12*, 40–51. [CrossRef]
19. Remaida, A.; Abdellaoui, B.; Moumen, A.; Idrissi, Y. Personality Traits Analysis Using Artificial Neural Networks: A Literature Survey. In Proceedings of the 1st International Conference on Innovative Research in Applied Science, Engineering and Technology (IRASET), Meknes, Morocco, 16–19 April 2020. [CrossRef]
20. Truong, V.T.; Nguyen, B.P.; Nguyen-Vo, T.-H.; Mazur, W.; Chung, E.S.; Palmer, C.; Tretter, J.T.; Alsaied, T.; Pham, V.T.; Do, H.Q.; et al. Application of Machine Learning in Screening for Congenital Heart Diseases Using Fetal Echocardiography. *Int. J. Cardiovasc. Imaging* **2022**, *38*, 1007–1015. [CrossRef]
21. Shahzad, M.N.; Suleman, M.; Ahmed, M.A.; Riaz, A.; Fatima, K. Identifying the Symptom Severity in Obsessive-Compulsive Disorder for Classification and Prediction: An Artificial Neural Network Approach. *Behav. Neurol.* **2020**, *2020*. [CrossRef]
22. Komatsu, H.; Watanabe, E.; Fukuchi, M. Psychiatric Neural Networks and Precision Therapeutics by Machine Learning. *Biomedicines* **2021**, *9*, 403. [CrossRef]
23. Dwyer, D.B.; Falkai, P.; Koutsouleris, N. Machine Learning Approaches for Clinical Psychology and Psychiatry. *Annu. Rev. Clin. Psychol.* **2018**, *14*, 91–118. [CrossRef] [PubMed]
24. Durstewitz, D.; Koppe, G.; Meyer-Lindenberg, A. Deep Neural Networks in Psychiatry. *Mol. Psychiatry* **2019**, *24*, 1583–1598. [CrossRef] [PubMed]
25. Gray, M.J.; Litz, B.T.; Hsu, J.L.; Lombardo, T.W. Psychometric Properties of the Life Events Checklist. *Assessment* **2004**, *11*, 330–341. [CrossRef] [PubMed]
26. McFarlane, A.C. PTSD and DSM-5: Unintended Consequences of Change. *Lancet Psychiatry* **2014**, *1*, 246–247. [CrossRef]
27. Blevins, C.A.; Weathers, F.W.; Davis, M.T.; Witte, T.K.; Domino, J.L. The Posttraumatic Stress Disorder Checklist for DSM-5 (PCL-5): Development and Initial Psychometric Evaluation. *J. Trauma Stress* **2015**, *28*, 489–498. [CrossRef]
28. Wortmann, J.H.; Jordan, A.H.; Weathers, F.W.; Resick, P.A.; Dondanville, K.A.; Hall-Clark, B.; Foa, E.B.; Young-McCaughan, S.; Yarvis, J.S.; Hembree, E.A.; et al. Psychometric Analysis of the PTSD Checklist-5 (PCL-5) among Treatment-Seeking Military Service Members. *Psychol. Assess.* **2016**, *28*, 1392–1403. [CrossRef]
29. Ho, T.K. Random Decision Forests. In Proceedings of the Third International Conference on Document Analysis and Recognition, Montreal, QC, Canada, 14–16 August 1995; Volume 1.
30. Nembrini, S.; König, I.R.; Wright, M.N. The Revival of the Gini Importance? *Bioinformatics* **2018**, *34*, 3711–3718. [CrossRef]

Article

Chicken Swarm-Based Feature Subset Selection with Optimal Machine Learning Enabled Data Mining Approach

Monia Hamdi [1], Inès Hilali-Jaghdam [2], Manal M. Khayyat [3], Bushra M. E. Elnaim [4], Sayed Abdel-Khalek [5,6] and Romany F. Mansour [7,*]

1. Department of Information Technology, College of Computer and Information Sciences, Princess Nourah Bint Abdulrahman University, P.O. Box 84428, Riyadh 11671, Saudi Arabia; mshamdi@pnu.edu.sa
2. Department of Computer Sciences and Information Technology, Applied College, Princess Nourah Bint Abdulrahman University, P.O. Box 84428, Riyadh 11671, Saudi Arabia; imalihilali@pnu.edu.sa
3. Department of Information Systems, College of Computers and Information Systems, Umm Al-Qura University, P.O. Box 7607, Makkah 24382, Saudi Arabia; mmkhayat@uqu.edu.sa
4. Department of Computer Science, College of Science and Humanities in Al-Sulail, Prince Sattam Bin Abdulaziz University, P.O. Box 173, Al-Kharj 16278, Saudi Arabia; b.elnaim@psau.edu.sa
5. Department of Mathematics, Faculty of Science, Sohag University, Sohag 82524, Egypt; sayedquantum@yahoo.co.uk or sabotalb@tu.edu.sa
6. Department of Mathematics, College of Science, Taif University, P.O. Box 11099, Taif 21944, Saudi Arabia
7. Department of Mathematics, Faculty of Science, New Valley University, El-Kharga 72511, Egypt
* Correspondence: romanyf@sci.nvu.edu.eg

Abstract: Data mining (DM) involves the process of identifying patterns, correlation, and anomalies existing in massive datasets. The applicability of DM includes several areas such as education, healthcare, business, and finance. Educational Data Mining (EDM) is an interdisciplinary domain which focuses on the applicability of DM, machine learning (ML), and statistical approaches for pattern recognition in massive quantities of educational data. This type of data suffers from the curse of dimensionality problems. Thus, feature selection (FS) approaches become essential. This study designs a Feature Subset Selection with an optimal machine learning model for Educational Data Mining (FSSML-EDM). The proposed method involves three major processes. At the initial stage, the presented FSSML-EDM model uses the Chicken Swarm Optimization-based Feature Selection (CSO-FS) technique for electing feature subsets. Next, an extreme learning machine (ELM) classifier is employed for the classification of educational data. Finally, the Artificial Hummingbird (AHB) algorithm is utilized for adjusting the parameters involved in the ELM model. The performance study revealed that FSSML-EDM model achieves better results compared with other models under several dimensions.

Keywords: feature subset selection; data mining; educational data mining; artificial intelligence; machine learning; metaheuristics

1. Introduction

Data mining (DM) is the procedure of understanding data through cleaning raw data, discovering patterns, producing models, and testing the models. It comprises of several fields such as statistics, machine learning (ML), and database systems. Education DM (EDM) is an emergent field with an arising strategy to investigate the various types of data which are obtained from an education background [1]. It is an interdisciplinary area which inspects data mining (DM), man-fabricated consciousness, and measurable demonstrating with the data produced using an academic organization [2]. EDM uses a calculation method for taking care of elucidating academic data considering a definitive point of examining academic enquiries. To make a nation stand out among different nations across the globe, education frameworks should encounter an essential advancement by re-planning their design. The concealed data and examples from various data sources can be extricated by adjusting the strategies for DM. For summing up the outcomes of students with their qualifications, they investigate the abuse of DM in the academic fields. Crude data can be altogether moved through DM models. The data achieved from an education organization go through examination of various DM strategies [3]. The strategy identifies the conditions wherein students can strive to have a positive impact [4].

Student performance prediction (SPP) has different definitions according to troublesome perspectives; however, the measured assessment assumes a significant part in current education establishments. SPP seems effective in aiding all partners in the education interaction. For students, SPP can assist them with picking reasonable courses or activities and make their arrangements for academic durations [5]. For educators, SPP can assist with changing learning material and presenting programs compatible with the students' capacity, and help identify struggling students. For education chiefs, SPP can assist with checking the education program and enhancing the course framework. Generally, partners in the education advancement have intentions to further develop the education outcome. Moreover, the data-driven SPP study provides a goal of reference for the education framework. Weka, a compelling DM technique was utilized to produce the outcome [6].

The increment of educational information from distinct sources has resulted in desperation for the EDM research [7]. This can help to further objectives and characterize specific goals of education and highlight subset determinations by disposing of the component that is repetitive/is not important. The set of components chosen should follow the Occam Razor rule to provide the best outcome in light of the goal [8]. The data size to be dealt with has expanded in the past five years; hence, the choice is turning into a necessity before any sort of arrangement happens. It is not quite the same as the element extraction strategy because the determination method does not change the first portrayal of the data [9]. The least complex method includes choice, where how much quality in an examination is diminished by choosing just the main view of the circumstances such as a more elevated level of exercises [10].

Since the high dimensionality raises computational costs, it is essential to define a way to reduce the number of considered features. Feature selection (FS) allows reducing a high dimensionality problem and selecting a suitable number of features. This study designed a Feature Subset Selection with optimal machine learning for the Educational Data Mining (FSSML-EDM) model. The proposed FSSML-EDM model involves the Chicken Swarm Optimization-based Feature Selection (CSO-FS) technique for electing feature subsets. Next, the extreme learning machine (ELM) classifier was employed for the classification of educational data. Finally, the Artificial Hummingbird (AHB) algorithm was utilized for adjusting the parameters involved in the ELM model. The performance study revealed the effectual outcomes of the FSSML-EDM model over the compared models under several dimensions. Our contributions are summarized as follows:

- We propose a model comprising data preprocessing, CSO-FS, ELM classification, and AHB parameter;
- We designed a new CSO-FS technique to reduce the curse of the dimensionality problem and enhanced the classification performance;
- We employed the ELM classification model with the AHB-based parameter optimization technique for the EDM process;
- We validated the performance of the FSSML-EDM model using the benchmark dataset from the UCI repository.

2. Literature Review

Injadat et al. [11] explored and analyzed two distinct datasets at two distinct phases of course delivery (20% and 50%) utilizing several graphical, statistical, and quantitative approaches. The feature analysis offers understanding as to the nature of distinct features regarded and utilizes in the selection of ML techniques and their parameters. Moreover, this work presents a systematic model dependent upon the Gini index and p-value for selecting an appropriate ensemble learner in a group of six potential ML techniques. Ashraf et al. [12]

progressed an accurate prediction pedagogical method, considering the pronounced nature and novelty of presented approach in Educational Data Mining. The base classifications containing RT, j48, kNN, and naïve Bayes (NB) were estimated on a 10-fold cross-validation model. In addition, the filter procedure as over-sampling (SMOTE) and under-sampling (Spread subsampling) were exploited to examine some important alterations in outcomes amongst meta and base classifications.

Dabhade et al. [13] forecasted student academic performance in a technical institution in India. The data pre-processed and factor analysis were executed on the attained dataset for removing the anomaly from the data, decreasing the dimensionality of the data, and attaining the most correlated feature. Nahar et al. [14] generated two datasets concentrating on two distinct angles. In the primary dataset classification and forecast, the type of students (bad, medium, and good) on a particular course was dependent upon its prerequisite course efficiency. This can be executed during the artificial intelligence (AI) course. The secondary dataset also classified and forecasted the last grade (A, B, C) of an arbitrary subject; our data can be established in such a way that the data are only concentrated on the efficiency of the midterm exam.

Despite all the studies performed on FS process, to the best of our knowledge, only few works have carried out an FS-based classification model for EDM. Earlier works have used ML models for EDM without contributing much significance to the FS process. At the same time, the parameters involved in the ML models (i.e., ELM) considerably affect the overall classification performance. Since the trial-and-error method for parameter tuning is a tedious and erroneous process, metaheuristic algorithms can be applied. Therefore, metaheuristic optimization algorithms can be designed to optimally tune the parameters related to the ML models to improve the overall classification performance.

3. The Proposed Model

In this study, a new FSSML-EDM technique was developed for mining educational data. The proposed FSSML-EDM model involves data preprocessing at the initial stage to transform the input data into a compatible format. Then, the preprocessed data are passed into the CSO-FS technique for electing feature subsets. Next, the ELM classifier can be employed for the effective identification and classification of educational data. Finally, the AHB algorithm is utilized for effectively adjusting the parameters involved in the ELM model. The outcome of the ELM model is the classification output. Figure 1 depicts the block diagram of FSSML-EDM technique.

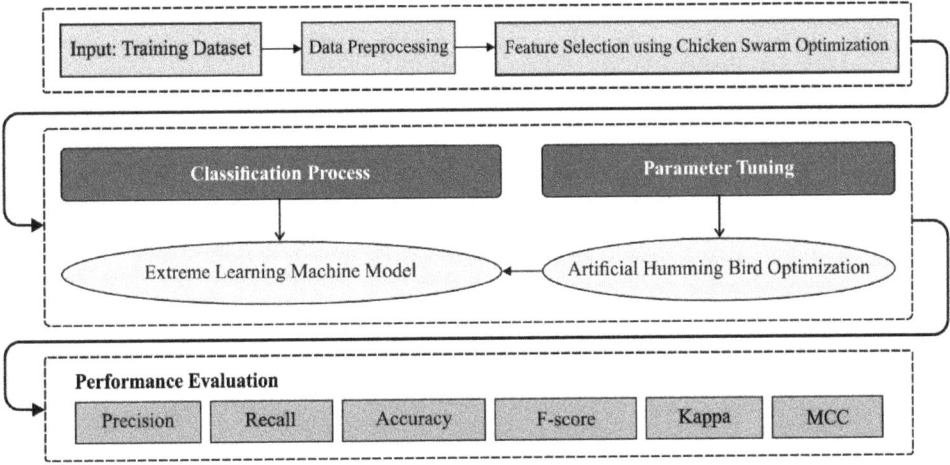

Figure 1. Block diagram of FSSML-EDM technique.

3.1. Process Involved in CSO-FS Technique

At the initial stage, the presented FSSML-EDM model incorporates the design of the CSO-FS technique for electing feature subsets. The CSO algorithm is chosen over other optimization algorithms due to its simplicity and high parallelism. The CSO simulates the chicken movement and the performance of the chicken swarm; the CSO is explained as follows: CSO has several groups, and all the groups have a dominant rooster, some hens, and chicks [15]. The rooster, hen, and chick from the group are found dependent upon their fitness value. The rooster (group head) is the chicken which is an optimum fitness value. However, the chick is the chicken which has the worse fitness value. The majority of chickens are hens and it can be selected arbitrarily to stay in that group. The dominance connection and mother–child connection from the group remain unaltered and upgrade during (G) time steps. The movement of chickens are expressed under the equation which utilizes to the rooster place upgrade provided by Equation (1):

$$X_{ij}^{r+1} = X_{i,j}^t \times \left(1 + randn\left(0, \sigma^2\right)\right) \qquad (1)$$

whereas:

$$\sigma^2 = \begin{cases} 1 & \text{if } f_i \leq f_k \\ \exp\left(\frac{f_k - f_i}{|f_i| + \varepsilon}\right) & \text{Otherwise} \end{cases}$$

In which $k \in [1, N_r]$, $k \neq i$, and N_r refers the amount of chosen roosters. $X_{i,j}$ signifies the place of rooster number i in jth dimensional under t and $t+1$ iteration, $randn(O, \sigma^2)$ is utilized for generating Gaussian arbitrary numbers with mean 0 and variance σ^2; ε refers to the constant with minimum value; and f_i is the fitness value to the equivalent rooster i. The equation which utilizes the hen place upgrade is provided by Equations (2)–(4):

$$X_{i,j}^{t+1} = X_{i,j}^t + S_1 randn\left(X_{r1,j}^t - X_{i,j}^t\right) + S_2 randn\left(X_{r2,j}^t - X_{i,j}^t\right) \qquad (2)$$

In which:

$$S_1 = \exp\left(\frac{f_i - f_{r1}}{|f_i| + \varepsilon}\right) \qquad (3)$$

and:

$$S_1 = \exp(f_{r2} - f_i) \qquad (4)$$

where $r1, r \in [1, \ldots, N]$, $r1 \neq rr$ refers to the index of the rooster, but $r2$ implies the chicken in the swarm which is a rooster or hen and a uniform arbitrary number is created by $randn$. Finally, the equation that utilizes the chick place upgrade is provided by Equation (5):

$$X_{i,j}^{t+1} = X_{i,j}^t + FL\left(X_{m,j}^t - X_{i,j}^t\right), \; FL \in [0, 2] \qquad (5)$$

where $X_{m,j}^t$ signifies the place of ith chick mother.

3.2. ELM Based Classification

At this stage, the ELM classifier can be employed for the effective identification and classification of educational data. The ELM model has n input layers, l hidden layers, and m output layers. Initially, considering the training instance $\{X, Y\} = \{x_i, y_i\} (i = 1, 2, \ldots, Q)$, and it is comprised of the input feature $X = [x_{i1} x_{i2} \ldots x_{iQ}]$ and matrix $Y = [y_{j1} y_{j2} \ldots y_{jQ}]$ with training instance, where the matrix X and Y are expressed by [16]:

$$X = \begin{bmatrix} x_{11} & x_{12} & \cdots & x_{1Q} \\ x_{21} & x_{22} & \cdots & x_{2Q} \\ \vdots & \vdots & \ddots & \vdots \\ x_{n1} & x_{n2} & \cdots & x_{nQ} \end{bmatrix}, \qquad (6)$$

$$Y = \begin{bmatrix} y_{11} & y_{12} & \cdots & y_{mQ} \\ y_{21} & y_{22} & \cdots & y_{mQ} \\ \vdots & \vdots & \ddots & \vdots \\ y_{m1} & y_{m2} & \cdots & y_{mQ} \end{bmatrix},$$

where n and m parameters denote the dimension of input and output matrix. Next, ELM set the weights amongst input and hidden layers randomly:

$$w = \begin{bmatrix} w_{11} & w_{12} & \cdots & w_{1n} \\ w_{21} & w_{22} & \cdots & w_{2n} \\ \vdots & \vdots & \ddots & \vdots \\ w_{l1} & w_{l2} & \cdots & w_{ln} \end{bmatrix}, \quad (7)$$

where w_{ij} denotes the weight from ith hidden and jth input layers. Figure 2 showcases the framework of ELM. Then, ELM considers the weight from output and hidden layers that can be shown below:

$$\beta = \begin{bmatrix} \beta_{11} & \beta_{12} & \cdots & \beta_{1m} \\ \beta_{21} & \beta_{22} & \cdots & \beta_{2m} \\ \vdots & \vdots & \ddots & \vdots \\ \beta_{l1} & \beta_{l2} & \cdots & \beta_{lm} \end{bmatrix}, \quad (8)$$

where β_{jk} indicates the weight from jth hidden and ith output layers. Next, ELM set a bias of hidden layers randomly:

$$B = [b_1 b_2 \cdots b_n]^T. \quad (9)$$

After that, ELM chooses the network activation function. According to, output matrix T is characterized by:

$$T = [t_1, t_2, \ldots, t_Q]_{m \times Q}. \quad (10)$$

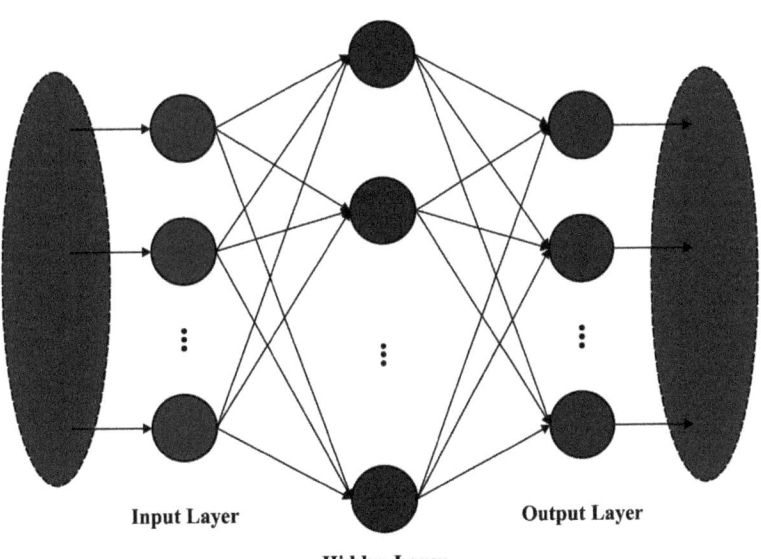

Figure 2. Framework of ELM.

The column vector of output matrix T is shown in the following:

$$t_j = \begin{bmatrix} t_{1j} \\ t_{2j} \\ \vdots \\ t_{mj} \end{bmatrix} = \begin{bmatrix} \sum_{i=1}^{l} \beta_{i1} g(w_i x_j + b_i) \\ \sum_{i=1}^{l} \beta_{i2} g(w_i x_j + b_i) \\ \vdots \\ \sum_{i=1}^{l} \beta_{im} g(w_i x_j + b_i) \end{bmatrix} (j = 1, 2, 3, \ldots, Q). \tag{11}$$

Moreover, considering Equations (10) and (11), it is modelled in the following:

$$H\beta = T', \tag{12}$$

where T' indicates transpose of T and H represents simulation outcomes of hidden neurons. To achieve better solution with less error, the least square model is employed for determining the weight matrix measure of β [17,18].

$$\beta = H^+ T'. \tag{13}$$

To enhance the normalization ability of the system and provide stable outcomes, the regularization parameter of β is used. The amount of hidden layers is minimal in contrast with the amount of training samples, β is shown in the following [19]:

$$\beta = \left(\frac{I}{\lambda} + H^T H\right)^{-1} H^T T'. \tag{14}$$

When the amount of hidden layers is maximal than the amount of training samples, β is denoted as follows [20]:

$$\beta = H^T \left(\frac{I}{\lambda} + H H^T\right)^{-1} T'. \tag{15}$$

3.3. AHB Based Parameter Optimization

Finally, the AHB algorithm is utilized for effectively adjusting the parameters involved in the ELM model with the goal of attaining maximum classification performance [21]. The AHB algorithm is an optimization approach stimulated from the foraging and flight of hummingbirds. The three major models are provided as follows: in a guided foraging model, three flight behaviors are utilized in foraging (axial, diagonal, and omnidirectional flight). It can be defined as follows:

$$v_i(t+1) = x_{i,ta}(t) + h \cdot b \cdot (x_i(t) - X_{i,ta}(t)) h \sim N(0,1) \tag{16}$$

where $x_{i,ta}(t)$ characterizes the location of the targeted food source, h signifies the guiding factor, and $x(t)$ represents the location of ith food source at time t. The location updating of the ith food source is provided by:

$$x_{Ai}(t) = \begin{cases} x_i(t) & f(x_i(t)) \leq f(v_i(t+1)) \\ v_i(t+1) & f(x_{i(t)}) > f(v_i(t+1)) \end{cases} \tag{17}$$

where $f(x_i(t))$ and $f(v_i(t+1))$ denote the value of function fitness for $x(t)$ and $v_i(t+1)$. the local search of hummingbirds in the territorial foraging strategy is provided in the following:

$$v_i(t+1) = x_{i(t)} + g \cdot b \cdot \left(x_{i(t)}\right) g \sim N(0,1) \tag{18}$$

where g represents the territorial factor. The arithmetical formula for the migration foraging of hummingbirds is provided by:

$$x_{wor}(t+1) = lb + r \cdot (ub - lb) \tag{19}$$

where x_{wor} indicates the source of food with worst population rate of nectar refilling, r represents a random factor, and ub and lb denote the upper and lower limits, respectively.

4. Experimental Validation

The proposed FSSML-EDM model was simulated using a benchmark dataset from UCI repository, which comprises of 649 samples with 32 features and 2 class labels as illustrated in Table 1. The parameter settings are provided as follows: learning rate, 0.01; dropout, 0.5; batch size, 5; and number of epochs, 50. For experimental validation, the dataset is split into 70% training (TR) data and 30% testing (TS) data.

Table 1. Dataset details.

Details	Values
Number of samples	649
Feature count	32
Class count	2
Source	https://archive.ics.uci.edu/ml/datasets/student+performance (accessed on 30 January 2022)

Figure 3 highlights a set of confusion matrices produced by the FSSML-EDM model on the test data. The figure indicates that the FSSML-EDM model resulted in effectual outcomes. On entire dataset, the FSSML-EDM model identified 545 samples into pass and 86 samples into fail. In addition, on 70% of the training dataset, the FSSML-EDM model identified 390 samples into pass and 53 samples into fail. Moreover, on 30% of testing dataset, the FSSML-EDM model identified 155 samples into pass and 33 samples into fail.

Table 2 offers a comprehensive EDM outcome of the FSSML-EDM model on test dataset. The experimental values indicated that the FSSML-EDM model accomplished maximum outcomes on all datasets. Figure 4 provides brief classification results of the FSSML-EDM model on entire dataset. It can be inferred from the figure that the FSSML-EDM model classified pass instances for $accu_y$, $prec_n$, $reca_l$, F_{score}, MCC, and kappa of 97.23%, 97.50%, 99.27%, 98.38%, and 89.08% respectively. Moreover, the figure shows that the FSSML-EDM model classified fail instances for $accu_y$, $prec_n$, $reca_l$, F_{score}, MCC, and kappa of 97.23%, 95.56%, 86%, 90.53%, and 89.08%, respectively.

Table 2. Result analysis of FSSML-EDM technique with distinct measures and datasets.

Class Labels	Accuracy	Precision	Recall	F-Score	MCC	Kappa Score
			Entire Dataset			
Pass	97.23	97.50	99.27	98.38	89.08	-
Fail	97.23	95.56	86.00	90.53	89.08	-
Average	97.23	96.53	92.64	94.45	89.08	88.91
			Training Set (70%)			
Pass	97.58	97.50	99.74	98.61	89.57	-
Fail	97.58	98.15	84.13	90.60	89.57	-
Average	97.58	97.82	91.94	94.60	89.57	89.22
			Testing Set (30%)			
Pass	96.41	97.48	98.1	97.79	88.22	-
Fail	96.41	91.67	89.19	90.41	88.22	-
Average	96.41	94.58	93.65	94.1	88.22	88.2

Figure 5 provides detailed classification results of the FSSML-EDM model on 70% of the training dataset. The figure reveals that the FSSML-EDM model classified pass instances for $accu_y$, $prec_n$, $reca_l$, F_{score}, MCC, and kappa of 97.58%, 97.50%, 99.74%, 98.61%, and 89.57%, respectively. In addition, the figure shows that the FSSML-EDM model classified fail instances for $accu_y$, $prec_n$, $reca_l$, F_{score}, MCC, and kappa of 97.58%, 98.15%, 84.13%, 90.60%, and 89.57% respectively.

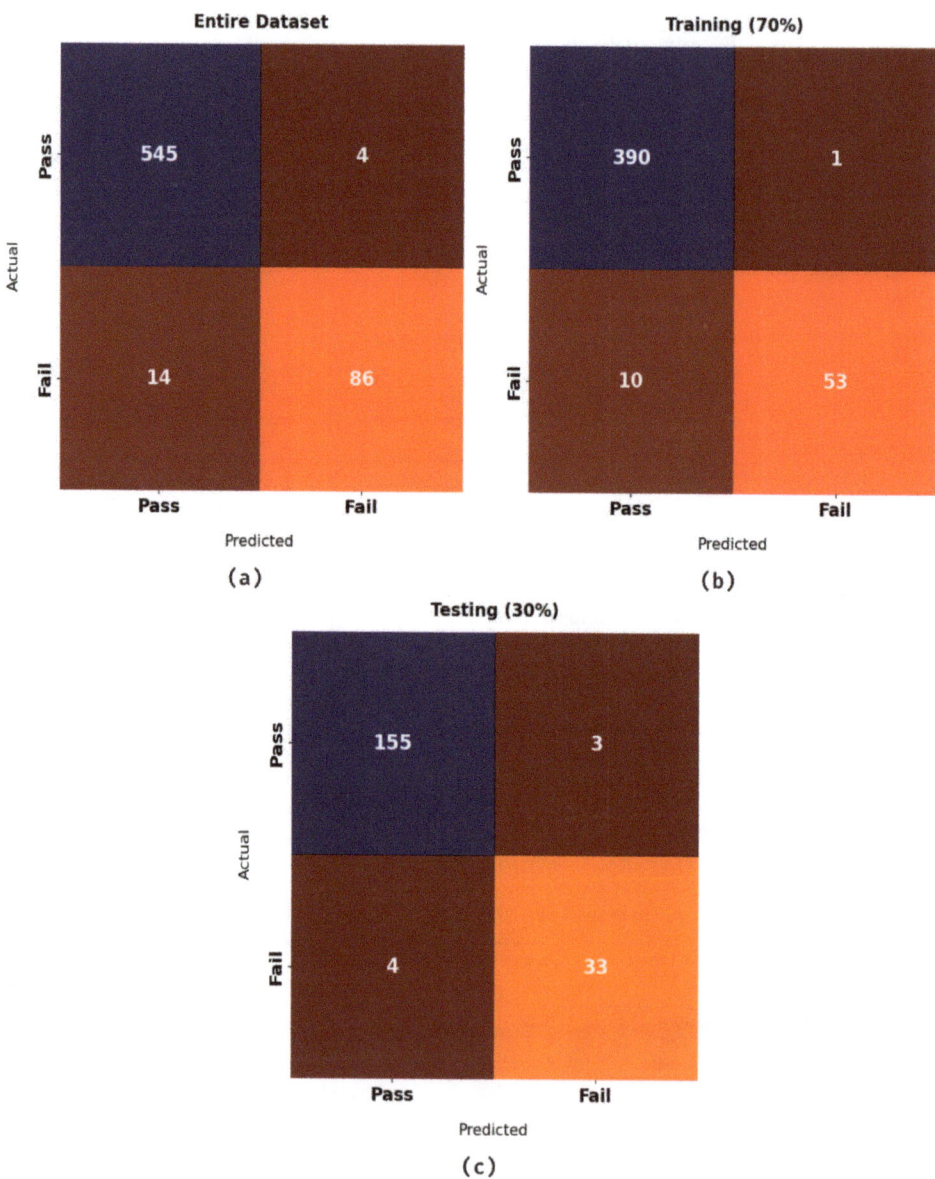

Figure 3. Confusion matrix of FSSML-EDM technique on test data. (**a**) Entire dataset, (**b**) 70% of training dataset, and (**c**) 30% of testing dataset.

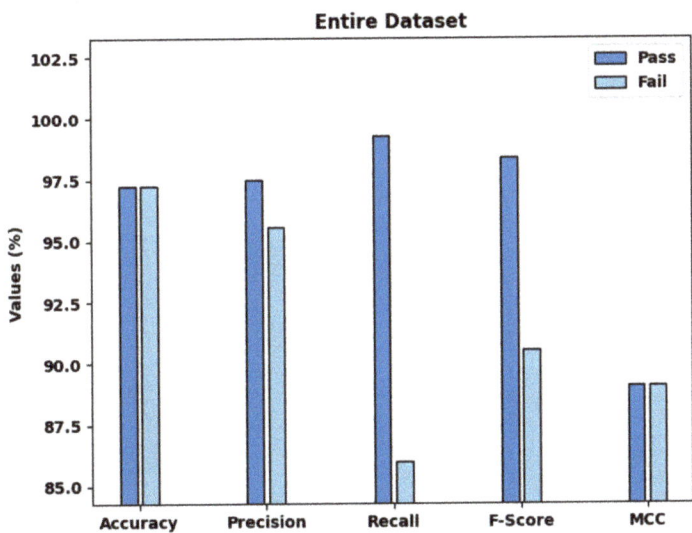

Figure 4. Result analysis of FSSML-EDM technique on entire dataset.

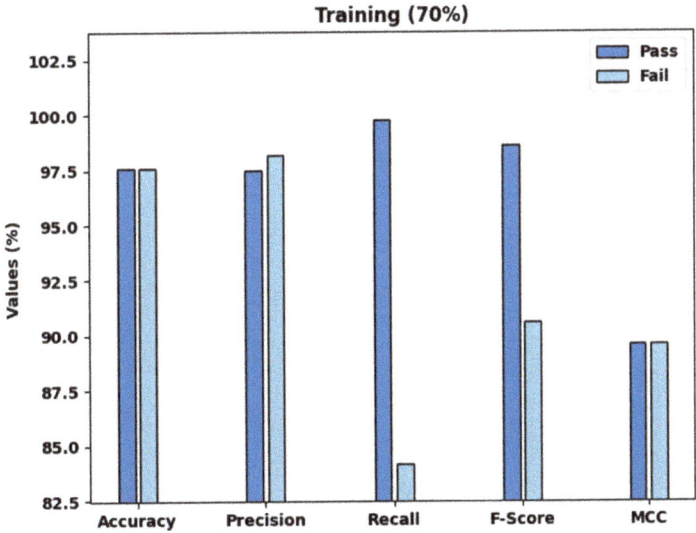

Figure 5. Result analysis of FSSML-EDM technique on 70% of training dataset.

Figure 6 offers brief classification results of the FSSML-EDM approach on 30% of testing dataset. The figure exposes that the FSSML-EDM algorithm classified pass instances for $accu_y$, $prec_n$, $reca_l$, F_{score}, MCC, and kappa of 96.41%, 97.48%, 98.1%, 97.798%, and 88.22%, respectively. Moreover, the figure shows that the FSSML-EDM approach classified fail instances for $accu_y$, $prec_n$, $reca_l$, F_{score}, MCC, and kappa of 96.41%, 91.67%, 89.19%, 90.41%, and 88.22%, respectively.

Figure 7 illustrates the training and validation accuracy inspection of the FSSML-EDM technique on the applied dataset. The figure of the FSSML-EDM approach offers maximum training/validation accuracy on the classification process.

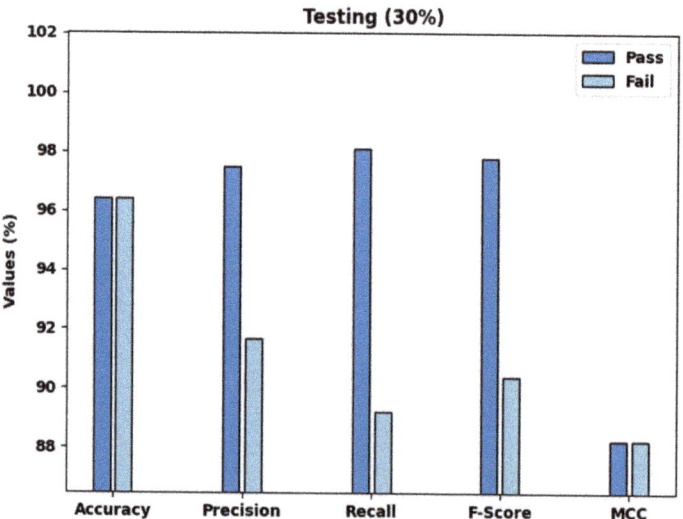

Figure 6. Result analysis of FSSML-EDM technique on 30% of testing dataset.

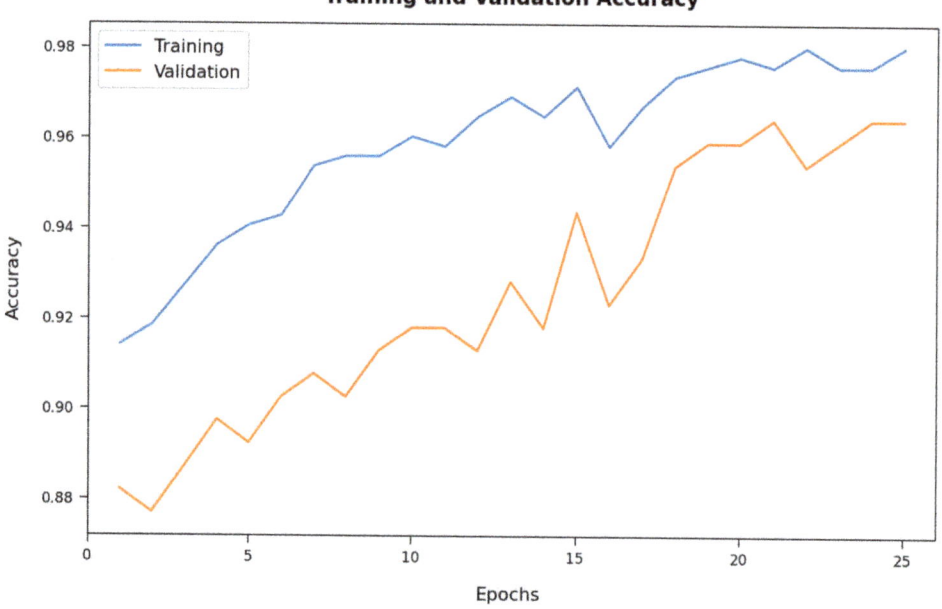

Figure 7. Accuracy graph analysis of FSSML-EDM technique.

Next, Figure 8 reveals the training and validation loss inspection of the FSSML-EDM approach on the applied dataset. The figure shows that the FSSML-EDM algorithm offers reduced training/accuracy loss on the classification process of the test data.

A brief precision-recall examination of the FSSML-EDM model on the test dataset is portrayed in Figure 9. By observing the figure, it is noticed that the DLBTDC-MRI model accomplished maximum precision-recall performance under all classes.

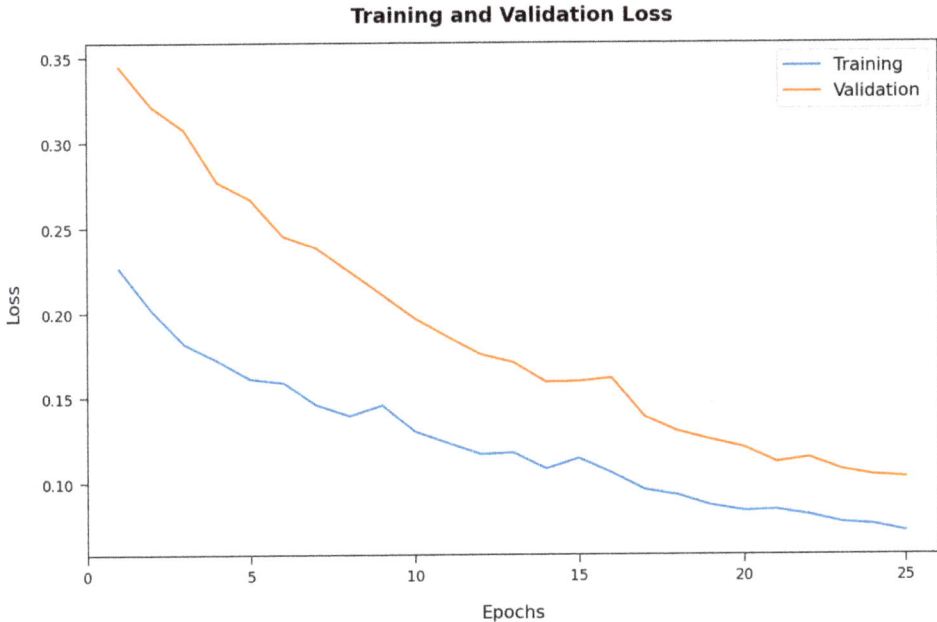

Figure 8. Loss graph analysis of FSSML-EDM technique.

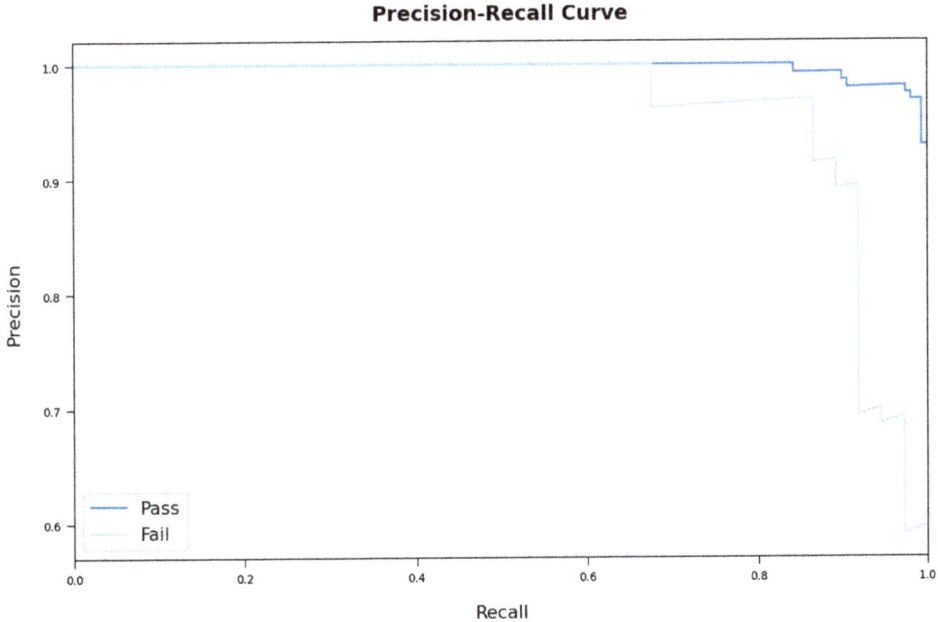

Figure 9. Precision-recall curve analysis of FSSML-EDM technique.

A detailed ROC investigation of the FSSML-EDM approach on the distinct datasets is portrayed in Figure 10. The results indicate that the FSSML-EDM technique exhibited its ability in categorizing two different classes such as pass and fail on the test datasets.

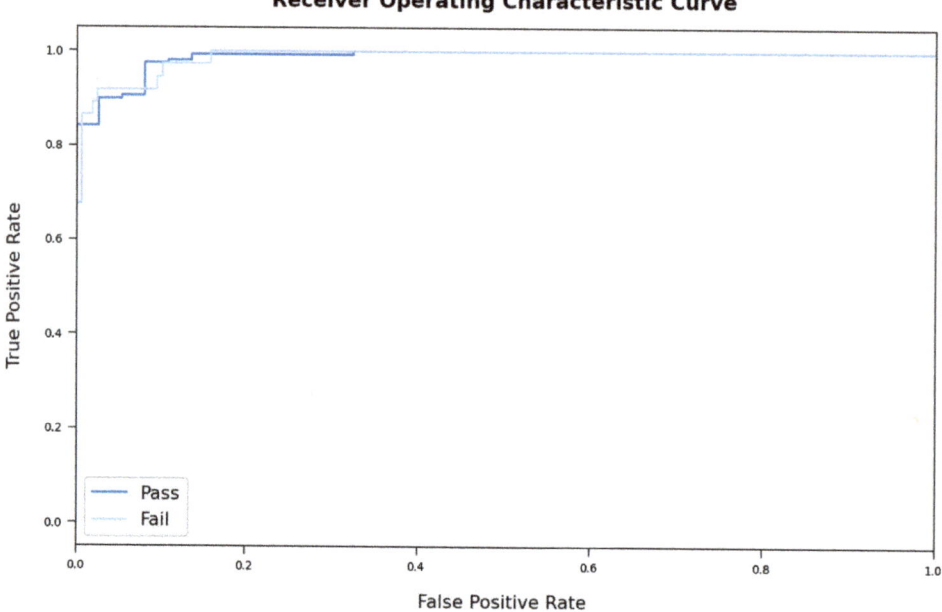

Figure 10. ROC curve analysis of FSSML-EDM technique.

Table 3 reveals an extensive comparative study of the FSSML-EDM model with existing models such as improved evolutionary algorithm-based feature subsets election with neuro-fuzzy classification (IEAFSSNFC) [22], neuro-fuzzy classification (NFC) [21], neural network (NN), support vector machines (SVM), decision tree (DT), and random forest (RF). Figure 11 inspects the comparative $prec_n$, $reca_l$, and $accu_y$ investigation of the FSSML-EDM model with recent methods. The figure reveals that the NN and SVM models showed poor performance with lower values of $prec_n$, $reca_l$, and $accu_y$. The NFC, DT, and RF models have showed slightly improved values of $prec_n$, $reca_l$, and $accu_y$. Moreover, the IEAFSS-NFC model resulted in reasonable $prec_n$, $reca_l$, and $accu_y$ of 93.81%, 92.39%, and 90.33%, respectively. Furthermore, the FSSML-EDM model accomplished effectual outcomes with maximum $prec_n$, $reca_l$, and $accu_y$ of 94.58%, 93.65%, and 96.41%, respectively.

Table 3. Comparative analysis of FSSML-EDM approach with existing methods [21].

Methods	Precision	Recall	Accuracy	F-Score	MCC	Kappa
FSSML-EDM	94.58	93.65	96.41	94.10	88.22	88.20
IEAFSSNFC	93.81	92.39	90.33	93.01	73.78	73.37
NFC Algorithm	81.76	91.41	81.66	86.99	56.21	50.10
NN Algorithm	67.58	85.76	64.30	76.03	57.52	67.82
SVM Algorithm	68.83	86.77	66.36	76.63	66.27	66.17
DT Algorithm	78.22	93.40	77.81	83.02	52.87	59.80
RF Algorithm	74.95	91.90	75.40	83.39	62.68	58.34

Figure 12 inspects the comparative F_{score}, MCC, and kappa analysis of the FSSML-EDM method with existing algorithms. The figure reveals that the NN and SVM methods showed poor performance with lower values of F_{score}, MCC, and kappa. Similarly, the NFC, DT, and RF approaches showed slightly improved values of F_{score}, MCC, and kappa.

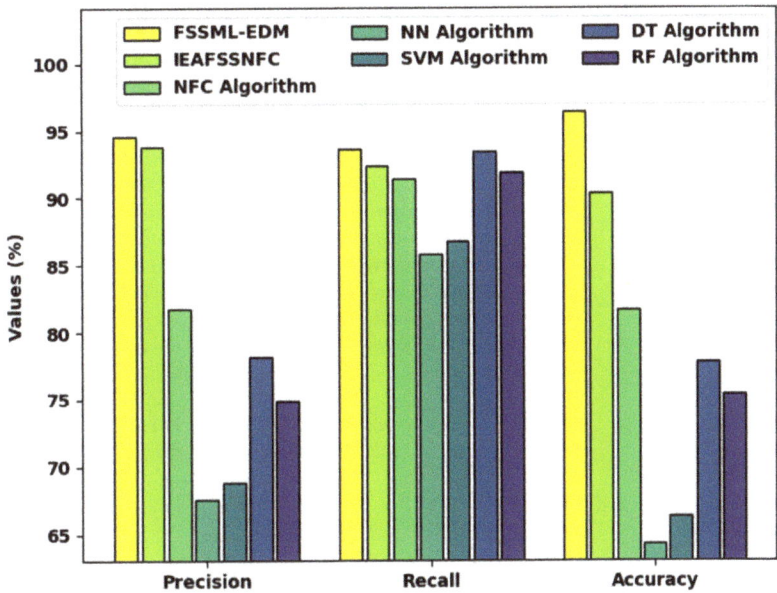

Figure 11. $Prec_n$, $reca_l$, and acc_y analysis of FSSML-EDM technique.

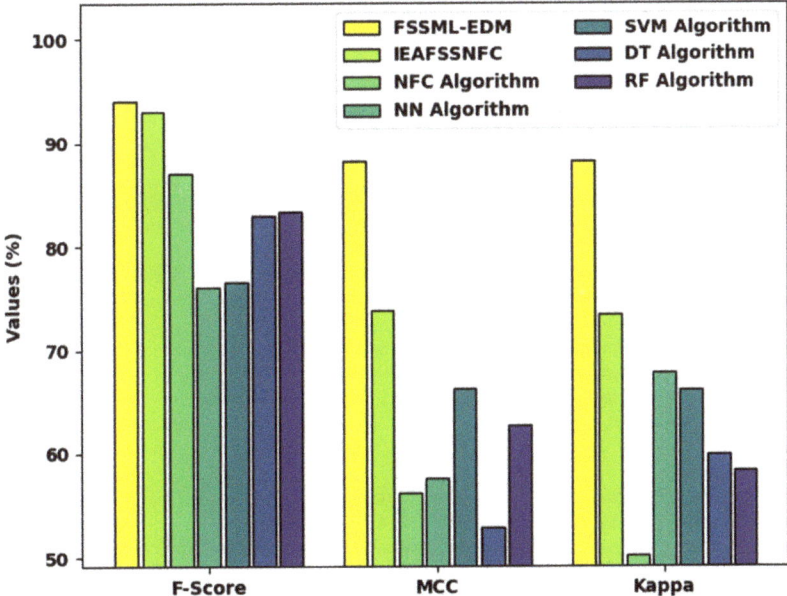

Figure 12. F_{score}, MCC, and kappa analysis of FSSML-EDM technique.

Moreover, the IEAFSSNFC model resulted a in reasonable F_{score}, MCC, and $kappa$ of 93.01%, 73.78%, and 73.37%, respectively. Additionally, the FSSML-EDM methodology accomplished effectual outcomes with maximum F_{score}, MCC, and $kappa$ of 94.10%, 82.22%, and 88.20%, respectively. Therefore, the FSSML-EDM model has the capability of assessing student performance in real time.

5. Conclusions

In this study, a new FSSML-EDM technique was developed for mining educational data. The proposed FSSML-EDM model involves three major processes. At the initial stage, the presented FSSML-EDM model incorporates the design of CSO-FS technique for electing feature subsets. Next, ELM classifier can be employed for the effective identification and classification of educational data. Finally, the AHB algorithm is utilized for effectively adjusting the parameters involved in the ELM model. The performance study revealed the effectual outcomes of the FSSML-EDM model over the compared models under several dimensions. Therefore, the FSSML-EDM model can be used as an effectual tool for EDM. In the future, feature reduction and outlier removal models can be employed to improve performance. In addition, the proposed model is presently tested on small-scale dataset, which needs to be explored. As a part of the future scope, the performance of the proposed model will be evaluated on a large-scale real-time dataset.

Author Contributions: Conceptualization, M.H.; Data curation, I.H.-J.; Formal analysis, I.H.-J.; Investigation, M.M.K.; Methodology, M.H. and R.F.M.; Project administration, M.M.K.; Resources, B.M.E.E.; Software, B.M.E.E.; Supervision, S.A.-K.; Validation, S.A.-K.; Visualization, S.A.-K.; Writing—original draft, M.H.; Writing—review & editing, R.F.M. All authors have read and agreed to the published version of the manuscript.

Funding: This research was funded by Princess Nourah bint Abdulrahman University Researchers Supporting Project number (PNURSP2022R125), Princess Nourah bint Abdulrahman University, Riyadh, Saudi Arabia; Also, the authors would like to thank the Deanship of Scientific Research at Umm Al-Qura University for supporting this work by Grant Code: (22UQU4400271DSR07).

Data Availability Statement: Data sharing not applicable to this article as no datasets were generated during the current study.

Conflicts of Interest: The authors declare that they have no conflict of interest. The manuscript was written through contributions of all authors. All authors have given approval to the final version of the manuscript.

References

1. Prakash, B.A.; Ramakrishnan, N. Leveraging Propagation for Data Mining: Models, Algorithms and Applications. In Proceedings of the 22nd ACM SIGKDD International Conference on Knowledge Discovery and Data Mining, San Francisco, CA, USA, 13–17 August 2016; pp. 2133–2134.
2. Jalota, C.; Agrawal, R. Analysis of Educational Data Mining Using Classification. In Proceedings of the 2019 International Conference on Machine Learning, Big Data, Cloud and Parallel Computing (COMITCon), Faridabad, India, 14–16 February 2019; pp. 243–247. [CrossRef]
3. Kenthapadi, K.; Mironov, I.; Thakurta, A.G. Privacy-preserving data mining in industry. In Proceedings of the Twelfth ACM International Conference on Web Search and Data Mining, WSDM'19: The Twelfth ACM International Conference on Web Search and Data Mining, Melbourne, VIC, Australia, 11–15 February 2019; pp. 840–841.
4. Yan, D.; Qin, S.; Bhattacharya, D.; Chen, J.; Zaki, M.J. 20th International Workshop on Data Mining in Bioinformatics (BIOKDD 2021). In Proceedings of the 27th ACM SIGKDD Conference on Knowledge Discovery & Data Mining, Singapore, 14–18 August 2021; pp. 4175–4176.
5. Aldowah, H.; Al-Samarraie, H.; Fauzy, W.M. Educational data mining and learning analytics for 21st century higher education: A review and synthesis. *Telemat. Inform.* **2019**, *37*, 13–49. [CrossRef]
6. Fernandes, E.; Holanda, M.; Victorino, M.; Borges, V.R.P.; Carvalho, R.; Van Erven, G. Educational data mining: Predictive analysis of academic performance of public school students in the capital of Brazil. *J. Bus. Res.* **2019**, *94*, 335–343. [CrossRef]
7. De Andrade, T.L.; Rigo, S.J.; Barbosa, J.L.V. Active Methodology, Educational Data Mining and Learning Analytics: A Systematic Mapping Study. *Inform. Educ.* **2021**, *20*, 171–204. [CrossRef]

8. Sáiz-Manzanares, M.; Rodríguez-Díez, J.; Díez-Pastor, J.; Rodríguez-Arribas, S.; Marticorena-Sánchez, R.; Ji, Y. Monitoring of Student Learning in Learning Management Systems: An Application of Educational Data Mining Techniques. *Appl. Sci.* **2021**, *11*, 2677. [CrossRef]
9. Anand, N.; Sehgal, R.; Anand, S.; Kaushik, A. Feature selection on educational data using Boruta algorithm. *Int. J. Comput. Intell. Stud.* **2021**, *10*, 27. [CrossRef]
10. Shrestha, S.; Pokharel, M. Educational data mining in moodle data. *Int. J. Inform. Commun. Technol. (IJ-ICT)* **2021**, *10*, 9. [CrossRef]
11. Injadat, M.; Moubayed, A.; Nassif, A.B.; Shami, A. Systematic ensemble model selection approach for educational data mining. *Knowl.-Based Syst.* **2020**, *200*, 105992. [CrossRef]
12. Ashraf, M.; Zaman, M.; Ahmed, M. An Intelligent Prediction System for Educational Data Mining Based on Ensemble and Filtering approaches. *Procedia Comput. Sci.* **2020**, *167*, 1471–1483. [CrossRef]
13. Dabhade, P.; Agarwal, R.; Alameen, K.; Fathima, A.; Sridharan, R.; Gopakumar, G. Educational data mining for predicting students' academic performance using machine learning algorithms. *Mater. Today Proc.* **2021**, *47*, 5260–5267. [CrossRef]
14. Nahar, K.; Shova, B.I.; Ria, T.; Rashid, H.B.; Islam, A. Mining educational data to predict students performance. *Educ. Inf. Technol.* **2021**, *26*, 6051–6067. [CrossRef]
15. Deb, S.; Gao, X.-Z.; Tammi, K.; Kalita, K.; Mahanta, P. Recent Studies on Chicken Swarm Optimization algorithm: A review (2014–2018). *Artif. Intell. Rev.* **2019**, *53*, 1737–1765. [CrossRef]
16. Zhang, L.; Yang, H.; Jiang, Z. Imbalanced biomedical data classification using self-adaptive multilayer ELM combined with dynamic GAN. *Biomed. Eng. Online* **2018**, *17*, 181. [CrossRef] [PubMed]
17. Roozbeh, M.; Arashi, M.; Hamzah, N.A. Generalized Cross-Validation for Simultaneous Optimization of Tuning. *Iran. J. Sci. Technol. Trans. A Sci.* **2020**, *44*, 473–485. [CrossRef]
18. Amini, M.; Roozbeh, M. Optimal partial ridge estimation in restricted semiparametric regression models. *J. Multivar. Anal.* **2015**, *136*, 26–40. [CrossRef]
19. Roozbeh, M. Optimal QR-based estimation in partially linear regression models with correlated errors using GCV criterion. *Comput. Stat. Data Anal.* **2018**, *117*, 45–61. [CrossRef]
20. Roozbeh, M.; Babaie-Kafaki, S.; Aminifard, Z. Improved high-dimensional regression models with matrix approximations applied to the comparative case studies with support vector machines. *Optim. Methods Softw.* **2022**, 1–18. [CrossRef]
21. Zhang, Z.; Huang, C.; Huang, H.; Tang, S.; Dong, K. An optimization method: Hummingbirds optimization algorithm. *J. Syst. Eng. Electron.* **2018**, *29*, 386–404. [CrossRef]
22. Duhayyim, M.A.; Marzouk, R.; Al-Wesabi, F.N.; Alrajhi, M.; Hamza, M.A.; Zamani, A.S. An Improved Evolutionary Algorithm for Data Mining and Knowledge Discovery. *CMC-Comput. Mater. Contin.* **2022**, *71*, 1233–1247.

Article

A High-Level Representation of the Navigation Behavior of Website Visitors

Alicia Huidobro [1], Raúl Monroy [1,*] and Bárbara Cervantes [2,†]

[1] School of Engineering and Science, Tecnologico de Monterrey, Atizapan de Zaragoza 52926, Mexico; a01749803@itesm.mx
[2] Virtus Be Real S.A. de C.V., Atizapan de Zaragoza 52987, Mexico; barb@virtus.mx
* Correspondence: raulm@tec.mx
† This research was carried while Dr. Cervantes was a Research Assistant at Tecnologico de Monterrey.

Abstract: Knowing how visitors navigate a website can lead to different applications. For example, providing a personalized navigation experience or identifying website failures. In this paper, we present a method for representing the navigation behavior of an entire class of website visitors in a moderately small graph, aiming to ease the task of web analysis, especially in marketing areas. Current solutions are mainly oriented to a detailed page-by-page analysis. Thus, obtaining a high-level abstraction of an entire class of visitors may involve the analysis of large amounts of data and become an overwhelming task. Our approach extracts the navigation behavior that is common among a certain class of visitors to create a graph that summarizes class navigation behavior and enables a contrast of classes. The method works by representing website sessions as the sequence of visited pages. Sub-sequences of visited pages of common occurrence are identified as "rules". Then, we replace those rules with a symbol that is given a representative name and use it to obtain a shrinked representation of a session. Finally, this shrinked representation is used to create a graph of the navigation behavior of a visitor class (group of visitors relevant to the desired analysis). Our results show that a few rules are enough to capture a visitor class. Since each class is associated with a conversion, a marketing expert can easily find out what makes classes different.

Keywords: web analytics; web log mining; clickstream analysis; sequence mining; sequitur; graph techniques

1. Introduction

The more knowledge a company has about visitors, the more effective its marketing strategies will be [1–3]. Therefore, it is valuable to know how visitors navigate the website [4–6]. This knowledge has to be obtained from the huge amount of data that are stored on a website [6–8]. Web analytics solutions (WAS) are widely used and provide useful metrics [9–17]. However, they have some limitations for describing the navigation behavior of visitors. Current web analytics software provides a page-by-page report [11,12]. This level of detail produces huge graphs that are difficult to analyze and compare. Numerous literature approaches analyze the sequence of visited pages [18–22] but they do not provide a high-level description of the navigation behavior. They are limited to cluster visitors based on different criteria; for example, the longest common subsequence of visited pages [20,23–27].

The objective of our research is to find out the navigation behavior that is common in a whole class of visitors. Each class of visitors should provide valuable knowledge in terms of business goals, specifically for marketing experts. Therefore, the segmentation of visitors is important. We used conversions as classes of visitors, as proposed by A. Huidobro et al. [28]. This approach eases the interpretation of results because conversions are specific visitor actions that contribute to business objectives [3,5,29], and it is a concept with which marketing experts are familiar. Examples of website conversions are: to pay for a product or a service, to fill in a form with contact details, or to post a positive product review.

To describe the navigation behavior of a whole class of visitors, we started by representing sessions as a sequence of visited pages. From the sequences representing sessions of a given class, we extracted the most frequent subsequences of pages. We called those sequences "rules". Each rule is formed by different pages and represents visitors actions. For example, making a payment or searching for the availability of a product. We named the rules and used them to obtain a reduced representation of each session; session reduction is a result of replacing sub-sequences (of length greater than or equal to two) for the name of the corresponding rule. The representation of sessions with rules drastically reduces the length of sessions (for example, from forty pages to two rules). Various types of analyses can be performed with the reduced representation of sequences. For example, comparing the frequency of a given rule in two different classes of visitors. We show the result of our analysis in a graph to facilitate the explanation oriented to marketing experts. Using the described method, we reduce hundreds of nodes and edges into a simplified graph that captures the navigation behavior of a whole class of visitors. The graph also assists in the comparison of the navigation behavior of different classes of visitors. It prevents the marketing expert from analyzing huge graphs to understand the navigation behavior of visitors. Our four-step methodology is shown in Figure 1.

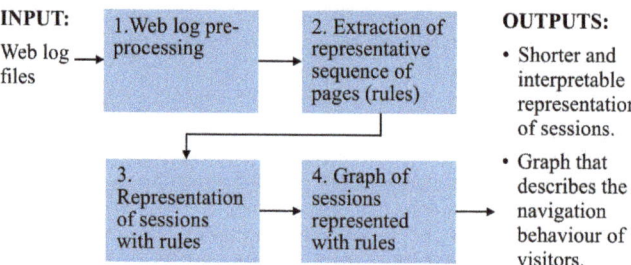

Figure 1. The four-step methodology for characterizing website visitors based on their navigation behavior.

1.1. Related Work

In this subsection, we explain the limitations of both popular commercial software and literature approaches for describing the navigation behavior of a whole class of visitors. Concerning commercial software, we focus on Google Analytics and Matomo, which have a similar functionality. Google Analytics is the most popular web analytics software [30–32] and Matomo is an alternative to overcome some limitations of Google Analytics [12].

1.1.1. Commercial Software

Google Analytics and Matomo provide a similar functionality for tracking the navigation behavior of visitors. In Google Analytics, it is called a "Behavior flow" report. In Matomo, it is the section "Goal conversion tracking", but it is only available in the premium version. Both consist of showing the sequence of the most visited pages in a period. It aims to measure the engagement page to page. Therefore, it is useful for finding pages where the traffic is lost, but it is difficult to follow a path with numerous pages. It is also difficult to visualize the path of 100% of visitors if they are numerous and behave differently. It is possible to track events instead of pages. Nevertheless, those events have to be previously configured. Therefore, events do not represent the natural navigation behavior of visitors. In Figure 2, we show an example of the behavior flow chart in Google Analytics. The page-by-page detail does not provide a high-level description of the navigation behavior [11,12]. Tens of pages would have to be reviewed to understand the navigation behavior of a whole class of visitors.

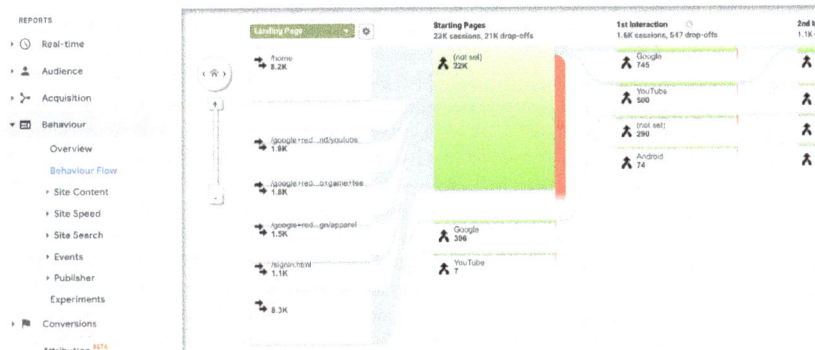

Figure 2. Example of the "Behavior flow" report in Google Analytics. It shows the sequence of most visited pages, from left to right. The thick red lines indicate traffic drop-offs. Each column corresponds to a web page or event. Therefore, this type of visualization does not show all the navigation in a single view but continues to the right, according to the number of pages or events.

1.1.2. Other Non-Commercial Approaches

There are diverse web log mining approaches in the literature. However, they are centered around identifying clusters of visitors, and not on obtaining a high-level description of their navigation behavior. The analysis of visited pages, called sequence mining, is commonly applied for discovering patterns with a frequency support measure [33]. Clickstream analysis is the most popular sequence mining approach used for clustering visitors [21]. Clickstream is the sequence of pages visited by a user in a given website and period [27]. In our approach, a rule is a sequence of pages frequently visited by visitors of the same class. Therefore, we reviewed clickstream approaches; below, we describe some of them.

S. Tiwari et al. [20] use previously visited pages to forecast online navigational patterns (finding the next page expectation). They apply agglomerative clustering to group visitors according to the previous web data accessed. They obtain the set of frequently visited pages in each group of visitors. This information is used to put in the cache pages with higher frequency in order to reduce the search time.

A. Banerjee et al. [27] propose finding the longest common sub-sequence of clickstreams using a dynamic programming algorithm. Then, they identify similar users by computing a similarity value that considers the time spent on each page. With the similarity values, they construct a weighted similarity graph. Finally, they find clusters on that graph. They found that, in some cases, there are no exact matches. As a solution, they propose to first group data into categories.

There are other clickstream pattern mining approaches, but they are focused on improving the runtime or memory consumption for clustering visitors [21,22]. Visualization tools have also been proposed to analyze the navigation behavior of visitors [34–39]. However, they provide a detailed analysis of web pages; for example, to find the percentage of visitors on each web page.

Our contribution is a high-level description of the navigation behavior of visitors. A distinguishing characteristic of our approach is that we extracted the natural navigation behavior of visitors instead of finding if visitors perform previously known actions. Another distinctive aspect is that we represented business functions (conversions) in a single node (rule); this data reduction is relevant because representing all of the sessions of an e-commerce website usually involves thousands of visitors and hundreds of pages. In Figure 3, we show an example of sessions represented with rules. Considering that each rule groups N web pages, the proposed representation reduces the information a business expert needs to analyze while keeping interpretability. The representation obtained by commercial software would involve much more nodes (see Figure 2). This would be difficult, for example, in the identification of loops that are worth analyzing and comparing different entry points to the website. We describe this in more detail in Sections 4 and 5.

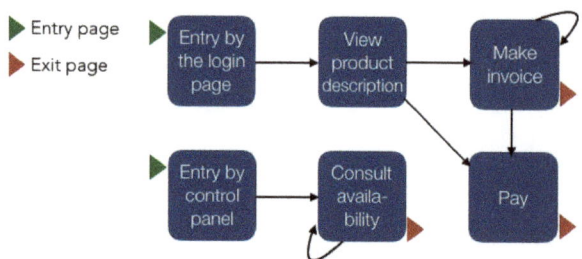

Figure 3. An example of sessions represented with rules. Each node represents a rule (business functions) that groups N web pages. We can see, for example, that visitors who arrive at the website by the login page have a greater chance of paying than those who enter through the control panel. We also identify loops. The loop in the "Consult availability" rule may be expected because visitors usually review the availability of N products. However, the loop in the "Make invoice" is worth investigating since it could be a cause of dropout.

1.2. Methodology

Web log mining is the use of data mining techniques to obtain information about the navigation behavior of visitors [40]. The main difficulties in web log mining are the huge amount of traffic on websites and the wide variety of paths that visitors could follow [41]. Understanding the navigation behavior of numerous visitors can be overwhelming. Therefore, we aim to describe the navigation behavior of visitors with a simplified representation. With a sequence mining approach, we captured the milestones of different classes of visitors and presented them as a graph. That reduced the amount of data that a marketing expert would have to analyze in order to understand the navigation behavior of visitors and contrast different classes of visitors. To achieve this goal, we represented the navigation behavior of the website visitors as the sequence of visited pages in each session. That representation allows us to find out the representative navigation milestones in each class of visitors. To this aim, we used a compression algorithm that allowed us to identify sequences of pages that are common among visitors from the same class. We called those common sequences "rules". The set of rules obtained in each class of visitors describes the navigation behavior of most of the visitors in that class. Having identified the rules for each class of visitors, it is possible to replace the session pages with rules. This results in a reduced representation of sessions that allows us to carry out different kinds of analyses. For example, sessions could be represented exclusively with rules or, conversely, the behavior that is not represented by rules could be analyzed further. Statistics of the sessions represented as rules would help a marketing expert to establish questions of interest. We analyzed those statistics and, due to our simplification purpose, we found it relevant to represent the navigation behavior of visitors only with the most frequent rules. For our target audience, who are marketing experts, a graph visualization of results would be more friendly. Therefore, we summarized all of the sessions of a given class in a graph. The representation of sessions with rules significantly reduced the amount of data that a marketing expert would have to analyze. The graph depiction assists in the understanding of the navigation behavior of visitors, even when our work was not focused on visualization techniques.

In Section 2, we explain the sequence mining process for identifying rules in each class of visitors. Then, in Section 3, we describe how we used rules for representing sessions. In Section 4, we present the graph that describes the navigation behavior of visitors and insights obtained from it. In Section 5, we summarize our contributions and compare them with previous work. Finally, in Section 6, we mention the advantages and limitations of the proposed methodology.

2. Identification of Rules in Each Class of Visitors

To find out the most common sub-sequences of visited pages for different classes of visitors, in the first place, one needs to represent the navigation behavior of website visitors. With that representation, it is then possible to find sequences of web pages that are commonly visited among visitors from a given class. Below we describe: (1) how we represented sessions with a sequence of symbols that contains the navigation behavior of interest, (2) the compression algorithm that we used to find common sub-sequences of pages, and (3) how we used that compression algorithm to find out the most common sub-sequences of visited pages, which are the milestones for each class of visitors.

2.1. Representation of Each Class of Visitors as a Sequence of Symbols

The input data consist of 50,820 sessions represented as the list of visited pages. There were thousands of different pages, but only a small subset was relevant for the proposed analysis. Once we identified relevant pages on sessions, we represented them as symbols to ease the sequence mining process.

2.1.1. Identification of Relevant Pages

We are interested in the navigation behavior that could be meaningful for marketing experts. Therefore, we identified relevant pages, which are described as follows:

1. Filtering of pages of interest: Our marketing partner prepared a list of 298 web pages that they were interested in analyzing. We removed from sessions all web pages that were not pages of interest. We eliminated the sessions that did not visit any page of interest (26%). The dataset was reduced to 37,400 sessions (74%).
2. Removing of pages that are automatically loaded: Those pages are not meaningful for marketing experts because they do not represent the intentional navigation behavior of visitors (for example, Java resources necessary for the proper functioning of the site).
3. Removing the subsequent repetition of the same page: Most sessions had pages subsequently repeated n times. For example, Home → Home → Home → Home → Login → Control panel → Control panel → Logout. Our information technology partner indicated to us that, in most cases, it is due to the functionality of the website, and not related to the navigation behavior of visitors. For example, if the visitor fulfils a form, the same page could be automatically reloaded whenever the visitor clicks on a different field. Therefore, we reduced the subsequent occurrences of the same page to one occurrence. The previous example would be reduced to Home → Login → Control panel → Logout.

The process to keep only relevant pages entailed some information loss. That information could be useful for some traffic analytics; for example, to measure the number of pages sent to the visitor, the amount of data transmitted, or the frequency of clicks. Nevertheless, that loss does not affect the objective of describing the navigation behavior of visitors. We only needed web pages intentionally visited.

2.1.2. Representation of Sessions as a Sequence of Symbols

To ease the sequence mining process, we represented each session as a sequence of symbols. Due to the fact that there are 298 pages of interest, we assigned a two-letter identifier to each of them. Then, in each session, we replaced the name of the page with its identifier; for example, the session Home → Login → Control panel → Logout became *AaAzBkBb*.

2.1.3. Segmentation of Data in Different Classes of Visitors

We are interested in describing the navigation behavior of different classes of visitors and contrasting them. Therefore, it is necessary to segment data. The input dataset was already labelled. We classified 100% of sessions into four disjoint classes:

- Visitors who made a payment: 7% of the sessions.
- Visitors who started the payment process but did not conclude it: 10% of the sessions.
- Visitors who made a conversion different to the made payment or started payment: 32% of the sessions.
- Visitors who did not perform any conversion: 52% of the sessions.

We will refer to the previous classes of visitors as "Made payment", "Started payment", "Other conversions", and "No conversion". We obtained a dataset for each class of visitors.

With sessions represented as a sequence of symbols and segmented into different classes of visitors, it is possible to identify the representative navigation milestones in each class of visitors. To this aim, we used a compression algorithm, which is described next.

2.2. Selection and Implementation of the Compression Algorithm

An objective of our research was to reduce the amount of data that have to be analyzed in order to understanding the navigation behavior of visitors. Our strategy was to find recurrent sub-sequences of visited pages. Therefore, we used a sequence mining approach. In this subsection, we explain how we selected the sequence mining algorithm, how it operates, and the implementation that we used.

2.2.1. Selection of the Sequence Mining Algorithm

We discarded algorithms that find the longest common sub-sequence, such as MAXLEN [27,42], because we are interested in all of the sub-sequences that are repeated, no matter if they are long. We evaluated compression algorithms such as Sequitur [42–44], Repair [45,46], and Bisection [42,47]. We selected the Sequitur algorithm because it is the most efficient. It runs in linear time. Below, we explain this algorithm.

2.2.2. Sequitur algorithm

Sequitur finds repetitive sub-sequences in a sequence by identifying rules. It creates a grammar based on repeated sub-sequences. Then, each repeated sub-sequence becomes a rule in the grammar. To produce a concise representation of the sequence, two properties must be met [48,49]:

- $p1$ (digram uniqueness) : there is no pair of adjacent symbols repeated in the grammar.
- $p2$ (rule utility): every rule appears more than once.

To clarify the operation of Sequitur, we will use the following definitions:

- Sequence: a string of symbols, e.g., "aghhhhbfababdchdttttyhhs".
- Rule: a sub-sequence that appears twice or more in a sequence and its minimum length is 2. The rules obtained with the Sequitur algorithm may be defined in terms of other rules.
- Base rule: a rule that does not contain other rules, e.g., rule 1 = "a b", rule 2 = "d c".
- Nested rule: a rule composed of base rule(s), e.g., if rule 3 = "f 1 1 2 h", it is a nested rule defined in terms of the base rules 1 and 2.
- Expanded rule: the result of recursively unfolding all the rules that are contained in a nested rule, e.g., the nested rule "f 1 1 2 h" is expanded as "f a b a b d c h".

We will use the sequence aghdfghmadfgh as an example to describe the operation of the Sequitur algorithm. For each symbol in the sequence, Sequitur verifies the properties of digram uniqueness and rule utility. In Table 1, in each row, we show the resulting grammar and the expanded rules, as each new symbol is reviewed. In the column "Resulting grammar", 1 to n are the found rules, and 0 is the result of using those rules in the original string. Grammar 0 is not expanded in the last column because it is not a rule. However, if we expand Grammar 0, we obtain the original string. We can see that Sequitur does not find any rule from rows 1 to 7. That is because there are no pairs of symbols that appear twice or more in the string. In row 8, the pair of symbols "gh" appears twice, so it is added to the grammar as rule 1. In row 11, the pair of symbols "aa" appears twice and it is added to the grammar as rule. In row 13, the pair of symbols "df" appears twice and it is added to the grammar as rule 3. In row 15, the rule "df" becomes a nested rule because "dfgh" is found twice, but the pair "gh" is already rule 2, so rule 3 changes from "df" to "df 2". All of the rules added to the grammar met properties $p1$ and $p2$.

2.2.3. Implementation of the Sequitur Algorithm

We used a publicly available implementation of Sequitur [50]. We adapted this implementation in order to use it with the two-letter identifier of each web page. That was necessary because the original implementation identifies each symbol as a different element in the sequence.

Table 1. Operation of the Sequitur algorithm. NRF = No rules found.

No.	New Symbol	The String so Far	Resulting Grammar	Expanded Rules
1	a	a	$0 \to a$	NRF
2	g	ag	$0 \to a\,g$	NRF
3	h	agh	$0 \to a\,g\,h$	NRF
4	d	aghd	$0 \to a\,g\,h\,d$	NRF
5	f	aghdf	$0 \to a\,g\,h\,d\,f$	NRF
6	g	aghdfg	$0 \to a\,g\,h\,d\,f\,g$	NRF
7	h	aghdfgh	$0 \to a\,1\,d\,f\,1\,1 \to g\,h$	gh
8	m	aghdfghm	$0 \to a\,1\,d\,f\,1\,m\,1 \to g\,h$	gh
9	a	aghdfghma	$0 \to a\,1\,d\,f\,1\,m\,a\,1 \to g\,h$	gh
10	d	aghdfghmad	$0 \to a\,1\,d\,f\,1\,m\,a\,d\,1 \to g\,h$	gh
11	f	aghdfghmadf	$0 \to a\,1\,2\,1\,m\,a\,2\,1 \to g\,h$ $2 \to d\,f$	gh df
12	g	aghdfghmadfg	$0 \to a\,1\,2\,1\,m\,a\,2\,g\,1 \to g\,h$ $2 \to d\,f$	gh df
13	h	aghdfghmadfgh	$0 \to a\,1\,2\,m\,a\,2\,1 \to g\,h\,gh$ $2 \to d\,f\,1$	dfgh

Next, we explain how we used this implementation of the Sequitur algorithm for finding recurrent sub-sequences of visited pages.

2.3. Rule Extraction

We used the Sequitur algorithm to find recurrent sub-sequences of visited pages (rules) in each class of visitors. In this subsection, we explain how we extracted, analyzed, and selected those rules.

2.3.1. Rule Finding

Sequitur identifies the sub-sequences that appear twice or more in a string as rules. Nevertheless, for our analysis, it was necessary to find all sub-sequences that are common among different sessions. Some of those sub-sequences may appear only once in each session. To this aim, we concatenated sessions of each class of visitors. Below, we explain this methodology.

1. Concatenate all sessions of a given class of visitors, adding a distinguishing pair of symbols between each session.
2. Apply the Sequitur algorithm.
3. Expand rules.
4. Exclude rules that include the pair of symbols mentioned in the first step.
5. Compute the frequency of each rule in sessions of the same class of visitors.

In Table 2, we show the percentage of sessions and the number of rules found in each class of visitors. We can see that the classes of visitors "Made payment", "Started payment", and "Other conversions" have a much higher number of rules than the "No conversion" class of visitors, even when "No conversion" has the highest percentage of visitors. This could indicate a more homogeneous behavior in visitors from the first three classes.

Table 2. Rules obtained in each class of visitors. Columns 2 to 5 indicate the class of visitor. Seven percent of the sessions are visitors from the class Made payment, where we found 764 rules. Conversely, fifty-two percent of the sessions are visitors from the class No conversion, where we found only 92 rules.

Metric	Made Payment	Started Payment	Other Conversions	No Conversion
Percentage of visitors	7%	10%	32%	52%
Number of rules	764	704	997	92

Rules should allow us to contrast classes. Therefore, we made an inter-class analysis to find out if the set of rules is different in each class of visitors.

2.3.2. Inter-Class Analysis

The objective of the inter-class analysis is to find out (1) if the rules are different for each class of visitors, and (2) if those rules are relevant. To this aim, we computed two metrics:

- Percentage of rules found in sessions: given a set of rules, it measures the percentage of those rules that are found in a group of sessions. It allows us to find out if a set of rules describes a specific class of visitors or not. A result of 100% in all classes of visitors for a given set of rules would mean that all those rules were found in the four classes of visitors. Thus, that set of rules would not describe a specific class of visitors.
- Inverse frequency of a rule: it measures the percentage of sessions in which a rule is found at least once. A high percentage indicates that the rule is relevant for describing the navigation behavior of visitors.

As an example of the inter-class analysis, in Table 3, we show the metrics of the rules found in visitors from the class "Made payment". Below, we summarize the interpretation of this table.

- A total of 100% of the rules were found in "Made payment" sessions because rules were extracted from those sessions. We can see that this percentage decreases to approximately 50% for the classes of visitors "Started payment" and "Other conversions". For the visitors from the class "No conversion", it reduces to 6%. These results indicate that approximately 50% of the rules specifically describe the navigation behavior of the visitors that belong to the class "Made payment".
- The highest inverse frequency indicates that one rule was found in up to 91% of sessions that belong to the class of visitors "Made payment". This metric is lower for the other three classes of visitors. Since we use this metric to measure the rule relevance, we can say that this set of rules is more relevant for the visitors that belong to the class "Made payment".

Table 3. Rules selected for each class of visitors: the nested rules with inverse frequency ≥5%.

Metric	Made Payment	Started Payment	Other Conversions	No Conversion
Percentage of "made payment" rules found in sessions	100%	57%	46%	6%
Highest inverse frequency of a "made payment" rule in a session	91%	68%	33%	2%

We made the inter-class analysis for the other three classes of visitors. Both metrics are higher when the set of rules and the sessions belong to the same class of visitors. Nevertheless, it was remarkable that the highest inverse frequency of No conversion rules was only 14% in the sessions of the same class. This indicates that the behavior of the visitors that belong to the class No conversion is less homogeneous.

The inter-class analysis confirmed that there are relevant and specific rules for each class of visitors. The next step was to select the best rules for describing the navigation behavior of visitors.

2.3.3. Rule Selection

A selection of rules is necessary because the rules obtained until now include base rules and nested rules. This is redundant because base rules are contained in nested rules. There could also be rules with too low an inverse frequency (e.g., rules that are found in just one session). These rules are not representative. Therefore, we applied two criteria for selecting rules:

1. Select only nested rules. This eliminates redundancy.
2. Select rules with inverse frequency ≥5%. A rule that describes less than 5% of the sessions does not generalize the navigation behavior of visitors; thus, it is not useful for the objectives of our research.

In Table 4, we show the number of rules obtained after applying these selection criteria. The inverse frequency of all of the nested rules extracted from the class of visitors No conversion was <5%. We concluded that the navigation behavior of this class of visitors is non-homogeneous. Thus, it could not be simplified using a small set of rules. In the next steps of the process, we only used the classes of visitors Made Payment, Started payment, and Other conversions. From now on, when we use the term "rule(s)", we refer to the set of rules presented in Table 4.

Table 4. Rules selected for each class of visitors: the nested rules with inverse frequency ≥5%.

Metric	Made Payment	Started Payment	Other Conversions	No Conversion
Number of rules	9	5	4	0

We assigned a name to each rule. In Table 5, we list that name and the number of pages that form each rule. We also mention the class of visitors in which the rule was found. The rules listed in Table 5 are the navigation milestones for each class of visitors. Now, those rules can be used to simplify the representation of sessions. That process is explained next in Section 3.

Table 5. Name of the rules found in each class of visitors. The rule length indicates the number of pages that form each rule. An "X" indicates that the rule was found in that class of visitors.

Rule Name	Rule Length	Made Payment	Started Payment	Other Conversion
Go to control panel	4	X	X	X
Pay via control panel	7	X		
Pay and modify product	5	X		
Consult availability and pay	8	X		
Modify product and pay	8	X		
Start payment	4	X		
Pay for a service	8	X		
Make invoice	4	X		
Login and modify product information	4	X		X
Modify product information	3		X	X
Consult payment details	3		X	
Make payments query	3		X	
Modify product information and start payment	3		X	
Consult availability	3			X

3. Representation of Sessions with Rules

At this point, we have already identified the rules for each class of visitors. These rules can be used for representing sessions. This reduced representation allows us to carry out different kinds of analyses. In Section 3.1, we explain how we select rules to create a reduced graph and we provide statistics of the sessions represented with rules. These statistics provide information that would help marketing or information technology experts to establish questions of interest. Then, in Section 3.2, we describe how we select the data to be shown based on the questions of interest. For our particular case study, it was relevant to represent the navigation behavior of visitors only with the most frequent rules.

3.1. Selection of Rules to Visualize

We used the rules identified in Section 2 to represent sessions. In each session or group of sessions, we only used the rules that belong to the same class of visitors, according to Table 5. For example, a session that belongs to the class of visitors "Made payment" is represented only with the nine rules found in the sessions of the same class of visitors. In Figure 4, we show an example of three representations of a session: (1) the original session, (2) the session we obtained by replacing in the original session frequently occurring sub-sequences with rules (we called it a shrinked session), and (3) the session we obtained by stripping off any symbol but a rule in a shrinked session (we called it a stripped session).

The rules represent the behavior that is common among visitors from the same class. Conversely, pages that do not form rules represent uncommon behavior. To determine which analysis is worth conducting, we obtained statistics about sessions represented with rules. These statistics would help a marketing or information technology expert to determine questions of interest. We computed statistics on the three representations exemplified in Figure 4: original session, shrinked session, and stripped session. We computed the length of each representation and the reduction rate with respect to the length of the original session. Using the example in Figure 4, the length of the original session is 12, the length of the shrinked session is 5, and the length of the stripped session is 3.

- The reduction rate of the shrinked session is equal to $1 - $ (length of the shrinked session/length of the original session); that is, $1 - (5/12) = 0.58$. The length of the session is reduced by 0.58 (58%) when it is expressed with rules and pages that do not form a rule.
- The reduction rate of the stripped session is equal to $1 - $ (length of the stripped session/length of the original session); that is, $1 - (3/12) = 0.75$. The length of the session is reduced by 0.75 (75%) when it is expressed only with rules.

For each class of visitors, we computed the length of the three representations and the reduction rate. As an example, in Table 6, we show the results for the class of visitors "Made payment". We can see that the average reduction rate is 0.54 in shrinked sessions. For stripped sessions, the average reduction rate is 0.95. To better understand how the reduction rate behaves, we obtained a histogram of the reduction rate. In Figure 5, we show the histogram for shrinked and stripped sessions.

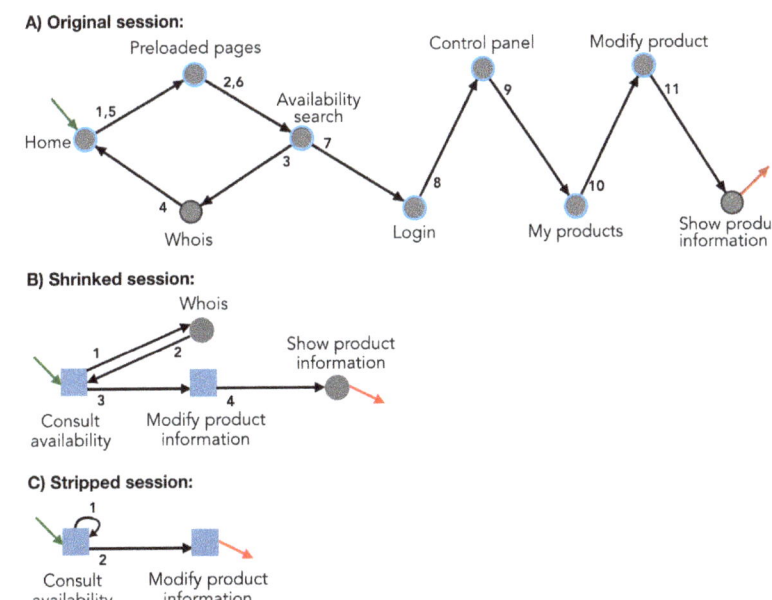

Figure 4. Example of a session represented with rules. (**A**) shows the original session. The green (respectively, red) arrow indicates the entry (respectively, exit) page. Circles with a blue border are pages that are part of a rule. This session belongs to visitors from the class "Other conversions". Therefore, we only used the rules identified in that class of visitors. We obtained (**B**) by representing the session with rules. (**C**) is the result of removing all pages that do not form a rule.

Table 6. Statistics of the length of sessions represented as rules. Metrics in rows 1 to 3 refer to the length of sessions in each representation. Metrics in rows 4 and 5 refer to the reduction rate with respect to the original session. In the last row, we indicate the percentage of sessions that we used in calculations. A total of 30% of sessions do not include any rule. Thus, in the last column, the percentage is reduced to 70%.

Metrics for Visitors from the Class "Made Payment"	Original Session	Shrinked Session	Stripped Session
Average session length	39.23	18.26	1.67
Maximum session length	572	181	24
Standard deviation of session length	30.81	16.46	1
Average reduction rate from original session	NA	0.54	0.95
Standard deviation of reduction rate from original session	NA	0.17	0.04
Percentage of sessions considered	100%	100%	70%

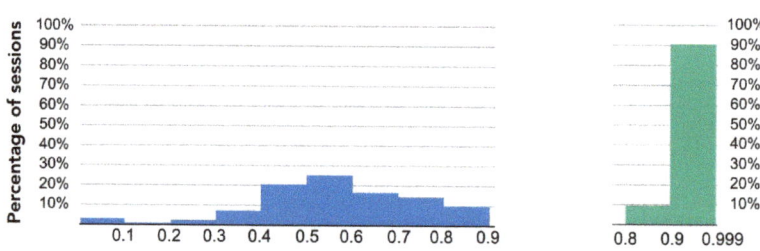

Figure 5. Histogram of the reduction rate of visitors from the class "Made payment". The reduction rate is calculated with respect to the length of the original session. The blue histogram corresponds to the shrinked sessions; their reduction rate varies from 0 to almost 1. The green histogram corresponds to the stripped sessions; their reduction rate varies from 0.8 to almost 1.

3.2. Selection of the Session Representation to Visualize

Previous statistics would help marketing or information technology experts to determine questions of interest; for example: what is the common navigation behavior in each class of visitors? what is different in the navigation behavior of each class of visitors? what navigation behavior is common among all classes of visitors? what are the relevant entry and exit milestones (rules) in each class of visitors?, etc. Different session representation is useful for each question.

In our case, the objective is to capture the milestones of different classes of visitors in a reduced representation of their navigation behavior. Therefore, for further analysis, we used the shrinked sessions. These allowed us to reduce the amount of data to analyze and contrast different classes of visitors. The elimination of pages that do not form rules does not affect our objective. On the contrary, including them would introduce information about the individual navigation behavior of visitors. Nevertheless, the analysis of pages that do not form rules could be relevant for other purposes; for example, to find out what distinguishes visitors from the same class.

Using shrinked sessions, we created a graph visualization that allows us to summarize the navigation behavior of each class of visitors. That visualization is presented next in Section 4.

4. Results

Shrinked sessions contain the milestones of the navigation behavior of visitors. In this section, we present those shrinked sessions in a graph visualization aimed at our target audience, marketing experts. Our work was not focused on visualization techniques, but the use of a graph is user friendly. It also assists in analyzing and comparing different rules or different classes of visitors. In Section 4.1, we explain how we built the graph. In Section 4.2, we describe the visualization of a whole class of visitors. Then, in Section 4.3, we exemplify the analysis of a single rule. Finally, in Section 4.4, we contrast different classes of visitors.

4.1. Graph Creation

In this subsection, we describe the concepts and calculations that we used to build a graph that describes the navigation behavior of visitors.

4.1.1. Definitions

Consider i and j rules in the class of visitors A:

- Entry rate of the rule i: this is the number of sessions that start in the rule i divided by the total number of sessions in the class A. It is denoted by $r(e_i)$.
- Exit rate of the rule i: this is the number of sessions that end in the rule i divided by the total number of sessions in the class A. It is denoted by $r(x_i)$.

- Frequency of the edge $e\{i,j\}$: this is the flow of visits from the rule i to the rule j. It is equal to the number of occurrences of the edge $e\{i,j\}$. It is denoted by f_{ij}.
- Out-degree frequency of the rule i: this is the flow of visits that goes out from the rule i. It is the sum of edge frequencies in which the source rule is i plus $r(x_i)$. It is denoted by O_i.
- Weight of the edge $e\{i,j\}$: this is the frequency of the edge $e\{i,j\}$ divided by the out-degree frequency of the source node i; that is, $\frac{f_{ij}}{O_i}$. It is denoted by w_{ij}.

4.1.2. Calculation Example

Consider the rules a and b found in the class of visitors "A". This class has 10 sessions. In addition, consider the following information:

- Entry rule: seven sessions started in rule a and three sessions started in rule b.
- Exit rule: two sessions ended in rule a and eight sessions ended in rule b.
- Edge frequency: $f_{ab} = 5$, $f_{aa} = 3$, and $f_{ba} = 6$.

In order to construct the graph, it is necessary to calculate the entry rates, the exit rates, and the weights.

- Entry rate: $r(e_a) = 7/10 = 0.7$ and $r(e_b) = 3/10 = 0.3$.
- Exit rate: $r(x_a) = 2/10 = 0.2$ and $r(x_b) = 8/10 = 0.8$.
- The calculation of weights is shown in Table 7.

Table 7. Example of weight calculation. The out-degree frequency O_i is the sum of frequencies f_{ij} of edges with the same source rule. Thus, $O_a = 5 + 3 + 2 = 10$ and $O_b = 6 + 8 = 14$.

Source Rule i	Target Rule j	f_{ij}	O_i	$w_{ij} = \frac{f_{ij}}{O_i}$
a	b	5	10	5/10 = 0.5
a	a	3	10	3/10 = 0.3
a	Exit	2	10	2/10 = 0.2
b	a	6	14	6/14 = 0.43
b	Exit	8	14	8/14 = 0.57

4.1.3. Graph Example

In Figure 6, we show the graph obtained in our example.

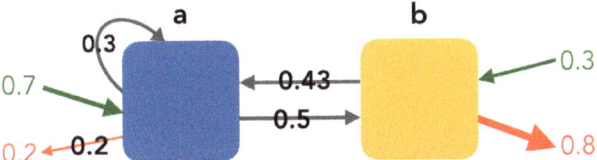

Figure 6. (a,b) Graph example. Yellow nodes are the rules where conversion occurs. The arrow thickness corresponds to the edge weight. The green (respectively, red) arrows indicate the entry (respectively, exit) rate. The values in the middle of the arrows indicate the weight of the edge (w_{ij}). If there were edges with a weight <0.05, they would be in a lighter grey, and their weight would not be shown.

4.2. Visualization of a Whole Class of Visitors

We created the graph for each class of visitors as described in Section 4.1. In Figure 7, we show the graph of visitors that belong to the class "Made payment". The marketing expert could determine if the observed behavior is expected or if there is suspicious or interesting behavior that is worth investigating. The interpretation of the graph depends on the business questions in which the marketing expert is interested. Below, we present our interpretation.

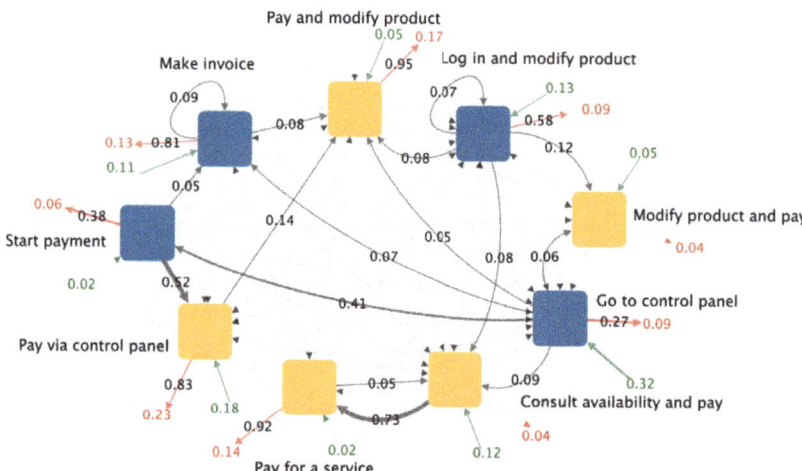

Figure 7. Graph of shrinked sessions for visitors from the class "Made payment". Yellow nodes are the rules where the payment is confirmed.

4.2.1. Relevant Entry and Exit Rules

In Figure 7, we can see that the rule "Go to control panel" has the highest entry rate (0.32). A total of 32% of the sessions have this rule as the entry point. The rule "Pay via control panel" has the highest exit rate (0.17). A total of 17% of the sessions have this rule as the exit point.

Based on the weight of the edges, there are three rules with a weight >0.90 on their red arrow. Those rules are "Pay and modify product", "Pay for a service", and "Modify product and pay". This means that almost all visitors who follow those rules leave the website after that. Contrarily, only 25% of visitors who follow the rule "Consult availability and pay" leave the website.

4.2.2. Most Frequent Path

If we follow the path of the highest entry rate and highest weights, we can see that 32% of visitors enter by the rule "Go to control panel". From there, 41% of visitors follow the rule "Start payment". Then, 52% of visitors follow the rule "Pay via control panel". In this rule, the payment is confirmed. After that, 83% of visitors leave the website. The marketing expert could evaluate if this path was expected. For example, is that sequence of 15 pages adequate? Could it be shorter? Was it expected that visitors leave the website immediately after the payment?

4.2.3. Rules in Which Conversion Occurs

From all of the rules in which the payment occurs, most visitors leave the website. The marketing expert could determine feasible strategies to retain visitors after a purchase; for example, a flash discount on the purchase of additional service. There is an exception in the rule "Consult availability and pay". From this rule, 73% of visitors continue with the rule "Pay for a service". Those visitors made two payments because, in both rules, the payment is confirmed.

Besides observing the "big picture" in the graph, it is also possible to analyze specific rules in more detail. Next, we exemplify it.

4.3. Analysis of Specific Rules

From the rules in which the payment does not occur, the rule "Make invoice" has the highest exit rate. Therefore, we will analyze this rule further. Visitors who follow this rule mainly come from the rules "Start payment" and "Go to control payment". In those rules, the payment has not been confirmed. Additional analysis from marketing expert is needed to determine the reasons for the described behavior. For example, is the making of the invoice clear? Is it a long process? Does it have an annoying bug? Does it require redundant information? Is it used by clients or competing companies to inquire about the prices of products or services?

After knowing the reasons for losing visitors in the rule "Make invoice", marketing experts could design strategies for retaining them; for example, proactive online help. If the marketing team does not have enough information to determine why visitors are leaving after this rule, different actions could be implemented; for example, a pop-up window to rate the process to make the invoice. Even users who confirm the payment may provide useful information about this process.

Besides reviewing rules in detail, the graph representation also allows us to compare different classes of visitors. This is exemplified next.

4.4. Contrasting Different Classes of Visitors

The comparison of different classes of visitors depends on the behavior in which the marketing expert is interested. Below, we present how we contrasted the classes of visitors "Made payment" (shown in Figure 7) and "Started payment" (shown in Figure 8).

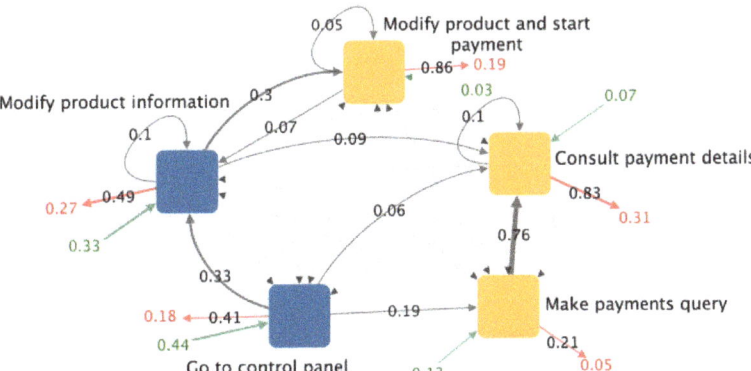

Figure 8. Graph of shrinked sessions for visitors from the class "Started payment". Yellow nodes are the rules where the payment is started.

4.4.1. Contrasting the Exit Rule

Most visitors from the class "Made payment" leave the website after following the rule "Pay via control panel". This is a rule in which the payment is confirmed. Most visitors from the class "Started payment" leave the website after following the rule "Consult payment details". This is a rule in which visitors start the payment. This indicates that most visitors who start a payment but do not confirm it leave the website immediately after consulting the payment details instead of navigating further or requesting online help.

In both classes, the highest exit rate is in the rules in which a conversion is performed, even though the conversion is different in each class of visitors.

4.4.2. Contrasting a Common Rule

In both classes of visitors, the rule "Go to control panel" has the highest entry rate. Nevertheless, the exit rate is double in visitors from the class "Started payment". After following the rule "Go to control panel", most visitors from the class "Made payment" start the payment process, whereas most visitors from the class "Started payment" modify the product information. This could be useful for encouraging the purchase in the pages where the product information is modified.

4.4.3. Contrasting the Most Frequent Path

The path with the highest entry rate and weights, in visitors from the class "Made payment", is "Go to control panel" (32%) → "Start payment" (41%) → "Pay via control panel" (52%) → Exit (83%). In visitors from the class "Started payment", the path with the highest entry rate and weights is "Go to control panel" (44%) → "Modify product information" (41%) → Exit (49%). This confirms the relevance of the rule "Modify product information" as an exit point.

5. Discussion

We presented the graph of shrinked sessions for different classes of visitors. This visualization reduces the amount of data that marketing experts would have to analyze for understanding the navigation behavior of visitors. It also assists in contrasting different classes of visitors. Our main contributions were: (1) to obtain results that are easy to interpret and could be meaningful for marketing experts. We achieved this by using classes of visitors associated with conversions of the sales funnel; and (2) to ease the analysis of results with a simplified description of the navigation behavior of visitors. This was created by using rules, which are the sequences of pages of common occurrence.

In Section 1.1 "Previous work", we describe previous commercial and non-commercial approaches related to our work. In Table 8, we summarize their differences with our method.

Table 8. Differences between our method and previous approaches.

Type	Author	Differences with Our Approach
Commercial software	Google Analytics (GA) [11] and Matomo [12]	They provide graphs with page-by-page detail. This helps to measure web page engagement; for example, to find pages where traffic is lost. However, this detail makes it difficult to visualize a trajectory with numerous pages or to visualize 100 percent of visitors. It is possible to track events instead of web pages, but since events are pre-configured, they do not necessarily represent the natural navigation behavior of visitors. In addition, GA does not allow you to analyze data generated prior to its use.
Non Commercial software	S. Tiwari et al. [20]	Its goal is to find the expectation of the next page using agglomerative clustering. Visitors are classified based on previous web pages they accessed, but web pages are not clustered or associated with conversions. Therefore, classes are not necessarily meaningful to a business expert and do not provide a high-level representation of the navigation behavior. It is useful in an online implementation to improve web response time, but is not intended to facilitate analysis for MKT experts.
	A. Banerjee et al. [27]	Its purpose is to find the longest common sub-sequence of clickstreams using a dynamic programming algorithm. They use a similarity graph to find clusters of visitors based on the time spent on each page. In our approach, the longest path is not necessarily the most relevant in terms of business goals. In fact, we found that, in general, visitors who make a payment visit fewer pages than those who do not. In our approach, the time spent on each webpage is not relevant. Finally, the similarity graph that they build is aimed to cluster visitors but is not to be used by marketing experts for further analysis.
	Huy M. et al. [21,22]	They present a novel data structure (pseudo-IDList) suitable for clickstream pattern mining. They also propose using the average weight measure for clickstream pattern mining and present an improved method named Compact-SPADE. Both approaches focus on improving runtime or memory consumption for clustering visitors, but no business knowledge is incorporated to create those clusters. In addition, they do not create a high-level graph of the clusters for further analysis by business experts.
	F. Gómez [34]	He presents a visualization tool for analyzing website traffic. It aims to distinguish bots from human visitors based on their navigation path. Like commercial software, it provides a page-by-page detail, which makes it difficult to analyze numerous pages.
	B. Cervantes [35]	They combine visualization and machine learning techniques for analyzing web log data. The visualization can be used by business experts to obtain insights by looking at key elements of the graph. However, visitors are not classified in terms of business goals. Furthermore, the visualization provides page-by-page detail, which makes it difficult to analyze visits with numerous nodes.

Web analytics software is essential for measuring website traffic and follow-up marketing campaigns. Nevertheless, its standard configuration and reporting options make it hard to extract high-level knowledge about the navigation behavior of different classes of visitors, especially due to the high amount of website traffic and the diversity of paths that visitors could follow. Most non-commercial approaches focus on finding clusters of visitors or improving the runtime performance, and proposed visualizations also provide a page-by-page detail that may lead to enormous graphs that are difficult to analyze. To highlight the advantages of the method that we propose, we compared the resultant visualization (Figure 8) with the visualization of Google Analytics (Figure 2) and a non-commercial approach (Figure 9). We will refer to the two last as CSW (commercial software) and NCA (non-commercial approach), respectively. Next, we list the most relevant differences:

- Both CSW and NCA provide page-by-page detail. Considering that most commercial websites have hundreds of pages, a graph that shows all website sessions in a given period would be (1) extremely long in CSW and (2) uninterpretable in NCA.
- Both CSW and NCA allow us to filter segments of visitors, but this is not enough to have an easy-to-interpret graph. CSW allows us to select the starting webpage in the graph. However, that leads to an incomplete graph. It allows for an analysis of engagement in the selected web pages but does not allow for a visualization of the complete path followed by visitors.
- CSW allows tracking pre-configured events instead of web pages but without the context of all of the web pages visited by the related visitors. Conversely, our approach makes no assumptions about the visitor behavior and provides the rules (sequences of visited pages) in the context of the complete navigation paths.
- Neither CSW nor NCA eases the identification of loops. Our proposed method clearly shows loops, in a single conversion and between different conversions.
- In CSW and NCA, it is hard to visualize the navigation behavior of a whole class of visitors. Therefore, it would be more difficult to compare different classes of visitors. Conversely, our approach would provide a moderately small graph for each class of visitors, and these graphs are easier to compare. This comparison of classes allows us to answer specific business questions. For example, what is the most common sequence of visited pages on which visitors of two different classes leave the website?
- Generally, achieving business objectives (conversions) involves the visiting of several pages. Some business goals may be partially identified as events in CSW, e.g., the sequence of web pages that a visitor must follow to make a payment. However, visitors may follow longer common sequences that help to reduce the number of nodes. In addition, some common navigation behavior is not predictable. For example, what do visitors who did not finish the payment process have in common?

Our method helps to identify points of interest whose interpretation is enriched by the opinion of a business expert. This approach assists in answering business questions in the context of the navigation behavior of all visitors in a given class, which is opposite to existing solutions that mainly aim to analyze the web page performance in detail. Next, we mention some examples of findings that would be difficult to obtain in a graph with page-by-page detail:

- The identification of unexpected loops or repetitions that could be avoided with website enhancements. For example, in Figure 7, we can see that 5% of the traffic in the node "Modify product and start payment" loops in this rule. The business expert could investigate the cause, e.g., a technical error, a non-intuitive site design, or a lack of clarity in the information shown.
- Identification of processes in which web traffic is lost. For example, in Figure 7, we can see that there are three rules in which the payment process can start: (1) "Modify product and start payment", (2) "Consult payment details", and (3) "Make payments query". However, the dropout rate is four times higher in the first two and they

have a loop. A call to action in the web pages of rules 1 and 2 could decrease their dropout rate.
- Finding the relationship between two conversions, regardless of whether they are subsequent or not. For example, we found that a high percentage of visitors who dropped out before confirming the payment did not request assistance at any point in their session. Thus, the online helpdesk is underutilized, as it could help to retain customers that leave before payment is finalized. A call to action on the pages prior to payment confirmation could increase the conversion rate.
- Comparing different website versions or different periods at a high level. If a website changes drastically, it can be difficult or even impossible to compare the impact of each page on the user experience. With our method, we can compare the versions at a high level. We could find, for example, how many steps the most common path has and if the new version reduced or increased the loops in navigation, and could compare the shortest path to make a payment versus the most common path to pay.
- Contrasting the navigation behavior of different classes of visitors. For example, new vs. recurrent; male vs. female; or visitors from different countries. All of them are in the context of the whole navigation behavior of the classes of interest. For example, the graphs in Figures 7 and 8 can be compared as discussed in Section 4.4. This comparison would not be easy in two graphs with hundreds of nodes and edges.

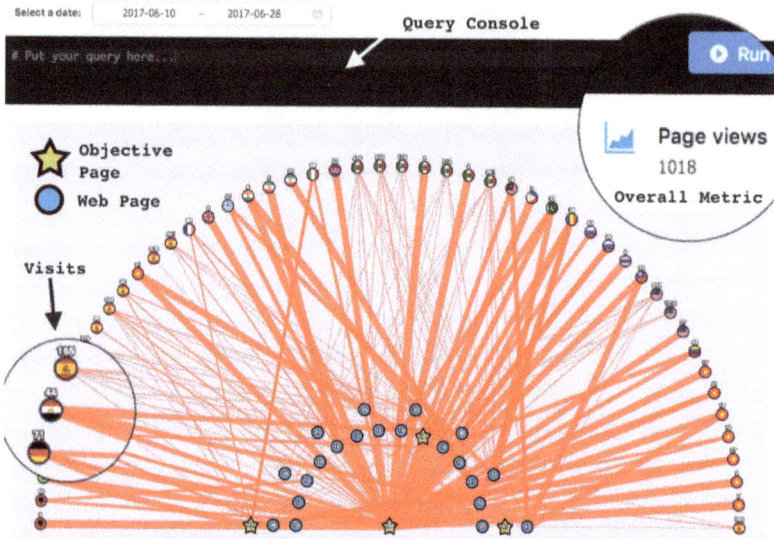

Figure 9. An example of the visualization proposed by B. Cervantes et al. [35]. Blue nodes are web pages, starts are objective pages, and nodes with country flags are visits of users from that country.

6. Conclusions

To describe the navigation behavior of visitors, we proposed a clickstream analysis. It is based on identifying actions that are repeated by users of the same class, considering an action as a sequence of visited pages. To assist in the interpretation of results to marketing experts, we created a graph representation. Our proposal is a starting point to further simplify the analysis of the navigation behavior of visitors or the extraction of knowledge for a marketing audience. Next, we summarize the contributions of our method, its limitations, and future work.

6.1. Contributions

There are three main advantages of our methodology over other existing solutions. The first advantage is that it reduces the amount of data to analyze for understanding the navigation behavior of visitors. The second advantage is that it extracts the natural navigation behavior of visitors. The third advantage is the use of web logs as entry data. Below, we explain them in more detail.

The increasing amount of data generated on websites makes it difficult to find relevant knowledge. With our method, we replace tens of pages with a single graph. Besides summarizing the navigation behavior of a whole class of visitors, our approach also allows us to compare different classes of visitors. This knowledge could be used to improve the effectiveness of marketing campaigns or website design. For example, an action (which is composed of a sequence of pages) could be especially successful to attract new visitors, but unsuccessful to make clients purchase. Marketing experts could design strategies for visitors to leap from the interest stage to the purchase stage (e.g., add proactive online help, provide more information about the benefits of the product, or a retargeting campaign for the visitors who performed visits of that sequence of pages).

With our methodology, we extracted the natural navigation behavior of visitors. This distinguishes our work from other solutions. Previous approaches group the web pages in tasks identified by the business expert. Therefore, they reflect the expected behavior, not the natural paths followed by visitors. Our approach, on the contrary, obtains the common sub-sequences of visited pages that visitors follow. This approach allowed us to find useful information; for example, that the making of the invoice is a relevant exit point. It also enabled us to contrast relevant entry and exit rules for different classes of visitors.

The use of web logs as entry data allows for the performance of a retrospective analysis. This is not possible in commercial software, where the configuration of conversions and market segments usually applies only for future traffic of the website. The use of web logs also allows us to prepare data according to different objectives. For example, we could compare different periods of a given class of visitors or different website versions.

6.2. Limitations

Our method focuses on a high-level understanding of navigation behavior. However, some business questions necessarily require a detailed web-page-level review. For those cases, commercial software is already effective; for example, if we want to know where traffic flows to after the visit of a specific web page.

Our approach can extract facts; for example: out of N possible ways to make a payment, which one is the shortest or the most frequent. However, in other cases, the findings are only the beginning of the discussion and require the intervention of a business expert. For example, a loop is not necessarily bad, but the interpretation of a human expert is needed to identify which ones are worth analyzing and correcting.

The effectiveness of our method relies on the existence of sequences of pages that are common among visitors to a website. However, there is a possibility that the navigation is too sparse for a particular class of visitors. In those cases, there will be no rules with a relevant frequency. While this would in itself be a finding, it would not be possible to construct a graph for further analysis by a business expert.

6.3. Future Work

There is a latent need for creative ways to help business experts evaluate the performance of a website. Next, we mention a few examples of how our method could be improved or extended:

- The effectiveness of our approach could be tested for improving metrics measurement, website design, and paid marketing effectiveness.
- Software aimed at marketing experts could be useful for autonomously replicating and personalizing the process that we followed. For example, the company could identify the five most relevant conversions and use them for describing the navigation

behavior of visitors. On the contrary, the company may find it useful to associate each page of interest with a conversion.
- It would be valuable to extract rules from the high-level visualizations that we obtained. For example, Acosta-Mendoza et al. propose a frequent approximate subgraph mining approach [51], which we could incorporate as the last step of our methodology.
- The use of rules that we propose can be applied after classifying visitors with different methods. We used conversions to classify visitors because we focused on a marketing audience. However, visitors could be classified with other techniques and purposes.
- After identifying rules of interest with our method, some of them could be configured in web analytics software for monitoring (e.g., such as events in Google Analytics). Although visitor behavior is dynamic, it could be useful for the marketing expert to monitor some rules autonomously.

Our approach responds to the need for a high-level description of the navigation behavior of website visitors. It does not replace the functionality of existing web analytics software; on the contrary, it can complement it. Our method can also be used with existing classification techniques. This work is a starting point for business questions that require understanding the navigating behavior of website visitors in a wide context. We believe that this is a very promising area of research.

Author Contributions: Conceptualization, R.M. and B.C.; methodology, A.H.; software, A.H.; validation, A.H.; formal analysis, A.H.; investigation, A.H.; resources, R.M. and B.C.; data curation, A.H.; writing—original draft preparation, A.H.; writing—review and editing, R.M. and B.C. visualization, A.H.; supervision, R.M. and B.C.; project administration, A.H. and R.M.; funding acquisition, R.M. All authors have read and agreed to the published version of the manuscript.

Funding: The research reported here was supported by Consejo Nacional de Ciencia y Tecnología (CONACYT) studentship 957562 to the first author.

Institutional Review Board Statement: Not applicable.

Data Availability Statement: We did not use publicly available datasets. We thank NIC Mexic for providing the data used in this research.

Acknowledgments: The authors acknowledge the technical support of Tecnologico de Monterrey, Mexico. We also thank NIC Mexico for providing the data used in this research.

Conflicts of Interest: The authors declare no conflict of interest.

Abbreviations

The following abbreviations are used in this manuscript:

WAS   Web analytics solutions
CSW   Commercial software
NCA   Non-commercial approach

References

1. Bondarenko, S.; Laburtseva, O.; Sadchenko, O.; Lebedieva, V.; Haidukova, O.; Kharchenko, T. Modern Lead Generation in Internet Marketing for the Development of Enterprise Potential. *Int. J. Innov. Technol. Explor. Eng. (IJITEE)* **2019**, *8*, 3066–3071.
2. Berman, R.; Israeli, A. The Value of Descriptive Analytics: Evidence from Online Retailers. Harvard Business School Working Paper, No. 21-067. 2020. pp. 1–56. Available online: https://www.hbs.edu/faculty/Pages/item.aspx?num=59259 (accessed on 20 January 2021).
3. Kotler, P.; Gary, A. *Principles of Marketing*, 12th ed.; Pearson Education: London, UK, 2007.
4. Hun, T.K.; Yazdanifard, R. The Impact of Proper Marketing Communication Channels on Consumer's Behavior and Segmentation Consumers. *Asian J. Bus. Manag.* **2014**, *2*, 155–159.
5. Kotler, P.; Kartajaya, H.; Setiawan, I. *Marketing 4.0. Moving from Traditional to Digital*, 3rd ed.; John Wiley & Sons, Inc.: Hoboken, NJ, USA, 2017.
6. Rahman, A.; Dash, S.; Luhach, A.K.; Chilamkurti, N.; Baek, S.; Nam, Y. A Neuro-fuzzy approach for user behaviour classification and prediction. *J. Cloud Comput. Adv. Syst. Appl.* **2019**, *8*, 1–15.

7. Kandpal, N.; Singh, H.P.; Shekhawat, M.S. Application of Web Usage Mining for Administration and Improvement of Online Counseling Website. *Int. J. Appl. Eng. Res.* **2019**, *14*, 1431–1437.
8. Bertero, C.; Roy, M.; Sauvanaud, C.; Tredan, G. Experience Report: Log Mining Using Natural Language Processing and Application to Anomaly Detection. In Proceedings of the IEEE 28th International Symposium on Software Reliability Engineering (ISSRE), Toulouse, France, 23–26 October 2017; pp. 351–360.
9. Velkumar, K.; Thendral, P. A survey on web mining techniques. In Proceedings of the 2nd International Conference on New Scientific Creations, Osaka, Japan, 7–9 April 2020; pp. 167–173.
10. Wang, Y.; Liu, H.; Liu, Q. Application Research of Web Log Mining in the E-commerce. In Proceedings of the Chinese Control And Decision Conference (CCDC), Hefei, China, 22–24 August 2020; IEEE: Piscataway, NJ, USA, 2020; pp. 349–352.
11. Google. Google Analytics-Knowledgebase. 2021. Available online: https://developers.google.com/analytics (accessed on 29 January 2021).
12. Matomo. Matomo-Open Analytics Platform. 2021. Available online: https://developer.matomo.org (accessed on 20 January 2021).
13. Omniture. Omniture Website. 2021. Available online: https://marketing.adobe.com/resources/help (accessed on 15 January 2021).
14. Leadfeeder. Leadfeeder Website. 2021. Available online: https://www.leadfeeder.com (accessed on 12 January 2021).
15. VMO. VMO Website. 2021. Available online: https://vwo.com (accessed on 18 January 2021).
16. Paveai. Paveai Website. 2021. Available online: https://www.paveai.com/referrer-spam-remover/ (accessed on 21 January 2021).
17. Woopra. Woopra Website. 2021. Available online: https://www.woopra.com (accessed on 25 January 2021).
18. Venugopal, K.R.; Nimbhorkar, S.S. Web Page Recommendations Based Web Navigation Prediction. In *Web Recommendations Systems*; Springer: Singapore, 2020; pp. 109–130.
19. El Aissaoui, O.; El Madani El Alami, Y.; Oughdir, L.; El Allioui, Y. Integrating web usage mining for an automatic learner profile detection: A learning styles-based approach. In Proceedings of the 2018 International Conference on Intelligent Systems and Computer Vision (ISCV), Fez, Morocco, 2–4 April 2018; pp. 1–6.
20. Tiwari, S.; Gupta, R.K.; Kashyap, R. To Enhance Web Response Time Using Agglomerative Clustering Technique for Web Navigation Recommendation. In Proceedings of the Computational Intelligence in Data Mining, Honolulu, HI, USA, 27 November–1 December 2017; Advances in Intelligent Systems and Computing; Springer: Singapore, 2019; Volume 711, pp. 659–672.
21. Huynh, H.M.; Nguyen, L.T.T.; Vo, B.; Oplatkova, Z.K.; Hong, T.P. Mining Clickstream Patterns Using IDLists. In Proceedings of the 2019 IEEE International Conference on Systems, Man and Cybernetics (SMC), Bari, Italy, 6–9 October 2019; pp. 2007–2012.
22. Huynh, H.M.; Nguyen, L.T.T.; Vo, B.; Nguyen, A.; Tseng, V.S. Efficient methods for mining weighted clickstream patterns. *Exp. Syst. Appl.* **2020**, *142*, 112993. [CrossRef]
23. Prakash, P.G.O.; Jaya, A. Analyzing and Predicting User Navigation Pattern from Weblogs using Modified Classification Algorithm. *Indones. J. Electr. Eng. Comput. Sci.* **2018**, *11*, 333–340. [CrossRef]
24. Abirami, K.; Mayilvaganan, P. Fuzzy Clustering with Artificial Bee Colony Algorithm using Web Usage Mining. *Int. J. Pure Appl. Math.* **2018**, *118*, 3619–3626.
25. Abirami, K.; Mayilvaganan, P. Similarity Measurement Of Web Navigation Pattern Using K-Harmonic Mean Algorithm. *Elysium J. Eng. Res. Manag.* **2017**, *4*, 1–6.
26. Aravindan, J.S.; Vivekanandan, K. An Overview of Pre-processing Techniques in Web usage Mining. *Int. J. Comput. Trends Technol. (IJCTT)* **2017**, *48*, 41–44. [CrossRef]
27. Banerjee, A.; Ghosh, J. Clickstream Clustering using Weighted Longest Common Subsequences. In Proceedings of the Web Mining Workshop at the 1st SIAM Conference on Data Mining, Chicago, IL, USA, 5–7 April 2001; Volume 143, p. 144.
28. Huidobro, A.; Monroy, R.; Cervantes, B. A Contrast-Pattern Characterization of Website Visitors in Terms of Conversions. In *Technology-Enabled Innovations in Education (CIIE) 2020*; Part of the Book Series: Transactions on Computer Systems and Networks (TCSN); Springer: Berlin/Heidelberg, Germany, 2022.
29. Armstrong, G.; Kotler, P.T.; Trifts, V.; Buchwitz, L.A. *Marketing: An Introduction*, 6th ed.; Pearson: London, UK, 2017.
30. Kumar, V.; Ogunmola, G.A. Web Analytics for Knowledge Creation: A Systematic Review of Tools, Techniques, and Practices. *Int. J. Cyber Behav. Psychol. Learn. (IJCBPL)* **2020**, *10*, 1–14. [CrossRef]
31. WTS. Web Technology Surveys (WTS) Website. 2021. Available online: https://w3techs.com (accessed on 13 January 2021).
32. G2. G2 Website. 2021. Available online: https://www.g2.com (accessed on 18 January 2021).
33. Gita, S.; Christopher, G.; Bui, H.H.; Pynadath, D.; Goldman, R.P. *Plan, Activity, and Intent Recognition. Theory and Practice. Chapter 5: Stream Sequence Mining for Human Activity Discovery*; Kauffmann Publishers: Waltham, MA, USA, 2014; pp. 123–148.
34. Gómez, F. Visualization and Machine Learning Techniques to Support Web Traffic Analysis. Master's Thesis, Tecnológico de Monterrey, Monterrey, Mexico, 2018.
35. Cervantes, B.; Gómez, F.; Loyola-González, O.; Medina-Pérez, M.A.; Monroy, R.; Ramírez, J. Pattern-Based and Visual Analytics for Visitor Analysis on Websites. *Appl. Sci.* **2019**, *9*, 3840. [CrossRef]
36. Igor, C.; David, H.; Christopher, M.; Padhraic, S.; Steven, W. Visualization of Navigation Patterns on a Web Site Using Model-Based Clustering. In Proceedings of the 6th ACM SIGKDD International Conference on Knowledge Discovery and Data Mining, Boston, MA, USA, 6–9 August 2000; pp. 280–284.

37. Dubois, P.M.J.; Han, Z.; Jiang, F.; Leung, C.K. An Interactive Circular Visual Analytic Tool for Visualization of Web Data. In Proceedings of the IEEE/WIC/ACM International Conference on Web Intelligence (WI), Omaha, NE, USA, 13–16 October 2016; pp. 709–712.
38. Ahmed, N.K.; Rossi, R.A. Interactive Visual Graph Analytics on the Web. In Proceedings of the 9th International AAAI Conference on Web and Social Media, Oxford, UK, 26–29 May 2015; pp. 566–569.
39. Bourobou, S.T.M.; Yoo, Y. User Activity Recognition in Smart Homes Using Pattern Clustering Applied to Temporal ANN Algorithm. *Dep. Electr. Comput. Eng. Pusan Natl. Univ.* **2015**, *15*, 11953–11971. [CrossRef] [PubMed]
40. Srivastava, J.; Cooley, R.; Deshpande, M.; Tan, P.N. Web Usage Mining: Discovery and Applications of Usage Patterns from Web Data. *SIGKDD Explor.* **2000**, *1*, 12–23. [CrossRef]
41. Malviya, B.K.; Agrawal, J. A Study on Web Usage Mining Theory and Applications. In Proceedings of the Fifth International Conference on Communication Systems and Network Technologies, Gwalior, India, 4–6 April 2015; pp. 935–939.
42. Nakamura, R.; Inenaga, S.; Bannai, H.; Funamoto, T.; Takeda, M.; Shinohara, A. Linear-Time Text Compression by Longest-First Substitution. *Algorithms* **2009**, *2*, 1429–1448. [CrossRef]
43. Charikar, M.; Lehman, E.; Ding Liu, R.P.; Prabhakaran, M.; Sahai, A.; Shelat, A. The Smallest Grammar Problem. *IEEE Trans. Inf. Theory* **2005**, *51*, 1–23. [CrossRef]
44. Galle, M. Investigating the Effectiveness of BPE: The Power of Shorter Sequences. In Proceedings of the Conference on Empirical Methods in Natural Language Processing and the 9th International Joint Conference on Natural Language Processing, Hong Kong, China, 3–7 November 2019; pp. 1375–1381.
45. Larsson, N.J.; Moffat, A. Offline Dictionary-Based Compression. In Proceedings of the Data Compression Conference, Snowbird, UT, USA, 29–31 March 1999; pp. 296–305.
46. Bille, P.; Gørtz, I.L.; Prezza, N. Space-Efficient Re-Pair Compression. In Proceedings of the Data Compression Conference, Snowbird, UT, USA, 4–7 April 2017, pp. 171–180.
47. Yang, E.H.; Kieffer, J.C. Efficient universal lossless data compression algorithms based on a greedy sequential grammar transform. I. Without context models. *IEEE Trans. Inf. Theory* **2000**, *46*, 755–777. [CrossRef]
48. Nevill-Manning, C.G.; Witten, I.H. Compression and Explanation using Hierarchical Grammars. *Comput. J.* **1997**, *40*, 3–116. [CrossRef]
49. Latendresse, M. Masquerade Detection via Customized Grammars. In *Lecture Notes in Computer Science, Proceedings of the Second International Conference (DIMVA), Vienna, Austria, 7–8 July 2005*; IEEE: Piscataway, NJ, USA, 2005; pp. 1–12.
50. Manninen, M. Public Implementation of Sequitur in Python. 2021. Available online: https://github.com/markomanninen/pysequitur (accessed on 30 January 2021).
51. Acosta-Mendoza, N.; Carrasco-Ochoa, J.A.; Martínez-Trinidad, J.F.; Gago-Alonso, A.; Medina-Pagola, J.E. Mining clique frequent approximate subgraphs from multi-graph collections. *Appl. Intell.* **2020**, *40*, 878–892. [CrossRef]

Article

A Deep Neural Network Technique for Detecting Real-Time Drifted Twitter Spam

Amira Abdelwahab [1,2,*] and Mohamed Mostafa [2]

[1] Department of Information Systems, College of Computer Science and Information Technology (CCSIT), King Faisal University, P.O. Box 400, Al-Ahsa 31982, Saudi Arabia
[2] Department of Information Systems, Faculty of Computers and Information, Menoufia University, Shibin Al Kawm 32511, Egypt; mohamed.saad@ci.menofia.edu.eg
* Correspondence: a.ahmed@kfu.edu.sa

Abstract: The social network is considered a part of most user's lives as it contains more than a billion users, which makes it a source for spammers to spread their harmful activities. Most of the recent research focuses on detecting spammers using statistical features. However, such statistical features are changed over time, and spammers can defeat all detection systems by changing their behavior and using text paraphrasing. Therefore, we propose a novel technique for spam detection using deep neural network. We combine the tweet level detection with statistical feature detection and group their results over meta-classifier to build a robust technique. Moreover, we embed our technique with initial text paraphrasing for each detected tweet spam. We train our model using different datasets: random, continuous, balanced, and imbalanced. The obtained experimental results showed that our model has promising results in terms of accuracy, precision, and time, which make it applicable to be used in social networks.

Keywords: spam detection; deep learning; semantic similarity; social network security

1. Introduction

Currently, many internet users can impart information and work together inside online social networks (OSNs). However, Twitter is viewed as the most well-known informal community which offers free blogging services for clients to publish their news and thoughts inside 280 characters. Clients can follow others through various platforms [1]. Consistently, a huge number of Twitter clients share their status and news about their disclosures [2]. Moreover, the Twitter platform additionally attracts criminal records (spammers) that can tweet spam substances, which may incorporate destructive URLs. This could divert clients to malevolent or phishing sites for bringing in cash misguidedly [3,4] by assaulting the client's profile. As Twitter set caps for the length of the characters of tweets, this makes spammer swindle clients by putting cheat content or malicious URL to divert them for the outside site [5]. In an investigation studying the correlation between both email and social spam, the click-through rate of Twitter spam was found to reach 0.13%, in spite of the fact that email spam arrives at 0.0003–0.0006% [6]. Moreover, social spam is viewed as increasingly perilous and cheats a lot of clients [7].

To tackle this problem, many researchers are focusing on detecting spammers by discovering the statistical features of spammers on both messaging and account levels. These messaging detection approaches focus on checking tweet content to find keyword patterns, hashtags, and URLs. These approaches are shown to be effective, but real-time detection is needed to solve the huge number of messages which are posted per hour. The account level approaches focus on extracting statistics and info about the behavior of each account to classify whether they are spam accounts or legitimate users. However, an experimental study was conducted to examine whether the statistical features changed over time. The experimental results proved that the statistical features are changed over time.

Most of the researchers are focusing on collecting these features and trying to experience spammers priorities, ignoring that these features drift over time. However, spammers will try to tackle all these features. In this paper, an effective technique has been proposed to tackle the aforementioned limitations. Our proposed technique focuses on the content of each tweet in addition to the statistical features. Moreover, it has an auto-learning capability to find the features which make it able to classify each tweet as spam or not with high accuracy in a reasonable time.

Accordingly, these challenges inspire us to investigate this problem to contribute to spam detection approaches. To cope with this problem, we maintain a framework that contains three stages to detect spammers:

- Fast filter mode classifier to determine whether each input tweet is spam or not.
- Every filtered spam tweet is paraphrased to generate a new spam sentence with different definition with the same meaning.
- Ensemble deep learning methods are collected in addition to the statistical features to decide the output of the classifier.

The rest of this manuscript is organized as follows. Section 2 briefly discusses the literature review on Twitter spam detection. Section 3 clarifies the problem statement of spam drift in detail. Section 4 explains our proposed detection framework. Section 5 discusses our experiments and results. Finally, conclusions are represented in Section 6.

2. Literature Review

Many studies have been performed to improve spam detection challenges. These studies can be organized into three categories [8], syntax analysis, feature analysis, and blacklist techniques, as shown in Figure 1.

Most of the research applied blacklisting techniques based on URLs in the tweets using any third-party tools, such as Trend Micro or Google safe browsing. However, S. Savage [9] creates a lightweight technique for spam detection, while [10] filtered tweets based on checking URLs in tweets, username patterns, and hashtags.

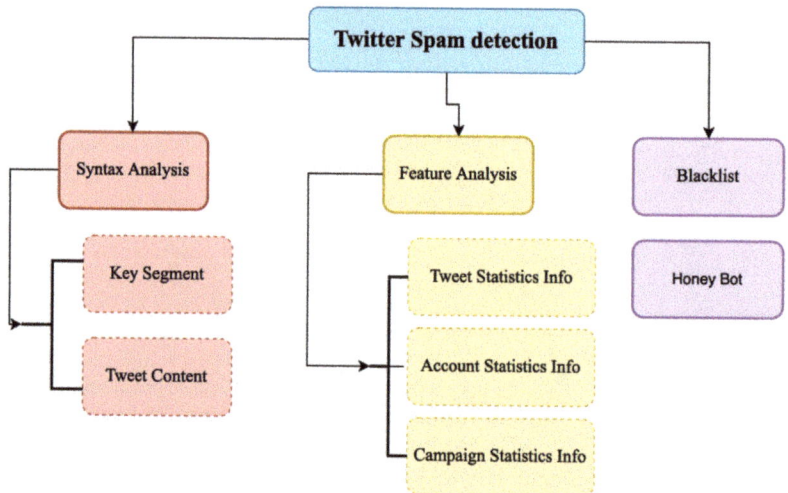

Figure 1. Twitter spam detection taxonomy.

Consequently, a lot of researchers have applied machine learning (ML) techniques in their works [11–14] and extracted some features of users, such as number of followings, username pattern, and account creation in addition to features of content, such as length of tweets, number of hashtags, and hashtags pattern. Authors in [11] employed honey pots to collect spammers' profiles to extract statistical features using different ML algorithms, such as Decorate and Random some space. However, Benevento et al. attempted to detect spammers by using a support vector machine (SVM) algorithm [12]. These features can be easily fabricated as spammers can buy fake spammers' followers and followings. Thus, some studies [15] depend on a social graph to tackle the problem of fabrication by calculating distance and connectivity of each tweet between sender and receiver to examine whether it is spam. Yang et al. [16] built a more robust feature using a bidirectional link ratio between centrality and local cluster coefficient with performance 99% true positive, while [17] provides a new solution that can detect most campaigns and classify each of them into spam or not spam using deep learning techniques and semantic similarity methods.

Most of the described methods focus on detecting spam tweets based on some statistical features. Some studies employ syntax analysis, while a spam dataset based on hashtags was created by [18], in which authors collected 14 million tweets and classified them using five different techniques. Sedhi and son [19] utilized a package of four lightweight techniques to detect spam at tweet level using part of speech tag, content-based, sentiment, and user-based features, using a word vector as the universal feature of their task. Le and Mikulov [20] have deployed a deep learning method by constructing a tweet vector by combining the word vector with the document vector to classify the neural network.

In [21], the authors employ the horse herd optimization algorithm (HOA), inspired by nature optimization algorithms. This algorithm emulates the social exhibitions of horses at various ages. The idea behind this study has a great performance result on complex problems, specifically with high dimensions, solving many dimension problems with low cost based on time, performance, and complexity (up to 10,000 dimensions). The researcher attempts to find the best solution by employing the multiobjective opposition-based binary which gave good results compared with similar approaches. However, it still depends on statistical functions which can deviate over time as explained.

The study by Abayomi-Alli [22] used the ensemble approach to detect SMS spam. This approach depends on two pipeline the BI-LSTM (Bidirectional Long-Short Term Memory) network which produce accurate results in text classification tasks and the classical machine learning methods. However, this approach does not employ any attention mechanism in the BI-LSTM network, which causes this approach to suffer in long sentences of more than 8 words.

Many different extraction methods have been used for representing tweets, such as [23]. In this reference, authors analyzed people's sentiments collected through tweets. They employed three different feature extraction methods, domain-agnostic, fastText-based, and domain-specific, for tweet representation. Then, an ensemble approach was proposed for sentiment analysis by employing three CNN models and traditional ML models, such as random forest (RF), and SVM using the Nepali Twitter sentiment dataset, called NepCOV19Tweets. Their models achieve 72.1% accuracy by employing a smaller feature size (300-D). However, these models have two limitations. First, they are complex and need high computational resources for implementation. Second, their methods are based on only semantic features.

In addition, authors in [24] analyzed people's sentiments using three feature extractions, term frequency-inverse document f(TF-IDF, fastText, and a combination of these two methods as hybrid features for representing COVID-19 tweets. Then, they validated their methods against different ML techniques. Their SVM model obtained the highest accuracy on both TF-IDF (65.1%) and hybrid features (72.1%). The major limitation of this model is its high computational complexity.

TF-IDF [25] may be used to vectorize text into a format that is more suitable for machine learning and natural language processing approaches. It is a statistical measure that we can apply to terms in a text and then use to generate a vector, whereas other methods, such as word2vec [26], will provide a vector for a term and then extra effort may be required to transform that group of vectors into a single vector or other format. Another approach is Bidirectional Encoder Representations from Transformers (BERT), which converts phrases, words, and other objects into vectors using a transformer-based ML model [27]. However, BERT's design also includes deep neural networks, which means it can be significantly more computationally expensive than TF-IDF.

Because our proposed framework will be used with highly intensive data applications, we had to choose a high-performance and quick feature extraction method. TF-IDF produces high accuracy relative to our framework, so we decided to build our model with it.

Most of the mentioned studies focus on extracting the features that can help them find the spammers, but they ignore a very important problem, which is "spam drift", meaning that these features are changed over time. Egele et al. [28] build a historical-based model, which does not suffer from this problem. Authors in [29] have built a model using a fuzzy model that attempts to adapt the features over time, but the accuracy is decreased. So, we will focus on this problem and then try to build a robust framework to cope with most of the challenges to detect Twitter spam.

3. Problem Statement

The problem revealed in this paper is detecting and classifying each tweet whether it is spam or not. So, we have the problem of "spam drift", which happened because most of the researchers focus on determining the spam tweets based on the statistical features. Most of them focus on selection of features as shown in Table 1. In the real world, these features are changing in an unpredictable way over time. Therefore, we attempted to build a framework that is robust against these changes.

Table 1. Comparative study of ten consequence days between spam and non-spam using KL-Divergence.

	D-1 vs. D-2		D-2 vs. D-3		D-3 vs. D-4		D-4 vs. D-5		D-5 vs. D-6		D-6 vs. D-7		D-7 vs. D-8		D-8 vs. D-9		D-9 vs. D-10	
F-1	0.37	0.05	0.35	0.04	0.45	0.05	0.25	0.04	0.27	0.04	0.28	0.04	0.30	0.06	0.27	0.04	0.35	0.05
F-2	0.25	0.11	0.23	0.11	0.27	0.11	0.20	0.11	0.22	0.11	0.22	0.11	0.18	0.11	0.39	0.11	0.36	0.11
F-3	0.29	0.08	0.23	0.08	0.33	0.08	0.16	0.08	0.23	0.08	0.21	0.08	0.21	0.09	0.27	0.09	0.24	0.09
F-4	0.17	0.08	0.14	0.08	0.15	0.09	0.15	0.08	0.18	0.08	0.20	0.08	0.14	0.08	0.28	0.09	0.20	0.09
F-5	0.03	0.02	0.03	0.02	0.04	0.02	0.03	0.02	0.02	0.02	0.03	0.02	0.02	0.02	0.06	0.02	0.06	0.02
F-6	0.99	0.36	0.53	0.36	0.64	0.36	0.37	0.36	0.46	0.35	0.41	0.35	0.46	0.36	0.51	0.36	0.53	0.37
F-7	0.11	0.05	0.09	0.04	0.05	0.05	0.05	0.05	0.06	0.04	0.08	0.05	0.07	0.05	0.11	0.05	0.09	0.05
F-8	0.20	0	0	0	0.05	0	0.04	0	0.03	0	0.04	0	0.02	0	0.05	0	0.03	0
F-9	0.10	0	0.04	0	0.02	0	0.03	0	0.02	0	0.02	0	0	0	0.05	0	0.02	0
F-10	0	0	0.04	0	0.04	0	0.02	0	0.11	0	0	0	0.02	0	0.33	0	0.28	0
F-11	0.27	0.02	0.07	0.02	0.07	0.02	0.12	0.02	0.11	0	0.1	0	0.27	0.02	0.29	0.03	0.21	0.03
F-12	0.05	0	0	0	0.03	0	0.04	0.02	0.04	0	0.05	0	0.05	0	0.47	0	0.47	0

At the beginning, we will try to prove this problem as in [29]. So, we have crawled data of tweets from Twitter Stream API for 10 consecutive days. We have to check a lot of tweets to determine which are spam. In this stage, we found that most of the spam tweets contain a URL, which most spammers use to spread their malicious content by sending the victim to mine or farm sites. Therefore, we use Trend Micro's Web Reputation Technology (WRT) to detect the tweet as spam or not based on the URL [22]. This WRT system helps users to identify the malicious sites in real-time with high reliability with an accuracy rate of 100% as reported in [30]. Moreover, we have made hundreds of manual inspections to ensure the reliability of this system.

As described previously, we found that the statistical features are changing from day to day with impressive effect as shown in Table 1. For example, we found that the average number of account followings changes from the 1st day (500–900) to the 9th day (950–1350). This means that the spammers try to collect the followings, but the average number of followings is confused whether this account is spam or not.

Therefore, to justify the problem of changing the statistical features, the distribution of the data should be modeled. There are two types of data: parametric and non-parametric. The parametric approaches are always used when the distribution of data is known as normal distribution, but the statistical features of Twitter are unknown [31,32]. So, we used the non-parametric approaches. One of the most common non-parametric approaches is the statistical test. The calculation of the statistical test is based on computing the distance between the two distributions to calculate the change between them. Distance is calculated using Kullback-Leibler (KL) divergence [31], which is also known as relative entropy, shown in Equation (1):

$$D_{kl}(P|Q) = \sum_i P(i) \log \frac{P(i)}{Q(i)} \quad (1)$$

This formula is used to measure the two probability distributions as reported in [33]. Let $s = \{x_1, x_2, \ldots, x_n\}$ be a multi-set from a finite set F containing numerical feature values, and $N(x|s)$ is the number of appearances of $x \in s$. Thus, the relative proportion of each x is shown Equation (2)

$$P_s(x) = \frac{N(x|s)}{n} \quad (2)$$

The ratio of the two variables P/Q is undefined, if we assume $Q(i) = 0$. Therefore, the estimation of $P_s(x)$ is changed to Equation (3)

$$P_s(x) = \frac{N(x|s) + 0.5}{n + |F|/2} \quad (3)$$

when variable $|F|$ is defined as the number of elements in the finite set F. The distance between two day's tweets, $D1$ and $D2$, is defined as shown in Equation (4)

$$D(D1|D2) = \sum_{x \in F} P_{D1}(x) \log \frac{P_{D1}(x)}{P_{D2}(x)} \quad (4)$$

We calculate the KL Divergence of spam and legitimate tweets of each feature in two adjacent days as shown in Table 1. The larger the distance, the more dissimilarity between the two distributions. So, according to the results in Table 1, the distance is large in most features in case of spam data. However, in non-spam data, the distance is very small in most of the features. According to this study, by examining the Number_of_tweet (f-6) feature from Table 1, we notice that the KL Divergence metric of spam tweets for Day 1 and Day 2 is 0.99. However, in non-spam tweets, it is 0.36, which means that the distribution of this feature is changed from Day 1 to Day 2 compared to non-spam tweets. As shown in Table 1, most features are changing unpredictably from one day to another, although the training data is fixed and is not affected by any changes. Therefore, the performance of the classifiers will become inaccurate if the decision boundary is not updated.

4. The Proposed Model

The process of classifying tweets as spam or not has three challenges. First, the tweet classification process can not only depend on statistical features because it drifts over time as described. So, our classifier considers the tweet content. Second, our proposed framework must struggle over the spammers because they try to change the tweet content, which helps them to evade from any monitor system [34]. Therefore, new spam tweets must be rephrased from the detected spam. Third, a robust framework must be built that is able to detect spam tweets in less execution time to cope with Twitter big data challenges. These three challenges motivated us to build the proposed framework. This framework consists of three layers as shown in Figure 2.

4.1. Learning from Detected Spam Tweets

This layer is used to filter Twitter as an initial step for fast detection of spam tweets. As described in Figure 2, our proposed framework is interested in spam tweets to regenerate a new semantic meaning of the same tweet by the next layer. Therefore, new information or words can be obtained that the spammer can use to paraphrase the tweet content and spread their spam again. In this step, the SVM classifier is utilized. First, this classifier is trained with a bi-gram (set of two words for each tweet) and transforms the tweets with TF-IDF. Then, the new unlabeled tweets are entered into this classifier to classify them (Spam, notSpam). This method focuses on the non-spam tweets, which will be the input for the next layer.

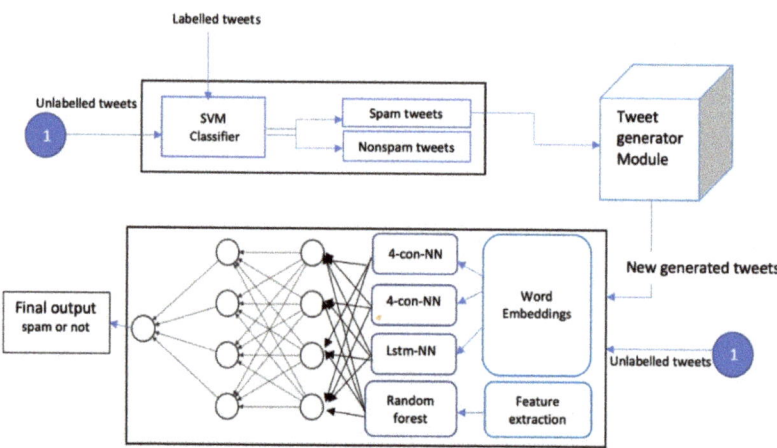

Figure 2. The proposed framework.

4.2. Generate New Tweets

In the real world, researchers try to build robust systems. However, smarter spammers are trying to tackle these solutions. Therefore, a system for tweet paraphrasing should be built using a method that generates text by preserving the same meaning and semantic, not only focusing on the correct grammar. Therefore, we used the encoder-decoder framework [35], which is embedded with an attention model network. The spam tweet paraphrasing model is shown in Figure 3.

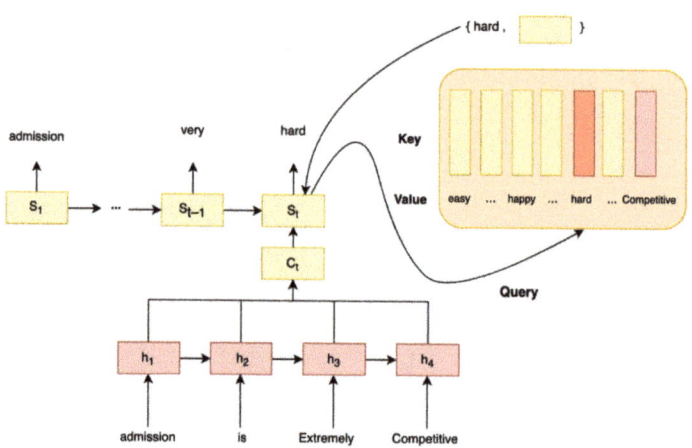

Figure 3. An overview of spam tweet paraphrasing model.

Given the source spam messages as input from the classifier layer, the encoder packs the source into dense representation vectors called context vector c_t, which captures the context information for this message. Then, the decoder tries to generate the paraphrased messages from the hot encoded vectors according to Equations (5) and (6).

$$c_t = \sum_{i=1}^{N} \alpha_{ti} h_i \qquad (5)$$

$$\alpha_{ti} = \frac{e^{g(s_t, h_i)}}{\sum_{j=1}^{N} e^{g(s_t, h_j)}} \qquad (6)$$

where $g(s_t, h_i)$ is an attractive score between the encoder state h_i and the decoder state s_t. Then, the dense representations are fed into an attention layer. For predicting words, the decoder utilizes the combination of source and target context vector as query q_t shown in Equation (7) to get the word embeddings

$$q_t = \tanh(W_c[s_t; c_t]) \qquad (7)$$

The candidate words W_i and its corresponding embedding vector e_i are stored as key-value pairs $\{e_i, W_i\}$. Therefore, our model uses q_t to query these key-value pairs by evaluating all the applicant words between the query q_t and the word vector W_i as shown in Equation (8)

$$f(q_t, e_i) = \begin{cases} q_t^T e_i \\ q_t^T W_a e_i \\ v^T \tanh(W_q q_t + W_e e_i) \end{cases} \qquad (8)$$

where W_q and W_e are two trainable parameter matrices, and v^T is a trainable parameter vector. Then return the word which has the highest matching. The chosen word is emitted as the generated token, and its embedding is then utilized as the contribution of the long short-term memory (LSTM) at the next step. The word embedding is affected by three sources: the input of the encoder, the input of the decoder, and the query of the output layer. In the training stage, we used the Adam optimizer method with these hyper-parameters $\beta 1 = 0.9$, $\beta 2 = 0.999$, $\alpha = 0.001$, and $\in = 1 \times 10^{-8}$

4.3. Ensemble Method

In this layer, we proposed a novel technique to classify the tweets as spam or non-spam as shown in Figure 4. We have combined three deep neural network classifier techniques together for content based on one classifier for user-based features, which contains two different architectures. First, we will explain the methodology for each component and then explain the whole technique as an ensemble classifier.

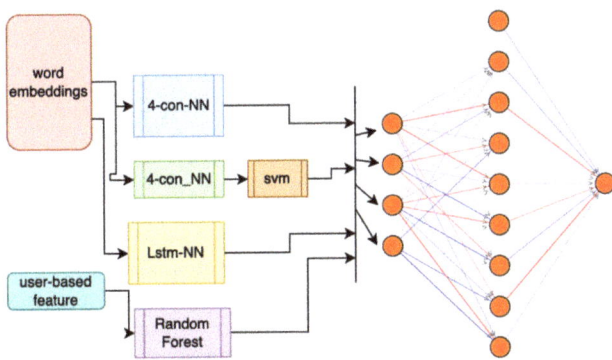

Figure 4. Ensemble neural network architecture.

4.3.1. Convolution Neural Network

In this section, the convolution neural network (CNN) will be discussed. Recently, this network was designed to be used in computer vision problems. However, it has been shown that it can be used in natural language processing (NLP) tasks as [36] proposed neural architecture used in many NLP tasks, such as part of speech tagging, chunk, and named entity recognition. Our model is inspired by [36] in that the layers of this architecture are divided into five parts, input layer, embedding layer, convolution layer, pooling layer, and output layer, as shown in Figure 5. The input layer receives tweet messages as words or embedding words using word2vec or glove [37]. Each tweet is split into words with max_length value 50 because the length of max tweet message is 280 characters, which is difficult to exceed this number of words. If the length is small, it should be padded with value 0. Thereafter, these words are split into features by performing kernel multiplication and then are fed into the next layer, the convolution layer. ReLU, sigmoid, and tanh activation functions are used to obtain the convolution feature map. Then, max pooling is used to select the maximum activation value. Max pooling is used with NLP tasks where min and mean pool is used with computer vision tasks. The fully connected hidden dense layer with sigmoid activation function is applied to classify the tweets. Twelve regularization is used to avoid overfitting. To build this architecture, we used loss function: binary cross entropy and optimizer parameters.

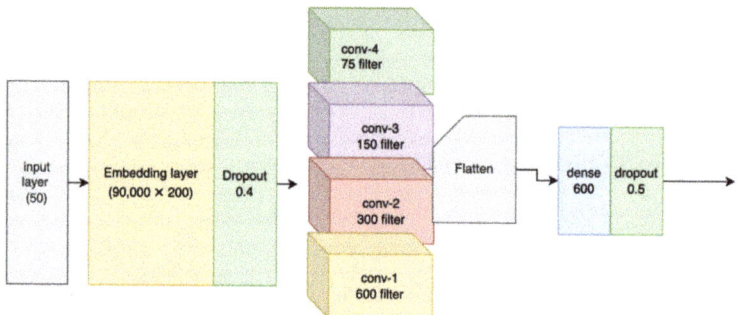

Figure 5. Neural network architecture with four conv. layers.

4.3.2. Recurrent Neural Networks

A recurrent neural network (RNN) is a network of directed connection between each node. The main feature of this network is the hidden state (memory) that can capture the sequential dependence in data. So, we utilized LSTM networks in our work rather than gated recurrent unit (GRU) [38], which has a problem with remembering long sequences. As shown in Figure 6, we used the same architecture as CNN, but we replaced the convolution layer with the LSTM layer which contains three main gates as follows: Forget gate is responsible for controlling what information should throw away from memory, Input gate is responsible for controlling what new information should be added to hidden state from the current input, Output gate decides what information to output from the memory. Then the output of this layer is entered to fully connected dense layer to produce the output.

4.3.3. Feature-Based Model

Statistical features in spam classifiers detection give good results [8]. Apart from using word embedding as described in the previous two sections, we also consider user-based features in our classifier.

A dataset with 6 million tweets is used to extract these features especially for user-based features [29]. We have presented the extracted features that can differentiate between spam or legitimate users as shown in Table 2. To represent the behavior of spam and legitimate accounts, a comparative study has been built between each extracted feature to represent the difference between them using the empirical cumulative distribution function (ECDF) as shown in Figure 7.

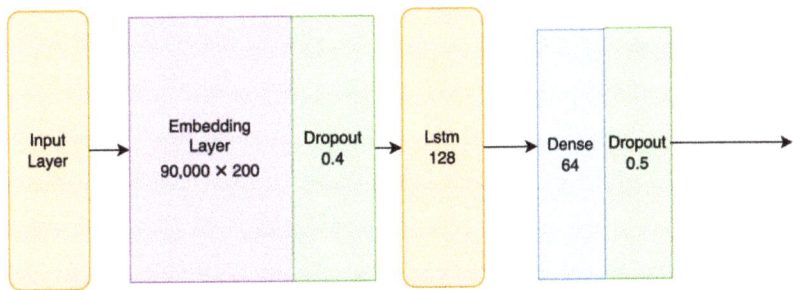

Figure 6. Recurrent neural network architecture.

Table 2. Extracted Features with the Corresponding Description.

Feature No.	Title	Description
F1	Age of account	The count of days of an account from the creation date until the last posted tweet
F2	Number of followers	The count of followers of this Twitter account
F3	Number of followings	The count of friends of this Twitter account
F4	Number of user favorites	The count of favorites this Twitter account added
F5	Number of lists	The size of lists this Twitter account added
F6	Number of tweets	The count of tweets this Twitter account post
F7	Number of retweets	The size of retweets for each tweet
F8	Number of hashtags	The count of hashtags added in this tweet
F9	Number of URLs	The count of user mentions added in this tweet
F10	Number of chars	The count of URLs added in this tweet
F11	Number of digits	The size of characters in this tweet
F12	Number of user mentions	The count of user mentions added in this tweet

The experimental study found that more than 53% of spam users have less than 500-day account age. However, 38% of non-spammers have less than 500 days. This means that they always try to create new accounts to spread their attacks, but they get blocked by spam detection techniques. Also, regarding the number of user mentions, most of the spammers must put more than one user mention to spread their data. Regarding number of capital words, most of the spammers use capital words to attract the users, and more than 70% of spammers use capital words in their tweets compared to only 30% of non-spammer users. In addition, we have also identified a new attribute called reputation of users, which is calculated as shown in Equation (9):

$$\text{Reputation} = \frac{\text{number of followers}}{\text{number of followers} + \text{number of followings}} \quad (9)$$

However, we found that the ratio of spammers is always small. They always have number of followings more than number of the followers because they try to make fake followers or following to show that this is a real account.

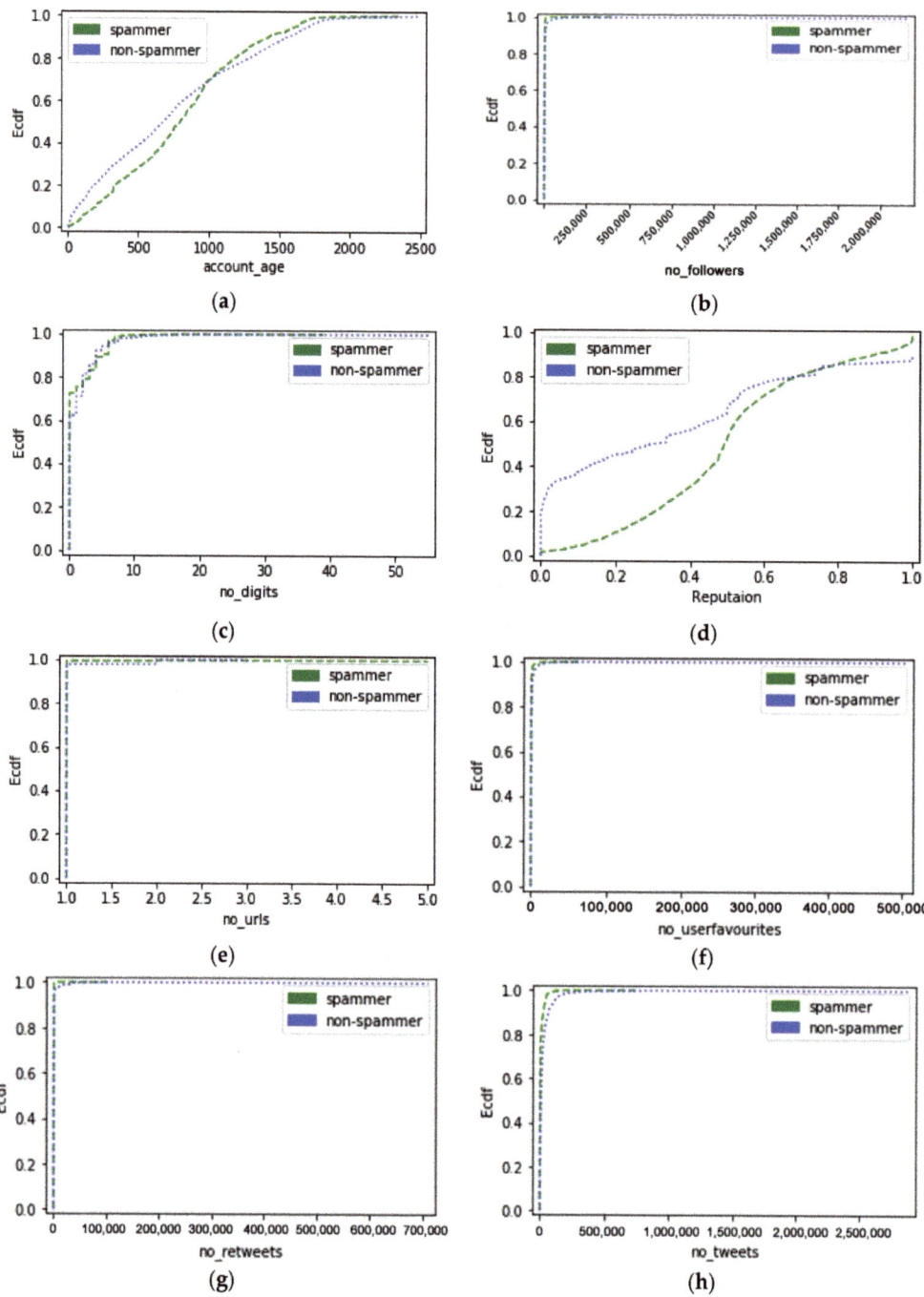

Figure 7. *Cont.*

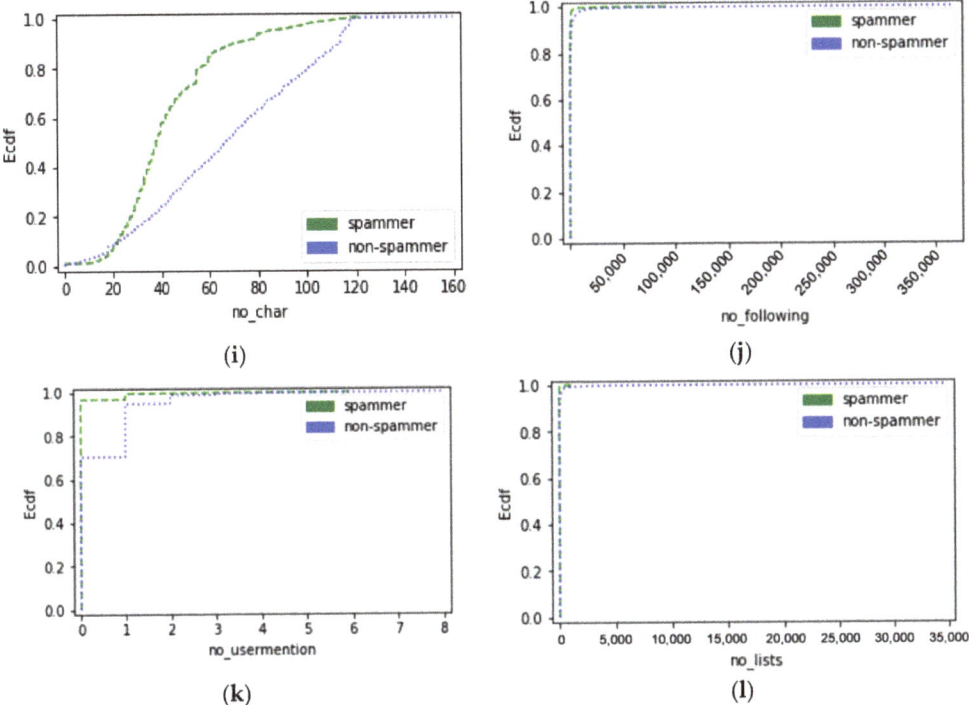

Figure 7. (ECDF) User-based features comparison: (**a**) account age; (**b**) number of followers; (**c**) number of digits; (**d**) reputation; (**e**) number of URLs; (**f**) number of user favorites; (**g**) number of retweets; (**h**) number of tweets; (**i**) number of characters; (**j**) number of followings; (**k**) number of user mentions; (**l**) number of lists.

4.3.4. Proposed Ensemble Approach

As shown in Figure 4, this architecture contains three different neural networks gathered with one classifier for a user-based feature and is described as follows:

- First, CNN is used with four convolution layers, which is trained with Twitter glove [37].
- Second, CNN is also used with four convolution layers to extract features and then classify them using the SVM algorithm. This CNN is trained with Twitter Glove in all dimensions.
- Third, the LSTM network is used and trained with the Hspam dataset, which contains 14 million tweets [18] and with Twitter Glove.
- Finally, random forest is used to classify the user-based features as it gives the best results according to [8,39]. It is trained using the icc dataset [40].

Furthermore, a neural network meta classifier is utilized and trained from the newly created data which consists of three-layers. It contains four input nodes and eight hidden nodes with a bias that is supported with the ReLU activation function. The output has only one node supported with the sigmoid activation function to generate value from 0 to 1.

5. Experiments and Results

In this section, we will present our experiments for each approach with different datasets for detecting the spam tweets in the Twitter platform. Firstly, we will give a brief description of our datasets and the evaluation metrics used in this study, then we will discuss our results of each approach.

5.1. Dataset

A ground truth dataset, which is called Hspam, is applied [18]. It contains 14 million tweets collected over two months and classified using many methods, such as manual annotation, KNN-based annotation, user-based annotation, domain-based annotation, and reliable ham tweet detection. For the privacy of the Twitter platform, we must grab the tweets using tweet_id, but there are some tweets that are deleted or missed. So, we focus only on the returned tweets. To evaluate our approaches over many datasets, we split our dataset into 4 samples as shown in Table 3. We made two balanced samples with random selection and another with continuous selection. Then, we selected another two samples and divided the ratio of spam to not spam to 20 times as it describes that, in real life, 5% only of tweets are spam [6]. So, we made two samples to simulate the real-life data. For testing our approaches, we selected a random sample of 0.5 million tweets to make a fair comparison between all dataset samples and all approaches.

Table 3. Dataset Samples.

Dataset No.	Type	Spam:Not-Spam
1	random	200 k:200 k
2	continuous	200 k:200 k
3	random	50 k:1000 k
4	continuous	50 k:1000 k

5.2. Evaluation Metrics

To evaluate our approach, we used the metrics of recall, precision, and F1-score which are shown in Equations (10)–(12), respectively. We supposed that spam tweets are positive while non-spam tweets are negative. Then, we constructed the confusion matrix accordingly as shown in Table 4, where TP (true-positive) refers to all spam tweets that are predicted correctly as spam tweets, FN (false-negative) denoted as all spam tweets which are predicted wrongly as non-spam tweets, TN (true-negative) denoted as all non-spam tweets which are predicted correctly as non-spam tweets, and FP (false-positive), which refers to all non-spam tweets predicted wrongly as spam tweets.

$$\text{Recall} = \frac{TP}{(TP + FN)} \tag{10}$$

$$\text{Precision} = \frac{TP}{(TP + FP)} \tag{11}$$

$$F1 - \text{score} = \frac{2 * \text{Precision} * \text{Recall}}{\text{Precision} + \text{Recall}} \tag{12}$$

Table 4. Confusion Matrix.

		Predicted	
		spam	Not-spam
Actual	spam	TP	FP
	Not-spam	FN	TN

5.3. Experiments Settings

We have run our experiments in Linux ubuntu 18 LTS, with Inter(R) core (TM) I7 CPU of 16 GB. For each run over each dataset with every model, we divide the dataset into 80% as a training set and 20% for testing. All basic parameters we use in each model are put in each figure in the last section, embedding layer, dropout, number of filters, and dense network.

6. Results and Discussion

In this subsection, we will discuss the results of each model in our proposed framework and compare it with the latest frameworks.

6.1. Primary Twitter Filter

In this section, maxentropy, random forest, and SVM are implemented. As shown in Table 5 and Figure 8, SVM achieved the best results in terms of recall, precision, and F1-score for most datasets. So, it is selected to be applied in our framework with parameters c = 0.1, kernel = linear, and penalty = 12.

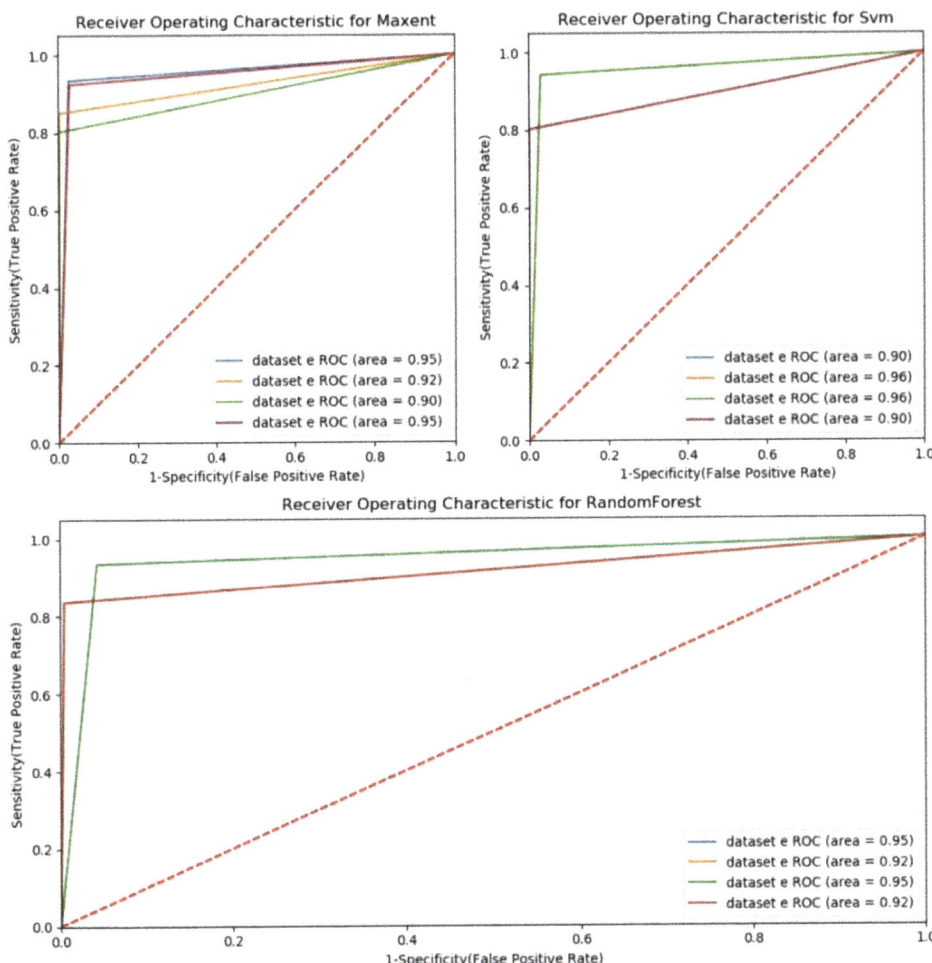

Figure 8. Roc curve for comparative study for SVM, MaxEntropy and Random Forest algorithms foreach dataset as the first module for filtering the tweets.

Table 5. Evaluation Results for Dataset 1.

Method		Precision	Recall	F-Measure
First module	MaxEntropy	0.96	0.95	0.95
	RandomForest	0.96	0.95	0.95
	SVM	0.97	0.96	0.96
LSTM		0.95	0.96	0.95
CNN		0.92	0.95	0.93
CNN + SVM		0.95	0.95	0.95
Random Forest (user-based feature)		0.96	0.90	0.93
SVM (user-based feature)		0.94	0.84	0.89
Chen et al. [41]		0.85	0.64	0.73
Wang et al. [40]		0.94	0.80	0.86
Madisetty et al. [42]		0.94	0.95	0.94
Proposed method		0.96	0.96	0.96

6.2. User-Based Features

As discussed earlier, the statistical features are changed over time, but this cannot prevent their abilities to detect spammers' actions with high accuracy and precision. Therefore, we attempt to find new user-based features. SVM and random forest are compared to get the best algorithm to be part of our detection framework. As shown in Tables 5 and 6, random forest achieves the best results in terms of precision and recall where trained with 6 million-tweet dataset [40] to get the user-based statistical features.

Table 6. Evaluation Results for Dataset 4.

Method		Precision	Recall	F-Measure
First module	MaxEntropy	0.96	0.95	0.95
	RandomForest	0.96	0.95	0.95
	SVM	0.96	0.96	0.96
LSTM		0.98	0.93	0.95
CNN		0.95	0.89	0.93
CNN + SVM		0.97	0.89	0.93
Random Forest (user-based feature)		0.60	0.70	0.65
Chen et al. [41]		0.58	0.67	0.62
Wang et al. [40]		0.79	0.76	0.77
Madisetty et al. [42]		0.92	0.94	0.93
Proposed method		0.97	0.95	0.96

6.3. Ensemble Method

This is the main module that consists of three main algorithms as discussed previously. They are trained with the Twitter Glove word embedding [37] dataset for all dimensions 25, 50, 100, 200. The results of each dimension are compared to our four datasets for each model as shown in Figures 9–11. We found that the results for the 200 dimensions are better in the three models, CNN, LSTM, and CNN with SVM.

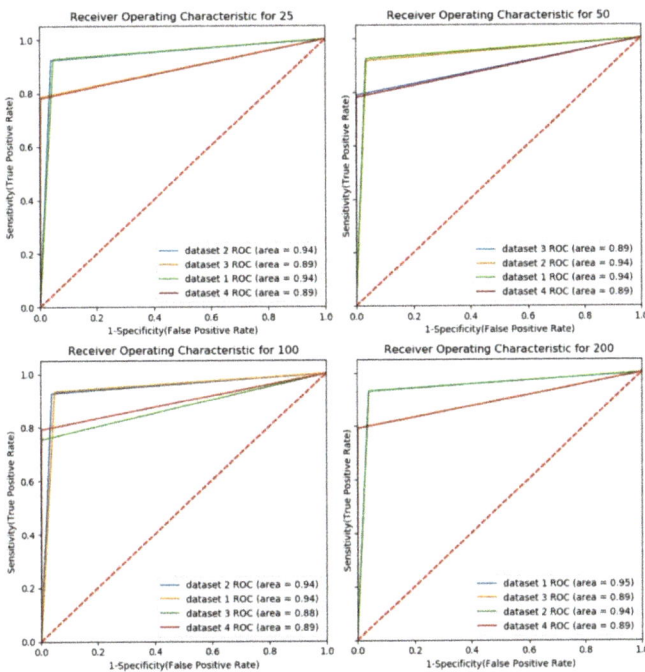

Figure 9. Roc curve for CNN model results for each dataset as a first component in our ensemble method.

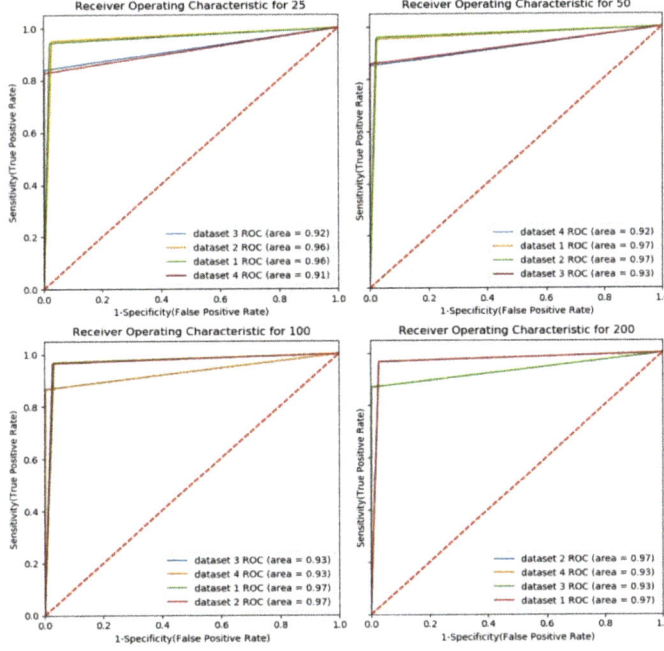

Figure 10. ROC curve for LSTM model results for each dataset as a third component in our ensembl method.

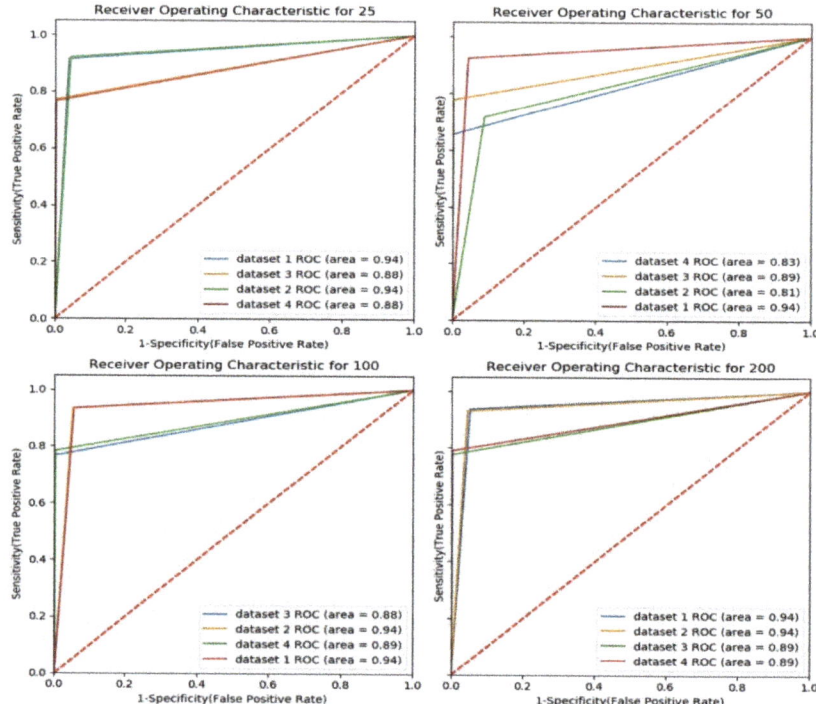

Figure 11. ROC curve for CNN features with SVM model results for each dataset as a second component in our ensemble method.

The CNN model is very good at finding the patterns. Each convolution will fire when a learned pattern is detected, but it suffers from long patterns or long tweets, which make the results of precision and F1-measure less. So, we embedded that LSTM model that is built using RNN, which is the strongest one with long sequences compared to CNN. Some studies [43] conducted an alternative for the last softmax function by SVM model. It aims to decide the optimal hyperplane for isolating the two classes in the dataset, and a multinomial case is apparently disregarded. With the utilization of SVM in a multinomial classification, the case turns into a one-versus-all, in which the positive class has the highest score, while the rest has the negative class.

6.4. Meta-Classifier

To achieve the results of our proposed framework, we build a sequential neural network that assembles the results of the utilized methods: LSTM, CNN, CNN feats with SVM, user-based features as presented in Figure 12. As shown in Tables 5 and 6, the proposed model achieved the best results in terms of accuracy, precision, and recall compared to the latest research in this field. Although [41] has the lowest execution time that it take 0.002 for each tweet, this execution time is very small compared to our proposed method as it takes longer, approximately 2 ms for each tweet. That is because of the number of features used to detect the spam and the combination of models that the tweet must pass to get the final result. However, this time can be optimized using clusters of nodes to decrease the time.

We also found that the results of the meta classifier are not boosted very much as they are too close to the ensemble model, but it is able to preserve the performance by a significant margin for this dataset. So, we can offer robust framework, that can be self-trained with the new words and hashtags, which the spammer can use as Twitter always has new subjects and interests of their users.

6.5. Performance of Learned Model

Twitter is considered a real-time platform. Therefore, it is extremely important to block spam tweets before it spread for preserving the safety of its users and preventing any potential damage. So, the proposed framework is designed to observe the execution time of the detection process. The processing time is calculated for the whole framework for each tweet. We found that each tweet takes 1:2 ms to detect whether it is spam or not. This value is very acceptable in real-time applications, although it can be decreased by using clusters of these models that help with the parallelization of the execution of the process of detecting spamming activities. However, most of the spammers are always thinking out of the box.

They try to deceive all detection strategies by changing the keywords and content and trying new features that can pass from detection methods and attract the users. On the other hand, there are legitimate users who are posting in new trending topics and new events happened immediately. So, we need to retrain the detection framework periodically to preserve the same accuracy and performance which we added in designing our framework, while all systems that depend only on the statistical features will be useless at later time. Our framework combined the statistical features with the deep learning features. So, it is very difficult for a spammer to fool our detection system. Furthermore, we have conducted four experiments with different datasets to test our framework. We concluded that our framework gives good results in both balanced and imbalanced datasets where the imbalanced dataset 4 has 1 million tweets and the balanced dataset 1 has 0.4 million tweets. They gave the same results in precision and F1-measure, which show the robustness of our detection framework as shown in Tables 5 and 6.

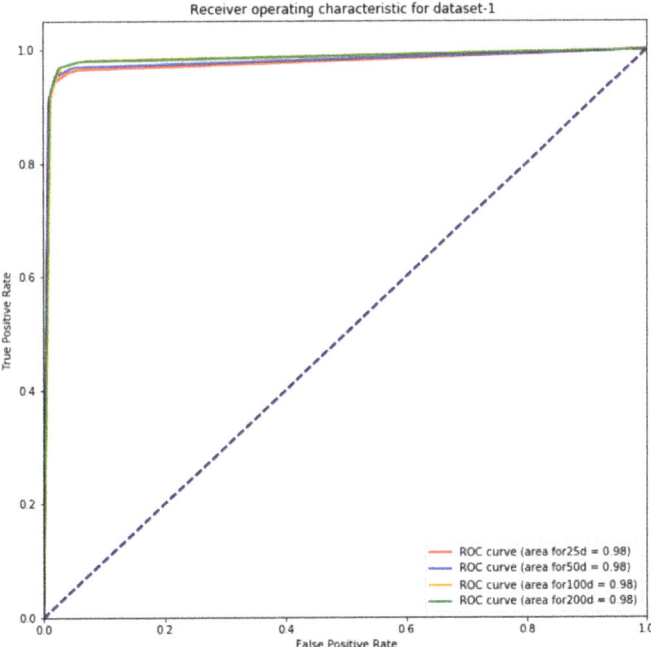

Figure 12. *Cont.*

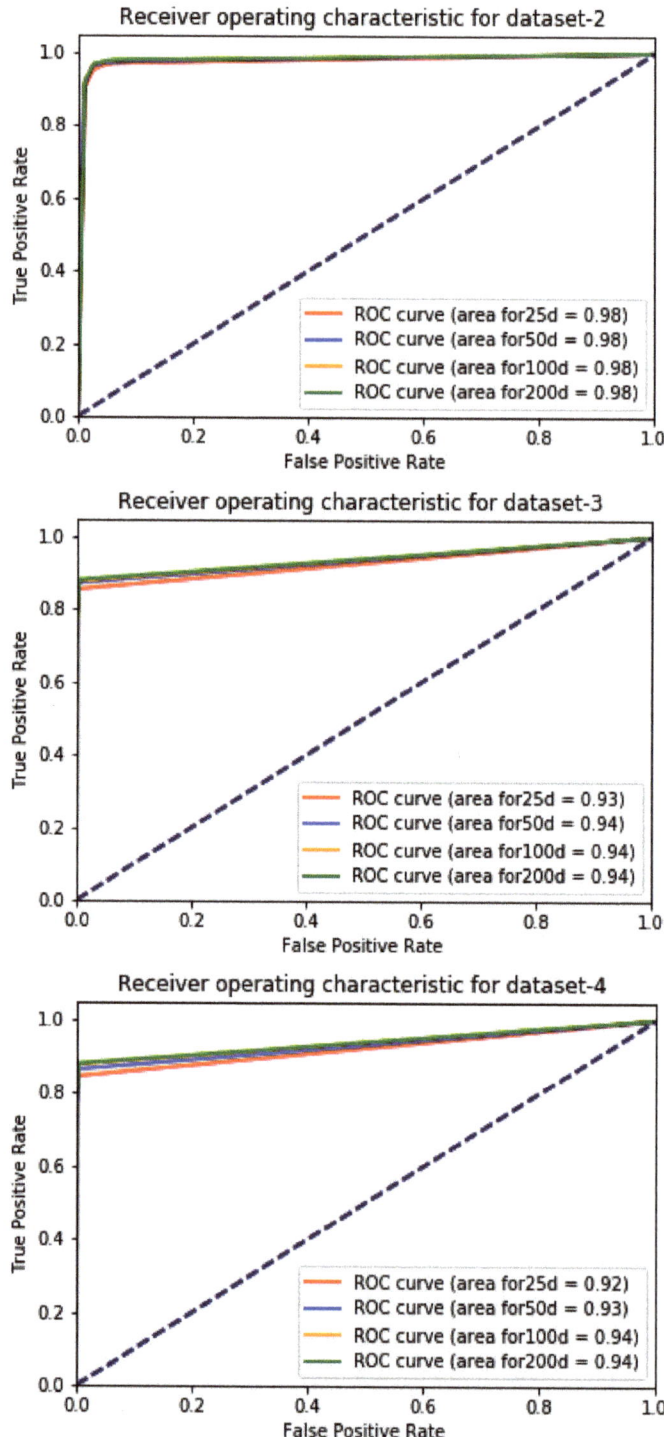

Figure 12. ROC curve for the results of our proposed framework for different datasets 1, 2, 3, and 4.

7. Conclusions

In this paper, we have proposed an ensemble learning framework based on deep learning technique that tries to detect spam tweets based on two methods: firstly, working at the tweet level by building three robust models; secondly, work with a user-based feature to gather information between the user information and the words in each tweet. We also tried to get ahead of step by generating new spam tweets to train our models to predict any spam paraphrasing those spammers can try to deceive our users. The proposed model has been trained using four datasets for more than 7 million tweets to build a robust framework. The experiments show that our proposed model gives excellent results compared to other methods in an acceptable time.

In future work, we will try to conduct more experiments in other online social networks rather than Twitter. Also, we will consider other data formats, such as images and videos that can affect OSN platforms. In addition, we need to try our model in new real data to study if our framework can be affected by the changing of data.

Author Contributions: Conceptualization, A.A. and M.M.; methodology, A.A.; software, M.M.; validation, A.A. and M.M.; formal analysis, M.M.; investigation, A.A.; resources, A.A.; data curation, M.M.; writing—original draft preparation, M.M.; writing—review and editing, A.A.; visualization, M.M.; supervision, A.A.; project administration, A.A.; funding acquisition, A.A. All authors have read and agreed to the published version of the manuscript.

Funding: This work was supported through the Annual Funding track by the Deanship of Scientific Research, Vice Presidency for Graduate Studies and Scientific Research, King Faisal University, Saudi Arabia [Project No. AN000417].

Institutional Review Board Statement: Not applicable.

Informed Consent Statement: Informed consent was obtained from all subjects involved in the study.

Data Availability Statement: The dataset is available on http://nsclab.org/nsclab/resources/?fbclid=IwAR2SkJQ9hN-0LCTb54UYdBCm7CS10zZqgywrh4lOtJo7M4JxjCr2D184QYk, (accessed on 20 April 2021).

Conflicts of Interest: The authors declare no conflict of interest.

References

1. Chu, Z.; Widjaja, I.; Wang, H. Detecting social spam campaigns on twitter. In Proceedings of the International Conference on Applied Cryptography and Network Security, Singapore, 26–29 June 2012; pp. 455–472.
2. Ghosh, S.; Viswanath, B.; Kooti, F.; Sharma, N.K.; Korlam, G.; Benevenuto, F.; Ganguly, N.; Gummadi, K.P. Understanding and combating link farming in the twitter social network. In Proceedings of the 21st International Conference on World Wide Web, Lyon, France, 16–20 April 2012; pp. 61–70.
3. Adewole, K.S.; Anuar, N.B.; Kamsin, A.; Varathan, K.D.; Razak, S.A. Malicious accounts: Dark of the social networks. *J. Netw. Comput. Appl.* **2017**, *79*, 41–67. [CrossRef]
4. Zhu, Y.; Wang, X.; Zhong, E.; Liu, N.N.; Li, H.; Yang, Q. Discovering spammers in social networks. In Proceedings of the Twenty-Sixth AAAI Conference on Artificial Intelligence, Toronto, ON, Canada, 22–26 July 2012.
5. Lee, S.; Kim, J. Warningbird: A near real-time detection system for suspicious urls in twitter stream. *IEEE Trans. Dependable Secur. Comput.* **2013**, *10*, 183–195. [CrossRef]
6. Grier, C.; Thomas, K.; Paxson, V.; Zhang, M. @ spam: The underground on 140 characters or less. In Proceedings of the 17th ACM Conference on Computer and Communications Security, Chicago, IL, USA, 4–8 October 2010; pp. 27–37.
7. Thomas, K.; Grier, C.; Ma, J.; Paxson, V.; Song, D. Design and evaluation of a real-time url spam filtering service. In Proceedings of the 2011 IEEE Symposium on Security and Privacy, Oakland, CA, USA, 22–25 May 2011; pp. 447–462.
8. Wu, T.; Wen, S.; Xiang, Y.; Zhou, W. Twitter spam detection: Survey of new approaches and comparative study. *Comput. Secur.* **2018**, *76*, 265–284. [CrossRef]
9. Ma, J.; Saul, L.K.; Savage, S.; Voelker, G.M. Learning to detect malicious urls. *ACM Trans. Intell. Syst. Technol.* **2011**, *2*, 1–24. [CrossRef]
10. Yardi, S.; Romero, D.; Schoenebeck, G. Detecting spam in a twitter network. *First Monday* **2010**, *15*. [CrossRef]
11. Lee, K.; Caverlee, J.; Webb, S. Uncovering social spammers: Social honeypots+ machine learning. In Proceedings of the 33rd International ACM SIGIR Conference on Research and Development in Information Retrieval, Geneva, Switzerland, 19–23 July 2010; pp. 435–442.
12. Benevenuto, F.; Magno, G.; Rodrigues, T.; Almeida, V. Detecting spammers on twitter. In Proceedings of the Collaboration, Electronic Messaging, Anti-Abuse and Spam Conference (CEAS), Redmond, WA, USA, 13–14 July 2010; Volume 6, p. 12.

13. Stringhini, G.; Kruegel, C.; Vigna, G. Detecting spammers on social networks. In Proceedings of the 26th Annual Computer Security Applications Conference, Austin, TX, USA, 6–10 December 2010; pp. 1–9.
14. Wang, A.H. Don't follow me: Spam detection in twitter. In Proceedings of the 2010 International Conference on Security and Cryptography (SECRYPT), Athens, Greece, 26–28 July 2010; pp. 1–10.
15. Song, J.; Lee, S.; Kim, J. Spam filtering in twitter using sender-receiver relationship. In Proceedings of the International Workshop on Recent Advances in Intrusion Detection, Menlo Park, CA, USA, 20–21 September 2011; pp. 301–317.
16. Yang, C.; Harkreader, R.; Gu, G. Empirical evaluation and new design for fighting evolving twitter spammers. *IEEE Trans. Inf. Forensics Secur.* **2013**, *8*, 1280–1293. [CrossRef]
17. Mostafa, M.; Abdelwahab, A.; Sayed, H.M. Detecting spam campaign in twitter with semantic similarity. *J. Phys. Conf. Ser.* **2020**, *1447*, 12044. [CrossRef]
18. Sedhai, S.; Sun, A. Hspam14: A collection of 14 million tweets for hashtag-oriented spam research. In Proceedings of the 38th International ACM SIGIR Conference on Research and Development in Information Retrieval, Santiago, Chile, 9–13 August 2015; pp. 223–232.
19. Sedhai, S.; Sun, A. Semi-supervised spam detection in Twitter stream. *IEEE Trans. Comput. Soc. Syst.* **2017**, *5*, 169–175. [CrossRef]
20. Le, Q.; Mikolov, T. Distributed representations of sentences and documents. In Proceedings of the International Conference on Machine Learning, Beijing, China, 21–26 June 2014; pp. 1188–1196.
21. Hosseinalipour, A.; Ghanbarzadeh, R. A novel approach for spam detection using horse herd optimization algorithm. In *Neural Computing & Applications*; Springer: New York, NY, USA, 2022. [CrossRef]
22. Abayomi-Alli, O.; Misra, S.; Abayomi-Alli, A. A deep learning method for automatic SMS spam classification: Performance of learning algorithms on indigenous dataset. In *Concurrency and Computation Practice and Experience*; Wiley: Hoboken, NJ, USA, 2022. [CrossRef]
23. Sitaula, C.; Basnet, A.; Mainali, A.; Shahi, T.B. Deep Learning-Based Methods for Sentiment Analysis on Nepali COVID-19-Related Tweets. *Comput. Intell. Neurosci.* **2021**, *2021*, 2158184. [CrossRef]
24. Shahi, T.B.; Sitaula, C.; Paudel, N. A Hybrid Feature Extraction Method for Nepali COVID-19-Related Tweets Classification. *Comput. Intell. Neurosci.* **2022**, *2022*, 5681574. [CrossRef]
25. Aizawa, A. An information-theoretic perspective of TF–IDF measures. *Inf. Process. Manag.* **2003**, *39*, 45–65. [CrossRef]
26. Church, K.W. Word2Vec. *Nat. Lang. Eng.* **2017**, *23*, 155–162. [CrossRef]
27. Fei, S.; Liu, J.; Wu, J.; Pei, C.; Lin, X.; Ou, W.; Jiang, P. BERT4Rec: Sequential recommendation with bidirectional encoder representations from transformer. In Proceedings of the 28th ACM International Conference on Information and Knowledge Management, Beijing, China, 3–7 November 2019; pp. 1441–1450.
28. Egele, M.; Stringhini, G.; Kruegel, C.; Vigna, G. Toward detecting compromised accounts on social networks. *IEEE Trans. Dependable Secure Comput.* **2017**, *14*, 447–460. [CrossRef]
29. Chen, C.; Wang, Y.; Zhang, J.; Xiang, Y.; Zhou, W.; Min, G. Statistical features-based real-time detection of drifted twitter spam. *IEEE Trans. Inf. Forensics Secur.* **2016**, *12*, 914–925. [CrossRef]
30. Whole Product Dynamic Real-World Protection Test. 2016. Available online: https://www.av-comparatives.org/testmethod/real-world-protection-tests/ (accessed on 12 August 2020).
31. Dasu, T.; Krishnan, S.; Venkatasubramanian, S.; Yi, K. An information-theoretic approach to detecting changes in multi-dimensional data streams. In Proceedings of the Symposium on the Interface of Statistics, Computing Science, and Applications, Pasadena, CA, USA, 24–27 May 2006.
32. Gama, J.; Žliobaitė, I.; Bifet, A.; Pechenizkiy, M.; Bouchachia, A. A survey on concept drift adaptation. *ACM Comput. Surv.* **2014**, *46*, 1–37. [CrossRef]
33. Csiszar, I.; Körner, J. *Information Theory: Coding Theorems for Discrete Memoryless Systems*; Cambridge University Press: Cambridge, UK, 2011.
34. Chen, C.; Zhang, J.; Xiang, Y.; Zhou, W.; Oliver, J. Spammers are becoming "Smarter" on Twitter. *IT Prof.* **2016**, *18*, 66–70. [CrossRef]
35. Ma, S.; Sun, X.; Li, W.; Li, S.; Li, W.; Ren, X. Query and output: Generating words by querying distributed word representations for paraphrase generation. *arXiv* **2018**, arXiv:1803.01465.
36. Kim, Y. Convolutional neural networks for sentence classification. *arXiv* **2014**, arXiv:1408.5882.
37. Pennington, J.; Socher, R.; Manning, C.D. GloVe: Global vectors for word representation. In Proceedings of the EMNLP 2014—2014 Conference on Empirical Methods in Natural Language Processing, Doha, Qatar, 25–29 October 2014; pp. 1532–1543.
38. Chung, J.; Gulcehre, C.; Cho, K.; Bengio, Y. Empirical evaluation of gated recurrent neural networks on sequence modeling. *arXiv* **2014**, arXiv:1412.3555.
39. Verma, M.; Sofat, S. Techniques to detect spammers in twitter—A survey. *Int. J. Comput. Appl.* **2014**, *85*. [CrossRef]
40. Zhang, J.; Chen, C.; Chen, X.; Xiang, Y.; Zhou, W. 6 million spam tweets: A large ground truth for timely Twitter spam detection. In Proceedings of the IEEE International Conference on Communications, London, UK, 8–12 June 2015; pp. 7065–7070.
41. Wang, B.; Zubiaga, A.; Liakata, M.; Procter, R. Making the most of tweet-inherent features for social spam detection on Twitter. *arXiv* **2015**, arXiv:1503.07405.
42. Madisetty, S.; Desarkar, M.S. A neural network-based ensemble approach for spam detection in Twitter. *IEEE Trans. Comput. Soc. Syst.* **2018**, *5*, 973–984. [CrossRef]
43. Agarap, A.F. An architecture combining convolutional neural network (CNN) and support vector machine (SVM) for image classification. *arXiv* **2017**, arXiv:1712.03541.

Article

Natural Time Series Parameters Forecasting: Validation of the Pattern-Sequence-Based Forecasting (PSF) Algorithm; A New Python Package

Mayur Kishor Shende [1], Sinan Q. Salih [2,3], Neeraj Dhanraj Bokde [4,*], Miklas Scholz [5,6,7], Atheer Y. Oudah [8,9] and Zaher Mundher Yaseen [10,11,12]

1. Defence Institute of Advanced Technology, Pune 411025, India; mayur.k.shende@gmail.com
2. Computer Science Department, Dijlah University College, Al-Dora, Baghdad 00964, Iraq; sinan.salih@duc.edu.iq
3. Artificial Intelligence Research Unit (AIRU), Dijlah University College, Al-Dora, Baghdad 00964, Iraq
4. Center for Quantitative Genetics and Genomics, Aarhus University, 8000 Aarhus, Denmark
5. Directorate of Engineering the Future, School of Science, Engineering and Environment, The University of Salford, Newton Building, Salford M5 4WT, UK; m.scholz@salford.ac.uk
6. Department of Civil Engineering Science, School of Civil Engineering and the Built Environment, University of Johannesburg, Kingsway Campus, P.O. Box 524, Auckland Park, Johannesburg 2006, South Africa
7. Department of Town Planning, Engineering Networks and Systems, South Ural State University, 76, Lenin Prospekt, 454080 Chelyabinsk, Russia
8. Department of Computer Sciences, College of Education for Pure Science, University of Thi-Qar, Nasiriyah 64001, Iraq; atheer@alayen.edu.iq
9. Scientific Research Center, Al-Ayen University, Thi-Qar 64001, Iraq
10. Department of Earth Sciences and Environment, Faculty of Science and Technology, Universiti Kebangsaan Malaysia, Bangi 43600, Selangor, Malaysia; yaseen@ukm.edu.my
11. Adjunct Research Fellow, USQ's Advanced Data Analytics Research Group, School of Mathematics Physics and Computing, University of Southern Queensland, Springfield, QLD 4350, Australia
12. New Era and Development in Civil Engineering Research Group, Scientific Research Center, Al-Ayen University, Thi-Qar 64001, Iraq
* Correspondence: neerajdhanraj@qgg.au.dk

Abstract: Climate change has contributed substantially to the weather and land characteristic phenomena. Accurate time series forecasting for climate and land parameters is highly essential in the modern era for climatologists. This paper provides a brief introduction to the algorithm and its implementation in Python. The pattern-sequence-based forecasting (PSF) algorithm aims to forecast future values of a univariate time series. The algorithm is divided into two major processes: the clustering of data and prediction. The clustering part includes the selection of an optimum value for the number of clusters and labeling the time series data. The prediction part consists of the selection of a window size and the prediction of future values with reference to past patterns. The package aims to ease the use and implementation of PSF for python users. It provides results similar to the PSF package available in R. Finally, the results of the proposed Python package are compared with results of the PSF and ARIMA methods in R. One of the issues with PSF is that the performance of forecasting result degrades if the time series has positive or negative trends. To overcome this problem difference pattern-sequence-based forecasting (DPSF) was proposed. The Python package also implements the DPSF method. In this method, the time series data are first differenced. Then, the PSF algorithm is applied to this differenced time series. Finally, the original and predicted values are restored by applying the reverse method of the differencing process. The proposed methodology is tested on several complex climate and land processes and its potential is evidenced.

Keywords: forecasting; univariate; time series; Python; PSF

1. Introduction

Time series forecasting is a field of interest in many research and society fields such as energy [1–3], economics [4,5], health [6,7], agriculture [8,9], education [10,11], infrastructure [12,13], defense [14], technology [15], hydrology [16,17], and many others. Time series are generally addressed in terms of stochastic processes in which values are placed at consecutive points in time [18]. Time series forecasting is the process of predicting values of a historical data sequence [19]. In the digitized development, with the increase in extensive historical data, more powerful and cross-platform-compatible forecasting methods are highly desirable [20,21].

Pattern-sequence-based forecasting (PSF) is a univariate time series forecasting method which was proposed in 2011 [22]. It was developed to predict a discrete time series and proposed to use clustering methods to transform a time series into a sequence of labels. To date, several researchers have proposed modifications for its improvement [23–26] and recently, its implementation in the form of an R package was also proposed [27,28]. PSF has been successfully used in various domains including wind speed [29], solar power [26], water demand [13], electricity prices [30], CO_2 emissions [31], and cognitive radio [32].

The PSF algorithm consists of various processes. These processes are broadly categorized into two steps, clustering of data and, based on this clustered data, performing forecasting. The predicted values are appended at the end of the original data and these new data are used to forecast future values. This makes PSF a closed-loop algorithm, which allows PSF to predict values for a longer duration. PSF has the ability to forecast more than one values at the same time, i.e., it deals with arbitrary lengths for the prediction horizon. It must be noted that this algorithm was particularly developed to forecast data which contain some patterns. Figure 1 shows the steps involved in the PSF method.

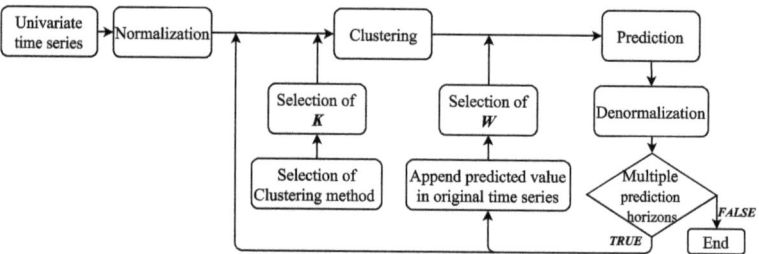

Figure 1. Block diagram of the PSF method (Source: [33]).

The goal of the clustering step is to discover clusters and label them accordingly in the data. It consists of the normalization of the data, the selection of the optimal number of clusters, and applying k-means clustering using the optimum number of clusters. Normalization is an important part of any data processing technique. The formula used to normalize the data is:

$$X'_j = \frac{X_j}{\frac{1}{N}\sum_{i=1}^{N} X_i} \quad (1)$$

where X_j is an input time series and X'_j denotes the normalized value for X_j and $i = 1, \ldots, N$. The k-means clustering technique is used to cluster and label the data. However, k-means requires the number of clusters (k) to be provided as an input. To calculate the optimum value of k, the silhouette index was used. The clustering step outputs the time series as a series of labels which are used for forecasting.

Then, the last "w" labels are selected from the series of labels outputted by the clustering step. This sequence of w labels is searched for in the series of labels. If the sequence is not found, then the search is repeated with the last $(w - 1)$ labels. The selection of the optimum value of w is crucial in order to get accurate prediction results. Formally, the size of the window for which the error in forecasting is minimum during the training process is called the optimum window size. The error function used is shown in (2).

$$\sum_{t \in TS} \|\hat{X}(t) - X(t)\| \tag{2}$$

where $\hat{X}(t)$ is a predicted value at time t, $X(t)$ is the measured data at same time instance, and TS represents the time series under study.

After the selection of the optimum window size (w), the last w values are searched for in a series of labels and labels next to the discovered sequence are stored in a new vector called ES. The data corresponding to these labels from the original time series are retrieved. The future time series value is predicted by averaging the retrieved data from the time series with the expression (3).

$$\hat{X}(t) = \frac{1}{size(ES)} \times \sum_{j=1}^{size(ES)} ES(j) \tag{3}$$

This predicted value is appended to the original time series and the process is repeated for predicting the next value as shown in Figure 2. This allows PSF to make long-term predictions.

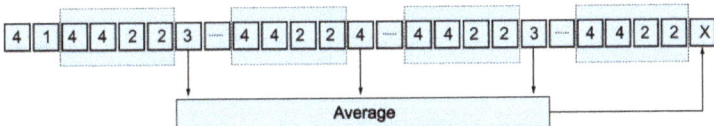

Figure 2. Prediction with PSF algorithm (Source: [27]).

In the current research, the main intention of the current investigation was to develop a new Python package for modeling univariate time series data that are characterized by natural stochasticity. This can contribute remarkably to the best knowledge of monitoring, assessment, and advisable support for decision makers that are interested with such time-series-related problems. Among several time series engineering problems, hydrological time series forecasting is one of the highly attractive topics recently discovered [34–36]. Hydrological time series processes are very complex and stochastic problems that require robust technologies to tackle their complicated mechanisms. Hence, in this research, several hydrological time series examples were tested to validate the proposed methodology.

2. Difference Pattern-Sequence-Based Forecasting (DPSF) Method

The PSF algorithm was particularly developed to forecast data for a time series which contains pattern or is seasonal, thus the prediction error is very small for such time series. However, if the time series follows some trends or is not seasonal, then the error increases. This can be observed in the illustrative examples provided in the later sections. The "nottem" dataset is very seasonal, thus the predictions of PSF are observed to be better than that of ARIMA. However, in the "CO_2" dataset, the result of PSF is not as good as that of ARIMA. This is because the "CO_2" dataset follows an upward trend. The forecasting results with the PSF method are degraded with positive or negative trends. To tackle this problem the DPSF model was proposed [3].

The DPSF method is a modification of the PSF algorithm. The time series is differenced once. These differenced data are then used for prediction using the PSF algorithm. The predicted values are then appended to the differenced time series, which was used for prediction using PSF. Finally, the original time series is attempted to be regenerated using the reverse method of the first-order differencing process.

The DPSF method gives better results for data where positive or negative trends can be observed in the data. However, the PSF method does not work well with such datasets and prefers seasonal datasets. This can also be observed in examples shown in Sections 4.1 and 4.2. An example in Section 4.1 uses a seasonal dataset (*nottem*), where the

PSF results are better than the DPSF results. In Section 4.2, the CO_2 dataset is used, which shows a positive trend. Here the results of DPSF are significantly better than those of PSF.

3. Description of the Python Package for PSF (PSF_Py)

The proposed Python package for PSF (PSF_Py) is available at the Python repository, describing license, version, and required package imports [37]. The package can be installed using command in Listing 1.

Listing 1. Command to install PSF_Py package.

```
pip install PSF_Py
```

The package makes use of "pandas", "numpy", "matplotlib", "sklearn" packages. The various tasks of the processes are accomplished by using various functions, such as psf(), predict(), psf_predict(), optimum_k(), optimum_w(), cluster_labels(), neighbour(), psf_model(), and psf_plot(). The code for all the functions was made available on GitHub [38]. All these functions were made private and are not directly accessible by the user. The user needs to create an object of the class Psf, which takes as inputs the time series, cycle, values for the window size (w), and the number of clusters (k) to be formed. The values of k and w are optional; if not specified by the user, then they are internally calculated using the optimum_k() and optimum_w() functions. Once the PSF model has been created, the predictions can be made using the predict() method. The predict() takes as its input the number of predictions to make (n_ahead). For the DPSF model, the user makes use of the class Dpsf. The remaining process is the same as that of Psf.

After the predictions are made using the predict() method of class Psf, the model can be viewed using the model_print() method. The original time series and predicted values are plotted using the psf_plot() or dpsf_plot() methods. Alternatively, the user can use "matplotlib" functions to plot the time series.

3.1. optimum_k()

The optimum_k function is used to calculate the optimum number of clusters for forecasting. The PSF uses the k-means algorithm to cluster the data, but the algorithm requires the number of clusters as an input. The function takes as inputs the time series and a tuple consisting of the desired values for k. The function performs k-means clustering using KMeans() from the sklearn package, calculates its silhouette score using the "the silhouette_score()" function and returns the value of k for which the score was maximum.

3.2. optimum_w()

The optimum_w function is used to calculate the optimum window size. The window size is a critical parameter for getting accurate predictions. A cross-validation is performed to find the optimum value for the window size. The time series is divided into a training and test set. The test set consists of the last cycle values of the time series and the training set consists of the remaining time series values. PSF is performed on the training set and cycle values are predicted. Then, the error is calculated for the predicted values and on the test set. The error is calculated using the mean absolute error (MAE). The function returns the value of w for which the error is minimum.

The functions for calculating the optimum window size and clustering the data may yield a different result in R and Python. Therefore, the predictions done in R and Python can vary in some cases. Furthermore, the default window values in optimum_w() range from 5 to 20 in Python. In R, they range from 1 to 10. In some cases, it was observed that the optimum number of clusters was calculated more accurately in Python. Overall, the predicted values were very similar to R.

3.3. get_ts()

In the Python package for PSF, some time series are included, namely, "nottem", "AirPassengers", "Nile", "morley", "penguin", "sunspots", and "wineind". It should be noted that the package does not provide the entire data frames (datasets). It only provides a 1D array that consists of the data for the time series. These can be accessed using the get_ts() function, which takes as an input the name of the time series.

3.4. predict()

The predict() method is used to perform the forecasting. This method returns a numpy array of values predicted according to the PSF algorithm (or DPSF algorithm, if the DPSF model is used). The actual calculations take place in the psf_predict() function, which was made private and not intended to be directly used by the user. The predict() method also calculates the optimum values of k and w, in case no values are given by the user, using the optimum_w() and optimum_k() functions described above. If a tuple of values is passed instead of an integer, then the optimum k and w are calculated from those values. Furthermore, the normalization of the data is done in this method.

Some other functions are available to the users. The model_print() function prints the actual time series, predicted values, values of k and w used for predictions, and value of cycle for the time series. This function does not return anything; it only prints the data and parameters. The functions psf_plot() and dpsf_plot() take the PSF model and predicted values as inputs and plot them. The functions make use of the "matplotlib" package.

4. Demonstration

Following several established research works from the literature, proposing a new soft-computing methodology must be validated with real time series datasets [39–42]. The proposed package in the current research was examined on six different time series dataset. The performance of forecasting methods were compared with the root-mean-square error ($RMSE$), mean absolute error (MAE), mean absolute percentage error ($MAPE$), and Nash–Sutcliffe efficiency (NSE) [43,44]. These error metrics are defined in Equations (4)–(7), respectively.

$$RMSE = \sqrt{\frac{1}{N}\sum_{i=1}^{N}|X_i - \hat{X}_i|^2} \quad (4)$$

$$MAE = \frac{1}{N}\sum_{i=1}^{N}|X_i - \hat{X}_i| \quad (5)$$

$$MAPE = \frac{1}{N}\sum_{i=1}^{N}\frac{|X_i - \hat{X}_i|}{X_i} \times 100\% \quad (6)$$

$$NSE = 1 - \frac{\sum_{i=1}^{N}(X_i - \hat{X}_i)^2}{\sum_{i=1}^{N}(X_i - X_{mean})^2} \quad (7)$$

where X_i and $\hat{X}_i$ are the measured and predicted data at time t. X_{mean} is the mean of the measured data and N is the number of predicted values.

For each of the examples demonstrated, the original dataset was divided into training and test data. The number of observation values used for the test data is mentioned in each example. Once the forecasted values were calculated, they were compared against the test data.

4.1. Example 1: Nottem Dataset

In the below example, the "nottem" time series was used for the model training, forecasting, and plotting. It contains the average air temperatures at Nottingham Castle in degrees Fahrenheit over 20 years [45]. The procedure is the same for other univariate time series. Table 1 reveals the statistical characteristics of the time series.

Table 1. Statistical characteristics of the "nottem" dataset.

Mean	Median	Min	Max	SD	Kurtosis	Skewness
280.3	265.5	104.0	622.0	119.9663	−0.429844	0.5710676

The package contains the `get_ts()` function, which can be used to access some univariate time series included in the package using command in Listing 2.

Listing 2. `get_ts()` function to access univariate time series included in the package.

```
# From the package import class PSF, and
# function get_ts() and psf_plot()
>>> from PSF_Py import Psf, get_ts, psf_plot

# Get the Time series 'nottem'
>>> ts = get_ts('nottem')
```

We split the time series into training and test parts. The test contained the last 12 values of the time series and the training part contained the remaining data. A `Psf` model was then created using the training set as shown in Listing 3.

Listing 3. Command to create a `Psf` model.

```
>>> train, test = ts[:len(ts)-12], ts[len(ts)-12:]

# Create a PSF model for prediction
>>> a = Psf(data=train, cycle=12)
```

The model can be printed using the `model_print()` method as shown in Listing 4.

Listing 4. Command to print the model.

```
>>> a.model_print()
Original time-series :
0      40.6
1      40.8
2      44.4
3      46.7
4      54.1
5      58.5
6      57.7
7      56.4
8      54.3
9      50.5
10     42.9
\dots
219    46.6
220    52.4
221    59.0
222    59.6
223    60.4
224    57.0
225    50.7
226    47.8
227    39.2
Length: 228, dtype: float64
k     =  2
w     =  12
cycle =  12
dmin  =  31.3
dmax  =  66.5
type  =  <class 'PSF_Py.psf.Psf'>
```

Then, Listing 5 shows how the actual prediction was performed using this PSF model.

Listing 5. Command to predict using PSF model.

```
# Perform prediction using predict method of
# class Psf.
>>> b = a.predict(n_ahead=12)
>>> b

array([39.62727273, 39.65454545, 41.87272727,
46.25454545, 52.87272727, 58.37272727, 62.40909091,
60.25454545, 56.38, 49.45, 43.02857143, 40.5])
```

where b contains the predicted values.

The model and predictions can be plotted using the psf_plot() function (shown in Listing 6) as shown in Figure 3.

Listing 6. Command to plot the original and predicted values.

```
>>> psf_plot(a, b)
```

A similar procedure was carried out to perform the prediction in R using the PSF library. Several error metrics was calculated for the predicted values and testing set. The performance of Python and R are compared in Table 2 and Figure 4.

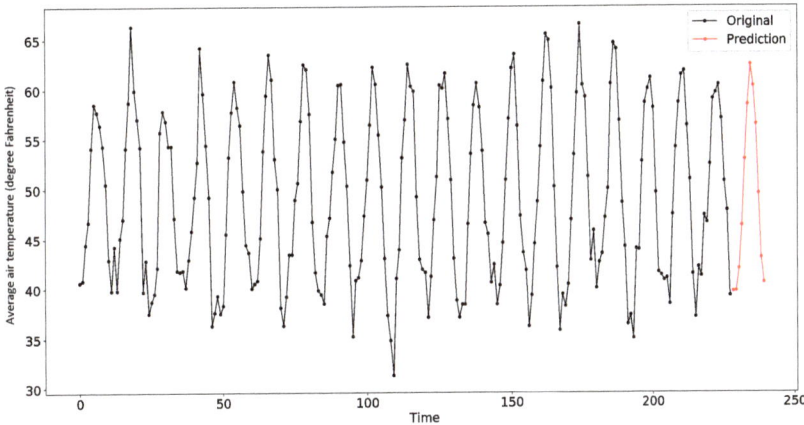

Figure 3. Result of psf_plot() for the "nottem" dataset.

Table 2. Comparison of forecast methods with different error metrics for the "nottem" dataset.

Function	Psf() (Python)	Dpsf() (Python)	psf() (R)	auto.arima() (R)
Models	$(k, w) = (2, 12)$	$(k, w) = (2, 12)$	$(k, w) = (2, 2)$	-
RMSE	1.84	5.27	2.24	2.34
MAE	1.54	4.77	1.94	1.93
MAPE	3.23	9.43	4.14	4.21
NSE	0.94	0.59	0.92	0.91

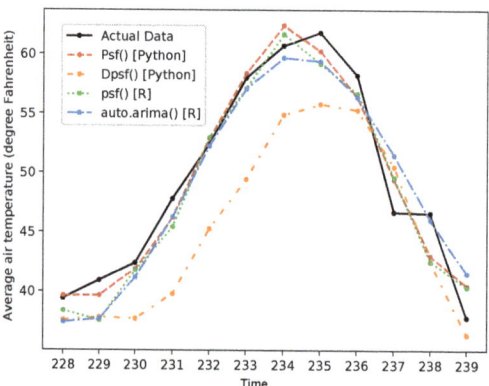

Figure 4. Plot showing the test data and values forecasted using various methods for the "nottem" dataset.

4.2. Example 2: CO_2 Dataset

This example demonstrates the use of the DPSF algorithm. The dataset consisted of atmospheric concentrations of CO_2 expressed in parts per million (ppm) and reported in the preliminary 1997 SIO manometric mole fraction scale [46]. The values for February, March, and April of 1964 were missing and were obtained by interpolating linearly between the values for January and May of 1964. Table 3 contains the statistical characteristics of the time series.

Table 3. Statistical characteristics of the "CO_2" dataset.

Mean	Median	Min	Max	SD	Kurtosis	Skewness
337.1	335.2	313.2	366.8	14.96622	−1.223013	0.2419156

The time series data were divided into training and testing datasets. The training set contained the time series data, excluding the last 12 values. The testing dataset contained the last 12 values. A Dpsf model was created using the training dataset, and the future 12 values were forecasted as shown in Figure 5. The corresponding commands are shown in Listing 7. These predictions were then compared with the testing dataset. The comparisons are provided in Table 4 and Figure 6.

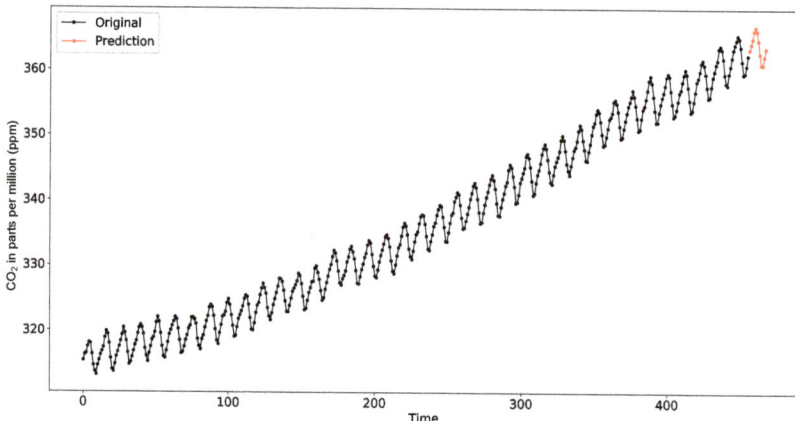

Figure 5. Result of `dpsf_plot()` for the "CO_2" dataset.

Listing 7. Commands to create and use Dpsf model.

```
# Import Dpsf, get_ts(), and dpsf_plot()
# from PSF_Py package
>>> from PSF_Py import Dpsf, dpsf_plot, get_ts

# Load the time series CO2
>>> ts = get_ts('co2')

# Divide the time series into training and testing
>>> train, test = ts[:len(ts)-12], ts[len(ts)-12:]

# Create Dpsf model
>>> a = Dpsf(data=train, cycle=12)

# The created model can be displayed using
# model_print() method
>>> a.model_print()
Original time-series :
0       315.42
1       316.31
2       316.50
3       317.56
4       318.13
5       318.00
6       316.39
7       314.65
8       313.68
9       313.18
10      314.66
\dots
448     365.45
449     365.01
450     363.70
451     361.54
452     359.51
453     359.65
454     360.80
455     362.38
Length: 456, dtype: float64
k = 2
w = 18
cycle = 12
dmin = 313.18
dmax = 365.45
type = <class 'PSF_Py.dpsf.Dpsf'>

# Perform prediction using predict() method
>>> b = a.predict(n_ahead=12)
>>> b
array([363.35347826, 364.19434783, 365.03521739,
366.27304348, 366.79695652, 366.19913043, 364.75913043,
362.73458498, 361.06708498, 361.03143281, 362.2740415,
363.51445817])

# Plot the model and predicted values
>>> dpsf_plot(a,b)
```

Table 4. Comparison of forecast methods with different error metrics for the "CO_2" dataset.

Function	Dpsf() (Python)	Psf() (Python)	psf() (R)	auto.arima() (R)
Models	$(k, w) = (2, 18)$	$(k, w) = (9, 19)$	$(k, w) = (2, 10)$	-
RMSE	0.41	1.48	5.93	1.63
MAE	0.32	9.27	5.91	1.40
MAPE	0.08	2.67	1.62	0.38
NSE	0.95	0.32	−8.15	0.302

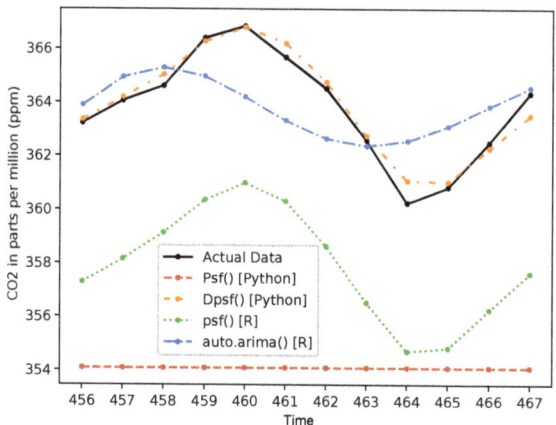

Figure 6. Plot showing the test data and values forecasted using various methods for the "CO_2" dataset.

4.3. Example 3: Water Demand Dataset

The PSF and DPSF algorithms were applied to forecast water demand on the given dataset. Investigating such high complex time series data is highly important for water management [47]. Table 5 contains the statistical characteristics of the time series.

Table 5. Statistical characteristics of the "Water Demand" dataset.

Mean	Median	Min	Max	SD	Kurtosis	Skewness
18.97	17.41	0.93	45.98	7.988099	0.3019151	0.6812421

Different error metrics comparison is listed in Table 6. The error for the `Psf()` function in python was found to be better than that of the other algorithms adopted in this study. The dataset and predictions using `Psf()` and `Dpsf()` are plotted in Figures 7 and 8. Further, the comparison of forecasted values using various methods are shown in Figure 9.

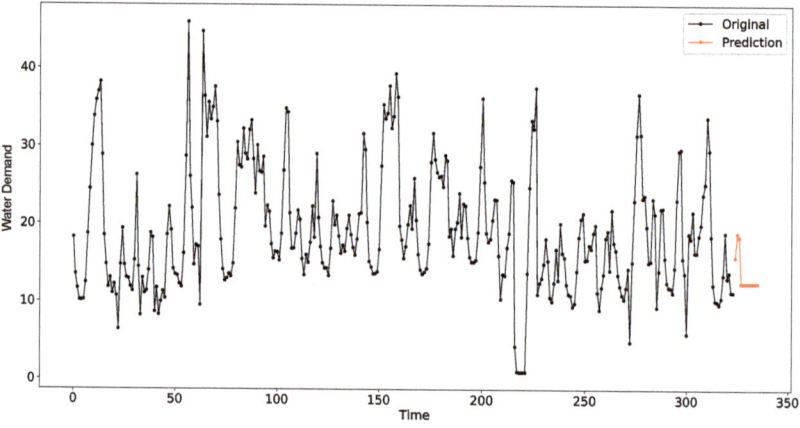

Figure 7. Result of `psf_plot()` for the "Water Demand" dataset.

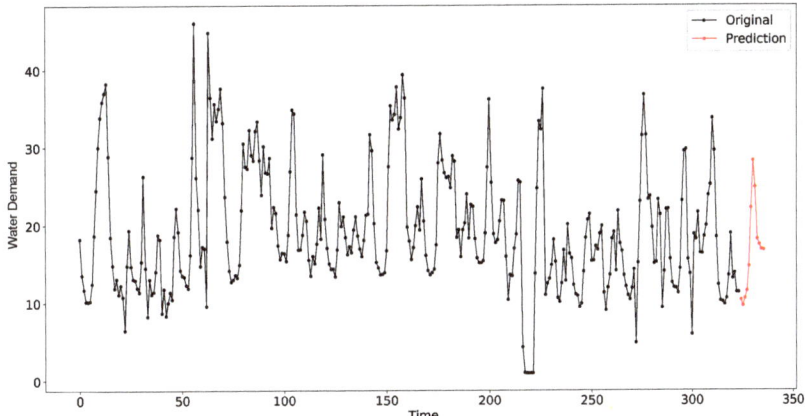

Figure 8. Result of `dpsf_plot()` for the "Water Demand" dataset.

Table 6. Comparison of forecast methods with different error metrics for the "Water Demand" dataset.

Function	Dpsf( ) (Python)	Psf( ) (Python)	psf( ) (R)	auto.arima( ) (R)
RMSE	6.16	5.92	6.45	7.55
MAE	4.98	4.37	5.07	5.93
MAPE	45.69	49.55	70.99	86.58
NSE	−1.79	−5.22	−0.17	−0.61

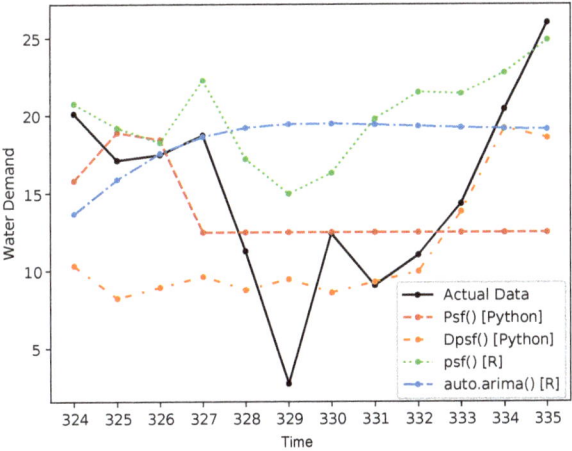

Figure 9. Plot showing the test data and values forecasted using various methods for the "Water Demand" dataset.

4.4. Example 4: Total Solar Radiation Dataset

Among several climatological time series, total solar radiation is one of the essential climatological processes. Providing a robust soft-computing methodology for solar radiation can contribute remarkably to clean and friendly sources of energy [48]. The dataset consisted of daily solar radiation readings for year 2010 to year 2018 at Baker station in North Dakota. Before applying the algorithms, the dataset was reduced by taking the mean of the values for each month. Table 7 presents the statistical characteristics of the time series. Performance of various methods are tabulated in Table 8. Results of `psf_plot()` and `dpsf_plot()` for the

"Total Solar Radiation" dataset are shown in Figures 10 and 11. Further, the comparison of forecasted values with different methods are shown in Figure 12.

Table 7. Statistical characteristics of the "Total Solar Radiation" dataset.

Mean	Median	Min	Max	SD	Kurtosis	Skewness
325.11	296.90	16.71	750.09	188.0211	−0.7063935	0.5369928

The error for `Psf()` was significantly less the that for `auto.arima()` and `Dpsf()`. The errors are listed in Table 8.

Table 8. Comparison of forecast methods with different error metrics for "Total Solar Radiation" dataset.

Function	Dpsf() (Python)	Psf() (Python)	psf() (R)	auto.arima() (R)
RMSE	446.48	121.84	137.73	233.17
MAE	345.22	108.20	104.66	197.16
MAPE	338.73	52.37	56.56	124.71
NSE	−4.58	0.25	0.63	−0.043

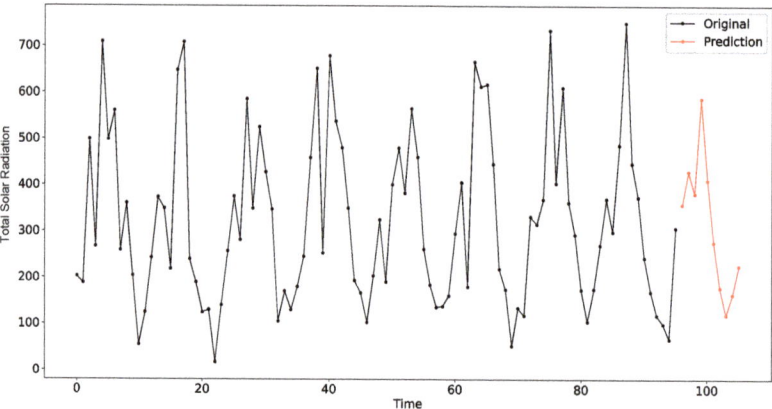

Figure 10. Result of `psf_plot()` for the "Total Solar Radiation" dataset.

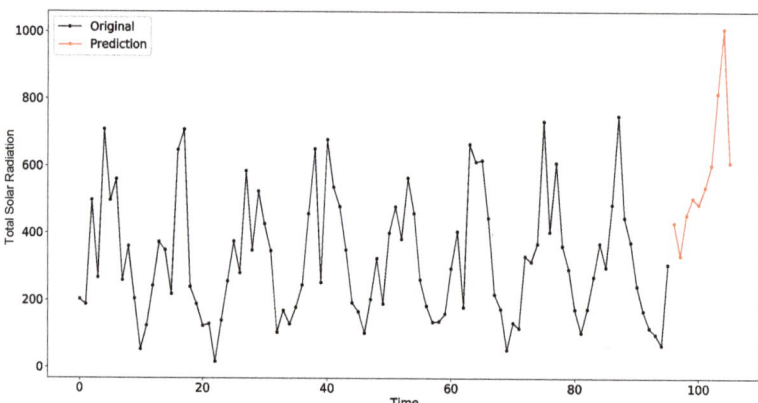

Figure 11. Result of `dpsf_plot()` for the "Total Solar Radiation" dataset.

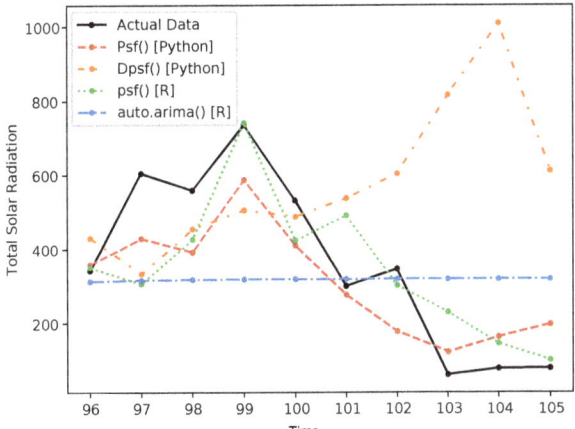

Figure 12. Plot showing the test data and values forecasted using various methods for the "Total Solar Radiation" dataset.

4.5. Example 5: Average Bare Soil Temperature

Soil temperature is an important process that is related to geoscience engineering [49]. Based on the factual mechanism, soil temperature has highly nonstationary features due to the influence of the soil morphology, climate, and hydrology information [50,51]. Hence, taking the soil temperature as a time series forecasting is highly useful for multiple geoscience engineering applications [52]. The data were obtained from the same region as in Example 4 ("Baker station") and using the same data span, "2010–2018". A similar modeling procedure was implemented as in Section 4.4. Table 9 reports the statistical characteristics of the soil temperature time series, and the performance of various methods are tabulated in Table 10. Results of `psf_plot()` and `dpsf_plot()` for the "Average Bare Soil Temperature" dataset are shown in Figures 13 and 14. Further, the comparison of forecasted values with different methods are shown in Figure 15.

Table 9. Statistical characteristics of the "Average Bare Soil Temperature".

Mean	Median	Min	Max	SD	Kurtosis	Skewness
46.65	42.38	21.48	78.21	17.18163	−1.395386	0.355737

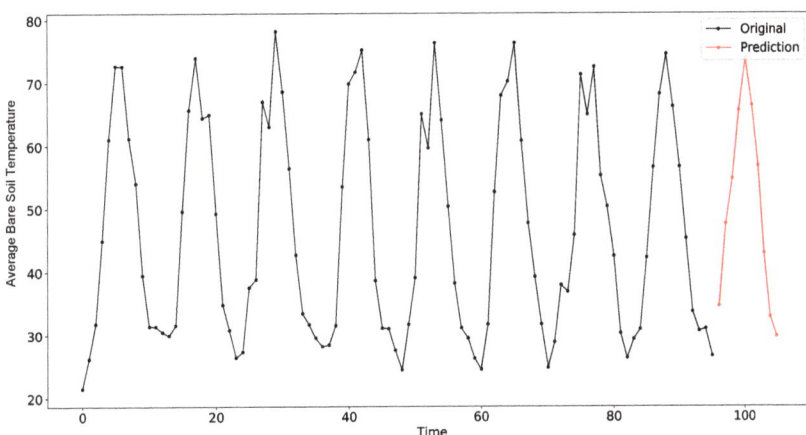

Figure 13. Result of `psf_plot()` for the "Average Bare Soil Temperature" dataset.

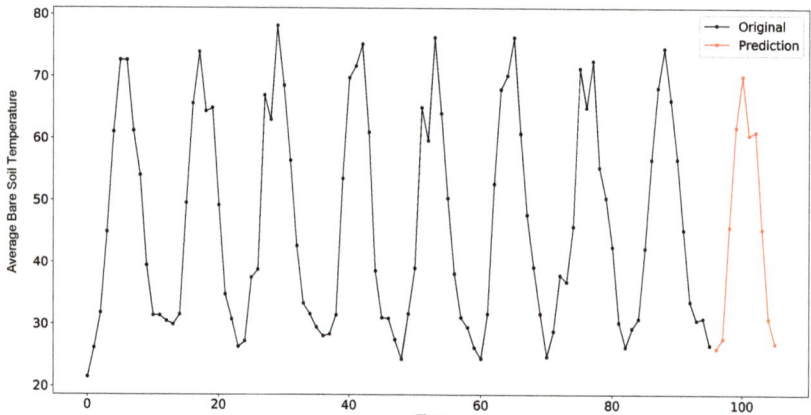

Figure 14. Result of `dpsf_plot()` for the "Average Bare Soil Temperature" dataset.

Table 10. Comparison of forecast methods with different error metrics for the "Average Bare Soil Temperature" dataset.

Function	Dpsf( ) (Python)	Psf( ) (Python)	psf( ) (R)	auto.arima( ) (R)
RMSE	12.70	7.92	9.38	8.75
MAE	9.40	5.79	7.69	7.32
MAPE	18.23	10.85	15.42	14.39
NSE	0.37	0.70	0.69	0.73

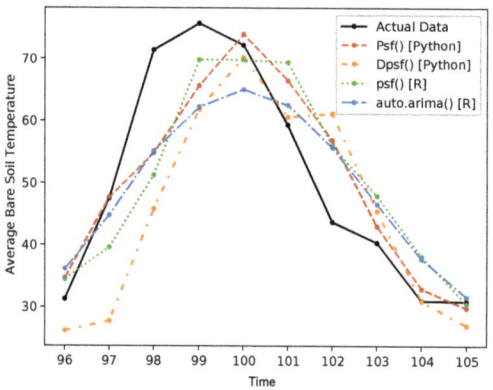

Figure 15. Plot showing the test data and values forecasted using various methods for the "Average Bare Soil Temperature" dataset.

4.6. Example 6: Average Temperature

The final example reported in this research is modeling the air temperature. Having a reliable and robust technique for air temperature is very essential for diverse water resources and hydrological processes [53,54], for instance, in agriculture, water body evaporation, crops production, etc. [55]. Similar to Examples 4 and 5, the air temperature data were from the same station, region, and data span. For these data, the procedure followed was the same as in Examples 4 and 5. Table 11 indicates the statistical characteristics of the time series. The performance of various methods are tabulated in Table 12. Result of psf_plot() for the "Average Temperature" dataset are shown in Figure 16. Further, the comparison of forecasted values with different methods are shown in Figure 17.

Table 11. Statistical characteristics of the "Average Temperature" dataset.

Mean	Median	Min	Max	SD	Kurtosis	Skewness
39.48	43.47	−15.70	77.85	24.23293	−0.85042	−0.4995846

Table 12. Comparison of forecast methods with different error metrics for the "Average Temperature" dataset.

Function	Psf( ) (Python)	Dpsf( ) (Python)	psf( ) (R)	auto.arima( ) (R)
RMSE	7.83	85.14	12.34	10.87
MAE	6.41	80.91	9.62	8.83
MAPE	22.29	207.16	22.03	22.03
NSE	0.69	−35.81	0.61	0.69

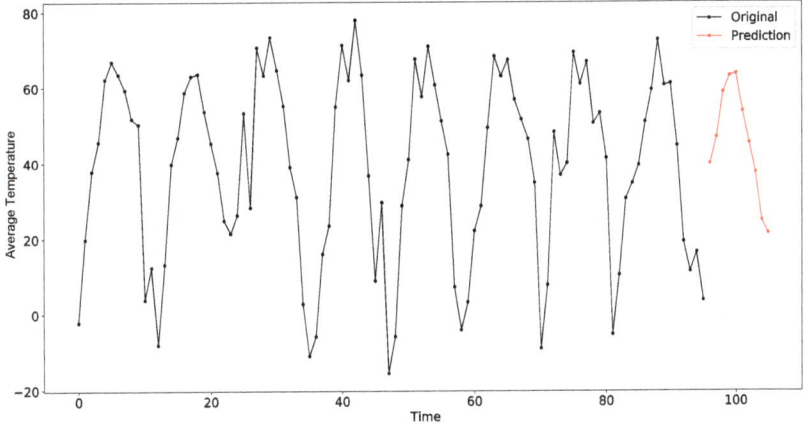

Figure 16. Plot showing result of psf_plot() for the "Average Temperature" dataset.

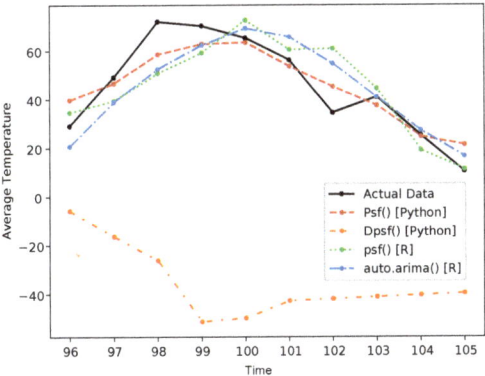

Figure 17. Plot showing the test data and values forecasted using various methods for the "Average Temperature" dataset.

5. Discussion and Conclusions

This paper described the PSF_Py package in detail and demonstrated its use for implementing the PSF and DPSF algorithms for diverse applications on real time series forecasting datasets. The package makes it very easy to make predictions using the PSF algorithm. The syntax is similar to that in R and is very easy to understand. The examples shown above suggested that the results from the Python package were comparable to those in R. The values of the window size and the number of clusters may differ in both packages. The algorithm worked exceptionally well for the time series containing periodic patterns. The forecasting error of the DPSF method, implemented in the proposed package, was much smaller and better than the benchmark ARIMA model. The complexity of a model is another critical aspect besides its accuracy. We compared the time and space complexities of the models in case studies with the GuessCompx tool. The GuessCompx tool [56,57] empirically estimates the computational complexity of a function in terms of Big-O notations. It computes multiple samples of increasing sizes from the given dataset and estimates the best-fit complexity according to the "leave-one-out mean squared error (LOO-MSE)" approach. The "nottem" dataset was used to calculate the complexities. The results of the tool are summarized in Table 13, and it shows that both PSF and DPSF models are computationally efficient and consumes an optimum amount of memory to achieve a better accuracy.

Table 13. Estimated complexities according to the GuessCompx tool [56].

	Psf()(Python)/psf()(R)	Dpsf( ) (Python)	auto.arima( ) (R)
Time Complexity	$\mathcal{O}(\log n)$	$\mathcal{O}(\log n)$	$\mathcal{O}(n^3)$
Space Complexity	$\mathcal{O}(\log n)$	$\mathcal{O}(\log n)$	$\mathcal{O}(1)$

It is worth to mention that this research proposed a reliable and robust computational technique that can be implemented for online and offline forecasting for diverse hydrological and climatological applications [58,59]. In future work, other hybrid models [33,60] of the PSF method can be incorporated into the proposed Python package, with which further improved accuracy in forecasting can be targeted. In addition, the application of the proposed package could be extended to several new data-driven research domains. Further, other hydrological processes dataset or other engineering time series data could be investigated for the possibility to generalize the proposed package.

Author Contributions: Conceptualization, M.K.S., S.Q.S., M.S. and N.D.B.; methodology, M.K.S., S.Q.S., M.S. and N.D.B.; software, M.K.S., A.Y.O., Z.M.Y. and N.D.B.; validation, Z.M.Y., M.S., A.Y.O. and N.D.B.; formal analysis, M.K.S., S.Q.S., Z.M.Y., M.S., A.Y.O. and N.D.B.; investigation, M.K.S., S.Q.S., Z.M.Y., M.S., A.Y.O. and N.D.B.; resources, S.Q.S., Z.M.Y., M.S., A.Y.O. and N.D.B.; data curation, M.K.S., S.Q.S., Z.M.Y., A.Y.O. and N.D.B.; writing—original draft preparation, M.K.S., S.Q.S., Z.M.Y., M.S., A.Y.O. and N.D.B.; writing—review and editing, M.K.S., S.Q.S., Z.M.Y., M.S., A.Y.O. and N.D.B.; visualization, M.K.S. and N.D.B.; supervision, Z.M.Y., M.S., A.Y.O. and N.D.B.; project administration, Z.M.Y., M.S., A.Y.O. and N.D.B.; funding acquisition, Z.M.Y., N.D.B. and M.S. All authors have read and agreed to the published version of the manuscript.

Funding: This work was financially predominantly supported by WATERAGRI (European Union Horizon 2020 research and innovation program under Grant Agreement Number 858375).

Institutional Review Board Statement: Not applicable.

Informed Consent Statement: Not applicable.

Data Availability Statement: The data presented in this study are available on request from the corresponding author.

Conflicts of Interest: The authors declare no conflict of interest.

Abbreviations

The following abbreviations are used in this manuscript:

1D	One-dimensional
ARIMA	Autoregressive integrated moving average
CO2	Carbon dioxide
DPSF	Differenced pattern-sequence-based forecasting
MAE	Mean absolute error
MAPE	Mean absolute percentage error
Max	Maximum value
Min	Minimum value
NSE	Nash–Sutcliffe efficiency
PSF	Pattern-sequence-based forecasting
RMSE	Root-mean-square error
SD	Standard deviation

References

1. Faskari, S.A.; Ojim, G.; Falope, T.; Abdullahi, Y.B.; Abba, S. A Novel Machine Learning based Computing Algorithm in Modeling of Soiled Photovoltaic Module. *Knowl.-Based Eng. Sci.* **2022**, *3*, 28–36.
2. Bokde, N.; Feijóo, A.; Villanueva, D.; Kulat, K. A review on hybrid empirical mode decomposition models for wind speed and wind power prediction. *Energies* **2019**, *12*, 254. [CrossRef]
3. Bokde, N.; Feijóo, A.; Kulat, K. Analysis of differencing and decomposition preprocessing methods for wind speed prediction. *Appl. Soft Comput.* **2018**, *71*, 926–938. [CrossRef]
4. Cao, J.; Li, Z.; Li, J. Financial time series forecasting model based on CEEMDAN and LSTM. *Phys. A Stat. Mech. Appl.* **2019**, *519*, 127–139. [CrossRef]
5. Arce, P.; Antognini, J.; Kristjanpoller, W.; Salinas, L. Fast and Adaptive Cointegration Based Model for Forecasting High Frequency Financial Time Series. *Comput. Econ.* **2019**, *54*, 99–112. [CrossRef]
6. Shih, H.; Rajendran, S. Comparison of time series methods and machine learning algorithms for forecasting Taiwan Blood Services Foundation's blood supply. *J. Healthc. Eng.* **2019**, *2019*, 6123745. [CrossRef]
7. Vázquez, M.; Melin, P.; Prado-Arechiga, G. Hybrid Neural-Fuzzy Modeling and Classification System for Blood Pressure Level Affectation. In *Hybrid Intelligent Systems in Control, Pattern Recognition and Medicine*; Springer: Berlin/Heidelberg, Germany, 2020; pp. 257–269.
8. Mithiya, D.; Datta, L.; Mandal, K. Time Series Analysis and Forecasting of Oilseeds Production in India: Using Autoregressive Integrated Moving Average and Group Method of Data Handling–Neural Network. *Asian J. Agric. Ext. Econ. Sociol.* **2019**, *30*, 1–14. [CrossRef]
9. Paliwal, V.; Ghare, A.D.; Mirajkar, A.B.; Bokde, N.D.; Feijoo Lorenzo, A.E. Computer Modeling for the Operation Optimization of Mula Reservoir, Upper Godavari Basin, India, Using the Jaya Algorithm. *Sustainability* **2020**, *12*, 84. [CrossRef]
10. Nguyen-Huy, T.; Deo, R.C.; Khan, S.; Devi, A.; Adeyinka, A.A.; Apan, A.A.; Yaseen, Z.M. Student Performance Predictions for Advanced Engineering Mathematics Course With New Multivariate Copula Models. *IEEE Access* **2022**, *10*, 45112–45136. [CrossRef]
11. Li, M.; Hinnov, L.; Kump, L. Acycle: Time-series analysis software for paleoclimate research and education. *Comput. Geosci.* **2019**, *127*, 12–22. [CrossRef]
12. Gonzalez-Vidal, A.; Jimenez, F.; Gomez-Skarmeta, A.F. A methodology for energy multivariate time series forecasting in smart buildings based on feature selection. *Energy Build.* **2019**, *196*, 71–82. [CrossRef]
13. Gupta, A.; Bokde, N.; Kulat, K. Hybrid leakage management for water network using PSF algorithm and soft computing techniques. *Water Resour. Manag.* **2018**, *32*, 1133–1151. [CrossRef]
14. Kim, J.; Lee, H. A study on predictive model for forecasting anti-aircraft missile spare parts demand based on machine learning. *Korean Data Inf. Sci. Soc.* **2019**, *30*, 587–596.
15. Bokde, N.; Beck, M.W.; Álvarez, F.M.; Kulat, K. A novel imputation methodology for time series based on pattern sequence forecasting. *Pattern Recognit. Lett.* **2018**, *116*, 88–96. [CrossRef]
16. Arikan, B.B.; Jiechen, L.; Sabbah, I.I.; Ewees, A.; Homsi, R.; Sulaiman, S.O. Dew Point Time Series Forecasting at the North Dakota. *Knowl.-Based Eng. Sci.* **2021**, *2*, 24–34. [CrossRef]
17. Cui, F.; Salih, S.Q.; Choubin, B.; Bhagat, S.K.; Samui, P.; Yaseen, Z.M. Newly explored machine learning model for river flow time series forecasting at Mary River, Australia. *Environ. Monit. Assess.* **2020**, *192*, 1–15. [CrossRef]
18. Bokde, N.D.; Feijóo, A.; Al-Ansari, N.; Yaseen, Z.M. A comparison between reconstruction methods for generation of synthetic time series applied to wind speed simulation. *IEEE Access* **2019**, *7*, 135386–135398. [CrossRef]
19. De Gooijer, J.G.; Hyndman, R.J. 25 years of time series forecasting. *Int. J. Forecast.* **2006**, *22*, 443–473. [CrossRef]
20. Zhang, G.P. Time series forecasting using a hybrid ARIMA and neural network model. *Neurocomputing* **2003**, *50*, 159–175. [CrossRef]

21. Hu, H.; Zhang, J.; Li, T. A Comparative Study of VMD-Based Hybrid Forecasting Model for Nonstationary Daily Streamflow Time Series. *Complexity* **2020**, *2020*, 4064851. [CrossRef]
22. Alvarez, F.M.; Troncoso, A.; Riquelme, J.C.; Ruiz, J.S.A. Energy time series forecasting based on pattern sequence similarity. *IEEE Trans. Knowl. Data Eng.* **2010**, *23*, 1230–1243. [CrossRef]
23. Jin, C.H.; Pok, G.; Park, H.W.; Ryu, K.H. Improved pattern sequence-based forecasting method for electricity load. *IEEJ Trans. Electr. Electron. Eng.* **2014**, *9*, 670–674. [CrossRef]
24. Shen, W.; Babushkin, V.; Aung, Z.; Woon, W.L. An ensemble model for day-ahead electricity demand time series forecasting. In Proceedings of the Fourth International Conference on Future Energy Systems, ACM, Berkeley, CA, USA, 21–24 May 2013; pp. 51–62.
25. Koprinska, I.; Rana, M.; Troncoso, A.; Martínez-Álvarez, F. Combining pattern sequence similarity with neural networks for forecasting electricity demand time series. In Proceedings of the 2013 International Joint Conference on Neural Networks (IJCNN), Dallas, TX, USA, 4–9 August 2013; pp. 1–8.
26. Fujimoto, Y.; Hayashi, Y. Pattern sequence-based energy demand forecast using photovoltaic energy records. In Proceedings of the 2012 International Conference on Renewable Energy Research and Applications (ICRERA), Nagasaki, Japan, 11–14 November 2012; pp. 1–6.
27. Bokde, N.; Asencio-Cortés, G.; Martínez-Álvarez, F.; Kulat, K. PSF: Introduction to R Package for Pattern Sequence Based Forecasting Algorithm. *R J.* **2017**, *9*, 324–333. [CrossRef]
28. Bokde, N.; Asencio-Cortés, G.; Martínez-Álvarez, F. *PSF: Forecasting of Univariate Time Series Using the Pattern Sequence-Based Forecasting (PSF) Algorithm*, R Package Version 0.4; R Foundation for Statistical Computing: Vienna, Austria, 2017.
29. Bokde, N.; Troncoso, A.; Asencio-Cortés, G.; Kulat, K.; Martínez-Álvarez, F. Pattern sequence similarity based techniques for wind speed forecasting. In Proceedings of the International Work-Conference on Time Series (ITISE), Granada, Spain, 27–29 June 2017; pp. 18–20.
30. Bokde, N.; Tranberg, B.; Andresen, G.B. A graphical approach to carbon-efficient spot market scheduling for Power-to-X applications. *Energy Convers. Manag.* **2020**, *224*, 113461. [CrossRef]
31. Bokde, N.D.; Tranberg, B.; Andresen, G.B. Short-term CO2 emissions forecasting based on decomposition approaches and its impact on electricity market scheduling. *Appl. Energy* **2021**, *281*, 116061. [CrossRef]
32. Patil, J.; Bokde, N.; Mishra, S.K.; Kulat, K. PSF-Based Spectrum Occupancy Prediction in Cognitive Radio. In *Advanced Engineering Optimization Through Intelligent Techniques*; Springer: Berlin/Heidelberg, Germany, 2020; pp. 609–619.
33. Bokde, N.; Feijóo, A.; Al-Ansari, N.; Tao, S.; Yaseen, Z.M. The hybridization of ensemble empirical mode decomposition with forecasting models: Application of short-term wind speed and power modeling. *Energies* **2020**, *13*, 1666. [CrossRef]
34. Song, T.; Ding, W.; Liu, H.; Wu, J.; Zhou, H.; Chu, J. Uncertainty Quantification in Machine Learning Modeling for Multi-Step Time Series Forecasting: Example of Recurrent Neural Networks in Discharge Simulations. *Water* **2020**, *12*, 912. [CrossRef]
35. Niu, W.J.; Feng, Z.K.; Chen, Y.B.; Zhang, H.R.; Cheng, C.T. Annual streamflow time series prediction using extreme learning machine based on gravitational search algorithm and variational mode decomposition. *J. Hydrol. Eng.* **2020**, *25*, 04020008. [CrossRef]
36. Mazher, A. Visualization Framework for High-Dimensional Spatio-Temporal Hydrological Gridded Datasets using Machine-Learning Techniques. *Water* **2020**, *12*, 590. [CrossRef]
37. PSF_Py. Python Package Version 0.1. Available online: https://pypi.org/project/PSF-Py/ (accessed on 1 December 2021).
38. GitHub PSF_Py. Available online: https://github.com/Mayur1009/PSF_py (accessed on 31 December 2019).
39. Hyndman, R.J.; Khandakar, Y. *Automatic Time Series for Forecasting: The Forecast Package for R*; Number 6/07; Department of Econometrics and Business Statistics, Monash University: Victoria, Australia, 2007.
40. Charte, F.; Vico, A.; Pérez-Godoy, M.D.; Rivera, A.J. predtoolsTS: R package for streamlining time series forecasting. *Prog. Artif. Intell.* **2019**, *8*, 505–510. [CrossRef]
41. Bokde, N.D.; Yaseen, Z.M.; Andersen, G.B. ForecastTB—An R Package as a Test-Bench for Time Series Forecasting—Application of Wind Speed and Solar Radiation Modeling. *Energies* **2020**, *13*, 2578. [CrossRef]
42. Shende, M.K.; Feijóo-Lorenzo, A.E.; Bokde, N.D. cleanTS: Automated (AutoML) tool to clean univariate time series at microscales. *Neurocomputing* **2022**, *500*, 155–176. [CrossRef]
43. Omeje, O.E.; Maccido, H.S.; Badamasi, Y.A.; Abba, S.I. Performance of Hybrid Neuro-Fuzzy Model for Solar Radiation Simulation at Abuja, Nigeria: A Correlation Based Input Selection Technique. *Knowl.-Based Eng. Sci.* **2021**, *2*, 54–66.
44. Yaseen, Z.M. An insight into machine learning models era in simulating soil, water bodies and adsorption heavy metals: Review, challenges and solutions. *Chemosphere* **2021**, *277*, 130126. [CrossRef]
45. Anderson, O. The Box-Jenkins approach to time series analysis. *RAIRO-Oper. Res.* **1977**, *11*, 3–29. [CrossRef]
46. Keeling, C.D.; Whorf, T.P. Scripps Institution of Oceanogra-phy (SIO) University of California, La Jolla. Data 2000. Available online: http://cdiac.esd.ornl.gov/trends/co2/sio-mlo.htm (accessed on 1 December 2021).
47. Abd Rahman, N.; Muhammad, N.S.; Abdullah, J.; Wan Mohtar, W.H.M. Model performance indicator of aging pipes in a domestic water supply distribution network. *Water* **2019**, *11*, 2378. [CrossRef]
48. Sharafati, A.; Khosravi, K.; Khosravinia, P.; Ahmed, K.; Salman, S.A.; Yaseen, Z.M.; Shahid, S. The potential of novel data mining models for global solar radiation prediction. *Int. J. Environ. Sci. Technol.* **2019**, *16*, 7147–7164. [CrossRef]
49. Razali, S.F.M.; Wahab, J.A.; Mukhlisin, M.; Arshad, I.; Mohamed, Z.S. Effectiveness of Electrical Capacitance Volume Tomography Method in Soil Water Content Measurement. *J. Teknol.* **2013**, *65*, 55–59

50. Guo, L.; Fu, P.; Shi, T.; Chen, Y.; Zhang, H.; Meng, R.; Wang, S. Mapping field-scale soil organic carbon with unmanned aircraft system-acquired time series multispectral images. *Soil Tillage Res.* **2020**, *196*, 104477. [CrossRef]
51. Penghui, L.; Ewees, A.A.; Beyaztas, B.H.; Qi, C.; Salih, S.Q.; Al-Ansari, N.; Bhagat, S.K.; Yaseen, Z.M.; Singh, V.P. Metaheuristic Optimization Algorithms Hybridized With Artificial Intelligence Model for Soil Temperature Prediction: Novel Model. *IEEE Access* **2020**, *8*, 51884–51904. [CrossRef]
52. Wei, X.; Zhang, L.; Yang, H.Q.; Zhang, L.; Yao, Y.P. Machine learning for pore-water pressure time-series prediction: Application of recurrent neural networks. *Geosci. Front.* **2020**, *12*, 453–467. [CrossRef]
53. Naganna, S.R.; Deka, P.C.; Ghorbani, M.A.; Biazar, S.M.; Al-Ansari, N.; Yaseen, Z.M. Dew point temperature estimation: application of artificial intelligence model integrated with nature-inspired optimization algorithms. *Water* **2019**, *11*, 742. [CrossRef]
54. Nearing, G.S.; Kratzert, F.; Sampson, A.K.; Pelissier, C.S.; Klotz, D.; Frame, J.M.; Prieto, C.; Gupta, H.V. What role does hydrological science play in the age of machine learning? *Water Resour. Res.* **2020**, *57*, e2020WR028091. [CrossRef]
55. Azad, A.; Kashi, H.; Farzin, S.; Singh, V.P.; Kisi, O.; Karami, H.; Sanikhani, H. Novel approaches for air temperature prediction: A comparison of four hybrid evolutionary fuzzy models. *Meteorol. Appl.* **2020**, *27*, e1817. [CrossRef]
56. Agenis-Nevers, M.; Bokde, N.D.; Yaseen, Z.M.; Shende, M.K. An empirical estimation for time and memory algorithm complexities: Newly developed R package. *Multimed. Tools Appl.* **2021**, *80*, 2997–3015. [CrossRef]
57. Agenis, M.; Bokde, N. *GuessCompx: Empirically Estimates Algorithm Complexity*, R Package Version 1.0.3; R Foundation for Statistical Computing: Vienna, Austria, 2019.
58. Ozkan, M.B.; Karagoz, P. Data mining-based upscaling approach for regional wind power forecasting: Regional statistical hybrid wind power forecast technique (RegionalSHWIP). *IEEE Access* **2019**, *7*, 171790–171800. [CrossRef]
59. Zsoter, E.; Cloke, H.; Stephens, E.; de Rosnay, P.; Muñoz-Sabater, J.; Prudhomme, C.; Pappenberger, F. How well do operational Numerical Weather Prediction configurations represent hydrology? *J. Hydrometeorol.* **2019**, *20*, 1533–1552. [CrossRef]
60. Bokde, N.; Feijóo, A.; Villanueva, D.; Kulat, K. A Novel and Alternative Approach for Direct and Indirect Wind-Power Prediction Methods. *Energies* **2018**, *11*, 2923. [CrossRef]

Article

Identification of Mobility Patterns of Clusters of City Visitors: An Application of Artificial Intelligence Techniques to Social Media Data

Jonathan Ayebakuro Orama [1,*], Assumpció Huertas [2], Joan Borràs [1], Antonio Moreno [3] and Salvador Anton Clavé [1,4]

1. Eurecat, Centre Tecnològic de Catalunya, C/Joanot Martorell, 15, 43480 Vila-Seca, Spain; joan.borras@eurecat.org (J.B.); salvador.anton@urv.cat (S.A.C.)
2. Department of Communication, Universitat Rovira i Virgili, Av. Catalunya, 35, 43002 Tarragona, Spain; sunsi.huertas@urv.cat
3. Intelligent Technologies for Advanced Knowledge Acquisition (ITAKA) Research Group, Escola Tècnica Superior d'Enginyeria, Departament d'Enginyeria Informàtica i Matemàtiques, Universitat Rovira i Virgili, Av. Països Catalans, 26, 43007 Tarragona, Spain; antonio.moreno@urv.cat
4. Department of Geography, Universitat Rovira i Virgili, C/Joanot Martorell, 15, 43480 Vila-Seca, Catalonia, Spain
* Correspondence: jonathan.orama@eurecat.org; Tel.: +34-674-885-859

Abstract: In order to enhance tourists' experiences, Destination Management Organizations need to know who their tourists are, their travel preferences, and their flows around the destination. The study develops a methodology that, through the application of Artificial Intelligence techniques to social media data, creates clusters of tourists according to their mobility and visiting preferences at the destination. The applied method improves the knowledge about the different mobility patterns of tourists (the most visited points and the main flows between them within a destination) depending on who they are and what their preferences are. Clustering tourists by their travel mobility permits uncovering much more information about them and their preferences than previous studies. This knowledge will allow DMOs and tourism service providers to offer personalized services and information, to attract specific types of tourists to certain points of interest, to create new routes, or to enhance public transport services.

Keywords: mobility patterns; social media data; artificial intelligence; tourist clusters; tourist flows

1. Introduction

Technological evolution has brought changes in tourists and their behavior [1–3], and it has catalyzed new information challenges for destinations. In this evolution, some destinations have started to become smart by integrating technological infrastructures and end-user devices [4–6]. However, the fulfillment of two of the main objectives of smart destinations, namely the enhancement of tourists' experiences and the improvement of their management, is still far from complete, and results from the destinations' efforts remain largely unreported [7]. Progress in this area requires Destination Management Organizations (DMOs) to know who their tourists are, what needs and travel preferences they have, what they visit the most, and which are their mobility patterns and flows around the destination [8].

Technological evolution has allowed some Destination Management Organizations to start to maintain personalized and real-time exchange of information with tourists [9] and, at the same time, to collect vast amounts of information from them (big data). The analysis of these data permits offering them even more personalized services [10,11] at the moment and place they need it [12,13]. This two-way communication between tourists and

DMOs helps to generate more satisfactory tourist experiences [5,14,15] and to improve the destination's management [16].

Many studies have focused on knowing who are the visitors of a destination [17]. These studies have classified tourists in clusters or profiles depending on their travel preferences and behaviors [18,19]. Some studies have analyzed the acceptance of technology by tourists [20], while others have focused on their degree of connectivity during the trip [21,22]. To find out their preferences and behaviors, some authors have analyzed their information searches during the trip [23–25] and others their movements at the destination (flow analysis) through GPS or other smart technologies [26,27]. Knowing the mobility patterns of tourists is one of the most important issues for the development of tourism planning and destination management [28,29].

Social media has brought a great transformation in the related tourism research [8,30,31]. Social media analytics use natural language processing and machine learning techniques to analyze social media content [32]. Geotagged Social Media Data (GSMD) offer information about tourist behavior, travel route choices, emotions, and satisfaction level [33]. Nowadays, technology and analytical tools are evolving and social media analytics allow us to know the movements or flows of tourists [34]. Twitter is a platform with global coverage, very useful for tourist mobility analysis [35] that even allows us to determine the most visited POIs (Points of Interest) at destinations [36].

Existing research in spatial data or mobility/flow analysis through GSMD still offers little information about mobility patterns of different sub-groups or clusters of tourists [37]. Nevertheless, the more DMOs know about the mobility, preferences and behavior of tourists, the more they will be able to offer personalized services, packages and information [11,38]. Additionally, the more they can automatize processes to obtain information from open social media data, the more efficient they will be when providing personalized information throughout travel recommender systems [39].

Therefore, the aim of the study is to develop a methodology that, through the application of Artificial Intelligence techniques to geotagged social media data, creates clusters of tourists according to their mobility patterns and visiting preferences at the destination. The analytical and managerial goal is to know the most visited points of interest and the main flows between them within a destination for each tourist cluster. This will allow the DMOs to uncover their tourists' profiles, their preferences, and their mobility patterns at the destination. This will also let them enhance the visitors experience through the personalization of tourist packages, services, public transport and also the information offered on each attraction or spot. Finally, this will also enhance the usefulness and efficiency of DMOs to mitigate the array of problems caused by the mobility of visitors towards and around the main points of interest through a better experience design management and interaction with the environment [40].

2. Theoretical Framework

2.1. Tourist Flow Analysis and Social Media Analytics

Prior to the technological developments, studies on tourist mobility were based on tourists' surveys [35], and they were rather limited. Tourist flow analysis grew enormously with the development of tracking mechanisms like GPS, cell-tower identification or Wi-Fi positioning [41], which have made it possible to obtain big data from the movement of tourists at destinations. Several studies have used GPS [27,42,43] to find out which were the most visited places in a particular destination and when they were visited. In destinations, the proliferation of sensor networks and portable devices like smartphones has also made it possible to obtain big data from tourists and to know their movements or flows [26]. In general, the increasing effectiveness and reliability of GPS data and the mobile positioning data have increased the possibilities of analyzing spatial-temporal behaviors, widening the research objectives beyond the initial aim to know where and when visitors went. In this vein, they have been used to identify seasonal demand patterns by Ahas et al. [44] or to improve the management of destination marketing by Kuusik et al. [45]. Other authors have considered data obtained from mobility services, such as the subway smart card [46] or bike sharing systems [47].

Social media also has very useful platforms for knowing the movements of tourists. Social media analytics (SMA) is a research field that has advanced heavily since 2014, but it is still in an early stage of development [32]. The potential of social media as sources for big data research in the field of tourism has increased in the last decade [8,30], and studies on big data, social media, UGC (User-Generated Content), and online reviews have proliferated in hospitality and tourism [30,32,34,48,49]. Moreover, the innumerable footprints that millions of tourists leave online using the technological platforms constitute an interesting source for knowing the tourists' movements and flows [49,50], although big data-based theoretical studies still remain limited [34].

Text analytics and data mining studies try to find out tourists' interests and to predict their decisions and behaviors [51]. Trend analysis studies also try to predict tourists' behaviors [52] or future trends in tourist behavior at destinations [53]. Nevertheless, one of the best ways to know the behavior of tourists during the trip is through spatial data analysis.

Spatial data analysis is a stream of studies within SMA that, through the analysis of GSMD [8], aim to ascertain the spatial distribution of tourists on a place or a destination [54] and even to know tourists' movements or flows [26,41,55]. Flow is the collective movement of people [26], and flow analysis shows the movement of tourists in a location [38]. GSMD are key sources of information to analyze tourists flows [56] in order to uncover their travel preferences and behaviors [26] or the tourists' experiences through a spatial analysis [33]. Provenzano et al. [50] compared GSMD results with the UNWTO record-based network demonstrating the usefulness of GSMD to discover tourist flows. However, there are still few publications that analyze Geotagged Big Data to examine the spatial distribution and flows of different types of tourists in the destinations [35].

GSMD analysis allows for knowing the dispersion of tourists and also the routes and activities they carry out in the destination [57–62], their density of movements [63], their flows [26,38,64,65], and the most popular resorts, attractions, or points of interest in the destinations [36,62,66,67].

Most studies that analyze GSMD have focused on Twitter because it is a platform that has global coverage and its data are available for free on the Internet from the moment the tweets are published [35]. Twitter is, along with Tripadvisor, one of the two most used platforms by SMA. It also allows the analysis of multi-modal data such as User Generated Content (including text, images, and even videos), and geotagged information [32,68]. However, studies based on geotagged photos and other social media like Flickr [38,69], Foursquare [60], or Instagram [70] have also proliferated showing tourists' flows, movements, and behaviors in destinations.

It has also been shown that analyzing different social media sources or platforms is useful because they provide complementary information and enrich the knowledge of different tourists' movements [35]. In this line, Dietz et al. [71] analyzed tourists' movements at destinations through three social media (Twitter, Foursquare, and Flickr) and identified different types of trips according to the origin of the tourists. A study by Sugimoto et al. [72] combined tracking technologies and surveys to study the relationship between visitor mobility and urban spatial structures. Salas-Olmedo et al. [35] analyzed the digital footprint of urban tourists through photos, check-ins, and tweets from three social media (Panoramio, Foursquare, and Twitter). In addition, they used a clustering methodology to identify certain areas of the destinations according to the tourist activities that visitors carried out in them. However, they did not cluster or segment tourists to know their different preferences, movements, and behaviors.

Many studies on GSMD have focused on tourists' mobility patterns [59,73–75]. However, the difference in mobility patterns between sub-groups or clusters of tourists has not been fully researched [37].

2.2. Uncovering the Mobility Patterns of Clusters of Tourists

Previous studies have shown that different types, sub-groups, or clusters of tourists may present different travel behaviors [76–79]. Domènech et al. [80], for instance, identified that cruise passengers with different expenditure levels have different mobility patterns in port destination cities. However, this kind of studies usually apply an ad-hoc combination of analytic techniques that is not easy to generalize.

From a complementary perspective, many researchers have followed the digital footprint of tourists [35] to know their mobility in destinations, but the current research shows that it is difficult to analyze all these data by segmenting tourists. In fact, many studies have analyzed tourists' mobility patterns [73,74] without taking into account the diversity of tourists [37] because of the difficulty of obtaining their socio-demographic data. This aspect can be considered only in those cases in which user information is available, such as the one described by Massimo and Ricci [81]. In that case, they use information produced by a recommender system to define patterns of visitors depending on the similarities in their observed visit trajectories.

Previous GSMD-based studies have focused on the clustering of tourists according to diverse factors. Following Liu et al. [37], studies that segment visitors according to their mobility patterns can be based on non-spatial factors (socio-economic status, gender, age, income, education, race) or on spatial factors. For instance, Manca et al. [82] focused on spatial data and Jin et al. [41] on spatial and temporal data. Nevertheless, very few studies have focused on the analysis of mobility patterns according to the socio-demographic data in order to segment visitors in a destination because, with the currently applied methods of analysis, very little socio-demographic data can be obtained from users. In this vein, several SMA studies based on GSMD analysis have claimed to obtain demographic data from tourists to better understand who they are and to be able to classify them [26,69,83]. However, the available information is still very limited [60] and, in some cases, it is even reduced to the country of origin [56].

To name some of those studies, Chua et al. [26] focused on spatial, temporal, and also demographic data from Twitter to discover the tourists flows in a destination, creating tourist profiles and segmenting them by country of origin. Similarly, Vu et al. [77] analyzed the different mobility patterns, popular locations, and routes in Hong Kong of Western and Asian tourists. In the same line, Paldino et al. [84] analyzed geo-tagged picture data from Flickr, segmenting domestic and foreign tourists, and Ma et al. [18] also analyzed the mobility of tourists in destinations and their most visited attractions by classifying tourists into foreign tourists and domestic tourists. Van der Zee and Bertocchi [85] analyzed the spatial behavior of visitors at a destination through a relational approach and Trip Advisor data, classifying visitors as local, national, European, and non-European. Vu et al. [86] analyzed the activities carried out in a destination by different groups of tourists also segmenting them by their country of origin. Xu et al. [87] analyzed mobility patterns of tourists in a country, South Korea, and its diverse destinations, according to their nationality or country of origin. Liu et al. [37] analyzed mobility via GSMD from Twitter by considering homogeneous segments of users (state visitors, national visitors, and international visitors), created according to their past visits.

However, despite the difficulty of obtaining other socio-demographic data than the origin of users from the GSMD, some mobility studies have tried to take a step further in segmenting visitors. Huang and Wong [88], for example, analyzed their mobility segmenting them by their socio-economic status through Twitter's GSMD. They identified this status from the home and work location of the users. In addition, they showed that socio-economic status and urban spatial structure are the factors that have a stronger influence on the mobility of visitors. On the other hand, Han et al. [89] analyzed the mobility patterns of visitors from the analysis of social media check-in. They used a deep learning method to try to classify tourists by the purpose of their travel.

Studies of mobility patterns that employ Artificial Intelligence techniques are still emerging, and very few of them try to identify meaningful clusters of tourists. Liao [90] obtained trajectory data from different location-based services and tourism applications, and then they applied cluster analysis to identify the most popular tourist attractions. DBSCAN clustering was used to identify spatial clusters of trajectories at the points of greatest interest, but not to identify clusters of tourists. Xu et al. [87] analyzed a mobile positioning data set in order to know the nationality and movement patterns of foreign tourists in South Korea. They used network analysis to identify the structure of tourism destinations based on patterns of travel flow, and clustering analysis to identify similar patterns. They identified areas of destinations with different visit patterns of tourists according to their nationality, but not clusters of tourists. Instead, Giglio et al. [91] used cluster analysis to identify automatically clusters of tourists around points of interest at destinations. They studied the relationship between human mobility and tourist attractions through geo-located images of Italian destinations provided by Flickr users. The results showed that social media data are a valuable source to understand the behavior of tourists in a destination. However, the study did not define or specify the different clusters of tourists and their different mobility flows between the most popular attractions.

Considering that, despite the difficulties and limitations, GSMD data can be analyzed in order to make segmentations more precise than the ones based on the country of origin, and also considering that mobility patterns are a key issue for DMOs; this study aims to make a contribution to the current challenges of analyzing tourism flows in destinations. Hence, its goal is to provide and test a methodology to create tourists' clusters (groups of visitors with similar characteristics, preferences, and patterns of travel) taking into account not only their personal and cultural interests, leisure activities, and the context, but also their mobility patterns on the destination. The authors' perception is that, from an academic perspective, this is a fundamental issue in order to better understand tourists spatial and temporal behavior. Additionally, from the point of view of the developers of tourists' experiences, this methodology is a new tool that can help to offer services to tourists in a more personalized way, enhancing the communication to the appropriate targets or the attraction of new ones [37]. Finally, it can help to improve the management of critical flows in certain points of interest of the tourism destinations, helping to minimize social stresses, built environment management difficulties, transportation issues, and frictions between tourists and local population in situations of congestion and overcrowding [40].

3. Methodology

3.1. Data Collection and Processing

Tourist mobility patterns can be analyzed by building user profiles, which group individuals with common visits to some points of interest or with similar travel behavior. These profiles can be discovered via a clustering process, which uncovers the common interests and habits of the visitors. The data required to cluster individuals based on their visited POIs for tourist mobility analysis can be obtained from various sources, including social media and mobile carriers (GPS). Social media data have become popular for this purpose in recent years.

The data used in this research were collected from the popular micro-blogging platform Twitter, using their application interface (API). The API allows developers to stream live tweets published at a specific location, which is provided as a JavaScript Object Notation (JSON) file that includes timestamps, texts, tweet IDs, user details, tweet language, coordinates, and place details. We streamed geo-located tweets published in the city of Barcelona in the year 2019, which amounted to over 1.5 million tweets from more than 100,000 users.

After the data collection, a cleaning process was applied. Users that had sent less than three tweets were discarded, along with their tweets. It was necessary to distinguish residents from visitors, as we were interested only in detecting visitor profiles. A tweet was considered to be from a tourist if Barcelona is not among his/her home locations. These home locations are specified explicitly in the individual's Twitter profile, or they are inferred from his/her tweets. Concretely, a place is considered to be a user's home location if he/she has posted daily tweets in a 20-day period (i.e., it is assumed that someone residing in a location for more than 20 consecutive days is not a tourist). Afterwards, tweets from residents were discarded.

In order to build the user profiles, it was crucial to identify the points of interest experienced by the tourists from their published tweets. The geographical coordinates of each tweet were sent to Overpass, a query engine for requesting specific features on the Open Street Map (OSM) server, in order to obtain points of interest in their proximity. The POIs returned from Overpass were then assigned to the tweets. OSM classifies physical features (buildings, parks, attractions, etc.) under certain tags that describe their type (e.g., nature: beach). We used these tags to build an activity tree, which has a hierarchical structure that categorizes activities. The activity tree contained 175 OSM tags, classified under nine main categories (Routes, Sports, Gastronomy, Leisure, Accommodation, Transportation, Nature, Events, and Culture) and 32 subcategories.

The activity tree allows us to categorize tweets based on an assigned POI visited in the tweet. This POI is chosen from the POIs returned from Overpass, by giving priority to POIs explicitly mentioned in the tweet and to POIs with OSM tags that belong to categories that are of higher interest to a tourist. For instance, we consider a museum to be more interesting to a tourist than a coffee shop, so the museum is prioritized over the coffee shop. The tweets that could not be assigned to any POI and activity were removed from the analysis. After the filtering process, the dataset had 37,302 tweets from 6066 individuals. The summary of the dataset is shown in Table 1.

Table 1. Dataset summary.

Statistics	Value
Total number of tweets in Barcelona	1,523,801
Total number of users in Barcelona	108,515
Statistics after filtering	
Total number of tweets in Barcelona	37,302
Total number of users in Barcelona	6066

Source: Authors, from a previous work [39].

3.2. Feature Engineering and Data Clustering

In order to cluster the users, each of them was represented by a numerical vector of features, which represents their interests and travel habits. Four types of features were considered:

- Activity interest features (25^1): these features represent different levels in the activity tree, which were chosen to show the categories more represented in the dataset. All tweets published by a user are assigned to activity categories as described in Section 3.1. The ratio of tweets in the highlighted activity interest features (Routes, Sports, Accommodation, Transportation, Nature, Food, Enotourism, AmusementParks, RecreationFacilities, Beach, Health&Care, NightLife, Shopping, Viewpoint, CulturalAmenities, Historic, Religious, Events, tourism_museum, amenity_arts_center, tourism_gallery, artwork_type_sculpture, artwork_type_architecture, artwork_type_statue, and other_artwork.) to the total number of tweets published by the user is taken to represent the user's degree of interest in those activities. They are in the range [0, 1].
- Travel features (3): these features give an idea of the degree of mobility of the user inside the city. They encode the length of the stay of the user in Barcelona (maximum consecutive days that the user sent tweets from this city), and the maximum and average distances between the location of published tweets. These values are computed by counting the days the user published tweets in Barcelona, eliminating gaps to find the maximum stretch of days with published tweets. They are normalized in the range [0, 1].

- Popularity features (5): these features show if the user is interested in the most popular places or if he/she prefers to visit places off the beaten track. They represent the percentage of tweets sent from the user from the top 10 most visited locations in Barcelona, the top 10–20, the top 20–50, the top 50–100, or from other POIs. These top visited locations are ranked by number of user visits in the dataset, and split into bins 1–10, 20–50, 50–100, and the rest (each bin represents a feature in this category). Then, the ratio of a user's tweets in each bin to his/her total number of tweets is used to represent the user in these features. They are in the range [0, 1].
- Temporal features (4): these features give an idea on the time of the day in which the user prefers to tour. They represent the percentages of tweets sent from the user at dawn (12:00 a.m.–7:00 a.m.), morning (7:00 a.m.–12:00 p.m.), afternoon (12:00 p.m.–8:00 p.m.), or night (8:00 p.m.–12:00 a.m.). As in the popularity features, bins are created to represent different time periods in the day (each bin represents a feature in this category). Then, the ratio of a user's tweets in each bin to his/her total number of tweets is used to represent the user in these features. They are in the range [0, 1].

Thus, each of the 6066 users was represented by a vector of 37 numbers, which codifies his/her leisure interests, moving ability, interest in popular places, and the preferred period of the day for visiting points of interest. All features were standardized using the *Z-score* scaler, and the k-means clustering algorithm was used to cluster this dataset into 25 clusters (this number was empirically decided after some experiments). Five of the 25 clusters had less than 50 users, so they were not considered to be very relevant, and they were dismissed from the posterior mobility analysis. Thus, at the end of the clustering process, there were 20 clusters with a minimum of 50 visitors. By averaging the values of the 37 features for the users in each cluster, we obtained a general description of the preferences of the users in that group.

In a previous work [39], you can find a more detailed technical explanation of the data collection, filtering, activity identification, and clustering steps.

4. Results

4.1. Characterization of the Visitors in Each Cluster

The analysis identified different clusters with a wide range of visit preferences. Figure 1 highlights the main characteristics shared by tourists in each of the 20 clusters, including their origin, the kind of leisure activities they visit, their preferred time of the day, and their interest in different kinds of activities. All clusters are associated with one or more types of activities, which match the activity features used in the clustering process.

As it can be seen in Figure 1, the historic and religious activities (columns A and B) are the ones associated with most clusters (0, 2, 5, 8, 11, 16, 17, and 19). In most of these clusters, users enjoy visiting the most popular POIs, revealing that the historic and religious attractions are among the most popular in the city of Barcelona. This also proves a direct correlation between tourist interests and their popularity, as it could be expected.

It can also be seen that the individuals in clusters 2 and 17 visit a larger number of popular POIs and have a wider spread of different kinds of activities. These clusters contain mostly non-Spanish tourists, who visit and experience many varieties of POIs that the city offers. On the other hand, clusters characterized mainly by Spanish nationals (clusters 1, 3, 9, 10, 15, 21, 23, and 24) focus on a small set of features and on unpopular POIs, indicating a higher specificity in their favorite POIs and their visits. People in cluster 1, for example, prefer to do scenic routes within the city. However, those in cluster 3 prefer to go to the beach or places near the beach, and some historic sites. Tourists on cluster 9 visit Barcelona mainly for health and care, although they also visit religious sites and cafes, whereas those in cluster 15 prefer food and enotourism, those in cluster 23 are mainly interested in visiting Camp Nou, the football stadium, and people in cluster 24 mainly visit museums.

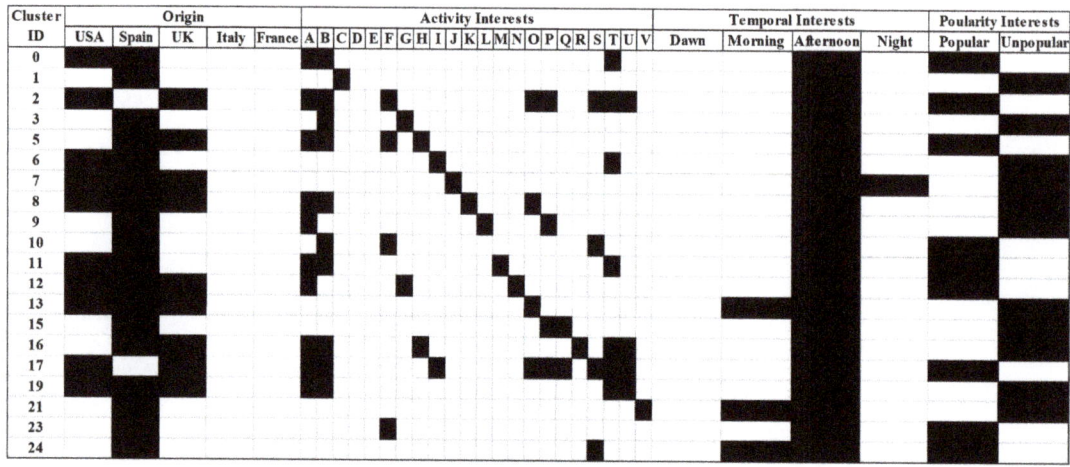

Figure 1. Cluster characteristics highlighting tourists' origin, preferred tour time, orientation towards popular POIs, and interests in different activities. * Note: A—Religious, B—Historic, C—Routes, D—Nature, E—Art Gallery, F— Recreational Facilities, G—Beach, H—Cultural Amenities, I—Shopping, J—Nightlife, K—Statues, L—Health & Care, M—Viewpoints, N—Sculptures, O—Accommodation, P—Food, Q—Enotourism, R—Amusement Parks, S—Museums, T—Architecture, U—Other Artworks, V—Art Centers.

The mobility analysis based on visitor clusters that was carried out also allows for knowing the specific POIs visited by the tourists of each cluster. Figure 2 shows the percentage of tourists from each cluster who visit the top 20 most visited POIs of the destination, highlighting in each row the values above the average. For example, Camp Nou, the Barcelona football stadium, is visited mostly by tourists from cluster 23, the religious architecture (as the Sagrada Família) and historic monuments (as the Palau de la Generalitat or the Casa Batlló) are mainly visited by tourists of clusters 0, 2, or 17, and beaches (like Barceloneta) or places near them by tourists of cluster 3. This figure also clearly identifies those clusters that are focused on the most popular POIs, and to what degree. Clusters 0 and 2 are heavily focused on popular POIs as they have an above average representation of 55% and 80% (respectively) in the popular POIs. In contrast, clusters 7, 12, 13, 15, 21, and 23 have very little representation in the popular POIs. This shows that the 20 clusters do not favor only popular or unpopular POIs.

	Attractions	0	1	2	3	5	6	7	8	9	10	11	12	13	15	16	17	19	21	23	24
0	Basilica de la Sagrada Família	25.04%	2.26%	11.48%	4.74%	7.61%	3.57%	1.42%	5.67%	4.02%	3.89%	6.63%	3.45%	1.43%	2.27%	5.08%	7.77%	5.20%	0.67%	1.50%	2.38%
1	Camp Nou	2.88%	1.23%	11.62%	2.42%	4.70%	2.80%	0.95%	3.72%	3.72%	3.01%	1.89%	3.79%	1.04%	1.08%	3.32%	4.57%	2.39%	0.33%	44.55%	1.19%
2	Park Güell	10.05%	1.29%	5.29%	1.43%	3.29%	2.51%	0.27%	3.01%	1.86%	2.22%	5.11%	2.41%	0.33%	0.67%	3.13%	3.75%	1.54%	0.33%	0.34%	0.56%
3	Palau de la Generalitat de Catalunya	6.02%	0.78%	1.89%	0.77%	1.13%	0.68%	0.27%	0.35%	1.55%	0.95%	2.27%	0.34%	0.46%	0.59%	0.59%	1.76%	1.47%	0.00%	0.31%	0.94%
4	Casa Batlló	5.37%	0.26%	1.95%	0.77%	0.85%	0.87%	0.27%	0.53%	0.31%	0.32%	0.95%	0.69%	0.59%	0.33%	1.37%	2.56%	1.90%	0.00%	0.17%	0.63%
5	Casa Milà	5.37%	0.39%	1.74%	0.11%	1.13%	0.48%	0.07%	0.71%	0.31%	0.56%	1.14%	0.34%	0.33%	0.59%	0.39%	2.59%	2.39%	0.33%	0.07%	1.00%
6	Arc de Triomf	3.78%	1.03%	1.66%	2.20%	1.60%	0.97%	0.20%	1.60%	0.93%	1.90%	2.08%	1.38%	0.52%	0.52%	1.95%	1.66%	1.12%	0.67%	0.20%	0.50%
7	Catedral de la Santa Creu i Santa Eulàlia	3.20%	0.45%	1.91%	0.55%	0.75%	0.58%	0.20%	1.77%	0.31%	0.40%	0.76%	0.69%	0.26%	0.41%	2.15%	1.52%	0.98%	0.00%	0.20%	0.25%
8	Platja de la Barceloneta	0.59%	0.26%	1.66%	15.97%	0.85%	0.29%	0.34%	1.60%	0.31%	0.56%	0.19%	0.69%	0.39%	0.33%	1.17%	1.19%	0.28%	0.33%	0.20%	0.19%
9	Font Màgica de Montjuïc	0.59%	0.00%	0.90%	0.44%	20.86%	0.29%	0.07%	0.35%	0.00%	0.79%	0.76%	1.03%	0.13%	0.19%	1.95%	0.93%	0.07%	0.00%	0.10%	0.00%
10	Plaça de Catalunya	1.15%	4.46%	1.26%	0.66%	0.66%	0.97%	0.14%	0.53%	1.24%	0.48%	0.57%	0.69%	0.39%	0.52%	0.00%	1.50%	0.98%	0.33%	0.31%	0.19%
11	Museu Nacional d'Art de Catalunya	0.48%	0.45%	1.36%	0.22%	1.88%	0.39%	0.34%	0.00%	0.93%	6.03%	0.57%	0.00%	0.00%	0.22%	0.39%	1.30%	0.28%	0.00%	0.14%	1.88%
12	Lillo	0.04%	0.39%	0.48%	1.87%	0.09%	1.16%	0.81%	0.00%	0.00%	0.56%	0.00%	0.00%	0.13%	8.84%	0.00%	0.01%	0.70%	0.00%	0.31%	0.25%
13	Palau Sant Jordi	0.10%	0.39%	0.25%	0.22%	0.66%	0.48%	0.14%	0.18%	0.31%	18.64%	1.14%	0.34%	0.26%	0.19%	0.00%	0.17%	0.28%	1.33%	0.41%	0.38%
14	Al actor Iscle Soler	1.36%	0.58%	0.65%	0.99%	0.66%	0.39%	0.14%	0.71%	0.31%	0.08%	0.19%	0.34%	0.39%	0.56%	1.17%	1.55%	1.40%	0.00%	0.03%	1.44%
15	Arenas de Barcelona	0.38%	0.19%	1.11%	0.33%	0.75%	11.29%	0.20%	0.71%	0.62%	1.27%	0.95%	0.34%	0.00%	0.19%	0.59%	0.82%	0.49%	0.00%	0.10%	0.31%
16	Parc de la Ciutadella	0.65%	0.52%	0.69%	0.88%	0.75%	0.48%	0.07%	0.71%	1.24%	6.58%	0.95%	1.72%	0.07%	0.37%	0.78%	1.14%	0.28%	0.00%	0.27%	0.44%
17	Castell de Montjuïc	0.48%	0.19%	1.26%	0.11%	1.22%	0.29%	0.07%	0.35%	0.00%	4.36%	0.57%	0.00%	0.07%	0.19%	0.39%	1.70%	0.14%	0.00%	0.00%	0.13%
18	Font de la Plaça d'Espanya	0.61%	0.58%	1.11%	0.33%	1.13%	1.74%	0.14%	0.53%	0.93%	5.47%	0.38%	0.00%	0.26%	0.26%	0.78%	0.87%	0.28%	0.00%	0.14%	0.50%
19	Museu Picasso	0.42%	0.00%	0.71%	0.44%	0.28%	0.29%	0.07%	0.35%	0.31%	3.25%	0.38%	0.34%	0.26%	0.30%	0.39%	1.48%	0.28%	0.00%	0.10%	2.19%

Figure 2. Top 20 most visited attractions and the percentage of their tweets per cluster, highlighting values above average in green.

In summary, the clusters present unique groups of tourists with different characteristics and preferences derived from the clustering features and allows knowing which are the visitors of the most popular tourist POIs. This information can be very useful for the marketing managers of destinations and tourist attractions of the place because it allows them to know the visiting preferences of their visitors. Moreover, these data can also be exploited for mobility analysis, as described in the next section.

4.2. Tourist Mobility/Flow Analysis

To analyze the mobility of tourists within each cluster, bigrams (A, B) were extracted from their sequences of visits. These bigrams are n-grams of size two that represent the movement of a tourist from A to B (i.e., the user sent a tweet from A and the next one from B). Given a sequence of items, n-grams are unique sets of n directly adjacent items. For example, a sequence $S = \{a, b, c, d\}$ has the following 2-grams (popularly known as bigrams) $2grams = \{(a, b), (b, c), (c, d)\}$. N-grams must maintain the order in the original sequence and must be unique.

Bigrams were extracted from the sequences of visited places of each tourist in a certain cluster, and we counted their frequency of occurrence (i.e., the number of times a bigram appeared in the cluster). The clusters 0, 2, 3, 7, and 16 were selected to illustrate this analysis because of their diversity. The top 20 bigrams with a higher frequency in each cluster were taken as the most relevant. Figure 3 shows heat map plots of the tourist mobility within clusters, where the color intensity represents the movement between POIs measured by the frequency of occurrence.

As it can be seen from Figure 3, *Basílica de la Sagrada Família* acts as a hub in cluster 0, as all other POIs are directly connected to it. In most cases, tourists are visiting the other POIs after visiting *Basílica de la Sagrada Família* because its outflows exceed its inflows from other locations, except *Casa Batlló, Catedral de la Santa Creu i Santa Eulàlia*, and *Al actor Iscle Soler*, which might be a result of route preference. The strongest connection can be seen between *Basílica de la Sagrada Família* and *Park Güell* with almost equivalent inflow and outflow between them. In the case of cluster 2, *Basílica de la Sagrada Família* is once again the most interconnected attraction but with more inflows than in cluster 0, and the strongest connection is between *Basílica de la Sagrada Família* and *Camp Nou*. The other selected clusters (3, 7, and 16) show connections between various attractions with no clear hub.

Figures 4 and 5 help to further understand tourist mobility with network graphs plotted on the Barcelona city map. Nodes represent POIs, and edges are the bigrams that connect them (the wider is the edge, the more tourists travel between those two locations). It can be seen that proximity plays a role in why *Basílica de la Sagrada Família* acts as a hub in clusters 0 and 2. In cluster 3, the focus is the Mediterranean Sea as most POIs are near the beach, except in the case of *Basílica de la Sagrada Família, Park Güell*, and *Camp Nou*, as tourists are willing to travel out of the way to see these POIs. Clusters 7 and 16 show two different kinds of tourists. The former is focused on bars near the city center, whereas the latter visits many different kinds of places all around the city, including amusement parks, shop malls, and the beach, but also the most popular venues.

In summary, the analyzed clusters showed inter-connected POIs which are of interest to certain groups of tourists. In some cases, they focus on the popular attractions, but in others they also visit places off the beaten track. The graphic representation in the map of the mobility of different clusters of tourists in a destination provides new knowledge to DMOs, who could take them into account to define new tourist routes, to create targeted marketing campaigns or to optimize transport routes between heavily connected POIs for different types of tourists.

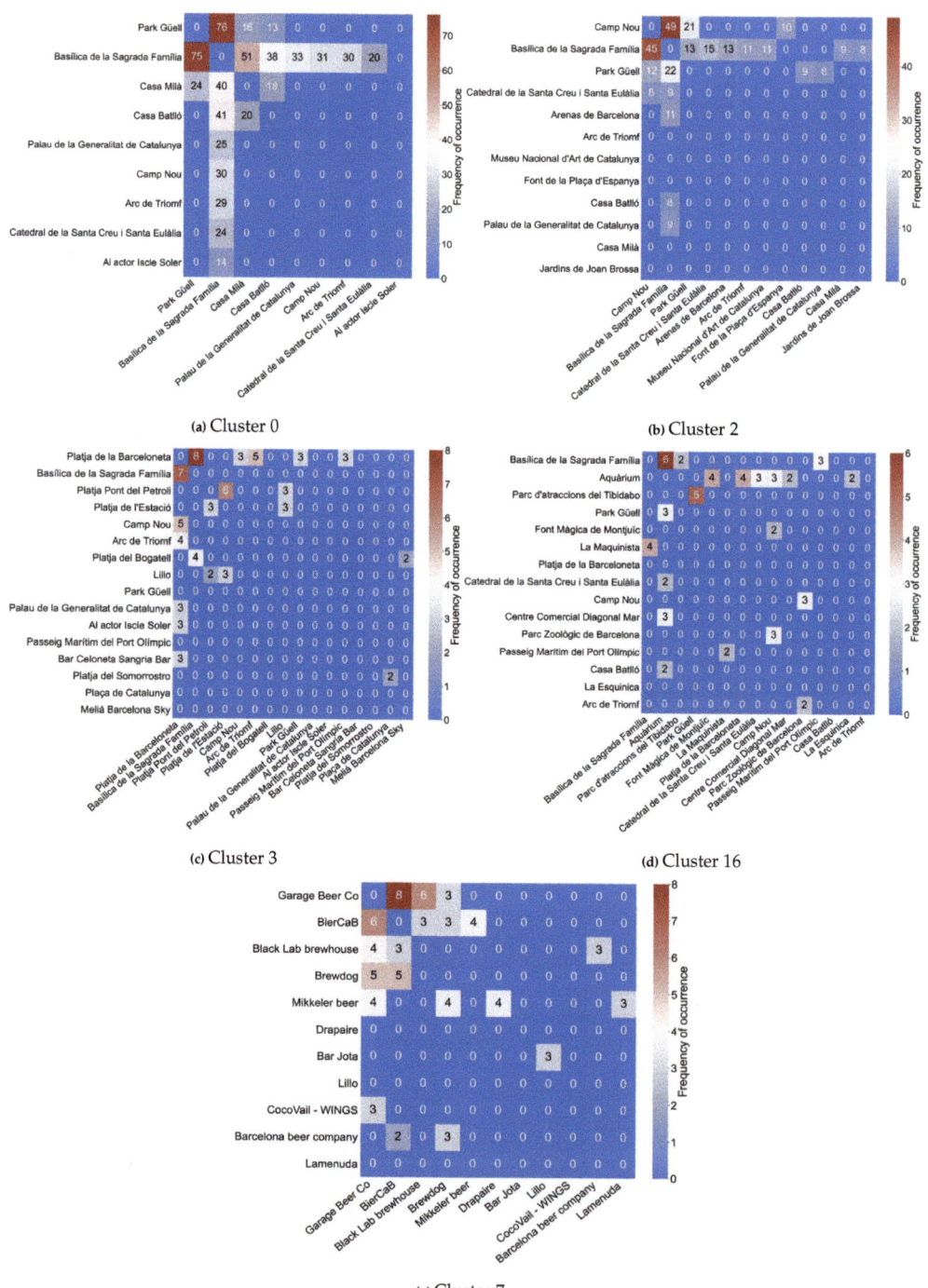

Figure 3. Mobility heat-maps for clusters 0, 2, 3, 16, and 7 representing bigrams with movement from left to bottom.

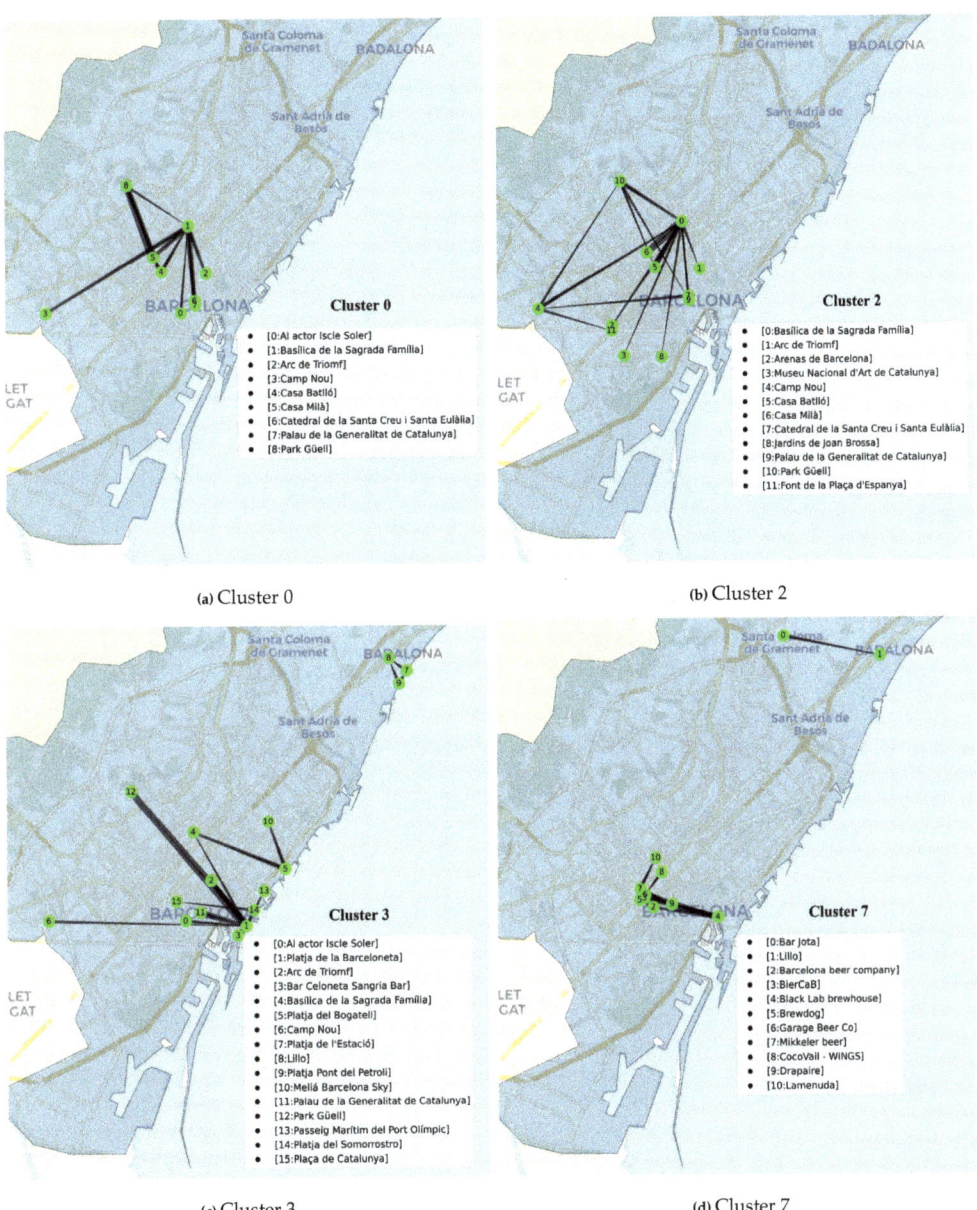

Figure 4. Tourist mobility pattern between attractions in Barcelona for clusters 0, 2, 3, and 7.

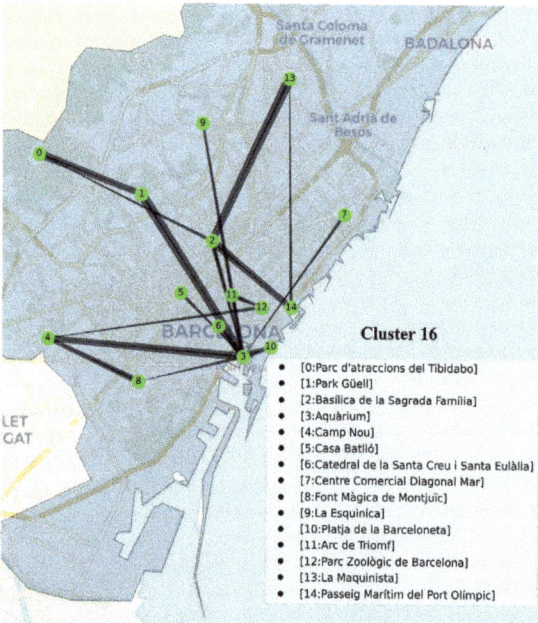

Figure 5. Tourist mobility pattern between attractions in Barcelona for cluster 16.

5. Discussion, Conclusions, and Implications

The main contribution of the study is the introduction of a method for analyzing social media data that create visitor profiles according to their travel preferences and mobility. This study corroborates that social media are very useful platforms as sources for big data research in the field of tourism [8,30], and they can also be used to study tourist mobility [26,35,41,55]. It also improves the knowledge about the different mobility patterns of tourists depending on who they are and what their preferences are [56]. Therefore, the study has shown that clustering visitors by their travel mobility permits uncovering much more information about visitors and their preferences than previous studies. It can also provide complementary information to DMOs, attraction operators, and developers of contextual and next-POI recommender systems [81].

Additionally, the study also reveals the most popular or the most visited points of interest at destinations. Previous studies had also found out the most popular tourist spots or the most visited routes by analyzing geo-tagged social media data [62,66], but their analysis did not allow for knowing which were the most visited POIs by the different tourists. Thus, interestingly, the applied method allows for knowing the percentages of tourists in each cluster who visit each attraction the most. This is crucial for the managers of the different tourist attractions that want to know who their majority visitors are as well as their interests; in that way, they will be able to adapt their service and information in an almost personalized way.

Another contribution of the study is to show the mobility of each cluster of tourists between POIs and to see graphically the movement that they make in the map of the destination. Previous studies have shown mobility with place maps and most visited points [26]. Many studies on GSMD only focused on tourists' mobility patterns [48,59,73]. However, the difference in mobility patterns between sub-groups or clusters of tourists has not been fully researched [37]. Therefore, GSMD analysis allows for knowing the dispersion and tourists' movements, the routes they follow, the activities they carry out in a territory [57–62], and their density of movements [63] and flows [38,64,65]. Hence, the resulting information is particularly valuable for city management, since it provides a better knowledge of the connections between points of interest related to different clusters of tourists according to their preferences and behaviors. This information can help DMOs to define new tourist routes, to create targeted marketing campaigns, to optimize transport routes between heavily connected POIs for different types of tourists, or to improve the management of congestion or overcrowding situations.

To sum up, through this application of Artificial Intelligence techniques to social media data creating clusters of tourists, it has been possible to know how to segment them according to their visitor behavior and visit preferences. This information is key to the DMOs and the different service providers of the destinations. The interest of DMOs in analyzing big data and knowing the maximum information about their tourists is based on being able to anticipate their interests and preferences [38]. This is precisely the information that this study provides. Therefore, the study can have a major impact on the marketing and flows management of tourist destinations. The exploration of the relationship between tourists' profiles, points of interest, and tourist mobility allows for gaining further insight into really concerning debates on tourism pressure in specific locations, and destination carrying capacity. Accordingly, it can be used by local and regional authorities, as well as by planners and urban designers, to deal with urban complexity, especially in successful tourist cities with contradictions and conflicts generated by overtourism [92].

From this perspective, the managerial implications of the study are diverse. Using these kinds of analytical tools, DMOs and tourism service providers could be able to offer the most personalized services and information, to attract specific types of tourists to certain points of interest [37], to propose the visit of new under-visited attractions to certain market segments, to create new routes or to optimize the existing ones, to enhance public transport services, to develop new POIs or tourist services for the busiest routes [93] or to create tourism development plans for the least visited areas [60].

In addition, it will allow destinations to encourage smart development, overcoming some of the existing gaps in the level of achievement of their objectives [7]. This includes the improvement of smart tourism developments such as the creation of differentiated attractive travel packages [86], the adaptation of the marketing and communication tactics to the preferences of visitors [10,11], the improvement of the satisfaction of tourists [5,14,15], and the co-creation of a more positive tourist destination image [94]. It will even have a major impact on travel recommendation systems, as shown in a previous study [39]. Finally, from the place management perspective, the detection of visitor flow patterns would help to regulate the carrying capacity of the visitors' points of interest avoiding overcrowding, improving allocation of visitor services and reducing tensions produced by the different tourist and residential uses of the city areas, infrastructures, and services around the points of interest.

Supplementary Materials: The following supporting information can be downloaded at: https://www.mdpi.com/article/10.3390/app12125834/s1.

Author Contributions: Conceptualization, A.H. and S.A.C.; methodology, J.A.O., J.B. and A.M.; software, J.A.O.; validation, J.B. and A.M.; formal analysis, J.A.O.; investigation, J.A.O.; resources, J.B. and A.M.; data curation, J.A.O. and J.B.; writing—original draft preparation, J.A.O. and A.H.; writing—review and editing, A.H., A.M. and S.A.C.; visualization, J.A.O.; supervision, J.B. and A.M.; project administration, J.B. and A.M.; funding acquisition, J.B. and A.M. All authors have read and agreed to the published version of the manuscript.

Funding: This research received no external funding.

Institutional Review Board Statement: Not Applicable.

Informed Consent Statement: Not Applicable.

Data Availability Statement: 3rd Party Data Restrictions apply to the availability of these data. Data were obtained from Twitter and are available at https://twitter.com (accessed on 1 January 2019) with the permission of Twitter. Research is allowed to provide Tweet IDs to other researchers to download using Twitter's API. The Tweet IDs of data presented in this paper are included in the supplementary material.

Acknowledgments: Jonathan Ayebakuro Orama is a fellow of Eurecat's "Vicente López" PhD grant program.

Conflicts of Interest: The authors declare no conflict of interest.

Abbreviations

The following abbreviations are used in this manuscript:

DMO	Destination Management Organization
GPS	Global Positioning System
GSMD	Geotagged Social Media Data
POI	Point of Interest
SMA	Social Media Analytics
UGC	User Generated Content
UNWTO	United National World Tourism Organization
OSM	Open Street Map

References

1. Buhalis, D.; Law, R. Progress in information technology and tourism management: 20 years on and 10 years after the Internet—The state of eTourism research. *Tour. Manag.* **2008**, *29*, 609–623. [CrossRef]
2. Hays, S.; Page, S.J.; Buhalis, D. Social media as a destination marketing tool: Its use by national tourism organisations. *Curr. Issues Tour.* **2013**, *16*, 211–239. [CrossRef]
3. Xiang, Z.; Gretzel, U. Role of social media in online travel information search. *Tour. Manag.* **2010**, *31*, 179–188. [CrossRef]
4. Buhalis, D.; Amaranggana, A. Smart Tourism Destinations Enhacing Tourism Experience Through Personalisation of Services. In *Information and Communication Technologies in Tourism*; Tussyadiah, I., Inversini, A., Eds.; Springer: Cham, Swizerland, 2015; pp. 377–389. [CrossRef]
5. Buonincontri, P.; Micera, R. The experience co-creation in smart tourism destinations: A multiple case analysis of European destinations. *Inf. Technol. Tour.* **2016**, *16*, 285–315. [CrossRef]
6. WTCF. WTCF Global Report on Smart Tourism in Cities. World Tourism Cities Federation. Beijing. 2019. Availble online: https://prefeitura.pbh.gov.br/sites/default/files/estrutura-de-governo/belotur/2020/wtcf-global-report-on-smart-tourism-in-cities.pdf (accessed on 25 January 2022)
7. Femenia-Serra, F.; Ivars-Baidal, J.A. Do smart tourism destinations really work? The case of Benidorm. *Asia Pac. J. Tour. Res.* **2021**, *26*, 365–384. [CrossRef]
8. Xiang, Z.; Fesenmaier, D.R. Big Data Analytics, Tourism Design and Smart Tourism. In *The future of tourism: Innovation and Sustainability*; Xiang, Z., Fesenmaier, D., Eds.; Springer: Cham, Swizerland, 2017; pp. 299–307. [CrossRef]
9. Wang, K.; Lin, C. The adoption of mobile value-added services: Investigating the influence of IS quality and perceived playfulness. *Manag. Serv. Qual. Int. J.* **2012**, *22*, 184–208. [CrossRef]
10. Kotoua, S.; Ilkan, M. Tourism destination marketing and information technology in Ghana. *J. Destin. Mark. Manag.* **2017**, *6*, 127–135. [CrossRef]
11. Lamsfus, C.; Martín, D.; Alzua-Sorzabal, A.; Torres-Manzanera, E. Smart Tourism Destinations: An Extended Conception of Smart Cities Focusing on Human Mobility. In *Information and Communication Technologies in Tourism 2015*; Tussyadiah, I.; Inversini, A., Eds.; Springer: Cham, Swizerland, 2015; pp. 363–375. [CrossRef]
12. Choe, Y.; Fesenmaier, D.R. The Quantified Traveler: Implications for Smart Tourism Development. In *Analytics in Smart Tourism Design*; Xiang, Z., Fesenmaier, D., Eds.; Springer: Cham, Swizerland, 2017; pp. 65–77. [CrossRef]
13. Wang, D.; Xiang, Z.; Fesenmaier, D.R. Adapting to the mobile world: A model of smartphone use. *Ann. Tour. Res.* **2014**, *48*, 11–26. [CrossRef]
14. Boes, K.; Buhalis, D.; Inversini, A. Conceptualising smart tourism destination dimensions. In *Information and Communication Technologies in Tourism*; Tussyadiah, I., Inversini, A., Eds.; Springer: Cham, Swizerland, 2015; pp. 391–403. [CrossRef]
15. Molinillo, S.; Anaya-Sánchez, R.; Morrison, A.M.; Coca-Stefaniak, J.A. Smart city communication via social media: Analysing residents' and visitors' engagement. *Cities* **2019**, *94*, 247–255. [CrossRef]
16. Soares, J.C.; Domareski Ruiz, T.C.; Ivars Baidal, J.A. Smart destinations: A new planning and management approach? *Curr. Issues Tour.* **2021**, 1–16. [CrossRef]

17. Gazley, A.; Watling, L. Me, My Tourist-Self, and I: The Symbolic Consumption of Travel. *J. Travel Tour. Mark.* **2015**, *32*, 639–655. [CrossRef]
18. Ma, A.T.H.; Chow, A.S.Y.; Cheung, L.T.O.; Lee, K.M.Y.; Liu, S. Impacts of Tourists' Sociodemographic Characteristics on the Travel Motivation and Satisfaction: The Case of Protected Areas in South China. *Sustainability* **2018**, *10*, 3388. [CrossRef]
19. Oh, J.Y.J.; Cheng, C.K.; Lehto, X.Y.; O'Leary, J.T. Predictors of tourists' shopping behaviour: Examination of socio-demographic characteristics and trip typologies. *J. Vacat. Mark.* **2004**, *10*, 308–319. [CrossRef]
20. Kim, D.Y.; Park, J.; Morrison, A.M. A model of traveller acceptance of mobile technology. *Int. J. Tour. Res.* **2008**, *10*, 393–407. [CrossRef]
21. Fan, D.X.F.; Buhalis, D.; Lin, B. A tourist typology of online and face-to-face social contact: Destination immersion and tourism encapsulation/decapsulation. *Ann. Tour. Res.* **2019**, *78*, 102757. [CrossRef]
22. Kirillova, K.; Wang, D. Smartphone (dis)connectedness and vacation recovery. *Ann. Tour. Res.* **2016**, *61*, 157–169. [CrossRef]
23. Almeida-Santana, A.; Moreno-Gil, S. New trends in information search and their influence on destination loyalty: Digital destinations and relationship marketing. *J. Destin. Mark. Manag.* **2017**, *6*, 150–161. [CrossRef]
24. Pan, B.; Xiang, Z.; Law, R.; Fesenmaier, D.R. The Dynamics of Search Engine Marketing for Tourist Destinations. *J. Travel Res.* **2011**, *50*, 365–377. [CrossRef]
25. Wang, D.; Xiang, Z.; Fesenmaier, D.R. Smartphone Use in Everyday Life and Travel. *J. Travel Res.* **2016**, *55*, 52–63. [CrossRef]
26. Chua, A.; Servillo, L.; Marcheggiani, E.; Moere, A.V. Mapping Cilento: Using geotagged social media data to characterize tourist flows in southern Italy. *Tour. Manag.* **2016**, *57*, 295–310. [CrossRef]
27. Orellana, D.; Bregt, A.K.; Ligtenberg, A.; Wachowicz, M. Exploring visitor movement patterns in natural recreational areas. *Tour. Manag.* **2012**, *33*, 672–682. [CrossRef]
28. Baggio, R.; Scaglione, M. Strategic visitor flows and destination management organization. *J. Destin. Mark. Manag.* **2018**, *18*, 29–42. [CrossRef]
29. Grinberger, A.Y.; Shoval, N. Spatiotemporal Contingencies in Tourists' Intradiurnal Mobility Patterns. *J. Travel Res.* **2019**, *58*, 512–530. [CrossRef]
30. Mariani, M.; Baggio, R.; Fuchs, M.; Höepken, W. Business intelligence and big data in hospitality and tourism: A systematic literature review. *Int. J. Contemp. Hosp. Manag.* **2018**, *30*, 3514–3554. [CrossRef]
31. Marine-Roig, E. Online travel reviews: A massive paratextual analysis. In *Analytics in Smart Tourism Design: Concepts and Methods*; Xiang, Z., Fesenmaier, D.R., Eds.; Springer: Cham, Swizerland, 2017; pp. 179–202. [CrossRef]
32. Mirzaalian, F.; Halpenny, E. Social media analytics in hospitality and tourism: A systematic literature review and future trends. *J. Hosp. Tour. Technol.* **2019**, *10*, 764–790. [CrossRef]
33. Zhang, X.; Yang, Y.; Zhang, Y.; Zhang, Z. Designing tourist experiences amidst air pollution: A spatial analytical approach using social media. *Ann. Tour. Res.* **2020**, *84*, 102999. [CrossRef]
34. Li, X.; Law, R. Network analysis of big data research in tourism. *Tour. Manag. Perspect.* **2020**, *33*, 100608. [CrossRef]
35. Salas-Olmedo, M.H.; Moya-Gómez, B.; García-Palomares, J.C.; Gutiérrez, J. Tourists' digital footprint in cities: Comparing Big Data sources. *Tour. Manag.* **2018**, *66*, 13–25. [CrossRef]
36. Hu, Y.; Li, Z.; Yang, C.; Jiang, Y. A graph-based approach to detecting tourist movement patterns using social media data. *Cartogr. Geogr. Inf. Sci.* **2019**, *46*, 368–382. [CrossRef]
37. Liu, Q.; Wang, Z.; Ye, X. Comparing mobility patterns between residents and visitors using geo-tagged social media data. *Trans. GIS* **2018**, *22*, 1372–1389. [CrossRef]
38. Miah, S.J.; Vu, H.Q.; Gammack, J. A big-data analytics method for capturing visitor activities and flows: The case of an island country. *Inf. Technol. Manag.* **2019**, *20*, 203–221. [CrossRef]
39. Orama, J.A.; Borràs, J.; Moreno, A. Combining Cluster-Based Profiling Based on Social Media Features and Association Rule Mining for Personalised Recommendations of Touristic Activities. *Appl. Sci.* **2021**, *11*, 6512. [CrossRef]
40. Anton Clavé, S. Urban Tourism and Walkability. In *The Future of Tourism: Innovation and Sustainability*; Fayos-Solà, E., Cooper, C., Eds.; Springer: Cham, Swizerland, 2019; pp. 195–211. [CrossRef]
41. Jin, C.; Cheng, J.; Xu, J. Using User-Generated Content to Explore the Temporal Heterogeneity in Tourist Mobility. *J. Travel Res.* **2018**, *57*, 779–791. [CrossRef]
42. Edwards, D.; Griffin, T. Understanding tourists' spatial behaviour: GPS tracking as an aid to sustainable destination management. *J. Sustain. Tour.* **2013**, *21*, 580–595. [CrossRef]
43. Shoval, N.; McKercher, B.; Ng, E.; Birenboim, A. Hotel location and tourist activity in cities. *Ann. Tour. Res.* **2011**, *38*, 1594–1612. [CrossRef]
44. Ahas, R.; Aasa, A.; Mark, Ü.; Pae, T.; Kull, A. Seasonal tourism spaces in Estonia: Case study with mobile positioning data. *Tour. Manag.* **2007**, *28*, 898–910. [CrossRef]
45. Kuusik, A.; Tiru, M.; Ahas, R.; Varblane, U. Innovation in destination marketing: The use of passive mobile positioning for the segmentation of repeat visitors in Estonia. *Balt. J. Manag.* **2011**, *6*, 378–399. [CrossRef]
46. Roth, C.; Kang, S.M.; Batty, M.; Barthélemy, M. Structure of Urban Movements: Polycentric Activity and Entangled Hierarchical Flows. *PLoS ONE* **2011**, *6*, e15923. [CrossRef]
47. Beecham, R.; Wood, J.; Bowerman, A. Studying commuting behaviours using collaborative visual analytics. *Comput. Environ. Urban Syst.* **2014**, *47*, 5–15. [CrossRef]

48. Li, J.; Xu, L.; Tang, L.; Wang, S.; Li, L. Big data in tourism research: A literature review. *Tour. Manag.* **2018**, *68*, 301–323. [CrossRef]
49. Lu, W.; Stepchenkova, S. User-Generated Content as a Research Mode in Tourism and Hospitality Applications: Topics, Methods, and Software. *J. Hosp. Mark. Manag.* **2015**, *24*, 119–154. [CrossRef]
50. Provenzano, D.; Hawelka, B.; Baggio, R. The mobility network of European tourists: A longitudinal study and a comparison with geo-located Twitter data. *Tour. Rev.* **2018**, *73*, 28–43. [CrossRef]
51. Sohrabi, B.; Raeesi Vanani, I.; Nasiri, N.; Ghassemi Rudd, A. A predictive model of tourist destinations based on tourists' comments and interests using text analytics. *Tour. Manag. Perspect.* **2020**, *35*, 100710. [CrossRef]
52. Del Vecchio, P.; Mele, G.; Ndou, V.; Secundo, G. Creating value from Social Big Data: Implications for Smart Tourism Destinations. *Inf. Process. Manag.* **2018**, *54*, 847–860. [CrossRef]
53. Pantano, E.; Priporas, C.V.; Stylos, N. 'You will like it!' using open data to predict tourists' response to a tourist attraction. *Tour. Manag.* **2017**, *60*, 430–438. [CrossRef]
54. Huang, A.; Gallegos, L.; Lerman, K. Travel analytics: Understanding how destination choice and business clusters are connected based on social media data. *Transp. Res. Part C Emerg. Technol.* **2017**, *77*, 245–256. [CrossRef]
55. Önder, I. Classifying multi-destination trips in Austria with big data. *Tour. Manag. Perspect.* **2017**, *21*, 54–58. [CrossRef]
56. Hawelka, B.; Sitko, I.; Beinat, E.; Sobolevsky, S.; Kazakopoulos, P.; Ratti, C. Geo-located Twitter as proxy for global mobility patterns. *Cartogr. Geogr. Inf. Sci.* **2014**, *41*, 260–271. [CrossRef]
57. Li, Y.; Xiao, L.; Ye, Y.; Xu, W.; Law, A. Understanding tourist space at a historic site through space syntax analysis: The case of Gulangyu, China. *Tour. Manag.* **2016**, *52*, 30–43. [CrossRef]
58. Önder, I.; Koerbitz, W.; Hubmann-Haidvogel, A. Tracing Tourists by Their Digital Footprints: The Case of Austria. *J. Travel Res.* **2016**, *55*, 566–573. [CrossRef]
59. Orsi, F.; Geneletti, D. Using geotagged photographs and GIS analysis to estimate visitor flows in natural areas. *J. Nat. Conserv.* **2013**, *21*, 359–368. [CrossRef]
60. Vu, H.Q.; Li, G.; Law, R.; Zhang, Y. Tourist Activity Analysis by Leveraging Mobile Social Media Data. *J. Travel Res.* **2018**, *57*, 883–898. [CrossRef]
61. Wood, S.A.; Guerry, A.D.; Silver, J.M.; Lacayo, M. Using social media to quantify nature-based tourism and recreation. *Sci. Rep.* **2013**, *3*, 1–7. [CrossRef] [PubMed]
62. Zhou, X.; Xu, C.; Kimmons, B. Detecting tourism destinations using scalable geospatial analysis based on cloud computing platform. *Comput. Environ. Urban Syst.* **2015**, *54*, 144–153. [CrossRef]
63. García-Palomares, J.C.; Gutiérrez, J.; Mínguez, C. Identification of tourist hot spots based on social networks: A comparative analysis of European metropolises using photo-sharing services and GIS. *Appl. Geogr.* **2015**, *63*, 408–417. [CrossRef]
64. Cheng, M.; Edwards, D. Social media in tourism: A visual analytic approach. *Curr. Issues Tour.* **2015**, *18*, 1080–1087. [CrossRef]
65. Miah, S.J.; Vu, H.Q.; Gammack, J.; McGrath, M. A Big Data Analytics Method for Tourist Behaviour Analysis. *Inf. Manag.* **2017**, *54*, 771–785. [CrossRef]
66. Chen, Z.; Shen, H.T.; Zhou, X. Discovering popular routes from trajectories. In Proceedings of the 2011 IEEE 27th International Conference on Data Engineering, Hannover, Germany, 11–16 April 2011; pp. 900–911. [CrossRef]
67. Zanker, M.; Fuchs, M.; Seebacher, A.; Jessenitschnig, M.; Stromberger, M. An Automated Approach for Deriving Semantic Annotations of Tourism Products based on Geospatial Information. In *Information and Communication Technologies in Tourism 2009*; Höpken, W., Gretzel, U., Law, R., Eds.; Springer: Vienna, Austria, 2009; pp. 211–221. [CrossRef]
68. Jurdak, R.; Zhao, K.; Liu, J.; AbouJaoude, M.; Cameron, M.; Newth, D. Understanding Human Mobility from Twitter. *PLoS ONE* **2015**, *10*, e0131469. [CrossRef]
69. Barchiesi, D.; Moat, H.S.; Alis, C.; Bishop, S.; Preis, T. Quantifying international travel flows using Flickr. *PLoS ONE* **2015**, *10*, e0128470. [CrossRef]
70. Ma, S.D.; Kirilenko, A.P.; Stepchenkova, S. Special interest tourism is not so special after all: Big data evidence from the 2017 Great American Solar Eclipse. *Tour. Manag.* **2020**, *77*, 104021. [CrossRef]
71. Dietz, L.W.; Sen, A.; Roy, R.; Wörndl, W. Mining trips from location-based social networks for clustering travelers and destinations. *Inf. Technol. Tour.* **2020**, *22*, 131–166. [CrossRef]
72. Sugimoto, K.; Ota, K.; Suzuki, S. Visitor Mobility and Spatial Structure in a Local Urban Tourism Destination: GPS Tracking and Network analysis. *Sustainability* **2019**, *11*, 919. [CrossRef]
73. Gabrielli, L.; Furletti, B.; Trasarti, R.; Giannotti, F.; Pedreschi, D. City users' classification with mobile phone data. In Proceedings of the 2015 IEEE International Conference on Big Data (Big Data), Santa Clara, CA, USA, 29 October–1 November 2015; pp. 1007–1012. [CrossRef]
74. Li, D.; Zhou, X.; Wang, M. Analyzing and visualizing the spatial interactions between tourists and locals: A Flickr study in ten US cities. *Cities* **2018**, *74*, 249–258. [CrossRef]
75. Wu, Y.; Li, Z.; Wu, W.; Zhou, M. Response selection with topic clues for retrieval-based chatbots. *Neurocomputing* **2018**, *316*, 251–261. [CrossRef]
76. Batra, A. Senior pleasure tourists: Examination of their demography, travel experience, and travel behavior upon visiting the Bangkok metropolis. *Int. J. Hosp. Tour. Adm.* **2009**, *10*, 197–212. [CrossRef]
77. Vu, H.Q.; Li, G.; Law, R.; Ye, B.H. Exploring the travel behaviors of inbound tourists to Hong Kong using geotagged photos. *Tour. Manag.* **2015**, *46*, 222–232. [CrossRef]

78. Ahn, M.J.; McKercher, B. The Effect of Cultural Distance on Tourism: A Study of International Visitors to Hong Kong. *Asia Pac. J. Tour. Res.* **2015**, *20*, 94–113. [CrossRef]
79. Phillips, W.J.; Jang, S. Destination image differences between visitors and non-visitors: A case of New York city. *Int. J. Tour. Res.* **2010**, *12*, 642–645. [CrossRef]
80. Domènech, A.; Gutiérrez, A.; Anton Clavé, S. Cruise Passengers' Spatial Behaviour and Expenditure Levels at Destination. *Tour. Plan. Dev.* **2020**, *17*, 17–36. [CrossRef]
81. Massimo, D.; Ricci, F. Clustering Users' POIs Visit Trajectories for Next,-POI Recommendation. In *Information and Communication Technologies in Tourism 2019*; Pesonen, J., Neidhardt, J., Eds.; Springer: Cham, Swizerland, 2019; pp. 3–14. [CrossRef]
82. Manca, M.; Boratto, L.; Morell Roman, V.; Martori i Gallissà, O.; Kaltenbrunner, A. Using social media to characterize urban mobility patterns: State-of-the-art survey and case-study. *Online Soc. Net. Media* **2017**, *1*, 56–69. [CrossRef]
83. Fuchs, M.; Höpken, W.; Lexhagen, M. Big data analytics for knowledge generation in tourism destinations—A case from Sweden. *J. Destin. Mark. Manag.* **2014**, *3*, 198–209. [CrossRef]
84. Paldino, S.; Bojic, I.; Sobolevsky, S.; Ratti, C.; González, M.C. Urban magnetism through the lens of geo-tagged photography. *EPJ Data Sci.* **2015**, *4*, 1–17. [CrossRef]
85. Van der Zee, E.; Bertocchi, D. Finding patterns in urban tourist behaviour: A social network analysis approach based on TripAdvisor reviews. *Inf. Technol. Tour.* **2018**, *20*, 153–180. [CrossRef]
86. Vu, H.Q.; Li, G.; Law, R. Cross-Country Analysis of Tourist Activities Based on Venue-Referenced Social Media Data. *J. Travel Res.* **2020**, *59*, 90–106. [CrossRef]
87. Xu, Y.; Li, J.; Belyi, A.; Park, S. Characterizing destination networks through mobility traces of international tourists — A case study using a nationwide mobile positioning dataset. *Tour. Manag.* **2021**, *82*, 104195. [CrossRef]
88. Huang, Q.; Wong, D.W.S. Activity patterns, socioeconomic status and urban spatial structure: What can social media data tell us? *Int. J. Geogr. Inf. Sci.* **2016**, *30*, 1873–1898. [CrossRef]
89. Han, S.; Ren, F.; Wu, C.; Chen, Y.; Du, Q.; Ye, X. Using the TensorFlow Deep Neural Network to Classify Mainland China Visitor Behaviours in Hong Kong from Check-in Data. *ISPRS Int. J. Geo-Inf.* **2018**, *7*, 158. [CrossRef]
90. Liao, Y. Hot Spot Analysis of Tourist Attractions Based on Stay Point Spatial Clustering. *J. Inf. Process. Syst.* **2020**, *16*, 750–759. [CrossRef]
91. Giglio, S.; Bertacchini, F.; Bilotta, E.; Pantano, P. Machine learning and points of interest: Typical tourist Italian cities. *Curr. Issues Tour.* **2020**, *23*, 1646–1658. [CrossRef]
92. Lew, A.; McKercher, B. Modeling Tourist Movements: A Local Destination Analysis. *Ann. Tour. Res.* **2006**, *33*, 403–423. [CrossRef]
93. Chancellor, H.C. Applying travel pattern data to destination development and marketing decisions. *Tour. Plan. Dev.* **2012**, *9*, 321–332. [CrossRef]
94. Jabreel, M.; Huertas, A.; Moreno, A. Semantic analysis and the evolution towards participative branding: Do locals communicate the same destination brand values as DMOs? *PLoS ONE* **2018**, *13*, e0206572. [CrossRef] [PubMed]

Article

Multivariate Time Series Deep Spatiotemporal Forecasting with Graph Neural Network

Zichao He, Chunna Zhao * and Yaqun Huang

School of Information Science and Engineering, Yunnan University, Kunming 650504, China;
hzc@mail.ynu.edu.cn (Z.H.); huangyq@ynu.edu.cn (Y.H.)
* Correspondence: zhaochunna@ynu.edu.cn

Abstract: Multivariate time series forecasting has long been a subject of great concern. For example, there are many valuable applications in forecasting electricity consumption, solar power generation, traffic congestion, finance, and so on. Accurately forecasting periodic data such as electricity can greatly improve the reliability of forecasting tasks in engineering applications. Time series forecasting problems are often modeled using deep learning methods. However, the deep information of sequences and dependencies among multiple variables are not fully utilized in existing methods. Therefore, a multivariate time series deep spatiotemporal forecasting model with a graph neural network (MDST-GNN) is proposed to solve the existing shortcomings and improve the accuracy of periodic data prediction in this paper. This model integrates a graph neural network and deep spatiotemporal information. It comprises four modules: graph learning, temporal convolution, graph convolution, and down-sampling convolution. The graph learning module extracts dependencies between variables. The temporal convolution module abstracts the time information of each variable sequence. The graph convolution is used for the fusion of the graph structure and the information of the temporal convolution module. An attention mechanism is presented to filter information in the graph convolution module. The down-sampling convolution module extracts deep spatiotemporal information with different sparsities. To verify the effectiveness of the model, experiments are carried out on four datasets. Experimental results show that the proposed model outperforms the current state-of-the-art baseline methods. The effectiveness of the module for solving the problem of dependencies and deep information is verified by ablation experiments.

Keywords: multivariate time series; deep spatiotemporal information; down-sampling convolution; attention; graph neural network

1. Introduction

With the development of the Internet, various sensors and data-storage devices have appeared in modern society. As a result, a large amount of time series data is generated by recording temperature, traffic, power consumption, and financial data. Multivariate time series data consists of time series data generated by multiple sensors or data storage devices, and there are dependencies among multiple time series. For example, a household's daily electricity usage and hourly electricity production from solar panels can be considered time series data. In most cases, the data usually come from the electricity consumed by multiple households or solar data generated at different locations. A multivariate time series is constructed from these data. There may be complex dynamic dependencies between multivariate time series data. Therefore, each time series in a multivariate time series is helpful for forecasting tasks. At the same time, multivariate time series data such as electricity and transportation have periodic characteristics. Multivariate time series forecasting has been studied for a long time in capturing the periodic characteristics and dynamic dependencies of variables [1–4]. For example, studies using the Harmonic regression method enhanced the prediction performance of $PM_{2.5}$ by capturing periodic information [5].

In recent years, some researchers have made efforts in time series analysis and forecasting. For example, traditional forecasting methods represented by statistical methods. Most rely on mathematical equations to describe the evolution of time series, such as the Autoregressive Integrated Moving Average Model (ARIMA) [6]. Therefore, various variants based on the ARIMA model have emerged. Models based on traditional methods are more computationally efficient. However, these models are mostly limited to linear models and univariate predictions. It is difficult to extend to multivariate time series problems.

In the era of big data, with the development of sensor technology and computing power, most of the time series data comes from data collected by various devices. However, the information of large-scale data is difficult to extract by traditional methods. Deep learning is the current popular information extraction method. Features of large-scale data can be obtained through deep learning techniques. In time series forecasting, deep learning techniques are employed to achieve better forecasting accuracy than traditional methods. At the same time, deep learning technology has made great progress in the research and application of image processing, audio processing and natural language processing [7–9]. Although traditional machine learning and statistical methods are often employed in time series forecasting tasks, deep learning techniques are gaining attention from researchers. With further development, there have been studies on applying graph neural networks and attention methods in time series forecasting [10–12]. Capturing spatial information by building a graph structure of multivariate time series. These methods have achieved certain results. A graph neural network allows each node in the graph to acquire information about the surrounding nodes. Multivariate time series can be considered from the perspective of graph nodes. Spatial information can be obtained between multivariate time series by constructing graphs. For periodic data, the information of adjacent nodes is more informative. Compared with vanilla neural networks, graph neural networks can capture the dependency information between different sequences, which is more suitable for the prediction of multivariate time series. Therefore, graph neural networks can achieve more accurate prediction results than vanilla neural networks by aggregating information from multiple sequences.

In this paper, a multivariate time series deep spatiotemporal forecasting model with a graph neural network (MDST-GNN) is proposed. The model consists of four core components: graph learning, temporal convolution, graph convolution, and down-sampling convolution. The local information and deep spatiotemporal information of multivariate time series data can be learned by the model. Dependencies between sequences can be captured by a graph learning module. The temporal information is captured by the 1D convolution of the temporal convolution module. In the graph convolution module, the spatial dependencies between variables are extracted through relational graphs. The spatiotemporal information in sequences with different sparsity is captured by down-sampling convolution modules. The experiments in this paper show that the model has good prediction performance and generalization ability.

The main contributions of this paper are as follows:

1. A more general time series forecasting model based on graph convolutional networks and deep spatiotemporal features is proposed in this paper.
2. The attention mechanism is added to the graph convolution module to realize the filtering of spatiotemporal information.
3. A down-sampling convolution module is proposed to extract deep spatiotemporal information of time series to improve the performance of the model.

The remainder of this paper is organized as follows: Section 2 presents the related work and research status. Section 3 introduces the definition of the problem and presents the overall framework and algorithmic flow of the model. Section 4 describes the experimental part and gives the experimental results of different methods in the dataset, analysis of experimental results, and ablation experiments. Finally, Section 5 is the conclusion of this paper.

2. Related Works

2.1. Time Series Forecasting with Traditional Methods

Time series forecasting has been studied for a long time. Most of the existing work can be divided into statistical methods and machine learning and deep learning methods. Such as Autoregressive Integrated Moving Average Model (ARIMA) [6] and a hybrid ARIMA and multilayer perception model (VARMLP) [13]. ARIMA obtained future forecast values by constructing polynomials of historical information and adding noise. VARMLP modeled linear and nonlinear data combining ARIMA with an artificial neural network model (ANN) [14]. Neural networks are often used to capture nonlinear relationships in time series forecasting [15,16]. However, the main limitations of ARIMA models are the pre-assumed linear patterns and the requirement for high stationarity of the data. Therefore, ARIMA is not suitable for modeling problems of multivariate time series. Furthermore, Linear Support Vector Regression (SVR) [17] treats the prediction problem as a typical regression problem with parameters changing over time. The vector autoregressive model (VAR) [18] extends the AR model and was a commonly used econometric model. However, these models are difficult to extend to multivariate time series forecasting problems.

2.2. Time Series Forecasting with Deep Learning

In recent years, with the improvement of data availability and computing power, deep learning techniques have been adopted to obtain better prediction accuracy than traditional methods. Nonlinear patterns of data can be captured by deep learning models and outperform traditional methods. The time series forecasting models LST-Net [19] and TPA-LSTM [20] excelled in capturing nonlinear information. LSTNet used Convolutional Neural Networks (CNN) and Recurrent Neural Networks (RNN) to extract short-term local dependence patterns and long-term patterns of time series. The former encoded the short-term local information of multivariate sequences into low-dimensional vectors. The latter decoded the vectors to capture long-term dependency information. Long Short-Term Memory (LSTM) [21] is a variant of RNN that is often used for time series forecasting tasks. LSTM also shows excellent performance in natural language processing tasks. TPA-LSTM extracted temporal patterns through the LSTM network, and a convolutional network and attention mechanism were used to calculate the attention score. However, LSTNet and TPA-LSTM cannot model the dependencies of multiple variables. RNN and LSTM cannot memorize the dependencies of multiple variables for a long time. Sample Convolution and Interaction Networks (SCINet) [22] use sequence sampling and convolutional neural network methods to capture temporal information. However, SCINet does not consider the dependencies among multiple variables, and the stacking of multiple layer structures results in huge time and space costs. Recently, Temporal Convolutional Networks (TCN) [23] have been applied to time series forecasting problems. In the TCN architecture, dilated convolutions can be used to flexibly adjust the receptive field, and its space complexity is lower than that of RNN. However, the causal convolution of TCN is not suitable for sliding window inputs. With the development of attention methods, the Transformer [24] model has replaced the RNN model in many sequence modeling tasks. Therefore, various time series forecast methods based on Transformers have emerged [25], which are quite effective in predicting long series. However, although time series models for reducing the spatial cost of Transformer have been proposed, the space cost is still large.

With further research, graph neural networks have shown great advantages in processing graph data [26–28]. In the structure of graph neural networks, each node is interconnected with its neighbors, and information is transmitted between nodes. The variables of a multivariate time series can be transformed into a graph-like structure. A variable represents a node in the graph. Nodes are interrelated through their hidden dependencies. Therefore, graphs in multivariate time series data modeling can better represent the interdependencies between time series. Currently, many people have used graph neural networks to deal with time series problems [29,30]. Multivariate Time Series Forecasting with Graph Neural Networks (MTGNN) [31] built a graph with variables as nodes. The spatiotemporal information of the data is captured by dilated convolutional networks [32] and relational graphs. However, the dilated convolutional structure of MT-GNN causes the loss of locally continuous and deep-level information. Although the above methods have been successfully applied to many forecasting problems, most of them have corresponding shortcomings.

By comparing traditional methods and classical deep learning models, a multivariate time series deep spatiotemporal forecasting model with graph neural network (MDST-GNN) is proposed in this paper. The model is able to learn relational graphs from multivariate time series data. Deep spatiotemporal information is extracted and filtered through down-sampling convolutional networks and attention methods. Our model can capture the deep nonlinear spatiotemporal features in the sequence and solve the problem of local and global information loss.

3. Methods

Firstly, this section presents the definition of the prediction problem. The MDST-GNN model consists of a graph-learning module, a temporal convolution module, a graph convolution module and a down-sampling convolution module. In this paper, an attention mechanism is introduced into the graph convolution module to filter spatiotemporal information. A down-sampling convolution module is proposed to extract deep spatiotemporal information to improve model performance. Finally, the overall frame diagram and algorithm steps of the MDST-GNN model are given.

3.1. Problem Definition

Definition 1. *There is a multivariate time series with sequence length m, given as a set $X = \{s_{m,1}, s_{m,2}, s_{m,3}, \ldots, s_{m,n}\}$, where $s_{m,1} = \{t_{1,1}, t_{2,1}, t_{3,1}, \ldots, t_{m,1}\}$ is the set of the first variable sequence and $t_{n,[i]} \in R$ is the value of the ith variable at time step n.*

Definition 2. *A graph can be defined as $G = \{V, E\}$. V represents the set of nodes. E represents the set of edges formed by the dependencies between variables. An adjacency matrix is a mathematical form that facilitates graph computation. It is $A \in R^{N \times N}$, assuming $\{vi, vj\} \in V$. If $(vi, vj) \in E$, then $A_{ij} = C > 0$, if $(vi, vj) \notin E$, then $A_{ij} = 0$.*

Definition 3. *The goal is to learn a model $F(\cdot)$ and build the mapping of F from X to Y by minimizing the L2 regularization loss function. Given a prediction step size h, it is possible to predict the future value $Y = \{s_{m+h,n}\}$ of X after h steps.*

3.2. Graph Learning Module

During the training of the model, the spatial information representation of the input data and the implicit relationships among multiple sequences are obtained by the graph learning module. In existing research, graphs are mostly constructed by the method of node similarity and distance, and these graphs are usually bidirectional or symmetric. For the prediction task in this paper, other nodes may be affected by the change in one node. For example, if the traffic roads in a certain area are congested, other roads in the area will also change. When solar power generation in a region rises, other sites in the region will also have certain changes. Therefore, a one-way relational graph structure is more suitable to be constructed:

$$A_1 = tanh(\alpha \times E_1 \times W_1) \qquad (1)$$

$$A_2 = tanh(\alpha \times E_2 \times W_2) \qquad (2)$$

$$B = A_1 \times A_2^T \qquad (3)$$

$$A = Relu(tanh(\alpha \times (B - B^T))) \tag{4}$$

According to the above formula, the initial adjacency matrix A can be obtained. E_1 and E_2 are learnable nodes encoding information. W_1 and W_2 are model-learnable parameters. The hyperparameter α is used to prevent the vanishing gradient problem caused by the saturation of the activation function. The adjacency matrix is converted to a one-way matrix by matrix subtraction and activation function Relu. When A_{ij} is a positive number, $A_{ij} = 0$:

$$A[i, not\ argtopk(A[i,:], k)] = 0 \tag{5}$$

Argtopk() extracts the indices of the top k maxima of the vector. In order to simplify the calculation amount, the k nodes with the largest value among the nodes are selected as the nodes with high relevant information during graph convolution. Unselected nodes are assigned the value 0. This method is more flexible in constructing graphs, and the internal information of the graph can be adjusted according to the data during the training process.

3.3. Temporal Convolution Module

The temporal convolution module consists of two Dilated Inception layers. Tanh and Sigmoid activation functions are used after the Dilated Inception layer. One dilated inception layer is followed by an activation function, and Tanh is used as a filter. The sigmoid function of the other layer is used as the gate unit. The gate unit controls the amount of information that the filter propagates to the next module.

The advantages of the Inception network and Dilated convolution are incorporated into the Dilated Inception layer. Information at different scales can be captured by the Inception network, while the dilated convolutional network ensures that long-term sequences can be processed. First, the receptive field of traditional convolutional networks is limited by the depth of the network and the size of the convolution kernels. Processing long-term sequences requires increasing convolution kernel size and network depth, which increases the cost of computational resources for the problem. For example, for a network with L one-dimensional convolutions and K convolution kernels, the size of the receptive field is:

$$R = (K - 1) \times L + 1 \tag{6}$$

In WaveNet [33], stacked dilated convolutions were used to make the network have a very large receptive field. Computational efficiency and input data integrity are guaranteed with only a few layers. In this paper, the dilated convolution method is used to reduce the cost of model computing resources. The dilation factor is doubled for each layer. With the increase in depth, the dilation factor can make the receptive field grow exponentially. For long time series, the advantage of dilated convolution is that the internal data structure can be preserved without reducing the length of the data input. However, models designed based on dilated convolutions also have some problems. Due to the discontinuity of the convolution kernel, all elements cannot be covered in the dilated convolution, so the continuity of information will be lost. Therefore, the Inception network is introduced into the model. Multiple convolution kernels of different sizes are used to cover the receptive field to retain more information.

In the Inception network, features of multiple scales are obtained by convolution kernels of different sizes. The sparse matrices output by multiple convolutional networks are aggregated into denser submatrices. For the Inception network, the size of the convolution kernel needs to be selected according to the characteristics of the data. According to the periodicity of the time series (2, 3, 6, 7), four convolution kernels are used by the Inception network in this paper. These convolution kernels can be combined to cover multiple time periods of different lengths. The input data X is processed using four convolution kernels of different scales. The outputs of different scale convolutions are fused to obtain complete temporal information.

$$X = concat(X \times I_{1\times 2}, X \times I_{1\times 3}, X \times I_{1\times 6}, X \times I_{1\times 7}) \quad (7)$$

Finally, the convolution results of different lengths are cropped to the same length. In Formula (7), the convolution results are concatenated by the channel dimension. Features of different scales are learned by each layer in the network. The adaptability of the network to different scales of information is increased by the concatenation of channel dimensions.

3.4. Graph Convolution Module

In the graph convolution module, dependency information is extracted from the input data through the adjacency matrix of the graph learning module. Each node of the adjacency matrix is fused with highly dependent node information to obtain the dependency information of each node and its related nodes.

The graph convolution module consists of two Attention Mixed Propagation layers for processing the inflow and outflow information of each node. The structure of the graph convolution module is shown on the left of Figure 1, and A is the adjacency matrix of the node relationship obtained by the graph learning layer. The inflow information of each node is processed by the Attention Mixed propagation layer. A^T is used to process the outflow information of the node. After the Attention Mixed propagation layer, the final node feature information is obtained by summing the inflow and outflow information of the nodes. The structure of the Attention Mixed Propagation layer is shown on the right in Figure 1, and A is the dependency matrix between nodes, D_{in} is the output information of the temporal convolutional layer, and $D^{(k)}$ represents the information that D_{in} propagates K times in the nodes of A. After the Concat connection, C is the channel dimension of the feature information, N is the number of variables in the feature information, and T is the sequence length of the feature information. The node information is weighted and filtered for different dimensions of the feature information, and the weighted sum is used as the output of the Attention Mixed propagation layer. The graph obtained by the graph learning layer is utilized to process the information flow of the relevant nodes in the Attention Mixed propagation layer. The Attention Mixed propagation layer consists of two parts: information propagation and information selection.

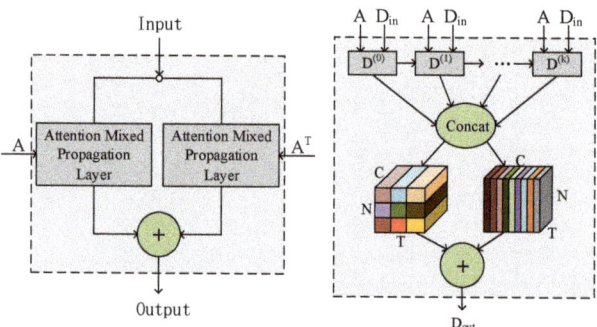

Figure 1. Graph Convolution Module and Attention Mixed Propagation.

The information propagation steps are as follows:

$$D^{(k)} = \beta D_{in} + (1-\beta) \frac{(A+I)}{\sum_{j=0}^{n} A_{ij}} D^{(k-1)} \quad (8)$$

$$D = Concat(D^{(0)}, D^{(1)}, ..., D^{(k)}) \times W^{(k)} \quad (9)$$

Among them, β in the Formula (8) is a hyperparameter used to control the retention rate of initial information. A is the graph adjacency matrix. K is the depth of information propagation. D_{in} is the output of the previous module. It can be seen from Formula (9) that $D^{(k)}$ is concatenated through the channel dimension after the information propagation process. Afterwards, the channel dimension is compressed to the dimension before concatenation by a convolutional network. D contains the features of spatial dependence after each node information is propagated.

However, initial information and new information are continuously fused in graph convolution. The initial information of the node will be continuously lost when reaching a certain depth, which will lead to unreliable data. Therefore, the β parameter is introduced to preserve part of the initial information. Make sure that local and deep-level information of nodes is preserved. At the same time, the cases where the spatial dependence is not obvious or there is no spatial dependence also need to be considered between the data. In this case, the important information of each node will be disturbed by the graph convolution operation instead.

Therefore, Spatial and Channel Squeeze and Excitation (scSE) [34] is used as an information-selection method to filter out some unnecessary information in this paper. The scSE attention method consists of two parts, namely, Channel Squeeze and Excitation (cSE) and Spatial Squeeze and Excitation (sSE). The attention mechanism is used to adjust the weights of features in the network. By weighting important feature maps or feature channels, the influence of unimportant features was reduced, thereby improving prediction results. The core idea of Squeeze and Excitation (SE) was to dynamically learn feature weights through network training. The effective feature weight was amplified and the invalid or small effect feature weights were reduced so that the model can achieve better results.

Among them, cSE refers to the compressed spatial dimension information and the adjusted channel dimension weights. After the data passed through the fully connected layer, the weight of each channel was multiplied with the original input in the channel dimension. Finally, the adjusted feature map was obtained.

Channel attention is defined as follows:

$$z_k = \frac{1}{H \times W} \sum_{i}^{H} \sum_{j}^{W} d_k(i,j) \tag{10}$$

$$\hat{z} = sigmoid(w_1 z), w_1 \in R^{c \times c} \tag{11}$$

$$\hat{D}_{cSE} = [\sigma(\hat{z}_1)d_1, \cdots, \sigma(\hat{z}_c)d_c] \tag{12}$$

The input feature map is $D = [d_1, d_2, \ldots, d_c]$, where each channel is $d_i \in R^{H \times W}$. D is converted to $z \in R^{1 \times 1 \times C}$ after going through a global pooling layer (GAP). In Formula (10), z_k is the global spatial information in each channel obtained through the global pooling layer. In Formula (11), global spatial information is transformed into channel weight values $\hat{z}$ (between 0 and 1) by sigmoid and fully connected layers. As the network continues to train, the input feature map is adaptively adjusted to emphasize important channels.

The sSE in the method referred to the compression of channel information and the adjustment of the weight of the spatial dimension. After the data passed through the fully connected layer, the weight of each point in the spatial dimension was multiplied with the original input in the spatial dimension. Finally, the adjusted feature map was obtained.

Spatial attention is defined as follows:

$$q = sigmoid(D \times w_1), q \in R^{H \times W} \tag{13}$$

$$\hat{D}_{sSE} = [\sigma(q_{1,1})d_{1,1}, \cdots, \sigma(q_{h,w})d_{h,w}] \tag{14}$$

$$D_{out} = \hat{D}_{cSE} + \hat{D}_{sSE} \tag{15}$$

The input feature maps are $D = [d_{1,1}, d_{1,2}, \ldots, d_{h,w}]$, where each $d_{i,j} \in R^{1 \times 1 \times C}$. In Formula (13), D is converted into a spatial weight value q (between 0 and 1) after passing through the convolutional network and the activation function Sigmoid. Finally, the channel attention feature map and the spatial attention feature map are added to obtain the weighted feature map D_{out}. In addition, D_{out} is the output after information filtering.

3.5. Down-Sampling Convolution Module

The down-sampling convolution module in this paper is a multilayer module. Multiple resolution temporal features are captured by down-sampling convolutions to improve model performance. The down-sampling convolution module consists of basic down-sampling blocks, each D-s Block contains a structure on the right of the figure. The last layer is connected via Concat. FC is a fully connected layer, which maps the output to the specified dimension, as shown on the left of Figure 2. The output of the previous module is used as the input of the binary tree structure, and multiple spatiotemporal short-sequence information is obtained after passing through L layers. The short-sequence information is rearranged into new deep spatiotemporal sequence information. Through residual connection, the original input is added to the newly extracted deep spatiotemporal information sequence to ensure the integrity of the information. A basic down-sampling block of a binary tree structure consists of sequence segmentation, convolution filtering, and information crossing. The output data of the previous module is divided into two subsequences in the down-sampling component as shown in Figure 2 right. The output D_{out} of the graph convolution module is used as input, and then each layer takes the output of the upper layer as input. D_{even} and D_{odd} represent sequences with odd and even subscripts, respectively. Conv1, Conv2, Conv3, and Conv4 are four identical 1D convolutional networks, respectively. The exp function is used to highlight peaks of information. Hadamard product is represented by $\odot$, which is the multiplication between the elements. Finally, the output of the current layer is obtained by subtracting the two sequences. Different convolutional filters are used to extract new sequence information from each sequence. In order to avoid the loss of information caused by dividing the sequence multiple times, the important information of multiple subsequences is preserved through information crossing.

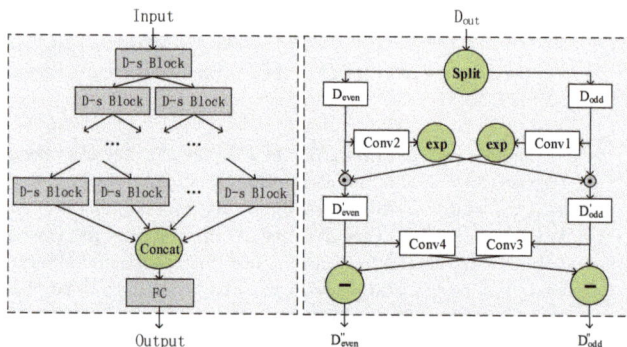

Figure 2. Down-sampling Convolution Module and Down-sampling block (D-s Block).

The input sequence is decomposed into odd and even sequences by the sequence decomposition operation in the down-sampling block of Figure 2. The odd sequences take data at positions 1, 3, 5, etc., in the input sequence. The even sequences take data at positions 0, 2, 4, etc., in the input sequence. The original sequence D_{out} is decomposed into two subsequences D_{even} and D_{odd}. Odd and even sequences reduce the amount of data while retaining most of the information of the original sequence. After that, different convolutional networks are employed to extract the feature information of the input sequence from the two sequences. The feature information obtained by different convolutional networks has stronger representation ability after fusion:

$$D_{even}, D_{odd} = split(D_{out}) \tag{16}$$

$$D'_{even} = D_{even} \odot \exp(conv_1(D_{odd})), \quad D'_{odd} = D_{odd} \odot \exp(conv_2(D_{even})) \tag{17}$$

$$D''_{even} = D'_{even} - conv_3(D'_{odd}), \quad D''_{odd} = D'_{odd} - conv_4(D'_{even}) \tag{18}$$

In Formula (16), D_{out} is split into D_{even} and D_{odd}. In Formula (17), D_{even} and D_{odd} are mapped to the hidden state through two convolutional networks and converted to exp format. In Formula (18), two other convolutional networks map D'_{even} and D'_{odd} to new hidden states, which are subtracted to obtain the final result. The mapping process of the hidden state can be viewed as a scaling transformation of the two subsequences. The scaling factor is learned during network training.

The down-sampling convolution module enlarges the receptive field compared to the dilated convolution used in the WaveNet architecture. More importantly, after the input is divided into two subsequences, the temporal information in D_{even} and D_{odd} are fused by different one-dimensional convolutions. In this process, the integrity of time information is ensured, and the ability to represent information is enhanced. The down-sampling convolution module consists of several basic modules. Among them, the basic module as a whole presents a tree structure. The information in the basic module is accumulated layer by layer. The deep feature information contains the small-scale temporal information transmitted by the shallow layer. In this way, both short-term and long-term dependencies of time series can be captured. In the last layer of the module, all the subsequences are recombined by inverse odd sequence and even sequence segmentation to obtain a new sequence representation. The new sequence information is fused with the original sequence through residual connection to ensure the integrity of the sequence information. Map to the specified output dimension using a fully connected layer.

The output part consists of skip connections and two 1×1 convolutional networks in this paper. Skip connections normalize the output of the down-sampling convolution module to have the desired predicted sequence length. A 1×1 standard convolutional network is used to convert the channel dimension to the desired dimension.

3.6. Experiment Model

The model structure of MDST-GNN is shown in Figure 3. It consists of four parts: a graph learning module, K temporal convolution modules, K graph convolution modules, and a down-sampling convolution module. The graph learning module is used to construct the spatial dependency graph of the data. The temporal convolution module captures the temporal information of the data. The spatiotemporal information is obtained by fusing the dependency graph and temporal information in the graph convolution module. The down-sampling convolution module extracts deep spatiotemporal information. Add residual connections to the model to avoid vanishing gradients during training. A skip connection is added after each temporal convolution module. To obtain the final output, the hidden features are projected onto the desired output dimension by convolution. Algorithm 1 shows the algorithm steps of the model.

Algorithm 1: Algorithm steps of the model.

Input: Dataset X, initialize model parameters, batch size B, the dimension of the variable N, time series length T, channel dimension C.

Output: Ŷ. Predicted result of train/test data X after h steps.

```
// Preprocessing of data:
```
1   (a) Normalize each sequence of a multivariate time series X.
2   (b) Divide X into training set (60%), validation set (20%) and test set (20%).

```
// Fitting of Model along with estimation:
```
3 **while** *not at end of epoch* **do**
4 | constructure learning graph A;
5 | **for** $x \in R^{B \times C \times N \times T}$ *in* $X \in$ (train, valid) **do**
6 | | Get high-dimensional features of Xtrain from channel dimension;
7 | | **for** *L in Layers* **do**
8 | | | add skip connection;
9 | | | The temporal features of x are extracted by temporal convolution;
10 | | | The spatiotemporal features are obtained by fusing the temporal features with A through graph convolution;
11 | | | Layer Norm normalized spatiotemporal features;
12 | | **end**
13 | | A downsampling convolution operation is performed to extract deep spatiotemporal information;
14 | | Concatenate deep spatiotemporal information and skip connections information;
15 | | Forecast the future time series $\hat{y}$;
16 | | Reverse normalize $\hat{y}$;
17 | | Compute loss and gradient;
18 | | Update model parameters by back propagation;
19 | **end**
20 **end**

```
// Prediction:
```
21 Ŷ = predict(x sample a batch from X), $X \in$ (test dataset)

- Input: The raw data X of the multivariate time series.
- Output: The prediction result of data X after h (Horizon) steps. The value of h can take 3, 6, 12, and 24.
- Line 1–2: Preprocess the input raw data X. Normalize each sequence of a multivariate time series X. Divide X into training set (60%), validation set (20%), and test set (20%). The Xtrain and Ytrain are obtained by splitting the sequence X with a fixed-length sliding window. Xtrain represents the input data for training, and Ytrain represents the labels of the training data.
- Line 4: Construct the graph structure A of the multivariate time series. A represents the dependencies between different sequences in a multivariate time series by an adjacency matrix.
- Line 6: A 1×1 convolutional network is used to obtain high-dimensional data in the channel dimension of Xtrain.
- Line 8: Add skip connection method to preserve part of the original information of each layer.
- Line 9: Perform a temporal convolution operation on the input data to obtain the temporal information of the data.
- Line 10: In the graph convolution, spatially weighted spatiotemporal information is obtained by multiplying the temporal information with an adjacency matrix A.
- Line 11: The output data are normalized using Layer Norm. Repeat Line 8 to Step 11 for L times. L represents the number of layers of the module.

- Line 13: Perform down-sampling convolution operation on the obtained spatiotemporal information to extract deep spatiotemporal information.
- Line 14–15: Concatenate deep spatiotemporal information and skip connections information. The final output result is obtained through 1 × 1 convolutional dimensionality reduction information.
- Line 16–18: Reverse normalize the output of the model. The mean value (MAE) of the difference between the output and the true value is used as the loss function. The model parameters are updated according to the gradient, and the steps from Step 3 to Step 10 are repeated until the model finally converges to the minimum error.
- Line 21: Finally, input the test set into the trained model to obtain the prediction result.

The above process can be divided into 4 parts. Line 1 to 2 is the data preprocessing part. Lines 4 to 15 are the MDST-GNN model training and fitting process. Line 16 to 18 is the loss function calculation part. Line 21 gives the final prediction result. The source code of the algorithm is available at https://github.com/yiminghzc/MDST-GNN (accessed on 28 May 2022).

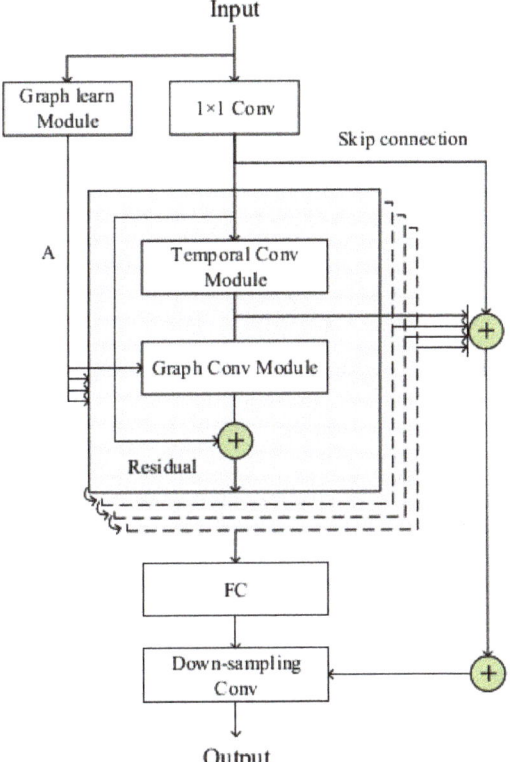

Figure 3. Model structure diagram of MDST-GNN.

4. Experiment Analysis

4.1. Experiment Dataset Analysis

In order to evaluate the effectiveness and generalization ability of the model, a classical multivariate time series dataset is adopted in this paper. The dataset comes from the experimental dataset given by LSTNet [19]. It contains multivariate time series datasets in four different domains:

- Solar Energy: Solar power generation data from Alabama State PV plants in 2006, sampled every 10 min from 137 PV plants;
- Traffic: Hourly road occupancy (between 0 and 1) on San Francisco Bay Area highways for 48 months (2015–2016) recorded by the California Department of Transportation, including data from 862 sensor measurements;
- Electricity: The hourly electricity consumption (kWh) of 321 users from 2012 to 2014;
- Exchange Rate: Daily exchange rate records for 8 countries (Australia, British, Canada, China, Japan, New Zealand, Singapore, and Switzerland) from 1990 to 2016.

Table 1 presents the statistical information of the experimental dataset in this paper. It includes four data sets. Time length represents the time length of a sequence. Variable represents the number of sequences in a multivariate sequence, and Sample rate represents the time interval of data recording. For example, there are 862 sequences with a length of 17,544 in the Traffic dataset, and the sequence data are recorded at an hourly interval.

Table 1. Dataset Statistics.

Dataset	Time Length	Variable	Sample Rate
Solar Energy	52,560	137	10 min
Traffic	17,544	862	1 h
Electricity	26,304	321	1 h
Exchange Rate	7588	8	1 day

The dataset contains linear and nonlinear interdependencies. The characteristics of the datasets are shown by selecting two variables from each dataset. The power consumption values of the two users at different times is shown in Figure 4. The traffic road occupancy values of the two roads at different times are shown in Figure 5. The horizontal axis represents the different time periods of each day. The vertical axis represents electricity consumption and road occupancy during this period.

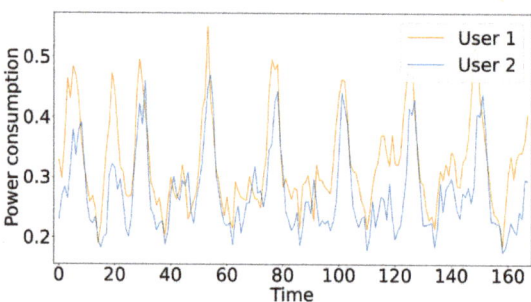

Figure 4. Consumer electricity consumption per hour.

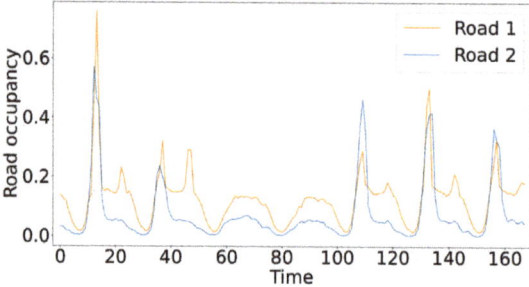

Figure 5. Road occupancy rate per hour.

The power generation values recorded every 10 min at both power stations are shown in Figure 6. Daily exchange rate values for the two countries are shown in Figure 7. The horizontal axis represents the time span in different units. The vertical axis represents power generation and exchange rate values during this period.

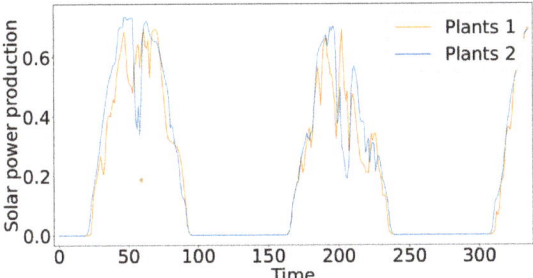

Figure 6. Solar power generation per 10 min.

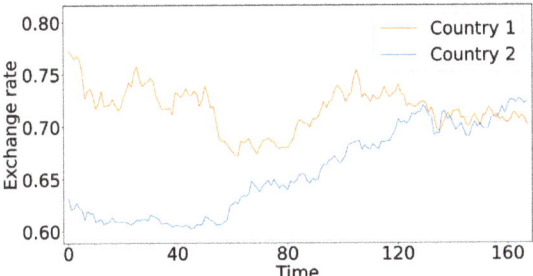

Figure 7. Daily exchange rates for two countries.

From the above data analysis, the data characteristics of the four data sets can be found. As can be seen from the figure, the Traffic, Electricity, and Solar Energy datasets have strong periodic patterns. The time series periods of multiple variables are not exactly the same, but the values of multiple variables at different periods are very similar. The above data analysis results are instructive to this paper. A multivariate time series forecasting model MDST-GNN is proposed in this paper, which can fully utilize the similarity information in the data. Information filtering is enhanced by incorporating attention methods, and the down-sampling convolution module is added to improve the deep information extraction ability. The relationship between multiple variables is modeled through a graph neural network to capture the dependency information between variables. The dependency information obtained by the graph neural network can enhance the forecasting ability of periodic time series.

4.2. Methods for Comparison

In order to effectively evaluate the experimental model and show the performance difference between different methods, the current state-of-the-art methods are compared with the model in this paper. The performance of the model on different dataset is shown by the diversity comparison of different methods.

The methods in our comparative evaluation are the follows:

- VAR-MLP: Hybrid model of multilayer perceptron (MLP) and autoregressive model (VAR) [13];
- GRU: Variant GRU model based on long short-term memory network;
- LSTNet: A hybrid model of deep neural network composed of convolutional neural network and recurrent neural network [19];

- TPA-LSTM: Recurrent Neural Network Model Based on Attention Mechanism [20];
- MTGNN: Hybrid model based on graph neural network and convolutional neural network [31];
- SCINet: Convolutional neural network model based on parity sequence segmentation and intersection [22].

4.3. Metrics

To evaluate the performance of our proposed MDST-GNN model, the same evaluation metrics are used for the comparison methods in this paper. The pros and cons of different methods can be clearly displayed by the same evaluation metrics. The evaluation metrics are the relative root mean square error (RRMSE) and the empirical correlation coefficient (CORR):

$$\text{RRMSE} = \frac{\sqrt{\sum_t \frac{1}{n}\sum_{i=0}^{n}(Y_{ti} - \hat{Y}_{ti})^2}}{\sqrt{\sum_t \frac{1}{n-1}\sum_{i=0}^{n}(Y_{ti} - (\overline{Y}))^2}}, t \in \Omega_{Test} \qquad (19)$$

$$\text{CORR} = \frac{1}{n}\sum_{i=1}^{n}\frac{\sum_t (Y_{ti} - (\overline{Y_i}))(\hat{Y}_{ti} - (\overline{\hat{Y}_i}))}{\sqrt{\sum_t (Y_{ti} - (\overline{Y_i}))^2 (\hat{Y}_{ti} - (\overline{\hat{Y}_i}))^2}}, t \in \Omega_{Test} \qquad (20)$$

In Formulae (19) and (20), Y and $\hat{Y}$ are the truth value and the predicted value, respectively. $\overline{Y}$ and $\overline{\hat{Y}}$ represent the mean of the truth and predicted values. Ω_{Test} represents numerical computation using the test set. For RRMSE, lower values are better, and for CORR, higher values are better.

4.4. Experimental Setup

This section describes the hardware and software environment of the experiment and the configuration of related parameters. Our models are built with the Pytorch open source deep learning library. The device configuration used in the experiment is Intel core i5 10400F 2.9 GHz, the GPU is NVIDIA GeForce RTX 3060 12 G, and the memory is 16 GB.

The four datasets are divided by time into training set (60%), validation set (20%), and test set (20%) in this paper. According to the performance difference of the model among different hyperparameters, the optimal hyperparameters are selected to validate the performance of the model on the test set.

The key hyperparameter settings of MDST-GNN are shown in Table 2. In this paper, the model adopts four graph convolution modules, four temporal convolution modules, and one down-sampling convolution module. Adam is used as the optimizer, and the gradient clipping is 5. The network model is converged to the optimal solution by the learning rate decay technique. The input sequence window length is 168, and the output sequence length is 1. Train the model to predict future target intervals (Horizon) 3, 6, 12, and 24. The starting 1×1 convolution has 1 input channel and 16 output channels. The activation function saturation rate of the graph learning module is 3, and the node-embedding dimension is 40. In the dataset Electricity, Traffic, and Solar Energy, the Number of neighbors (K of Formula (5)) of each node is set to 20. Neighboring node information is not considered for the Exchange Rate. The dilation factor of the convolutional network in the temporal convolution module is 2. A dropout of 0.3 is employed after each temporal convolution module. Layer Norm is used after each graph convolution module. The propagation depth of the Attention Mixed propagation layer is 2. The information retention rate of the propagation layer is 0.05. Both the graph convolution module and the temporal convolution module have 16 output channels. The number of layers (Num layers) of the down-sampling convolution module is shown in Table 2. The input channel of the down-sampling convolution module is 16, and the dropout is 0.3. Two skip connection layers have 32 output channels. In the output part of the model, two standard 1 × 1 convolutional networks with 64 output channels and 1 output channel are used. The training Epoch is 30. More detailed hyperparameters can be found in Table 2.

Table 2. Hyperparameter Settings.

Model Setting	Solar Energy				Traffic				Electricity				Exchange Rate			
Horizon	3	6	12	24	3	6	12	24	3	6	12	24	3	6	12	24
Batch size	8				16				32				4			
Learning rate	1×10^{-4}				1×10^{-4}				1×10^{-3}				5×10^{-4}			
Window length	168				168				168				168			
Layers	4				4				4				4			
Num nodes	137				862				321				8			
Weight decay	1×10^{-4}				1×10^{-5}				1×10^{-4}				1×10^{-4}			
Num layer	4				3				3				3			

Hyperparameters are obtained by changing the research parameters and fixing other parameters to obtain the optimal hyperparameters in this paper. Each experiment was repeated 5 times with 30 Epochs per run, and the hyperparameter that minimized the RRMSE among the 5 experiments was chosen. We investigate the hyperparameters that affect the results of the MDST-GNN model. The number of neighbors and layers were selected from the parameters. The parameters are analyzed by the results obtained from 5 experiments on the dataset Exchange Rate. Figure 8 shows the experimental results of the parameters. It can be seen from Figure 8a that fewer related nodes have better results, which indicates that the spatial dependence among multiple exchange rates is weak, and increasing the information of adjacent nodes will only increase the noise. Figure 8b shows that increasing the number of layers can achieve good results, but the change in the RRMSE tends to be flat when the number of layers is greater than 4, which is because the overfitting phenomenon occurs when the number of layers is too large.

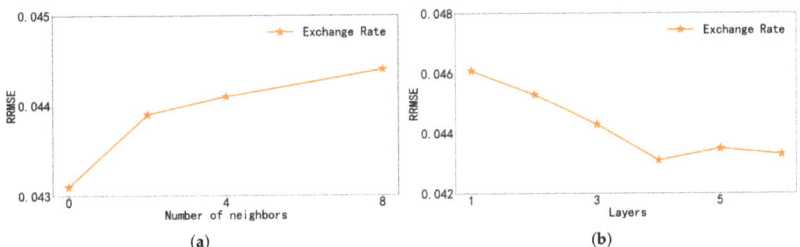

Figure 8. Number of neighbors and Layers parameter analysis in Exchange Rate. Left (a) is the RRMSE result of the parameter Number of neighbors taking 0, 2, 4, and 8 respectively, and right (b) is the RRMSE result of the parameter Layers from 0 to 6.

4.5. Results

The experiments are carried based on four test sets for the validation of the MDST-GNN model. And the evaluation results of all methods are summarized in Table 3. The horizon is set to 3, 6, 12, and 24 to predict the value after a specified time period in the future. For example, it represents forecasting 3 to 24 h into the future for electricity and traffic values in the Traffic and Electricity datasets. In Solar Energy, it means forecasting solar energy values 30 to 240 min into the future. In Exchange Rate, it represents the forecasted exchange rate value for the next 3 to 24 days. When the value of Horizon is larger, the prediction task is more difficult. The optimal results for forecast are highlighted in the table in bold black, and the suboptimal results are shown in red. Finally, the comparison results between the MDST-GNN model and other related models are shown in Table 3.

Table 3. Comparison of forecasting methods for multivariate time series methods.

Dataset		Solar Energy				Traffic				Electricity				Exchange Rate			
		Horizon				Horizon				Horizon				Horizon			
Methods	Metrics	3	6	12	24	3	6	12	24	3	6	12	24	3	6	12	24
VARMLP	RRMSE	0.1922	0.2679	0.4244	0.6841	0.5582	0.6579	0.6023	0.6146	0.1393	0.162	0.1557	0.1274	0.0265	0.0394	0.0407	0.0578
	CORR	0.9829	0.9655	0.9058	0.7149	0.8245	0.7695	0.7929	0.7891	0.8708	0.8389	0.8192	0.8679	0.8609	0.8725	0.828	0.7675
GRU	RRMSE	0.2058	0.2832	0.3726	0.464	0.4928	0.499	0.5037	0.5045	0.0776	0.0903	0.0971	0.102	0.0195	0.0258	0.0347	0.0447
	CORR	0.98	0.9601	0.9289	0.8857	0.851	0.8465	0.8431	0.8428	0.9412	0.9222	0.9088	0.9079	0.9768	0.9686	0.9534	0.9355
LSTNet-skip	RRMSE	0.1843	0.2559	0.3254	0.4643	0.4777	0.4893	0.495	0.4973	0.0864	0.0931	0.1007	0.1007	0.0226	0.028	0.0356	0.0449
	CORR	0.9843	0.969	0.9467	0.887	0.8721	0.869	0.8614	0.8588	0.9283	0.9135	0.9077	0.9119	0.9735	0.9658	0.9511	0.9354
TPA-LSTM	RRMSE	0.1803	0.2347	0.3234	0.4389	0.4487	0.4658	0.4641	0.4765	0.0823	0.0916	0.0964	0.1006	0.0174	0.0241	0.0341	0.0444
	CORR	0.985	0.9742	0.9487	0.9081	0.8812	0.8717	0.8717	0.8629	0.9439	0.9337	0.925	0.9133	0.979	0.9709	0.9564	0.9381
MTGNN	RRMSE	0.1778	0.2348	0.3109	0.427	0.4162	0.4754	0.4461	0.4535	0.0745	0.0878	0.0916	0.0953	0.0194	0.0259	0.0349	0.0456
	CORR	0.9852	0.9726	0.9509	0.9031	0.8963	0.8667	0.8794	0.881	0.9474	0.9316	0.9278	0.9234	0.9786	0.9708	0.9551	0.9372
SCINet	RRMSE	0.1775	0.2301	0.2997	0.4081	0.4216	0.4414	0.4495	0.4453	0.0748	0.0845	0.0926	0.0976	0.018	0.0247	0.034	0.0442
	CORR	0.9853	0.9739	0.955	0.9112	0.892	0.8809	0.8772	0.8825	0.9492	0.9386	0.9304	0.9274	0.9739	0.9662	0.9487	0.9255
MDST-GNN	RRMSE	0.1764	0.2321	0.3082	0.4119	0.4162	0.4461	0.4377	0.4452	0.0738	0.0833	0.0884	0.0922	0.0172	0.0245	0.0337	0.0431
	CORR	0.9855	0.9735	0.9519	0.9103	0.8958	0.8803	0.8841	0.8792	0.9454	0.9346	0.9264	0.9222	0.9811	0.9727	0.9578	0.9392

Note: The predicted optimal results are in bold black, and the suboptimal results are shown in red.

We plot the RRMSE results for all methods of Electricity and Traffic, as shown in Figure 9. From the figure, it can be found that the method using neural network significantly outperforms the VARMLP model in the dataset. Obviously, neural networks have more advantages in time series forecasting. Subsequent models using neural networks have improved their prediction accuracy. Among them, MTGNN combined with spatial information outperforms LSTNet and TAP-LSTM models in results. The SCINet model also has good results in some datasets. Figure 9a shows that the RRMSE of multiple models is relatively stable, and the prediction accuracy of each model is improved. At the same time, Figure 9b can see that the MTGNN model fluctuates when the horizon is 6, which indicates that the spatial dependence of the dataset is weak when the horizon is 6, which interferes with the model. Compared with MTGNN, the MDST-GNN model has smaller fluctuations in this part, which shows that the attention method plays a role in filtering information and reduces the interference of irrelevant information. When the horizon is other values, the RRMSE tends to be stable.

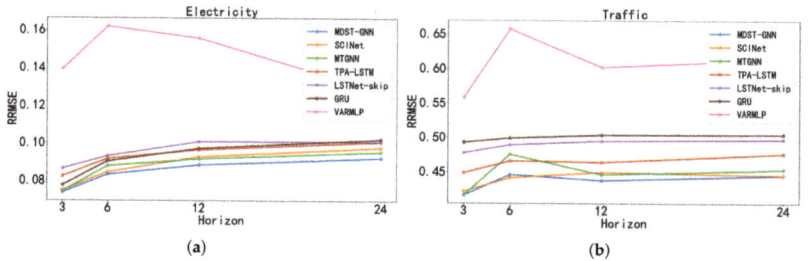

Figure 9. RRMSE comparison of all methods in Electricity and Traffic. Left (a) is the RRMSE result of all methods in Electricity, right (b) is the RRMSE result of all methods in Traffic, and horizon takes 3, 6, 12, and 24 respectively.

The RRMSE metric of our model is improved by 1%, 1.4%, 3.5%, and 3.3% on the Electricity dataset compared to the state-of-the-art method. Furthermore, on the Traffic dataset, when the horizon is 12, the RRMSE metric is 1.9% higher than the best baseline method, which proves the effectiveness of the model. More importantly, forecasts have also improved for noncyclical exchange rate data. This is because the change trend of the exchange rate is relatively stable. In this paper, the temporal information of the exchange rate is well captured by the model's deep information extraction. It is demonstrated that the framework can capture deep spatiotemporal information well, even in data with weak periodicity.

To illustrate the effectiveness of MDST-GNN in modeling spatiotemporal features in time series data, Figures 10–12 show the performance of the MDST-GNN on a specific time series (one of the output variables). Our model obtains results that are consistent with the truth value in the periodic pattern of the data. The comparative prediction results and truth values on the test set Electricity are shown in Figure 10. The comparison of the prediction results on the test set Traffic is shown in Figure 11. The comparison of the prediction results on the test set Solar Energy is shown in Figure 12. Our model achieves excellent performance on prediction tasks. The error is small between the predicted result and the truth value.

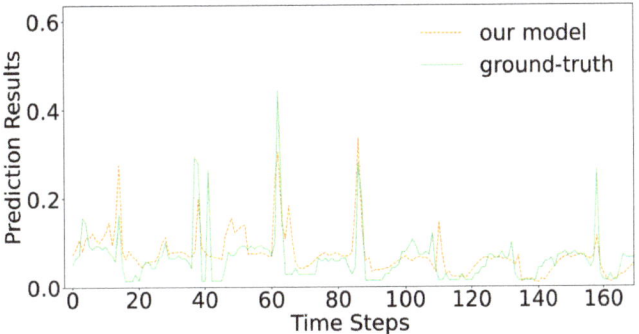

Figure 10. Electricity (Horizon = 24) forecast results.

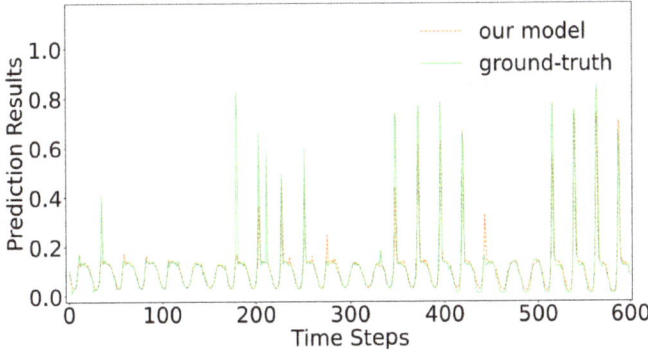

Figure 11. Traffic (Horizon = 24) forecast results.

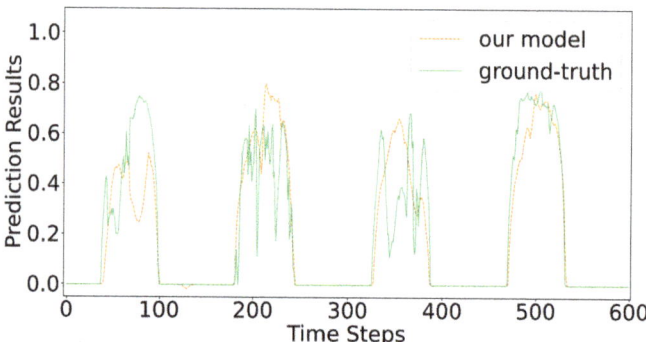

Figure 12. Solar Energy (Horizon = 24) forecast results.

However, the model performed slightly worse on the prediction task of Solar Energy data. As can be seen from Figure 12, the periodic pattern is captured by the model well, but there is an error between the results and the truth value within the periodic time. This is because the fluctuation in the data at a certain moment causes the periodic information to be disturbed. In Figure 6, it can be seen that the data remain periodic, but the data fluctuate greatly in a certain period of time. At the same time, the power generation of solar power plants is also affected by many other factors. For example, the local weather and temperature.

Overall, the model is more dominant on most tasks, achieving excellent performance on the exchange rate, traffic, and electricity datasets.

4.6. Ablation Study

A model combining an attention mechanism and time series segmentation is proposed in this paper. In this section, an ablation experiment is performed on this model, and the effectiveness of the above method will be verified. Among them, the models containing different modules are named as follows:

- w/o A: The attention mechanism part is removed from the information selection process of the graph convolution module. The output of the information selection step is passed directly to the next section.
- w/o S: Remove the down-sampling convolution module from the model and replace that part with a fully connected layer.

The effectiveness of the module is verified by removing the attention method and the down-sampling convolution module. The results of the ablation experiments on the test set are shown in Table 4. Ablation experiments verify the effectiveness of the modules in four datasets. The best results are shown in bold black. The overall model outperforms the ablation model by comparison. In Table 4, the attention method has advantages on Electricity and Traffic, and the down-sampling convolution method is more effective on Exchange Rate and Solar Energy. The effectiveness of integrating these two parts into the model is verified in Table 4. Among them, the data are filtered by the attention method, so that the data retain more important information and enhance the robustness. Down-sampling convolution captures the deep spatiotemporal information of the sequence and enhances the predictive power of the data on cyclical trends. Overall, the accuracy of model predictions is improved. To verify the effectiveness of the module, we plot the one-dimensional time series (one variable) of the Electricity test set in Figure 13, where the green curve is the real data and the yellow dashed line is the predicted value. We can see that the full model captures the spikes in the data better, and the w/o S model does not capture this change.

Table 4. Ablation study (Horizon = 24).

Dataset	Metrics	w/o A	w/o S	MDST-GNN
Solar Energy	RRMSE	0.4279	0.429	**0.4119**
	CORR	0.903	0.9042	**0.9103**
Traffic	RRMSE	0.4584	0.4577	**0.4452**
	CORR	0.8732	0.87	**0.8792**
Electricity	RRMSE	0.0952	0.095	**0.0922**
	CORR	0.9212	0.9213	**0.9222**
Exchange Rate	RRMSE	0.0444	0.0459	**0.0431**
	CORR	0.939	0.9344	**0.9392**

Note: The optimal results are in bold black.

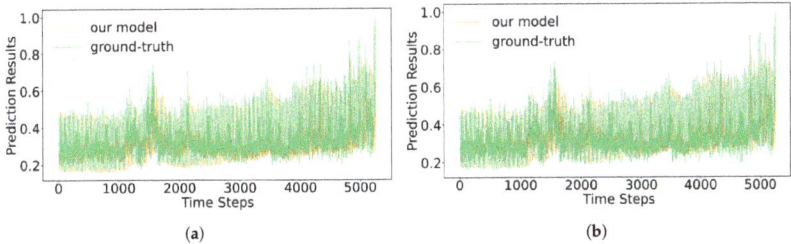

Figure 13. Time series (one variable) predicted and true values for the Electricity test set (Horizon = 24). Left (**a**) is the w/o S model result, right (**b**) is the result of the full model.

In summary, time series forecasting involves temporal, spatial, and periodic information. Of course, introducing the modules proposed in this paper will incur additional computational costs. However, it is very helpful to consider the above information. The improvement of this information on the prediction task is demonstrated by the results of the ablation experiments.

5. Conclusions

Multivariate time series have complex spatiotemporal information, and there are dependencies among multiple series. In addition, the time series has a periodic pattern. According to the characteristics of multivariate time series, a multivariate time series deep spatiotemporal forecasting model with a graph neural network (MDST-GNN) is proposed in this paper. It comprises four modules: graph learning, temporal convolution, graph convolution, and down-sampling convolution. In order to deal with complex information better, the model adopts a graph neural network to transform complex information into processable graph information. Furthermore, the model utilizes a temporal convolutional network to extract temporal information in the predicted sequence. Graph convolutional networks are used to extract spatiotemporal information of predicted sequences. The attention method is added to improve the information filtering ability. Down-sampling convolutional networks are used to extract deep spatiotemporal information. The MDST-GNN model can filter out irrelevant dependency information between graph nodes and is more suitable for multivariate time series forecasting. The prediction accuracy of data peaks can be enhanced by capturing deep spatiotemporal information. In experiments, the proposed model predicts future values at different intervals for four datasets. Based on the above discussion and experimental results, the advantages of MDST-GNN are verified in the experimental results on four sets of public datasets, and the attention method and down-sampling convolutional network proposed in this paper improve the prediction accuracy of the model.

The MDST-GNN model has achieved significant improvements on multiple datasets, but there are still certain problems in predicting data with large short-term fluctuations such as Solar Energy. This is mainly caused by the insensitivity of convolutional networks to local fluctuations and the lack of long-term memory information. At the same time, the model has many parameters, and how to reduce the model parameters while maintaining good prediction performance is a problem worth pondering. Our next research will revolve around the problem of model lightweight and insensitivity to local fluctuations.

Author Contributions: Conceptualization, Z.H., C.Z. and Y.H.; data curation, Z.H.; methodology, Z.H. and C.Z.; software, Z.H.; supervision, C.Z. and Y.H.; validation, Z.H.; writing—original draft, Z.H. and C.Z.; writing—review and editing, Z.H., C.Z. and Y.H. All authors have read and agreed to the published version of the manuscript.

Funding: This research was funded by the National Natural Science Foundation of China (Nos. 61862062, 61104035).

Institutional Review Board Statement: Not applicable.

Informed Consent Statement: Not applicable.

Data Availability Statement: The data presented in this study are openly available in Github (https://github.com/laiguokun/multivariate-time-series-data, accessed on 2 February 2022).

Conflicts of Interest: The authors declare no conflict of interest.

References

1. Taylor, J.W.; McSharry, P.E. Short-Term Load Forecasting Methods: An Evaluation Based on European Data. *IEEE Trans. Power Syst.* **2007**, *22*, 2213–2219. [CrossRef]
2. Du, S.; Li, T.; Yang, Y.; Horng, S.J. Deep Air Quality Forecasting Using Hybrid Deep Learning Framework. *IEEE Trans. Knowl. Data Eng.* **2021**, *33*, 2412–2424. [CrossRef]
3. Chen, J.L.; Li, G.; Wu, D.C.; Shen, S. Forecasting Seasonal Tourism Demand Using a Multiseries Structural Time Series Method. *J. Travel Res.* **2019**, *58*, 92–103. [CrossRef]
4. Zhuang, D.E.H.; Li, G.C.L.; Wong, A.K.C. Discovery of Temporal Associations in Multivariate Time Series. *IEEE Trans. Knowl. Data Eng.* **2014**, *26*, 2969–2982. [CrossRef]
5. Akdi, Y.; Glveren, E.; Nlü, K.; Yücel, M. Modeling and forecasting of monthly PM 2.5 emission of Paris by periodogram-based time series methodology. *Environ. Monit. Assess.* **2021**, *193*, 622. [CrossRef] [PubMed]
6. Box, G.E.P.; Jenkins, G.M.; MacGregor, J.F. Some Recent Advances in Forecasting and Control. *J. R. Stat. Soc. Ser. Appl. Stat.* **1974**, *23*, 158–179. [CrossRef]
7. Chouhan, V.; Singh, S.K.; Khamparia, A.; Gupta, D.; Tiwari, P.; Moreira, C.; Damaševičius, R.; de Albuquerque, V.H.C. A Novel Transfer Learning Based Approach for Pneumonia Detection in Chest X-ray Images. *Appl. Sci.* **2020**, *10*, 559. [CrossRef]
8. Lin, T.H.; Akamatsu, T.; Tsao, Y. Sensing ecosystem dynamics via audio source separation: A case study of marine soundscapes off northeastern Taiwan. *PLoS Comput. Biol.* **2021**, *17*, e1008698. [CrossRef] [PubMed]
9. Li, Q.; Li, S.; Zhang, S.; Hu, J.; Hu, J. A Review of Text Corpus-Based Tourism Big Data Mining. *Appl. Sci.* **2019**, *9*, 3300. [CrossRef]
10. Li, G.; Nguyen, T.H.; Jung, J.J. Traffic Incident Detection Based on Dynamic Graph Embedding in Vehicular Edge Computing. *Appl. Sci.* **2021**, *11*, 5861. [CrossRef]
11. Simeunovic, J.; Schubnel, B.; Alet, P.J.; Carrillo, R.E. Spatio-Temporal Graph Neural Networks for Multi-Site PV Power Forecasting. *IEEE Trans. Sustain. Energy* **2022**, *13*, 1210–1220. [CrossRef]
12. Abbasimehr, H.; Paki, R. Improving time series forecasting using LSTM and attention models. *J. Ambient Intell. Humaniz. Comput.* **2022**, *13*, 673–691. [CrossRef]
13. Zhang, G. Time series forecasting using a hybrid ARIMA and neural network model. *Neurocomputing* **2003**, *50*, 159–175. [CrossRef]
14. Zhang, G.; Patuwo, B.E.; Hu, M.Y. Forecasting with artificial neural networks: The state of the art. *Int. J. Forecast.* **1998**, *14*, 35–62. [CrossRef]
15. Kaur, T.; Kumar, S.; Segal, R. Application of artificial neural network for short term wind speed forecasting. In Proceedings of the 2016 Biennial International Conference on Power and Energy Systems: Towards Sustainable Energy (PESTSE), Bengaluru, India, 21–23 January 2016; pp. 1–5. [CrossRef]
16. Bukhari, A.H.; Raja, M.A.Z.; Sulaiman, M.; Islam, S.; Shoaib, M.; Kumam, P. Fractional Neuro-Sequential ARFIMA-LSTM for Financial Market Forecasting. *IEEE Access* **2020**, *8*, 71326–71338. [CrossRef]
17. Cao, L.J.; Tay, F.E.H. Support vector machine with adaptive parameters in financial time series forecasting. *IEEE Trans. Neural Netw.* **2003**, *14*, 1506–1518. [CrossRef]
18. Qin, D. Rise of VAR modelling approach. *J. Econ. Surv.* **2011**, *25*, 156–174. [CrossRef]

19. Lai, G.K.; Chang, W.C.; Yang, Y.M.; Liu, H.X. Modeling Long–Short-Term Temporal Patterns with Deep Neural Networks. In Proceedings of the 41st International ACM SIGIR Conference on Research and Development in Information Retrieval, Ann Arbor, MI, USA, 8–12 July 2018; pp. 95–104. [CrossRef]
20. Shih, S.Y.; Sun, F.K.; Lee, H.Y. Temporal pattern attention for multivariate time series forecasting. *Mach. Learn.* **2019**, *108*, 1421–1441. [CrossRef]
21. Hochreiter, S.; Schmidhuber, J. Long Short-Term Memory. *Neural Comput.* **1997**, *9*, 1735–1780. [CrossRef] [PubMed]
22. Liu, M.; Zeng, A.; Xu, Z.; Lai, Q.; Xu, Q. Time Series is a Special Sequence: Forecasting with Sample Convolution and Interaction. *arXiv* **2021**. [CrossRef]
23. Bai, S.; Kolter, J.Z.; Koltun, V. An empirical evaluation of generic convolutional and recurrent networks for sequence modeling. *arXiv* **2018**. [CrossRef]
24. Vaswani, A.; Shazeer, N.; Parmar, N.; Uszkoreit, J.; Jones, L.; Gomez, A.N.; Kaiser, Ł.; Polosukhin, I. Attention is all you need. *Adv. Neural Inf. Proces. Syst.* **2017**, *30*, 5999–6009. [CrossRef]
25. Zhou, H.; Zhang, S.; Peng, J.; Zhang, S.; Li, J.; Xiong, H.; Zhang, W. Informer: Beyond efficient transformer for long sequence time-series forecasting. *arXiv*. [CrossRef]
26. Wu, Z.; Pan, S.; Chen, F.; Long, G.; Zhang, C.; Yu, P.S. A Comprehensive Survey on Graph Neural Networks. *IEEE Trans. Neural Netw. Learn. Syst.* **2021**, *32*, 4–24. [CrossRef]
27. Mai, W.; Chen, J.; Chen, X. Time-Evolving Graph Convolutional Recurrent Network for Traffic Prediction. *Appl. Sci.* **2022**, *12*, 2824. [CrossRef]
28. Cui, Z.; Henrickson, K.; Ke, R.; Wang, Y. Traffic Graph Convolutional Recurrent Neural Network: A Deep Learning Framework for Network-Scale Traffic Learning and Forecasting. *IEEE Trans. Intell. Transp. Syst.* **2020**, *21*, 4883–4894. [CrossRef]
29. Khodayar, M.; Wang, J. Spatio-Temporal Graph Deep Neural Network for Short-Term Wind Speed Forecasting. *IEEE Trans. Sustain. Energy* **2019**, *10*, 670–681. [CrossRef]
30. Qi, Y.; Li, Q.; Karimian, H.; Liu, D. A hybrid model for spatiotemporal forecasting of PM2.5 based on graph convolutional neural network and long short-term memory. *Sci. Total Environ.* **2019**, *664*, 1–10. [CrossRef]
31. Wu, Z.; Pan, S.; Long, G.; Jiang, J.; Chang, X.; Zhang, C. Connecting the dots: Multivariate time series forecasting with graph neural networks. In Proceedings of the 26th ACM SIGKDD International Conference on Knowledge Discovery & Data Mining, Virtual Event, 6–10 July 2020; pp. 753–763. [CrossRef]
32. Yu, F.; Koltun, V. Multi-scale context aggregation by dilated convolutions. *arXiv* **2016**. [CrossRef]
33. Oord, A.V.D.; Dieleman, S.; Zen, H.; Simonyan, K.; Vinyals, O.; Graves, A.; Kalchbrenner, N.; Senior, A.; Kavukcuoglu, K. WaveNet: A generative model for raw audio. *arXiv* **2016**. [CrossRef]
34. Roy, A.G.; Navab, N.; Wachinger, C. Concurrent Spatial and Channel 'Squeeze & Excitation' in Fully Convolutional Networks. *Lect. Notes Comput. Sci.* **2018**, *11070*, 421–429. [CrossRef]

Article

Performance Evaluation of Sequential Rule Mining Algorithms

Amira Abdelwahab [1,2,*] and Nesma Youssef [3]

[1] Information Systems Department, College of Computer Sciences and Information Technology (CCSIT), King Faisal University, P.O. Box 400, Al-Ahsa 31982, Saudi Arabia
[2] Information Systems Department, Faculty of Computers and Information, Menoufia University, Shibin Al Kawm 32511, Egypt
[3] Department of Information System, Sadat Academy for Management Science, Cairo 12411, Egypt; nesmayousef1811@gmail.com
* Correspondence: a.ahmed@kfu.edu.sa

Abstract: Data mining techniques are useful in discovering hidden knowledge from large databases. One of its common techniques is sequential rule mining. A sequential rule (SR) helps in finding all sequential rules that achieved support and confidence threshold for help in prediction. It is an alternative to sequential pattern mining in that it takes the probability of the following patterns into account. In this paper, we address the preferable utilization of sequential rule mining algorithms by applying them to databases with different features for improving the efficiency in different fields of application. The three compared algorithms are the TRuleGrowth algorithm, which is an extension sequential rule algorithm of RuleGrowth; the top-k non-redundant sequential rules algorithm (TNS); and a non-redundant dynamic bit vector (NRD-DBV). The analysis compares the three algorithms regarding the run time, the number of produced rules, and the used memory to nominate which of them is best suited in prediction. Additionally, it explores the most suitable applications for each algorithm to improve the efficiency. The experimental results proved that the performance of the algorithms appears related to the dataset characteristics. It has been demonstrated that altering the window size constraint, determining the number of created rules, or changing the value of the minSup threshold can reduce execution time and control the number of valid rules generated.

Keywords: sequential rule mining; non redundant sequential rules; TRuleGrowth; top-k non redundant rules; closed sequential patterns

1. Introduction

There is a fundamental issue in extracting useful information from the temporal relations in large sequence datasets. It helps a user to acquire useful knowledge for making a prediction. Many methods are emerging for finding the temporal relations in datasets. One of the foremost popular methods is mining sequential patterns to discover, as often as possible, patterns in sequence datasets [1,2]. Mining sequential patterns rely on one measure called support measure. The support measure means the number of presence items in a dataset. It can be misleading and inadequate for making a prediction. Mining sequential rules is an extension of sequential patterns mining that addresses the previous problem by considering additional measures [3,4].

Mining sequential rules take another measure besides the support into consideration, called the confidence measure, which means that the probability of executing the next pattern is calculated. There are many challenges for mining sequential rules, such as classifying similar rules differently. Additionally, some rules have been discovered that lose their importance when appearing separately. Therefore, particular rules are losing their use in predicting. All previous reasons impact the generation of a large number of redundant rules that affect the efficiency of the mining process. Numerous analysts have proposed upgraded methods of sequential rule mining (SRM) to decrease redundant rules and progress the proficiency of these algorithms. SRM is divided into two categories: partially ordered and standard sequential rules. The proposed enhanced algorithms concentrate on two directions:

The first type is a common type for mining the sequential rules named standard. It helps to enhance efficiency through the process of mining. The mining process consists of two procedures; the first is mining sequential patterns that appear frequently. The second is producing sequential rules that rely on the first procedure. Therefore, numerous researchers give consideration to the first procedure to enhance the performance through disposing of grouping that does not affect the ultimate result. Mining closed sequential patterns is an example of the previous idea. It helps to produce rules based on more compact data. In this study, we make a reference to this type with the non-redundant dynamic bit-vector algorithm.

The second type is the newest type for mining the sequential rules named partially ordered rules. It helps to enhance efficiency by extending the mining of sequential rules algorithms by adding constraints or by finding a specified number of the most visit rules in a database. In the partially ordered mining, there is no arrangement between items in the prior and posterior sides. The pattern growth approach is applied to discover all rules incrementally. There are improved algorithms that acknowledge an extra constraint to enhance the overall performance. The TRuleGrowth algorithm adds a window size parameter. It makes a difference to decrease the number of rules produced, as it diminishes the runtime, and diminished disk space is a prerequisite to store generating rules, so that users are able to analyze the rules in an easy manner. Additionally, we have another approach to produce non-redundant rules. We find the most frequent rules (the top-k) that achieved the minConf threshold. Therefore, we have only two parameters, K and minConf. Like the TNS algorithm, we did not take the minSup into consideration due to the difficulty of determining the valid values that suit each dataset's features.

In this paper, we present a broad consider of two sorts of SRM: partially ordered and standard sequential rules. We study three algorithms named TRuleGrowth, TNS, and non-redundant with a dynamic bit-vector algorithm. All these algorithms generate non-redundant rules and we compare the results of their implementation to decide the most reasonable areas for each of them. We assess the final results according to these criteria: runtime, number of produced rules, and memory utilization.

2. Literature Review

Numerous research has been suggested to enhance the mining process of sequential patterns. The primary obstacle in mining sequential patterns is producing unessential sequential patterns when setting the support measure with a very low value. Mining the sequential rules is an alternative to sequential patterns that assist the users in having knowledge of sequence items for making a prediction. It has been found in numerous zones like electronic learning [5], manufacturing simulation [6], the analysis of customer behavior [7], and decision systems [8].

The primary algorithm proposed for mining the sequential rules by Mannila and Verkano is studying the sequence behavior for the prediction process. It helps in finding all items that occurred as often as possible in a sequence dataset [9]. Then, most research has been proposed to produce sequential patterns that appear frequently and remove repetitive rules within the following stage of the mining process. They had to check the database numerous times to find the support of each itemset that induces minimum complexity and extra cost like RuleGen algorithm [10]. After that, the researchers have found rules with no consideration of their arrangement; refer to partially ordered sequential rules (POSR). It stands up on those items in the predecessor, and forerunner sides are unarranged. Two primary algorithms for the POSR are named CMRule and CMDeo [11,12]. The CMRule is the baseline algorithm that expels the temporal information and generates rules that accomplish the support threshold. It relies on the produced number of sequential rules that cause ineffectual performance [13]. The second baseline algorithm is CMDeo, which acts as more proficient than the CMRule. It discovers all substantial rules size $1*1$ by expanding both sides of the rules. To address the previous obstacles, RuleGrowth has been proposed. It can extend rules amid guarantees as it was necessary for rules in sequence datasets [14–16].

Various algorithms have been developed based on the prefix tree to realize superior efficiency. The CNR, IMSR, and MNSR algorithms rely on enhancing the rules by eliminating non-redundant rules [17–19]. They sort the sequences according to the support value ascendancy before producing rules. In this way, it diminishes the scan's number and minimizes complexity to $o(n^2)$.

TRuleGrowth is an extension of RuleGrowth. It has been developed to control the maximum consecutive items by applying an additional constraint called window size. This constraint helps to produce much fewer number of rules. So, it enhances the performance due to diminishing the request space used to store the generated rules [20–23].

The researchers proposed the Top-k sequential rule mining to overcome the problem of the difficulty of determining the valid minSup value that suits each database features [24,25]. It depends on two parameters: k is the number of rules that users want to generate, and the minConf that is easy to determine due to user satisfaction. The TopSeqRules is the first algorithm that addresses the Top-k sequential rule mining. It depends on the same strategy as the RuleGrowth algorithm. It integrates the two procedures to expand the left and the right sides of the rule with the general procedure for mining the top-k pattern. Researchers enhanced many algorithms to reduce disk space and generate interesting sequential rules. The Top-k non-redundant sequential rule (TNS) utilizes the TopSeqRules for mining the top-k to eliminate the redundancy on the generated rules [26,27].

A proficient algorithm named non-redundant with dynamic bit-vector has been suggested. It is used to remove unnecessary rules early through utilizing dynamic bit-vector with pruning techniques, so that it improves the performance by reducing the execution time and memory utilization [28–30].

3. Methods of Applying Comparative Algorithms

There are two categories for mining the sequential rules. The first category is called standard sequential rules that discover relations between two patterns that act sequentially. It depends on two measures, support and confidence, which are selected by the user. It exists in many algorithms like RuleGen, IMSR (Improved Mining Sequential Rule), and NRD-DBV (Non-Redundant-Dynamic Bit Vector) algorithm. It produced the result only in integer's format, and it proves its efficiency in creating an imperative choice or expectation. The second category is called POSR, which is the newest type of SRM that discovers relations between two unarranged item-sets. It does not care about the relations between the predecessor and forerunner of rules. The POSR is based on the pattern growth approach, which starts with two items and expands the rules one element at a time recursively. It can expand the mining process by including extra constraints to improve the performance of the general rules like the TRuleGrowth algorithm. Therefore, it can control the number of generated rules, which helps in saving more space and being more specific. The POSR can also satisfy the user's desire by producing a predefined number of the rules like the Top-k algorithm. Each type has its benefits to generate the non-redundant rules. In this paper, we present the most frequent recent algorithms that help in discovering the non-redundant rules by applying them to different dataset's features to reach the best efficiency.

3.1. The Fundamental Operations of the TRuleGrowth Algorithm

The TRuleGrowth algorithm is a type of POSR that does not need to arrange its items. It is an extension of the RuleGrowth algorithm that proves its efficiency compared to the last one. It is similar to RuleGrowth based on an approach called pattern growth. It performs incrementally, begins with two elements, and grows one item at a time by expanding the right and the left side of the rule. The TRuleGrowth utilizes an extra constraint called window size to control the number of rules generated. It helps in producing more accurate results and saving more space by generating much fewer sequential rules. The value of a window size constraint can be an obstacle when its value increases. The best solution, in this case, is using the RuleGrowth algorithm instead of TRuleGrowth to eliminate the high computations due to emerging large number of rules.

The construction of the TRuleGrowth algorithm is formed by three stages. The primary stage is transforming the database to the sequential list, and then setting the support value. The moment stage is creating a rule size $1 * 1$ and executing two procedures to extend the rule on the right and the left sides. The final stage is determining the window size and the confidence value, and after that, testing the legitimacy of the rules to produce the non-redundant sequential rules, as shown in Figure 1.

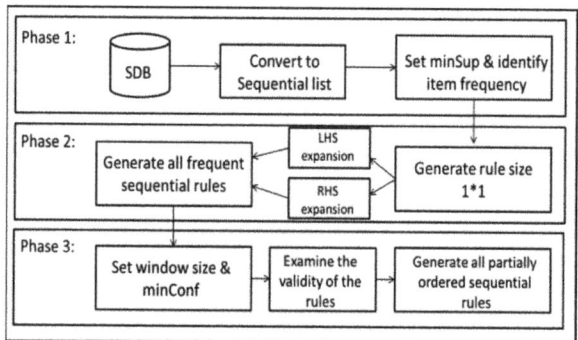

Figure 1. The RuleGrowth algorithm framework based on [31].

The TRuleGrowth Application Algorithm

This algorithm begins with scanning the dataset once to discover each item on each side. At that point, it distinguishes every item achieving the support value threshold to produce all accurate rules with size $1 * 1$. To computing sides (x→z) and sides (z→x), it filters the dataset to generate the first sequence and calculate each duo of items individually. Then we compute the support value by partitioning |sides (x→z)| / |s|. If the support values of the item are not lower than the minSup, then the two strategies have been executed to grow each side of the rule [14]. We have guaranteed that the value of the sliding window has applied for all the rules. It saves all events of each item and shows their position by including that item. For the events of c in the sequence {a,c}, {b,c}, {c}, and {a,b,e} are 1, 2, and 3. At that point, utilize the hash table for searching each item found before item z and items found before x in a sequence dataset. It can be done inside a window size parameter, as appeared in Appendix A Algorithm A1 [22].

The operation of the two procedures is accomplished in the following steps: begin by establishing a hash table and assign the null value. Then, check the item-set to dispose of all items that do not accomplish the sliding window predetermined value. If the measure of 'hash x' = size 'x', then include each item $z \in y \cap n$ in the hash table. In case 'hash table' < 'x' at the point, contain each item with the position of n as DB ϵ x $\cap$ n. At last, if 'hash y' = size 'y' and size 'hash x' = size 'x', include side to accessible side (y U {z}→x) for each item $z \notin y \cup x$ that contains ID, to begin with an item of 'x' inside window size.

An extra parameter called sliding window can be included which has the following characteristics:

1. Controlling the number of produced rules, so less space and time is required to search the desired sequential rules.
2. Reducing the amount of memory space required to store the generated rules by developing fewer rules. Therefore, it gives the facility to analyze the output to the user.

3. Favoring its significance in practical for temporal transactions like analyses data for shares market.

3.2. The Operation of the Top-k Non-Redundant Sequential Rule (TNS)

The TNS algorithm adopts TopSeqRules to mine the Top-k rules after eliminating redundancy of sequential rule. It depends on the same search procedure of the RuleGrowth algorithm. The TopSeqRules has two parameters: the number of rules that is determined by the user needs (K), and the minConf threshold that also satisfies the user requirements. It also utilizes three main variables; the first is minSup that is set to initial value = 0 and raises with regard to the number of rules generated. The second variable is L, which helps to perform Top-k rules by keeping each item that achieved the threshold value. The third variable is R having the rule with the maximum support values that helps in choosing the most candidate rules.

The TNS Algorithm Implementation

The TNS algorithm firstly scans the dataset only once to identify each item, as seen in Figure 2. It considers an integer parameter K, minConf value, and initializes a value of minSup with zero. Then it generates a rule recursively by growing the valid rule size $1 * 1$. After that, it performes two procedures to extend the right and the left side of the rule to generate the Top-k sequential rules. It is followed by removing all redundant rules which means that if r_a is equal to r_b with the same support, we will absorb r_a. Then it verifies the result by setting parameter delta Δ with a value higher than the all removed rules, so the Top-k non-redundant rules will be generated as shown in Algorithm A2 [24].

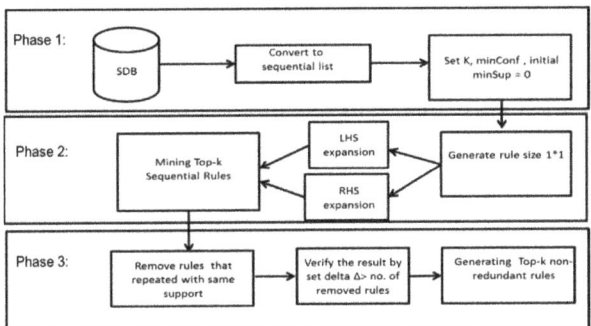

Figure 2. Framework of TNS algorithm.

Applying the TNS algorithm solves the trouble of generating either a large number of sequential rules or fewer numbers which may lose valuable information. It also addresses the challenge of generating redundant sequential rules. It has more advantages as:

1. It saves more time by depending on another parameter to generate the wanted number of sequential rules. Therefore, it does not rely on minSup value that is difficult to be determined regarding database features.
2. Removes the redundant rules and verifies the result by the delta parameter that was set higher than the removed sequential rules.

3.3. The Operation of the Non-Redundant with Dynamic Bit Vector Algorithm

The main idea of the NRD-DBV algorithm is to mine more compact data without losing any information or distorting the final result. It is based on mining closed patterns that depend on a vertical format. It performs efficiently in large datasets since it generates a smaller number of rules. Additionally, it utilizes pruning techniques to enhance overall performance.

The NRD-DBV Application Algorithm

The implementation of the NRD-DBV is performed in the following steps, as shown in Figure 3:

1. Transforming the dataset to a bit vector by removing zeroes from the front and the end of the sequence. It is followed by using a dynamic bit vector structure to determine the position of each item.
2. Setting the support threshold to find all items that achieve the threshold value and storing them in a prefix tree structure as the parent node of the tree.
3. Performing the check downward closer checking means removing all prefixes that do not expand the rule. For instance, item c ordinarily happens after item b with a similar support value of b; at that point c ought to be ingested such as A(BC) = 60% and A(BC)DE = 60%. By applying this approach, we will remove sequence A (BC).
4. Setting all found frequent sequences as a sub-node and analyzing it, whether prefix generator or closed patterns.
5. Applying the sequence extension technique for every sub-node by applying two methods. The first is called item extension. It expands the patterns by including new items at the final item-set by regarding that item as larger than the last element of the item-set. The second one is called a sequence extension item-set expansion by inserting the item as a new item-set after the final existing, as displayed in Algorithms A3 and A4.
6. Producing the NRD-DVB by applying a condition to halt producing rules that do not achieve the confidence threshold. This is indicated as, in the case (($\frac{sup(Sequence\ of\ Sn)}{sup(Sequence\ of\ pre)}$) $\geq minconf$), the point nr-SeqRule, even with nr-SeqRule union with R. Additionally, cease to produce the rules for the sub-nodes. Conjointly, cease producing the rules when support (n1) < support (n) and if $\frac{sup(n1)}{sup(n2)}$ < minConf, then $\frac{sup(n2)}{sup(n)}$ < minConf.

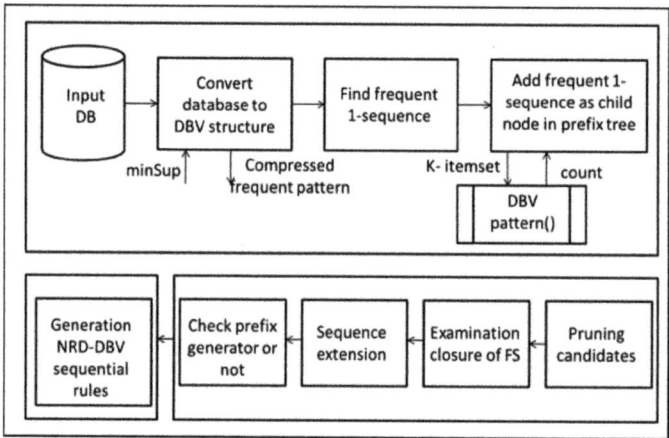

Figure 3. The NRD-DBV algorithm framework based on [31].

The NRD-DVB algorithm helps to compact the dataset by eliminating any super sequence with a similar support value to the root. Therefore, it is more proficient, as:

1. It diminishes the memory utilization, and the runtime demanded to mine large sequence datasets.
2. Furthermore, it embraces the prefix tree to store all sequences that produce more proficient non-redundant rules.

4. Experiments and Results

Experiments were processed to assess the runtime, memory usage for each algorithm, and the number of generated rules. Additionally, the influence of the minSup on both NRD-DBV and TRuleGrowth algorithms was measured and the TNS algorithm was compared with the other two algorithms after producing the same number of rules for each of them. Three algorithms were implemented on a PC with an Intel Core i5 2.3 GHz and free RAM running with 6.58 GB. We utilized Python language encoded on Jet Brains PyCharm.

Four real databases with diverse characteristics were executed to assess the results obtained from SPMF. The first dataset is named BMSwebview1 (Gazelle) [32] which consists of 59,601 clickstream data sequences from an e-commerce website. There are 497 separate items and the foremost vital issue that distinguishes their items reiterated in a seldom manner. The second database is a database of a sign dialect articulation consisting of 800 sequences transcript from recordings [33]. It includes 267 particular sets of items. The Korsarak is the third database; it is regarded as one of the biggest sequential databases. It has 990,000 sequences of click-stream information from a Hungarian news entrance. It incorporates 41,270 items. Because of the trouble connected on TRuleGrowth that caused the overhead limitation to be surpassed, we used a subset of the global database of Korsarak that contained only 25,000 items, which include non-reputation of position on the news. The BMSWebView2 (Gazelle) is the fourth database; it utilizes the information set within the KDD CUP 2000. It includes click-stream data of e-commerce in range 77,512 with 3340 particular items with an average length of 4.62. All experiments have been analyzed regarding to runtime, generated rules, and memory usage. The impact of the minSup on the previously stated criteria is studied.

The utilized datasets have different features useful for our comparison. In the first dataset (BMSwebview1), due to the variance of sequences, we selected a lower minSup value, which means that items are not repeated frequently in the dataset. We did not have any rules during the mining process while setting minSup like other attempts. In all studies, the minConf threshold was set to 0.5 for all states. The parameters' values were determined after several preliminary experiments to achieve the most preferable results.

4.1. Compared the TRuleGrowth with the NRD-DBV Algorithm

From the first dataset (BMS web view1), it is clear that the run time increased with decreasing minSup. It is a reversed relationship between the minSup and the runtime. The clarification of the relationship appears with raising values of window size and in the NRD-DBV algorithm. When the window size constraint esteem diminishes, we take note that it takes less time and has fewer number of rules. That is due to eliminating the complex computations of produced rules. It is similar to the outcome for the generated rules. Additionally, there is moreover a reversed relationship between the minSup and the generated rules' number. With the high esteem of window size constraint in the TRuleGrowth algorithm, there is an additional increment in the number of rules produced. As the window size esteem diminishes and increments minSup esteems simultaneously, the generated rules of the NRD-DBV are adjacent to the number of generated rules from the TRuleGrowth algorithm. Figures 4 and 5 show the runtime, no. of rules with minConf = 0.5% and minSup set from (0.09 to 0.06%), and Figure 6 shows the memory usage.

Additionally, it is found that when minimizing the value of window size, the time and number of sequence rules required are decreased. This is because producing sequential rules does not need very much computing.

On the other hand, in the sign dataset, we unrestricted with a low value for minSup. As before, we observed that the runtime increased with decreasing minSup value. The gap between the two parameters increased, especially for the TRuleGrowth algorithm when assigning lower values of window size constraint. This is a result of generating a large number of rules at smaller minSup values and higher window size value. It is an opposite relation between minSup and the generated rules. Figures 7 and 8 show the runtime, number of rules with minConf = 0.5% and minSup set from (0.2% to 0.8%), and Figure 9 presents the memory usage.

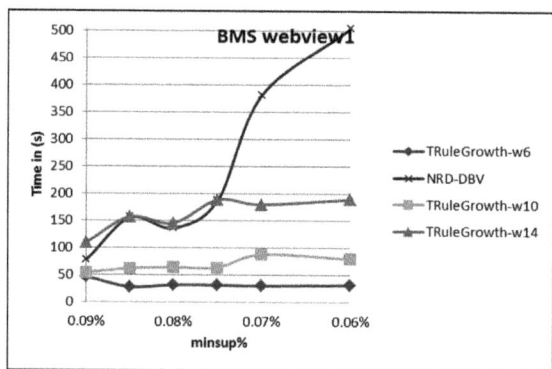

Figure 4. Comparison of the runtime of the TRuleGrowth with the NRD-DBV for (BMS webview1) dataset.

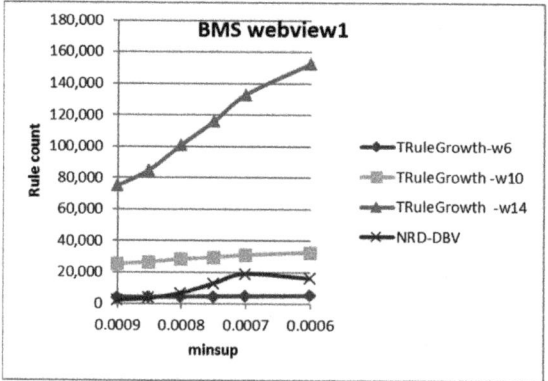

Figure 5. Comparison between the No. of rules generated for the TRuleGrowth and the NRD-DBV for (BMS webview1) dataset.

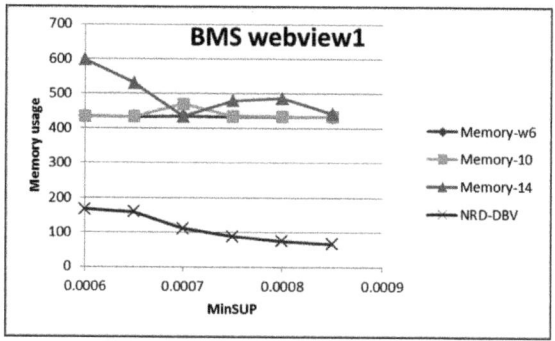

Figure 6. Comparison of memory usage for the TRuleGrowth with the NRD-DBV algorithm for (BMS webview1) dataset.

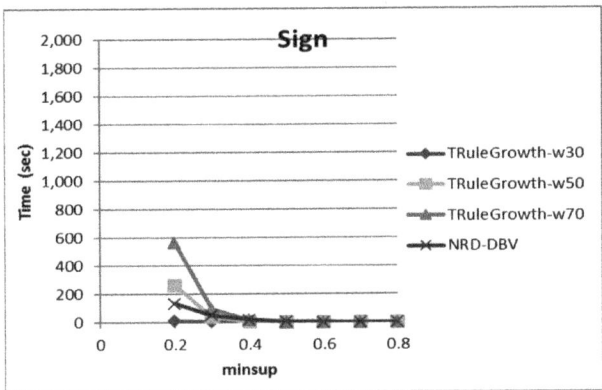

Figure 7. Comparison of the runtime of the TRuleGrowth with the NRD-DBV for (Sign) dataset.

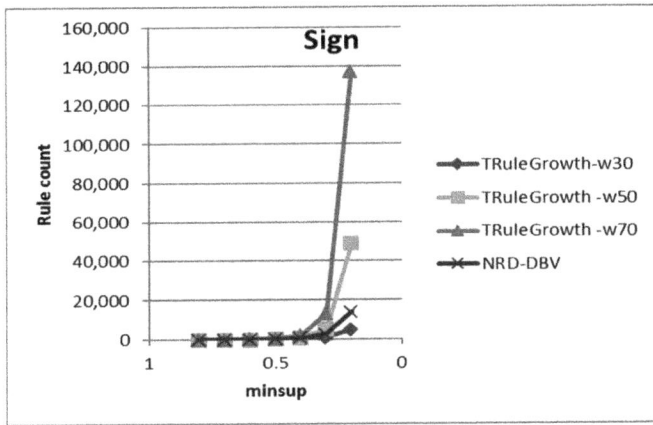

Figure 8. Comparison between the No. of rules generated for the TRuleGrowth and the NRD-DBV for (Sign) dataset.

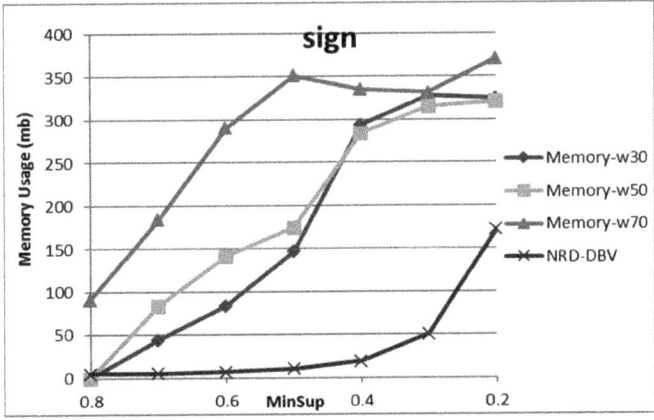

Figure 9. Comparison of memory usage for the TRuleGrowth with the NRD-DBV algorithm for (Sign) dataset.

TRuleGrowth algorithm with lower window size constraint still achieved the least time required for generating the sequential rules. This is because of lower computations needed for the smallest number of rules. NRD-DBV takes more time than TRuleGrowth as it generates more sequential rules based on ordering.

While in the Korsarak database, the NRD-DVB proved its efficiency in producing the sequential rules. It generated approximately 21 rules in 200 (s), whereas the TRuleGrowth stopped generating any sequential rules, as it was restrained by the overhead. We managed this issue by employing a subset of the Korsarak with 25,000 groupings.

By applying the alternative solution to solve the problem with stops generating rules in the TRuleGrowth algorithm, the subset of the Korsarak database with only 25,000 sequences is used. The results demonstrated the availability of the TRuleGrowth algorithm, especially when assigning a low value to the minSup threshold. It generates rules faster than the NRD-DBV algorithm. The high speed of the TRuleGrowth algorithm is evident in generating rules when diminishing the minSup value, whereas the NRD-DBV takes three times more time than the TRuleGrowth. The runtime and the number of the generated rules are not affected by different values of window size, as shown in Figures 10 and 11. The NRD-DBV achieved the best utilization of memory as shown in Figure 12.

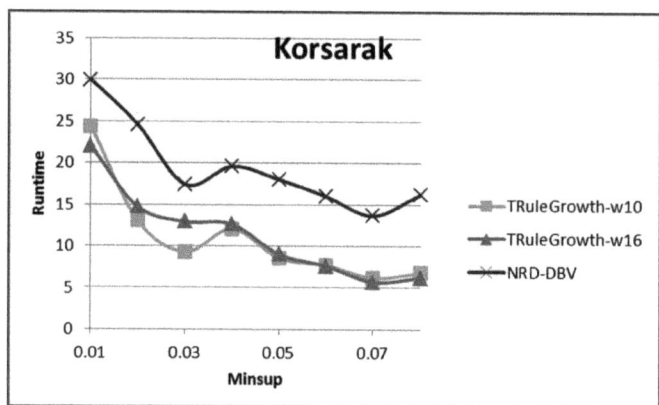

Figure 10. Comparison of the runtime of the TRuleGrowth with the NRD-DBV for (Korsarak) dataset.

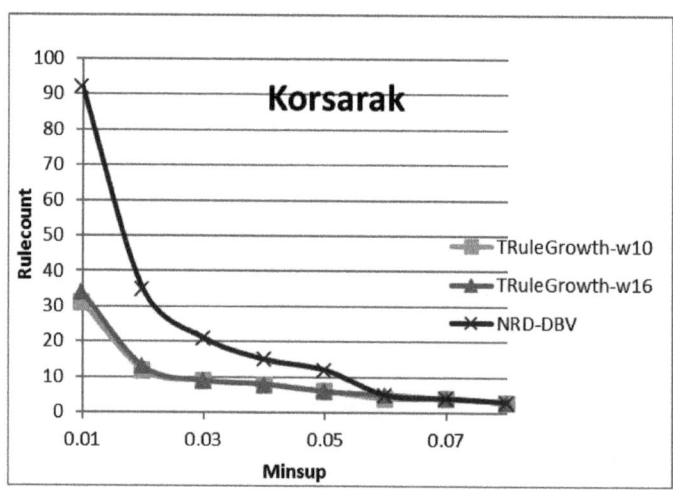

Figure 11. Comparison between the No. of rules generated for the TRuleGrowth and the NRD-DBV for (Korsarak) dataset.

The last database is named BMSwebview2; it has different features from the first database, BMSwebview1. It has 358,278 overall instances of items, whereas the BMSwebview1 has only 149,639 that forced us to assign fewer values to minSup as mentioned before. The higher the values assigned to the window size parameter, the more time taken to generate the rules, particularly when assigning a very low value to the minSup at the same time. However, the TRuleGrowth still achieved the most parcel of the execution time to produce the sequential rules, as clarified in Figure 13.

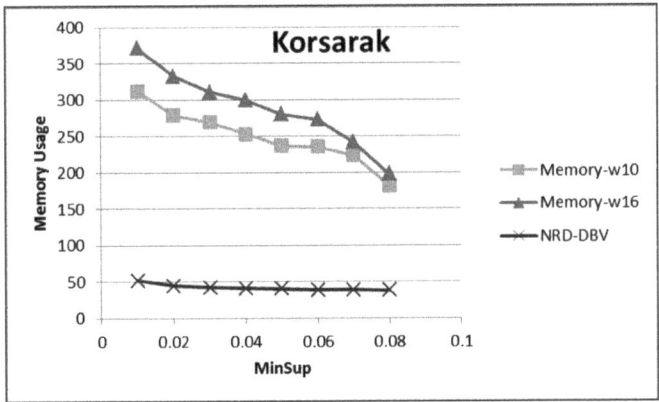

Figure 12. Comparison of memory usage for the TRuleGrowth with the NRD-DBV algorithm for (Korsarak) dataset.

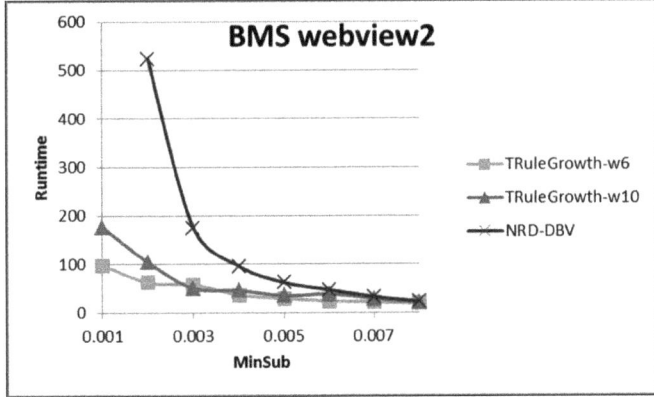

Figure 13. Comparison of the runtime of the TRuleGrowth with the NRD-DBV for (BMS webview2) dataset.

Concerning the number of rules, the TRuleGrowth algorithm generated the lowest number of rules with a low window size constraint value. With a larger window size or a higher minSup value, the number of consecutive rules in TRuleGrowth grew in the NRD-DBV algorithm because computations take longer time on a large number of rules, as shown in Figure 14, and the NRD-DBV algorithm still achieved the least memory usage as shown in Figure 15.

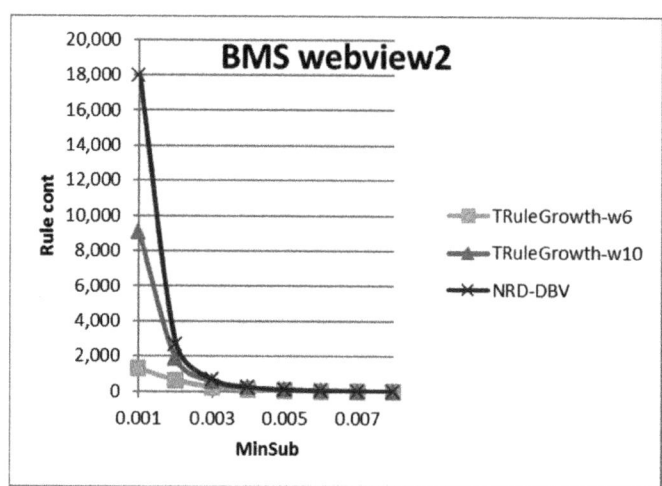

Figure 14. Comparison between the No. of rules generated for the TRuleGrowth and the NRD-DBV for (BMS webview2) dataset.

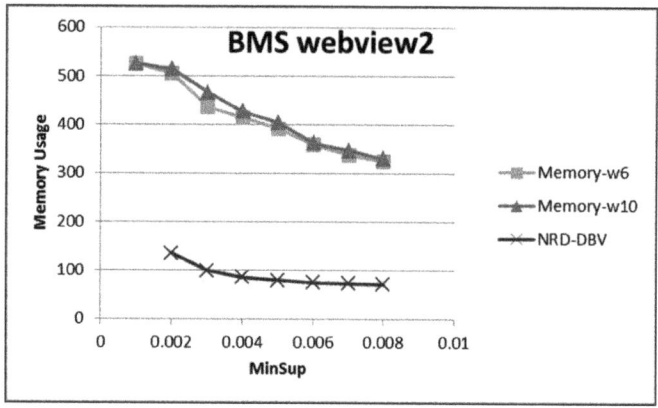

Figure 15. Memory usage for the BMS webview2 dataset with different minSup values and (minConf = 0.5).

Likewise, when using the TRuleGrowth algorithm with a small value of window size constraint or high values of minSup, the smallest number of rules was generated. When the minSup value was reduced or values of window size constraint were increased, the number of rules in TRuleGrowth increased and it took longer to make a computation.

4.2. Comparing the TNS Algorithm with the Other Two Algorithms

We compared the TNS algorithm with the other two algorithms by setting the K parameter equal to the number of rules generated from each of the other algorithms, either with different window size constraints or different minSup values.

The TNS algorithm stopped generating any rules with (BMSwebview1). That is because of the nature of this database's features: its items are rarely repeated.

In the sign database, the TRuleGrowth algorithm generated sequential rules in less time than the TNS algorithm, as shown in Figure 16. The TNS achieved its efficiency in generating sequential rules faster than the NRD-DBV algorithm (see Figure 17), and NRD-DBV achieved good performance in memory usage at the maximum value of minSup as presented in Figure 18.

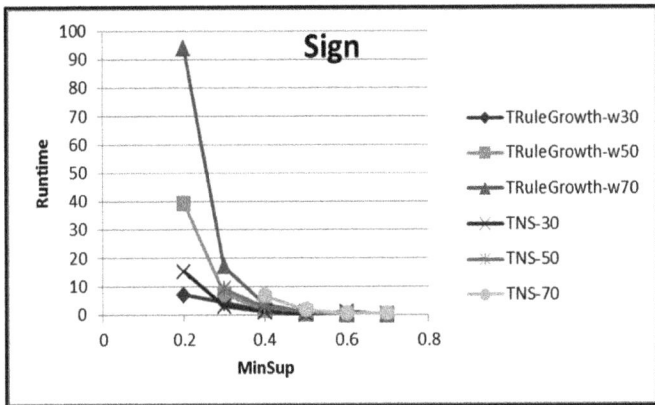

Figure 16. Comparison of the runtime of the TNS with the TRuleGrowth for (Sign) dataset.

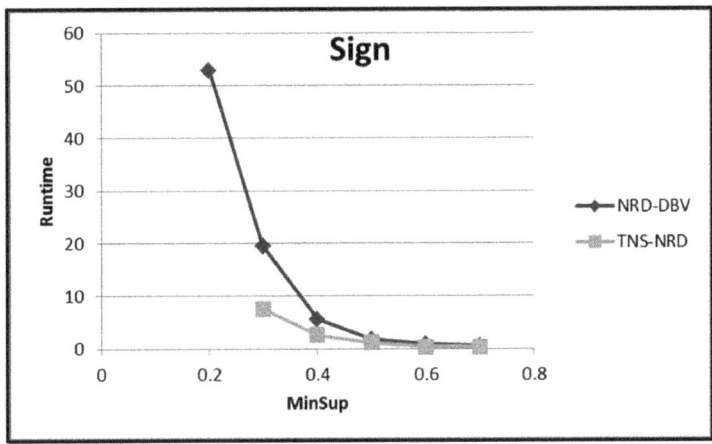

Figure 17. Comparison of the runtime of the TNS with the NRD-DBV for (Sign) dataset.

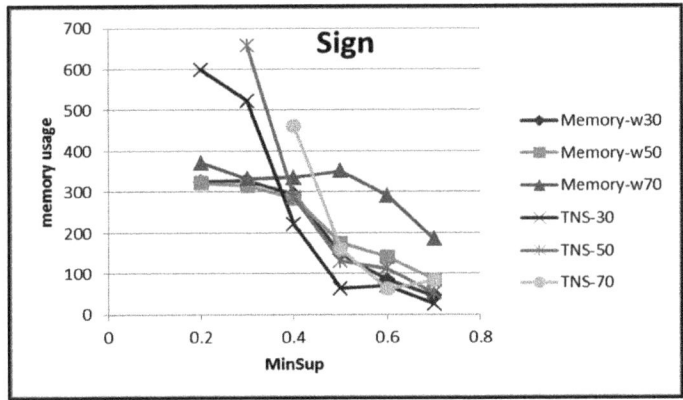

Figure 18. Comparison of memory usage for the TNS with the TRuleGrowth algorithm for (Sign) dataset.

As seen in Figures 19 and 20 in the Korsarak dataset, the TNS algorithm generated almost four times fewer sequential rules than the two other algorithms.

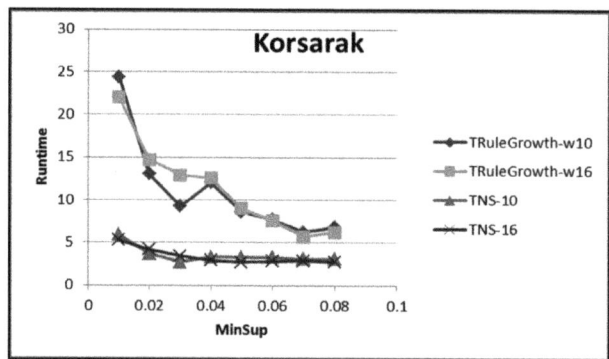

Figure 19. Comparison of the runtime of the TNS with the TRuleGrowth for (Korsarak) dataset.

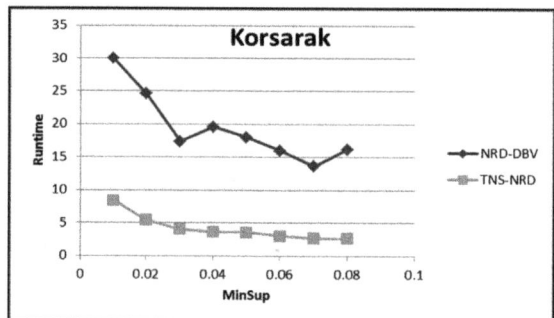

Figure 20. Comparison of the runtime of the TNS with the NRD-DBV for (Korsarak) dataset.

In the BMSwebview2 dataset, rules were generated in half the time taken for generating rules with the NRD-DBV algorithm. Additionally, rules were generated in less or approximately close to the time taken for the TRuleGrowth algorithm, as shown in Figures 21 and 22.

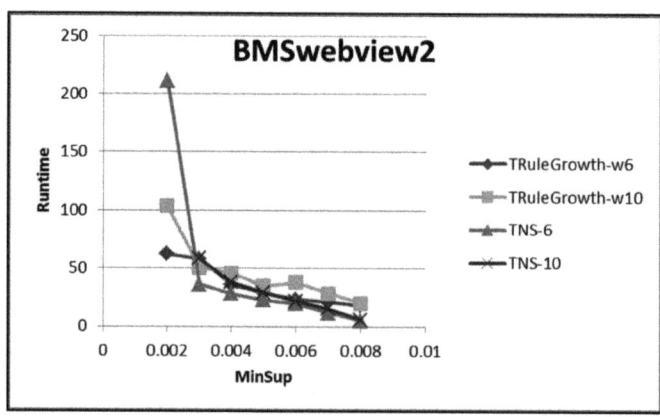

Figure 21. Comparison of the runtime of the TNS with the TRuleGrowth for (BMS webview2) dataset.

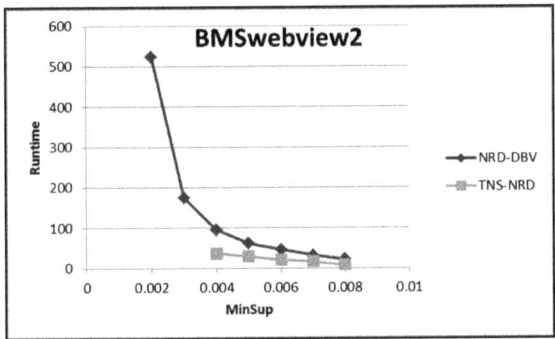

Figure 22. Comparison of the runtime of the TNS with the NRD-DBV for (BMS webview2) dataset.

Regarding the memory usage for each algorithm, it makes sense that the amount of memory demanded increased with the lowering of the minSup value, since the number of sequential rules is growing. However, in all experiments, the NRD-DBV method was demonstrated to be more memory efficient than the TRuleGrowth and TNS algorithms. This is because it has the advantage of the DBV structure and prunes all prefix child nodes to remove unnecessary rules, as shown before in Figures 6, 9, 12, 15 and 18, and also the following Figures 23–27.

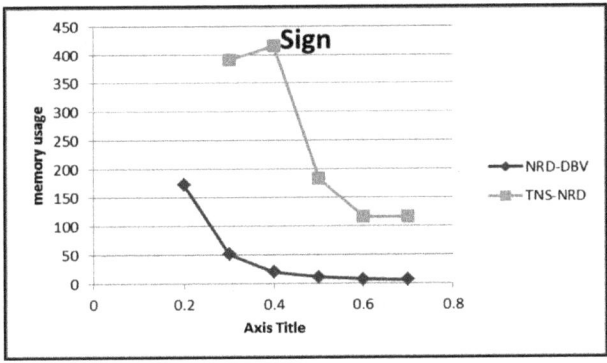

Figure 23. Comparison of memory usage for the TNS with the NRD-DBV algorithm for (Sign) dataset.

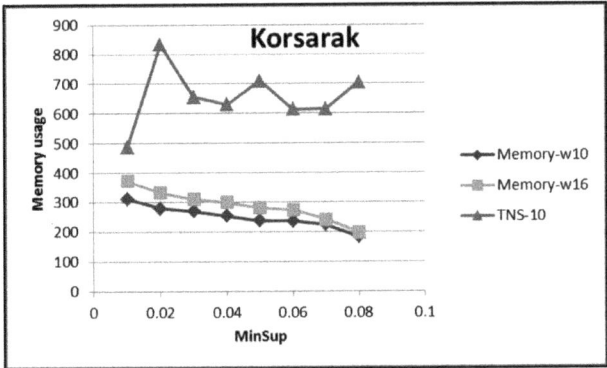

Figure 24. Comparison of memory usage for the TNS with the NRD-DBV algorithm for (Korsarak) dataset.

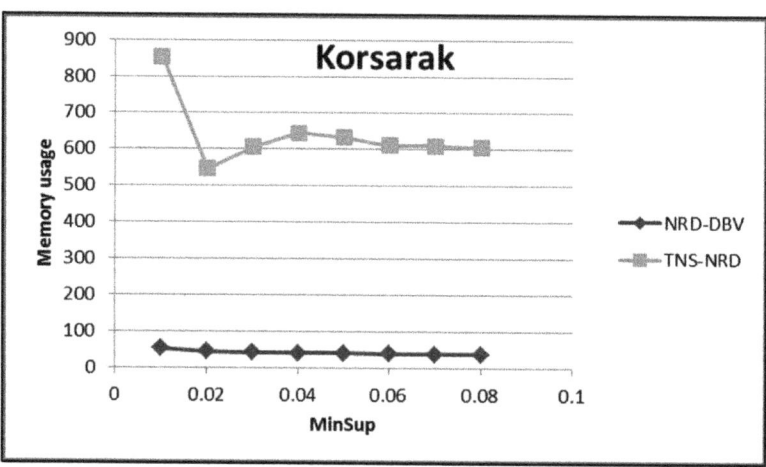

Figure 25. Comparison of memory usage for the TNS with the NRD-DBV algorithm for (Korsarak) dataset.

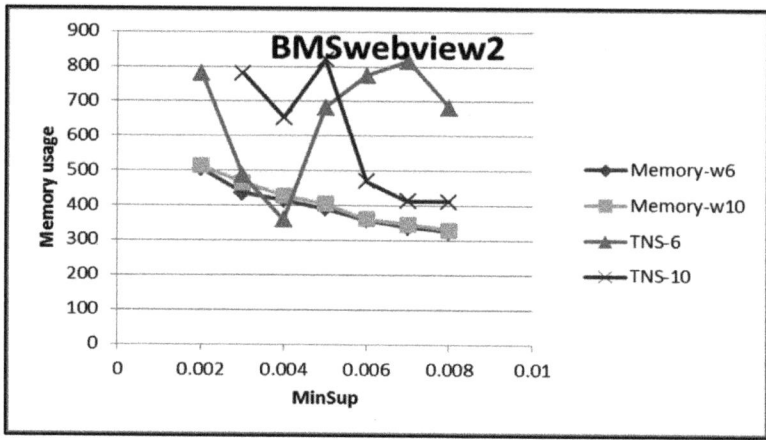

Figure 26. Comparison of memory usage for the TNS with the TRuleGrowth algorithm for (BMS webview2) dataset.

Computational complexity has been measured for each algorithm; we found that both the TRuleGrowth and NRD-DBV algorithms are less complex. The complexity of the TRuleGrowth algorithm is linear regarding the number of sequential rules in the dataset; either one or two recursive calls are applied to expand the right and left sides.

In the NRD-DBV, producing non-redundant rules has a complexity of $o(n*c)$, where n is the number of nodes and c is the average number of child nodes. We must implement $(n-1)$ procedures for validating and producing sequential rules such as $k \ll n$ for each sequence. As a result, NRD-DBV complexity is $\approx o(n)$. TNS algorithm is efficient when setting the parameter k up to 2000 rules. Otherwise, it performs more complexity because of high computational expenses on mining sequential rules.

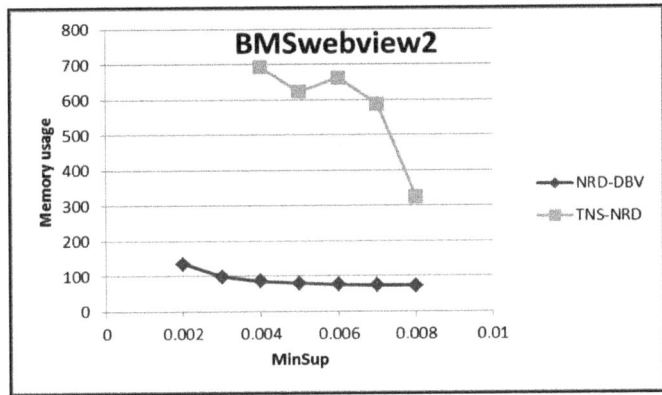

Figure 27. Comparison of memory usage for the TNS with the NRD-DBV algorithm for (BMS webview2) dataset.

5. Conclusions

This paper presents a meaningful comparison of three algorithms designed for the task of sequential rule mining, which is especially common to several sequences. Each algorithm was analyzed utilizing four real datasets with different features. For example, one dataset had long sequential patterns with low diversity of items that forced us to use a low minSup value to generate the sequential rules. Another dataset had short sequential patterns with a high diversity of items. Another one was a huge dataset that caused an overhead limit excess, which made us resort to using a subset of the original dataset.

Our experiments indicated that the performance of the algorithms is associated with the features of the datasets. Moreover, experience shows that it can reduce the execution time and control the number of valid rules generated by several orders of size restrictions such as adjusting the window size constraint or determine the number of generated rules or change the value of the minSup threshold.

With a specified value of a window size constraint, mining the TRuleGrowth algorithm can run faster and the correctness of discovered sequential rules that are not constrained by the arrangement can be increased.

The NRD-DBV algorithm could be used to reduce the number of sequential rules and memory requirements. It relies on a DBV structure with a prefix-tree that leads to early pruning of child nodes to reduce the search space. In addition, the NRD-DBV method generates more rules for taking item arrangement into account than the TRuleGrowth algorithm.

The researchers conclude that each algorithm has its own use in the fields of application of sequential rule mining to achieve the highest possible efficiency. NRD-DBV algorithm has many applications in error detection, intervention, and bugs. It is useful in domains that require the arrangement of items such as in medical area (for example, if the patient is suffering from a fever, which is followed by a decrease in the level of coagulation, followed by the appearance of red marks on the body, it is reasonable that the patient will need to be treated for dengue fever. This order in events is important in predicting an appropriate type of treatment). Additionally, it can be used in marketing to design the most personalized strategy, and also in software engineering where ordering is mostly important to accomplish its tasks.

The TRuleGrowth algorithm implementation allows the allocation of optional parameters like maximizing the number of items that appear in the antecedent and consequent of a rule. It can be useful in making product recommendations and performing fast decision making.

For future work, we intend to improve the NRD-DBV algorithm by using another concise representation, such as maximal or generator patterns, to improve performance in the large sequences database.

Author Contributions: Conceptualization, A.A. and N.Y.; methodology, A.A.; software, N.Y.; validation, A.A. and N.Y.; formal analysis, N.Y.; investigation, A.A.; resources, A.A.; data curation, N.Y.; writing—original draft preparation, N.Y.; writing—review and editing, A.A.; visualization, N.Y.; supervision, A.A.; project administration, A.A.; funding acquisition, A.A. All authors have read and agreed to the published version of the manuscript.

Funding: This work was supported through the Annual Funding track by the Deanship of Scientific Research, Vice Presidency for Graduate Studies and Scientific Research, King Faisal University, Saudi Arabia [Project No. AN000519].

Institutional Review Board Statement: Not applicable.

Informed Consent Statement: Informed consent was obtained from all subjects involved in the study.

Data Availability Statement: The dataset is available on https://www.philippe-fournier-viger.com/spmf/index.php?link=datasets.php, accessed on 20 April 2021.

Conflicts of Interest: The authors declare no conflict of interest.

Appendix A

Algorithm A1: The TRuleGrowth algorithm

Input
Sequence database
Minimum support
Minimum confidence
Output
Set of sequential rules
The executed time and memory usage of the generated rules
Algorithm
Begin
scanning dataset
For (each item m in DS) do {
Store each side that contains item m
If sup of each pair of item x,y $\geq$ minSup {
Set sides (x$\rightarrow$y) equal to zero}}
Calculate sides for generating rule (x$\rightarrow$y)
else If (sup of rule (x$\rightarrow$y) $\geq$ minSup) then
If (size of left side of rule $\leq$ maxleft && size of
right side of rule $\leq$ maxright) then
else If (rule <= window size Constraint)
Then Expand left & Expand right
End if
If confidence of rule (x$\rightarrow$y) $\geq$ minConf
Then generate rule {x}{y} with its confidence Support
End if
End for
End

Algorithm A2: TNS algorithm

Input
Sequence database
K= specified numbers of rules
Minimum support
Minimum confidence

Output
Set of sequential rules
The executed time and memory usage of the generated rules

Algorithm
Begin
R = ø. L= ø. minSup = 0.
Scan DB once & Record each item in variable(s)
FOR each pair of items I, j such that $|sids(i)| \geq$ minsup and ∩ 4. $|sids(j)| \geq$ minsup: sids(i⇒j) := Ø. sids(j⇒i) := Ø.
FOR each sid s ∈ (sids(i) ∩ sids(j):
IF i occurs before j in s THEN sids(i⇒j) := sids(i⇒j)∪7. {s}.
IF j occurs before i in s THEN sids(j⇒i) := sids(j⇒ i) ∪ 9.{s}.
END FOR
IF $|sids(i \Rightarrow j)| / |S| \geq minsup$ THEN $conf(\{i\} \Rightarrow \{j\}) := |sids(i \Rightarrow j)| / |sids(i)|$.
IF $conf(\{i\} \Rightarrow \{j\}) \geq minconf$ THEN SAVE({i}⇒{j}, L, k, minsup).
Set flag expandLR **of** {i}⇒{j}to true.
R := R∪{{i}⇒{j}}.
END IF
... [lines 11 to 17 are repeated here with *i* and *j* swapped] ...
END FOR
WHILE $\exists r \in R$ AND $sup(r) \geq minsup$ DO
Select the rule *rule* having the highest support in R
IF *rule*.expandLR = true THEN
EXPAND-L(*rule*, L, R, k, *minsup, minconf*).
EXPAND-R(*rule*, L, R, k, *minsup, minconf*).
ELSE EXPAND-R(*rule*, L, R, k, *minsup, minconf*).
REMOVE *rule* from R. REMOVE from R all rules r ∈ R | $sup(r) <minsup$.
END WHILE
SAVE(*r, R, k, minsup*)
L := L∪{r}.
IF $|L| \geq k$ THEN
IF $sup(r) > minsup$ THEN
WHILE $|L| > k$ AND $\exists s \in L | sup(s) = minsup$
REMOVE s from L.
END IF
Set *minsup* to the lowest support of rules in L.
END IF
FOR (NRD = 1, NRD < Δ, NRD + +) Do
The result is exact (generated TNS)
ELSE Return with higher Δ value
END FOR
End

Algorithm A3: NRD-DBV algorithm

Input
Sequence database
Minimum support
Minimum confidence
Output
Set of sequential rules
The executed time and memory usage of the generated rules
Algorithm
Begin
Initialize a root→ null
NRD-seqRule→∅
Find out frequent closed sequence (FCS) by converting pattern into DBV pattern |x| in DS &
sup(x) ≥ minSup
Set FCS as child node of a root
For (each child node cn) do
Call Closed Pattern-Extension (cn, minSup);
For (each child node cn) do
Call Generate-NRD-SeqRule (cn, minConf, NRD-SeqRule)
End

Algorithm A4: Closed Pattern-Extension method

Input
Frequent sequential patterns
Minimum support
Minimum confidence
Output
Set of sequential rules
The executed time and memory usage of the generated rules
Algorithm
Begin
Set listNode →child nodes of root
For (each prefix Sequence in listNode) do
If sequential patterns not pruned, then
for (each prefix sequential patterns in listNode) do
If (sup (PrefixSp →Sequence-extension ≥ minSup) then
Add prefixSP as a new itemset after the last itemset of the sequence
Else If (sup (Sp →Itemset-extension ≥ minSup)
Add prefixSP as a new item in the last itemset of sequence
End For
Call Closed Pattern-Extension (prefixSP, minSup);
End If
Check & put the attribute of SP: closed pattern, prefixed generator or NULL;
End For
End

References

1. Mooney, C.H.; Roddick, J.F. Sequential pattern mining—Approaches and algorithms. *ACM Comput. Surv.* **2013**, *45*, 1–39. [CrossRef]
2. Hemeida, A.; Alkhalaf, S.; Mady, A.; Mahmoud, E.; Hussein, M.; Eldin, A.M.B. Implementation of nature-inspired optimization algorithms in some data mining tasks. *Ain Shams Eng. J.* **2020**, *11*, 309–318. [CrossRef]
3. Huynh, B.; Bay, V.O.; Vaclav, S. An efficient parallel method for mining frequent closed sequential patterns. *IEEE Access* **2017**, *5*, 17392–17402. [CrossRef]
4. Kour, A. Sequential Rule Mining, Methods, and Techniques: A Review. *Int. J. Comput. Intell. Res.* **2017**, *13*, 1709–1715.

5. Toussaint, B.-M.; Luengo, V. Mining surgery phase-related sequential rules from vertebroplasty simulations traces. In Proceedings of the Conference on Artificial Intelligence in Medicine in Europe, Pavia, Italy, 17–20 June 2015; pp. 35–46.
6. Werke, M. Principles for Modelling of Manufacturing Sequences. Ph.D. Thesis, KTH Royal Institute of Technology, Stockholm, Sweden, 2015.
7. Noughabi, E.A.Z.; Albadvi, A.; Far, B.H. How Can We Explore Patterns of Customer Segments' Structural Changes? A Sequential Rule Mining Approach. In Proceedings of the 2015 IEEE International Conference on Information Reuse and Integration, San Francisco, CA, USA, 13–15 August 2015; pp. 273–280.
8. Jannach, D.; Jugovac, M.; Lerche, L. Adaptive recommendation-based modeling support for data analysis workflows. In Proceedings of the 20th International Conference on Intelligent User Interfaces, Atlanta, GA, USA, 29 March–1 April 2015; pp. 252–262.
9. Leemans, M.; van der Aalst, W.M. Discovery of frequent episodes in event logs. In *International Symposium on Data-Driven Process Discovery and Analysis*; Springer: Cham, Switzerland, 2014; pp. 1–31.
10. Bhoomika, A.P.; Selvarani, R. A Survey on Web Page Recommender Systems. In Proceedings of the Alliance International Conference on Artificial Intelligence and Machine Learning (AICAAM), Bangalore, India, 26–27 April 2019.
11. Jamshed, A.; Mallick, B.; Kumar, P. Deep learning-based sequential pattern mining for progressive database. *Soft Comput.* **2020**, *24*, 17233–17246. [CrossRef]
12. Bajaj, S.B.; Garg, D. Survey on Sequence Mining Algorithms. *Int. J. Eng. Appl. Sci. Technol.* **2016**, *1*, 58–64.
13. Alja'am, J.M.; El Saddik, A.; Sadka, A.H. (Eds.) *Recent Trends in Computer Applications: Best Studies from the 2017 International Conference on Computer and Applications, Dubai, UAE*; Springer: Berlin/Heidelberg, Germany, 2018.
14. Kiran, R.U.; Kitsuregawa, M.; Reddy, P.K. Efficient discovery of periodic-frequent patterns in very large databases. *J. Syst. Softw.* **2016**, *112*, 110–121. [CrossRef]
15. Setiawan, F.; Yahya, B.N. Improved behavior model based on sequential rule mining. *Appl. Soft Comput.* **2018**, *68*, 944–960. [CrossRef]
16. Senthilkumar, R.; Deepika, R.; Saranya, R.; Govind, M.D. Generating adaptive partially ordered sequential rules. In Proceedings of the International Conference on Informatics and Analytics, Pondicherry, India, 25–26 August 2016; ACM: New York, NY, USA, 2016; pp. 1–8.
17. Pham, T.T.; Luo, J.; Hong, T.P.; Vo, B. An efficient method for mining non-redundant sequential rules using attributed prefix-trees. *Eng. Appl. Artif. Intell.* **2014**, *32*, 88–99. [CrossRef]
18. Tran, M.T.; Le, B.; Vo, B.; Hong, T.P. Mining non-redundant sequential rules with dynamic bit vectors and pruning techniques. *Appl. Intell.* **2016**, *45*, 333–342. [CrossRef]
19. Van, T.T.; Vo, B.; Le, B. IMSR_PreTree: An improved algorithm for mining sequential rules based on the prefix-tree. *Vietnam. J. Comput. Sci.* **2014**, *1*, 97–105. [CrossRef]
20. Fournier-Viger, P.; Wu, C.W.; Tseng, V.S.; Cao, L.; Nkambou, R. Mining partially-ordered sequential rules common to multiple sequences. *IEEE Trans. Knowl. Data Eng.* **2015**, *27*, 2203–2216. [CrossRef]
21. Pujari, M.S.D.; Mane, M.R.; Ghorpade, V.R. Analysis of TRuleGrowth algorithm for discovery of sequential rules. *Int. J. Eng. Res. Technol.* **2017**, *10*, 396–399.
22. Indhumathi, V.; Karthika, S.K. An Efficient Way to Handle the High Dimensional Problem with Fuzzy Association Rule. *Int. J. Eng. Res. Technol.* **2016**, *4*, 1–6.
23. Saritha, P.C.; Senthil Prakash, T.; Rajesh, M.; Remya, K.S. Discovering Sequential Rules for Web Usage Analysis. *Int. J. Eng. Technol. Sci.* **2015**, *II*, 57–62.
24. Fournier-Viger, P.; Tseng, V.S. Mining top-k sequential rules. In Proceedings of the International Conference on Advanced Data Mining and Applications, Beijing, China, 17–19 December 2011; Springer: Berlin/Heidelberg, Germany, 2011; pp. 180–194.
25. Mollenhauer, D.; Atzmueller, M. Sequential Exceptional Pattern Discovery Using Pattern-Growth: An Extensible Framework for Interpretable Machine Learning on Sequential Data Minign. In Proceedings of the XI-ML@ KI, Bamberg, Germany, 21 September 2020.
26. Bou Rjeily, C.; Badr, G.; Al Hassani, A.H.; Andres, E. Overview on Sequential Mining Algorithms and Their Extensions. In *Recent Trends in Computer Applications*; Springer: Cham, Switzerland, 2018; pp. 3–16.
27. Fournier-Viger, P.; Tseng, V.S. TNS: Mining top-k non-redundant sequential rules. In Proceedings of the 28th Annual ACM Symposium on Applied Computing, Coimbra, Portugal, 18–22 March 2013; pp. 164–166.
28. Jamsheela, O.; Raju, G.K. Parallelization of Frequent Itemset Mining Methods with FP-tree: An Experiment with PrePost + Algorithm. *Int. Arab J. Inf. Technol.* **2021**, *18*, 208–213.
29. Nguyen, H.Q.; Pham, T.T.; Vo, V.; Vo, B.; Quan, T.T. The predictive modeling for learning student results based on sequential rules. *Int. J. Innov. Comput. Inf. Control* **2018**, *14*, 2129–2140.
30. Wang, C.-S. Mining Non-Redundant Inter-Transaction Rules. *J. Inf. Sci. Eng.* **2015**, *31*, 1849–1865.
31. Youssef, N.; Abdulkader, H.; Abdelwahab, A. Evaluating Non-redundant Rules of Various Sequential Rule Mining Algorithms. In Proceedings of the International Conference on Advanced Intelligent Systems and Informatics, Cairo, Egypt, 19–21 October 2020; Springer: Cham, Switzerland, 2020.

32. Wu, Y.; Zhu, C.; Li, Y.; Guo, L.; Wu, X. NetNCSP: Nonoverlapping closed sequential pattern mining. *Knowl.-Based Syst.* **2020**, *196*, 105812. [CrossRef] [PubMed]
33. Fournier-Viger, P.; Lin, J.C.W.; Gomariz, A.; Gueniche, T.; Soltani, A.; Deng, Z.; Lam, H.T. The SPMF open-source data mining library version 2. In Proceedings of the Joint European Conference on Machine Learning and Knowledge Discovery in Databases, Riva del Garda, Italy, 20–22 September 2016; pp. 36–40.

Article

User Trust Inference in Online Social Networks: A Message Passing Perspective

Yu Liu * and Bai Wang *

Beijing Key Laboratory of Intelligence Telecommunication Software and Multimedia, Beijing University of Posts and Telecommunications, Beijing 100876, China
* Correspondence: imyuliu@outlook.com (Y.L.); wangbai@bupt.edu.cn (B.W.)

Abstract: Online social networks are vital environments for information sharing and user interactivity. To help users of online social services to build, expand, and maintain their friend networks or webs of trust, trust management systems have been deployed and trust inference (or more generally, friend recommendation) techniques have been studied in many online social networks. However, there are some challenging issues obstructing the real-world trust inference tasks. Using only explicit yet sparse trust relationships to predict user trust is inefficient in large online social networks. In the age of privacy-respecting Internet, certain types of user data may be unavailable, and thus existing models for trust inference may be less accurate or even defunct. Although some less interpretable models may achieve better performance in trust prediction, the interpretability of the models may prevent them from being adopted or improved for making relevant informed decisions. To tackle these problems, we propose a probabilistic graphical model for trust inference in online social networks in this paper. The proposed model is built upon the skeleton of explicit trust relationships (the web of trust) and embeds various types of available user data as comprehensively-designed trust-aware features. A message passing algorithm, loop belief propagation, is applied to the model inference, which greatly improves the interpretability of the proposed model. The performance of the proposed model is demonstrated by experiments on a real-world online social network dataset. Experimental results show the proposed model achieves acceptable accuracy with both fully and partially available data. Comparison experiments were conducted, and the results show the proposed model's promise for trust inference in some circumstances.

Keywords: trust inference; trust propagation; online social network; social network analysis; probabilistic graphical model; message passing; belief propagation; model interpretability

1. Introduction

Trust exists in many different forms in various disciplines. For instance, the trust on the World Wide Web can be trust in content, trust in services, and trust in people [1]. Although different disciplines take different definitions and forms of trust, they commonly aim to solve the problem of accurately evaluating trust between two entities, to help complex systems make informed decisions. For example, some peer-to-peer system may take advantage of trust to curb malicious attacks and maintain network robustness [2]. A complex model selection system could evaluate the trustworthiness of a cloud-based machine learning model-as-a-service (MaaS) for industrial Internet of Things and smart city services [3]. Some online social service could use trust to improve the quality of recommendations [4]. Some researchers leveraged a trust network to study the relational antecedents of members' influence in organizations [5].

Without loss of generality, we focus on user trust in online social networks (OSNs) in this paper, which is one of the most common types of trust. We followed [6] to define user trust in OSNs: a subjective expectation an OSN user has about another user's future behavior. Social trust is a basic social construct [7], and it enables people to collectively live

and work in groups. In social networks, trust helps people find whom to trust, to build beneficial or even reciprocal social relationships, so that the quality of interindividual interactions could be improved and the risks of social activities reduced.

Many online social services embrace trust management systems to help their users to build and expand their webs of trust so that users can keep being engaged in their services [8]. For example, Twitter has deployed a user recommendation service called "Who to Follow" to use a user's "circle of trust" for recommending new connections to the user [9]. Being a key contributing factor in many complex systems, trust has been elaborately explored and researched, and it has been proven to be helpful in securing social commerce [10], recommending trustworthy users [11], providing accurate and personalized recommendations [4,12–14], filtering trustworthy authorities or users [15], finding opinion leaders or trolls [16], maximizing influence diffusion [17], and decision making [18–20]. However, data of trust information, such as trust relationships, do not always explicitly or abundantly exist for the above-mentioned tasks to use. Therefore, the study of trust inference is necessary and practical for social network analysis and relevant decision making tasks.

The process of inferring an unknown trust relationship in OSNs, which is often referred to as trust inference, involves exploitation of social construct elements. The sources of relevant trust information that assembles social constructs in OSNs include but are not limited to existing trust relationships and data created by the users involved in the relationships, such as their activities, including posting reviews and casting votes, and other content generated by them (user-generated contents, UGC).

Various algorithms and models have been proposed to infer trust in OSNs [21]. Some of them make use of topological data, i.e., the web of trust relationships or the trust network, to predict trust relationships. However, due to the ever-present issue that observable trust relationships in OSNs are often sparse, some vanilla algorithms for predicting trust are prevented from achieving more accurate predicted results in large real OSNs. With the aim of tackling the issue, other methods use both the web of trust and UGC data to achieve more accurate results in inferring trust.

Nevertheless, there are three major problems holding back existing trust inference models. Firstly, if additional UGC data are available, some of them and various types of interplay among them are discarded when the trust inference framework integrates them with the trust network, making the model prone to generating less accurate results. Secondly, lesser types of data from OSN users are permitted to use, given the fact that the privacy and data protection of online users are being much more respected nowadays. Online service users may opt out of using some of or all of their data for certain data analysis tasks conducted by online services—especially with the regulations and laws being implemented and enforced, such as General Data Protection Regulation (EU) (GDPR) [22], the California Consumer Privacy Act (CCPA) [23], and the Personal Information Protection Law of the People's Republic of China (PIPL) [24]. Thus, some crucial data may be unobtainable for trust inference. Last but not least, most trust inference models are poorly interpretable. The interpretability of a trust inference model should be improved alongside achieving better performance, not only for inferring trust itself but for making other relevant informed decisions.

Bearing the aforementioned problems in mind, we propose creating a probabilistic graphical model in which various types of UGC data are built and then integrated as features in such a way that not only are most of their characteristics preserved, but that the interaction among features can also be captured and embedded. The contributions of this paper are as follows.

- The proposed model takes advantage of the integration of the trust network and user-generated contents in the network; the latter is embedded into a probabilistic graphical model built upon the former. The model permits the directionality of trust relationships and preserves various facets and properties of trust. The way of both

building features from UGC data and embedding them into the probabilistic graph preserves as much information as the data may contain.
- To infer trust, the proposed model uses a message passing algorithm, loopy belief propagation, for the model's probabilistic inference. This inference algorithm can be viewed as a reproduction of the propagative and incomplete transitive characteristics of trust. By using the message passing algorithm, the resulting probability for each predicted user-to-user trust relationship can be well interpreted.
- As a binary classification task, the performance of the proposed method to infer trust is demonstrated with a dataset derived from a real online social network in comparison with some state-of-the-art binary classifiers. Experimental results show the proposed model achieves better accuracy and F_1 score with the whole data presented and maintained higher recall and acceptable precision with some of data absent. Thus, one can conclude that the proposed model shows its promising ability for trust inference in nowadays privacy-constrained online social analysis where available data are often limited. To address the data limitation, the problem that a model should have higher precision or higher recall is also discussed.

Although this paper only focuses on inferring user trust in online social networks, the proposed model may also be adopted to fulfill other inference tasks to better assist decision making in other complex systems. The least work required for other similar tasks is to properly define a concrete graphical model and a set of reasonably-built features, if additional data exist.

The rest of the paper is organized as follows. In Section 2, we briefly review the literature of related works on trust inference. In Section 3, we elaborate the prerequisites, define the problem, and then propose the model. In Section 4, we present experiments conducted with a dataset derived from a real-world online social network, and then analyze the performance of the proposed model. Finally, we conclude our work in Section 5.

2. Related Work

The problem of trust inference or trust prediction between two users in online social networks or two nodes in general networks bears some similarity with the link prediction problem, and thus it can be modeled as a link prediction task. However, using a link prediction method to predict trust links requires the method to work with directional links or even signed links, which complicates the link prediction method itself.

For example, Schall [25] leverages micro-structural patterns and the resulting node similarity to retrieve the probability of a missing directional link existing between two users in a social network. The method's drawback is that the micro-structural pattern is limited to a triad, and consequently it may fail in finding links between any two arbitrary nodes that do not have a common neighbor.

The work by Barbieri et al. [26] also employed link prediction techniques to infer friend or trust relationships. In this work, they proposed a generative model, one of the stochastic topic models, to generate social links for users with the consideration of user's interests in "topical" and "social" resources, e.g., whether a targeted user is an authority on a topic or he/she is recognized by an acquaintance in the real world.

Trust inference models based on the trust propagation theory are often called "walk-based" methods. In [27], Mao et al. developed a trust inference framework which obtains the trust rate between any pair of users by aggregating a set of strong trust paths generated with the knowledge of their weighted similarity about commonly interesting topics and their trust propagation ability in the social network. If the trust rate is above a user-defined threshold, the framework determines that there should be a trust link between the users.

The work by Oh et al. [28] included a unified model combining both explicit and implicit trust, and infers trust links by using different trust propagation strategies. The three primary trust propagation strategies include direct propagation, transposed trust, and global trust propagation. Other complex strategies, such as co-citations and trust coupling, are combinations of the primary propagation strategies. Other walk-based methods include ModelTrust [29], TidalTrust [30], AssessTrust [31], OpinionWalk [32], etc.

Trust prediction can also be achieved and improved by using collaborative filtering techniques, particularly the matrix factorization (MF)-based methods. It is also quite convenient for MF-based methods to integrate other types of data that carry trust information. hTrust [33] incorporates low-rank matrix factorization and homophily regularization to infer trust links. The homophily regularization controls how user rating similarity affects predicting user trust relationships. MATRI [34] extracts user trust tendency using matrix factorization from the user trust rating matrix and incorporates trust propagation with trust tendency into a collective matrix factorization framework to infer trust. Another MF-based trust inference model [35] takes advantage of not only matrix-factorized trust tendency and propagated trust, but also similarities of users' rating habits, and achieves good performance.

Neural networks are also employed for trust evaluation. NeuralWalk [36] employs a neural network named WalkNet to model single-hop trust propagation, and then iteratively assesses unknown multi-hop trust relationships. Although NeuralWalk can achieve good accuracy in trust prediction, it is inefficient due to the massive matrix operations involved in training and test set selection. Besides, the interpretability for such methods based on neural networks is an obvious drawback.

3. The Proposed Model

In this section, we propose our model for user trust inference in OSNs. Firstly, we state the relevant assumptions and prerequisites on which the proposed model is based; secondly, we describe our modeling approach in detail; and finally, we briefly discuss the implementation of the model.

3.1. Prerequisites

A variety of studies and literature [6,21,37,38] have found that trust has many unique features and characteristics, and they are embedded in user profiles and other UGC data in OSNs. Based on relevant findings of trust and OSNs, we give some key principles and assumptions on which our proposed model stands in this section, without formal proofs.

Assumption 1. *Through activities of users in online social networks, user-generated content, such as reviews, posts, votes, issued trust, and so on, represent and bear the user's attitude, credibility, and trustworthiness.*

A survey [37] suggests that numerous factors, including logical trust attributes (e.g., experience, frequency, stability, and rationality), emotional trust attributes (e.g., hope, fear, and regret) and relational trust attributes (e.g., similarity), contribute to construct individual trust through social capital and social activities. Meanwhile, in online social networks, the above factors are expressed through various types of user-generated contents and user activities. Therefore, trust can be harvested through a variety of UGC data that exists in OSNs, such as their posted reviews or articles, cast ratings and votes, and issued trust relationships.

Assumption 2. *For a trust relationship between a trustor and a trustee, not only the trustee but also the trustor contributes to the relationship formation.*

The formation of a trust relationship involves the trustor who evaluates and issues trust, and the trustee who presents and receives it, which makes trust asymmetric and subjective. The issuance of a trust relationship is determined by the trustor through their perception of the trustee's trustworthiness and how others perceive it. However, due to the difficulty of modeling trust's subjectivity, many studies only focus on making use of

UGC data that represent trustees' credibility [39–41], leaving trust an objective concept and measure.

Based on this point, we bear the mind in this paper that although same types of user data are being used for collecting trust information, they could serve different purposes for the trustor and the trustee involved in a trust relationship. For example, the same characteristics extracted from one of a user's reviews may serve as different features: the type of attitude features that suggest how the user trusts others, or the type of trustworthiness features which indicate how he is being trusted by others.

Assumption 3. *Users bearing similarities in their profiles or activities have a higher likelihood to establish trust relationships.*

That is suggested by the homophily effect, which is one of the most important theories that attempt to explain why people establish trust relations with each other [42]. For example, in the situation of product reviewing, people with similar tastes about items are more likely to trust each other.

Taking the previous two assumptions into consideration, we could further state that a group of similar users may build trust relationships with similar users from another group, if there exists a trust relationship between a pair of users from each group. This also implies trust's incomplete transitivity property.

Assumption 4. *In datasets from online social networks, no observable or explicit trust relationship between two users does not truly guarantee there will not be any trust between them.*

For example, we may infer a trust relationship issued by Alice to Bob, provided that (1) there are many other users who have certain similar characteristics as Alice has, and they also trust Bob, or (2) Alice trusts many other users who have traits in common with Bob. However, it is worth noting that there are quite a few reasons that the relationship of Alice and Bob is not present in the network. It can be explained from three perspectives:

- Due to some particular or unknown facts, Alice does not trust Bob; the trust relationship does not exist, and therefore, it will never be observed.
- It might be possible that Alice would trust Bob at some time later, but at the time we observe the social network or capture a snapshot of the network as a dataset, Alice does not know Bob yet or Alice does not claim to trust Bob yet, so the trust relationship from Alice to Bob does not exist.
- Alice does trust Bob and the trust relationship does exist in the real network, but it is missing from the dataset we observe. The cause could be the inability of capturing the whole network or capturing their relationship data being prohibited by the privacy preference settings of relevant users.

This uniqueness of trust in OSNs makes trust inference in OSNs quite different from general link prediction problems and general binary classification tasks. Since we only focus on inferring trust relationships in online social networks without any distrust information, as a binary classification task, the goal of our proposed model is to find as many trust relations as possible, and in the meantime, maintain considerable overall accuracy. Further discussion on this assumption is beyond the scope of this paper, and it will be left for future work.

Assumption 5. *Trust is propagative but not fully transitive, so it will be beneficial for us to learn under what criteria trust can be transferable from one user to another.*

For example, if Alice trusts Bob and Bob trusts Chris, Alice can derive some amount of trust on Chris based on how much she trusts Bob and how much Bob trusts Chris, but Alice may not trust Chris or even she does not know Chris. However, under some particular circumstances which is what we need to learn, Alice will trust Chris. Based on this assumption, we propose two primary trust propagation strategies below so that our model can learn from more complex trust relationship topology that commonly exists in real-world datasets:

- Direct trust propagation may exist from Alice to Chris when Alice trusts Bob and Bob trusts Chris.
- Transposed trust propagation may exist from Alice to Chris when Alice trusts Bob and Chris also trusts Bob.

The proposed trust propagation strategies are demonstrated in Figure 1. Some more complex propagation schemes can be derived from the above two primary ones. For example, if Alice trusts Bob and Chris, and Daniel also trusts Bob and Chris, there might be an increase in the trust between Alice and Daniel, which is a cascaded result of two transposed trust propagation instances. In the field of citation network analysis, this very same scheme is called *co-citation* and has been greatly studied. It is worth noting that the co-citation propagation conforms to Assumption 3, but, differently from it, we derived the "co-citation"-equivalent trust propagation from the topology perspective. The same above-mentioned trust propagation strategies of direct trust propagation and transposed trust propagation were also leveraged in [28], which helped the researchers build a better trust prediction model.

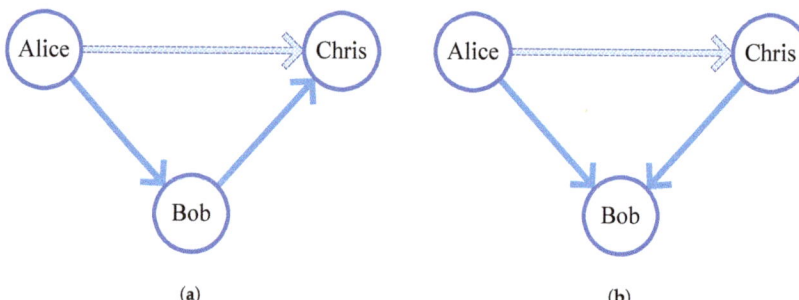

Figure 1. Two primary trust propagation strategies. (a) Direct trust propagation. (b) Transposed trust propagation.

3.2. Model Construction

Many modern online social services have deployed a feature which allows their users to build friend networks. It is common understanding that trust has a dedicated role in forming friendships between two individuals, and thus many trust-related studies also use friend networks in OSNs as trust networks. In particular, there are several online services that have explicitly implemented trust networks as web of trust—such online services include Epinion (http://www.epinions.com/ (accessed on 28 February 2018)) and Ciao (http://www.ciao.co.uk/ (accessed on 19 June 2021)).

We modeled our learning and inference tasks through a conditional random field (CRF), one of probabilistic graphical model variations. The structure of the probabilistic graphical model was built upon the trust network of an OSN, and the features that were to be added to the model were extracted and then built from the UGC data from the OSN. Due to the way that the UGC and topological features are embedded into the trust network, the CRF model not only uses both the explicit trust information (the trust network) and the user-generated contents from the social network, but also has the capability of capturing the interplay among various types of features extracted from the UGC and the network topology.

Differently from the conventional link prediction problem in which edges between nodes represent trust relationships, our method represents relationships as nodes. In other words, we model a real-world directional trust link as a trust relationship node in the model.

Therefore, the random variables in the CRF model are the predefined states or labels of users and trust relationships. (In this paper, we use "state" and "label" interchangeably.) In the CRF model, the two types of random variable nodes in the probabilistic graph are:

- **user** node. It can be either a *trustor* node or a *trustee* node;
- **trustRelation** node. It represents an observable or a nonexistent trust link in the network.

Figure 2 demonstrates the difference between a trust relationship commonly represented in real social networks and one modeled by our approach.

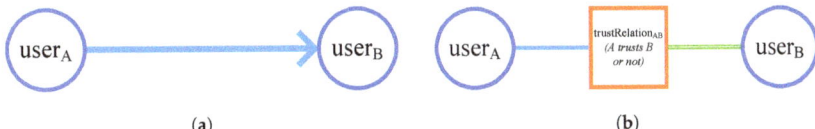

Figure 2. Demonstration of one user trusting another in the real world and in the proposed model. (a) Real-world trust relationship representation: $user_A$ trusts $user_B$. (b) $user_A$ trusting $user_B$ rendered in the proposed model.

For a user-user pair whose trust relationship is un-observed in the OSN, the objective of the model in this paper is to infer the probabilities of labels of the corresponding *trustRelation* node whose state is unknown in the probabilistic graph, so that the trust relationship can be predicted.

It is worth looking at how we handle edges in the model. Edges in a CRF are usually homogeneous in type. That means edges in the graph do not have to be type-specific. However, without breaking any conventional rule for model inference, we may particularly mark edges with dedicated types so that different edges can delegate different types of meanings and thus serve different purposes. In our model, the type of an edge between a *trustor* node and a *trustRelation* node is different from the type of an edge between a *trustRelation* node and a *trustee* node. It is also worth noting that involving different edge types grant the model the possibility of recognizing directional trust between a pair of two users. An example of modeling the mutual relationship between two users is demonstrated in Figure 3.

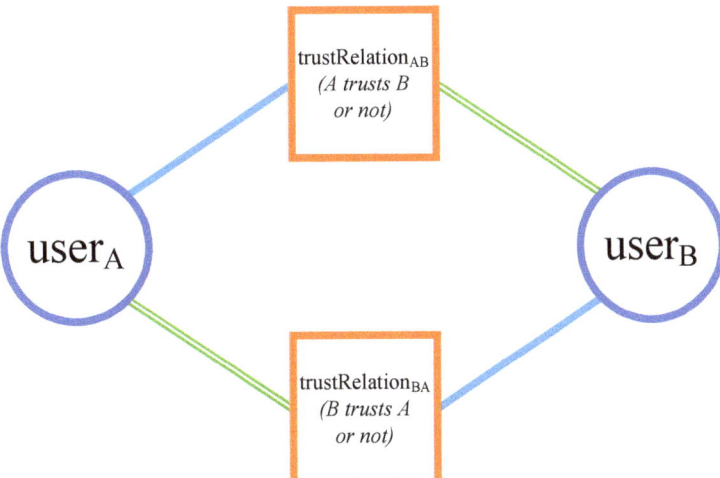

Figure 3. A demonstration of modeling two users' mutual relationship in the proposed model.

3.2.1. Notation and Problem Definition

Let U_i denote the user random variable at node i and T_j or T_{ab} (or $T_{a \to b}$) denote the trustRelation random variable at node j or the node representing the trust relationship from user U_a to user U_b. The notation of nodes and edges is detailed in Table 1.

Table 1. Notation of (random variable) nodes and edges in the proposed model.

		Notation	Description
Nodes			
		V	The set of all (random variable, r.v.) nodes.
user		U_u	R.v. for a user node u, either a trustor or a trustee.
		T_t	R.v. for a trustRelation node t.
trustRelation		T_{ab}	R.v. for a trustRelation node representing the trust relationship from user U_a to user U_b.
Edges			
		E	The set of all edges.
trustor ↔ trustRelation		E_{ut}	An edge between a trustor node U_u and a trustRelation node T_t.
trustRelation ↔ trustee		E_{tu}	An edge between a trustRelation node T_t and a trustee node U_u.

Now, we examine two users, for example, Alice and Bob, in a trust network and use a binary variable $T_{\text{Alice} \to \text{Bob}}$ to represent the possible trust relationship from Alice to Bob. If a trust relationship from Alice to Bob is present in the network, it means that Alice trusts Bob and we label the variable with value 1. If no trust relationship from Alice to Bob is observed in the dataset, we label the variable with value 0. As trust is directional and asymmetry, a different variable $T_{\text{Bob} \to \text{Alice}}$ also exists, and its value, which is also binary, represents the observational result of the trust relationship from Bob to Alice. Furthermore, we use probabilities to indicate trust relationships. For any two users A and B:

$$P(T_{A \to B} = 1) > P(T_{A \to B} = 0) \quad , \quad \text{if A trusts B;} \\ otherwise \quad , \quad \text{if A does not express trust in B.} \tag{1}$$

Additionally, particularly for trust relationships being observed in the dataset:

$$\left. \begin{array}{l} P(T_{A \to B} = 1) = 1 \\ P(T_{A \to B} = 0) = 0 \end{array} \right\} \quad , \quad \text{if A trusts B;} \tag{2}$$

$$\left. \begin{array}{l} P(T_{A \to B} = 1) = 0 \\ P(T_{A \to B} = 0) = 1 \end{array} \right\} \quad , \quad \text{if A does not express trust in B.} \tag{3}$$

The notation can be easily extended to support distrust, a concept that differs from either trust or no trust being observed in the dataset. However, distrust is beyond the scope of this paper, hence we would like to leave it for future research.

With the notation, the trust inference problem can be stated as follows. Given all user nodes U and a set of observed existing and nonexistent trustRelation nodes (their probability representations are either $P(T = 1) = 1$ or $P(T = 1) = 0$), the method predicts a set of un-observed trust relationships T^* by comparing their probability representations $P(T^* = 1)$ and $P(T^* = 0)$ that are calculated during the model inference.

3.2.2. Features

As stated in Assumption 1, trust information can be obtained, and trust can be harvested and evaluated through a user's generated contents in online social networks, including reviews, posts, connections, etc., as they are the representation and bearer of the user's attitude, credibility and trustworthiness, i.e., the trust constructs. Therefore, we extract various types of features from the dataset and embed them to the probabilistic graphical model to aid trust inference.

In our conditional random field, an arbitrary number of features of any arbitrary type can be attached to any node or any edge. All the features used in the proposed model are discrete, and they can be *label-observation features* for nodes, *label-label-observation features* for edges or *label-label features* for edges. In other words, the feature function of each feature is non-zero for a single state per node or a single state per edge (the state of an edge is determined by the state-pair of the two nodes connected by the edge), and the type and value of the feature are derived from observations in the UGC data from the OSN dataset. For example, we observe in the OSN dataset that a user has 57 trustors and the corresponding user node will be associated with a feature, whose type is "nTrustors" and value is 57. Table 2 lists typical sets of features used in this paper and we briefly describe them below.

Table 2. Sets of features used in the proposed model.

Feature Set	Description of Features in the Set
$\mathcal{F}_{PRF}$	Statistical features for user profiles (User Profile Features)
$\mathcal{F}_{UGC}$	Linguistic and stylistic features for reviews (UGC Features)
$\mathcal{F}_{TP}$	Propagative features for trust propagation (TP Features)
$\mathcal{F}_{TAUX}$	The first category of Auxiliary features
$\mathcal{F}_{TPAUX}$	The second category of Auxiliary features

Statistical features for user profiles (User profile features)

A user's profile is the most direct depiction of the user's social capital that reflects their identity and status which in turns reflect their attitude, credibility and trustworthiness. A set of typical statistical features for user profiles built from UGC data are used in this paper. As [43] suggests, an Internet celebrity, who is in fact an active and vigorous source for disseminating information, usually have a great many followers or trustors. Thus, the *number of trustors* of a user is an obvious indicator of the evidence that how the user's being trusted by others. In the meantime, the *number of trustees* of a user also shows their engagement and importance in the online social network. The *number of reviews* posted by a user and the *number of ratings* cast by a user is a reflection of their experience, frequency and involvement in the online social network. Some online social services also have a rank system for user reviews' helpfulness, and the *numbers of a user's reviews' helpfulness being rated* as *exceptional helpful, very helpful, helpful, somewhat helpful* or *not helpful* are intuitive hints for the user's experience, expertise and credibility.

In the proposed model, for each user, we build the statistical features from the user's profile data and attach them to the user node; for each trust relationship, we build the statistical features from the two involving users' profiles as edge features and attach them to the corresponding edge between the user node and the trustRelation node. As explained previously, an edge between a user node and a trustRelation node may have two different types. Herein, for either type of such edges, each user profile feature has a designated type, either as a feature denoted by "u2TrU" for edges between a trustor node and a trustRelation node, or as a feature denoted by "Tr2uU" for edges between a trustRelation node and a trustee node. In this way, the model is guaranteed to distinguish the features for a user as a trustor in a trust relationship from those features for the same user acting as a trustee in another trust relationship, which conforms to our Assumption 2.

Feature vector construction. Using features listed in Table 3:

- For each user U_u, we create a feature vector $F_{PRF}^{U}(U_u)$. Each feature of this type is a *label-observation feature*.
- For each trustor ↔ trustRelation edge or trustRelation ↔ trustee edge, we create a feature vector $F_{PRF}^{u2TrU}(E_{u \leftrightarrow t})$ or $F_{PRF}^{Tr2uU}(E_{t \leftrightarrow u})$, respectively. Each feature of this type is a *label-label-observation feature*.

Table 3. Statistical features for user profiles used in the proposed model.

Feature Name	Description
nRatings	The number of ratings a user has cast.
nRated	The number of ratings a user's reviews received.
nRated5	The number of *exceptional helpful* ratings a user's reviews received.
nRated4	The number of *very helpful* ratings a user's reviews received.
nRated3	The number of *helpful* ratings a user's reviews received.
nRated2	The number of *somewhat helpful* ratings a user's reviews received.
nRated1	The number of *not helpful* ratings a user's reviews received.
nReviews	The number of reviews posted by a user.
nTrustors	The number of trustors a user has.
nTrustees	The number of trustees a user has.

Linguistic and stylistic features for reviews (UGC features)

As previous studies [6,39,40] suggest, the linguistic characteristics and stylistic features of a review deliver the attitude, emotional status and part of expertise of the author, the quality of it implies whether or not the author is objective and unbiased, and the textual content of the review conveys the author's experience and expertise. According to Assumption 1, features extracted from reviews contribute to each user's attitude and trustworthiness, and thus affect their probability of trusting others and being trusted by others. Furthermore, according to Assumption 3, investigating this type of features also helps in finding similar users and suggesting trust relations to similar users. The linguistic and stylistic features for posts used in this paper include:

- *Parts-of-speech* (POS) used in this paper include nouns, verbs, adjectives, adverbs and conjunctions. These POS are mostly-used classes of words and may have different impacts across reviews. We use the ratio of the number of words in each POS type to the number of segments in a review as the feature value.
- The *Subjectivity* and *Polarity* of a word or a phrase describes whether the segment expresses either a *positive* or a *negative* meaning in either *strong* or *weak subjective* way. These words can have various parts-of-speech. We use the ratio of the number of these words or phrases to the number of segments in a review as the feature value.
- *Indicative* words could imply whether a post will be more credible or less convincing. They're functioning as *assertives, factives, implicatives, report verbs, hedges* or *biased words*. The lexicons are from [40,44]. Similarly, we use the ratio of the number of these words to the number of segments in a review as the feature value.

The *Affective words* (http://wndomains.fbk.eu/wnaffect.html (accessed on 1 June 2021)) and *Sentimental words* [45], which express an author's emotions, traits, sensations, attitudes or behaviors, can also be served as features for reviews. Using them may slightly increase the model's performance, however, for the sake of simplicity, we do not leverage them as features in this work.

All UGC features are attached to edges between user nodes and trustRelation nodes. Similarly as how we did with user profile features, we also mark UGC features with either type "u2TrR" or type "Tr2uR" to respect the two distinct types of edges to which they are attached.

Feature vector construction. Using features listed in Table 4:

- For each trustor ↔ trustRelation edge or trustRelation ↔ trustee edge, we create a feature vector $F_{UGC}^{u2TrR}(E_{u\leftrightarrow t})$ or $F_{UGC}^{Tr2uR}(E_{t\leftrightarrow u})$, respectively. Each feature of this type is a *label-label-observation feature*.

Table 4. Linguistic and stylistic features for reviews used in the proposed model.

Feature Type	Feature Name	Description: the Ratio of the Number of Specified Elements to All Segments in One of a User's Reviews
–	rPuncs	Punctuation marks
POS	rNouns	Nouns
	rAdjs	Adjectives
	rVerbs	Verbs
	rAdvs	Adverbs
	rConjs	Conjunctions
Subjectivity & Polarity	rPositives	Positive words and phrases
	rNegatives	Negative words and phrases
Indicative	rAssertives	Assertive verbs
	rFactives	Factive verbs
	rImplicatives	Implicative words and phrases
	rReports	Report verbs
	rBiases	Biased words
	rHedges	Mitigating words

Propagative features for trust propagation (TP features)

According to the trust propagation strategies described in Assumption 5, we propose two types of propagative features for trust propagation. Still take Alice, Bob and Chris for example, the proposed features are as follows.

- Direct trust propagation feature will try to capture how much Alice will trust Chris if Alice trusts Bob and Bob trusts Chris.
- Transposed trust propagation feature will try to describe how much Alice will trust Chris if Alice and Chris both trust Bob.

For any arbitrary trustRelation node T_1, we observe the state occurrence combinations of all motifs where each motif consists of three trustRelation nodes satisfying the following criteria:

- One of the three nodes in the motif is trustRelation node T_1. The other two *different* trustRelation nodes T_2 and T_3 are in the set of trustRelation nodes that are present in the dataset.
- The trustor node linked to T_1 is also linked to T_2 as a trustor node.
- The trustee node linked to T_1 is also linked to T_3 as
  - either a trustee node (for direct trust for trustRelation node T_1) while the trustee node of T_2 is the trustor node of T_3,
  - or a trustor node (for transposed trust for trustRelation node T_1) while the trustee node of T_2 is also the trustee node of T_3.

In other words, for each motif, the observing target including the motif itself consists of a trustor node, a trustee node, their corresponding trustRelation node, a third user in whose trust relationships either the trustor/trustee or trustor/trustor are shared, and their corresponding trustRelation nodes. Figure 4 illustrates the topological diagram for direct trust and transposed trust in the proposed model.

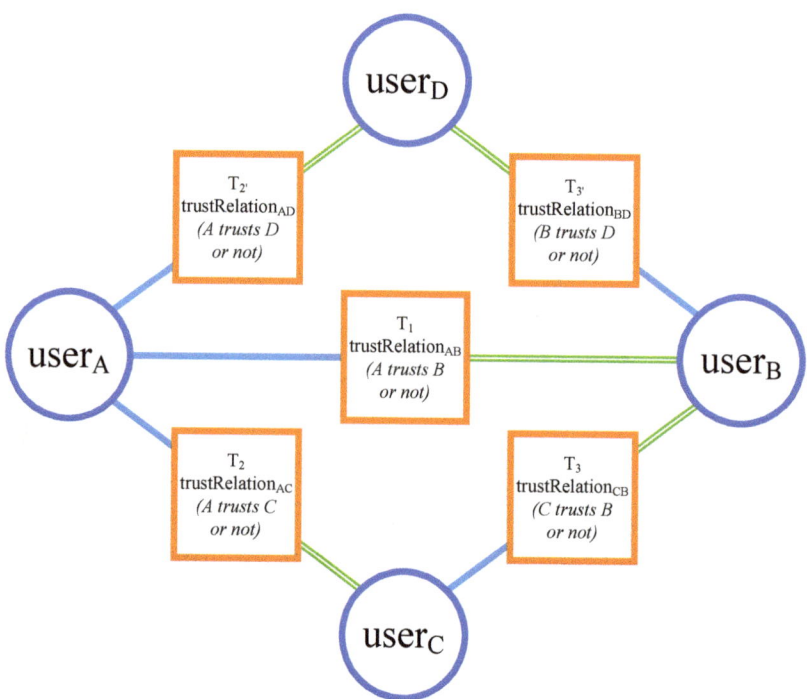

Figure 4. Illustration of direct trust and transposed trust for a trustRelation node in a 3-trustRelation-nodes motif. (T_2 and T_3 contribute direct trust to T_1; and $T_{2'}$ and $T_{3'}$ contribute transposed trust to T_1).

We build a trustRelation node's trust propagation features based on the numbers of state sequence occurrences of the three trustRelation nodes in each motif that the node has. Use the notation from the above criteria, for a trustRelation node T_1 and all its possible 3-trustRelation-nodes motifs that meet the criteria, a total of 16 trust propagation features are built, through the eight state sequences of the three trustRelation nodes in a motif in the specific order of T_1, T_2 and T_3. The feature values are either 1, if at least one motif with a corresponding state sequence exists, or 0, otherwise. Note that only trustRelation nodes representing trust or no trust relationships that exist in the observed dataset will get accounted for generating trust propagation feature values. As listed in Table 5, eight of the 16 features in this type are for direct trust propagation and the other eight are for transposed trust propagation.

Feature vector construction. Trust propagation features of each type will be generated as node features and get attached to trustRelation nodes. Using features listed in Table 5:

- For each trustRelation node T_t, we check if any instance of the 16 state sequences exists to generate trust propagation features, by applying the above criteria to all 3-trustRelation-nodes motifs in which T_t acts as T_1, and then create a feature vector $F_{TP}^T(T_t)$ to include these features. Each of them is a *label-observation feature*.

Table 5. Trust propagation features used in the proposed model.

Feature Type	Feature Name	Sequenced "Labels" of Nodes in Motif		
		$T_{A \to B}$ / T_1	$T_{A \to C}$ / T_2	$T_{C \to B}$ / T_3
Direct Trust	d000	N	N	N
	d001	N	N	Y
	d010	N	Y	N
	d011	N	Y	Y
	d100	Y	N	N
	d101	Y	N	Y
	d110	Y	Y	N
	d111	Y	Y	Y
		$T_{A \to B}$ / T_1	$T_{A \to D}$ / T_2	$T_{B \to D}$ / T_3
Transposed Trust	t000	N	N	N
	t001	N	N	Y
	t010	N	Y	N
	t011	N	Y	Y
	t100	Y	N	N
	t101	Y	N	Y
	t110	Y	Y	N
	t111	Y	Y	Y

Refer to Figure 4 for $T_{A \to B}$, $T_{A \to C}$, $T_{C \to B}$, and $T_{B \to D}$. For a trustRelation node: "Y" indicates an existing trust and "N" a nonexistent one.

Auxiliary features

For better modeling real-world correlations among users and trust relationships and for the proposed method to work properly in the model's probabilistic inference, certain auxiliary edge features are built and attached to the model. They are called auxiliary in this paper because the proposed model and the trust inference approach will still work without adding them, though inefficiently.

We build the auxiliary edge features through the inspiration of the *Ising model* [46] (or more generally the *Potts model*) in statistical mechanics. These models imply that two directly connected nodes of the same type tend to be in the same state. This inspires us that the state–state pair of two directly connected nodes of different types might also follow certain statistical rules. In this paper, two categories of auxiliary edge features are proposed as follows.

1. One category of auxiliary edge features will be attached to each edge between a user node and a trustRelation node. Their labelnames are, respectively, prefixed with "u2TrT" and "Tr2uT" for features on a *trustor–trustRelation edge* and features on a *trustRelation–trustee edge*. This setting matches the construction of our probabilistic graphical model where edges between user nodes and trustRelation nodes have different types. Such an setting allows the model to distinguish how differently a trustor or a trustee affects a trust relationship's formation.
   Feature vector construction. For each trustor ↔ trustRelation edge or trustRelation ↔ trustee edge, we create a feature vector $F_{TAUX}^{u2TrT}(E_{u \leftrightarrow t})$ or $F_{TAUX}^{Tr2uT}(E_{t \leftrightarrow u})$, respectively. Each feature in this category is a *label-label feature*.
2. The other category of auxiliary edge features will be attached to edges between trustRelation nodes that are involved in the motif structure explained previously. Similarly to trust propagation features, features in this category follow the concept of propagative trust, i.e., direct trust propagation and transposed trust propagation, and grant values of each of them with either 0 for direct trust or 1 for transposed trust. However, different from the trust propagation features which are node features, they are edge features trying to "filter out similarly behaving trustRelation nodes".

Feature vector construction. For each trustRelation ↔ trustRelation edge, we create a feature vector $F^T_{\text{TPAUX}}(E_{t \leftrightarrow t'})$. Each feature in this category is a *label-label-observation feature*.

The current implementation of the proposed model does not support inference on cliques yet, which will be discussed below. And thus, it hinders the employment of the second category of auxiliary features (*label-label-observation features*) on edges between trustRelation nodes, which require the prerequisite of the existence of trustRelation–trustRelation edges. However, we use the same inference method for pairwise graph structure approximately for cliques, and we'd like to leave the inference on cliques as future work to complete.

3.2.3. Model Formulation

The random variables in our model are the states or labels of corresponding nodes. For a user node, its state is a predefined measurement for the user from the original online social network. It can be direct statistics of this user or carefully handcrafted measurement calculated from information obtained from their OSN data. For demonstration purpose and brevity, we use user categories defined by the online social service as user node states in this paper. For a trustRelation node, which represents the trust relationship between the trustor user and the trustee user, the random variable's state is the trust relationship's existence in the OSN dataset. As each node has a state, each edge has a state–state pair (or a transition state) that is determined by the states of the two nodes connected by it. Table 6 summarizes state configurations used in this paper.

Table 6. Configurations of node state and edge state–state pair.

Type	States	Description
Node		
user (u)	0, 1, 2	User categories defined by the OSN.
trustRelation (t)	0	Such an relationship is observed.
	1	Such an relationship is un-observed.
Edge (U: state of user node, T: state of trustRelation node)		
$E_{u \leftrightarrow t}$	UT: 00, 01, 10, 11, 20, 21	state–state pair consisting of U and T.
$E_{t \leftrightarrow u}$	TU: 00, 01, 02, 10, 11, 12	state–state pair consisting of T and U.
$E_{t \leftrightarrow t'}$	TT: 00, 01, 10, 11	state–state pair consisting of T and T.

Due to the way that we model trust relationships as random variable nodes in the probabilistic graph, the smallest significant structure in the resulting graph is pairwise. (Although there will be smallest cliques that consist of three trustRelation nodes if the second category of auxiliary features is leveraged, we still model the conditional random field and run probabilistic inference on it pairwisely.) Different pairwise structures are connected via the common user nodes or trustRelation nodes. It is worth noting that each node, if connected by a dummy node, can also be viewed as a pairwise structure, and thus we call each node a unitary structure.

Each unitary structure has a set of associated *node feature functions* and each pairwise structure has a set of *edge feature functions*. In our problem setting, we attach features to each node and edge. The features used in this paper are the user profile features, UGC features, and trust propagation features.

We use T and T* to denote the set of all known trust relationships and the set of trust links whose states are unknown, respectively. Let Ψ denote the set of feature weights, and the proposed model that computes a conditional distribution can be defined as

$$P(T^*|U, T; \Psi) = \frac{1}{Z(U, T)} \prod_i \varphi_i(U, T; \Psi), \qquad (4)$$

where $Z(\cdot)$ is the normalization constant, and φ_i is the i_{th} potential function for either a unitary structure or a pairwise structure.

For any node $V_i \in (U, T, T^*)$ or any edge $E_{j:\langle V_s, V_t \rangle}$ connecting nodes V_s and V_t, the potential functions for either unitary structures or pairwise structures used in this paper are, respectively, defined in the log-linear form as follows.

$$\varphi_i(V_i; \Psi_V) = \exp\left(\sum_k \psi_k f_{ik}(V_i)\right), \qquad (5)$$

$$\varphi_j(E_{j:\langle V_s, V_t \rangle}; \Psi_E) = \exp\left(\sum_k \psi_k f_{jk}(E_{j:\langle V_s, V_t \rangle})\right), \qquad (6)$$

where $f_{ik}(\cdot)$ is the k_{th} feature function in the i_{th} structure. In the way that features are weighted and then linearly aggregated, the interplay among features of a same node or edge is collectively numericalized.

3.3. Probabilistic Model Inference and Interpretation

From the above-mentioned model construction, we know that there will be loops in the probabilistic graph if bidirectional trust relations exist. That means if Alice and Bob trust each other, which is common in the real world, then the graph containing only the two users and their trust relationships is no longer a linear-chain or a tree, as shown in Figure 3.

For the probabilistic model inference, collectively predicting all needed trust relationships from the online social network involves iterating through an exponential number of possible label combinations, and thus requires exponential time. Furthermore, as the probabilistic graph contains loops, and exact inference on such a general graphical model is thus intractable, approximations are employed. We propose to solve the inference problem using the *loopy belief propagation* (LBP) technique. As a *belief propagation* (BP) method variant, the LBP is a *message passing* algorithm but requires a slightly different schedule of message updating rules from the vanilla BP method.

It is worth noting that each pairwise structure in the probabilistic graph only connects two random variable nodes, and a unitary structure can be viewed as if there is a dummy node linked to it so that a pseudo-pairwise structure exists. Therefore, we can safely skip the factor graph framework and send messages directly between each pair of nodes connected by an edge. This way of handling message passing is equivalent to the original BP algorithm.

We chose to update messages synchronously, i.e., in each time epoch, each pair of nodes exchange messages, if they are connected by an edge. In the iterative message updates, each node's belief is normalized so that the normalized belief approximates the node's marginal probability and is further considered as the new local evidence (also called compatibility or potential) at this node. Similarly, for an edge and the two nodes connected by it, we use the normalized belief of the pairwise structure as its local evidence. In the model inference, passing messages, calculating node/edge beliefs, and updating messages are repeated until message convergence or an allowed maximum number of iterations is reached.

When the LBP is done, we normalize each node's belief so that it approximates the node's marginal distribution. Through the marginal probabilities of all possible labels for a selected trustRelation node, the trust relationship indicated by this node can be determined by Equation (1). Such probabilities for the trustRelation node can be further interpreted from the message passing perspective.

Let m_{ji} denote a message sent from node i's neighboring node j to it, x_i be the random variable at node i, and $\varphi_i(x_i)$ and $\varphi_{ij}(x_i, x_j)$ be the local evidence at node i (unitary structure) and edge $\langle i, j \rangle$ (and its connected nodes i and i, pairwise structure). According to BP, the belief $b_i(x_i)$ at a node i before normalization, which will then approximate the variable's marginal probability, is proportional to the product of the local evidence at this node and all the messages coming to it:

$$b_i(x_i) \propto \varphi_i(x_i) \prod_{j \in N(i)} m_{ji}(x_i), \qquad (7)$$

where $N(i)$ denotes the set of nodes directly neighboring node i. The messages are determined by message update rules as follows,

$$m_{ji}(x_i) \leftarrow \sum_{x_j} \varphi_j(x_j) \varphi_{ji}(x_j, x_i) \prod_{k \in N(j) \setminus i} m_{kj}(x_j). \qquad (8)$$

Analogously to Equation (7), the pairwise belief $b_{ij}(x_{ij})$ at a pairwise structure will be

$$b_{ij}(x_{ij}) \propto \varphi_{ij}(x_i, x_j) \varphi_i(x_i) \varphi_j(x_j) \prod_{k \in N(i) \setminus j} m_{ki}(x_i) \prod_{k \in N(j) \setminus i} m_{kj}(y_j), \qquad (9)$$

Without loss of generality, we take Figure 5 as an example for the following discussion. U_A, U_B, T_{AB} are the random variables of the trustor node A, the trustee node B and the trustRelation node linked to them, respectively. Since the trustRelation node is linked to a trustor node and a trustee node by only two edges, with Equation (7), the belief at it is proportional to

$$b_{T_{AB}}(T_{AB}) \propto \varphi_{T_{AB}}(T_{AB}) \prod_{i \in N(T_{AB})} m_{i \to T_{AB}}(T_{AB}), \qquad (10)$$

and the two messages (M_A and M_B in the figure) sent to the trustRelation node are, respectively

$$m_{U_A \to T_{AB}}(T_{AB}) \leftarrow \sum_{U_A} \varphi_{U_A}(U_A) \varphi_{U_A, T_{AB}}(U_A, T_{AB}) \prod_{k \in N(U_A) \setminus T_{AB}} m_{k \to U_A}(U_A), \qquad (11)$$

$$m_{U_B \to T_{AB}}(T_{AB}) \leftarrow \sum_{U_B} \varphi_{U_B}(U_B) \varphi_{U_B, T_{AB}}(U_B, T_{AB}) \prod_{k \in N(U_B) \setminus T_{AB}} m_{k \to U_B}(U_B). \qquad (12)$$

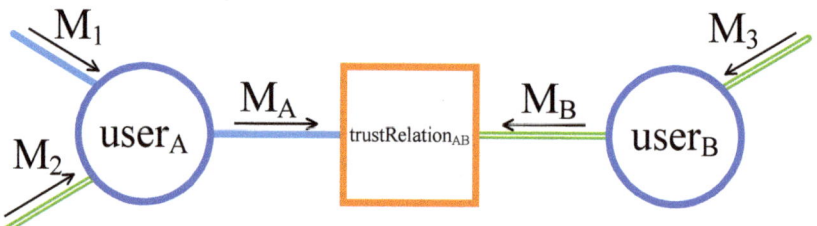

Figure 5. An illustration of passing messages through a trustor node U_A and a trustee node U_B to a trustRelation node T_{AB}.

Let $\Lambda_x(y)$ be the multiplication of the local evident at node x and edge $\langle x, y \rangle$, and substitute Equations (11) and (12) and the messages demonstrated in the figure into Equation (10). The belief at the trustRelation node amounts to

$$b_{T_{AB}}(T_{AB}) = \kappa \varphi_{T_{AB}}(T_{AB})(M_A M_B) \tag{13}$$

$$= \kappa \varphi_{T_{AB}}(T_{AB}) \left[\sum_{U_A} \Lambda_{U_A}(T_{AB})(M_1 M_2) \right] \left[\sum_{U_B} \Lambda_{U_B}(T_{AB}) M_3 \right], \tag{14}$$

where κ is a normalization constant.

It follows that the trustRelation node's belief is proportional to all local evidence at this node and two messages sent by the trustor node and the trustee node. The local evidence is the calculated potential through the compatibility function (energy function, refer to Equations (5) and (6). Based on the trustor's attitude, experience, awareness of other users' expertise and trustworthiness, etc., collected by Equation (11), the message M_A sent by the trustor node tells the trustRelation node how much the trustor believes they will issue or not issue a trust relationship to the trustee. Likewise, through the trustee's expertise, experience and evidential suggestions from other users' trust, etc., constituted by Equation (12), the message M_B sent from the trustee node tells the trustRelation node how much the trustee thinks their behaviors should be recognized by the potential trustor so that the trustor will trust them or not.

One can conclude that both the trustor and the trustee are involved in forming a trust relationship, obviously, in a real-world social network, and they have different contributions to the relationship formation, which is in accordance with Assumption 2, which we made previously.

3.4. Parameter Estimation

For the model to be able to infer trust, we need to know each parameter in the model, i.e., the weights for all features. In this section, we embrace the simple but effective gradient descent method to minimize the model's negative likelihood so that the training data will achieve locally highest probability under the model.

From Equations (4)–(6), the conditional log-likelihood with respect to the set of feature weights Ψ to be maximized can be obtained as follows.

$$l(\Psi) = -\log Z(\cdot) + \sum_i \log[\varphi_i(U, T; \Psi)] \tag{15}$$

$$= -\log Z(\cdot) + \sum_i \left(\sum_k \psi_k f_{ik}(V_i) \right) + \sum_j \left(\sum_k \psi_k f_{jk}(E_{j:\langle V_s, V_t \rangle}) \right), \tag{16}$$

and with the LBP algorithm, the approximated gradients of the likelihood (the partial derivatives with respect to feature ψ_k) are

$$\frac{\partial l}{\partial \psi_k} = \sum_i \sum_k f_{ik}(X_i) - \sum_i \sum_k f_{ik}(X_i) q(X_i) + \frac{\psi_k}{\sigma^2}, \tag{17}$$

where X_i can be either a unitary or a pairwise structure; $q(\cdot)$ is the approximated marginal, i.e., the belief of the unitary or pairwise structure, which can be determined by running a pass of the LBP algorithm on the graph; and the last term is the regularization term to prevent over-fitting.

As was discussed in the previous section, calculating the logarithm of the normalizing constant $\log Z(\cdot)$ is intractable, and thus we use Bethe Energy [47] to further approximate it:

$$\log Z(\cdot) \approx l_{\text{BETHE}}(\psi, q)$$
$$= -\sum_{s,t} \sum_{V_s, V_t} q(V_s, V_t)[\log q(V_s, V_t) - \log P(V_s, V_t)] \tag{18}$$
$$+ \sum_s \sum_{V_s} [d(V_s) - 1] q(V_s)[\log q(V_s) - \log P(V_s)]$$

where $d(V_s)$ is the degree of node V_s; $P(V_s)$ and $P(V_s, V_t)$ are, respectively, the initial potentials of their unitary and pairwise structures; and $q(\cdot)$ and $q(\cdot, \cdot)$ are corresponding optimal marginal distributions of approximated beliefs through LBP.

Between gradient descent epochs, the new feature weight vector $\psi^{(m)}$ is computed from the old vector $\psi^{(m-1)}$ by

$$\psi^{(m)} = \psi^{(m-1)} + \alpha_m \nabla l(\psi^{(m-1)}), \tag{19}$$

where $\nabla l(\cdot)$ is the partial derivatives calculated through Equation (17), and $\alpha_m > 0$ is a step size controlling the distance the parameter moves in the direction of the gradient, which is also called the learning rate.

3.5. Implementation

Our implementation of the proposed model, including the model construction, inference, and relevant training and predicting procedures, was based on the framework introduced in our previous work [48]. For the sake of brevity, we only discuss some concerns on the model implementation in this section which may greatly affect the model's performance.

Numerical overflows and underflows. These are very common in BP and other message passing algorithms. For example, some terms in the potential functions of unitary or pairwise structures (e.g., Equations (5) or (6)) may be overflowed due to the exponential calculations; in message passing (e.g., Equation (8)), if the messages passed via each edge are not constrained, then some messages will exhibit underflow after certain iterations of message updates; and calculating beliefs (e.g., Equation (7) and (9)) may cause overflow or underflow or both. The trick to tackling the overflow problem here is to shift every exponent in the calculated potential by subtracting the largest exponent. For the underflow issue during message passing, it is necessary to normalize messages frequently.

Parameter learning rate in model training. According to Equation (19), if the learning rate α_m for step m is too large, the new parameters will move too far in the direction of the gradient; if it is too small, the training procedure will be very slow to accomplish. Thus, it is essential to properly schedule learning rates in the whole model training process. A simple common approach is to let α_m decrease slowly to 0 as step m grows, which is

$$\alpha_m = \frac{1}{\sigma^2(\alpha_0 + m - 1)}, \tag{20}$$

where α_0 is the initial learning rate and σ^2 is the L2 regularization. The initial learning rate α_0 can be manually set or obtained by running a few passes of gradient descent over the graph [49].

Implementation of bi-directional message passing. For bi-directionally passing messages via each edge, the implementation of a non-directional edge in the model is built as two mutually opposite directional edges. Consequently, the number of *real functioning edges* in the implementation will be doubled and the number of calculations in the probabilistic inference procedure will greatly increase. In order for the model to perform LBP efficiently, parallelism could be deployed in synchronous message passing. It is also beneficial to offload the LBP algorithm to *graphics processing unit* (GPU) devices to further accelerate the model inference and training.

4. Experiments

We performed experiments with data (the dataset is publicly accessible via https://www.cse.msu.edu/~tangjili/trust.html (accessed on 10 June 2017)) from a typical online social network, Ciao, where users are allowed to build trust network, cast ratings, post reviews on a variety types of items, and rate other's reviews. We chose Ciao because of the availability of a relatively full web of trust and abundant user-generated content for explicit and inexplicit trust for trust inference.

4.1. Data

For fast model evaluation and comparison with other binary classifiers, we extracted a portion from the full data as our dataset used for experiments. As user links in social networks are often sparse, it is obvious that the observed trust relationships takes up only a very small fraction, whereas unobserved ones are common, which means the data are unbalanced. To deal with the imbalance in the dataset and for the sake of simplicity, we undersampled unobserved relationships. The statistics for the dataset used in experiments are listed in Table 7.

Table 7. Dataset specification.

Number of users	14,317	
Number of reviews	24,406	
Number of reviews per user	1.7	
Number of trust relationships	Y: 87,804	N: 78,863
Web of trust density	Y: 0.00043	N: 0.00038

For a trust relationship: "Y" indicates an existing trust and "N" a nonexistent one.

Features introduced in Section 3.2.2, including contextual features and relational features, were constructed with information extracted from the dataset. For reviews, we deployed an annotator by CoreNLP (https://stanfordnlp.github.io/CoreNLP/ (accessed on 20 June 2017)) to extract words and phrases from texts and build stylistic and linguistic features. Detailed feature statistics are listed in Supplementary Materials.

Although we carried out the experiments on only one dataset, the proposed method is universally applicable to various online social networks. With only a set of users and the set of trust relationships from other data sources, the model can still be built successfully and then infer trust, though without adequate relevant features the inference may perform unsatisfactorily. If additional features are available, the proposed method will prove its efficiency in trust relationship prediction.

4.2. Experimental Settings

4.2.1. Comparison Methods

We chose several easy-to-implement state-of-the-art binary classifiers as baseline comparison methods, including *support vector machine* (SVM) with a radial basis function (RBF) kernel, *decision tree* (DT), and *random forest* (RF). Generally speaking, linear SVMs are interpretable but less efficient than SVMs with an RBF kernel that are partially interpretable; DTs provides interpretable results, and RFs deliver better results than DTs do but decrease interpretability.

We did not compare our model with the methods proposed in [33–35], as ours is supervised learning. We also did not conduct comparison experiments between ours and models based on neural networks. Although these models probably could, and most likely would, achieve better performances than ours, to interpret these models is still a problem.

4.2.2. Evaluation Metrics

As we construct our mission of trust relationship inference as a binary classification task in this paper, we used the common metrics for classification evaluation. In detail, we used *Accuracy*, *Precision*, *Recall*, and F_1 *score* for evaluations.

For the set of user trust relationships that are to be inferred by a model or a method, we denote the number of all elements in the set by C; the number of observed trust relationships that were also predicted to be existent (true positive data points) by tp; and the numbers of false negative, false positive, and true negative ones by fn, fp, and tn, respectively. Then, the Accuracy is defined as

$$\text{Accuracy} = \frac{\text{tp} + \text{tn}}{C}, \qquad (21)$$

and Precision, Recall, and F_1 score are, respectively, defined as

$$\text{Precision} = \frac{tp}{tp + fp}, \tag{22}$$

$$\text{Recall} = \frac{tp}{tp + fn}, \tag{23}$$

$$F_1 = \frac{2tp}{2tp + fp + fn}. \tag{24}$$

From the metric definitions, the higher one metric is, the better performance a model or a method has.

4.2.3. Experiment Setup

In this paper, two sets of experiments were conducted.

1. For model validation and comparisons, we conducted experiments using the proposed model and comparison methods with different feature set combinations on the split training and test datasets, and then compared the resulting performances with the evaluation metrics.
2. For privacy-restrict online social network analysis, experiments were carried out with partially reduced data to further explore the proposed model's trust inference capability in a real-world scenario. Hereinafter, the reduced data means that features from a certain set for a portion of users were missing for a specific experiment. As stated earlier in Section 1, in real-world online social networks, some users may choose to opt out of part of or all of their data being used by online social services.

As was discussed in Section 3.2.2, the proposed model will still work without auxiliary features. Nevertheless, the types of auxiliary features are a particular coexistent by-product of how the proposed model was built, and also reflect the real-world mechanism of trust relationship formation. Therefore, these features were used in all experiments for the proposed model, acting as part of the foundation of the model. Note that these features only work with the proposed model.

In all experiments for model validation and comparison, we used different combinations of feature sets to show each method's ability in trust inference. Table 8 lists the different feature sets for experiments. (Refer to Table 2 for the types of features used in this paper.) For the comparison methods, the feature set combinations available for them are similar but without any auxiliary features from $\mathcal{F}_{TAUX}$ or $\mathcal{F}_{TPAUX}$.

For model learning and predicting, the set of user trust relationships was randomly split into a training set and test set, and the ratios of sizes of the two sets were 50–50%, 0–40%, 70–30%, 80–20%, and 90–10%. (A better way to split the data is to split data according to trust relationship creation time. However, in the chosen dataset, such information of trust relationship creation time was missing, and thus we resorted to splitting the data randomly.) All the second set of experiments used the 90–10% split for training and test datasets.

For the second set of experiments, the reduced feature data were generated by randomly removing one type of features from a certain percentage of users. The percentages for feature removal are 20%, 40%, 60% and 80%, respectively. If two types of features are used at the same time for an experiment, the random removal for each type of features is independent.

Other experiment setup included: in all experiments for the proposed model, we set the maximum number of gradient descent epochs to 20 and the maximum number of LBP iterations to 10.

Table 8. Sets of features used for experiments.

# of Experiment Set		# of Experiment	Feature Set Contents			
1st	2nd		$\mathcal{F}_{PRF}$	$\mathcal{F}_{UGC}$	$\mathcal{F}_{TAUX}$	$\mathcal{F}_{TP} + \mathcal{F}_{TPAUX}$
✓		1			✓	
✓	✓	2	✓		✓	
✓	✓	3		✓	✓	
✓	✓	4			✓	✓
✓	✓	5	✓	✓	✓	
✓	✓	6	✓		✓	✓
✓	✓	7		✓	✓	✓
✓		8	✓	✓	✓	✓

4.3. Results and Discussion

4.3.1. The First Set of Experiments with All Possibly Usable Feature Data

Performance of the proposed method with different feature sets

Firstly, we report the trust inference performance of the proposed method. The experiments were conducted with eight different feature set combinations on the five split training and test datasets, and accuracy and F_1 score are reported for each of them. As shown in Figure 6, the results are organized into three groups by how the feature sets were composed: the first group contains results from experiments 1, 2, 5, 6, and 8, which illustrates how integrating the user profile feature set $\mathcal{F}_{PRF}$ into the model affects the model's performance; similarly, the second group contains experimental results from experiments 1, 3, 5, 7, and 8 to show the power of using UGC feature set $\mathcal{F}_{UGC}$; the third group of 1, 4, 6, 7, and 8 depicts the effect of trust propagation feature set $\mathcal{F}_{TP} + \mathcal{F}_{TPAUX}$.

With either a single feature set or a combination of feature sets, the proposed method outperformed three naive classifiers, *uniformly random guess*, *random selected class*, and *majority class*, which, respectively, achieved accuracies of 0.5000, 0.5014, and 0.5269 according to the dataset specification (refer to Table 7). From the reported results evaluated by the accuracy metric, one can conclude that the proposed method is efficient and capable of inferring trust relationships.

As was previously discussed, with only the first category of auxiliary features, the proposed method will still worked, and it also achieved above-average performance. They are special features that only work with our model but not for other comparison methods. This makes our model with this set of features promising as a supervised learning model, when abundant data, such as user-generated content, are available as data input.

A quick glance over the performance results regarding both accuracy and F_1 score shows that substituting additional features into the model does improve the model's performance. However, the results differ a bit when the added combination of additional feature sets varies. The observations are as follows.

1. On top of the first category of auxiliary features ($\mathcal{F}_{TAUX}$), adding a single feature set ($\mathcal{F}_{PRF}$, $\mathcal{F}_{UGC}$, or $\mathcal{F}_{TP} + \mathcal{F}_{TPAUX}$) into the model will improve the model's performance. The use of the UGC feature set $\mathcal{F}_{UGC}$ improves the model's accuracy (and F_1 score) greatly by 42.45% to 50.22% (27.80% to 30.76%), followed by the user profile feature set $\mathcal{F}_{PRF}$ by 14.92% to 20.87% (1.16% to 6.60%), and then the trust propagation feature set $\mathcal{F}_{TP} + \mathcal{F}_{TPAUX}$ by 0.35% to 1.01% (0.34% to 1.32%).
2. Although adding a single feature set $\mathcal{F}_{TP} + \mathcal{F}_{TPAUX}$ did not greatly improve the performance, it could help another single feature set $\mathcal{F}_{PRF}$ to achieve better results. This can be seen from experiment 6 and experiment 2, where the model performance was improved by 11.26% to 14.27% in accuracy (Figure 6a) and 13.60% to 18.09% in F_1 score (Figure 6d).
3. Using all types of features (in experiment 8) does not always promise the best result. The performance for the proposed model with such feature sets was close to the

performance of the model with the UGC feature set $\mathcal{F}_{UGC}$ with or without other feature sets.

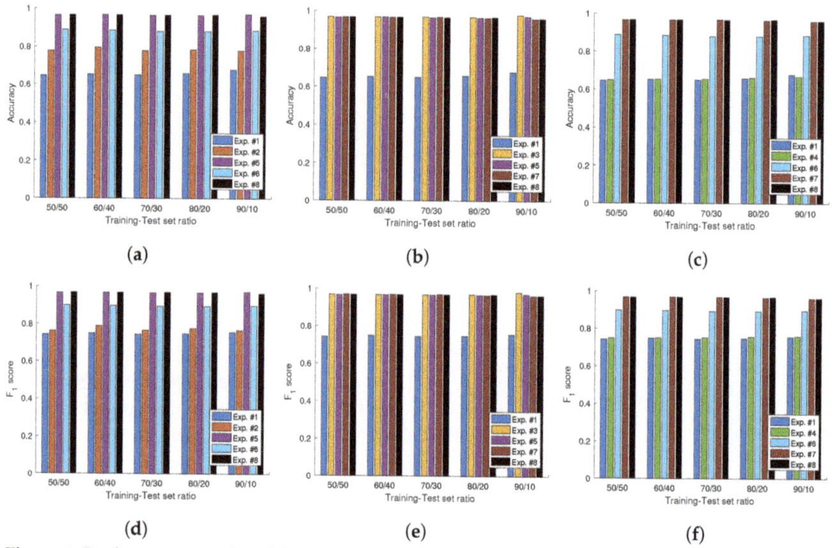

Figure 6. Performance results of the proposed model evaluated by Accuracy (Acc) and F_1 score for the first set of experiments. (**a**) Experiments 1, 2, 5, 6, 8 (Acc). (**b**) Experiments 1, 3, 5, 7, 8 (Acc). (**c**) Experiments 1, 4, 6, 7, 8 (Acc). (**d**) Experiments 1, 2, 5, 6, 8 (F_1). (**e**) Experiments 1, 3, 5, 7, 8 (F_1). (**f**) Experiments 1, 4, 6, 7, 8 (F_1).

It is expected to see the model get better results when additional features are added into it. It is also foreseeable that using UGC features ($\mathcal{F}_{UGC}$) should work better than using other types of features, as UGC data are usually more abundant than other types of features, both from a dataset and in the real world. The expected result will in turn validate Assumption 1, that a user's generated contents hold the representation of the user's trust information. All the good performance results came from a rich amount of UGC data, and so, a legitimate question arises, "What if some of the UGC data are missing possibly due to any privacy-related constraints?" Or more precisely, "What would the model performance become if some of the UGC data are not available?" The second set of experiments conducted with reduced feature data will shed light on the answers to them.

As for the trust propagation features, apart from the data imbalance, there is another possible reason that they do not always improve the model's performance: the probabilistic inference is performed on pairwise structures rather than cliques. Nevertheless, the trust propagation features do improve the model's performance when working with the statistical user profile features.

Performance Comparisons

Secondly, we report the comparative performance results achieved by using our model and other methods discussed in the previous section. For these experiments, all available feature datasets and their combinations are free to use for experimenting. The performances for each method evaluated by the accuracy and F_1 score metrics, and experiments in which the best performances were achieved are reported in Tables 9 and 10. Full results, including precision and recall for each experiment, are reported in the Supplementary Materials. As has been already stated, the auxiliary features only fit in the proposed model, and all the other types of features can be used for all methods.

Table 9. First experiment set: best performance comparison for different methods by Accuracy.

Training–Test	Our Model	SVM	DT	RF
50–50%	0.9678 (#3)	0.9106 (#6)	0.8778 (#6)	0.9212 (#8)
60–40%	0.9673 (#3)	0.9139 (#6)	0.8847 (#6)	0.9239 (#8)
70–30%	0.9675 (#7)	0.9120 (#6)	0.8853 (#6)	0.9215 (#8)
80–20%	0.9684 (#3)	0.9093 (#6)	0.8729 (#6)	0.9152 (#8)
90–10%	0.9804 (#3)	0.9143 (#6)	0.8741 (#6)	0.9198 (#8)

Table 10. First experiment set: best performance comparison for different methods by F_1 score.

Training–Test	Our Model	SVM	DT	RF
50–50%	0.9688 (#7)	0.9160 (#6)	0.8850 (#6)	0.9247 (#8)
60–40%	0.9684 (#7)	0.9190 (#6)	0.8923 (#6)	0.9275 (#8)
70–30%	0.9698 (#7)	0.9170 (#6)	0.8925 (#6)	0.9250 (#8)
80–20%	0.9691 (#3)	0.9141 (#6)	0.8793 (#6)	0.9188 (#8)
90–10%	0.9810 (#3)	0.9193 (#6)	0.8812 (#6)	0.9238 (#8)

From the experimental results listed in the tables and the Supplementary Materials, the first observation is that our proposed method outperforms other comparison methods in terms of accuracy and F_1 score, if all types of features are free to use.

The second observation is that UGC features ($\mathcal{F}_{UGC}$) were always involved in the used features when all methods achieved their respective best or second best performances. The fact that there is trust construct embedded in UGC data is proved again, but through the results by comparison methods this time. Consequently, one can harvest a user's trust information from UGC data from the user and his "friends" including trustors and trustees, which thus bears witness to Assumption 1 we made in Section 3.1.

Last but not least, in contrast to the results achieved by our proposed model, SVM and decision tree generated worse results by adding UGC features than user profile features, and all three comparison methods had improved results by using trust propagation features. One possible reason for the performance divergence's cause is the very large number and dimensions of UGC features employed in the three comparison methods; meanwhile, a few yet powerful trust propagation features greatly improved their performance when working with either UGC features or user profile features. Another reason that our model behaved differently in these experiments is that ours can balance a massive number of features which may counter each other, and can also "capture and numericalize" interplayed features.

A peek at Recall: higher Precision or higher Recall for trust relationship prediction in OSNs?

For a classification task, the outcome for it determines the expectations for the precision and recall in the task's result. For the task of trust relationship prediction, or more generally friend recommendation, in an online social network that exists in an online social service, there are some considerations that might help with making the decision.

In OSNs, friend relationship or trust relationship recommendation is an efficient way for users to get started and engaged more in the online social service's activities so that the online social service's revenue could gain.

From the user's perspective, the recommendation should provide users with accurate sets of users based on their homophily and existing friend/trust networks, and the expected precision of the recommendation or the prediction is to be high ideally.

On the other hand, it is probable that the number of candidates being recommended to a user will be few due to the user's strict criteria, or nearly none, which would eventually make the recommendations less effective; and thus, from the online service's operating and managing perspective, in addition to suggested users who satisfy the user's criteria, it is essential to recommend extra possible candidates to the user, although these candidates may not strictly match the user's criteria fed to the inference algorithm. Therefore, a higher recall for such a recommender or a predictor of a model will benefit an online social network. Additionally, of course, the model should maintain acceptable precision.

Another reason for a higher recall comes from the fact that the dataset used for friend recommendation or trust relationship prediction tasks is usually incomplete. As previously discussed, part of an "ideally complete" dataset would be missing due to various actual reasons. Consequently, even though a model generates good prediction results with high precision, the results may still be far away from a "real ideal." Thus, as a trade-off, a prediction result with a higher recall is acceptable.

Taking the above considerations into account, one of the best models that fit in the trust relationship prediction tasks in this paper would achieve a higher recall while still maintaining an acceptable precision. From the results for the first experiment set, our proposed model had an average recall of 0.9327 in all 40 experiments; and for SVM, decision tree, and random forest in their respective 35 experiments, the average recalls were 0.8239, 0.7950, and 0.8382.

4.3.2. The Second Set of Experiments with Reduced Feature Data

From a quick look at the experiment setup, the second set of privacy-aware experiments conducted with reduced feature data revealed some similarities with the first set of experiments in the training set and test set split configuration. It is true that if we are to conduct another group of experiments in which users choose to opt out of usages of all their profile data and UGC data and even some of users deny the usage of their trust relationships in trust inference tasks, the experiments will be exactly the same as the ones in the first set of experiments using only the first category of auxiliary features ($\mathcal{F}_{TAUX}$) with specific training and test datasets.

However, the fact is that they are not the same from the management perspective. The split training set and test set configuration is for model verification. On one hand, the aforementioned experiments are only particular ones in trust relationship inference in this paper. On the other hand, real-world privacy settings vary a lot from service to service, OSN to OSN, and it is worth exploring how a model performs in close to real conditions.

Overall performance results

Figures 7 and 8 show the results of the second experiment set with reduced feature data evaluated by the Accuracy and the F_1 score metrics, respectively. In general, for different feature set combinations, the performance of the proposed model and the comparison methods decreases when the ratio of removed features increases.

Similarly to the results of experiments with full feature data, the proposed model works well with UGC features and outperformed other methods greatly in these experiments. This is the answer to the early question about the model's performance with partially available UGC data.

A second peek at Recall with reduced feature data

This set of experiments were a simulation of the real-world scenario where obtainable online social network datasets are incomplete due to various reasons. In particular, one whole category or certain types of data from a certain number of users are unavailable, when the users choose to limit the usage of their data by online social services through privacy settings. Although such an experimental setup in this paper does not cover all possible scenarios, it may shed some light on the study about how a model might work when some of the privacy-restricted data are unavailable.

As previously discussed, a higher recall with acceptable precision achieved by a method to infer trust in OSNs is one of the ideal objects for online social services. In all 30 experiments from the second set, our proposed model achieved an average recall of 0.9409; 27 in 30 recalls were ≥ 0.90. The results for SVM, Decision Tree and random forest were, respectively: 0.7682 (2 recalls were ≥0.90), 0.7444 (none was ≥0.90), and 0.7844 (two recalls were ≥0.90). Refer to Supplementary Materials for the full results.

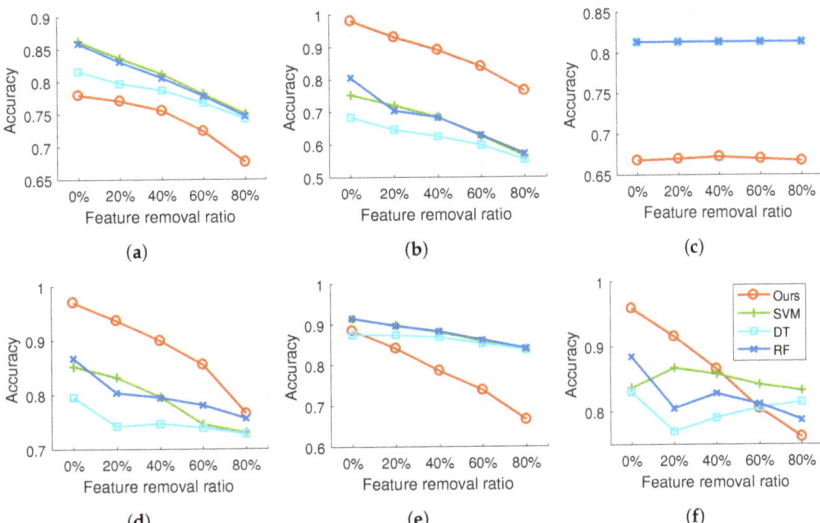

Figure 7. Performance results of the proposed model and comparison methods evaluated by accuracy for the second set of experiments. (**a**) Experiment 2s (Acc). (**b**) Experiment 3s (Acc). (**c**) Experiment 4s (Acc). (**d**) Experiment 5s (Acc). (**e**) Experiment 6s (Acc). (**f**) Experiment 7s (Acc).

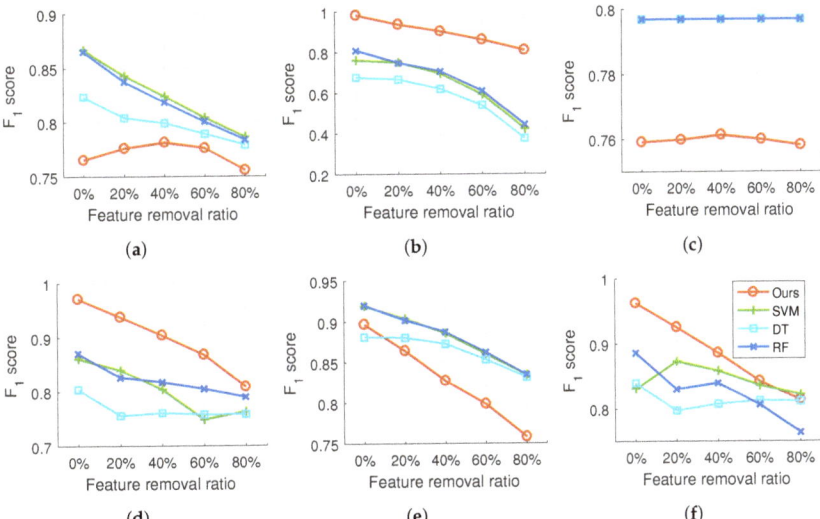

Figure 8. Performance results of the proposed model and comparison methods evaluated by F_1 score for the second set of experiments. (**a**) Experiment 2s (F_1). (**b**) Experiment 3s (F_1). (**c**) Experiment 4s (F_1). (**d**) Experiment 5s (F_1). (**e**) Experiment 6s (F_1). (**f**) Experiment 7s (F_1).

5. Conclusions

In this paper, we explored the problem of collecting trust information and exploiting trust's various properties to infer trust in online social networks. Both explicitly presented trust relationships and information inexplicitly embedded in user-generated contents that bear users' attitude, experience, expertise, credibility, trustworthiness, etc., are harvested as trust information. A probabilistic graphical model based on a conditional random field for trust inference was proposed, which can effectively take advantage of trust's asymmetric, propagative, non-transitive, and subjective properties. With loopy belief propagation, a message passing algorithm, the model inference was presented and well interpreted. Experiments were conducted to evaluate the proposed model on a real-world online social trust dataset, and the experimental results demonstrated the effectiveness of the proposed model for trust inference.

Further improvements to the proposed model can be achieved. Implementing the model inference on cliques rather than pairwise structures may help the model to capture interplay among trust relationships that have same trustors or same trustees more accurately, making it possible to integrate more types of features that convey users' beliefs through complex interactions between users. Our handling of class imbalance for classifications, the underlying fact of which is the sparsity in user relationships in online social networks, is quite simple, and it may be further addressed by introducing penalties.

The study presented in this paper is primitive, but the proposed model is promising. Distrust is also a trust relationship type that can be supported by adding an extra label to the trustRelation node in the proposed model. Then, with a proper dataset, a model that can infer relationships of both trust and distrust can be trained. The proposed model also supports quantitative and context-specific trust evaluation, which could be an interesting future study with a proper dataset. By using each user's probability of trusting another user, an individual-oriented personalized trust management system can be built, and many social recommendation tasks will benefit from it.

With respect to trust's subjectivity and asymmetric properties, the concept of distinguishing the trustor's attitude, experience and belief from the trustee's expertise, trustworthiness, and credibility when forming a trust relationship—which was shown to be helpful for supervised trust inference in this paper—may help to improve unsupervised methods for trust inference. Finally, it will also be crucial to study the model's sensitivity against attacks.

Supplementary Materials: The following supporting information can be downloaded at: https://www.mdpi.com/article/10.3390/app12105186/s1. Detailed feature statistics used in this paper and full experimental results, including performances evaluated by accuracy, precision, recall and F_1 score for each experiment conducted in this paper, are enclosed in Supplementary Materials.

Author Contributions: Conceptualization, Y.L. and B.W.; data curation, Y.L.; methodology, Y.L.; software, Y.L.; validation, Y.L.; writing, Y.L.; funding acquisition, B.W. All authors have read and agreed to the published version of the manuscript.

Funding: This research was partly funded by the National Key Research and Development Program of China under grant 2018YFC0831500, the National Natural Science Foundation of China under grant 61972047, and the NSFC-General Technology Basic Research Joint Funds under grant U1936220.

Institutional Review Board Statement: Not applicable.

Informed Consent Statement: Not applicable.

Data Availability Statement: The full data of the results used to support the findings of this study are enclosed in the Supplementary Materials. The source code for our model implementation and raw data for the experiments conducted in this paper are available from the corresponding author upon request.

Acknowledgments: Yu Liu would like to thank Sergey Kosov for the inspiration for CRF network implementations and inference algorithms. The authors also would like to thank Yunlei Zhang and Jinna Lv for their kind and supportive suggestions for model implementation with accelerated computing using GPUs, and Bin Wu for providing a free test environment for GPU computing.

Conflicts of Interest: The authors declare no conflict of interest.

Abbreviations

The following abbreviations are used in this paper:

OSN	Online Social Network
UGC	User-Generated Contents
CRF	Conditional Random Field
r.v.	random variable
TP	Trust Propagation
POS	Parts-of-Speech
BP	Belief Propagation
LBP	Loopy Belief Propagation
GPU	Graphics Processing Unit
SVM	Support Vector Machine
RBF	Radial Basis Function
DT	Decision Tree
RF	Random Forest

References

1. Golbeck, J. Trust on the World Wide Web: A Survey. *Found. Trends® Web Sci.* **2008**, *1*, 131–197. [CrossRef]
2. Meng, X.; Zhang, G. TrueTrust: A feedback-based trust management model without filtering feedbacks in P2P networks. *Peer-Netw. Appl.* **2020**, *13*, 175–189. [CrossRef]
3. Qolomany, B.; Mohammed, I.; Al-Fuqaha, A.; Guizani, M.; Qadir, J. Trust-Based Cloud Machine Learning Model Selection for Industrial IoT and Smart City Services. *IEEE Internet Things J.* **2021**, *8*, 2943–2958. [CrossRef]
4. Zhao, J.; Wang, W.; Zhang, Z.; Sun, Q.; Huo, H.; Qu, L.; Zheng, S. TrustTF: A tensor factorization model using user trust and implicit feedback for context-aware recommender systems. *Knowl.-Based Syst.* **2020**, *209*, 106434. [CrossRef]
5. Sparrowe, R.T.; Liden, R.C. Two Routes to Influence: Integrating Leader-Member Exchange and Social Network Perspectives. *Adm. Sci. Q.* **2005**, *50*, 505–535. [CrossRef]
6. Sherchan, W.; Nepal, S.; Paris, C. A Survey of Trust in Social Networks. *ACM Comput. Surv.* **2013**, *45*, 33. [CrossRef]
7. Searle, J.R.; Willis, S. *The Construction of Social Reality*; Simon and Schuster: New York, NY, USA, 1995.
8. Jøsang, A.; Ismail, R.; Boyd, C. A survey of trust and reputation systems for online service provision. *Decis. Support Syst.* **2007**, *43*, 618–644. Emerging Issues in Collaborative Commerce. [CrossRef]
9. Gupta, P.; Goel, A.; Lin, J.; Sharma, A.; Wang, D.; Zadeh, R. WTF: The Who to Follow Service at Twitter. In Proceedings of the 22nd International Conference on World Wide Web (WWW '13), Rio de Janeiro, Brazil, 13–17 May 2013; Association for Computing Machinery: New York, NY, USA, 2013; pp. 505–514. [CrossRef]
10. Sharma, S.; Menard, P.; Mutchler, L.A. Who to trust? Applying trust to social commerce. *J. Comput. Inf. Syst.* **2019**, *59*, 32–42. [CrossRef]
11. Golzardi, E.; Sheikhahmadi, A.; Abdollahpouri, A. Detection of trust links on social networks using dynamic features. *Phys. A Stat. Mech. Its Appl.* **2019**, *527*, 121269. [CrossRef]
12. Bathla, G.; Aggarwal, H.; Rani, R. A graph-based model to improve social trust and influence for social recommendation. *J. Supercomput.* **2020**, *76*, 4057–4075. [CrossRef]
13. Wu, L.; Sun, P.; Fu, Y.; Hong, R.; Wang, X.; Wang, M. A Neural Influence Diffusion Model for Social Recommendation. In Proceedings of the 42nd International ACM SIGIR Conference on Research and Development in Information Retrieval (SIGIR'19), Paris, France, 21–25 July 2019; Association for Computing Machinery: New York, NY, USA, 2019; pp. 235–244. [CrossRef]
14. Zuo, L.; Xiong, S.; Qi, X.; Wen, Z.; Tang, Y. Communication-Based Book Recommendation in Computational Social Systems. *Complexity* **2021**, *2021*, 6651493. [CrossRef]
15. Elbeltagi, I.; Agag, G. E-retailing ethics and its impact on customer satisfaction and repurchase intention: A cultural and commitment-trust theory perspective. *Internet Res. Electron. Netw. Appl. Policy* **2016**, *26*, 288–310. [CrossRef]
16. Vosoughi, S.; Roy, D.; Aral, S. The spread of true and false news online. *Science* **2018**, *359*, 1146–1151. [CrossRef] [PubMed]
17. Zhang, B.; Zhang, L.; Mu, C.; Zhao, Q.; Song, Q.; Hong, X. A most influential node group discovery method for influence maximization in social networks: A trust-based perspective. *Data Knowl. Eng.* **2019**, *121*, 71–87. [CrossRef]
18. Chui, M.; Manyika, J.; Bughin, J. The Social Economy: Unlocking Value and Productivity through Social Technologies. McKinsey Global Institute. 1 July 2012. Available online: https://www.mckinsey.com/industries/technology-media-and-telecommunications/our-insights/the-social-economy (accessed on 14 May 2022).
19. Wu, J.; Xiong, R.; Chiclana, F. Uninorm trust propagation and aggregation methods for group decision making in social network with four tuple information. *Knowl.-Based Syst.* **2016**, *96*, 29–39. [CrossRef]
20. jiao Du, Z.; yang Luo, H.; dong Lin, X.; min Yu, S. A trust-similarity analysis-based clustering method for large-scale group decision-making under a social network. *Inf. Fusion* **2020**, *63*, 13–29. [CrossRef]

21. Ghafari, S.M.; Beheshti, A.; Joshi, A.; Paris, C.; Mahmood, A.; Yakhchi, S.; Orgun, M.A. A Survey on Trust Prediction in Online Social Networks. *IEEE Access* **2020**, *8*, 144292–144309. [CrossRef]
22. General Data Protection Regulation (EU) 2016/679 (GDPR). Available online: https://en.wikipedia.org/wiki/General_Data_Protection_Regulation (accessed on 10 April 2022).
23. California Consumer Privacy Act (CCPA). Available online: https://en.wikipedia.org/wiki/California_Consumer_Privacy_Act (accessed on 10 April 2022).
24. Personal Information Protection Law of the People's Republic of China. Available online: https://en.wikipedia.org/wiki/Personal_Information_Protection_Law_of_the_People's_Republic_of_China (accessed on 10 April 2022).
25. Schall, D. Link prediction in directed social networks. *Soc. Netw. Anal. Min.* **2014**, *4*, 157. [CrossRef]
26. Barbieri, N.; Bonchi, F.; Manco, G. Who to Follow and Why: Link Prediction with Explanations. In Proceedings of the 20th ACM SIGKDD International Conference on Knowledge Discovery and Data Mining (KDD '14), New York, NY, USA, 24–27 August 2014; ACM: New York, NY, USA, 2014; pp. 1266–1275. [CrossRef]
27. Mao, C.; Xu, C.; He, Q. A cost-effective algorithm for inferring the trust between two individuals in social networks. *Knowl.-Based Syst.* **2019**, *164*, 122–138. [CrossRef]
28. Oh, H.K.; Kim, J.W.; Kim, S.W.; Lee, K. A unified framework of trust prediction based on message passing. *Clust. Comput.* **2018**, *22*, 2049–2061. [CrossRef]
29. Massa, P.; Avesani, P. Controversial users demand local trust metrics: An experimental study on epinions.com community. *AAAI* **2005**, *1*, 121–126.
30. Golbeck, J.; Hendler, J.A. FilmTrust: Movie recommendations using trust in web-based social networks. *CCNC. Citeseer* **2006**, *2006*, 282–286.
31. Liu, G.; Yang, Q.; Wang, H.; Lin, X.; Wittie, M.P. Assessment of multi-hop interpersonal trust in social networks by Three-Valued Subjective Logic. In Proceedings of the IEEE INFOCOM 2014—IEEE Conference on Computer Communications, Toronto, ON, Canada, 27 April–2 May 2014; pp. 1698–1706. [CrossRef]
32. Liu, G.; Chen, Q.; Yang, Q.; Zhu, B.; Wang, H.; Wang, W. OpinionWalk: An efficient solution to massive trust assessment in online social networks. In Proceedings of the IEEE INFOCOM 2017—IEEE Conference on Computer Communications, Atlanta, GA, USA, 1–4 May 2017; pp. 1–9. [CrossRef]
33. Tang, J.; Gao, H.; Hu, X.; Liu, H. Exploiting Homophily Effect for Trust Prediction. In Proceedings of the Sixth ACM International Conference on Web Search and Data Mining (WSDM '13), Rome, Italy, 4–8 February 2013; Association for Computing Machinery: New York, NY, USA, 2013; pp. 53–62. [CrossRef]
34. Yao, Y.; Tong, H.; Yan, X.; Xu, F.; Lu, J. MATRI: A Multi-Aspect and Transitive Trust Inference Model. In Proceedings of the 22nd International Conference on World Wide Web (WWW '13), Rio de Janeiro, Brazil, 13–17 May 2013; Association for Computing Machinery: New York, NY, USA, 2013; pp. 1467–1476. [CrossRef]
35. Zheng, X.; Wang, Y.; Orgun, M.; Zhong, Y.; Liu, G. Trust Prediction with Propagation and Similarity Regularization. In Proceedings of the AAAI Conference on Artificial Intelligence 2014, Québec City, QC, Canada, 27–31 July 2014; Volume 28.
36. Liu, G.; Li, C.; Yang, Q. NeuralWalk: Trust Assessment in Online Social Networks with Neural Networks. In Proceedings of the IEEE INFOCOM 2019—IEEE Conference on Computer Communications, Paris, France, 29 April–2 May 2019; pp. 1999–2007. [CrossRef]
37. Cho, J.H.; Chan, K.; Adali, S. A Survey on Trust Modeling. *ACM Comput. Surv.* **2015**, *48*, 1–40. [CrossRef]
38. Wang, J.; Jing, X.; Yan, Z.; Fu, Y.; Pedrycz, W.; Yang, L.T. A Survey on Trust Evaluation Based on Machine Learning. *ACM Comput. Surv.* **2020**, *53*, 1–36. [CrossRef]
39. Mukherjee, S.; Weikum, G.; Danescu-Niculescu-Mizil, C. People on Drugs: Credibility of User Statements in Health Communities. In Proceedings of the 20th ACM SIGKDD International Conference on Knowledge Discovery and Data Mining (KDD '14), New York, NY, USA, 24–27 August 2014; ACM: New York, NY, USA, 2014; pp. 65–74. [CrossRef]
40. Mukherjee, S.; Weikum, G. Leveraging Joint Interactions for Credibility Analysis in News Communities. In Proceedings of the 24th ACM International on Conference on Information and Knowledge Management (CIKM '15), Melbourne, Australia, 18–23 October 2015; ACM: New York, NY, USA, 2015; pp. 353–362. [CrossRef]
41. Mao, Y.; Shen, H. Web of Credit: Adaptive Personalized Trust Network Inference From Online Rating Data. *IEEE Trans. Comput. Soc. Syst.* **2016**, *3*, 176–189. [CrossRef]
42. Liu, H.; Lim, E.P.; Lauw, H.W.; Le, M.T.; Sun, A.; Srivastava, J.; Kim, Y.A. Predicting Trusts among Users of Online Communities: An Epinions Case Study; Association for Computing Machinery: New York, NY, USA, 2008; EC '08, pp. 310–319. [CrossRef]
43. Liu, Y.; Wang, B.; Wu, B.; Shang, S.; Zhang, Y.; Shi, C. Characterizing super-spreading in microblog: An epidemic-based information propagation model. *Phys. A: Stat. Mech. Its Appl.* **2016**, *463*, 202–218. [CrossRef]
44. Recasens, M.; Danescu-Niculescu-Mizil, C.; Jurafsky, D. Linguistic models for analyzing and detecting biased language. In Proceedings of the 51st Annual Meeting of the Association for Computational Linguistics, Sofia, Bulgaria, 4–9 August 2013; Volume 1: Long Papers, pp. 1650–1659.
45. De Albornoz, J.C.; Plaza, L.; Gervás, P. SentiSense: An easily scalable concept-based affective lexicon for sentiment analysis. In Proceedings of the Eight International Conference on Language Resources and Evaluation (LREC'12), Istanbul, Turkey, 23–25 May 2012; European Language Resources Association (ELRA): Istanbul, Turkey, 2012.

46. Friedli, S.; Velenik, Y. *Statistical Mechanics of Lattice Systems: A Concrete Mathematical Introduction*; Cambridge University Press: Cambridge, UK, 2017. [CrossRef]
47. Yedidia, J.S.; Freeman, W.T.; Weiss, Y., Understanding belief propagation and its generalizations. In *Exploring Artificial Intelligence in the New Millennium*; Gerhard, L., Bernhard, N., Eds.; Morgan Kaufmann Publishers Inc.: Burlington, MA, USA, 2003; pp. 239–269.
48. Liu, Y.; Li, J.; Zhang, Y.; Lv, J.; Wang, B. A High Performance Implementation of A Unified CRF Model for Trust Prediction. In Proceedings of the 2018 IEEE 20th International Conference on High Performance Computing and Communications; IEEE 16th International Conference on Smart City; IEEE 4th International Conference on Data Science and Systems (HPCC/SmartCity/DSS), Exeter, UK, 28–30 June 2018; pp. 848–853. [CrossRef]
49. Bottou, L. Stochastic Gradient Descent Examples on Toy Problems. 2010. Available online: https://leon.bottou.org/projects/sgd (accessed on 16 September 2017).

Article

Parallel Frequent Subtrees Mining Method by an Effective Edge Division Strategy

Jing Wang [1,*] and Xiongfei Li [2]

[1] School of Media Science, Northeast Normal University, Changchun 130024, China
[2] Key Laboratory of Symbolic Computation and Knowledge Engineering of Ministry of Education, Jilin University, Changchun 130012, China; xiongfei@jlu.edu.cn
* Correspondence: wangj755@nenu.edu.cn

Abstract: Most data with a complicated structure can be represented by a tree structure. Parallel processing is essential to mining frequent subtrees from massive data in a timely manner. However, only a few algorithms could be transplanted to a parallel framework. A new parallel algorithm is proposed to mine frequent subtrees by grouping strategy (GS) and edge division strategy (EDS). The main idea of GS is dividing edges according to different intervals and then dividing subtrees consisting of the edges in different intervals to their corresponding groups. Besides, the compression stage in mining is optimized by avoiding all candidate subtrees of a compression tree, which reduces the mining time on the nodes. Load balancing can improve the performance of parallel computing. An effective EDS is proposed to achieve load balancing. EDS divides the edges with different frequencies into different intervals reasonably, which directly affects the task amount in each computing node. Experiments demonstrate that the proposed algorithm can implement parallel mining, and it outperforms other compared methods on load balancing and speedup.

Keywords: frequent subtree; parallel algorithms; data partitioning; load balancing

---

Citation: Wang, J.; Li, X. Parallel Frequent Subtrees Mining Method by an Effective Edge Division Strategy. *Appl. Sci.* **2022**, *12*, 4778. https:// doi.org/10.3390/app12094778

Academic Editor: Federico Divina

Received: 13 April 2022
Accepted: 6 May 2022
Published: 9 May 2022

Publisher's Note: MDPI stays neutral with regard to jurisdictional claims in published maps and institutional affiliations.

Copyright: © 2022 by the authors. Licensee MDPI, Basel, Switzerland. This article is an open access article distributed under the terms and conditions of the Creative Commons Attribution (CC BY) license (https:// creativecommons.org/licenses/by/ 4.0/).

1. Introduction

The era of big data has arrived with the advent of massive data. Semi-structured data [1,2] plays a crucial role in massive data with the non-strict structure feature. Most data with a complicated structure, including semi-structured data, can be represented by a tree structure. Data mining methods are used to find hidden relationships among massive data [3,4]. Frequent subtree mining has become an important field of data mining research [5–7]. It is the process of mining a subtree set from a given data set that satisfies user attention (support or frequent degree). Frequent subtree mining can be applied in many fields. For example, RNA molecule structure can be represented by a tree structure where, in order to obtain information about a new RNA molecule, the new one must be compared to the known RNA structures. The function information of new RNA can be obtained by looking for the same topology [8].

CFMIS (compressed frequent maximal induced subtrees) [9] is an efficient method for the frequent subtree mining we proposed earlier. The CFMIS algorithm can find all frequent induced subtrees without throwing solutions in less time. Parallel frequent subtree mining processing is essential for mining massive volumes of data in a timely manner. MapReduce is an ideal software framework to support distributed computing on large data sets on clusters of computers [10,11]. However, not all algorithms could be transplanted to the MapReduce framework, in fact, only a few algorithms could. Assigning data into appropriate blocks is crucial for paralleling algorithms in MapReduce [12]. In this paper, three parallel CFMIS (PCFMIS) algorithms, PCFMIS1, PCFMIS2 and PCFMIS3, are proposed. PCFMIS1 parallels CFMIS, transplanting CFMIS to MapReduce framework by GS. Furthermore, PCFMIS2 is proposed by optimizing the compression to reduce the running time on each slave node. Based on PCFMIS1 and PCFMIS2, PCFMIS3 is proposed to achieve load balancing by using an effective EDS.

In summary, the contributions of our work are as follows:

1. A grouping strategy is proposed to achieve effective data partitioning in order to parallel the frequent subtrees mining method.
2. The compression is optimized by avoiding all candidate subtrees to reduce the mining time on nodes.
3. An effective edge division strategy is proposed to achieve load balancing.
4. The proposed algorithm PCFMIS3 is outstanding on load balancing and running time.

The rest of the paper is organized as follows: in Section 2, related work is reviewed; the proposed PCFMIS1, PCFMIS2 and PCFMIS3 are presented in Section 3; in Section 4, experimental results are displayed and discussed; conclusions are made in Section 5.

2. Related Work

With the extensive application of semi-structured data, the research priority of frequent pattern mining has expanded from frequent item set mining [13,14] to frequent subtree mining [15]. L. Wang et al. proposed a novel framework for mining temporal association rules, which mainly represent the temporal relation among numerical attributes [16]. A new structure called a frequent itemsets tree is proposed to avoid generating candidate item sets in mining rules. Building the tree and mining the temporal relation between the frequent itemset proceed simultaneously. V. Huynh et al. proposed an improved version for IPPC tree, called IPPC+, to increase the performance of the tree construction [17]. IPPC+ improves the poor performance of IPPC tree in the case of datasets comprising a large number of distinguishing items but just a small percentage of frequent items. W. Pascal et al. proposed an algorithm mining probabilistic frequent subtrees with polynomial delay, but by replacing each graph with a forest formed by an exponentially large implicit subset of its spanning trees [18]. The algorithm overcomes the drawback that the number of sampled spanning trees must be bounded by a polynomial of the size of the transaction graphs, resulting in less impressive recall even for slightly more complex structures beyond molecular graphs. J. Wang et al. proposed a compression tree sequence (CTS) to construct a compression tree model and saved the information of the original tree in the compression tree. CFMIS [9] was proposed based on CTS to mine frequent maximal induced subtrees. For each iteration, compression could reduce the size of the data set, thus, the traversal speed was faster than that of other algorithms.

Out of memory and computing resources lead massive data mining to difficulties. Parallel data mining can be an effective solution to this problem [19–21]. In recent years, researchers have made some achievements in frequent item mining. S. Shaik et al. presented a scalable parallel algorithm for big data frequent pattern mining [22]. Three key challenges are identified to parallel algorithmic design: load balancing, work partitioning and memory scalability. D. Yan et al. proposed a general-purpose framework PrefixFPM for FPM that is able to fully utilize the CPU cores in a multicore machine [23]. PrefixFPM follows the idea of prefix projection to partition the workloads of PFM into independent tasks by divide and conquer. The state-of-the-art serial algorithms are adapted for mining frequent patterns including subsequences, subtrees, and subgraphs on top of PrefixFPM. D. Yan et al. extend PrefixFPM to provide the complete parallel algorithms by adopting four new algorithms so that a richer set of pattern types are covered, including closed patterns, ordered and unordered tree patterns, and a mixture of path, free tree, and graph patterns [24]. PrefixFPM exposes a unified programming interface to users who can readily customize it to mine their desired patterns. Xun. Y. et al. proposed FiDoop to achieve compressed storage and avoid building conditional pattern bases [25]. Hong T. P. et al. proposed a parallel genetic-fuzzy mining algorithm [26] based on the master–slave architecture to extract both association rules and membership functions from quantitative transactions. C. FB et al. proposed a frequent itemset mining method using sliding windows capable of extracting tendencies from continuous data flows [27]. They develop this method using Big Data technologies, in particular, using the Spark Streaming framework enabling distribution of the computation along several clusters and thus improving the algorithm speed. Sicard. N. et al. proposed a parallel fuzzy tree mining method (PaFuTM) [28]. In some of their approaches, the level-wise architecture is preserved but tasks are parallelized within each level. All candidates from each frequent subtree are assigned to specific tasks where they are generated and tested against the database.

3. PCFMIS Algorithm

In this section, we provide the definitions for some concepts that will be used in the remainder of the paper. The proposed parallel algorithm will also be explained in detail.

3.1. Prepared Knowledge

3.1.1. Definitions for Concepts

The CFMIS algorithm deals with the tree in which sibling nodes are unordered with labels and the sibling nodes of the same parent node have no repeats. The 'tree' mentioned below is the same tree as the CFMIS processes, assuming that there is no repeat label in a same tree. CFMIS focuses on frequent maximal induced subtree mining.

Definition 1. *Induced subtree. A tree $T' = (V', E', r')$ is an induced tree of $T = (V, E, r)$, denoted as $T' \subset T$ if $V' \subset V$, $E' \subset E$, where V is the set of nodes; E is the set of edges in which $(x,y) \in E$ represents that x is the parent of y; r is the root node.*

Definition 2. *Frequent subtree. $D = \{T_1, T_2, \ldots, T_n\}$ is a tree set, ε is the frequency threshold, $Occ(T_i, T')$ represents whether T' occurs in T_i, if $T' \subset T_i$, then $Occ(T_i, T') = 1$, else $Occ(T_i, T') = 0$. $Frq(T') = \sum_{i=1}^{n} Occ(T_i, T')$. T' is frequent subtree if $Frq(T') \geq \varepsilon$.*

Definition 3. *Maximal subtree. F is the frequent subtree set of D. T' and T'' are two frequent subtrees in F, T' maximize T'' (denoted as $T'' \xrightarrow{m} T'$) if and only if $T'' \subset T'$, there is no T''' in F to make $T'' \xrightarrow{m} T'''$ happen. T' is called maximal subtree.*

Definition 4. *Compression tree sequence(CTS). CTS is an ordered sequence composed by $node^{pd}$, $CTS = (node_0^{pd_0}, node_1^{pd_1}, \ldots, node_n^{pd_n})$, pd is the index pointing to the parent node for each node except the root node. Let the parent of $node_i^{pd_i}$ be $node_j^{pd_j}$, and then $pd_i = |i - j|$, where $node_0^{pd_0}$ is the root node.*

For example, the CTS of the example tree in Figure 1 can be $a^0 b^1 c^2 d^1 e^2 f^3$. a^0 is the root element. a is the parent element of b, due to the difference between the positions of a and b in the CTS is 1 while the index superscript of b is 1. c is the parent element of f, due to the difference between the positions of c and f in the CTS being 3 while the index superscript of f is 3. The same rule applies to other nodes, so the information about tree structure and all the edges in the tree can be obtained from CTS.

Definition 5. *Tree list length. The number of $node^{pd}$ in CTS is the length of CTS.*

3.1.2. CFMIS Algorithm

A simple review of the CFMIS algorithm is described below (more details in [9]), and it is primarily performed via four stages:

Stage 1. Construct the compression tree model: the original data set is constructed as a compression tree model using CTS;

Stage 2. Cutting edge: this stage is divided into two subprocesses, trim edges and clean-up edges. First, trim the edges for which the edge frequent degree is less than threshold. Then, delete the single node.

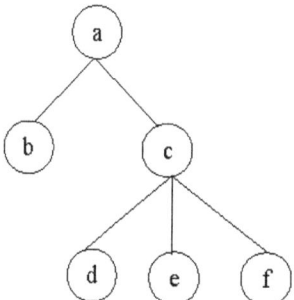

Figure 1. An example tree.

Stage 3. Find frequent subtrees: Compress them according to the descending edge frequent degree to obtain CTSs, and sort CTSs according to the tree list length from shortest to longest. Match the CTS_i with the CTSs following it; if matched (the CTS_i is obtained in another CTS_j), then the frequent degree of the T' represented by CTS_i is incremented by 1.

Stage 4. Maximal Stage: Run the frequent subtree sets maximal processing. The frequent maximal induced subtree set of the original data set are obtained.

3.2. Grouping Strategy

Data partitioning is the premise of the parallel algorithm. An effective data partitioning method can greatly reduce the data communication between different slave nodes, thereby reducing the parallel computing time. Based on the above findings, the grouping strategy (GS) of PCFMIS used to divide all the trees in original data set D into different groups is described below:

(1) If given m slave nodes, we should divide all the trees in D into m groups, and the number of the group is denoted as $Gnum$. For the edge (x,y) in D, divide (x,y) into the set $A = \{A_k\}, k \in [1, m]$.

(2) For $T_i \in D$, all the edges in T_i may belong to several A_k according to (1). Take the minimum of these k as the $Gnum$ of T_i, $Gnum = \min k$, so T_i is put into the group which $Gnum = \min k$. Then, for T_i, cut the edges which belong to $A_{\min k}$. Some new trees T_i' will appear after cutting edges.

(3) For these new trees T_i', repeat (2) until no new trees are produced.

(4) For $T_j \in D$, repeat (2) and (3).

(5) All the trees in original data set D are divided into different groups, and the different groups will be put in different slave nodes.

Definition 6. *Related Tree. Given a tree $T = (V, E, r)$, for $\forall (x, y) \in E$, there is $(x, y) \in A_k$. min k is the minimum of k. When $(x, y) \in A_{\min k}$, T is a related tree of (x, y), denoted as $(x, y) \to T$. The set of $t(x, y) \to T$ is denoted as $\Gamma(x, y)$.*

Property 1. *According to grouping strategy, a tree in original data set only belongs to one group.*

Property 2. *According to grouping strategy, if $(x, y) \in A_k$, all $\Gamma(x, y)$ will be put into the group which $Gnum = k$.*

According to Property 1, the trees in the original data set are grouped into different groups, which can reduce the scale of the data each slave node needs to process. Although in (2), new trees may be generated during the grouping process, the new trees are trimmed and less complex than the original tree.

We can conclude from Property 2, for $(x, y) \in A_k$, all the induced subtrees of $\Gamma(x, y)$ containing (x, y) can be found in the group in which $Gnum = k$. So frequent induced subtrees of $\Gamma(x,y)$ containing (x,y) can be found only in group k instead of the whole original data set. This avoids communication between groups and realizes real parallelism.

Definition 7. *Frequent Edge Degree.* $D = \{T_1, T_2, ..., T_n\}$, *the frequent edge degree of (x,y) is the number of times (x,y) appears in D, denoted as $EFrq(x,y)$.*

How to divide the edge (x,y) into set $\{A_k\}$ in (1) directly affects the $Gnum$ of $\Gamma(x,y)$. One feasible method is described below:

Given an evenly divided interval $A_{div} = (a_1, ..., a_i, ..., a_m)$, $a_1 > ... > a_i > ... > a_m$, $a_1 = EFrq_{min}(x,y)$, $a_m = EFrq_{max}(x,y)$. If $a_{i+1} > EFrq(x,y) \geq a_i$, the edge (x,y) is divided into A_i, then $\Gamma(x,y)$ will be put into the group in which $Gnum = k$. For example, in Figure 2, suppose that the number of slave nodes is 3. Divide the trees T_0, T_{00} into 3 groups (G_1, G_2, G_3). Given dividing interval $A_{div} = (a_1, a_2, a_3)$, $a_1 > a_2 > a_3$. $EFrq(a,b)$, $EFrq(c,d)$, $EFrq(d,f) \geq a_1$, $a_1 > EFeq(h,d)$, $EFrq(d,e) \geq a_2$, $a2 > EFrq(a,c) \geq a3$, so $(a,b)(c,d)(d,f)$ are divided into A_1; $(h,d)(d,e)$ are divided into A_2; (a,c) is divided into A_3. Take T_0 in Figure 2 as an example. For A_3, $\Gamma(a,c)$ (in Figure 2) is divided into $G3$. Then delete (a,c) from A_3 and cut (a,c). For A_2, $\Gamma(a,c)$ (Ti in Figure 2) are divided into $G2$. Then delete (d,e) from A_2 and cut (d,e). For A_1, $\Gamma(ab)$ (T_3 in Figure 2), $\Gamma(cd)$ ($T4$ in Figure 2) and $\Gamma(df)$ (T_4 in Figure 2) are divided into G_1. T_{01}, T_{02} are obtained after applying GS on T_{00}.

By using the above grouping strategy on the original data set and applying CFMIS algorithm in each group, the CFMIS algorithm is implemented in parallel. The new parallel algorithm is called PCFMIS1. However, the experiment results shown in Section 4.2 indicate that the parallel computing time and speedup did not achieve the desired results. Further improvements on PCFMIS1 will be discussed below.

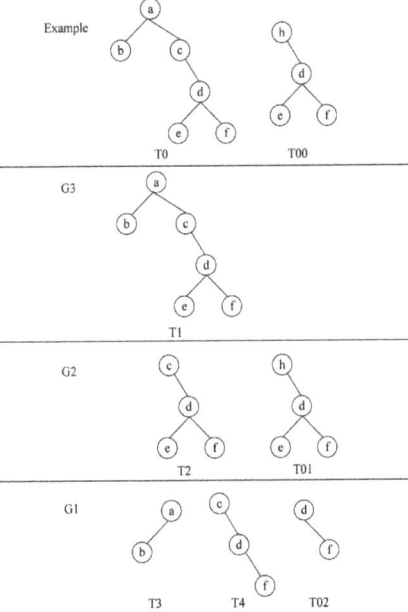

Figure 2. An example of weight tree dividing.

3.3. Improvements on Parallel Algorithm

3.3.1. Optimized Compression in CFMIS

Stage 3 is the central step of the CFMIS algorithm, and it also takes most of the time in CFMIS. The subsequence processing of Stage 3 must find all subtrees of a compression tree to determine whether each of them is frequent. In fact, it consumes up to 70% of the execution time in this stage. Optimizing Stage 3 can greatly reduce time consumption of the algorithm, particularly when the data size is large. In this section, CFMIS is refined by optimizing Stage 3.

According to Property 2, for any edges $(x,y) \in A_k$, all the induced subtrees of $\gamma(x,y)$ containing (x,y) can be found in the group k, so frequent induced subtrees of $\gamma(x,y)$ can also be found. For other edges $(p,q) \notin A_k$, $(p,q) \in A_f$, all the induced subtrees of $\gamma(p,q)$ containing (p,q) can be found in the group f. For the reasons above, we only need to find all the frequent induced subtrees of $\gamma(x,y)$ which contain (x,y) instead of all the frequent induced subtrees in group k. Other frequent induced subtrees could be found in other groups. If a CTS in group k does not contain (x,y), this CTS does not have to match with the CTSs following it. That is, this improvement in Stage 3 avoids finding all subtrees of a compression tree to determine whether each of them is frequent. The improvement in compression in groups makes the running time shorter. The improved parallel algorithm is called PCFMIS2. Although the time has been reduced, the load on slave nodes is not balanced.

3.3.2. Load Balancing

An effective edge division strategy (EDS) is proposed in this section. If $(x,y) \in A_k$, $\Gamma(x,y)$ will be put into the group k. The division of edges in the original data set affects the load of the slave nodes. Take the frequent edge degree as the basis for the edge division strategy. Abstract edge division strategy as a math problem, it can be described as below: Suppose that there are w different edges in the original data set, and their frequent edge degree is denoted as $EFrq(i)$, $1 \leq i \leq w$. Record $EFrq(i)$ in the array $x[i]$. Divide different edges from the original data set into the set $\{A_k\}$, ensuring that the sum of the frequent edge degree in each A_k is approximately equal. The improved parallel algorithm is called PCFMIS3.

The steps of EDS are described below:

1. Get the mean of array X, $u = \frac{\sum X[i]}{k}$.
2. Traverse the array X, if $X[i] > u$, then it is assigned separately to a group. Suppose there are s groups like that.
3. Now, the problem is translated into such a problem: divide $(w-s)$ different edges into $(k-s)$ sets, ensuring that the sum of the frequent edge degree in each group is approximately equal.
4. For the rest $X[j]$, $1 \leq j \leq w-s$, get the mean of array X, $u' = \frac{\sum X[j]}{k-s}$.
5. Translate the step (3) and (4) problem to 0–1 Knapsack Problem in order to solve it.

An example of the EDS method is given here to show how it works: suppose that the frequent edge degree of the original data set is 50, 60, 80, 100, 150, 200, 400, 1000, and $k = 3$. The mean value $u = \frac{50+60+80+100+150+200+400+1000}{3} = 680$. As $1000 > 680$, 1000 is assigned separately to A_1. Now, the problem is translated into such a problem: Divide the rest of the edges into two sets, ensuring that the sum of the frequent edge degree in each set is approximately equal. Get the mean value $u = \frac{50+60+80+100+150+200+400}{2} = 520$. Translate the problem to 0–1 Knapsack Problem in order to solve it. The weights of these items are 50, 60, 80, 100, 150, 200, 400 and the backpack capacity is 520. The answer is that 50, 60, 400 make the total value biggest in the backpack. 50, 60, 400 are assigned to A_2, and the rest are assigned to A_3.

PCFMIS3 solved the problem of load balancing and introduced the optimized compression. The flowchart of PCFMIS3 is shown in Figure 3. Three steps including two Map-reduce operations are completed during parallel computation.

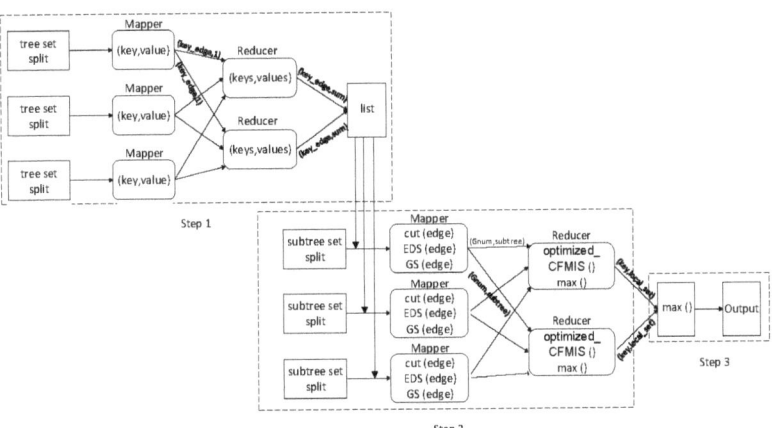

Figure 3. Parallel algorithm PCFMIS3 flowchart.

Step1: Calculate edge frequent degree of each edge in original tree set. In Map 1 (Algorithm 1), record each occurrence of each edge in a tree set split, which is the input of Reduce 1 (Algorithm 2). In Reduce 1, the edge frequent degree of each edge is counted out.

Step 2: Cut edge and find frequent subtree. In Map 2 (Algorithm 3), trim the edges for which the edge frequent degree is less than according to the list; divide the edges into different sets according to EDS; divide the subtrees into different groups according to GS. Then which group the subtree is divided to is the input of Reduce (Algorithm 4). In Reduce 2, find frequent subtrees in each group. The maximal frequent subtrees of each group could be obtained.

Step 3: Find the maximal subtrees of original tree set. In this step, run the frequent subtree sets maximal processing to obtain the final maximal frequent subtrees.

Algorithm 1: Map 1 $(key, value)$

    Input: //*key*: document name
           //*value*: subtree set
    Output: $(key\_edge, 1)$ // the key_edge is the edge in the subtree set.
1 **for** *each edge in subtree set* **do**
2 | Emit $(key\_edge, 1)$
3 **end**

Algorithm 2: Reduce 1 $(keys, values)$

    Input: //*key*: the set of the same edge
           //*values*: the list of the edge value
    Output: (key_edge, sum) // sum is the frequency of the edge
1 $sum = 0$;
2 **for** *each edge value in values* **do**
3 | $sum = sum + value$; Emit (key_edge, sum)
4 **end**

Algorithm 3: Map 2 $(key, value)$

Input: //$split$: subtree set split
//$list$: the list of the edges
Output: key // key is the $Gnum$
$value$ // value is the subtree in different $Gnum$

1 **for** *each edge in list* **do**
2     $subtree\_group = cut(edge)$
3   // cut edges that do not meet the threshold requirements, group is the remaining subtree set
4 **end**
5 **for** *each edge in subtree_group* **do**
6     $A(edge) = EDS(edge)$
7   // EDS is the edge division strategy; A(edge) is the division set
8 **end**
9 **for** *each subtree in subtree_group* **do**
10     $Gnum(subtree) = GS(subtree)$ // GS is the grouping strategy
11     $value = subtree$
12     $key = Gnum$
13     $Emit(key, value)$
14 **end**

Algorithm 4: Reduce 2 $(key, local\_set)$

Input: // $Gnum$: the group number
// $Gnum\_subtrees$: all the subtrees which group number is $Gnum$
Output: key // null
$local\_set$ // the frequent subtree set which belongs to this group

1 $frequent\_list = get\_edges(Gnum)$
2 // $get\_edges(Gnum)$ is used to get the list of the frequent edges of this group
3 **for** *the edges in frequent_list* **do**
4     $v = optimized\_CFMIS(Gnum\_subtrees)$
5   // optimized_CFMIS is used to find the frequent subtrees in this group
6     $local\_set = max(v)$
7   // max(v) is used to maximize the frequent subtrees
8     $Emit\ (key, local\_set)$
9 **end**

4. Experiments and Results

Paralleling the CFMIS algorithm only affects execution time, and it has no effect on the accuracy of the calculation results. The corresponding validity of the algorithm could consult to [9]. The number of groups in the GS is the number of the slave nodes in this paper. In order to prove that EDS is an effective method to solve load balancing, the load balancing tests are compared between PCFMIS1 and PCFMIS3. The experiments on computational time and speedup are done among PCFMIS1, PCFMIS2, PCFMIS3 and PaFuTM [28].

4.1. Experimental Environment

All of the experiments were conducted on a PC cluster connected with 100M Ethernet. Each PC was equipped with a 3.20 GHz Intel Core i5 and 4 GB main memory, running the Centos6.6 operating system. The version of the platform is Hadoop 2.6.2. The system configuration is shown in Figure 4. The synthetic data set used in this paper was generated by tree generator using the method in [29]. Parameters of the synthetic dataset are set as follows: f = 10 (f represents fan-out), d = 10 (d represents the depth of the tree), n = 100 (n represents the number of labels), m = 100 (m represents the number of tree nodes), and t (t represents the number of trees). While t = 50,000, the data set is denoted as D5; t = 100,000, denoted as D10; t = 200,000, denoted as D20; t = 500,000, denoted as D50; t = 1,000,000, denoted as D100; t = 2,000,000, denoted as D200. The real data set was obtained from CSLOGS data set, which is from a month-log of the data of the Rensselaer Polytechnic Institute's web site. CSLOGS10 contains 100,000 trees and CSLOGS100 contains 1,000,000 trees. The support thresholds for D5, D10, D20 and CSLOGS10 are 0.01 and 0.05. For D50, D100, D200 and CSLOGS100, the support thresholds are 0.01 and 0.001.

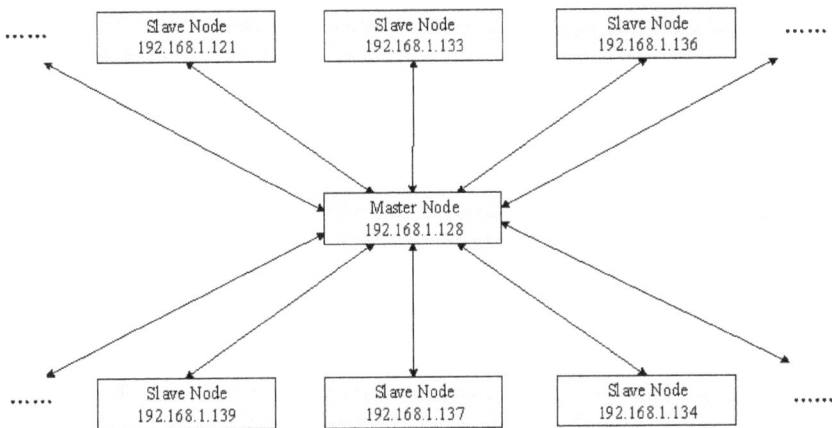

Figure 4. System configuration diagram.

4.2. Experiments and Analysis

During the experiments, it was found that for the data sets with large data volume, time cost increases dramatically when the number of nodes is too small. The reason is that the computation of the tree structure needs to constantly operate the stack. If the JVM stack is not enough, it can only keep replacing the stack. In this paper, experiments have been done on a small number of nodes for small data sets and on a large number of nodes for large data sets.

4.2.1. Comparison of Load Balancing

We performed the load balancing evaluation on both real data set CSLOGS10 and synthetic data set D50. For CSLOGS10, the number of nodes is set to 1–5; for D50, the number is set to 1–8.

Table 1 shows the amount of subtrees and computing time in different groups of CSLOGS10 in Reduce 2 while the total number of nodes are 3, 4, 5 and the support threshold is 0.01. The subtree amounts in each group divided by PCFMIS1 and PCFMIS3 are shown in Table 1. For PCFMIS1, when the number of nodes is 3, the amount of subtrees in the most loaded group ($Gnum = 3$) is 3.66 times that of the least loaded group ($Gnum = 1$); when the number of nodes is 4 and 5, the ratio is 4.54 and 6.96. For PCFMIS3, when the number of nodes is 3, the amount of subtrees in the most loaded group ($Gnum = 1$) is 1.32 times that of the least loaded group ($Gnum = 2$); when the number of nodes is 4 and 5, the ratio is 1.30 and 1.31. For the computing time, when the number of nodes is 3 in PCFMIS1, the longest computing time ($Gnum = 3$) is 3.31 times that of the shortest computing time ($Gnum = 1$). The corresponding amount ratio and time ratio are shown in Table 2. The closer the ratio is to 1, the better the effect of the load balancing. The same load balancing test is done on D50 (the support threshold is 0.01) which is shown in Table 3, and the corresponding amount ratio and time ratio are shown in Table 4. The experiments indicate that the efficient division of edges in the original data set affects the load of the slave nodes. The proposed EDS can achieve load balancing.

Table 1. The amount of subtrees and computing time in different $Gnum$ groups of CSLOGS10.

Number of Nodes	Gnum	PCFMIS1 Amount	PCFMIS1 Time (s)	PCFMIS3 Amount	PCFMIS3 Time (s)
3	1	18,395	22.73	53,466	40.01
	2	41,369	41.65	40,564	38.37
	3	67,365	75.34	50,084	37.72
4	1	15,463	18.39	49,826	28.58
	2	52,369	27.76	49,819	29.49
	3	67,428	55.56	38,462	25.28
	4	70,254	42.84	38,352	25.91
5	1	10,630	13.27	34,657	21.46
	2	32,745	21.36	38,724	23.11
	3	62,156	41.2	45,396	22.31
	4	47,563	32.58	42,683	22.12
	5	73,947	37.25	40,567	21.89

Table 2. The amount ratio and time ratio in different $Gnum$ groups of CSLOGS10.

Number of Nodes	PCFMIS1 Amount	PCFMIS1 Time (s)	PCFMIS3 Amount	PCFMIS3 Time (s)
3	3.66	3.31	1.32	1.06
4	4.54	3.02	1.3	1.17
5	6.96	3.1	1.31	1.08

Table 3. The amount of subtrees and computing time in different $Gnum$ groups of D50.

Number of Nodes	Gnum	PCFMIS1 Amount	PCFMIS1 Time (s)	PCFMIS3 Amount	PCFMIS3 Time (s)
4	1	96,386	82.36	134,526	118.63
	2	113,695	113.67	101,637	113.6
	3	155,692	136.98	116,985	123.64
	4	277,258	187.63	114,329	117.25
6	1	75,264	52.69	96,452	86.66
	2	65,897	53.76	93,658	84.32
	3	193,648	122.25	107,612	83.59
	4	85,638	85.96	84,369	83.12
	5	84,567	93.21	83,695	83.72
	6	156,942	110.67	92,418	84.87
8	1	87,526	67.77	54,960	63.89
	2	40,236	45.63	76,147	62.14
	3	73,658	62.37	58,426	63.45
	4	54,269	43.73	66,545	64.77
	5	86,352	58.23	65,471	62.95
	6	125,621	87.12	64,774	64.01
	7	97,634	81.69	70,425	63.52
	8	177,563	93.28	69,998	62.59

Table 4. The amount ratio and time ratio in different *Gnum* groups of D50.

Number of Nodes	PCFMIS1		PCFMIS3	
	Amount	Time (s)	Amount	Time (s)
3	2.88	2.29	1.32	1.09
4	2.94	2.32	1.29	1.04
5	4.41	2.13	1.39	1.04

4.2.2. Comparison of Running Time and Speedup

The speedup is used to measure the parallelization performance of parallel systems or programs. It is the ratio of the time that the same task runs in uniprocessor and parallel processor systems. The speedup is defined by the following formula [30]:

$$S_p = \frac{T_1}{T_p} \quad (1)$$

where p is the number of nodes, T_1 is the execution time on a single node, and T_p is the execution time on p nodes.

When $S_p = p$, the speedup is a linear speedup. It is the ideal speedup that the parallel algorithm tries to achieve. However, the linear speedup is difficult to achieve because the communication cost increases with the increasing number of cores.

Figure 5 shows the computational time of four algorithms for four data sets on a small number of nodes. Figure 6 shows the computational time of four algorithms for four data sets on large number of nodes. As the number of the nodes increases, the computational time of the four parallel methods becomes shorter. Due to the use of optimized compression, PCFMIS2 has less computational time than PCFMIS1. PCFMIS3 performs best, saving half the time compared to PCFMIS1. It indicates that the improvements on optimized compression and load balancing are effective. In particular, the EDS strategy proposed by PCFMIS3 divides the edges more rationally to provide a basis for grouping. As PaFuTM has to find all the candidate subtrees and duplicate redundant subtrees exist among nodes, PaFuTM has longer computational time than PCFMIS3.

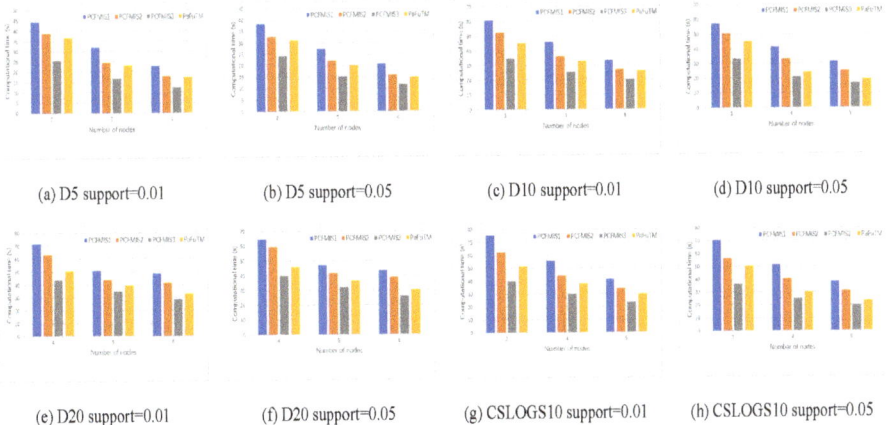

(a) D5 support=0.01 (b) D5 support=0.05 (c) D10 support=0.01 (d) D10 support=0.05

(e) D20 support=0.01 (f) D20 support=0.05 (g) CSLOGS10 support=0.01 (h) CSLOGS10 support=0.05

Figure 5. Computational time of four algorithms for four data sets on a small number of nodes.

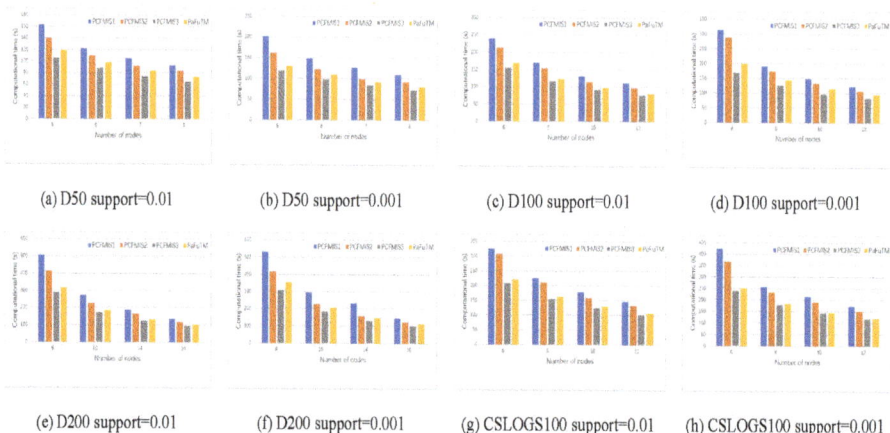

Figure 6. Computational time of four algorithms for four data sets on a large number of nodes.

Figure 7 shows the speedups on four data sets with a small number of nodes. Figure 8 shows the speedups on another four data sets with a large number of nodes. As the results show, the speedup of PCFMIS1 performs worst on all data sets. PCFMIS2 performs better than PCFMIS1. The speedups of PCFMIS3 and PaFuTM are closest to the linear one, but PCFMIS3 performs better. As the number of nodes increases, the speedup keeps growing. However, in Figure 7e,f, when the nodes increase from 5 to 6, the speedup of PCFMIS1 and PCFMIS2 grow slowly. There is a clear salient point. This also appears in Figure 8a,b,f. PCFMIS3 maintains a steady growth.

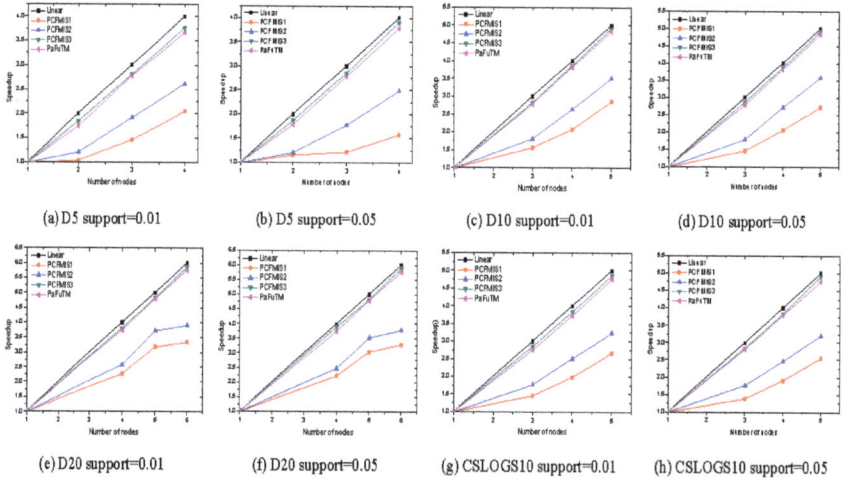

Figure 7. The speedups of four algorithms for four data sets on a small number of nodes.

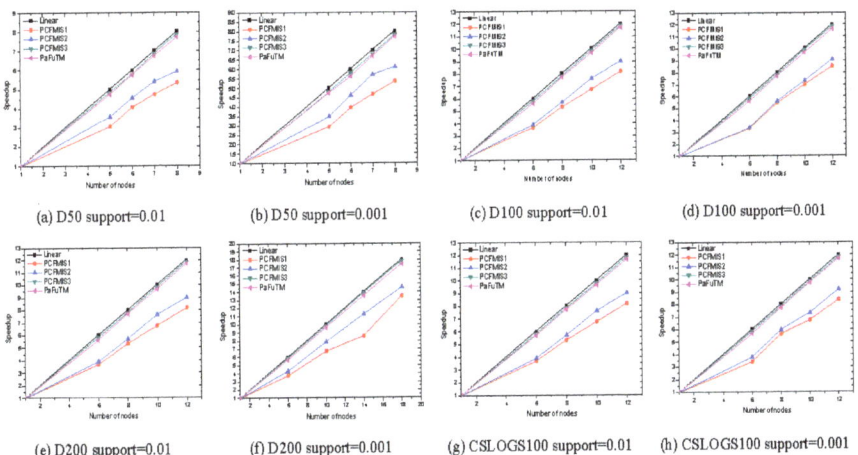

Figure 8. The speedups of four algorithms for four data sets on a large number of nodes.

5. Conclusions

A paralleling algorithm PCFMIS3 with GS and EDS is proposed in MapReduce framework to parallel CFMIS to mine frequent subtrees efficiently. The GS method divides the subtrees into different groups, which solves the data division problem in parallel computing. It avoids inter-group communication while mining frequent subtrees in each group to reduce parallel computing time. In PCFMIS3, load balancing is achieved by using EDS. Additionally, the compression stage in mining frequent subtrees is optimized by avoiding all candidate subtrees of a compression tree, which reduces the calculation time of nodes. Experiments demonstrate that the PCFMIS3 algorithm performs best on the comparison of load balancing and running time on both the real data set and synthetic data set. The maximum load is 1.3 times the minimum load, while it is up to 7 times without EDS. The time ratio of PCFMIS3 is only about 1.1, while the time ratio exceeds 2.0 without EDS. PCFMIS3 also performs best on different support values, saving half the computational time compared to PCFMIS1. The PCFMIS3 achieves the optimal speedup which is closest to the linear one on both small and large number of nodes.

Serial computing technology is difficult to meet the needs of massive data processing. Parallel computing can take advantage of multi-node computing resources to reduce problem resolution time. The proposed GS and EDS methods solve the two important issues of data partitioning and load balancing in parallel computing. To apply GS and EDS method in the mining of other frequent item sets is our future work.

Author Contributions: Conceptualization, J.W. and X.L.; methodology, J.W. and X.L.; software, J.W.; validation, J.W.; formal analysis, X.L.; writing—original draft preparation, J.W.; visualization, J.W. All authors have read and agreed to the published version of the manuscript.

Funding: This research was funded by the Technology Development Plan of Jilin Province (Jing Wang 2022) and the Fundamental Research Funds for the Central Universities.

Institutional Review Board Statement: Not applicable.

Informed Consent Statement: Not applicable.

Data Availability Statement: Not applicable.

Conflicts of Interest: The authors declare no conflict of interest.

References

1. Tekli, G. A survey on semi-structured web data manipulations by non-expert users. *Comput. Sci. Rev.* **2021**, *40*, 100367. [CrossRef]
2. Du, Y. Massive Semi-structured Data Platform Based on Elasticsearch and MongoDB. In *Signal and Information Processing, Networking and Computers*; Springer: Singapore, 2021; pp. 877–884.
3. Hong, T.P.; Lin, C.Y.; Huang, W.M.; Li, S.M.; Wang, S.L.; Lin, J.C. A One-Phase Tree-Structure Method to Mine High Temporal Fuzzy Utility Itemsets. *Appl. Sci.* **2022**, *12*, 2821. [CrossRef]
4. Lee, C.; Baek, Y.; Lin, J.C.; Truong, T.; Yun, U. Advanced uncertainty based approach for discovering erasable product patterns. *Knowl.-Based Syst.* **2022**, *24*, 108134. [CrossRef]
5. Black, F.; Drellich, E.; Tymoczko, J. Valid Plane Trees: Combinatorial Models for RNA Secondary Structures with Watson–Crick Base Pairs. *SIAM J. Discret. Math.* **2017**, *31*, 2586–2602. [CrossRef]
6. Welke, P. *Efficient Frequent Subtree Mining Beyond Forests*; IOS Press: Amsterdam, The Netherlands, 2020.
7. Li, H.; Lee, J.; Mi, H.; Yin, M. Finding good subtrees for constraint optimization problems using frequent pattern mining. *Proc. AAAI Conf. Artif. Intell.* **2020**, *34*, 1577–1584. [CrossRef]
8. Banchhor, C.; Srinivasu, N. Integrating Cuckoo search-Grey wolf optimization and Correlative Naive Bayes classifier with Map Reduce model for big data classification. *Data Knowl. Eng.* **2020**, *127*, 101788. [CrossRef]
9. Wang, J.; Liu, Z.; Li, W.; Li, X. Research on a frequent maximal induced subtrees mining method based on the compression tree sequence. *Expert Syst. Appl.* **2015**, *42*, 94–100. [CrossRef]
10. Neshatpour, K.; Malik, M.; Sasan, A.; Rafatirad, S.; Mohsenin, T.; Ghasemzadeh, H.; Homayoun, H. Energy-efficient acceleration of MapReduce applications using FPGAs. *J. Parallel Distrib. Comput.* **2018**, *119*, 1–17. [CrossRef]
11. Es-Sabery, F.; Hair, A. Big data solutions proposed for cluster computing systems challenges: A survey. In Proceedings of the 3rd International Conference on Networking, Information Systems & Security, Marrakech, Morocco, 31 March–2 April 2020; pp. 1–7.
12. Chen, F.; Deng, P.; Wan, J.; Zhang, D.; Vasilakos, A.V.; Rong, X. Data mining for the internet of things: Literature review and challenges. *Int. J. Distrib. Sens. Netw.* **2015**, *11*, 431047. [CrossRef]
13. Vo B.; Le T.; Coenen, F.; Hong, T.P. Mining frequent itemsets using the N-list and subsume concepts. *Int. J. Mach. Learn. Cybern.* **2016**, *7*, 253–265. [CrossRef]
14. Mao, Y.; Geng, J.; Deborah, S.M.; Yaser, A.N.; Zhang, C.; Deng, X.; Chen, Z. PFIMD: A parallel MapReduce-based algorithm for frequent itemset mining. *Multimed. Syst.* **2021**, *27*, 709–722.
15. Welke, P.; Seiffarth, F.; Kamp, M.; Wrobel, S. HOPS: Probabilistic subtree mining for small and large graphs. In Proceedings of the 26th ACM SIGKDD International Conference on Knowledge Discovery & Data Mining, Virtual Event, CA, USA, 23–27 August 2020; pp. 1275–1284.
16. Wang, L.; Meng, J.; Xu, P.; Peng, K. Mining temporal association rules with frequent itemsets tree. *Appl. Soft Comput.* **2018**, *62*, 817–829. [CrossRef]
17. Huynh, V.; Küng, J. Higher Performance IPPC+ Tree for Parallel Incremental Frequent Itemsets Mining. In Proceedings of the 5th International Conference FDSE, Ho Chi Minh City, Vietnam, 28–30 November 2018.
18. Pascal, W.; Tamas, H.; Stefan, W. Probabilistic and exact frequent subtree mining in graphs beyond forests. *Mach. Learn.* **2019**, *108*, 1137–1164.
19. Wang, C.S.; Chang, J.Y. MISFP-Growth: Hadoop-Based Frequent Pattern Mining with Multiple Item Support. *Appl. Sci.* **2019**, *9*, 2075. [CrossRef]
20. Upadhyay, N.M.; Singh, R.S.; Dwivedi, S.P. Prediction of multicore CPU performance through parallel data mining on public datasets. *Displays* **2022**, *71*, 102112. [CrossRef]
21. Hashem, I.A.; Yaqoob, I.; Anuar, N.B.; Mokhtar, S.; Gani, A.; Khan, S.U. The rise of big data on cloud computing: Review and open research issues. *Inf. Syst.* **2015**, *47*, 98–115. [CrossRef]
22. Shaik, S.; Subhani, S.; Devarakonda, N.; Nagamani, C. Parallel Computing Algorithms for Big data frequent pattern mining. In Proceedings of the International Conference on Computational Intelligence & Data Engineering ICCIDE, Vijayawada, India, 14–15 July 2017.
23. Yan, D.; Qu, W.; Guo, G.; Wang, X. PrefixFPM: A Parallel Framework for General-Purpose Frequent Pattern Mining. In Proceedings of the IEEE 36th International Conference on Data Engineering (ICDE), Dallas, TX, USA, 20–24 April 2020.
24. Yan, D.; Qu, W.; Guo, G.; Wang, X.; Zhou, Y. PrefixFPM: A parallel framework for general-purpose mining of frequent and closed patterns. *VLDB J.* **2021**, *31*, 253–286. [CrossRef]
25. Xun, Y.; Zhang, J.; Qin, X. Fidoop: Parallel mining of frequent itemsets using mapreduce. *IEEE Trans. Syst. Man Cybern. Syst.* **2016**, *46*, 313–325. [CrossRef]
26. Hong, T.P.; Lee, Y.C.; Wu, M.T. An effective parallel approach for genetic-fuzzy data mining. *Expert Syst. Appl.* **2014**, *41*, 655–662. [CrossRef]
27. Fern, ez-Basso, C.; Francisco-Agra, A.J.; Martin-Bautista, M.J.; Ruiz, M.D. Finding tendencies in streaming data using Big Data frequent itemset mining. *Knowl.-Based Syst.* **2019**, *163*, 666–674.
28. Sicard, N.; Laurent, A.; López, F.D.; Flores, P.M. Towards multi-core parallel fuzzy tree mining. In Proceedings of the 2010 IEEE International Conference on Fuzzy Systems (FUZZ), Barcelona, Spain, 18–23 July 2010; pp. 1–7.

29. Zaki, M.J. Efficiently Mining Frequent Trees in a Forest: Algorithms and Applications. *IEEE Trans. Knowl. Data Eng.* **2005**, *17*, 1021–1035. [CrossRef]
30. Zhang, J.; Wong, J.S.; Li, T.; Pan, Y. A comparison of parallel large-scale knowledge acquisition using rough set theory on different MapReduce runtime systems. *Int. J. Approx. Reason.* **2014**, *55*, 896–907. [CrossRef]

Article

Interested Keyframe Extraction of Commodity Video Based on Adaptive Clustering Annotation

Guangyi Man * and Xiaoyan Sun *

School of Information and Control Engineering, China University of Mining and Technology, Xuzhou 221116, China
* Correspondence: mgy_paper@163.com (G.M.); xysun78@126.com (X.S.)

Abstract: Keyframe recognition in video is very important for extracting pivotal information from videos. Numerous studies have been successfully carried out on identifying frames with motion objectives as keyframes. The definition of "keyframe" can be quite different for different requirements. In the field of E-commerce, the keyframes of the products videos should be those interested by a customer and help the customer make correct and quick decisions, which is greatly different from the existing studies. Accordingly, here, we first define the key interested frame of commodity video from the viewpoint of user demand. As there are no annotations on the interested frames, we develop a fast and adaptive clustering strategy to cluster the preprocessed videos into several clusters according to the definition and make an annotation. These annotated samples are utilized to train a deep neural network to obtain the features of key interested frames and achieve the goal of recognition. The performance of the proposed algorithm in effectively recognizing the key interested frames is demonstrated by applying it to some commodity videos fetched from the E-commerce platform.

Keywords: key interested frame; commodity video; clustering; deep neural network

---

1. Introduction

Videos have been successfully used in an increasing number of fields due to the development of video technology, including video retrieval [1], recommending interested videos to users in the personalized recommendation [2], recognizing and tracking moving targets based on surveillance videos as pattern recognition [3], and so on. The greatest advantage of applying videos in many scenarios is to continuously record what is happening and provide important information when required. However, it is also quite difficult to directly and efficiently find valuable frames due to the continuously recording. For example, when searching for a hit-and-run vehicle based on a traffic video, the police may spend several days watching every frame to find the target and may also suffer a great failure. If interesting keyframes can be recognized by removing redundant video frames, the workload of the users can be greatly reduced and the success rate of finding key information can be improved. Therefore, extracting the key and valuable frames from video has become one of the research hotspots in video processing [4,5].

In the existing relevant work on keyframe extraction, the keyframe of a video is generally defined as the frame containing the key action changing of the object [6]. The purpose of keyframe extraction is to find a set of images from the original video to represent the main action changes. Through the keyframe, users can understand the behavioral features of the main character or object in a relatively short time [7], and it can provide important information for users to make decisions. There are four kinds of keyframe extraction algorithms—that is, based on target, clustering algorithm, dictionary, and image features. Target-based keyframe extraction transforms the problem into the detection of important objects or people and extracts frames containing important elements from the video as the keyframe. Lee et al. [8] proposed a crucial person or target detection method based on the photographer's perspective and predicted the importance of new targets in video according to the significance region. This kind of algorithm is mainly used to detect important targets from the video. Another kind of keyframe extraction is based on clustering algorithm, which gathers each frame into different categories by designing an appropriate clustering method and selects one or more images in each category as the keyframe [9,10]. This kind of algorithm is simple, intuitive, and easy to implement but often needs to specify parameters such as clustering number or clustering radius, which limits its practical applicability. Dictionary-based keyframe extraction adopts a dictionary to reconstruct video, assuming that the video keyframe sequence is the best dictionary [11]. This kind of algorithm turns the keyframe selection into dictionary learning. Mademils et al. [12] proposed a keyframe extraction algorithm for human motion video based on significance dictionary and reconstructed the whole video using the benchmark of human activity; then, they extracted keyframes according to the dictionary. Furthermore, this sort of frame extraction algorithm pays more attention to the characteristics of the whole video but ignores the uniqueness of individual frames. Feature-based keyframe extraction generally uses the color, texture, or motion feature to realize the recognition of motion information. Zhang et al. [13] put forward a kind of keyframe extraction based on the image color histogram strategy. Yeung and Liu [14] come up with a fast keyframes recognition method based on the maximum distance of feature space. Meanwhile, Lai and Yi [15] extracted movement, color, and texture characteristics of frames and built dynamic and static significant mapping, improving the priority of movement information, which enhanced the extraction effect of motion information. Li et al. [11] mapped the video frame features into the abstract space, and then extracted keyframes in it. Existing keyframe extraction algorithms have achieved good results in motion target detection, key figure detection, creating video abstracts, and other fields but these algorithms either lack static feature extraction or pay attention to the overall features of the video while ignoring the uniqueness of a single frame or needing prior parameters that greatly limits the application value of keyframe extraction. In addition, these studies mainly focused on the movement information in the video and did not consider individual demands.

In fact, different users have different concerns when browsing a video, so extracting keyframes only by motion information is difficult to meet user's demands. For instance, on the e-commerce platform [16], the commodity video provides vital information for users searching for their needs, and the key is how the user can obtain the interesting information about the video in a very short time. Such information goes beyond movement changes, as representing global and local content about products is more crucial. Besides, the commodity video is commonly short video and movement of the object is not obvious, so traditional keyframe extraction algorithms based on motion changes no longer apply. At the same time, the definition of keyframe regarding the commodity video varies from person to person. Therefore, how to extract video keyframes according to the needs of different users has become a challenge to the traditional algorithm.

In recent years, many keyframe extraction algorithms have focused on adding an attention mechanism. Shih [17] designed an attention model based on semantic and visual information to mark frames, and selected frames with high scores as keyframes. Although the attention mechanism is integrated, there is no solution to deal with different users' interests.

Aiming at the above problems, we propose an algorithm of commodity video keyframe recognition based on adaptive clustering annotation to solve commodity video keyframe extraction. First of all, from the perspective of users' demands, the keyframe is defined as the frame containing global and local information that users are interested in, and these frames could not include noise and blur. Then, the frame-to-frame difference method is used to obtain the differential frame set by looking for the maximum difference between frames, where a differential frame is defined as the frame that has the greater difference and object movement compared to adjacent frames. For the set, an efficient and adaptive clustering strategy with few parameters based on frame difference degree and category scale is designed to realize the clustering of different frames and the differential frame sets are divided and annotated based on the keyframe definition defined by users' requirements. Furthermore, a small number of marked commodity keyframe samples are utilized to train the deep neural network by means of transfer learning [18] to realize accurate keyframe recognition and extraction.

Contributions of this paper mainly include the following four parts: (1) From the perspective of users' attention and interest in commodities, we propose the definition of commodity video keyframe. (2) An adaptive image clustering strategy based on the frame-to-frame difference and keyframe labeling method are proposed. (3) A deep neural network model is presented fusing the frame-to-frame difference with the transfer mechanism to realize the extraction of commodity video keyframes. (4) The proposed algorithm is applied to the self-built video library of clothing commodities, and the results show its effectiveness in meeting the personalized needs of users. Figure 1 shows the algorithm framework of our work.

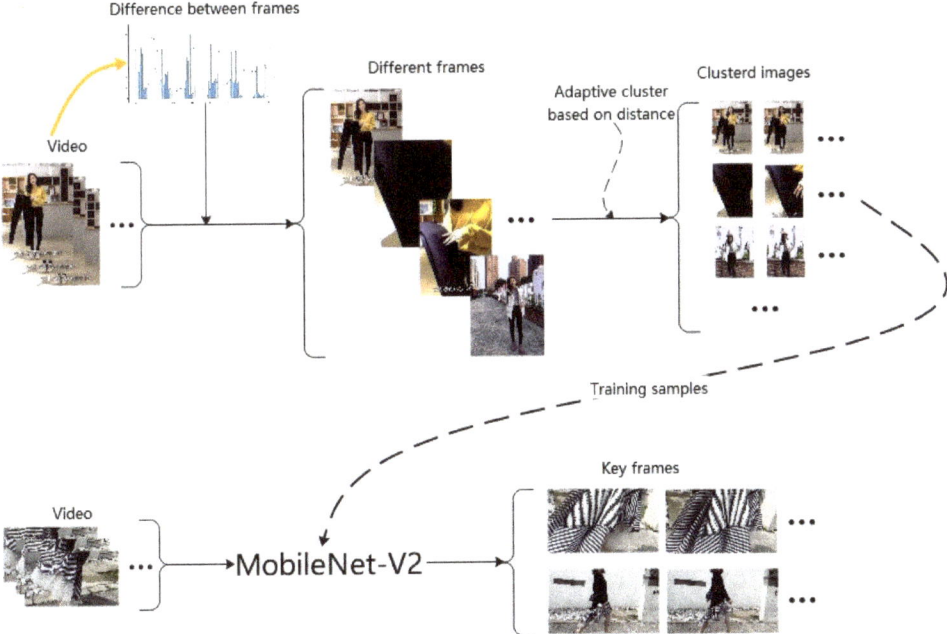

Figure 1. Proposed algorithm framework.

The paper is organized as follows: In Section 2, we provide a review of related work about keyframe extraction, image clustering, and deep neural network algorithm. In Section 3, we introduce algorithms proposed in this paper in detail, including the adaptive clustering strategy (Adaptive Cluster Based on Distance, ACBD), commodity video keyframe labeling algorithm, and keyframe extraction strategy. In Section 4, we evaluate the algorithm on the commodity dataset and analyze the results. In the Discussion section, we discuss the advantages and significance of our algorithm. In the Conclusion section, we conclude the paper.

2. Related Work

Keyframe extraction has become a hotspot in video processing technology nowadays and mainly uses clustering strategies, such as K-means clustering [19], mean-Shift clustering, density clustering [20], fuzzy C-mean clustering [21], etc. to generate video summaries and retrieve information. Generally, in the field of video retrieval, the video is usually transformed into keyframes so as to improve the efficiency. Sze et al. [22] proposed a keyframe extraction algorithm based on pixel features, which improved the retrieval performance compared with the traditional algorithm based on histogram feature. Pan et al. [21] proposed a keyframe extraction algorithm based on improved fuzzy C-means clustering, extracting frame images from each class as keyframes according to the maximum entropy. Xiao et al. [23] dynamically divided frames into different classes in accordance with the captured content and selected the frame closest to the class center as the keyframe. Wang and Zhu [24] extracted a moving target from the original video as keyframes through lens boundary detection. Chen et al. [25] used posture information to identify and select keyframes with abrupt posture changes on the basis of human targets, in order to make the network have adaptive ability in attitude changes and, thus, extract keyframes having motion information.

Normally, in the field of generating video summary, the extracted keyframe is used as the video summary. Ren et al. [26] divided the video into different segments according to lenses; then, they clustered different video segments, and finally, selected several frames from every category as keyframes of the video. In general, image features are usually fused into the keyframe extraction algorithm based on clustering. For instance, Gharbi et al. [10] extracted SURF features from video frames and then clustered features to extract keyframes. Likewise, Mahmoud et al. [27] extracted and clustered color features, and sequentially selected the center of each category as keyframes of the video. Liu et al. [28] designed feature description windows to extract the objects and reduced the number of windows through prior knowledge to reduce the possibility of overfitting. Gygli et al. [29] considered multiple target detection; they extracted the features of different targets through supervised learning and fused multiple features to extract the keyframe. Li et al. [11] extracted a frame per second to greatly shorten the length of the video, thus improving the efficiency of the algorithm.

With the rapid development of deep learning in the field of video processing, some scholars applied it to extract and recognize keyframe feature. Zhao et al. [30] used Recurrent Neural Networks (RNN) to extract video keyframes, which make the keyframe sequence represent the semantic information about the original video better. Agyeman et al. [31] extracted video features by 3D-CNN and ResNet and then recognized keyframes using a Long Short-Term Memory (LSTM) network trained by these features. Universally, RNN and LSTM are used to process time series data. Although video is a kind of time series data, for commodity video keyframe extraction, users do not focus on the temporal characteristics between two frames and pay more attention to the contents of each image. Therefore, we should consider other neural network models to extract image features that users are interested in to improve the accuracy of keyframe extraction.

At present, the convolutional neural network is mainly used to extract image features. Since AlexNet [32] made a breakthrough, the architecture of convolutional neural network (CNN) has been getting deeper and deeper. For example, VGG [33] network and GoogleNet [34] have reached 19 and 22 layers, respectively. However, with the increase in network depth, the problem of ineffective learning caused by gradient vanishing will lead to the saturation or even degradation of the performance of the deep convolutional neural network. Hence, He K. et al. proposed a deep residual network (ResNet) [35], adding the identity mapping and relying on the residual module to overcome the gradient disappearance and enhance the convergence of the algorithm. There are five models of ResNet network, including 18 layers, 34 layers, 50 layers, 101 layers, and 152 layers. With the network layers being deepened, the fitting ability of models is gradually improving but the training complexity is increasing sharply. From the perspective of reducing the complexity of deep convolutional neural network, Howard et al. proposed the structure of MobileNet [36], which greatly reduced the number of training parameters through the use of deep separable convolution. Further, on the basis of this network, Sandler et al. integrated the residual module and proposed MobileNet-V2 [37] with higher accuracy. On this basis, Gavai et al. [38] used MobileNet to classify flower images, and Yuan et al. [39] used Mobilenet-V2 to detect surface defects of galvanized sheet. Fu et al. [40] extracted text information from natural scenes by combining Mobilenet-V2 and U-NET. On account of the high efficiency and accuracy of Mobilenet-V2 in image feature extraction, we apply MobileNet-V2 to extract image features of commodity video keyframes in order to obtain frame features reflecting users' interest.

3. Keyframe Extraction by Adaptive Clustering Annotation Facing User's Interestingness

3.1. Keyframe Definition for User's Interest

In commodity videos, users will concentrate on images that reflect the global and local information of commodities. In addition, the clarity and quality of images will also greatly affect user experience and decision-making. Therefore, we first provide quantitative descriptions of image quality and the information mentioned previously and then define the keyframe based on the descriptions.

Figure 2 illustrates the global and local information of two frames. Visibly, the image containing global commodity information has many contour features and, oppositely, the other image lacks these features. Thus, we adopt the Laplace operator, which can embody contour features of images to define the global and local features of images that express user's interest.

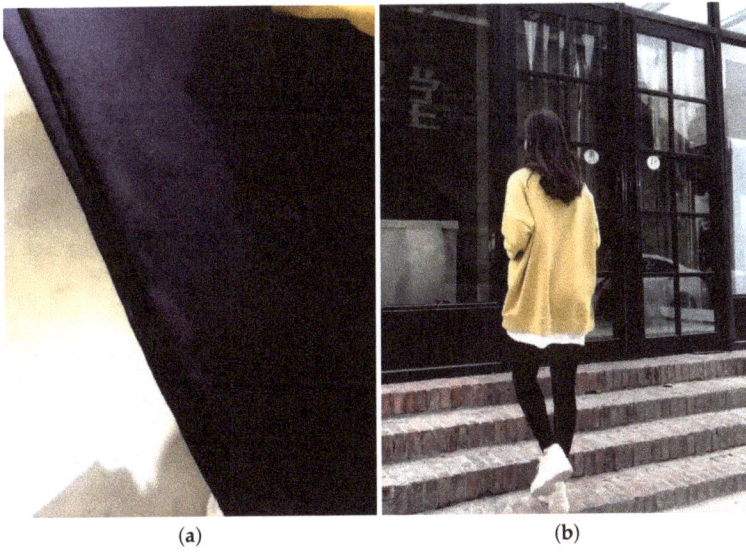

(a) (b)

Figure 2. (a) Local feature, (b) Global feature. Local features reflect commodity details including texture, material, workmanship, etc. and global features reflect the overall effect of the commodity on the model.

The pixel point matrix of the commodity video frame is denoted as $f(u,v)$, where u and v represent the row and column of the image, and its Laplace transform is shown in Equation (1) [41].

$$\nabla^2 f(u,v) = [f(u+1,v) + f(u-1,v) + f(u,v+1) + f(u,v-1)] - 4f(u,v), \quad (1)$$
$$u \in \{1,2,\ldots,h\}, v \in \{1,2,\ldots,w\}$$

In the Equation (1), h and w represent the sum of row and column, respectively. Further, we binarize the image after Laplace transform and then count the number of white points in the binary image to calculate the ratio denoted as $\eta = \frac{N_w}{N_t}$, which reflects the richness of contour information, where N_w and N_t represent the number of white points and total pixels, respectively. When η is large, it indicates that the frame of commodity video contains more contour features and likely reflects the global feature of the commodity. On the contrary, the frame may only contain the local features of goods. For example, for two frames in Figure 2, the η is 0.0029 and 0.028, respectively, showing large differences.

Mean value, standard deviation, and mean gradient are commonly used to measure image quality and describe the brightness, the color saturation, and the clarity of image, respectively. In commercial video frames, poor image quality is caused by blur and lack of the main object due to lens conversion, so the mean gradient can be used. Meanwhile, lack of the main object results in a large area of blank and the average gradient of blank part is 0, resulting in a small average mean of the whole image. For this reason, we adopt mean gradient to evaluate the quality of commodity video frames, as in Equation (2). In the equation, respectively, w and h represent the width and height of the picture; $\frac{\partial f(u,v)}{\partial x}$ and $\frac{\partial f(u,v)}{\partial y}$ represent horizontal gradient and vertical gradient. When the mean gradient of a frame is greater than the mean value of all frames' gradients, the image quality is higher.

$$G = \frac{1}{w \times h} \sum_{u=1}^{h} \sum_{v=1}^{w} \sqrt{\frac{(\frac{\partial f(u,v)}{\partial x})^2 + (\frac{\partial f(u,v)}{\partial y})^2}{2}} \quad (2)$$

Nonetheless, we encounter two problems using the above quantitative description in practical application. That is, (1) when a commodity has many designs, its image has abundant local and global contour features. At this condition, the η of every frame are similar to each other, so the global and local features cannot be completely divided by η. (2) When mean gradient is used to measure the image quality, the mean gradient of frames without complicated designs is similar to the value of frames that lack the main object, and these frames may be misclassified into low-quality. Therefore, we introduce user's interest to make up for the deficiency of the quantitative descriptions—that is, on the basis of these descriptions, every user participates in the judgment of the global information, local information, and image quality. In general, the commodity video keyframe is determined by η, G and the correction operations of the user.

In order to accurately identify keyframes in commodity video, our algorithm is divided into the following steps: (1) We extract a part of frames according to frame-to-frame difference and design an efficient automatic clustering strategy to cluster these frames. (2) We calculate η and G based on categories to make the clustering result more accurate by means of introducing local features, global features, and quality evaluation and then submit them to users for correction. Finally, we obtain reliable keyframe labels. (3) Aiming to extract keyframe features, we utilize a small number of keyframes containing labels to train Mobilenet-V2 by transfer learning and, finally, we can obtain keyframes using the network trained before.

3.2. Personalized Keyframe Adaptive Clustering Based on Frame-to-Frame Difference

Before extracting keyframes reflecting personalized demands, frames should be annotated. Obviously, it is time-consuming and difficult for users to annotate each frame. Thus, we expect to reduce this burden with the method of frame-to-frame difference, which can be used to identify the frames of shot transition and model's movements as the important information of the video. Therefore, we use it to measure the difference between two adjacent frames, and then design the Adaptive Cluster Based on Distance (ACBD) to shorten the labeling process.

3.2.1. Differential Frames Extraction

We define the set of all video frames as $\Psi = \{X_1, X_2, \ldots, X_n\}$, and after grayscaling the Ψ, it is expressed as $\Psi' = \{X'_1, X'_2, \ldots, X'_n\}$. Then, the frame-to-frame difference between frame i and frame $i-1$, denoted as $D(i)$, is shown in Equation (3).

$$D(i) = \frac{\sum_{m=1}^{w}\sum_{j=1}^{h} \|X'_i(j,m) - X'_{i-1}(j,m)\|}{w \times h}, i \in \{2,3,\ldots,n\} \quad (3)$$

Frame-to-frame difference is often used to detect object movement. The frame having larger difference value than the threshold is selected as a keyframe. In our work, we adopt a differential frame selection strategy based on maximum value. For example, $D(i) \geq \frac{D(i-1)+D(i+1)}{2}$ reveals that the frame X_i has great difference from other frames in $\{X_{i-2}, X_{i-1}, X_i, X_{i+1}\}$, so we consider that X_i is a differential frame. The set of differential frames is denoted as $\Psi_d = \{X_1, X_2, \ldots, X_L\}$. In order to filter redundant information ulteriorly, we set the threshold α, and when $L \leq \alpha$, the algorithm outputs the result; otherwise, the algorithm repeats the above process of differential frame extraction on Ψ_d.

3.2.2. Adaptive Clustering of Differential Frames

In order to improve annotation efficiency, we propose an Adaptive Cluster Based on Distance (ACBD) to cluster the set of differential frames and select the class center for user annotation. The ACBD algorithm uses Euclidean distance to measure the similarity between images and divides the categories through dynamic threshold to achieve accurate clustering of images. Assume that the set to be clustered is a differential frame set, as $\Psi_d = \{X_1, X_2, \ldots, X_L\}$. The ACBD algorithm is completed in four steps: (1) Obtain the initial classes—that is, calculate the similarity of the images and group L images into $L - 1$ classes. (2) Remove noise. (3) Combine related categories and delete abnormal images by intraclass difference. (4) According to the number of samples of every class, dynamically adjust the cluster threshold to optimize the clustering results. The details are shown as follows.

(1) Obtain the initial classes. We transform the image X_i to row vector, as $x_i = [x_{i,1}, x_{i,2}, \ldots, x_{i,(w \times h)}]$, and the Euclidean distance between any two frames is shown in Formula (4).

$$dis(X_m, X_l) = \sqrt{\sum_{i=1}^{w \times h} (x_{m,i} - X_{l,i})^2}, \quad (4)$$

$$m \in \{1, 2, \ldots, L\}, l \in \{1, 2, \ldots, L\}$$

Thus, we can obtain the image distance matrix of Ψ_d represented by $Dis(\Psi_d)$.

$$Dis(\Psi_d) = \begin{bmatrix} 0 & dis(X_1, X_2) & \cdots & dis(X_1, X_L) \\ dis(X_2, X_1) & 0 & \cdots & dis(X_2, X_L) \\ \vdots & \vdots & \ddots & \vdots \\ dis(X_L, X_1) & dis(X_L, X_2) & \cdots & 0 \end{bmatrix}$$

Afterwards, we calculate the mean of $Dis(\Psi_d)$ by Formula (5).

$$E = \frac{\sum_{j=i+1}^{L}\sum_{i=1}^{L} dis(X_i, X_j)}{C_L^2} \quad (5)$$

$$dis(X_p, X_q) < K \quad (6)$$

For each image, we gather its similar images into a group. According to Formula (6) in which K equals E for the first time, we group Ψ_d into $L - 1$ classes denoted as $A = \{A_1, A_2, \ldots, A_{L-1}\}$. For example, the clustering result of image i is represented as $A_i = \{A_{i,1}, A_{i,2}, \ldots, A_{i,p}\}, i = 1, 2, \ldots, L - 1$. $A_{i,p}$ represents that the image p is similar to the image i.

(2) Remove noise. Firstly, we calculate the number of elements in A_i denoted as a_i and set the threshold β to divide noise. If $a_i < \beta$, it means that images in A_i are quite different from most other images and the number of elements in it is not enough to be considered a separate cluster, so we determine A_i as a noise and delete it. Besides, for $A_{i,q}, q = 1, 2, \ldots, p$ we seek similar elements in A_i and count them denoted as $Count_q$ to delete $A_{i,q}$ if $Count_q$ is less than β.

(3) Merge categories based on associated images: We assume that sets with the same elements describe the same class, and therefore merge the intersecting sets. For example, a sample belongs to A_i and A_j, so we merge them to a category. And the result is denoted as $A' = \{A'_1, A'_2, A'_3, \ldots, A'_m\}$.

(4) Optimize cluster based on dynamical cluster threshold. In Formula (6), K is usually unable to accurately cluster different clusters, so we have to update K to improve accuracy. For this, we count the number of elements in $A'_t, t = 1, 2, \ldots, m$ denoted as Num_t and we set a threshold μ to change Formula (6) into Formula (7) so as to recalculate A and redo step (2) and step (3) if $\frac{Num_t}{L} > \theta, t = 1, 2, \ldots, m$. θ is a decimal representing the percentage of each category in the video.

$$dis(A_p, A_q) < \mu K \tag{7}$$

Finally, we can obtain the result until K stops changing or the number of iteration ε is reached. After clustering, we calculate η and G to separate images into containing local features, containing global features, and containing distorted information. Then, these images are sent to users to correct labels, so this process integrates user's preferences to achieve personalized keyframe extraction. The ACBD algorithm framework is shown in Algorithm 1.

Algorithm 1 The process of ACBD.

Input: The image set $\Psi_d = \{X_1, X_2, \ldots, X_L\}$
Output: Clustered images
 Step 1: Transform the image X_i to row vector x_i and get $Dis(\Psi_d)$ and E. Obtain the initial classes $A = \{A_1, A_2, \ldots, A_{L-1}\}$ according to Formula (6)
 Step 2:
 for i from 1 to $L - 1$ **do**
  Count a_i of $A_i = \{A_{i,1}, A_{i,2}, \ldots, A_{i,p}\}$
  if $a_i < \beta$ **then**
   Delete A_i
  for q from 1 ti p **do**
   Count $Count_q$
   if $Count_q < \beta$ **then**
    Delete $A_{i,q}$
 Step 3: Merge categories that have same elements and get the result $A' = \{A'_1, A'_2, A'_3, \ldots, A'_m\}$
 Step 4:
 for t from 1 to m **do**
  Count Num_t
  if $\frac{Num_t}{L} > \theta$ **then**
   According to Formula (7), change K to μK to recalculate A and redo step (2) and step (3)
  else
   return $A' = \{A'_1, A'_2, A'_3, \ldots, A'_m\}$

3.3. The Extraction of Keyframes of Interest Combined with Frame-to-Frame Difference and Deep Learning

After obtaining labeled images, it is time to train the network used for keyframe extraction. Considering the practicability of the network on mobile, the MobileNet-V2 network model is used in this paper, because under the condition of high accuracy, compared with Resnet-50, MobileNet-V2 runs faster and has fewer parameters.

However, the network may not be adequately trained only using a self-built dataset. Therefore, inspired by transfer learning [42], we use the pretrained model of ImageNet to retrain and fine-tune the network parameters on our dataset. After differential frame extraction and neural network classification, the keyframe containing user interest information is finally obtained.

4. Experiment

In this part, we verify the effectiveness and rationality of the algorithm proposed in this paper through experiments. Firstly, we design experiments to verify the effectiveness of the differential frame extraction algorithm and the adaptive clustering algorithm, and compare the difference between MobileNet-V2 and RESNET-50 in commodity video keyframe recognition. Finally, we give the overall output of the proposed algorithm. The experiment will be run and tested on the Clothes Video Dataset constructed in this paper.

4.1. The Experiment Background

In recent years, the volume of commodity video data has grown rapidly, but there is no publicly available commodity video dataset. Therefore, we downloaded 30 videos of each jacket, pants, shoes, and hat from Taobao (www.taobao.com) to construct a new Clothes Video Dataset, which contains 120 videos, and the length of videos ranging from ten seconds to one minute. The basic parameters of the dataset are shown in Table 1.

Table 1. Basic parameters of the Clothes Video Dataset.

	Number	Length
jacket	30	1 m 12 s
pants	30	49 s
hat	30	53 s
shoes	30	47 s

We consider that for the product, the details are the most important part, and the overall effect is second. Therefore, commodity video frames are divided into four categories: the first category shows commodity details reflecting texture, material, workmanship, etc.; the second category shows the overall effect of the commodity on the model; the third category contains a lot of information unrelated to commodities, such as scenes and models' faces; the fourth category is the distorted image. Thus, the first and second categories are defined as the keyframe of the video. We randomly selected 3 videos from each category in the dataset, a total of 12 videos, and then obtained the initial clustering by ACBD algorithm. Next, we corrected and divided the clustering results into the four categories mentioned before to obtain 790 images of the first category, 247 images of the second category, 58 images of the third category, and 45 images of the fourth category.

We used an Intel Core i7-8700K CPU with 64 GB RAM and an NVIDIA GeForce GTX 1080Ti graphics card. For the software environment, we used Python version 3.7. The parameters α, β, μ, θ, ε used in the experiment are 200, 3, 0.95, 1/3, and 5, respectively, through many experiments.

4.2. Differential Frame Extraction

We compared the algorithm proposed by Li et al. [11] with our algorithm for differential frame extraction to analyze the advantages and disadvantages. The algorithm proposed by Li et al. extracts one frame of image per second. The essence of the algorithm is to extract video frames at the same time interval. In this experiment, we set the extraction interval as 4 frames; the duration of the experiment video is 60 s and contains 1501 frames.

As can be seen in Figure 3, the video of 1501 frames is reduced to 176 frames, which greatly reduces the amount of data for subsequent processing and retains the main information of the video. By comparing Figures 4 and 5, a large number of frames remain after equal interval extraction, so it can be seen that the interval size of 4 frames is not reasonable, and the extraction interval should be expanded to improve the result. In practical application, the video length is often unknown, so it is impossible to determine the size of the extracted interval. Therefore, the differential frame extraction algorithm is more applicable.

Figure 3. Extraction results of differential frames.

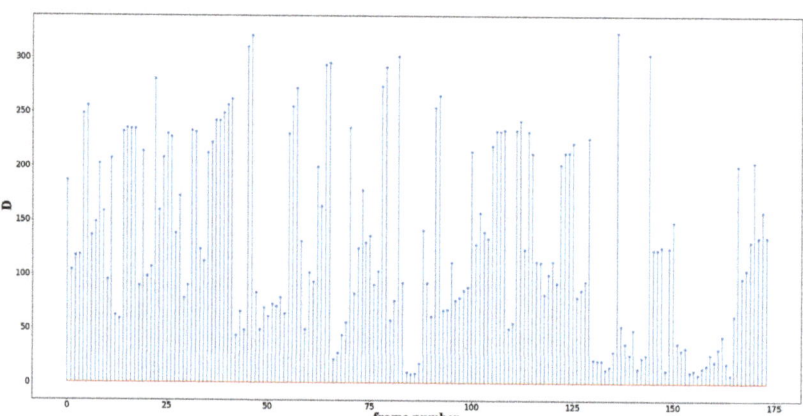

Figure 4. Interframe difference after differential frame extraction.

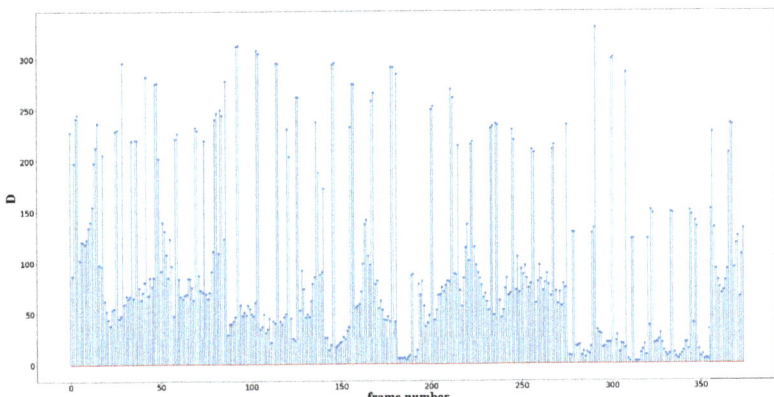

Figure 5. Interframe difference after equal interval extraction.

4.3. Acbd Algorithm

We designed three experiments to verify the effectiveness of our proposed ACBD algorithm. First, we conducted experiments about the effect of ACBD, then compared the effect of the ACBD algorithm with the DBSCAN algorithm on the commodity dataset constructed in this paper and tested its applicability with DBSCAN and K-Means on the UCI dataset.

4.3.1. Effect of ACBD

We used the above video for experiment and used the ACBD algorithm to cluster the obtained differential frames.

From the distribution of Figure 6b, it can be clearly seen that compared with Figure 6a, the ACBD algorithm deletes some differential frames and leaves 106 frames. The deleted frames are mainly the shot transition frames shown in Figure 7, and the transition frames contain a lot of useless and even misleading information, which cannot be used for subsequent algorithm processing. The removal of transition frames can improve the accuracy and efficiency; thus, the ACBD algorithm has the function of removing noise. Comparing the clustering results shown in Figure 8 with the difference frames in Figure 3, the ACBD algorithm removes the 128th to 136th pictures in Figure 3. According to statistics, the proportion of this scene in the video is 5.1%. For commodity videos, it can be considered that the scene with a low proportion is less descriptive for the commodity, so it can be deleted. From the clustering results, the ACBD algorithm can distinguish each cluster and achieve accurate clustering of differential frames.

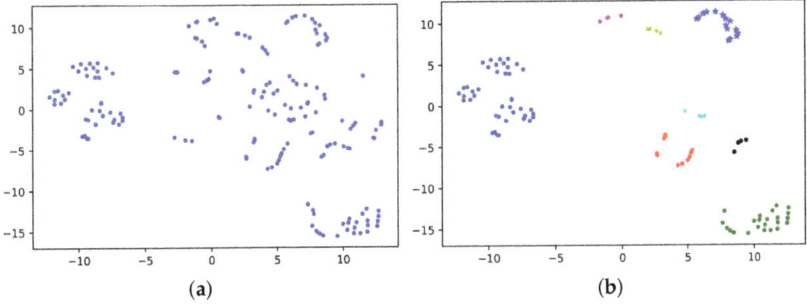

Figure 6. (**a**) Differential frame distribution. (**b**) Distribution after clustering.

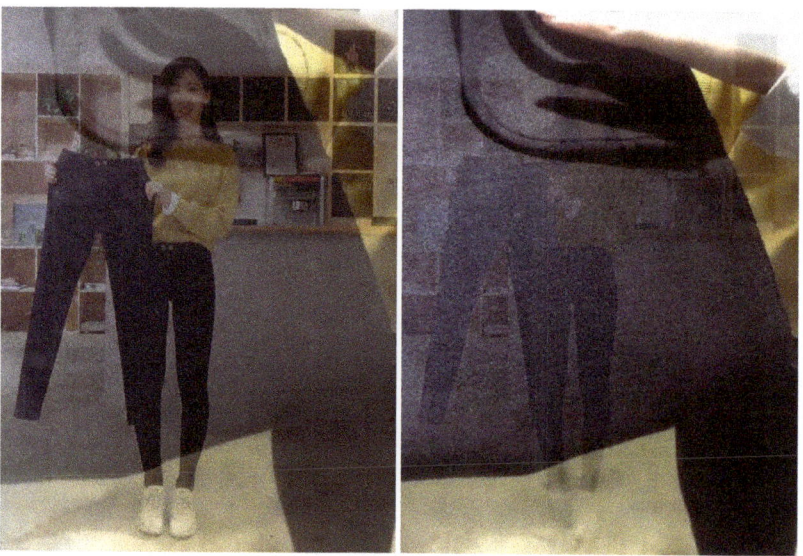

Figure 7. Transition frames.

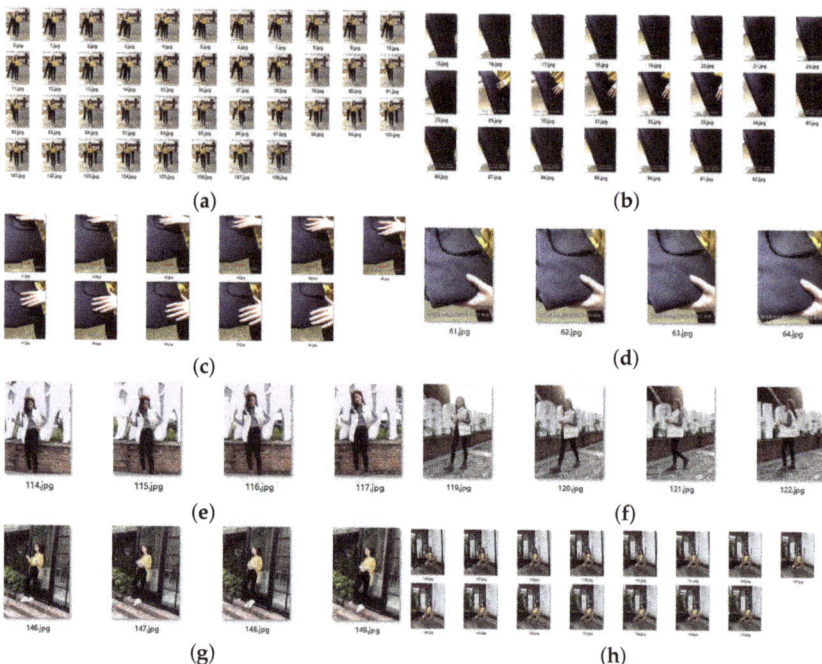

Figure 8. ACBD clusters the differential frames into 8 clusters (a–h).

4.3.2. Compared with DBSCAN and K-Means

In the commodity dataset, we compared ACBD with the common clustering algorithms K-means and DBSCAN to judge whether the ACBD algorithm is superior. We randomly selected a video from the dataset for experiment, and the clustering radius of DBSCAN was determined according to the mean distance of all images. The radius in this experiment was 20,000, and the minimum number of sample points was set to 3 after repeated debugging. The number of K-means clustering was set as 4.

From Figure 9a,b, we can see that, compared with the original video, DBSCAN algorithm abandoned many differential frames resulting in the loss of some important information. In addition, the DBSCAN algorithm needs to adjust the clustering radius and density artificially, and readjust the parameters for different videos, which greatly increases the workload. By comparing (c) and (d), the number of categories represented by "+" in the K-means clustering results is far greater than other categories, so the results are not accurate enough. However, the categories represented by "·" and "×" may be misclassified due to the long distance within classes. We also cannot determine the number of clusters for different videos in advance. It can be seen from the result presented in (d) that ACBD can solve the problems existing in K-means well. For the outliers in the upper right corner of Figure 9, the image has a small number of transition regions due to the scene transition and becomes an outlier after dimensionality reduction. However, this image should be classified into the green "·" category in Figure (d) after comparison one by one.

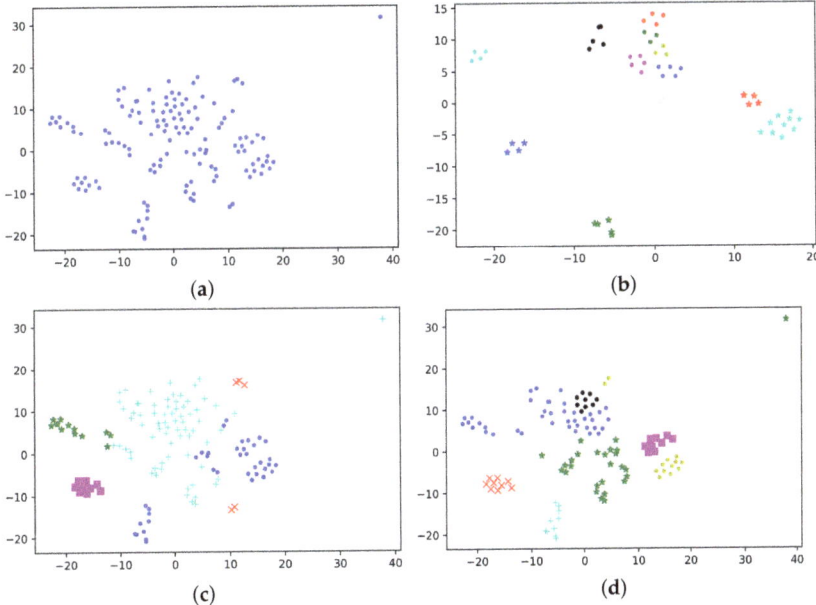

Figure 9. Comparison of clustering effects between the ACBD algorithm and DBSCAN algorithm. (**a**) Differential frame distribution. (**b**) DBSCAN algorithm clustering results. (**c**) K-means algorithm clustering results. (**d**) ACBD algorithm clustering results.

4.3.3. Effects on the UCI Dataset

In order to test the applicability of the ACBD algorithm, we verified the effect on IRIS, WINE, and HAPT datasets and compared it with K-means algorithm and DBSCAN algorithm. We used Adjusted Rand index (ARI) [43], Fowlkes–Mallows index (FMI) [44], and Adjusted Mutual Information (AMI) [45] to evaluate the clustering results, and these evaluation criteria are defined as follows. For a given set S of n instances, assume that $U = \{u_1, u_2, \ldots, u_R\}$ represents the ground-truth classes of S and $V = \{v_1, v_2, \ldots, v_C\}$ represents the result of the clustering algorithm. n_{ij} represents the number of instances in u_i and v_j. $n_{i.}$ and $n_{j.}$ represent the number of instances in u_i and v_j, respectively. Rand index (RI) is calculated by $\sum_{i,j} \binom{n_{ij}}{2}$, and thus, ARI Can be expressed as below.

$$ARI = \frac{RI - E(RI)}{max(RI) - E(RI)} \qquad (8)$$

In Formula (8), $E(RI) = \frac{[\sum_i \binom{n_i}{2}\sum_j \binom{n_j}{2}]}{\binom{n}{2}}$, $max(RI) = \frac{1}{2}[\sum_i \binom{n_i}{2} + \sum_j \binom{n_j}{2}]$. ARI is used to measure the degree of consistency between the two data distributions, and its range is [−1,1]. In order to measure the effect of the clustering algorithm more comprehensively, FMI and AMI are introduced for evaluation through different methods. Their value range is [0,1] and, the larger the value is, the more similar are the clustering results to the ground-truth. FMI and AMI can be expressed by Formulas (9) and (10), respectively.

$$FMI = \frac{\sum_{i,j} \binom{n_{ij}}{2}}{\sqrt{\sum_i \binom{n_{i.}}{2} \sum_j \binom{n_{.j}}{2}}} \qquad (9)$$

$$AMI = \frac{I(U,V) - E\{I(U,V)\}}{max\{H(U), H(V)\} - E\{I(U,V)\}} \qquad (10)$$

In Formula (10), $I(U,V) = \sum_{i=1}^{R} \sum_{j=1}^{C} \frac{n_{i,j}}{n} \log \frac{\frac{n_{ij}}{n}}{\frac{n_i n_j}{n^2}}$, $H(U) = -\sum_{i=1}^{R} \frac{n_i}{n} \log \frac{n_i}{n}$. The results are shown in the following table.

It can be seen from Tables 2–4 that the K-means algorithm performs the best on the Iris, Wine, and HAPT datasets, and ACBD can compete with K-means on the HAPT dataset. The DBSCAN algorithm did not obtain available clustering results after adjusting parameters many times on the WINE and HAPT datasets, so its clustering evaluation index was 0 on these two datasets. From the experimental results, the performance of the proposed algorithm (ACBD) on the large datasets, such as HAPT, is far better than that on the small datasets, such as IRIS and WINE.

Table 2. Comparison of IRIS experimental results.

	ARI	FMI	AMI
DBSCAN	0.4175	0.6723	0.5476
K-means	**0.7302**	**0.8208**	**0.7483**
ACBD	0.5681	0.7715	0.5768

Table 3. Comparison of Wine experimental results.

	ARI	FMI	AMI
DBSCAN	0	0	0
K-means	0.3711	0.5835	0.4226
ACBD	0.2451	0.4576	0.2708

Table 4. Comparison of HAPT experimental results.

	ARI	FMI	AMI
DBSCAN	0	0	0
K-means	0.3878	0.4713	0.5524
ACBD	0.3259	0.5182	0.3908

4.4. Neural Network Comparison and Overall Algorithm Effects

After ACBD clustering, user auxiliary annotation was carried out for each category to divide images into the above four categories, which greatly reduced the workload of manual annotation. The four labeled images were divided into training set and testing set according to 7:3, so as to train the deep neural network. The hyperparameters are set as follows: batch size, 32; epoch, 400; learning rate, 0.0001. Finally, the trained network is used to classify the video frames. The first category showing commodity details and the second category showing commodity overall effect are the video keyframes. Considering the deep network layer of ResNet, the accuracy is higher, but if the network layer is too deep, the machine is difficult to load. So, we verified whether MobileNet-v2 meets practical requirements while ensuring accuracy compared with ResNet-50. In the experiment, the batch size was set to 64.

As can be seen in Figures 10 and 11, the accuracy rates of ResNet-50 and MobileNet-V2 were similar, both at around 90%. Therefore, in consideration of applicability, we compared the training time and storage space of the two models.

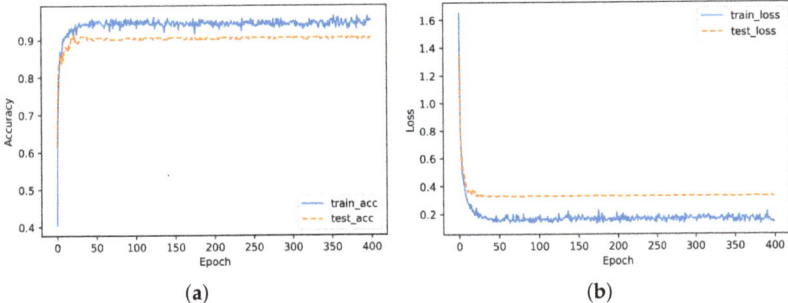

Figure 10. ResNet-50 training accuracy and loss (a,b).

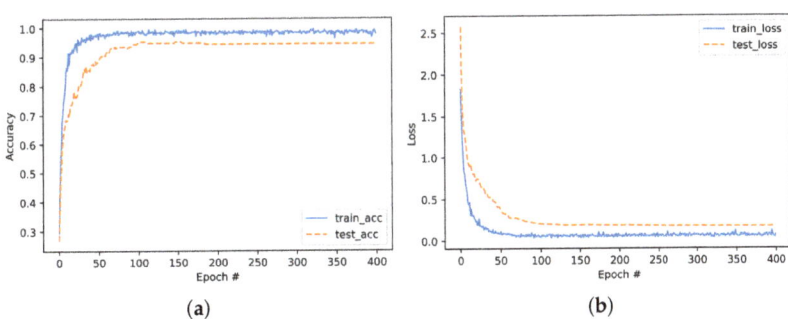

Figure 11. MobileNet-V2 training accuracy and loss (a,b).

Compared with ResNet-50, the training speed of MobileNet-v2 increased by 14.3% and the number of parameters decreased by 66.9%, shown in Table 5. Therefore, MobileNet-v2 has a wider available range from the applicability of mobile terminal, so we adopted the MobileNet-v2 network.

Table 5. Comparison of ResNet-50 and MobileNet-V2.

	ResNet-50	MobileNet-V2
Time spent per epoch (s)	7 ± 0.5	6 ± 0.05
Number of weights	42,472,325	14,064,709
Storage (MB)	324	107

Finally, we randomly selected one video from the remaining 108 videos in the database and inputted it into the MobileNet-V2 after training. Figure 12 shows the final classification results; (a), (b), (c), and (d) correspond to the first, second, third, and fourth categories, respectively, demonstrated in "Supplementary Materials". The first and second categories are the keyframes defined in this paper. From the experimental results, it can be concluded that the algorithm proposed in this paper can achieve the purpose of extracting keyframes, user preferences are reflected in the auxiliary annotation stage, and the ACBD clustering algorithm can greatly improve the efficiency of annotation. Therefore, the overall framework of the algorithm in this paper is reasonable and has good results.

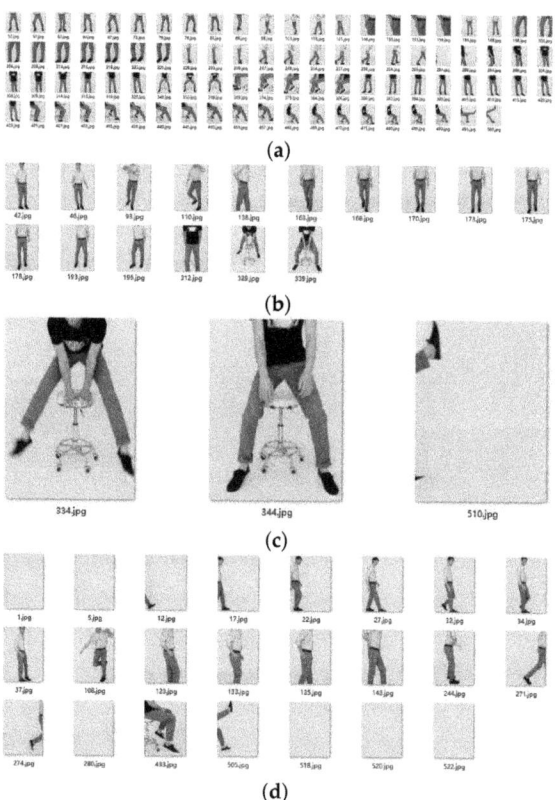

Figure 12. Final result of algorithm. (**a**–**d**) correspond to the first, second, third, and fourth categories, respectively.

5. Discussion

Since different users have different preferences, the existing keyframe extraction algorithms do not provide solutions for different interests. For this reason, we propose an algorithm of commodity video keyframe extraction based on adaptive clustering annotation. Compared with the existing keyframe extraction algorithms, our algorithm reflects the preferences of different users through the process of user annotation, and achieves accurate and personalized keyframe extraction. It provides a feasible method for users to find products faster and more accurately.

6. Conclusions

In order to solve the problem that different users have different definitions of keyframes in commodity video, this paper proposes a keyframe recognition algorithm of commodity video that integrates transfer learning and interest information, and extracts the keyframes of different users' preferences. First, the differential frames were extracted from commercial videos by frame-to-frame difference; then, the ACBD algorithm was used to cluster these frames to simplify the user annotation process. The data annotated by the user were used to train the Mobilenet-V2 network, and finally, the keyframes for individuals were extracted. The experimental results on the commodity video dataset constructed in this paper show that the proposed algorithm is effective and extracts the keyframes accurately. However, user preferences tend to change over time, which is not considered in this paper, so how to cater to the changing interests of users is the focus of our next research.

Supplementary Materials: The following are available online at https://www.mdpi.com/article/10.3390/app12031502/s1, Video S1: Demonstration.

Author Contributions: Conceptualization, G.M. and X.S.; methodology, G.M.; software, G.M.; validation, G.M. and X.S.; writing—original draft preparation, G.M.; funding acquisition, X.S. All authors have read and agreed to the published version of the manuscript.

Funding: This research was funded by National Natural Science Foundation of China under grants No. 61876184.

Institutional Review Board Statement: Not applicable.

Informed Consent Statement: Not applicable.

Conflicts of Interest: The authors declare no conflict of interest.

Abbreviations

The following abbreviation is used in this manuscript:

ACBD   Adaptive Cluster Based on Distance

References

1. Araujo, A.; Girod, B. Large-Scale Video Retrieval Using Image Queries. *IEEE Trans. Circuits Syst. Video Technol.* **2017**, *28*, 1406–1420. [CrossRef]
2. Wang, S.; Cao, L.; Wang, Y. A Survey on Session-based Recommender Systems. *ACM Comput. Surv.* **2021**, *54*, 1–38. [CrossRef]
3. Bi, F.; Lei, M.; Wang, Y.; Huang, D. Remote Sensing Target Tracking in UAV Aerial Video Based on Saliency Enhanced MDnet. *IEEE Access* **2019**, *7*, 76731–76740. [CrossRef]
4. Liu, X.; Song, M.; Zhang, L.; Wang, S.; Bu, J.; Chen, C.; Tao, D. Joint shot boundary detection and key frame extraction. In Proceedings of the 21st International Conference on Pattern Recognition (ICPR2012), Tsukuba, Japan, 11–15 November 2012; pp. 2565–2568.
5. Liu, H.; Pan, L.; Meng, W. Key frame extraction from online video based on improved frame difference optimization. In Proceedings of the 2012 IEEE 14th International Conference on Communication Technology, Chengdu, China, 19–21 October 2012; pp. 940–944.
6. Gygli, M.; Grabner, H.; Riemenschneider, H.; Van Gool, L. Creating summaries from user videos. In *European Conference on Computer Vision*; Springer: Cham, Switzerland, 2014; pp. 505–520.
7. Santini, S. Who needs video summarization anyway? In Proceedings of the International Conference on Semantic Computing (ICSC 2007), Laguna Hills, CA, USA, 27–29 January 2007; pp. 177–184.
8. Lee, Y.J.; Ghosh, J.; Grauman, K. Discovering important people and objects for egocentric video summarization. In Proceedings of the 2012 IEEE Conference on Computer Vision and Pattern Recognition, Providence, RI, USA, 16–21 June 2012; pp. 1346–1353.
9. Wu, J.X.; Zhong, S.H.; Jiang, J.M.; Yang, Y.Y. A novel clustering method for static video summarization. *Multimed. Tools Appl.* **2017**, *76*, 9625–9641. [CrossRef]
10. Gharbi, H.; Bahroun, S.; Massaoudi, M.; Zagrouba, E. Key frames extraction using graph modularity clustering for efficient video summarization. In Proceedings of the 2017 IEEE International Conference on Acoustics, Speech and Signal Processing (ICASSP), New Orleans, LA, USA, 5–9 March 2017; pp. 1502–1506.
11. Li, X.; Zhao, B.; Lu, X. Key Frame Extraction in the Summary Space. *IEEE Trans. Cybern.* **2017**, *48*, 1923–1934. [CrossRef]
12. Mademlis, I.; Tefas, A.; Pitas, I. Summarization of human activity videos using a salient dictionary. In Proceedings of the 2017 IEEE International Conference on Image Processing (ICIP), Beijing, China, 17–20 September 2017; pp. 625–629.
13. Zhang, H.J.; Wu, J.H.; Zhong, D.; Smoliar, S.W. An integrated system for content-based video retrieval and browsing. *Pattern Recognit.* **1997**, *30*, 643–658. [CrossRef]
14. Yeung, M.M.; Liu, B. Efficient matching and clustering of video shots. In Proceedings of the IEEE International Conference on Image Processing, Washington, DC, USA, 23–26 October 1995; pp. 338–341.
15. Lai, J.L.; Yi, Y. Key frame extraction based on visual attention model. *J. Vis. Commun. Image Represent.* **2012**, *23*, 114–125. [CrossRef]

16. Cong, Y.; Yuan, J.; Luo, J. Towards Scalable Summarization of Consumer Videos Via Sparse Dictionary Selection. *IEEE Trans. Multimed.* **2012**, *14*, 66–75. [CrossRef]
17. Shih, H.C. A Novel Attention-Based Key-Frame Determination Method. *IEEE Trans. Broadcast.* **2013**, *59*, 556–562. [CrossRef]
18. Yosinski, J.; Clune, J.; Bengio, Y.; Lipson, H. How transferable are features in deep neural networks? *Int. Conf. Neural Inf. Process. Syst.* **2014**, *27*, 3320–3328.
19. Tomasz, H. Key Frames Detection in Motion Capture Recordings Using Machine Learning Approaches. *Int. Conf. Image Process. Commun.* **2016**, *525*, 79–86.
20. Tang, H.; Liu, H.; Xiao, W.; Sebe, N. Fast and robust dynamic hand gesture recognition via key frames extraction and feature fusion. *Neurocomputing* **2019**, *331*, 424–433. [CrossRef]
21. Pan, R.; Tian, Y.; Wang, Z. Key-frame Extraction Based on Clustering. In Proceedings of the 2010 IEEE International Conference on Progress in Informatics and Computing, Shanghai, China, 10–12 December 2010; Volume 2, pp. 867–871.
22. Sze, K.W.; Lam, K.M.; Qiu, G. A New Key Frame Representation for Video Segment Retrieval. *IEEE Trans. Circuits Syst. Video Technol.* **2005**, *15*, 1148–1155.
23. Xiao, Y.; Xia, L. Key Frame Extraction Based on Connectivity Clustering. In Proceedings of the 2010 Second International Workshop on Education Technology and Computer Science, Wuhan, China, 6–7 March 2010.
24. Wang, Z.; Zhu, Y. Video Key Frame Monitoring Algorithm and Virtual Reality Display Based on Motion Vector. *IEEE Access* **2020**, *8*, 159027–159038. [CrossRef]
25. Chen, Y.; Huang, T.; Niu, Y.; Ke, X.; Lin, Y. Pose-Guided Spatial Alignment and Key Frame Selection for One-Shot Video-Based Person Re-Identification. *IEEE Access* **2019**, *7*, 78991–79004. [CrossRef]
26. Ren, J.; Jiang, J.; Feng, Y. Activity-driven content adaptation for effective video summarization. *J. Vis. Commun. Image Represent.* **2010**, *21*, 930–938. [CrossRef]
27. Mahmoud, K.M.; Ghanem, N.M.; Ismail, M.A. Unsupervised Video Summarization via Dynamic Modeling-based Hierarchical Clustering. In Proceedings of the 2013 12th International Conference on Machine Learning and Applications, Miami, FL, USA, 4–7 December 2013; pp. 303–308.
28. Liu, D.; Hua, G.; Chen, T. A Hierarchical Visual Model for Video Object Summarization. *IEEE Trans. Pattern Anal. Mach. Intell.* **2010**, *32*, 2178–2190. [CrossRef]
29. Gygli, M.; Grabner, H.; Gool, L.V. Video summarization by learning submodular mixtures of objectives. In Proceedings of the IEEE Conference on Computer Vision and Pattern Recognition, Boston, MA, USA, 7–12 June 2015; pp. 3090–3098.
30. Zhao, M.; Guo, X.; Zhang, X. Key Frame Extraction of Assembly Process Based on Deep Learning. In Proceedings of the 2018 IEEE 8th Annual International Conference on CYBER Technology in Automation, Control, and Intelligent Systems (CYBER), Tianjin, China, 19–23 July 2018; pp. 611–616.
31. Agyeman, R.; Muhammad, R.; Choi, G.S. Soccer Video Summarization using Deep Learning. In Proceedings of the 2019 IEEE Conference on Multimedia Information Processing and Retrieval (MIPR), San Jose, CA, USA, 28–30 March 2019; pp. 270–273.
32. Krizhevsky, A.; Sutskever, I.; Hinton, G.E ImageNet classification with deep convolutional neural networks. *Adv. Neural Inf. Process. Syst.* **2012**, *25*, 1097–1105. [CrossRef]
33. Simonyan, K.; Zisserman, A. Very Deep Convolutional Networks for Large-Scale Image Recognition. *arXiv* **2015**, arXiv:1409.1556.
34. Szegedy, C.; Liu, W.; Jia, Y.; Sermanet, P.; Rabinovich, A. Going deeper with convolutions. *IEEE Conf. Comput. Vis. Pattern Recognit.* **2015**, *1*, 1–9.
35. He, K.; Zhang, X.; Ren, S.; Sun, J. Deep Residual Learning for Image Recognition. In Proceedings of the IEEE Conference on Computer Vision and Pattern Recognition, Las Vegas, NV, USA, 27–30 June 2016; pp. 770–778.
36. Howard, A.G.; Zhu, M.; Chen, B.; Kalenichenko, D.; Wang, W.; Weyand, T.; Andreetto, M.; Adam, H. MobileNets: Efficient Convolutional Neural Networks for Mobile Vision Applications. *arXiv* **2017**, arXiv:1704.04861.
37. Sandler, M.; Howard, A.; Zhu, M.; Zhmoginov, A.; Chen, L.C. MobileNetV2: Inverted Residuals and Linear Bottlenecks. In Proceedings of the IEEE Conference on Computer Vision and Pattern Recognition, Salt Lake City, UT, USA, 18–22 June 2018; pp. 4510–4520.
38. Gavai, N.R.; Jakhade, Y.A.; Tribhuvan, S.A.; Bhattad, R. MobileNets for Flower Classification using TensorFlow. In Proceedings of the 2017 International Conference on Big Data, IOT and Data Science (BID), Pune, India, 20–22 December 2017; pp. 154–158.
39. Shen, Y.; Sun, H.; Xu, X.; Zhou, J. Detection and Positioning of Surface Defects on Galvanized Sheet Based on Improved MobileNet v2. In Proceedings of the 2019 Chinese Control Conference (CCC), Guangzhou, China, 27–30 July 2019; pp. 8450–8454.
40. Fu, K.; Sun, L.; Kang, X.; Ren, F. Text Detection for Natural Scene based on MobileNet V2 and U-Net. In Proceedings of the 2019 IEEE international conference on mechatronics and automation (ICMA), Tianjin, China, 4–7 August 2019; pp. 1560–1564.
41. Tian, Q.; Xie, G.; Wang, Y.; Zhang, Y. Pedestrian Detection Based on Laplace Operator Image Enhancement Algorithm and Faster R-CNN. In Proceedings of the 2018 11th International Congress on Image and Signal Processing, BioMedical Engineering and Informatics (CISP-BMEI), Beijing, China, 13–15 October 2018; pp. 1–5.
42. Pan, S.J.; Yang, Q. A Survey on Transfer Learning. *IEEE Trans. Knowl. Data Eng.* **2010**, *22*, 1345–1359. [CrossRef]
43. Hubert, L.; Arabie, P. Comparing partitions. *J. Classif.* **1985**, *2*, 193–218. [CrossRef]
44. Ramirez, E.H.; Brena, R.; Magatti, D.; Stella, F. Topic model validation. *Neurocomputing* **2012**, *76*, 125–133. [CrossRef]
45. Vinh, N.X.; Epps, J.; Bailey, J. Information Theoretic Measures for Clusterings Comparison: Variants, Properties, Normalization and Correction for Chance. *J. Mach. Learn. Res.* **2010**, *11*, 2837–2854.

Article

Optimal Tests for Combining *p*-Values

Zhongxue Chen

Department of Epidemiology and Biostatistics, School of Public Health, Indiana University Bloomington, 1025 E. 7th Street, Bloomington, IN 47405, USA; zc3@indiana.edu; Tel.: +1-812-855-1163

Abstract: Combining information (*p*-values) obtained from individual studies to test whether there is an overall effect is an important task in statistical data analysis. Many classical statistical tests, such as chi-square tests, can be viewed as being a *p*-value combination approach. It remains challenging to find powerful methods to combine *p*-values obtained from various sources. In this paper, we study a class of *p*-value combination methods based on gamma distribution. We show that this class of tests is optimal under certain conditions and several existing popular methods are equivalent to its special cases. An asymptotically and uniformly most powerful *p*-value combination test based on constrained likelihood ratio test is then studied. Numeric results from simulation study and real data examples demonstrate that the proposed tests are robust and powerful under many conditions. They have potential broad applications in statistical inference.

Keywords: chi-square test; constrained likelihood ratio test; Fisher test; gamma distribution; uniformly most powerful test

Citation: Chen, Z. Optimal Tests for Combining *p*-Values. *Appl. Sci.* **2022**, *12*, 322. https://doi.org/10.3390/app12010322

Academic Editor: Pentti Nieminen

Received: 16 November 2021
Accepted: 27 December 2021
Published: 29 December 2021

Publisher's Note: MDPI stays neutral with regard to jurisdictional claims in published maps and institutional affiliations.

Copyright: © 2021 by the author. Licensee MDPI, Basel, Switzerland. This article is an open access article distributed under the terms and conditions of the Creative Commons Attribution (CC BY) license (https:// creativecommons.org/licenses/by/ 4.0/).

1. Introduction

In statistical inference and decision making, it is critical but challenging to appropriately aggregate information from different sources. *p*-value combination approaches provide possible solutions. A *p*-value combination method usually combines the transformed statistics via the original individual *p*-values, and then, an overall *p*-value is obtained. The development of combining *p*-value has a long history. Many pioneer statisticians, including R. A. Fisher [1] and K. Pearson [2], had important contributions in this area. Their methods (e.g., Fisher test), along with others, such as the z-test [3] and the minimal *p*-test [4], are still widely used in today's statistical practice. Many studies have been conducted to compare the performances among those *p*-value combination tests [5–7]; it turned out that no test is uniformly most powerful although some methods may perform better than others under certain conditions. Combining dependent *p*-values is another research direction, as many robust and powerful methods have been proposed in the literature, including a recently proposed test based on Cauchy distribution (CCT) [8]. Although the CCT can be applied to both independent and dependent *p*-values, it has been shown that this test can never obtain a *p*-value less than the smallest *p*-value to be combined, and therefore, is not recommended for combining independent *p*-values [9]. In this paper, we focus on the situation where we have independent *p*-values to be combined.

It is well known that combining *p*-value methods have important applications in meta-analysis [10,11]. However, it is less recognized that combining *p*-value methods are more frequently but implicitly used in statistical testing. For instance, the commonly used chi-square tests, including the likelihood ratio test, the score test, and the Wald test, with degrees of freedom (df) greater than one can be viewed as *p*-value combination methods, which are special cases of our proposed gamma distribution-based tests (see Section 2). In other words, the popular chi-square tests only provide possible and special ways to combine *p*-values that are not necessarily optimal; more powerful methods for combining *p*-value may be found and used instead.

With recent technical developments, larger volume data, such as genome-wide genomic data, are generated more easily and rapidly. Consequently, advanced statistical methods, including p-value combination tests, are highly desirable [12–20]. For instance, meta-analyses, which combine information from different genome-wide association studies (GWASs), have identified many associated genetic variants that could not be identified from a single GWAS [21,22]. It is expected that with more powerful p-value combination tests being developed and available, more and more significant associated genetic variants will be discovered in cancer genomics.

Unfortunately, as Birnbaum [23] already noticed, there exists no uniformly most powerful (UMP) p-value combination test for all alternative hypotheses. However, it is possible that a method is UMP under a certain condition. Moreover, if the true condition is unknown, it is desirable to choose a robust p-value combination method in the sense that it has reasonable detection power under many conditions.

In this paper, we first propose a class of p-value combination methods based on gamma distribution. We show that several existing popular methods are equivalent to certain special cases of this class of tests. Then, we show that the proposed tests are UMP when the p-values to be combined are from certain distributions. When the p-values to be combined are from certain type of distributions whose parameters are partially or fully unknown, asymptotically UMP tests based on constrained likelihood ratio test (CLRT) are proposed and studied.

The rest of the manuscript is organized as follows: In Section 2, we first introduce some existing popular p-value combination tests, describe our proposed tests based on gamma distributions, and then study their connections to existing popular methods and their properties as of UMP tests. Finally, some asymptotically UMP tests based on CLRT are proposed and studied. In Section 3, we compare the performances of the proposed tests with some existing popular methods through a simulation study. In Section 4, two examples of real data applications are demonstrated to illustrate the desired performance of the proposed tests. This paper concludes in Section 5 with discussion and conclusions.

2. Methods

Suppose we have n independent p-values, denoted as $P_i(i = 1, \cdots, n)$, obtained from testing the individual null hypothesis H_{i0} versus the alternative hypothesis H_{i1}, respectively. In addition, throughout this paper, we assume $P_i \sim U(0,1)$ under H_{i0}, where $U(0,1)$ stands for the uniform distribution between 0 and 1. For a combining p-value test, in this paper, we consider testing the global null hypotheses, $H_0 = \cap H_{i0}$ vs. the global alternative hypothesis, $H_1 = \cup H_{i1}$. In statistical literature, several p-value combination tests were proposed long time ago but are still widely used today. We introduce some of the most popular ones as follows.

2.1. Some Existing Popular Tests

2.1.1. The Minimal p-Value (Min p) Test

This test is denoted as T_p, with the test statistic defined as [4]:

$$\min(P_1, P_2, \cdots, P_n) \quad (1)$$

whose null distribution is the beta distribution $Beta(1,n)$ and its p-value is defined as $1 - \left(1 - P_{(1)}\right)^n$, where $P_{(1)} = \min(P_1, P_2, \cdots, P_n)$. The Tippett's Min p test in (1) is closely related to the Bonferroni method [24]. When the minimal p-value $p_{(1)}$ is small, the two tests obtain similar results, and both are close to $np_{(1)}$.

2.1.2. The Chi-Square Test with n Degrees of Freedom

Denoted as χ_n^2, it has the test statistic [25,26]:

$$\sum_{i=1}^{n}\left(\Phi^{-1}(1-P_i)\right)^2 \qquad (2)$$

where $\Phi^{-1}(\cdot)$ is the inverse function of the cumulative distribution function (CDF) of the standard normal distribution, $N(0,1)$. The null distribution of the test χ_n^2 in (2) is the chi-square distribution with n df.

2.1.3. The Fisher Test

Denoted as F_p, it has the following test statistic [1]:

$$-2\sum_{i=1}^{n}\ln(P_i) \qquad (3)$$

whose null distribution is χ_{2n}^2, the chi-square distribution with $2n$ df.

2.1.4. The z Test

Denoted as Z_p, it has the test statistic [3]:

$$\sum_{i=1}^{n}\Phi^{-1}(1-P_i)/\sqrt{n} \qquad (4)$$

whose null distribution is $N(0,1)$.

Note that for all of the above tests, their overall one-sided p-values are calculated based on the right-tails, i.e., the areas beyond the test statistics from the right sides of their null distributions, to reflect the fact that smaller individual p-values provide stronger evidence to support the global alternative hypothesis.

2.2. New Tests Based on Gamma Distribution

We use $Gamma(\alpha, \beta)$ to denote a random variable that has a gamma distribution with shape parameter α and rate parameter β, where both parameters are positive. The probability density function (PDF) of $Gamma(\alpha, \beta)$ is:

$$f_{G(\alpha,\beta)}(x) = \beta^\alpha x^{\alpha-1}\exp(-\beta x)/\Gamma(\alpha) \qquad (5)$$

for $x > 0$, where the gamma function $\Gamma(z) = \int_0^\infty x^{z-1}e^{-x}dx$. Denote the corresponding CDF as $F_{G(\alpha,\beta)}(x)$. We can combine n independent p-values using $Gamma(\alpha, \beta)$ and obtain an overall p-value accordingly.

2.2.1. Gamma Distribution-Base Test $T_{G(\alpha,\beta)}$

Define the following test statistic:

$$T_{G(\alpha,\beta)}(P_1, P_2, \cdots, P_n) = \sum_{i=1}^{n} F_{G(\alpha,\beta)}^{-1}(1-P_i), \qquad (6)$$

where $F_{G(\alpha,\beta)}^{-1}(y)$ is the inverse function of the CDF $F_{G(\alpha,\beta)}(x)$.

We also define the following right-tailed p-value for $T_{G(\alpha,\beta)}$:

$$P = \Pr(Gamma(n\alpha, \beta) > t) = 1 - F_{G(n\alpha,\beta)}(t) = S_{G(n\alpha,\beta)}(t) \qquad (7)$$

where t is the observed value for the test $T_{G(\alpha,\beta)}$, and $F_{G(n\alpha,\beta)}(\cdot)$ and $S_{G(n\alpha,\beta)}(\cdot)$ are the CDF and the survival function of $Gamma(n\alpha, \beta)$, respectively.

The above test determined by the test statistic $T_{G(\alpha,\beta)}$ in (6) and the p-value P in (7) is called $T_{G(\alpha,\beta)}$. The p-value for a specific test T is also denoted as P_T. Therefore, the p-value in (7) can also be written as $P_{T_{G(\alpha,\beta)}}$. Based on the properties of gamma distributions, we have the following result for the test $T_{G(\alpha,\beta)}$:

Proposition 1. *The test $T_{G(\alpha,\beta)}$ with statistic defined in (6) and p-value defined in (7) controls type I error rate exactly at given significance level.*

To study the properties of the new tests, we use the following definitions:

Definition 1. *Two tests T_1 and T_2 are called equivalent and denoted as $T_1 \equiv T_2$ if $p_{T_1}(x) = p_{T_2}(x)$ for any observed data x, where $p_{T_i}(x)$ is the p-value obtained by test $T_i (i = 1, 2)$ from given data x.*

Based on the properties of the gamma distributions, we can easily verify the following result:

Proposition 2. *For any $\alpha > 0$ and $\beta > 0$, $T_{G(\alpha,\beta)} \equiv T_{G(\alpha,1)}$.*

Therefore, the rate parameter of the gamma distribution has no effect on the test $T_{G(\alpha,\beta)}$. For convenience, in this paper, we set $\beta = 1$ and use $T_{G(\alpha)}$ to denote $T_{G(\alpha,1)}$ hereafter unless otherwise specified.

Definition 2. *A positively-valued function $c(\theta)$ is called the exact slope of the sequence of tests T_n if $\lim_{n \to \infty} [(-2/n)ln(1 - F_n(T_n))] = c(\theta)$ with probability 1, where $F_n(T_n)$ is the CDF of T_n. A test is called asymptotically Bahadur optimal (ABO) if its exact slope is maximal at every $\theta \in \Theta - \Theta_0$, where Θ is the parameter space, and Θ_0 is the parameter space under the null hypothesis. The exact slope is a measure of the rate at which the attained p-value of a test statistic tends to 0 and is a measure of asymptotic efficiency.*

It has been proven that $T_{G(\alpha,1/2)}$ is ABO for any $\alpha \in (0, \infty)$ [27]. Hence, from proposition 2, we have the following property:

Proposition 3. *The test $T_{G(\alpha)}$ is ABO for any $\alpha \in (0, \infty)$.*

Previously, we proposed a different p-value combination test based on gamma distribution with the test statistic $T = \sum_{i=1}^{n} F_{G(1/P_i,1)}^{-1}(1 - P_i)$, which uses the random shape parameter $a_i = 1/P_i$ for p-value P_i, and its null distribution is intractable, and a resampling method is used to estimate the p-value. While in the current proposed tests, the same shape parameter is used for all individual p-values.

2.2.2. Connections between $T_{G(\alpha)}$ and Existing Popular Tests

Although the existing popular tests described in Section 2.1 were proposed a long time ago, and their theoretical properties and empirical performances have been extensively studied and compared [6,7,25,28,29], surprisingly, their relationships have not been fully investigated, and the theoretical explanation on the differences of their performances is lacking. In this subsection, we show that they are connected to the aforementioned gamma distribution-based tests $T_{G(\alpha)}$ with different α values. In fact, we have the following results:

Theorem 1. *The class of gamma distribution-based tests $T_{G(\alpha)}$ include special cases that are equivalent to the aforementioned existing popular methods. More specifically,*

$$T_{G(0)} \triangleq \lim_{\alpha \to 0+} T_{G(\alpha)} \equiv T_p;$$
$$T_{G(0.5)} \equiv \chi_n^2;$$
$$T_{G(1)} \equiv F_p; \text{ and}$$
$$T_{G(\infty)} \triangleq \lim_{\alpha \to \infty} T_{G(\alpha)} \equiv Z_p.$$

The proof of Theorem 1 is given in the Appendix A.

2.2.3. $T_{(\alpha)}$ as the Uniformly Most Powerful Test

Besides the ABO property, there is another attractive property for the gamma distribution-based test $T_{G(\alpha)}$: under certain conditions, it is UMP. We thus have the following theorem:

Theorem 2. *Suppose $P_1, P_2, \cdots, P_n$ are iid from the following common density function with parameters $\alpha > 0$ and $0 < c < 1$*

$$f_{\alpha,c}(p) = (1-c)^\alpha \exp\left[cF_{G(\alpha)}^{-1}(1-p)\right] \text{ for } p \in (0,1), \tag{8}$$

If both α and c are known, then test $T_{G(\alpha)}$ is UMP.

The proof is given in the Appendix A.

Remark 1. (i) For $p \in (0,1)$, when $c = 0$, $f_{\alpha,0}(p) = 1$. Therefore, $f_{\alpha,0}(p)$ corresponds to the global null hypothesis. (ii) Under the condition $f_{\alpha,c}(p) = (1-c)^\alpha \exp\left[cF_{G(\alpha)}^{-1}(1-p)\right]$ with $0 < c < 1$, from Theorem 1, the existing tests $T_p, \chi_n^2, F_p,$ and Z_p defined in (1)–(4) are UMP for given $\alpha = 0, 0.5, 1,$ and ∞, respectively. (iii) Along with Theorem 1, Theorem 2 provides insightful explanations on when and why an existing popular test described in Section 2.1 is preferred. For instance, when the p-values are extremely heterogeneous (e.g., a very small α in (8)), the Min p test (i.e., $T_{G(0)}$) s more powerful than the other gamma distribution-based tests. On the other hand, when the p-values are more homogeneous (e.g., a large α in (8)), the z test (i.e., $T_{G(\infty)}$) is preferred. (iv) The function $f_{\alpha,c}(p) = (1-c)^\alpha e^{cF_{G(\alpha)}^{-1}(1-p)}$ with two parameters α ($\alpha > 0$) and c ($0 < c < 1$) represents a large class of densities and can be used to approximate the true density functions under the alternative hypotheses. Based on simulation study, we found that under many situations, the true density functions under the alternative hypotheses can be closely approximated by $f_{\alpha,c}(p)$ with the two parameters being estimated from the data (see Figures S1–S19 in the Supplementary File).

2.3. Constrained Likelihood Ratio Tests

In Section 2.2, we have shown that $T_{G(\alpha)}$ is UMP if the p-values to be combined are from the common density as described in (8) with known constants α and c. When c is unknown, or both α and c are unknown, constrained likelihood ratio tests (CLRTs) can be constructed accordingly. In this subsection, we study those CLRT-based tests when parameter c is unknown with α being known or unknown.

2.3.1. CLRT-Based Tests with Known α Values

Under (8), with known $\alpha = \alpha_0$, the CLRT-based tests can be constructed based on the constrained MLE of c obtained through maximizing $l(\alpha_0, c) = l(c) = n\alpha_0 ln(1-c) + c\sum_{i=1}^n F_{G(\alpha_0)}^{-1}(1-P_i)$. More specifically, we define the following test statistic:

$$T_{CLRT,\alpha_0}(P_1, \cdots, P_n) = 2\alpha_0 n \ln(1 - \hat{c}_{CLRT,\alpha_0}) + 2(\hat{c}_{CLRT,\alpha_0}) \sum_{i=1}^n F_{G(\alpha_0)}^{-1}(1-P_i), \tag{9}$$

where $\hat{c}_{CLRT,\alpha_0}$ is the constrained MLE of c through maximizing the log-likelihood $l(\alpha_0, c)$ with the constrain $0 < c < 1$. We will reject the overall null hypothesis if the test statistic is large. In other words, a one-sided p-value will be calculated from the test.

For the above CLRT-based test T_{CLRT,α_0} in (9), we have the following result [30]:

Proposition 4. *The asymptotic distribution of the test T_{CLRT,α_0} is a mixture of chi-square distributions $\sum_{i=0}^{1} w_i \chi_i^2$, where χ_i^2 is the chi-square distribution with $df = i$, χ_0^2 is the random variable with probability 1 of being 0, and the weights w_0, w_1 are determined by the null and the alternative hypothesis.*

In practice, the p-values of the test T_{CLRT,α_0} can be estimated through resampling methods (e.g., see Section 2.3.2 for an example). However, the following result shows that this test is tightly connected with the gamma distribution-based test $T_{G(\alpha_0)}$, whose p-value can be calculated directly.

Theorem 3. *Let t_{CLRT,α_0} be the observed statistic of test T_{CLRT,α_0}; the p-value of T_{CLRT,α_0} is determined by the gamma distribution-based test $T_{G(\alpha_0)} = \sum_{i=1}^{n} F_{G(\alpha_0)}^{-1}(1 - P_i)$ as follows:*

$$Pr[T_{CLRT,\alpha_0} > t_{CLRT,\alpha_0}] = \begin{cases} P_{T_{G(\alpha_0)}} & \text{if } t_{CLRT,\alpha_0} > 0 \\ Pr\left[T_{G(\alpha_0)} < n\alpha_0\right] & \text{if } t_{CLRT,\alpha_0} = 0 \end{cases} \quad (10)$$

The proof is given in the Appendix A.

Proposition 5. *Under the conditions specified in (8), if the parameter $\alpha = \alpha_0$ is known, then asymptotically $T_{G(\alpha_0)} \equiv T_{CLRT,\alpha_0}$.*

Proof. From the proof of Theorem 3, we know that under (8), when $0 \leq c < 1$, $Pr[T_{G(\alpha_0)} < n\alpha_0] = Pr[\hat{c}_{\alpha_0} \leq 0] \to 0$ (as $n \to \infty$), and hence, the two p-values from tests $T_{G(\alpha_0)}$ and T_{CLRT,α_0} are asymptotically equal with probability 1. □

Theorem 4. *Under the conditions specified in (8), if the parameter $\alpha = \alpha_0$ is known, then the gamma distribution-based test $T_{G(\alpha_0)}$ and the CLRT-based test T_{CLRT,α_0} are both asymptotically UMP.*

Proof. When $\alpha = \alpha_0$ is known, it can be shown that the constrained MLEs for c is consistent (see, for instance, Theorem 1 of Self and Liang [30]). Hence, from Theorem 2, $T_{G(\alpha_0)}$ is asymptotically UMP. From Proposition 5, T_{CLRT,α_0} is asymptotically UMP. □

2.3.2. The Optimal CLRT-Based Test When α Is Unknown

When both parameters α and c in (8) are unknown, they need to be estimated via the constrained MLEs, from which the following constrained likelihood ratio test is defined:

$$T_{CLRT}(P_1, \cdots, P_n) = 2\hat{\alpha}_{CLRT} n \ln(1 - \hat{c}_{CLRT}) + 2(\hat{c}_{CLRT}) \sum_{i=1}^{n} F_{G(\hat{\alpha}_{CLRT})}^{-1}(1 - P_i) \quad (11)$$

where $\hat{\alpha}_{CLRT}$ and $\hat{c}_{CLRT}$ are the constrained MLEs for parameters α and c, respectively, through maximizing the log-likelihood function $l(\alpha, c) = n\alpha \ln(1-c) + c\sum_{i=1}^{n} F_{G(\alpha)}^{-1}(1-P_i)$ with the constrains $0 < c < 1$ and $\alpha > 0$. The R function "nlminb" can be applied to find the constrained MLEs and the corresponding test statistic. The proposed test was implemented using R; the R package "opt" (optimal p-value combination test) can be freely download from https://github.com/zchen2020/opt (accessed on 15 November 2021).

For the above CLRT-based test T_{CLRT}, similar to Proposition 4, we have the following result [30]:

Proposition 6. *The asymptotic distribution of the test T_{CLRT} is a mixture of chi-square distributions $\sum_{i=0}^{2} w_i \chi_i^2$, where χ_i^2 is the chi-square distribution with $df = i$, χ_0^2 is the random variable with probability 1 of being 0, and the weights w_0, w_1, w_2 are determined by the null and the alternative hypothesis.*

The above asymptotic result may not be directly applicable to estimate the p-value for this test, as the number of p-values n is usually small, and more seriously, the weights w_i's are difficult to obtain. Instead, a simple resampling method can be used to approximate the null distribution and to estimate the p-value of T_{CLRT}. More specifically, for given sample size n, randomly sample n null p-values evenly distributed between 0 and 1, then calculate the test statistic using (10). Repeat this process many times (e.g., 10^5); then, the empirical distribution of the test statistic can be used to approximate the null distribution and therefore the p-value of T_{CLRT}.

Similar to Theorem 4, we have the following result for T_{CLRT}:

Theorem 5. *Under the conditions specified in (8), the CLRT-based test T_{CLRT} is asymptotically UMP.*

Proof. Under conditions (8), it can be shown that the constrained MLEs for α and c are consistent (see, for instance, Theorem 1 of Self and Liang [30]). Hence, T_{CLRT} is asymptotically equivalent to T_{CLRT,α_0} for known $\alpha = \alpha_0$ in (8). Then from Theorem 4, T_{CLRT} is asymptotically UMP. □

Remark 2. (i) *When $\alpha = \alpha_0$ is known, compared with test T_{CLRT,α_0}, the test $T_{G(\alpha_0)}$ is preferred because (a) its test statistic and p-value are easier to get and (b) the two tests in general have very similar performances. (ii) When both α and c are unknown, the test T_{CLRT} is asymptotically UMP, while, in general, neither T_{CLRT,α_0} nor $T_{G(\alpha_0)}$ for preset $\alpha = \alpha_0$ is UMP or asymptotically UMP. Therefore, it is expected that T_{CLRT} is more robust, and overall, it has better performance than each individual gamma distribution-based test $T_{G(\alpha)}$, including the existing popular ones described in Sections 2.1.1–2.1.4.*

3. Numeric Studies

In this section, we assess the performances of the proposed tests through a simulation study. In the simulation, we compare the optimal CLRT-based test T_{CLRT} with the popular and representative gamma distribution-based tests, $T_{G(0)}$, $T_{G(1)}$, and $T_{G(\infty)}$ (i.e., the Min p, Fisher, and z test, respectively).

In the simulation study, fifty ($n = 50$) independent p-values are simulated and combined. Among these 50 p-values, m ($m = 0, 10, 20, 40, 50$) are assumed from the true individual alternative hypotheses, and the rest ($n - m$) are from the true individual null hypotheses. When $m = 0$, all 50 individual null hypotheses are true, and the empirical power obtained under this condition is the empirical type I error rate. The p-values from the true null hypotheses are randomly sampled between 0 and 1 from the uniform distribution. For a true individual alternative hypothesis H_{i1} ($i = 1, \cdots, m$), we assume the p-value p_i is obtained via a random variable $z_i \sim N(\mu_i, 1)$. We randomly set k of the m u_i's as positive or negative (those alternative hypotheses with the same direction of the effects are called concordant alternatives) and the rest of $m - k$ having the other direction. A two-sided p-value for each true individual alternative hypothesis are obtained via the standard z test by comparing the test statistic with the standard normal distribution $N(0,1)$.

For the true alternative hypotheses, we consider three different scenarios for the effects of μ_i's. Scenario 1: $|\mu_i| = \mu v_i / \sum_{i=1}^{m} v_i$, where $v_i = 10^{r_i}$; $r_i \sim N(0.3, 1)$; and $\mu = 0.8, 0.6, 0.4, 0.3$ when there are 10, 20, 40, and 50 true individual alternatives, respectively. Scenario 2: $|\mu_i| = \mu v_i / \sum_{i=1}^{m} v_i$, where $v_i \sim U(1, 100)$ and $\mu = 1.2, 1.0, 0.6, 0.5$ when the number of true individual alternatives is $m = 10, 20, 40,$ and 50, respectively. Scenario 3: $|\mu_i| = \mu/m$, and $\mu = 1.5, 1.2, 0.8,$ and 0.6 when $m = 10, 20, 40,$ and 50, respectively. Note that (i) the constants (e.g., μ, the parameters in the normal distribution for r_i and the uniform distribution for v_i) are chosen in the way so that the empirical powers are appreciable for comparison. (ii) For all the three scenarios, the sum of the absolute effect sizes is equal to μ; and (iii) for given m, the degree of heterogeneity of the effect sizes among the true individual alternatives decreases from Scenario 1 to Scenario 3. More specifically, in scenario 1, the effect sizes are extremely heterogenous when the number of the true individual alternatives is small. In Scenario 3, the effect sizes are more homogenous. The situations in Scenario 2 are between those in Scenarios 1 and 3. By considering those different conditions, we tried to conduct a reasonable and realistic simulation study to fairly compare our proposed tests with others.

The empirical power values of the tests are estimated using the rejection proportions based on 1000 replicates at the significance level of 0.05. For the new tests, T_{CLRT} 10^5 replicates are used to estimate their p-values from the resampling method described in Section 2.3.2. Under the overall null hypotheses (i.e., all individual null hypotheses are true), the empirical type I error rates for all methods with different significance levels were obtained. From the simulation study, all methods controlled type I error rate quite well (see Table S4 in the Supplementary File).

Figures 1–3 plot the empirical power values of the Min p (Min), Fisher (Fisher), z test (Z), and the proposed CLRT-based test T_{CLRT} (LRT_CS) when p-values are combined under Scenarios 1 to 3, respectively. We have the following observations: First, for Scenario 1 (Figure 1), where the effect sizes from the true individual alternative hypotheses are extremely heterogeneous, the Min p test (i.e., $T_{G(0)}$) usually performs better than the Fisher test ($T_{G(1)}$), which in turn performs better than the z test ($T_{G(\infty)}$). Second, when the degree of heterogeneity of the effect sizes among individual alternative hypotheses are less extreme, as in Scenarios 2 and 3 (Figures 2 and 3), Fisher test and the z test usually perform better or much better than the Min p test. Third, for the Min p, Fisher, and z test, one may perform very well for some conditions but very poorly under others. For instance, under Scenario 1 (extremely heterogeneous effect sizes among the alternatives), the Min p test is more powerful than the other two, while it is much less powerful under scenario 3 (homogeneous effect sizes among the alternatives). The opposite direction was observed for the z test. Fourth, under all conditions considered, the new test T_{CLRT} is either the best or very comparable to the best one. When the number of p-values to be combined is small, we observed similar patterns (see the simulation results in Tables S1–S3 in the Supplementary Materials when $n = 10$). This demonstrates that, as expected, T_{CLRT} is a robust test in the sense that under many conditions, it has reasonable detection power compared with other tests. We would like to point out that, as expected, the empirical power values from the CLRT-based test T_{CLRT,α_0} are very close to those from the corresponding gamma distribution-based tests $T_{G(\alpha)}$, with $\alpha = 0, 1, \infty$ being fixed (data not shown).

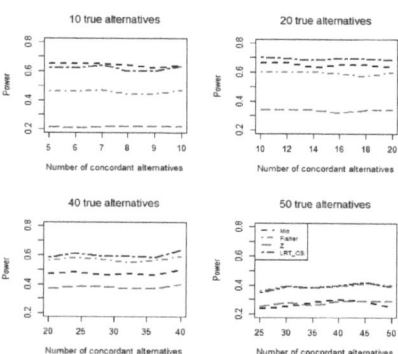

Figure 1. Empirical power values of the tests based on two-sided p-values under Scenario 1: $|\mu_i| = \mu v_i / \sum_{i=1}^m v_i$, where $v_i = 10^{r_i}$, $r_i \sim N(0.3, 1)$, and $\mu = 0.8, 0.6, 0.4, 0.3$ when there are 10, 20, 40, and 50 true individual alternatives, respectively.

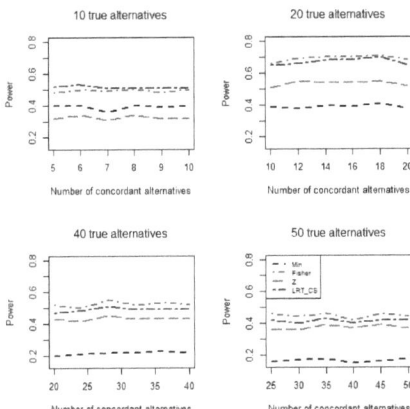

Figure 2. Empirical power values of the tests based on two-sided p-values under scenario 2: $|\mu_i| = \mu v_i / \sum_{i=1}^{m} v_i$, where $v_i \sim U(1, 100)$, and $\mu = 1.2, 1.0, 0.6, 0.5$ when the number of true individual alternatives is $m = 10, 20, 40,$ and 50, respectively.

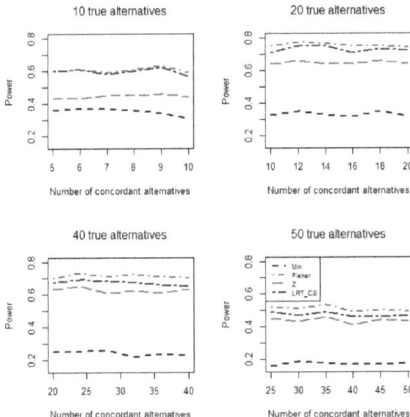

Figure 3. Empirical power values of the tests based on two-sided p-values under scenario 3: $|\mu_i| = \mu/m$, and $\mu = 1.5, 1.2, 0.8,$ and 0.6 when $m = 10, 20, 40,$ and 50, respectively.

4. Real Data Examples

In this section, we apply the proposed tests along with others to two real-world problems to demonstrate the usefulness of the proposed test.

4.1. Example 1: A Meta-Analysis

In a meta-analysis, 12 randomized trials examining the effect of patient rehabilitation designed for geriatric patients versus usual care on improving functional outcome at 3–12 month follow-up were used [31,32]. The estimated odds ratios (ORs) from the 12 trials are listed in Table 1.

The p-value from the Cochran's test for homogeneity was 0.021, indicating that the commonly used fixed effect model of meta-analysis was inadequate for this data set. Therefore, the authors ran the meta-analysis with a random effect model and estimated the overall OR as 1.36 with 95% CI (1.08, 1.71) [32]. However, the goodness-of-fit test for the random effect model obtained a p-value of 0.025 [33], indicating the lack of fit of the random effect model for this data set. Therefore, instead of using the problematic fixed or random effect models to combine information from the 12 trials, we use p-value combination methods to test whether there is an overall effect.

Table 1. Estimated odds ratio and its 95% CI from each study in a meta-analysis with 12 trials. Data were taken from Bachmann et al. and Riley et al.

Study	OR	95% CI	Study	OR	95% CI	Study	OR	95% CI
1	1.11	0.51, 2.39	5	0.88	0.39, 1.95	9	1.06	0.63, 1.79
2	0.97	0.78, 1.21	6	1.28	0.71, 2.30	10	2.95	1.54, 5.63
3	1.13	0.73, 1.72	7	1.19	0.69, 2.08	11	2.36	1.18, 4.72
4	1.08	0.42, 2.75	8	3.82	1.37, 10.60	12	1.68	1.05, 2.70

In order to use the p-value combination methods, for each trial, we calculate its p-value based on its reported 95% CI. Denote U and L the upper and lower limits of the 95% CI; the test statistic can be approximated as $t = \ln(U \times L)/\sqrt{4\ln(U/L)/3.92}$, whose asymptotic null distribution is $N(0,1)$. The sample sizes of these 12 trials were relatively large, ranging from 108 and 1388; therefore, we can reasonably estimate their p-values using the asymptotic null distribution. We calculate the two-sided p-value for each trial and apply the gamma distribution-based tests. The p-values from the Min p (i.e., $T_{G(0)}$), Fisher ($T_{G(1)}$), z test ($T_{G(\infty)}$), and T_{CLRT} for combining those two-sided p-values are 0.013, 0.0068, 0.075, and 0.0047, respectively. Except for the z test, which is known to be less powerful for this heterogeneous situation, all methods obtained p-values less than 0.05, and the proposed test T_{CLRT} had the smallest p-value, indicating that the proposed test is more powerful than the other tests under this specific situation.

4.2. Example 2: A Survival Analysis from a Clinical Trial

The second data set is from the randomized, double-blinded Digoxin Intervention Trial [34]. In this trial, patients with left ventricular ejection fractions of 0.45 or less were randomly assigned to digoxin (3397 patients) or placebo (3403 patients) groups. A primary outcome was the mortality due to worsening heart failure (see Figure S20 in the Supplementary Materials). In the original study, the authors used the log-rank (LR) test and obtained a p-value of 0.061, indicating that the evidence of the effectiveness of digoxin, in terms of reducing the mortality due to worsening heart failure, is at most marginal.

However, it is well known that the LR test may fail to detect the difference between two survival functions if their hazard rate functions are crossing [35,36]. We apply the two-stage approach [35,36] to this data set and obtained two p-values of 0.06 and 0.04 for the two stages. Since, under the null hypothesis, the two p-values from the two stages are asymptotically independent [35,36], we can combine them using the proposed test T_{CLRT} and the gamma distribution-based tests. The p-values are 0.078, 0.017, 0.0099, and 0.011 from the Min p, Fisher, z test, and T_{CLRT}, respectively. The proposed test obtained the second smallest p-value, which is slightly larger than the smallest one obtained by the z test.

In addition, the drug effect may differ between males and females. To investigate the possible interaction between sex and treatment, we divide the data into four groups based on the combinations of sex and treatment: Male—Placebo (MP), Male—Drug (MD), Female—Placebo (FP), and Female—Drug (FD). The sample sizes for the four groups are 2639, 2642, 764, and 755, respectively. We then compare the survival functions in the following three pairs of groups: MP vs. MD, (MP + MD) vs. FP, and (MP + MD + FP) vs. FD, where (MP + MD) is a new group with pooled data from groups MP and MD, and (MP + MD + FP) includes all the subjects from groups MP, MD, and FP (see Figure S21 in the Supplementary Materials). For each comparison, the two-stage approach is applied. We obtain the following six p-values: 0.019, 0.026, 0.504, 0.092, 0.975, and 0.050. It has been shown that under the null hypothesis, the six p-values obtained from the above approach are asymptotically independent [36]. Applying the gamma distribution-based tests, along with T_{CLRT}, to the six asymptotically independent p-values, we obtain p-values of 0.11, 0.0067, 0.020, and 0.013 from the Min p, Fisher, z test, and T_{CLRT}, respectively. It noticeable that the proposed test obtained the second smallest p-value, while Fisher test obtained the smallest one among those methods. These results show that except for the Min p test, all other tests obtain p-values less than 0.05. In addition, the p-values from T_{CLRT} in general are close to the smallest ones, while the popular tests, Fisher and z test, may get quite different p-values under different situations (two groups vs. four groups).

Compared with the original analysis, the results of the proposed optimal test T_{CLRT} using p-values from the two-stage approach applied to either two groups (placebo vs. drug) or four groups (combinations of sex and drug) provide stronger evidence against the null.

5. Discussion and Conclusions

In this paper, we studied a class of gamma distribution-based p-value combination methods, which include special cases that are equivalent to some existing popular methods. This class of tests provide unlimited choices for combining independent p-values. However, under a given situation, some of them may perform very poorly. Therefore, arbitrarily picking one of them may result in failing to detect true alternatives. On the other hand, if we try many different methods and report the smallest p-value, we need to adjust this p-value due to multiple comparison issue; otherwise, we will have more false findings than expected due to inflated type I error rate. Therefore, it is desirable to develop methods that can adaptively find the optimal approach from candidate tests. Our proposed CLRT-based test T_{CLRT} is one of such methods. We have shown that if the p-values to be combined are from a common density function $f_{\alpha,c}(p) = (1-c)^\alpha e^{cF_{G(\alpha)}^{-1}(1-p)}$ for $p \in (0,1)$, the gamma distribution-based test $T_{G(\alpha)}$ is UMP when both parameters α and c are known. When $\alpha = \alpha_0$ is known but c unknown, both $T_{G(\alpha)}$ and the CLRT-based test T_{CLRT,α_0} are asymptotically UMP. Furthermore, when both α and c are unknown, the proposed CLRT-based test T_{CLRT} is asymptotically UMP.

In a meta-analysis, it is natural to assign different weights to individual studies [5,7,37,38]. For instance, a larger weight can be assigned to a study with more subjects; hence, in the z test, a p-value from a larger study may receive a greater weight. Weights can also be assigned based on other quantities, such as the variances of the estimated effect sizes. However, there is no consensus on weight assignment. For our proposed tests, we can easily incorporate weights assigned to each individual p-value. For instance, the weighted gamma distribution-based tests can be constructed using $T_{G(\alpha)}^w = \sum_{i=1}^n F_{G(w_i\alpha)}^{-1}(1-P_i)$, where w_i is the weight assigned to study i ($i = 1, \cdots, n$). Based on the properties of gamma distributions, it is not difficult to show that $\lim_{\alpha \to \infty} T_{G(\alpha)}^w \equiv \sum_{i=1}^n w_i \Phi^{-1}(1-P_i)/\sqrt{\sum_{i=1}^n w_i^2}$, the weighted z test. Therefore, the class of weighted gamma distribution-based tests $T_{G(\alpha)}^w$ are generalizations of the weighted z test. Likewise, the weighted log-likelihood function with given weights becomes $l^w(\alpha,c) = \alpha \ln(1-c) \sum_{i=1}^n w_i + c \sum_{i=1}^n F_{G(w_i\alpha)}^{-1}(1-p_i)$, from which the corresponding weighted CLRT-based optimal test T_{CLRT}^W can be constructed accordingly.

Our proposed tests have much broader applications than in meta-analysis. In fact, they can be applied to almost all statistical testing problems when (asymptotically) independent p-values from individual components are available. For instance, in model selection, a typical step is to test whether a set of variables (or a single categorical variable with multiple levels) should be included in the final model. Often the time, the parameters, and the covariances of their estimates are estimated simultaneously through maximum likelihood estimation. Then the LRT via comparing the log-likelihood values from two models with and without the candidate variables, or the Wald chi-square test of the weighted sum of the squared estimated effect sizes, can be applied. For both LRT and the Wald test, a set of asymptotically independent p-values can be obtained through their asymptotically independent components (see, e.g., Chapter 16 of [39]). Hence, our proposed p-value combination methods, such as T_{CLRT}, can be applied and may result in a better final model.

Another example is the association test for two categorical variables in a two-way contingency table to which the Pearson chi-square test is usually applied. It is known that the Pearson's chi-square test statistic with k df can be partitioned into k asymptotically independent components whose null distributions are asymptotically iid chi-square distribution with 1 df [40]. For instance, the partition can be done through the Lancaster approach [41]. Hence, we can calculate a set of asymptotically independent p-values to which our proposed CLRT-based test is applicable.

The performance of the proposed approaches can be improved if the p-values to be combined are obtained from an individual study using more powerful tests. For instance, if we already know the direction of the effect (positive or negative) when we compare two group means, we can use a one-sided rather than a two-sided test to obtain the individual p-value. However, it should be pointed out that sometimes one-sided tests may not be always applicable to individual studies. Nevertheless, our proposed approaches can still be used.

In this paper, we focus on using gamma distribution to combine independent p-values. Our future direction will be developing gamma distribution-based methods to combine dependent p-values. The difficulty in this direction is how to choose the "optimal"-shape parameter so that the resulting test has good detection power and can control type I error rate for arbitrary dependency structure of the p-values to be combined. Our preliminary results indicate that this direction is promising. A follow-up paper will be published.

Supplementary Materials: The following are available online at https://www.mdpi.com/article/10.3390/app12010322/s1, Figure S1: some densities of $f_{a,c}(t)$; Figure S2: Histogram and the estimated density from simulated data when $\mu_i = 0$; Figures S3–S21: Histograms and the estimated densities from simulated data; Table S1: Empirical power from simulation under scenario 1 using $n = 10$ and $\alpha = 0.05$; Table S2: Empirical power from simulation under scenario 2 using $n = 10$ and $\alpha = 0.05$; Table S3: Empirical power from simulation under scenario 3 using $n = 10$ and $\alpha = 0.05$; Table S4: Empirical type I error rates from simulation study with 10,000 replicates using different significant levels.

Funding: This work was partially supported by the National Institutes of Health grants 1R03DE030259, UL1TR002529, and the Indiana University Open Access Article Publishing Fund.

Data Availability Statement: Data is contained within the article or supplementary material.

Conflicts of Interest: The author declares no conflict of interest.

Appendix A Proof of Theorems

To prove Theorem 1, we need the following results:

Lemma A1 (Theorem 1 of Liu, Martin, and Syring 2017). *If $Y_\alpha = Gamma(\alpha, 1)$, then $\lim_{\alpha \to 0+} -\alpha \ln(Y_\alpha) \sim Exp(1)$ in distribution* [42].

Corollary A1. $Pr\left(\lim_{\alpha \to 0+} Y_\alpha > 1\right) = 0.$

Proof of Corollary A1. From Lemma A1, $Pr\left(\lim_{\alpha \to 0+} Y_\alpha > 1\right) = Pr\left(\lim_{\alpha \to 0+} \ln(Y_\alpha) > 0\right) = Pr\left(\lim_{\alpha \to 0+} -\alpha \ln(Y_\alpha) < 0\right) = Pr(Exp(1) < 0) = 0.$ □

Corollary A2. *Let $Y = \lim_{\alpha \to 0+} Y_\alpha^{-\alpha}$, where $Y_\alpha = Gamma(\alpha, 1)$, then the PDF of Y is $f_Y(y) = 1/y^2$ for $y \in (1, \infty)$.*

Proof of Corollary A2. Notice that $Y = \lim_{\alpha \to 0+} Y_\alpha^{-\alpha} = \exp\left[\ln(\lim_{\alpha \to 0+} Y_\alpha^{-\alpha})\right] = \exp[\lim_{\alpha \to 0+} -\alpha \ln(Y_\alpha)]$. But from Lemma A1, $\lim_{\alpha \to 0+} -\alpha \ln(Y_\alpha) \sim Exp(1)$. Hence, the PDF of Y is $f_Y(y) = \exp(-\ln(y))/y = 1/y^2$ for $y \in [1, \infty)$. □

Lemma A2. Let $0 < p_1 < p_2 < 1$ and $q_i^{(\alpha)} = F_{G(\alpha)}^{-1}(p_i)$ $(i = 1, 2)$. Denote $r_\alpha = q_2^{(\alpha)} / q_1^{(\alpha)}$, then we have $\lim_{\alpha \to 0+} r_\alpha = \infty$. □

Proof of Lemma A2. Suppose $\lim_{\alpha \to 0+} r_\alpha = \infty$ does not hold; then, there exists a constant R such that $r_\alpha < R$ for any $\alpha > 0$. However, $0 < p_2 - p_1 = \Pr\left(q_1^{(\alpha)} < Y_\alpha < q_2^{(\alpha)}\right) = \Pr\left[-\alpha \ln\left(q_2^{(\alpha)}\right) < -\alpha \ln(Y_\alpha) < -\alpha \ln\left(q_1^{(\alpha)}\right)\right] = \Pr[-\alpha \ln\left(q_1^{(\alpha)}\right) - \alpha \ln(r_\alpha) < -\alpha \ln(Y_\alpha) < -\alpha \ln\left(q_1^{(\alpha)}\right)] < \Pr[-\alpha \ln\left(q_1^{(\alpha)}\right) - \alpha \ln(R) < -\alpha \ln(Y_\alpha) < -\alpha \ln\left(q_1^{(\alpha)}\right)] \to \Pr[-\alpha \ln\left(q_1^{(\alpha)}\right) < -\alpha \ln(Y_\alpha) < -\alpha \ln\left(q_1^{(\alpha)}\right)] = 0$ $(\alpha \to 0+)$, a contradiction. □

Corollary A3. $\lim_{\alpha \to 0+} T_{G(\alpha)}(P_1, P_2, \cdots, P_n) = \lim_{\alpha \to 0+} F_{G(\alpha)}^{-1}\left(1 - P_{(1)}\right)$, where $P_{(1)}$ is the smallest value of $P_1, P_2, \cdots, P_n$.

Proof of Corollary A3. This is a direct consequence of Lemma A2. □

Proof of Theorem 1. Now, we prove Theorem 1:

(i) Denote $Q_1 = \lim_{\alpha \to 0+} F_{G(\alpha)}^{-1}\left(1 - P_{(1)}\right)$. From Lemma A1 and Corollary A3, $P_{T_{G(0)}} = \lim_{\alpha \to 0+} \Pr(\text{Gamma}(n\alpha, 1) > Q_1) = \lim_{\alpha \to 0+} \Pr(Y_{n\alpha} > Q_1) = \lim_{\alpha \to 0+} \Pr(-n\alpha \ln(Y_{n\alpha}) < -n\alpha \ln(Q_1)) = 1 - \exp[n\alpha \ln(Q_1)]$. But, $\exp[n\alpha \ln(Q_1)] = \exp\left[\ln(Q_1^{n\alpha})\right] = Q_1^{n\alpha} = (Q_1^\alpha)^n = \{\exp[\alpha \ln(Q_1)]\}^n = \left[\lim_{\alpha \to 0+} \Pr(-\alpha \ln(Y_\alpha) > \alpha \ln(Q_1))\right]^n = \left[\lim_{\alpha \to 0+} \Pr(Y_\alpha < Q_1)\right]^n = \left(1 - P_{(1)}\right)^n$. Hence, $P_{T_{G(0)}} = 1 - \left(1 - P_{(1)}\right)^n = P_{T_p}$, and $T_{G(0)} \equiv T_p$.

(ii) From the property of gamma distribution, we know that $\text{Gamma}(\nu/2, 2) = \chi_\nu^2$, a chi-square distribution with ν df. However, the sum of n iid χ_ν^2 is $\chi_{n\nu}^2$. Hence, let $\nu = 1$ or $\alpha = 0.5$, $T_{G(0.5,2)} \equiv \chi_n^2$. However, from Proposition 2, $T_{G(0.5,2)} \equiv T_{G(0.5)}$; therefore, $T_{G(0.5)} \equiv \chi_n^2$.

(iii) As in (ii), when $\nu = 2$ and $\alpha = 1$, $\text{Gamma}(1, 2) = \chi_2^2$; therefore, $T_{G(1)} \equiv T_{G(1,2)} \equiv F_p$.

(iv) From the property of gamma distribution, we know that $\text{Gamma}(\alpha, \beta) \to N(\alpha/\beta, \alpha/\beta^2)$ $(\alpha \to \infty)$. Hence, for $\beta = 1$, $\text{Gamma}(\alpha, 1) \to N(\alpha, \alpha)$, and $\text{Gamma}(n\alpha, 1) \to N(n\alpha, n\alpha)$. If we define $T'_{G(\alpha)} = \left(T_{G(\alpha)} - n\alpha\right)/\sqrt{n\alpha} = \sum_{i=1}^n \left[F_{G(\alpha)}^{-1}(1 - P_i) - a\right]/\sqrt{n\alpha}$, then $T'_{G(\alpha)} \to N(0, 1)$ $(\alpha \to \infty)$. On the other hand, since $T'_{G(\alpha)}$ is a linear transformation of $T_{G(\alpha)}$, it is easy to show that $T_{G(\alpha)} \equiv T'_{G(\alpha)}$ for any $\alpha > 0$. Hence, $T_{G(\infty)} \equiv \lim_{\alpha \to \infty} T'_{G(\alpha)} = Z_p$. □

Proof of Theorem 2.

First, we show that $f_{\alpha,c}(p) = (1 - c)^\alpha \exp\left[c F_{G(\alpha)}^{-1}(1 - p)\right]$ is a PDF. Let $y = F_{G(\alpha)}^{-1}(1 - x)$, then $x = 1 - F_{G(\alpha)}(y) = \int_y^\infty t^{\alpha-1} \exp(-t)/\Gamma(\alpha) dt$, and $dx = -y^{\alpha-1} \exp(-y)/\Gamma(\alpha) dy$. Hence, $\int_0^1 f_X(x) dx = \int_0^1 (1 - c)^\alpha \exp\left[c F_{G(\alpha)}^{-1}(1 - x)\right] dx = \int_0^\infty (1 - c)^\alpha \exp(cy) y^{\alpha-1} \exp(-y) / \Gamma(\alpha) dy = 1$ as $(1 - c)^\alpha \exp(cy) y^{\alpha-1} \exp(-y)/\Gamma(\alpha) = (1 - c)^\alpha y^{\alpha-1} \exp[-(1 - c)y]/\Gamma(\alpha)$, the PDF of $\text{Gamma}(\alpha, 1 - c)$. However, under the global null hypothesis, $P_i \sim U(0, 1)$, the log-likelihood ratio under the global null and alternative hypotheses is $\sum_{i=1}^n \ln(f_{\alpha,c}(P_i)) = a(\alpha) + c \sum_{i=1}^n F_{G(\alpha)}^{-1}(1 - P_i)$, where $a(\alpha) = -n\alpha \ln(1 - c)$, a constant. Therefore, by the Neyman–Pearson lemma [43], $T_{G(\alpha)}$ is UMP under the specified condition. □

Proof of Theorem 3. Since the unconstrained MLE for c is $\hat{c}_{\alpha_0} = 1 - n\alpha_0 / \sum_{i=1}^n F_{G(\alpha_0)}^{-1}(1 - p_i)$, when $\hat{c}_{\alpha_0} \leq 0$, $T_{CLRT, \alpha_0} = 0$. On the other hand, when $\hat{c}_{\alpha_0} > 0$, i.e., $T_{G(\alpha_0)} = \sum_{i=1}^n F_{G(\alpha_0)}^{-1}(1 - p_i) > n\alpha_0$, $\hat{c}_{CLRT, \alpha_0} = \hat{c}_{\alpha_0}$, and $T_{CLRT, \alpha_0} = 2n\alpha_0 \ln\left(n\alpha_0 / \sum_{i=1}^n F_{G(\alpha_0)}^{-1}(1 - p_i)\right) + 2 \sum_{i=1}^n F_{G(\alpha_0)}^{-1}(1 -$

$p_i) - 2n\alpha_0 = 2n\alpha_0 \ln\left(n\alpha_0/T_{G(\alpha_0)}\right) + 2T_{G(\alpha_0)} - 2n\alpha_0 = 2n\alpha_0 \ln(n\alpha_0) - 2n\alpha_0 \ln\left(T_{G(\alpha_0)}\right) + 2T_{G(\alpha_0)} - 2n\alpha_0$. For any $t > 0$, let $A = \{t|t < T_{CLRT,\alpha_0}\}$; it is easy to show that $A = \{t|t < T_{CLRT,\alpha_0}\} = \{t|2n\alpha_0\ln(n\alpha_0) - 2n\alpha_0\ln\left(T_{G(\alpha_0)}\right) + 2T_{G(\alpha_0)} - 2n\alpha_0 > t\} = \{t|2\left(T_{G(\alpha_0)} - n\alpha_0\right) > t + 2n\alpha_0\ln\left(T_{G(\alpha_0)}/n\alpha_0\right)\}$. Let $f(x) = x - n\alpha_0\ln(x) - n\alpha_0 - t/2 + n\alpha_0\ln(n\alpha_0)$, then for $x > n\alpha_0$, $f'(x) = 1 - n\alpha_0/x > 0$, and $f(x)$ is an increasing function of x, but $\lim\limits_{x\to(n\alpha_0)+} f(x) = -t/2 < 0$, and $f(kn\alpha_0) = (k-1-\ln(k))n\alpha_0 - t/2 > 0$ for large k. Hence, there must exist a unique $x_0 \in (n\alpha_0, \infty)$ such that $f(x_0) = 0$. Accordingly, $Pr[T_{CLRT,\alpha_0} > t] = Pr[T_{CLRT,\alpha_0} > t, \hat{c}_{CLRT,\alpha_0} > 0] = Pr[2n\alpha_0\ln(n\alpha_0) - 2n\alpha_0\ln\left(T_{G(\alpha_0)}\right) + 2T_{G(\alpha_0)} - 2n\alpha_0 > t$ and $T_{G(\alpha_0)} > n\alpha_0] = Pr[T_{G(\alpha_0)} - n\alpha_0\ln\left(T_{G(\alpha_0)}\right) - n\alpha_0 - t/2 + n\alpha_0\ln(n\alpha_0) > 0, T_{G(\alpha_0)} > n\alpha_0] = Pr[T_{G(\alpha_0)} > t_0]$, where t_0 is the root of $f(x)$, i.e., $f(t_0) = 0$. This shows that when $T_{G(\alpha_0)} > n\alpha_0, T_{CLRT,\alpha_0}$ and $T_{G(\alpha_0)}$ have the same p-value. On the other hand, when $T_{G(\alpha_0)} \leq n\alpha_0$, $T_{CLRT,\alpha_0} = 0$; hence, $Pr[T_{CLRT,\alpha_0} = 0] = Pr[T_{G(\alpha_0)} < n\alpha_0]$. □

References

1. Fisher, R.A. *Statistical Methods for Research Workers*, 4th ed.; Oliver and Boyd: Edinburgh, UK, 1932.
2. Pearson, K. On a New Method of Determining "Goodness of Fit". *Biometrika* **1934**, *26*, 425.
3. Stouffer, S.A.; Suchman, E.A.; DeVinney, L.C.; Star, S.A.; Williams, R.M., Jr. *The American Soldier: Adjustment during Army Life. (Studies in Social Psychology in World War II)*; Princeton University Press: Princeton, NJ, USA, 1949; Volume 1.
4. Tippett, L.H.C. *Methods of Statistics*; Williams Norgate: London, UK, 1931.
5. Chen, Z. Is the weighted z-test the best method for combining probabilities from independent tests? *J. Evol. Biol.* **2011**, *24*, 926–930. [CrossRef]
6. Loughin, T.M. A systematic comparison of methods for combining p-values from independent tests. *Comput. Stat. Data Anal.* **2004**, *47*, 467–485. [CrossRef]
7. Whitlock, M.C. Combining probability from independent tests: The weighted Z-method is superior to Fisher's approach. *J. Evol. Biol.* **2005**, *18*, 1368–1373. [CrossRef]
8. Liu, Y.; Xie, J. Cauchy combination test: A powerful test with analytic p-value calculation under arbitrary dependency structures. *J. Am. Stat. Assoc.* **2020**, *115*, 393–402. [CrossRef] [PubMed]
9. Chen, Z. Robust tests for combining p-values under arbitrary dependency structures. 2021; unpublished.
10. Owen, A.B. Karl Pearson's meta-analysis revisited. *Ann. Stat.* **2009**, *37*, 3867–3892. [CrossRef]
11. Hedges, L.; Olkin, I. *Statistical Methods for Meta-Analysis*; Academic: San Diego, CA, USA, 1985.
12. Chen, Z.; Wang, K. Gene-based sequential burden association test. *Stat. Med.* **2019**, *38*, 2353–2363. [CrossRef] [PubMed]
13. Chen, Z.; Liu, Q.; Wang, K. A novel gene-set association test based on variance-gamma distribution. *Stat. Methods Med. Res.* **2018**, *28*, 2868–2875. [CrossRef]
14. Chen, Z.; Liu, Q.; Wang, K. A genetic association test through combining two independent tests. *Genomics* **2019**, *111*, 1152–1159. [CrossRef] [PubMed]
15. Chen, Z.; Lu, Y.; Lin, T.; Liu, Q.; Wang, K. Gene-based genetic association test with adaptive optimal weights. *Genet. Epidemiol.* **2018**, *42*, 95–103. [CrossRef]
16. Chen, Z.; Wang, K. A gene-based test of association through an orthogonal decomposition of genotype scores. *Hum. Genet.* **2017**, *136*, 1385–1394. [CrossRef]
17. Chen, Z.; Ng, H.K.T.; Li, J.; Liu, Q.; Huang, H. Detecting associated single-nucleotide polymorphisms on the X chromosome in case control genome-wide association studies. *Stat. Methods Med. Res.* **2017**, *26*, 567–582. [CrossRef]
18. Chen, Z.; Lin, T.; Wang, K. A powerful variant-set association test based on chi-square distribution. *Genetics* **2017**, *207*, 903–910. [CrossRef] [PubMed]
19. Chen, Z.; Han, S.; Wang, K. Genetic association test based on principal component analysis. *Stat. Appl. Genet. Mol. Biol.* **2017**, *16*, 189–198. [CrossRef]
20. Chen, Z. Testing for gene-gene interaction in case-control GWAS. *Stat. Its Interface* **2017**, *10*, 267–277. [CrossRef]
21. Choquet, H.; Melles, R.B.; Anand, D.; Yin, J.; Cuellar-Partida, G.; Wang, W.; Hoffmann, T.J.; Nair, K.S.; Hysi, P.G.; Lachke, S.A.; et al. A large multiethnic GWAS meta-analysis of cataract identifies new risk loci and sex-specific effects. *Nat. Commun.* **2021**, *12*, 3595. [CrossRef]
22. Schwantes-An, T.H.; Darlay, R.; Mathurin, P.; Masson, S.; Liangpunsakul, S.; Mueller, S.; Aithal, G.P.; Eyer, F.; Gleeson, D.; Thompson, A.; et al. Genome-wide Association Study and Meta-analysis on Alcohol-Associated Liver Cirrhosis Identifies Genetic Risk Factors. *Hepatology* **2021**, *73*, 1920–1931. [CrossRef]

23. Birnbaum, A. Combining Independent Tests of Significance. *J. Am. Stat. Assoc.* **1954**, *49*, 559–574.
24. Bonferroni, C. Il calcolo delle assicurazioni su gruppi di teste. In *Studi in Onore del Professore Salvatore Ortu Carboni*; Bardi: Rome, Italy, 1935; pp. 13–60.
25. Lancaster, H. The combination of probabilities: An application of orthonormal functions. *Aust. J. Stat.* **1961**, *3*, 20–33. [CrossRef]
26. Chen, Z.; Nadarajah, S. On the optimally weighted z-test for combining probabilities from independent studies. *Comput. Stat. Data Anal.* **2013**, *70*, 387–394. [CrossRef]
27. Berk, R.H.; Cohen, A. Asymptotically optimal methods of combining tests. *J. Am. Stat. Assoc.* **1979**, *74*, 812–814. [CrossRef]
28. Birnbaum, A. Characterizations of complete classes of tests of some multiparametric hypotheses, with applications to likelihood ratio tests. *Ann. Math. Stat.* **1955**, *26*, 21–36. [CrossRef]
29. Bahadur, R.R. Rates of Convergence of Estimates and Test Statistics. *Ann. Math. Stat.* **1967**, *38*, 303–324. [CrossRef]
30. Self, S.G.; Liang, K.Y. Asymptotic properties of maximum likelihood estimators and likelihood ratio tests under nonstandard conditions. *J. Am. Stat. Assoc.* **1987**, *82*, 605–610. [CrossRef]
31. Bachmann, S.; Finger, C.; Huss, A.; Egger, M.; Stuck, A.E.; Clough-Gorr, K.M. Inpatient rehabilitation specifically designed for geriatric patients: Systematic review and meta-analysis of randomised controlled trials. *BMJ* **2010**, *340*, c1718. [CrossRef]
32. Riley, R.D.; Higgins, J.; Deeks, J. Interpretation of random effects meta-analyses. *BMJ* **2011**, *342*, d549. [CrossRef]
33. Chen, Z.; Zhang, G.; Li, J. Goodness-of-fit test for meta-analysis. *Sci. Rep.* **2015**, *5*, 16983. [CrossRef]
34. The Digitalis Investigation Group. The effect of digoxin on mortality and morbidity in patients with heart failure. *N. Engl. J. Med.* **1997**, *336*, 525–533. [CrossRef]
35. Qiu, P.; Sheng, J. A two-stage procedure for comparing hazard rate functions. *J. R. Stat. Soc. Ser. B* **2007**, *70*, 191–208. [CrossRef]
36. Chen, Z.; Huang, H.; Qiu, P. Comparison of multiple hazard rate functions. *Biometrics* **2015**, *72*, 39–45. [CrossRef]
37. Mosteller, F.; Bush, R.; Lindzey, G. *Handbook of Social Psychology*; Addison-Wesley: Cambridge, MA, USA, 1954; pp. 289–334.
38. Good, I. On the weighted combination of significance tests. *J. R. Stat. Soc. Ser. B* **1955**, *17*, 264–265. [CrossRef]
39. Van der Vaart, A.W. *Asymptotic Statistics*; Cambridge University Press: Cambridge, UK, 2000; Volume 3.
40. Agresti, A. *Categorical Data Analysis*; Wiley-Interscience: Hoboken, NJ, USA, 2002.
41. Lancaster, H. The derivation and partition of χ^2 in certain discrete distributions. *Biometrika* **1949**, *36*, 117. [CrossRef] [PubMed]
42. Liu, C.; Martin, R.; Syring, N. Efficient simulation from a gamma distribution with small shape parameter. *Comput. Stat.* **2017**, *32*, 1767–1775. [CrossRef]
43. Casella, G.; Berger, R.L. *Statistical Inference*; Duxbury: Pacific Grove, CA, USA, 2002; Volume 2.

MDPI
St. Alban-Anlage 66
4052 Basel
Switzerland
www.mdpi.com

Applied Sciences Editorial Office
E-mail: applsci@mdpi.com
www.mdpi.com/journal/applsci

Disclaimer/Publisher's Note: The statements, opinions and data contained in all publications are solely those of the individual author(s) and contributor(s) and not of MDPI and/or the editor(s). MDPI and/or the editor(s) disclaim responsibility for any injury to people or property resulting from any ideas, methods, instructions or products referred to in the content.

www.ingramcontent.com/pod-product-compliance
Lightning Source LLC
LaVergne TN
LVHW070223100526
838202LV00015B/2078